AID AND THE POLITICAL ECONOMY OF POLICY CHANGE

The 1980s saw increased use of conditionality (exerting financial leverage by linking the availability of aid to promises of policy reforms by recipient governments) by the World Bank and bilateral aid donors, in addition to that long employed by the IMF. But how effective has this been and what role should it have in the future?

This study in political economy charts the growth of conditionality and challenges the official view that it is not coercive. Utilizing evidence on World Bank and IMF adjustment programmes, it shows that these have often not brought decisive improvements in policies or economic outcomes. Through detailed case studies of twenty-one developing countries, regional studies and other evidence since the 1980s, the study employs a principal–agent framework to explore the reasons for this failure.

The study concludes that implementation of policy conditions is poor when donor and government objectives differ, as is often the case. The incentives offered by donors are inadequate to ensure implementation of conditions, especially because of the donors' reluctance to punish non-implementation. It further concludes that there are deep-rooted obstacles to making conditionality more effective and proposes instead a model of donor–recipient relationships based on principles of ownership, selectivity, support and dialogue.

Principal author **Tony Killick** is Senior Research Fellow of the Overseas Development Institute, London, and Visiting Professor at the University of Surrey.

AID AND THE POLITICAL ECONOMY OF POLICY CHANGE

Tony Killick
with Ramani Gunatilaka
and Ana Marr

London and New York

First published 1998
by Routledge
11 New Fetter Lane, London EC4P 4EE

Simultaneously published in the USA and Canada
by Routledge
29 West 35th Street, New York, NY 10001

© 1998 Overseas Development Institute, London

Typeset in Garamond by Routledge
Printed and bound in Great Britain by T.J. International Ltd,
Padstow, Cornwall

British Library Cataloguing in Publication Data
A catalogue record for this book is available from the British Library

Library of Congress Cataloguing in Publication Data
Killick, Tony
Aid and the political economy of policy change / Tony Killick.
1. Economic assistance. 2. Structural adjustment (economic policy). 3.
Economic history—1971–1990. 4. Economic history—1990–
I. Title.
HC60.K4475 1998
338.91–dc21
98–9572 CIP

ISBN 0–415–18704–4 (hbk)
ISBN 0–415–18705–2 (pbk)

FOR ANDI AND BOBE.
UNCONDITIONALLY.

CONTENTS

List of tables   ix
Preface   xi
List of abbreviations   xiv

1 **The practice and justification of conditionality**   1
I The spread of conditionality   1
II The modalities of conditionality   6
III The nature of conditionality: co-operative or involuntary?   9
IV The legitimation of conditionality   12

2 **What has adjustment conditionality achieved?**   19
I Introduction and caution   19
II Programme effects   21
III Implementation and policy leverage   27
IV Implementation and results   41
V Social effects and the management of change   43
VI Conclusions   49

3 **Conditionality and adjustment in South-east Asia and Latin
America**   53
RAMANI GUNATILAKA AND ANA MARR

I South-east Asia   54
II Latin America   70

4 **The 'ownership' problem**   85
I Introduction   85
II Meaning and measurement of ownership   86
III The effects of ownership   88
IV Ownership matters because interests conflict   91

CONTENTS

V National resentment and the erosion of sovereignty   93
VI The extent of interest conflicts   97
VII Conclusion   98

5 The model, the research, some results   100
I Conditionality as an agency problem   100
II The nature of the evidence   104
III Participation constraints   110
Appendix: The selection procedures for the country sample   124

6 Rewards, punishments and the influence of national politics   129
I Rewards and punishments   129
II Why does delinquency go unpunished?   140
III The dominance of domestic politics   151

7 Alternatives to conditionality   160
I A paradox revisited   160
II The failure of conditionality   161
III Alternatives to conditionality   176

Master Table   199
Summary results on conditionality and economic policy
reforms in twenty-one developing countries, 1980–94

Bibliography   201
  Works cited in the main text   201
  Chapter 3 regional references   209
Index   214

TABLES

1.1   Subject coverage of World Bank conditions, 1994   3
1.2   IMF and World Bank adjustment lending, 1980–94   4
1.3   Average number of policy conditions per World Bank
      adjustment loan   5
1.4   The growth of performance criteria in IMF programmes   5
1.5   Regional breakdown of IMF and World Bank adjustment
      programmes, 1994   6
2.1   Effects of World Bank structural adjustment programmes:
      summary of results   22
2.2   Time between a programme coming into effect and the release
      of the second tranche for World Bank adjustment operations,
      1989–90 to 1993–4   30
2.3   Balance of payments viability and central government budget
      deficits   33
2.4   Balance of payments viability and GDP growth   33
2.5   Adjustment programmes and the quality of macro policies   35
2.6   Macroeconomic policy stances, 1990–1 and 1991–2, and the
      incidence of structural adjustment programmes in 1992   37
2.7   Policies and results in forty-two adjusting countries   42
2.8   Potential impact of selected adjustment measures on various
      poverty groups   44
3.1   Criteria of adjustment programmes – level of implementation   58
3.2   Influences on policy reform in Latin America   78
4.1   Correlating programme outcome with borrower ownership   88
5.1   Statistical summary of hypothesis tests in the Master Table 106

Master Table   Summary results on conditionality and   199
economic policy reforms in twenty-one developing
countries, 1980–94

PREFACE

A word on the origins of this study. At the beginning of the 1980s, colleagues and I examined the operations of the International Monetary Fund (IMF) in developing countries (published as Killick *et al.*, 1984a and 1984b). Things were not going too well, we decided. In particular, we saw Fund programmes as too narrow, too short-term to meet the needs of many developing countries with balance of payments problems. Not wishing merely to criticize, we advocated an alternative, 'real economy', approach. This was intended to reduce the Fund's reliance on its traditional demand–control policies, extending the potential scope of its policy influence to a wide range of instruments bearing on the supply-side of the economy and its institutional base. We held up the World Bank's then recently-introduced programmes of 'structural adjustment' as a model to follow. Although we also urged the importance of working for consensus with borrowing governments, the thrust of our recommendations undoubtedly implied a broadening of IMF conditionality.

Various influences have since moved the Fund a substantial distance in the direction we advocated (a development I trace in Killick, 1995b – especially Chapter 2). Over the same period, the World Bank greatly expanded the move into what it called 'policy-based lending' which was just beginning in the early 1980s. Others have since jumped onto the policy bandwagon: regional development banks (usually reluctantly and under pressure from those who provide their capital) and bilateral donor agencies. These developments too I have been in a position to observe rather closely.

But while the policy aspirations of the international financial institutions (IFIs) and national aid donors have burgeoned, I have grown more doubtful about the efficacy of their 'conditionality' and of the approach we advocated for the Fund in the early 1980s. This book is an attempt to confront the theory of conditionality with its limitations in practice, to analyse the reasons for these limitations, and (in the hope of doing better this time) again to suggest constructive alternatives.

Note that this book does not enter into much debate about the policy content of conditionality. There is a large literature on the design of

xi

adjustment already. My concern here is with the efficacy of conditionality as a means of achieving policy change, whatever the results of that change, although its influence on policy processes cannot be wholly divorced from the appropriateness of the policies being stipulated. I agree broadly with the policy thrust of donor-sponsored adjustment programmes; the issue this book is devoted to is whether their present heavy reliance on conditionality is an effective way for the IFIs and other donors to promote this strategy.

As it relates to developing countries, most published material on conditionality relates to the adjustment programmes of the IFIs and that is reflected in the evidence presented here. In principle, however, we are concerned generically with policy conditionality in whatever context it occurs: in project aid, in environmental issues, in the promotion of democracy and so on. This study is not just about adjustment, nor is it just about the IMF and World Bank. Note, however, that the focus is on *policy* conditionality, as distinct from the requirements that the IFIs and other donor agencies attach to their grants and credits for the purposes of procurement tying, financial accounting, progress reporting, auditing and so on.

I have run up some large debts in the course of this study. The largest is to Ramani Gunatilaka, now Research Fellow of the Institute of Policy Studies, Colombo, Sri Lanka, who undertook the large amount of work underlying the country survey reported chiefly in Chapters 5 and 6 with huge enthusiasm and imagination. She also undertook an additional survey of Latin American experiences, paralleled by an equivalent, equally notable, study of the South-east Asian case by my colleague Ana Marr; between them, they are the authors of Chapter 3. Professor T.C.I. Ryan and Douglas Zormelo contributed valuable background papers on Kenya and Ghana, respectively, and Douglas Zormelo also prepared a paper looking at the consistency of policy conditionality with the concept of national sovereignty (Zormelo, 1996a). Jane Horsfield and Matty Thwaites contributed greatly by bringing the manuscript into publishable form, and ODI's librarians, as always, were enormously helpful in tracking down sometimes obscure sources.

I am indebted too to the many officials of the Bretton Woods institutions, as well as of bilateral donors, who were invariably generous with their time and were the source of much of the official documentation referred to in the text – but who might prefer it if I did not name them all individually. Graham Bird and Joan Nelson are among my fellow-researchers who provided helpful and constructive comments on early drafts. Even more crucial was the contribution of the UK's Department for International Development (formerly Overseas Development Administration) which generously provided the grant which enabled this study to be undertaken while scrupulously abjuring any attempt to influence its findings.

To all of them and to my ever-patient wife, Inge, my thanks, and my apologies that it all took so much longer than expected. None of those mentioned necessarily agree with the conclusions arrived at; some definitely disagree.

Tony Killick
Overseas Development Institute, London
November 1997

LIST OF ABBREVIATIONS

BoP	Balance of payments
DAC	Development Assistance Committee (of the OECD)
EFF	Extended fund facility
ESAF	Enhanced structural adjustment facility
GDP	Gross domestic product
GNP	Gross national product
HIPC	Heavily indebted poor country
IDA	International Development Association
IFI	International financial institution
IMF	International Monetary Fund
ISI	Import-substituting industrialization
MDB	Multilateral Development Bank
NGO	Non-governmental organization
OECD	Organization for Economic Co-operation and Development
SAC	Structural adjustment condition
SAF	Structural adjustment facility
SAL	Structural adjustment loan
SAP	Structural adjustment programme
SDR	Special drawing right
SEA	South-east Asia
SECAL	Sectoral adjustment loan
SIP	Sector investment programme

HE THAT COMPLIES AGAINST HIS WILL,
IS OF HIS OWN OPINION STILL.

Samuel Butler

1

THE PRACTICE AND JUSTIFICATION OF CONDITIONALITY

The task of this chapter is to set the scene for what follows. We first trace the spread of conditionality in recent years and then briefly describe the modalities of conditionality. This leads to a discussion of the meaning and nature of conditionality and is followed by examination of the arguments in legitimation of the principle of applying conditionality. The chapter concludes by providing brief *prima facie* reasons for thinking that conditionality is not working well – and why, therefore, it seemed worthwhile to write this book.

I The spread of conditionality

It is only a modest exaggeration to say that in the 1970s the only substantial policy conditionality applied to developing country governments in search of assistance was that of the International Monetary Fund (IMF). The World Bank was yet to move far into 'policy-related' lending and the same was true of other donor agencies. Moreover, the Fund conditionality of that time was designedly of quite limited scope, confined to a few macroeconomic policy variables such as the exchange rate and domestic credit.

Since then, however, the position has been transformed. First the scope of IMF conditionality has been greatly extended (Killick, 1995b: 22–7). It began to take trade liberalization measures much more seriously. It increasingly insisted on delving below aggregate targets of budgetary deficit reductions to examine the specific revenue and expenditure measures envisaged to produce these outcomes, which it has rightly been observed 'unobtrusively introduces microconditionality' (Polak, 1991: 40).

The Fund's move into 'structural' conditionality has had three thrusts:

1   to increase the role of markets and private enterprises relative to the public sector, and to improve incentive structures;
2   to improve the efficiency of the public sector; and
3   to mobilize additional domestic resources.

This has broadened the content of its conditionality into such areas as the reduction or elimination of public subsidies and the removal of price controls, with the pricing of petroleum products and agricultural producer prices particularly frequent targets. The operation of the market mechanism has also been promoted through the liberalization of trade and payments; and the realm of the private relative to the public sector has been extended by numerous requirements for the privatization of public enterprises. The efficiency of the public sector has additionally been promoted through stipulations requiring some chronically inefficient public enterprises to go into liquidation. Improved domestic resource mobilization has been promoted by tax measures, and by provisions for the reform and strengthening of the financial sector, including the recapitalization and restructuring of banking institutions and de-control of interest rates.

Evidently, then, the previous principle of restricting IMF conditionality to a few macroeconomic variables has been abandoned in favour of a far more ambitious agenda. By contrast, once it got started in the business of policy conditionality the World Bank was never anything other than ambitious. Indeed, one of the first internal evaluations of its structural adjustment lending experiences criticized its staff for attempting too much, for being too unselective in the policy stipulations they wrote into programmes, and that has been a recurring theme in later evaluations.

If we take together the Bank's (increasingly rare) economy-wide structural adjustment programmes and its (still numerous) sectoral adjustment programmes, the aggregate coverage of its policy conditions is enormous, extending to all economic sectors and to the very wide range of policy instruments that can be deployed within these, as may be judged from the distribution of the 117 adjustment operations in being at mid-1994, shown in Table 1.1.

Of course, at any one time a borrowing government will only be confronted with conditions relating to some sub-set of the possible total. Nevertheless, the range of stipulations can be extraordinarily large, as is suggested by the not unusual example of Uganda, a country still trying to rebuild its public administration after the ravages of prolonged civil war. An unpublished Bank report sets out a total of *eighty-six* specific policy commitments for 1991–2 to 1993–4, of which *seventy-nine* should have been undertaken or initiated in FY 1991–2 alone. That this was not an extreme case is suggested by information showing that the *average number of conditions per adjustment loan in 1989 was fifty-six* (see Table 1.3), having risen steeply during the decade.

Even this account does not do full justice to the broadening of conditionality which has occurred over the last decade.[1] Measures to reduce poverty, or to alleviate the social costs of adjustment, have featured increasingly, with even the IMF changing tack to take a more active interest in this area. Policies for the protection of the environment have also begun to feature increasingly, particularly among some bilateral donors. Other policy causes promoted by

Table 1.1 Subject coverage of World Bank conditions, 1994

Economic sector	Number of programmes
Multi-sectoral	58
Agriculture	15
Education	6
Energy and power	4
Financial	18
Industrial	4
Mining	1
Population	2
Public sector management	9

Source: World Bank, 1995a: 115.

bilateral conditionality include reduced military spending, enhancement of the position of women and human development.

Various pressures have contributed to this explosion. Much of it has come from publics in the industrial countries, weary of the seemingly insatiable appetite of developing countries for aid and alarmed by media stories of corruption. Some, perhaps surprisingly, has come from NGOs who, while often highly critical of IFI-style conditionality, have not shrunk from advocating their own nostrums – to enforce protection of the environment, or of the poor, or of women, etc. Partly in response to these changing public attitudes but due also to their growing reluctance to aid developing countries in economic difficulties, government representatives on the Executive Boards of the IFIs have also exerted large pressures for conditionality, asking of proposals for new adjustment credits 'what policy changes are we buying with this money?'.

Also underlying this question are the intellectual influences, as well as practical experiences, which led to a growing belief that past government policy interventions in developing countries had often had malign effects and that aid applied within a distorted policy framework was likely to be wasted. The gradual fading of colonial guilt brought further changes in relations between the metropolitan powers and their former colonies. The demise of communism in Eastern Europe and the former USSR was a further important influence. By altering foreign policy objectives and devaluing the security-cum-foreign policy motive for aiding strategically placed countries, the ending of the Cold War brought further changes in relationships between donors and many recipients, increasing the self-confidence of the former and making them bolder in pressing their views.

These views were not, of course, confined to the economic sphere. There has also been a powerful move to link aid with the promotion of 'good governance' (accountability, transparency, the rule of law, the prevention of corruption, etc.), the observance of human rights and the promotion of multi-party democracy. There has been a growing use of conditionality in these areas, particularly by bilateral donors but also by the World Bank (which has tried, with only mixed success, to limit its stipulations in this area to the tenets of good governance).[2]

Table 1.2 shows the rapid growth in policy-oriented adjustment lending by the Bank since the early 1980s, with the number of new loans increasing five-fold during the 1980s, although there has been some reduction since. The trend is less clear in the case of the Fund but by the last period shown it was making an unprecedented large number of *high-conditionality* (i.e. excluding structural adjustment facility (SAF)) structural adjustment loans.

In addition to the growing number of governments entering into structural adjustment arrangements with the IFIs, the number of policy stipulations per credit has also been increasing (see Table 1.3).

In the IMF, the tendency towards proliferation is most obvious with its ESAF programmes. The range of policy conditions in these is considerably wider than in traditional stand-bys. There has been extensive use of precondi-

Table 1.2 IMF and World Bank adjustment lending, 1980–94 (average new credits and commitments per annum)

	IMF All credits		Structural adjustment [a]		World Bank	
	No.	Value[b]	No.	Value[b]	No.	Value[c]
1980–2	28	8.24	7	4.64	7	0.81
1983–5	27	7.24	2	2.92	17	2.18
1986–8	27	3.51	9	0.86	28	4.48
1989–91	23	7.17	10	4.17	35	6.31
1992–4	27	5.28	10	2.30	n/a	4.09

Source: World Bank, 1992a, Annex 1, and *Annual Reports, 1993, 1994*; IMF *Annual Report, 1994*, Table II.1.
Notes:
[a] Includes EFF, SAF and ESAF credits
[b] In SDR billions
[c] In US$ billions
These figures relate to the respective fiscal years of the two agencies.

Table 1.3 Average number of policy conditions per World Bank adjustment loan

	1980–8	*1989–91*
Preconditions (prior actions)	9	18
Legal requirements[a]	12	17
Other policy commitments	18	21
Total	39	56

Source: World Bank, 1992a, Table A2.3.
Note:
[a] Legal in the sense that their observance is required if a loan tranche is to be released, i.e. similar in status to IMF performance criteria.

Table 1.4 The growth of performance criteria in IMF programmes

1968–77	below 6
1977–84	7
1984–7	9½

Source: Polak, 1991: 14.

tions but additional evidence on proliferation can be seen in the averages of the number of performance criteria per programme presented in Table 1.4.

The substantial use of conditionality by bilateral donors is quite a recent development, although it has some history in the case of the USA and has never been entirely absent among other donors.[3] So far as adjustment conditionality is concerned, the bilaterals have mostly contented themselves with 'piggy-backing' on the conditionality of the IFIs, although with varying degrees of enthusiasm. The UK has gone furthest, with the USA, Germany and the Netherlands also firm supporters but with France, Japan and the European Union slower to come fully on board.

Overall, then, there has over the last one-and-a-half decades been an explosive growth in the use of conditionality, which has left few developing country governments untouched (see Table 1.5). Note the special concentration on sub-Saharan Africa: the extent to which policies in that region are under the direct influence of the IFIs and bilateral donors is without historical parallel. In enquiring into the effectiveness of conditionality we are therefore examining a phenomenon of no little importance.

Table 1.5 Regional breakdown of IMF and World Bank adjustment programmes, 1994

	World Bank	*IMF*
East Asia and Pacific	5	5
Europe and Central Asia	14	13
Middle East and North Africa	6	3
Latin America and Caribbean	21	8
South Asia	10	4
Sub-Saharan Africa	61	24
Totals	117	57

Source: World Bank, 1995a: 112; and *IMF Memorandum*, 6 February 1995, using World Bank country classifications.

II The modalities of conditionality[†][4]

In formal terms, conditionality of the type considered here refers to a mutual arrangement by which a government takes, or promises to take, certain policy actions, in support of which an IFI or other agency will provide specified amounts of financial assistance. However, the various policy requirements do not all have equal status.

The most binding are *preconditions*, or 'prior actions' as the IFIs prefer to call them. These are policy actions agreed in the course of a credit negotiation but which must be undertaken before the agency will present the credit agreement for the approval of its Board. These are quite extensively used by the Bank, as the figures in Table 1.3 show, and by the IMF. However, only a limited set of policy changes is amenable to this type of treatment. If there is not to be inordinate delay, prior actions must relate to actions over which those parts of government with which the IFI has been negotiating have direct control and which they can undertake quickly. The actions must be quite unambiguous, in the sense of being precisely specified and readily monitored.

In the context of a crawling peg regime, the exchange rate is a classic example of an instrument that passes these tests and, indeed, devaluation has probably been the most common prior action stipulated by the IMF. A specified change in some other price directly controlled by the Treasury has similar qualities, as do changes in tax rates, or in commodity subsidies. Policy shifts

† NB: Those familiar with the procedures of the IMF and World Bank could skip this section.

that have to be mediated through other levels of government, or those which are more qualitative in nature, or which involve institutional reforms which can only be implemented gradually, are clearly unsuitable for treatment as preconditions.

Once an agreement is worked out and any preconditions have been implemented, the way is clear for the government to draw upon the supporting line of credit. However, only very exceptionally will all the agreed amount become available 'up front', upon signature of the agreement. Any leverage which the lender (or giver) may have over the recipient government's policies wanes rapidly once the money has changed hands. The IFIs therefore usually only release their credits in instalments, or 'tranches'.

In the case of the IMF, stand-by credits are normally made available in quarterly tranches, while credits from its Enhanced Structural Adjustment Facility (ESAF) are normally subject to six-monthly tranches, although these terms can be varied according to country circumstances (there have even been instances of monthly tranching). The leash on World Bank structural adjustment credits is usually somewhat longer. Two tranches (i.e. an up-front payment plus one further instalment) are the general rule but three or four are not uncommon. Tranches are not necessarily of equal amounts, nor equidistant in time. Where it is desired to exert maximum leverage over a government, a credit may be 'back-loaded', with a large proportion payable in later tranches. Where there is high confidence in the intentions of a government and it needs finance urgently, there may be 'front-loading', with a large proportion of the credit being paid up-front. Both IFIs can vary tranching arrangements in these ways.

This brings us back to the hierarchy of policy conditions. After preconditions come certain *trigger actions* – what the IMF calls performance criteria and the Bank benchmark criteria or legal requirements (see Table 1.3). It is compliance with these which trigger governments' continuing access to the next outstanding tranche of the credit. IMF performance criteria typically include ceilings on the expansion of domestic credit, or on credit to the government, minimum levels of foreign exchange reserves and maxima on non-concessional foreign borrowings. Exceeding a ceiling or falling below a floor will normally result in the withholding of the next credit tranche until the government can come back into compliance or new targets can be agreed. The benchmark criteria of the Bank are more varied, depending on the nature of the credit in question, but commonly relate to such measures as trade liberalization, financial sector reforms, the composition of public expenditures, various aspects of agricultural policy and the reform or privatization of public enterprises. All should have the quality of being precisely defined and readily monitorable.

The third, and least binding, of the policy provisions within an agreement comprise the residual element of commitments contained in the overall programme but which are neither preconditions nor trigger criteria. Such policy commitments are often quite numerous but, since there is no direct linking of their implementation to access to finance, the degree of IFI leverage over them is fairly slight. It is not completely absent, however, for it may well be that implementation of some of these measures is important for the success of the programme. In principle, the IFIs can punish governments which take a casual attitude to the execution of these residual provisions by withholding credits in the future, or drawing up tighter conditionality provisions in any future agreements.

The trigger and residual conditions just described (but not usually the prior actions) are formalized in letters addressed by the borrowing government to the IFI in question, called 'Letters of Intent' by the IMF and 'Letters of Development Policy' by the World Bank. These letters will usually also describe the economic background to the credit in question and its objectives.

Trigger conditions have the defect of creating an inflexible strait-jacket for economies subject to sudden shocks, to say nothing of miscalculations on the part of those who draw up the programmes. The IMF's performance criteria have been particularly criticized along these lines. Both IFIs have developed techniques for reducing this inflexibility, however. Both, for example, are willing to grant waivers (which, however, have to be approved by their Boards) in the case of minor departures (or more substantial variations resulting from external shocks) from trigger conditions, although their willingness to do this varies from country to country and over time (see Killick, 1995b, Chapter 5 for a discussion of this in relation to the Fund).

There are also 'review clauses', which are intended to give IFI staff the ability to judge progress with a programme on the basis of the overall record, rather than simply in terms of compliance with trigger criteria. Increased use of review missions has been an important development for the Fund in recent years. Six-monthly review missions have become more or less standard practice in both stand-by and medium-term programmes, with the purpose to assess progress with a programme over the preceding half-year and to reconsider or determine performance criteria and other provisions for the following half-year. As such, they reduce the Fund's reliance on predetermined quantitative indicators and facilitate the modification of programmes in the light of changing circumstances. Bank missions are also supposed to assess overall programme progress, although a Bank report stated that this requirement is rarely taken seriously and sometimes ignored, with reviews tending in practice to concentrate on compliance with the legal trigger criteria (World Bank, 1991: 60). It is similarly unclear how much difference the introduction of more review missions has made to the *de facto* flexibility of the IMF.

There is also *cross-conditionality*. This refers to a situation in which access to one agency's finance is made conditional upon compliance with the stipulations of a second agency. There is a good deal of this, although this is not always formally stated and sometimes denied. A well-known (although non-formal) example is the requirement of the World Bank that for a country to be

8

eligible for a structural adjustment credit it must also have an agreement with the IMF, and remain in compliance with that agreement, or in some other way obtain the *imprimatur* of the Fund for its macroeconomic policies. Another example is provided by the practices of the Paris Club. This is the forum through which mainly OECD creditor governments co-ordinate their responses to debtor-country requests for relief on the servicing of official bilateral credits. The Paris Club has adopted the principle that a debtor government must have a programme with the IMF in order to be eligible for debt relief.

Bilateral aid agencies also make extensive use of cross-conditionality, commonly linking their programme aid to the conditionality of the IFIs. In such situations, the tasks of monitoring and enforcement are effectively delegated to the staff of the IFIs. In other respects, however, there is much variation in the approaches of bilateral agencies. The American agency, USAID, has probably been the most ambitious in developing policy conditionality which goes beyond that of the IFIs, particularly in the areas of privatization and the freeing of markets, as well as in the more overtly political area of the promotion of democracy and 'good government'. Most other major bilateral aid donors have travelled some distance in deploying conditionality which goes beyond that of the IFIs, particularly in support of democracy and human rights, although the practical import of this has been limited so far. There is too much variation to be able to generalize usefully about the modalities of bilateral donors (see Hewitt and Killick, 1996, for a survey of bilateral conditionality).

III The nature of conditionality: co-operative or involuntary?

A consensual view

The official view of the IFIs, in particular the view of their respective Boards, is that conditionality is consensual. The bulk of the commitments written into Letters of Intent or Development Policy, they insist, are the outcome of often long periods of consultation and discussion. The Letters are thus devices for setting out in a systematic and clearly defined way a package of measures which is mutually agreed as necessary to achieve the chosen objectives of the programme, codifying what should be done and in what sequence; serving as a kind of institutionalized memory against the possibility of changes among key ministers, officials, perhaps even the government itself; and providing a vehicle through which the agencies can undertake their programme lending. In the words of one Bank official:

> The Bank's policy assistance has been essentially a co-operative venture with the recipient countries. Successful country programmes

must be homegrown and cannot be standardized or externally imposed; they should be designed and perceived as central to the countries' own interests. The Bank plays a supplemental role, backing up and helping to implement sound policy initiatives.

(cited by Kahler, 1992: 101)

There are some serious difficulties with this benign view, however. For one thing, if the policy content of programmes is indeed consensual there seems no reason for the overt linking of implementation with credit releases, for tranching and trigger criteria. If consensus were the rule, why should credits not be paid 100 per cent up-front, as indeed they have been in a few cases? Similarly, the benign view sits ill with the use of prior actions, which both IFIs admit have increased over the years. The setting of preconditions might rather be seen as the ultimate signal of distrust and absence of consensus, a device for maximizing financial leverage which would be redundant if there were a genuine meeting of minds.

The view of IFI conditionality as playing 'a supplemental role, backing up and helping to implement sound policy initiatives' is similarly at odds with the evidence of an important study of the 'ownership' of World Bank structural adjustment programmes by two Bank staff members (Johnson and Wasty, 1993). Their results feature prominently in Chapter 4, so suffice it to report here that they studied the extent of government identification with programmes in some eighty-one cases, showing that in half (forty) of these ownership was classified *by Bank staff* as either 'low' or 'very low', and 'very high' in only sixteen cases. Such results flatly contradict the notion that programmes are normally consensual. We suspect that more of the reality is caught by President Moi of Kenya's threat that unless donors stopped complaining about civil rights abuses he would reverse the country's programme of economic reforms. So much for consensus!

The involuntary nature of stipulated policies

An alternative view – the view taken in this study – starts with semantics. In its relevant sense, a condition, according to *The Oxford English Dictionary*, is 'something demanded or required as a prerequisite to the granting or performance of something else; a stipulation'. This throws a quite different light on the matter, viewing conditionality as essentially coercive: the use of financial strength to promote donor objectives. A condition attached to a loan or grant sets out a requirement for action of some sort by the recipient government, without which assistance will not be granted or continued. Seen in this light, the technology of preconditions, tranching and trigger criteria is easy to understand. There is also no problem in reconciling this view with low levels of government programme ownership. Indeed, weak ownership becomes predictable because there is a presumption that the borrowing government would not voluntarily undertake the changes being stipulated, for otherwise writing them in as conditions is otiose and probably counterproductive.

What is implied here is a distinction between 'pro forma' and 'hard core' conditionality. If we consider the wide range of policy measures typically written into a Letter of Intent or of Development Policy, some of them will indeed be consensual, written in for the reasons given earlier and in order to persuade managements and Boards in Washington of the adequacy of the programme. We might think of this as pro forma conditionality. The proportion of policy commitments falling into this category is liable to vary greatly from case to case, and will be strongly correlated with ownership: high ownership = consensus = pro forma conditionality.

Hard core conditionality, by contrast, consists of actions, or promises of actions, made only at the insistence of the lender. They are a sub-set of the total policy content of the programme in question, a sub-set which is likely to include all or most preconditions, a substantial proportion of trigger criteria and some of the residual components. These, we suggest, are the essence of policy conditionality: measures that would not otherwise be undertaken or not within the time frame desired by the lender, promised involuntarily by governments in urgent need of the money to which the measures are attached. On this view, the exercise of conditionality introduces a species of economic sanction: the withholding of resources as punishment for noncompliance with the stipulations of the lending agency. (Chapter 7 compares the results of conditionality with those of economic sanctions in general.)

The position just described is the view taken in the remainder of this book. In general, when we refer to conditionality we are referring to the involuntary, 'hard core' aspect of it, which we regard as its essence (although it is acknowledged that there is a grey area between the hard core and pro forma varieties, when measures emerge after a long process of negotiations and it is practically impossible to disentangle the consensual from the involuntary). This view of conditionality as essentially coercive sharply differentiates it from various loose usages to which the word has sometimes been put. Some have written of 'positive' or 'ex post' conditionality, referring to the use of aid to reward governments for policies they have already voluntarily undertaken, but such usage stretches the use of the word quite beyond its meaning in everyday language and is unhelpful. Our view of conditionality also differentiates it sharply from the processes of consultation, advice and 'policy dialogue' which is also an important feature of relations between donor agencies and developing country governments. 'Dialoguing' implies no necessary linkage with financial assistance. Indeed, creating such a link, with its implications of unequal bargaining power, may well get in the way of persuasion.

We shall find later that this differentiation of conditionality from persuasion is important for the policy arguments of this book. It must be admitted, though, that it is often difficult to know where persuasion ends and conditionality takes over. There are multiple and frequent points of contact between agencies and borrowing governments, which means that only those with the most intimate awareness of the facts will know what is promised on the basis of consensus and what involuntarily – knowledge that outside researchers will only rarely acquire.

IV The legitimation of conditionality

It is possible to view the fact of conditionality as a simple expression of *force majeure*, summed up in the popular saying that 'he who pays the piper calls the tune'. On this view, the IFIs and other donor agencies are merely flexing their financial muscles in order to achieve their own objectives, without necessarily paying much heed to the interests of recipients. The donors have the resources which some developing country governments are desperate to obtain and this gives the donors the economic power to impose their own wills.

It will be shown later that quite a lot of the evidence is consistent with this rather cynical view. There is, for example, a clear inverse relationship between the use of conditionality and recipient governments' access to alternative sources of finance. This helps explain the upsurge in conditionality in Latin America during the 1980s, after the breaking of the debt crisis effectively cut the region off from private capital markets. It also explains why there has been such a high concentration of conditionality in sub-Saharan Africa, a region with acute financial difficulties and little access to alternative sources of capital. We will also see later that there is quite a lot of evidence that the governments of donor countries have used their financial power to promote their own foreign policy, security and trading interests (although this quite often works to loosen conditionality, rather than intensify it).

However, conditionality needs a justification which is more persuasive than the brutalism of *force majeure*. It requires legitimation, not least because of the ways in which it limits the freedom of governments internationally recognized as sovereign, and because the policies required often impose political and economic costs on these governments and their peoples. How might such legitimation be conferred?

One strand of such a justification sees conditionality as *a substitute for the collateral assets* which a private lender would require as a safeguard against default by the borrower (see Mosley, 1992, for a statement along these lines). If we concentrate for the moment on the IFIs, they are providing loans, not grants, and therefore need to assure themselves of the likelihood that borrowing governments will be in a position to repay, maintaining the 'revolving fund' nature of their operations and thus ensuring that they will be able to continue lending from repayments of past credits. One way in which they have protected themselves here is to establish the convention that they are to be treated as 'preferred creditors', with a first call on a country's resources, superior to the claims of creditor governments. Conditionality can be seen as an additional safeguard, designed to make sure that policies are put in place in borrowing countries that will raise their debt-servicing capacities, through improved export performance and the creation of a favourable policy climate for direct investment from abroad. In the IMF, which has seen a number of countries slip into arrears in the servicing of past credits, quite explicit attention is paid in the design of its programmes to ensuring the future ability of the borrowing government to repay the credit on schedule.

A closely related argument presents conditionality as *a safeguard against moral hazard*, i.e. against the danger that the provision of a loan or grant, by providing additional resources, will actually diminish governments' incentives to undertake (often politically risky) economic policy reforms. So long as the conditionality can be enforced, that possibility should be ruled out.

These arguments shade into another, which is valid for grant-giving bilateral donors as well as the IFIs. This refers to *the influence of recipient-country policies on aid effectiveness* (as well as on future debt-servicing capacities). The argument here can be expressed as follows. Both bilateral donors and IFIs (at least in their dealings with the poorer countries) are providing finance either as gifts (grants) or on sub-commercial terms, with substantial subsidy elements. Directly or indirectly, they are dispensing public monies paid by the taxpayers of the richer countries. As such, the governments of those countries (and the IFIs which they effectively control) have an obligation to ensure that these resources are well used. This obligation goes beyond the important tasks of requiring proper financial accounting and the avoidance of corrupt practices, to ensuring that the aid is effective in achieving the objectives for which it was provided.

There is a large empirical literature on aid effectiveness. Regarding developmental (as against humanitarian) aid, one of the clearest lessons learned is the large influence of recipient countries' policy environments. In a study of aid and development Krueger *et al.* conclude that

> The most important lesson learned about economic development, and therefore about the role of assistance, is the significance of the overall macroeconomic environment for economic growth. Over the past thirty years appreciation of the importance of appropriate trade and exchange rate policies, of fiscal and monetary policies, and of the overall incentive structure provided by government policies has increased continuously. . . . Experience indicates that the macroeconomic setting is an important determinant of the success of sectoral and project assistance. In countries where the macroeconomic framework is appropriate, real rates of return to investment projects tend to be high.
>
> (Krueger *et al.*, 1989: 306)

More recent research by Hadjimichael *et al.* (1995: 51, 55) and Burnside and Dollar (1997) provide strong corroboration for this. Taking all countries together, they found that aid receipts had little measurable impact on economic growth. However, both studies take the analysis further by developing (largely macroeconomic) indicators of the quality of country policies and investigating the influence of this factor, obtaining 'a robust finding . . . that aid has a positive impact on growth in a good policy environment' (Burnside and Dollar, 1997: 33).

Contrasting performances between otherwise similar economies seem largely explicable in terms of differing policy environments.[5] Reynolds' (1985) survey of long-run development experiences concludes that 'political organisation and the administrative competence of governments' is the single most important explanation of variations in developing countries' growth records and Bleaney (1996: 476) is among several researchers who have found macroeconomic instability to retard economic growth, which, he suggests, occurs by reducing the productivity of capital formation. On similar grounds, Isham and Kaufmann (1995: 22) describe its positive effects on the productivity of investment as 'the forgotten rationale' of policy reform.

Consistent with this, the policy environment has been found to exert a decisive influence on the effectiveness of *project* aid. This emerges strongly from a World Bank evaluation of its past projects (1989a: 30): 'The experience evaluated for this review emphasizes the great extent to which the fate of projects depends on sectoral and macroeconomic policies . . . .' Indeed, it was partly because it saw ill-chosen policies as causing increasing numbers of its projects to fail that the World Bank moved into conditionality-related lending at the end of the 1970s.

Of course, the quality of policy is not the sole determinant, not least because many developing country economies are highly vulnerable to terms of trade and other exogenous shocks. Easterly *et al.* (1993) conducted an econometric examination of the sources of differences in country growth rates and found that shocks exerted as much influence on outcomes as policies, and cautioned against over-emphasis on what can be achieved through policy improvements alone. Nonetheless, there is no serious challenge to the proposition that the quality of the policy environment matters a great deal for economic performance and, therefore, for the ability of aid to achieve its developmental purposes. This gives donors a legitimate interest in the policies of recipient governments and provides a justification for conditionality – always assuming that conditionality actually results in better policies.

Donors' stipulations are, of course, intended to improve the policy environment. However, it can additionally be argued that they have beneficial effects on this beyond their direct impact on the content of policy, and that these additional influences add further to the justification of conditionality. This can be argued along a number of lines.

First, the money and support of donor agencies can be used as *a political resource by reformers* within a government and this may be decisive when reformers and their opponents are fairly evenly balanced. In such situations, the fact that reformers can enlist the staffs of the IFIs and other donor agencies as supporters may give them additional clout in the Cabinet and other legendary smoke-filled rooms where policy decisions are taken. That they can unlock access to large amounts of finance gives them a further standing which is likely to be decisive in circumstances of economic crisis. Conditionality, then, can be seen as strengthening the hands of those within government who support the approach to policy favoured by the donor community. That often amounts to supporting those who place a larger weight on economic, as against political, rationality; and upon improved economic performance in the longer term as against the avoidance of short-term political discomfort.

Conditionality can further be argued to raise the quality and effectiveness of domestic economic policies by *inducing greater consistency over time*.[6] This is important in situations where a government's policies lack credibility among the general population and those outside the country (such as potential investors) whose decisions will impact on the economic results obtained. People may suspect the government's sincerity or its staying-power, expecting today's policy signals to be reversed sooner rather than later. The credibility problem is likely to be particularly large in countries which are in economic crisis and/or have a history of economic instability. In such situations, government measures will be rendered less effective because of countervailing public responses, forcing governments to go further than they would otherwise choose to do in order to counteract these responses and to persuade the public of their seriousness. Such 'over-kill' will, in turn, result in avoidable social and economic costs, and may place the political sustainability of the reforms in jeopardy.

Donor conditionality may be a way of solving the credibility problem. As Collier and his associates have been stressing in their writings, governments which appear, from low international credit ratings and other evidence, to lack credibility could gain substantially from the possibility of using an external 'agency of restraint' as a way of locking into policies which, without such a mechanism of commitment, may not command much confidence (e.g. see Collier *et al.*, 1997). Many of the governments of Africa might fall into this category. The problem arises because investors, and others, see the government as having discretionary power to change course at any time and suspect that it will use that power. The adjustment programmes of the IFIs can be seen as providing a government with a 'commitment technology', allowing it to surrender its discretionary powers in order to pre-commit itself to a defined set of policies for some time into the future. The government may thus be able to enlist the IFIs as tacit guarantors of the time consistency of its policies, raising the credibility and effectiveness of its measures, and lowering their associated costs.

For IFI credits to have such a reputational effect their conditionality must itself be believable, and they must have an adequate array of rewards and penalties to back up their implicit guarantee. Whether or not these conditions are satisfied is one of the main questions taken up in later chapters. However, there is no doubt that governments do often turn to the IFIs, and try hard to comply with policy conditions, for reputational reasons, particularly in the hope of impressing international investors. Moreover, there is some historical evidence that conditionality can indeed play this role. Santaella (1993) develops a model along the lines sketched above and then tests it against the records of six European currency stabilizations sponsored by the League of Nations in the 1920s. That these programmes achieved an impressive record of success he attributes to the League's ability to control and monitor execution of the programmes. 'The control machinery, together with the League's concern to protect its own reputation, appears to have assured the League's reconstruction schemes constituted credible changes of regime' (Santaella, 1993: 618).

Finally, there is *scapegoating*. The IMF in particular has long been inured to a tendency for borrowing governments to use it as a convenient whipping-boy, as a foreign force for the government to blame for unpopular measures in order to deflect criticism from itself. For a long time the Fund quite cheerfully saw itself as a provider of scapegoat services, although it has since become less content with this practice. The argument here, then, is that conditionality, by establishing a readily identifiable scapegoat, can ease the path of reform in political situations where a government regards acceptance of responsibility for policy changes as more risky than the charge that it is subservient to the IFIs.

This is a weak justification for conditionality, however. The prospects for the sustained implementation of reform measures must be poor where governments are so weak as to blame others, to say nothing of their credibility with the public and the perceived legitimacy of the measures in question. The IFIs have therefore come to discourage scapegoating, with the IMF in particular now urging governments to accept responsibility for their own actions and not to pass the buck to the Fund.

In summary, if we view the range of arguments outlined above we can see that the principle of conditionality does not lack legitimating arguments. Essentially, these all boil down to the claim that conditionality contributes directly and indirectly to the improvement of economic policies, which improvements will promote development as well as raising countries' abilities to repay the credits received. The corollary of this, however, is that *the justification of conditionality stands or falls on its ability to change policies for the better*.

There has, in fact, been little controversy about the principle of conditionality, even though there have been fierce disputes about the merits of particular measures. This has perhaps more been due to a pragmatic acknowledgement of the *force majeure* situation than to any intellectual conviction of the policy-improving qualities of conditionality. But the arguments deployed above have considerable force and it is not part of the purpose of this book to challenge the principle of conditionality *per se*.

16

There is one other argument which we should record here. It is not actually an argument in justification of conditionality as such but rather relates to the justification (or rationale) for the IFIs themselves. With the development and increased efficiency of (private) international capital markets, the question has been increasingly asked, why international agencies like the IMF and World Bank are needed (e.g. see Walters, 1994). A number of writers have responded by seeking to justify continuation of these institutions in terms of their superior ability to enforce conditionality, by comparison with private lenders (Sachs, 1989; Rodrik, 1996a; Hopkins *et al*., 1997). So in testing the efficacy of their conditionality in the following chapters we will also be throwing light on the desirability of the continued operations of the Fund and Bank in their present forms.

The justification of conditionality, we have concluded, stands or falls on its ability to improve policies within recipient countries. But does the reality of conditionality live up to the promise of the abstract arguments? The rest of this study is addressed to this question, to an analysis of the effectiveness of conditionality, and to consideration of alternative modes of operation.

The next chapter addresses the experiences of the IFIs with conditionality, largely on the basis of a survey of already-published research. Chapter 3 takes a regional approach, examining the adjustment experiences of South-east Asia and Latin America and the part played by conditionality in these. The next three chapters analyse sources of weakness in the use of conditionality, relating the problem to the idea of 'ownership' (Chapter 4), setting out a principal–agent framework of analysis, and drawing on country case studies to present evidence on effectiveness and sources of weakness (Chapters 5 and 6). Chapter 7 presents the conclusions of the study and discusses alternative modalities for the IFIs and other donor agencies.

Notes

1 See Nelson and Eglinton, 1993 Part I, and Hewitt and Killick, 1996, for fuller discussions.

2 In fact, it may have stopped trying because at the Bank's 1996 Annual Meeting, its President, James Wolfensohn, is reported as having urged a programme of political and social reform in Africa comprising a sustained attack on corruption, nepotism and patrimonialism, devolving power to regional and local administrations, revitalizing civil services, emphasizing professionalism and meritocracy, and acceptance of community groups, NGOs, trades unions and journalists as part of 'the economic development process' (*Africa Confidential* 37(20), 4 October 1996: 8).

3 In his study of American aid to India, Goldsmith documents the substantial attempts USAID made in the mid-1960s to use conditionality to influence India's agricultural policies and remarks (1988: 179) that in this respect policies have come full circle. We should recall too that President Kennedy's 1961 'Message to Congress on Foreign Aid' specified that American aid would henceforth be

contingent on the adequacy of domestic efforts of resource mobilization, self-help and internal reform (Ohlin, 1970: 32) – language that has a decidedly modern ring. Nelson and Eglinton (1992: 26–8) similarly detail the development of American aid conditionality linked to recipients' human rights records during the 1970s, chiefly by the Carter administration. There are also antecedents to present-day approaches to sectoral conditionality in the EC, in its 1960s programme to support agricultural production.

4   The following account relates to economy- or sector-wide conditionality of the type associated with IMF and World Bank adjustment loans. In addition, the Bank attaches policy conditions to all or most of its *projects*, which it calls 'covenants'. A recent report described these in the following terms:

> Loan and credit covenants are legal agreements . . . to achieve agreed objectives or to create conditions considered essential for project success. Covenants typically describe the nature and timing of actions to be taken by the Borrower, providing an opportunity for the parties imple-menting a project to reconsider their obligations if the agreed actions are not taken.
>
> (World Bank, 1994b: 9)

This source reviews the record of thirty-three completed forestry projects and reveals that a total of eighty-seven covenants were attached to these.

5   Thus, Krueger's 1987 comparison of the post-war economic histories of South Korea and Turkey attributes the greater economic progress of the former, starting from a poorer base, to the superior quality of economic policies in Korea. Within Africa, similar explanations have been given for the contrasting economic fortunes in the 1960s and 1970s of the Côte d'Ivoire and Ghana (although more recently it is a comparison that goes against Côte d'Ivoire) and between Kenya and Tanzania in the same period. At a different level, we may get an idea of the importance of policy from the regular exercises undertaken by the World Bank and some other agencies for forecasting alternative future scenarios for the world economy, finding large differences in expected outcomes depending on the assumptions made about the policies adopted.

6   For a presentation of this argument see Santaella, 1993. See also Sachs, 1989; and Rodrik, 1996a.

2

WHAT HAS ADJUSTMENT CONDITIONALITY ACHIEVED?

I Introduction and caution

In a sense, this chapter is about why a study of conditionality is necessary. Were all going well with this way of improving policies there would be little point in the project. The purpose of this chapter, therefore, is to examine the evidence on the effectiveness of conditionality, to examine the extent to which this falls short of the ideal, and to throw light on those aspects which work best and worst.

Virtually all the evidence surveyed below is derived from already-published multi-country, cross-section studies of the effects of the adjustment programmes of the IMF and the World Bank. It is therefore important for readers to be aware of the methodological pitfalls besetting such studies. I have described these in some detail elsewhere (Killick, 1995b: 37–43 – see also Khan, 1990; and Mosley *et al.*, 1991a: 181–7), so will here deal with them in only summary fashion.

There are various problems. Analytically, it can be very difficult to disentangle the several determinants at work in order to isolate the precise effects of an IFI programme. It is, for example, important for our purposes to differentiate the effects of policy changes induced by programmes from those effects resulting from the extra finance that comes with the programmes. It is sometimes difficult to identify satisfactory statistical proxies for the results it is desired to measure. The balance of payments is an example of a 'dependent variable' that is impossible to capture satisfactorily with a single indicator. There are problems, too, with the period over which the analysis is undertaken, with results highly sensitive to the choice made. And, as will be shown later, distortions are introduced by the failure of most studies to adjust for the extent to which programmes are actually implemented: poorly executed programmes cannot be expected to have as much economic impact as fully implemented ones, but most studies do not adjust for this factor.

Above all, there is *the problem of the counterfactual*. We are interested in the extent to which IFI programmes bring about economic improvements. In order to assess that we need to take a view of what would have happened in the absence of the programmes. But the counterfactual is unknowable. All we can do is to find ways of simulating what might have happened, and one of the most important questions that can be asked of any particular method of evaluating programme effects is, how well does it cope with the problem of the counterfactual? It is particularly important to deal with this because, otherwise, results can be seriously distorted by differences in countries' initial situations and by the intervention of exogenous shocks.

Alternative methodologies approach this in different ways:

With–without tests compare the records of two country groups, only one of which has adopted programmes, with the other group used as a control, i.e. as a proxy for the counterfactual. All hinges on the possibility of finding a truly comparable control group and of avoiding the bias arising from the fact that these countries have not agreed programmes with the IFIs, even though, by definition, their economic problems are as serious as those of the programme group.

Before–after tests simply compare the economic situations before and after adoption of a programme, imputing all changes as programme consequences. Although this approach has the merits of ease of implementation and of providing an indication of the extent to which the borrowing governments' desire to achieve economic improvements through adjustment programmes are actually realized, it does not cope well with the problem of the counterfactual, for it rests on the tacit assumption that the counterfactual is represented by a continuation of pre-programme conditions and trends, even though such continuation is often not a viable possibility.

Model-based tests are, in principle, a superior alternative, for it is possible to use models to simulate the outcomes of alternative policy mixes and to present a range of possible results to compare with those of the programme. However, such tests are no better than the models they rest upon, with the risk that the results will reflect model specifications rather than reality. Moreover, the models have to make the risky assumption that parameter values will be unaffected by the policies adopted.

Country case studies, being based on an intimate knowledge of the economies under study, should be able to cope best with the counterfactual problem, providing a locally-informed view of what would have happened in the absence of a programme. Apart from the variable quality of such studies, the chief limitation here is the danger of generalizing from a single case, or even a few. Evidence presented later, in Chapters 5 and 6, attempts to combine the virtues of the in-depth case-study approach with the agglomeration of a substantial number of observations (see also Killick, 1995b: 86–119 for an application of this technique to the appraisal of IMF programmes).

The methodological difficulties just outlined are real and serious. At the same time, they do not entail that there is nothing we can say about the effects of IFI programmes. What they do mean is that we have to be properly cautious in interpreting the results obtained and should not rely heavily on the outcomes of any one study unless substantiated elsewhere. It is possible in this way to build up a 'menu of information', where the results of different studies and methods point to similar conclusions – as is often the case. That is the approach adopted below.

The remainder of this chapter is arranged as follows. Part II makes a first approach to the issue of the effectiveness of conditionality by briefly summarizing the evidence on the economic effects of IFI programmes. It concludes, however, by pointing out the dangers of equating programme results with the effectiveness of conditionality and proceeds, in Part III, to examine evidence on programme implementation and on their revealed influence over economic policies. Part IV then examines the evidence on the connections between programme implementation and economic results, while Part V offers a short note on the social costs associated with adjustment programmes. Part VI summarizes the conclusions.

II Programme effects

The literature

To start with the World Bank, there has surprisingly only been one major independent study of the effects of Bank structural and sectoral adjustment programmes. Published in two volumes, this was undertaken by Paul Mosley, Jane Harrigan and John Toye (1991a and 1991b)[1] and used a combination of in-depth country studies and multi-country statistical and econometric methods in order, *inter alia*, to assess the impact of programmes on growth, exports and other key target variables.

This apart, all other multi-country studies of which we are aware have either been internal evaluations by the World Bank as an institution or by members of the World Bank staff, utilizing similar sources and often sharing methodological approaches.[2] It is proper for readers to approach in-house evaluations with a degree of caution. At worst, such undertakings can take on the character of *ex post* justifications of the Bank's record (an example will be cited later). Even when that element is not present, there may be unintended biases towards over-optimism, and there may be constraints on what the Bank and its staff are free to say to the public about programme failings, so that a misleadingly favourable picture may be painted. With two of the studies reported in Table 2.1 (Corbo and Rojas, 1992; and World Bank, 1992a) there is the added limitation that these appear to be drawn from almost the same data base, even though they undertake somewhat different tests. It is hardly surprising that these two studies yield very similar results; it might be better to regard these as a single set of results.

Table 2.1 Effects of World Bank structural adjustment programmes: summary of results

| The studies | | | | Performance indicators[a] | | | | |
Authorship	Nature	Country coverage	Period	Economic growth[b] (A)	Domestic saving (B)	Capital formation[c] (C)	Exports (D)	Inflation (E)
Corbo and Rojas, 1992	With–without	All	1985–8 compared with:					
			(i) 1970–80	**Positive**	None	Negative	**Positive**	None
			(ii) 1981–84	**Positive**	**Positive**	None	Positive	Accelerated
Elbadawi, 1992	With–without	(i) low-income	1980s	**Positive**	None	Negative	Positive	None
		(ii) Sub-Saharan Africa		None	Negative	**Negative**	**Positive**	Accelerated
Faini et al., 1991	With–without	(i) middle-income	mid-1980s	Positive		Negative	None	Slowed
		(ii) low-income		None	Negative	None	Positive	Accelerated
Mosley et al., 1991	Various methods[d]	All	1980s	None		Negative	**Positive**	
World Bank, 1992a	With–without[e]	(i) middle-income	1986–90 compared with 1971–80	**Positive**	**Positive**	Positive	**Positive**	
		(ii) low-income		**Positive**	Positive	Negative	**Positive**	

Notes:
a Variables tested are usually defined in first differences. Statistically significant results at the 95 per cent level or better are in bold.
b Generally, changes in constant-price GDP.
c Generally, changes in ratio of capital formation to GDP.
d Since multiple methods were employed, the entries here attempt to summarize the authors' overall results.
e Results after correcting for the degree of programme implementation.

Against that, a number of these studies do report results distinctly less positive than the Bank would have wished. Indeed, one of the studies reported below (Elbadawi *et al.*, 1992) was initially published as a Bank *Working Paper* under the title of 'Why Structural Adjustment has not Succeeded in Africa' before someone in the Bank blew the whistle and had the title changed. Also, one of the official Bank studies was commissioned by its Operations Evaluation Department (Jayarajah and Branson, 1995), which, although not entirely free of constraints, is constituted so as to give it maximum independence of the Bank's line departments in going about its work.

Some of the Bank-based studies reported on below are unsatisfactory for other reasons. Most of them are based on the with–without technique, usually comparing 'intensive' adjuster countries with others. The intrinsic limitations of this approach are considerable, with the danger that the results obtained may be an artefact of the sample and comparator countries chosen.[3] It also introduces questions concerning the criteria employed for identifying 'intensive' adjusters and the dangers of introducing additional biases by this route.

There is a larger and on the whole more satisfactory literature on the effects of IMF programmes, and one less dominated by researchers from within the institution. This has recently been described (in Killick, 1995b: Chapter 3), drawing upon the results of a large number of separate studies (see especially pp. 40–3 and accompanying footnotes), so we will not repeat the description here, although the results obtained are briefly summarized below. Staff members of the Fund (particularly of its Research Department, who have demonstrably been given a good deal of freedom in undertaking their tests and publishing their results) and independent academic researchers (including the present writer) have contributed substantially to this literature, using a variety of techniques of greater or lesser sophistication. As will be shown, this research has allowed a substantial body of evidence to be built up concerning the effects of Fund programmes.

A menu of information about programme effects

World Bank programmes

Notwithstanding the limitations of the literature mentioned above, the results of the various tests, summarized in Table 2.1, are sufficiently similar that it is possible to offer some generalizations with reasonable confidence.

The strongest results relate to export performance. All but one of the entries in Column (D) of Table 2.1 indicate a positive association between World Bank programmes and export growth, and most of these relationships are tested as statistically significant (marked in bold). As we will see shortly, a similar result is obtained for IMF programmes. Overall and changing from the positive language of 'correlation' to the normative language of causation, there is a sufficient accumulation of evidence to say with some confidence that in this respect Bank programmes exert a considerable influence in the desired direction.

The second most consistent result, however, is far from being in the desired direction: a negative association between programmes and investment levels (Column (C)). This too is a fairly consistent result (again replicated in the IMF case), although the frequency of statistical significance is lower in this case. There is, however, some evidence for middle-income countries that after an initial dip investment begins to rise again, a result that does not hold for the poorer countries (Jayarajah and Branson, 1995: 126–7). Although this has not been subjected to statistical testing, the usual proximate explanation of the generally negative outcome is that programmes are associated with budgetary cuts which fall disproportionately on public sector capital formation, and that the decline in certain types of public investment may also have a discouraging effect on private sector capital formation (tending to offset the improved private sector incentives flowing from the general reduction in economic distortions).[4]

The results on economic growth are more mixed. Taken together, the Corbo and Rojas and World Bank studies find significantly positive effects (although they also find that growth remains very low in low-income countries). Elbadawi obtains a positive and significant association for low-income countries taken together (but not for sub-Saharan Africa), while Faini *et al.* find no consistent influence in either direction for low-income countries and only a non-significant positive association for middle-income countries. Mosley *et al.* find no consistent association in either direction. The implication of the less negative findings on growth, as compared with investment, is that programmes are associated with improvements in the productivity or utilization of existing resources. However, experience and common sense tell us that growth based on getting more out of existing resources is unlikely to be sustained over the long-term, when growth will necessitate investment (and the technological progress embodied in it). The fall in investment apparently induced by programmes, if it were sustained, could scarcely fail to retard growth eventually.

The results on domestic saving are also mixed, and there are too few of them to permit generalization, as is also the case with the inflation variable.

One other feature to note from these and other studies is that the results tend to vary according to countries' income levels (or stage of development). One of the most consistent results coming out of the World Bank (1992a) study is that responses are slower and weaker in low-income, as compared with middle-income, countries – a point not fully conveyed by the summarization in Table 2.1. As that report noted:

> Among low-income countries . . . [e]xport and saving responses have been much weaker, total investment has fallen on average, and private investment has grown significantly in only a few cases and remains generally at inadequate levels.

> . . . The evidence to date for low-income countries suggests that adjustment lending is a necessary – but not a sufficient – condition for transition to a sustainable growth path.
>
> (World Bank, 1992a: 3)

A second major World Bank study, not included in Table 2.1 because its approach was not comparable, observes a similar difference:

> After several years of adjustment operations, countries seem to fall into two broad categories: those that have emerged from severe disequilibria into sustained growth, and those that are trapped in a cycle of low savings, low investment and low growth. . . . Those countries that have successfully adjusted have had better developed infrastructure; their educational levels have been higher, institutions in their public and private sectors were more mature, and their trade regimes were less highly distorted to begin with.
>
> (Jayarajah and Branson, 1995: 20)

In another study not reported above, Faini and de Melo (1990) found that adjustment packages had been more successful among (mainly middle-income) exporters of manufactures than in (mainly low-income) primary product exporters, where investment had been harder hit and growth had not been resumed.

IMF programmes

The more substantial literature on Fund programmes has yielded a rather richer 'menu of information' about their effects. This has quite recently been surveyed in some detail elsewhere (Killick, 1995b: Chapter 3),[5] and it is therefore unnecessary to set it all out again here. The following are the main relevant generalizations which emerge from the evidence surveyed there. Readers wanting substantiation and further detail are referred to that source and the references it provides. The chief findings on programme effectiveness included:

1   Overall, IMF programmes were associated with a strengthening of countries' balance of payments. Before–after tests on the IMF's ability to improve on the balance of payments (BoP) situations existing immediately prior to programme adoption provide conflicting evidence. Tests for the 1980s suggested moderate improvements in export, current account and overall balance of payment performances in the short-term, but substantial improvements thereafter (despite deteriorating terms of trade); earlier studies obtained weaker results. Before–after evidence on ESAF is also weak but positive. With–without and other approaches

which seek to estimate the counterfactual situation are more encouraging to the Fund, indicating that BoP performance is stronger as a result of programmes than it would otherwise have been.

2   The bulk of the evidence suggests little association between Fund programmes and reduced inflation, with price-reducing and price-raising effects tending to cancel out.

3   A substantial proportion of countries have frequent recourse to Fund credits, contrary to its objectives. From this it may be inferred that programmes are often unable to achieve sustained stabilization.[6] However, study of the situation of frequent-user countries suggests that a majority of them had somewhat stronger BoPs and lower inflation than ten years earlier, although the record on other performance indicators was variable.

4   Tests which analysed changes beyond the first year did not support the view that programme effects were short-lived. Indeed, impact was at its smallest in the twelve months immediately following adoption of a programme but larger in the following two years. A corollary, however, is that governments which turn to the IMF for a quick fix are apt to be disappointed.

5   Most tests indicated that adoption of an IMF programme was not associated with any systematic change in the rate of economic growth, although a minority suggest that there was a significant negative correlation. Simulations suggest that growth will be more favourable with programmes which incorporate investment-raising supply-side measures. Consistent with this, SAF programmes appeared to have done well but ESAFs less well. Overall, there was little evidence that programmes generally had substantial growth effects, positive or negative.

6   Any slow-down in growth may be the result of the substantial and sustained depression of investment rates, which (in common with findings on World Bank programmes) tests rather firmly linked with the adoption of Fund programmes. There was also evidence that some Fund programmes are associated with reductions in import volumes. This was also liable to worsen economic performance, although country studies uncovered little evidence of severe 'import strangulation'.

7   In the case of the Fund, there was little evidence that results varied systematically according to country income level.

Overview

No extreme conclusions emerge from this survey. It would be as inconsistent with the evidence to assert that adjustment programmes have proved wholly ineffective as it would be to claim that this is a success story. The IFIs have only limited revealed power to secure programme objectives. By the same token, they have limited power to do the harm their critics allege. Both Fund and Bank programmes appear to have been instrumental in strengthening export and BoP performance; they seem largely powerless to make much difference to inflation; they do not typically accelerate growth much, nor do they usually force economies into recession; however, the programmes of both agencies are clearly and consistently associated with reduced investment levels, which, if sustained, must exert a drag on economic progress in the longer term.

What does this mixture of success and failure tell us about the effectiveness of IFI policy conditionality? We should tread warily here, for we have so far said nothing about the extent to which 'agreed' programmes are actually executed. On the one hand, it would be accurate to equate programme results with the effectiveness of conditionality only if agreed policies were fully implemented – which is far from being the case. On the other hand, the extent of implementation, determining IFI influence over key policy instruments, itself provides evidence on the potency of this way of trying to improve policy environments. After all, it is through policy improvements that adjustment programmes attempt to achieve their objectives.

The next step, therefore, is to examine the evidence on programme implementation and on the extent to which the lending institutions are able to exercise leverage over the policy variables they need to change if their programmes are to induce the economic outcomes desired of them.

III Implementation and policy leverage

Evidence on implementation

Here again, it is necessary to begin by pointing out some of the pitfalls in interpreting the data on programme implementation. It was argued in Chapter 1 that conditionality should be understood to refer to a requirement for involuntary action of some sort on the part of the recipient government, without which assistance would not be granted or continued. A distinction was introduced between 'pro forma' and 'hard core' conditionality, with the latter consisting of promises of actions which are made only at the insistence of the lender. They are a sub-set of the total policy content of the programme in question, a sub-set likely to include almost all preconditions, a substantial proportion of trigger criteria and some other programme components.

If the validity of this distinction is accepted, it follows that official data on programme implementation, which will include observance of pro forma as well as hard core conditionality, are likely to give a seriously over-stated view of the extent of execution of the *measures the government would not otherwise have introduced*. Unfortunately, there is no way of isolating the hard core element from the general data. Even if we could, there would be the further complication that we would need to differentiate between implementation of preconditions, which by definition must be satisfied, and the others.

27

The task is rendered more complex by the supervention of *shocks* – unexpected shifts in world prices, extreme weather conditions, etc. These are common and sometimes severe and require programmes to be redesigned. Both the Fund and Bank acknowledge this necessity and are accustomed either to grant waivers for minor deviations, or to negotiate new programmes in the event of larger shocks. It would impart an unfairly adverse bias to implementation data to include measures that were not undertaken because they had been overtaken by events, but the data do not necessarily make adequate allowance for this factor.

Biasing the data in the opposite direction is an inclination in some cases for lender and borrower to conspire to pretend that conditions have been complied with when the reality is otherwise. Berg *et al.* provide an example from Senegal:

> One of the conditions of second tranche release in SAL III was that the GOS [Government of Senegal] offer for sale shares in 10 PEs [public enterprises] by September 1987. In fact, nothing had been done by the due date. The GOS met the condition by announcing in the local press that 10 enterprises were for sale. In fact, none were really ready for sale. . . . Even the decision to privatize the firms in question had not been fully discussed within GOS. . . . The Bank in any case accepted the announcement of intention to sell as equivalent to putting up for sale, and thus as meeting the condition for tranche release.
>
> (Berg *et al.*, 1990: 44)

As will become clear in Chapters 5 and 6, such pretence is by no means uncommon, for often both parties have reasons for pretending that failing programmes are on track.

Yet another way in which compliance data may give a misleadingly favourable impression relates to situations – again not uncommon – whereby the government, while formally complying, negates programme conditions by countervailing actions intended to restore the *status quo ante*, or regress after a while. On the basis of their studies of Francophone African countries, Guillaumont and Guillaumont found this was common in the area of trade liberalization:

> For example, a country commits itself to a certain degree of liberalisation of imports, i.e. to eliminate quantitative restrictions: the high percentage of the goods falling under such liberalisation will obviously pertain to those goods for which the quantitative restrictions were not binding. Or, under the pretext of collecting statistical information, administrative permits will persist . . . which, owing to

administrative delays, will have a restrictive effect similar to that of the import licences previously required.

(Guillaumont and Guillaumont, 1994: 86)

A very similar example was uncovered by the country study reported on in Chapter 5, with the Colombian government appearing to comply with requirements to liberalize imports by crossing off the prohibited list items that were not in any case actually imported, leaving the effective coverage of import controls little reduced (Urrutia, 1994: 291–2). Kenya has played similar tricks on import licensing, and has been similarly deceptive regarding its commitments on privatization (Mosley *et al.*, 1991b: 294–5).

A further complication in the measurement of compliance is indicated by the question, compliance by when? Should we be measuring it against the deadlines by which the actions were supposed to be undertaken, or is action at any time acceptable? As will be shown shortly, there is firm evidence of extensive slippage and yet the World Bank produces high implementation statistics, a combination which suggests that action at any time is treated as 'compliance'.

Lastly we should repeat the earlier warning about over-optimism arising from self-evaluation. The World Bank (1995a: 119) itself warns of bias in the high levels of satisfaction expressed in project managers' reports and cites the example of an agricultural adjustment credit in Sierra Leone, which was delayed by 240 per cent, whose disbursements lagged 50 per cent behind schedule but for which the task manager rated implementation as satisfactory.

Subject to the above cautions, on the face of it World Bank data appear to show good levels of implementation. An evaluation of experiences up to 1987 recorded that 60 per cent of all conditions had been fully implemented during the loan period, that there was 'substantial progress' with a further 24 per cent of conditions, and that 68 per cent of key policy conditions were implemented during the loan period (World Bank, 1988, Tables 4.3 and 4.4). The next Bank evaluation (World Bank, 1992a, Table A2.4) shows an even better record, with nearly three-quarters (73 per cent) of all conditions fully implemented and 88 per cent at least substantially so. Even Mosley *et al.* (1991a: 135–6) found 54 per cent of programme provisions fully implemented in the nine countries which they studied, and their study could not be accused of a pro-Bank bias.

Such favourable statistics are, however, hard to reconcile with the general perception within the Bank that programme execution has been poor and that structural adjustment lending has proved a good deal more problematical than its traditional project lending. That this may be a correct impression is supported by evidence on tranche delays. Recall from Chapter 1 that credit tranches are released when the Bank is satisfied with the borrowing government's compliance with trigger conditions. Delays in tranche releases are thus an indication of tardy programme execution.

The data in Table 2.2 relate to the time elapsed between a programme coming into effect and the Bank's release of the second tranche. Since not all trigger conditions are precisely time bound, it is not possible to give an exact measure of slippage. However, most second tranche trigger conditions are expected to occur within 12 months, so a one-year cut-off is regarded by Bank staff as a reasonable measure of delays.

By this standard, then, tranche-release conditions are sufficiently implemented to allow tranche release according to the intended schedule in only a quarter of the cases. Half of programmes are either seriously delayed or, in a minority of cases, abandoned altogether. From another source, we can gauge that both second and third tranche releases, on average, take twice as long as intended (World Bank, 1995a: 119).

Taking this information, adding in the biases imparted by the inclusion of pro forma provisions, by cosmetic implementation and by the non-recording of countervailing actions, and it appears a reasonable inference that weak implementation is indeed a serious problem for the Bank, as indeed it believes itself.

Implementation is a problem for the IMF too. A test somewhat analogous to the data on World Bank tranche delays (Table 2.2) is undertaken for Fund programmes in Killick (1995b: 61–3). The approach there was to analyse the record on programmes which broke down before the end of their intended lives, usually as a result of non-implementation of performance criteria. This

Table 2.2 Time between a programme coming into effect and the release of the second tranche for World Bank adjustment operations, 1989–90 to 1993–4

	Numbers of operations and percentage
1 Within schedule (elapsed time up to 12 months)	25
2 Delayed (12–18 months)	25
3 Seriously delayed (18–24 months)	15
(over 24 months)	27
4 Cancelled	8
Total	100

Source: I am grateful to the Bank for making this unpublished information available.

Note:
It so happens that the number of operations to which these data related adds up to 100, so that the results can be read either as absolute numbers or percentages.

found that of the 305 Fund programmes examined for the period 1979–93 more than half (53 per cent) had broken down in this way. Further analysis revealed that 18 per cent of all stand-bys (or 36 per cent of the discontinued ones) broke down almost immediately, with little or no utilization of the credit beyond the first tranche. Moreover, the trend appeared to be a deteriorating one, with a 61 per cent breakdown rate among programmes in the period from 1990–1 to 1992–3. The analysis excluded ESAF programmes because of the absence of a time series. However, analysis of data as at end-April 1993 revealed that of the twenty-five ESAF programmes that should have been completed by that date, only five had actually been concluded within the original timetable, a further fourteen had been extended and two had apparently been abandoned outright. Data on a further four were impossible to interpret.

There is other evidence of poor execution of IMF conditionality. Edwards (1989, Table 4) examined the compliance record for thirty-four Fund programmes approved in 1983 in respect of the government budget deficit, total domestic credit and domestic credit to government, and found that, overall, less than half (45 per cent) of all such conditions were observed. An unpublished 1991 staff review of experiences with SAF and ESAF programmes threw some additional light, with only slightly over half of all benchmark (i.e. trigger) criteria on schedule, or two-thirds within a few months thereafter.

Much of the above evidence relates to the Fund's programmes in developing countries but it appears that it has encountered similar difficulties in the 'transition' economies of Eastern Europe. A study undertaken for the Economist Intelligence Unit concludes (a) that aggregate indicators of the quality of policy were not significantly related to whether a country had an IMF programme in place or not; and (b) that 'the tendency to backslide has been all-pervasive', with an orthodox policy stance 'rarely sustained for two successive years in any country in this region' (Kekic, 1995: 8).

Two misleading reports

Given these difficulties, there is no presumption that IFI programmes are instrumental in achieving major improvements in the policy environments of borrowing countries. In the absence of direct evidence and given highly imperfect implementation, we cannot assume that adjustment conditionality leads to improved policies. Still less can we take policy improvements as indicating the influence of IFI stipulations. It is necessary to make this point because a publication of the IMF conveys the impression that its ESAF programmes are doing well by associating the existence of programmes with trends in the quality of country policies.

The reference here is to an IMF staff report on its experiences with ESAF programmes, authored by Schadler et al. (1993).[7] This examined the record of the nineteen countries that had undertaken ESAF programmes as of mid-1992. These countries, all but four of which were African, between them had had a total of fifty-one ESAF programmes by that date. The study was particularly concerned with the extent to which programmes were associated with improvements in financial and structural policies and with changes in external and domestic performance; its conclusions were broadly positive. It found important improvements in economic policies – particularly in the areas of trade and exchange liberalization, decontrol of agricultural prices and marketing boards and the liberalization of interest rates – although it added that in most of the countries reviewed reforms remain incomplete. It also found that, on average, ESAF countries had seen improvements in a range of performance indicators, although it acknowledged that there had been disappointments. They found a particularly strong increase in the growth of export volumes, although the current account BoP deficit actually rose from an average of 12.3 per cent of GDP in the pre-programme period to 16.8 per cent in the most recent year, and the report cautioned that external viability remained elusive, with visible improvements in only eleven of the nineteen.

These conclusions were influential. They were welcomed and endorsed by the Executive Board, with the IMF's 1993 *Annual Report* (p. 61) inferring that ESAF 'had proved an effective mechanism for Fund involvement in low-income countries', and they may well have played a crucial role in the Board's decision to renew ESAF in 1994. However, if indeed the Board was swayed by the findings of this report it was probably misguided to be so influenced.

From the perspective of this chapter, the study had the basic weakness of not differentiating outcomes according to the extent of programme implementation – important because we have already shown major slippages in ESAF programmes. Schadler *et al.* shy away from this, however. Instead, they divide the 19 countries into two groups, according to progress made towards BoP viability, and compare these sub-groups in respect of changes in domestic policies and in macroeconomic performance. The rationale for this approach is that if programmes are effective greater action on policy should lead to more progress towards viability. Unfortunately, the evidence for this turns out to be weak, as the authors acknowledge:

> Generally, the countries with the best external and domestic performance undertook stronger financial adjustment measures than those where progress towards external viability and domestic performance was weaker. However, except in the area of fiscal policy, differences were not great.
>
> (Schadler *et al.*, 1993: 37)

Even in the case of fiscal policy the differences were less than 'great' (see Table 2.3).

Table 2.3 Balance of payments viability and central government budget deficits (percentage of GDP)

	Three years before programme	Most recent year
Countries making more progress towards viability		
median	−9.1	−3.0
mean	−12.6	−5.7
Countries making less progress towards viability		
median	−7.2	−4.1
mean	−8.2	−3.9

Source: From Schadler *et al.*, 1993, Table 12.

No statistical testing was undertaken in the report but enough information was presented to permit it. A standard two-tailed test indicated that the differences in the means of the two groups fell well short of normally acceptable significance levels, so this evidence provides little support for the claim that those countries which secured the greatest progress towards viability undertook the strongest measures.

What now of the domestic economic performance of the two sub-groups? On this the authors are clear: 'Those countries that made the most progress in improving their debt position were also those that showed the strongest improvement in their domestic economic performance' (Schadler *et al.*, 1993: 34). Here the evidence seems stronger, as indicated by GDP growth rates (see Table 2.4).

But what light do such results throw on the effectiveness of conditionality? Not much, it appears, unless we can equate the 'progressors' as 'strong

Table 2.4 Balance of payments viability and GDP growth (percentage p.a.)

	Three years before programme	Most recent year
Countries making more progress towards viability		
median	1.4	4.0
mean	1.3	3.7
Countries making less progress towards viability		
median	3.0	2.5
mean	3.3	1.9

Source: Schadler *et al.*, 1993, Table 11.

implementers'. As we have seen, the grounds for doing so are slight but the authors seem to view things that way.

In fact, external influences emerge as the dominant influence on the comparative performances of the two sub-groups. The report shows that the terms of trade experiences of the 'non-progressors' were a good deal worse than their comparators, and that the former received much smaller increases in net financial resource transfers. Not surprisingly, therefore, they suffered far more compression in import volumes, with a 9 per cent annual *decline* against a 3 per cent *rise* for the 'progressors'.

Within the methodology of this report it is impossible to disentangle the influences of policy, resource flows and other factors affecting economic performance. Overall, it is hazardous to infer from it *anything* about the success or otherwise of ESAF programmes. We can accept, and there is supporting evidence elsewhere, that there have been policy improvements in the countries studied, in directions of which the Fund would approve. We can (just) accept that there is evidence (consistent with data presented earlier in this chapter) of some improvement in external performance, perhaps in domestic economic performance too. What we cannot do is to accept that the authors have demonstrated any systematic connection between these changes and implementation of ESAF conditionality.[8]

Although its approach is different and less unsatisfactory, a World Bank study of *Adjustment in Africa* (World Bank, 1994a) similarly conveys a misleadingly positive message. This study is based on the records of twenty-nine sub-Saharan African countries, all of which had received at least one structural adjustment credit during 1987–91, and focuses on the connections between changes in their economic performance and the extent to which they implemented policy reforms of the type associated with Bank structural adjustment programmes. This study has since been up-dated by the principal authors of the original and a colleague, refining the analysis and bringing in data for 1992 (Bouton *et al.*, 1994).

Neither of these reports is addressed directly to the question of the effectiveness of the Bank's structural adjustment conditionality *per se*. However, this self-imposed limitation does not stop the main report from generalizing about the efficacy of adjustment:

> In the African countries that have undertaken and sustained major policy reforms, adjustment is working. But a number of countries have yet to implement the reforms needed to restore growth. And even among the strongest adjusters, no country has gone the full distance in restructuring its economy.
>
> (World Bank, 1994a: 1)

Bouton *et al.* (1994: 1) conclude in the same vein ('improved policies are still associated with better performance, but countries still fall short of having sound policies') but report some deterioration in policy stances during 1992.

We will return later to the connection between performance and policy change. Our interest here is rather with the connection, if any, between adjustment conditionality and policy reform. Fortunately, enough information is available from these and other World Bank sources to allow us to juxtapose the results of this pair of studies with the incidence of World Bank structural adjustment programmes.

First, note the finding of the main report concerning the quality of macro-economic policies in the twenty-six countries investigated. These were assessed both as to the direction of change in macro policies between 1981–6 (roughly the pre-adjustment period) and 1987–91, and the judged quality of policy stance as at 1990–1. The results are set out in Table 2.5, alongside information about the number of Bank programmes in each category.

The most startling result is that the Bank viewed only one country as having achieved even 'adequate' macro policies by 1990–1 even though over the whole period in question this group of countries had between them obtained no less than ninety-three structural adjustment credits (they had also had a total of ninety-five high-conditionality IMF programmes). Even the countries with 'poor' or 'very poor' policies had received thirty adjustment loans. Evidently, the Bank's structural adjustment conditionality has exerted a less than vice-like grip over policies. While it is true that those with the better policies have had more programmes per country, we can see from the assessment of changes in policy in 1987–91 that these were judged to have

Table 2.5 Adjustment programmes and the quality of macro policies

Macro policy change, 1981–6 to 1987–91	Numbers of countries	Numbers of SACs
Large improvement	6	15
Small improvement	9	25
Deterioration	11	19

Macro policy stance, 1990–1	Numbers of SACs	1980–91
Adequate	1	11
Fair	13	52
Poor	6	14
Very poor	6	16

Source: World Bank, 1994a, Table 2.5 and Figure 2.3.

35

deteriorated in eleven countries even though they had received a total of nineteen programmes during the period of deterioration.

The Bouton *et al.* (1994) paper updating the main study also throws further interesting, if unencouraging, light on the subject. The authors undertook some reclassification of countries' 1990–1 policy stances on the basis of a refinement in methods and more up-to-date information, and undertook a reclassification based on 1992 information. Their results are set out in Table 2.6. To their results we have added indications of those countries which had Bank adjustment programmes during 1992 (for at least half of the year, but in most cases much more than half, and often dating back before 1992).

For 1990–1 the results of the earlier study were largely confirmed, with relatively minor changes in the groupings. However, comparison of the 1990–1 and 1991–2 results produced more dramatic results:

- There was an overall deterioration in policies, with more countries in the bottom group and fewer with 'fair' policies. Eight countries moved down (two all the way from 'fair' to 'very poor'), while only two moved up.
- Twelve of the fifteen bottom countries had adjustment programmes during 1992, while only five of the top ten countries had programmes. Furthermore, eight of the eligible thirteen bottom countries (i.e. excluding Sierra Leone and Zambia) had programmes with the IMF for the same period.
- Seven of the eight countries whose policy stances are shown as having deteriorated had Bank programmes in 1992, indicating that programme conditionality was unable to prevent policies worsening. Of these seven, five had also signed programmes with the IMF covering 1992.

This analysis shows the ineffectiveness of the Bank's (and the IMF's) adjustment conditionality. It would be impossible to predict the likely direction of change in the quality of policies from information about the IFIs' adjustment lending. As much was hinted at in the original Bank study, with the well-hidden and opaque statement (World Bank, 1994a: 216) that 'there was no clear relationship between change in net external transfers per capita and change in macroeconomic policies' – a passage which came a little clearer in a pre-publication draft: 'the intensity of adjustment lending is not strongly correlated with policy reform.' Indeed not. Properly understood, the main conclusion of *Adjustment in Africa*, that 'In the African countries that have undertaken and sustained major policy reforms, adjustment is working', is defensible, but it is clear from the evidence just presented that it would be quite wrong (but temptingly easy)[9] to infer from this that adjustment *programmes* are working. Whatever is working does not appear to bear much systematic relationship to adjustment lending. This conclusion is supported by the important work on the influence of the policy environment on aid effectiveness by two Bank staff members, Burnside and Dollar (1997, footnote 10),

Table 2.6 Macroeconomic policy stances, 1990–1 and 1991–2, and the incidence of structural adjustment programmes in 1992

	1990–1	*1991–2*[a]
Policies adequate	The Gambia	The Gambia
Policies fair	Burundi	⇑**Burkina Faso**
	Ghana	Burundi[*]
	Kenya	**Ghana**
	Madagascar	
	Malawi	⇑ ⇑Mozambique[*]
	Mali	Niger
	Mauritania	**Senegal**[*]
	Niger	**Tanzania**[*]
	Senegal	**Uganda**[*]
	Tanzania	
	Togo	
	Uganda	
Policies poor	Benin	**Benin**
	Burkina Faso	**Central Africa Republic**
	Gabon	⇓ Madagascar
	Nigeria	⇓ **Mali**
	Rwanda	⇓ **Togo**[*]
	Zimbabwe	
Policies very poor	Congo	Cameroon[*]
	Côte d'Ivoire	Congo[*]
	Cameroon	**Côte d'Ivoire**[*]
	Mozambique	⇓ ⇓**Kenya**[*]
	Sierra Leone	⇓ ⇓**Malawi**[*]
	Zambia	⇓ **Nigeria**[*]
		⇓ **Rwanda**
		Sierra Leone[#]
		Zambia[#]
		⇓ **Zimbabwe**[*]

Source: Adapted from Bouton *et al.*, 1994, Table 17; and from unpublished World Bank information on adjustment lending in 1992.

Notes:

[a] Countries in the 1991–2 column shown in bold had a World Bank adjustment programme for at least six months during 1992. Arrows indicate movements during 1992 (two arrows indicate a movement by two categories, e.g. from 'fair' to 'very poor')

[*] denotes countries which agreed IMF stand-by, Extended Facility or ESAF programmes to cover at least six months of 1992

[#] denotes countries ineligible for IMF credits during 1992 as a result of being in arrears with payments on previous credits cited in the previous chapter, 'who found no association between the volume of aid and improvements in policy'.

We will try to make sense of these results later in this volume but should already signal one possible explanation of the weakness of the observed relationship between adjustment programmes and policy improvements: moral hazard. It is a long-standing argument of some critics of the IFIs that their lending may actually retard reform, by providing money that allows governments to continue to defer politically painful but economically necessary measures. All depends on the motivation and strength of borrowing governments. Haggard and Webb studied the influence of external support on the reform process in a number of countries and concluded that

> When resources are made available to governments disposed *against* reform, such as Mexico in the late 1970s, Turkey in the late 1980s (on fiscal reform) and Senegal during parts of the 1980s, the financing allowed government to postpone, rather than pursue, adjustment.
>
> (Haggard and Webb, 1994: 27)

If such behaviour is common, the overall connection between programmes and policy change becomes quite unpredictable, and it may well be that this factor helps to explain the absence of clear connections between adjustment credits and policy change, as described above.

Direct evidence on policy leverage

There is other evidence which provides a more nuanced view on the extent of influence of adjustment conditionality over specific aspects of policy. From this some rather clear generalizations emerge.

Three key determinants of the extent of leverage emerge from empirical studies:

1 the *simplicity* of the policy instrument in question;
2 the ease with which it can be *monitored*; and
3 its amenability to *treatment as a precondition* (or prior action – see Chapter 1).[10]

The latter point is obvious: it is difficult, if not impossible, to evade preconditions, so leverage is likely to be at a maximum over policy variables that can be treated in this way. The relevance of the ease with which implementation of a measure may be monitored is also clear: governments may be tempted to dissimulate if they are in a position to conceal what is really going on.

As regards simplicity, this is determined by the extent of direct control exerted over an instrument by the government, the number of individuals and agencies through which a change has to be negotiated and effectuated, and by the strength and ability to organize of those opposed to change.

The exchange rate (which is principally within the sphere of influence of the IMF, rather than the World Bank) is the policy instrument that best passes these tests and indeed the evidence points to strong association between adjustment programmes and devaluations. It is well known that the Fund has frequently insisted on a devaluation as a programme precondition and Killick (1995b: 127) shows IMF programmes to be correlated with substantial, significant and sustained exchange rate depreciations, in both nominal and real terms. Two World Bank evaluations of experiences with structural adjustment lending (World Bank, 1992a; and Jayarajah and Branson, 1995) similarly report a strong association of programmes with currency devaluations (although it is likely that this was a coat-tail effect, resulting from the cross-conditionality with the IMF).

There is evidence that programmes exert leverage over other price-based policy instruments, although it is less strong than for the exchange rate. Killick's (1995b: 127) survey of the evidence on IMF programmes concludes that these probably exert considerable influence over such variables as interest rates and public enterprise pricing, and Jayarajah and Branson (1995: 145) report a general reduction in the occurrence of negative real interest rates.[11]

When attention is turned to the less amenable policy variables, the results are more problematical. Take first programme influence on governments' budget deficits – arguably the single most important macroeconomic policy variable. As regards the Fund, the evidence has been summarized as showing that, while there is a tendency for budget deficits to be reduced, this effect is weak and variable, and there is much slippage in the implementation of programmes' fiscal provisions (Killick, 1995b: 127). Conway (1994: 380–1) produces a more positive result, with programmes associated with a significant reduction in the budget-deficit-to-GNP ratio. This was achieved, however, on the basis of reductions in public sector capital formation (recall the result reported earlier of negative programme effects on investment), with no significant reductions in government current expenditures.

The evidence on the budgetary effects of Bank programmes is quite mixed. Faini *et al.* (1991) found some deterioration in fiscal indicators, while the World Bank (1992a) found evidence of declining budget deficits. Jayarajah and Branson's evaluation (1995: 120) for the World Bank also found that twenty-eight out of forty-two programme countries reduced their fiscal deficit ratios, but this too was achieved by cutting back on public investment, rather than through more fundamental fiscal reforms: 'On the expenditure side, the relatively poor performance has been the result of failure to reform in any meaningful way the expenditure planning, evaluation and monitoring mechanisms. In this sense structural adjustment is yet to come' (1995: 67). A report by the Bank's Operations Evaluation Department is brutally frank in coming to the same judgement:

fiscal adjustment has not resulted in more efficient spending in most countries. In many countries, expenditure reductions have worsened existing biases and inefficiencies. The extent of public expenditure restructuring has been very limited during the adjustment era. In most countries for which data are available, more resources were allocated to services that benefit the non-poor. The bias towards higher education appears to have worsened during adjustment, and significant imbalances between spending for hospital care and primary care have also remained in the health sector.

(World Bank, 1995c: 15)

Toye and Jackson (1996: 9) suggest one reason why the IFIs have had problems achieving expenditure improvements: their conditionalities have focussed much too exclusively on budgeted figures which, however, 'tend to be symbolic figures' and in many cases are 'pure fiction'.

The record with trade liberalization also appears unsatisfactory, for Oyejide *et al.*'s (1997) study of this in African countries found that of ten countries which had undertaken liberalization there had been subsequent reversals in seven of them.

The control of domestic credit creation is, of course, at the theoretical core of the IMF's approach to the strengthening of the BoP, so we might expect its programmes to exert a particularly strong influence over this variable. The facts suggest otherwise, however, probably because of programmes' limited power over budgetary outcomes. My own tests indicated some reduction in the rate of credit expansion and in the value of credit relative to GDP, but the effects were small and non-significant (Killick, 1995b: 73). Contrary both to expectations and Fund intentions, there was no significant reduction in the share of total credit going to the central government *vis-à-vis* the private sector. Conway (1994: 380–1) actually found IMF programmes to be associated with an increase in the expansion of domestic credit, although this result was not statistically significant.

Institutional reforms lie at the opposite end of the simplicity–complexity spectrum by comparison with currency devaluations: they are not for the most part amenable to treatment as preconditions; donor agencies are liable to have difficulties in keeping track of the extent of compliance; and such reforms are often imperfectly under the control of the central authorities, take time, typically involve a number of agencies and are liable to encounter opposition from well-entrenched beneficiaries of the *status quo*. It is hardly surprising, therefore, that the literature is virtually unanimous in agreeing that progress in this area has been the most imperfect and slowest. In the area of privatization, for example, conditionality has little revealed ability to achieve the implementation of a vigorous and efficient programme when this is against the inclinations of the government in question (see Berg, 1993: 26, on experiences in Africa). Much the same is true of civil service reorganizations, and the reform of agricultural marketing or of financial systems.

To sum up, then, the last two sections have shown that both IFIs experience considerable difficulties in ensuring the timely implementation of their policy stipulations, with little apparent connection between the existence of IFI-supported programmes and improvements in policy stance. With the exception of a small family of instruments with rather special characteristics, revealed leverage over policies is quite limited, particularly over the more 'structural' aspects of adjustment.

How much does this matter? Were programme provisions more fully and promptly executed, would this be likely to make much difference to the performance of the adjusting economies? To put the question another way, is the response of economies a function of the degree of programme implementation?

IV Implementation and results

The answer is in the affirmative, although with some qualifications.

To start with the World Bank's own evidence, we have earlier noted that the connections between programmes and economic results found in World Bank (1992a, Table A4) and reported in Table 2.1 were stronger and more favourable when the data were corrected for the degree of programme implementation. In fact, this was true in fifteen out of sixteen pairs of tests, although the differences were not typically large and the significance level was satisfactory in only two cases.

While cautioning that country compliance with Bank conditionality was no guarantee of successful adjustment,[12] the second World Bank report (Jayarajah and Branson, 1995, Table 2.2), based on a study of forty-two countries, included an interesting exercise showing that, when undertaken, programme measures generally moved economic performance in the desired direction, as is shown in the results reproduced in Table 2.7. Reduced fiscal deficits generally resulted in reduced inflation, devaluation improved resource balances, interest rates reforms raised foreign exchange reserves.

The Bank's report on *Adjustment in Africa* (1994a) also marshals evidence in support of its basic argument that economic performance was improved in countries which undertook and sustained appropriate macroeconomic policies (see especially pp. 140–1). The tests applied were fairly rudimentary. Schatz (1994) has shown that there were many exceptions to the general result, and Mosley *et al.* (1995) also point to substantial methodological weaknesses in the Bank's approach, although their own tests agree with the Bank on the importance of exchange rate and certain fiscal measures for economic growth. The Bank's results have been defended by White (1997), however, whose re-estimations for the same sample of countries concur in finding improved macroeconomic policies to have promoted faster growth, even though he too is

41

Table 2.7 Policies and results in forty-two adjusting countries (number of countries)

	Internal balance	*Resource balance*	*External balance*
Policy indicator	Reduce fiscal deficit	Real devaluation	Reduce negative interest differential
Desired outcome	Reduce inflation	Increase resource balance	Increase net foreign exchange reserves
Right policy/ Right outcome	24	32	31
Wrong policy/ Wrong outcome	10	2	5
Right policy/ Wrong outcome	4	3	6
Wrong policy/ Right outcome	4	5	–

Source: Jayarajah and Branson, 1995, Table 2.2.

critical of shortcomings in the Bank's approach. The thrust of the Bank's findings is further reinforced in the follow-up study by Bouton *et al.* (1994: 25–6) mentioned earlier, which again showed an apparently rather robust statistical connection between changes in growth rates and changes in macro policies, with exchange rate and fiscal (but not monetary) policy variables confirmed as having significant explanatory power.

The independent investigation by Mosley *et al.* (1991a, Chapter 7) broadly confirmed the positive influence of programme implementation on economic outcomes, with compliance having favourable effects on GDP growth and (more temporarily) on export growth. In their case, however, they found trade liberalization to provide the strongest policy explanation for the improvement in economic outcomes (1991a: 228).[13] Overall, they concluded that adjustment policy packages did promote GNP and export growth but *'if and only if the conditions are implemented'* (1991a: 282 [italics in original]).

The results relating to IMF programmes are less favourable. While Conway (1994: 385) found evidence that programme effects (positive and negative) were stronger where there was evidence of programme implementation, my own investigations were less reassuring (Killick, 1995b: 75). Comparisons of outcomes between programmes that were completed and those that were not (generally because of noncompliance with conditions) indicated that, focusing on the BoP record as the main target variable, it was not obvious that governments which completed their programmes got superior results. The various BoP indicators pointed in different directions and variations in results as between the completers and non-completers were statistically non-significant. It is possible that this result is connected to the non-significance of monetary policy variables found by Bouton *et al*. I have argued at length elsewhere that the Fund is mistaken to place so much faith in monetary policy variables because these are unlikely to influence outcomes in the ways that the Fund's model postulates (Killick, 1995b, Chapter 4).

Overall, a positive correlation between programme implementation and economic performance could be expected. Quite apart from the results just summarized, there is a good deal of evidence that the types of policy change which adjustment programmes seek to secure do indeed result in higher rates of growth and other economic benefits.[14] Openness and export success tend to have this effect. So does the avoidance of large macroeconomic imbalances. So does a policy strategy which seeks to work through, and strengthen, market mechanisms. In other words, the problem is not with the general thrust of the policies the IFIs are promoting but with the poor execution of these – with the modalities not the policy strategy.

V Social effects and the management of change

Few changes of economic policy do not affect the distribution of incomes within society and many of the measures commonly written into adjustment programmes are liable to impact powerfully on the welfare of different social groups. Economic policy reform is hence liable to have major political ramifications, creating risks for reforming governments and necessitating sensitive political management.

In later chapters we will be much concerned with the ways in which conditionality impacts upon political processes and how it affects politicians' calculations of the likely costs and benefits of reforms. As will be shown later, domestic politics are likely to have a dominant influence on what reforms are undertaken and persisted with. It will be useful here, therefore, to bring together such generalizations as are possible on programmes' social consequences, as they impact upon politicians' expectations of cost–benefit outcomes.

A factor which gives added weight to the importance of the social effects of programmes is what has been called 'the classical asymmetry'. This refers to the common situation in which the economic gains from a programme of reform are diffused among wide sections of society while the losses that occur are sharply concentrated on well-defined groups who are often well organized.[15] Such situations obviously create special requirements for skilful political management or, in its absence, can be a potent reason for the indifferent implementation record described earlier.

Against this background, what generalizations can be offered about the social effects of programmes as they impact upon the political calculus?[16] The first of these is tedious but necessary: *the effects are likely to be complex and varied.*

43

Some of the complexities of assessing the likely social effects of structural adjustment are illustrated in Table 2.8, which is reproduced from a survey of the poverty effects of adjustment programmes (Killick, 1995d). Although the effects will vary from economy to economy, the Table attempts to illustrate for a 'typical' developing economy the impact of those measures commonly incorporated in adjustment programmes which are most likely to affect the welfare of poverty groups.

Note that the effects are liable to vary across different groups of the poor. Import liberalization, for example, is liable to harm the urban working poor by forcing the closure of inefficient local import-substituting industries which

Table 2.8 Potential impact of selected adjustment measures on various poverty groups

Adjustment measures	Urban poor		Smallholders			Rural poor
	Working poor	Un-employed	Cash crop	Food exporters	Food importers	Landless/ working poor
Devaluation	N	P	P	?	?	P
Other export promotion		P	P			P
Import liberalization	N	P	P	?	P	?
Government food subsidy reductions	N	N	N	P	N	N
Civil service retrenchment	N					
Cuts in social services	N	N	N	N	N	N
Increased indirect taxes	N	N	N	N	N	N
Cost recovery measures	N	N	N	N	N	N
Public enterprise reform/privatization	N	P	P	P		
Wage freeze	N	P		N		?
Credit squeeze	N	?				

Notes:
N = substantial and negative
P = substantial and positive
? = potentially substantial but sign indeterminate
Blank entries indicate no substantial effect

can no longer compete, throwing them out of work. Those who are already unemployed in the urban economy, on the other hand, are liable to gain through improved availability and quality of imported supplies. The same goes for smallholders growing cash crops, who may benefit from lower prices and more dependable availability of such inputs as fertilizers, insecticides and farm equipment. Smallholders who grow food but still need to buy some of their requirements ('food importers') may also gain through lower prices as a result of import competition. The welfare outcome for smallholders who market a surplus of foodstuffs ('exporters') is indeterminate, with both welfare-raising and welfare-reducing influences at work; this is also liable to be the situation with the landless who rely on agricultural employment and off-farm sources of income. And so on: the exercise could be repeated for each of the policy measures selected. It could also be extended to include various groups of the not-so-poor with a similar outcome: from any one measure there are likely to be some losers, some gainers.

Table 2.8 also suggests a second generalization: *social outcomes are likely to be strongly influenced by the initial situation.* One aspect of this is the way in which programme effects are likely to be affected by the distribution of asset ownership. For example, the outcome in the rural economy will be much affected by whether smallholders participate in cash crop production or whether this is largely confined to estate production.

Another key aspect of the initial situation is the severity of the economic situation which leads to the adoption of a programme in the first place. For example, in Latin America during the 1980s severe reductions in absorption (consumption and investment) became *inevitable* after the debt crisis broke in 1982–3, given governments' decisions to honour their countries' debt commitments and the policies adopted by creditors.[17] Much the same can be said about Africa, where the deep-seated reasons for that continent's economic malaise impact severely on what, or how fast, improvements can be achieved through adjustment programmes. However, a severe economic crisis can cut the other way, by demonstrating the inescapable necessity for a change of direction, raising people's tolerance of a policy transformation and the hardships it is liable to bring, particularly when it brings to power a regime not tainted with the failures of the past. This factor operated powerfully in Eastern Europe, for example, at the time of the overthrow of communist regimes.

A third general result suggested by Table 2.8 is that *the burdens of adjustment are liable to fall disproportionately on members of the urban population.* The Table concentrates on poverty groups and shows major differences in impact as between the urban and rural poor (compare the first two columns with the rest). Indeed, so strong is this effect that adjustment has been observed to have significantly narrowed urban–rural inequalities in a number of countries. Among the countries studied in Killick (1995d), this was observed for Côte d'Ivoire, Ghana, Morocco and Tanzania. The importance of urban and rural effects of adjustment can be gauged from data in Psacharopoulos *et al*. (1992, Table 4.4) showing that during the 1980s absolute poverty in Latin America and the Caribbean changed from being predominantly rural to a majority of the poor becoming urban-based.

Looking beyond poverty groups, the anti-urban bias is still likely to hold. As a rule, many of the benefits of the interventionist policies which adjustment programmes generally seek to end accrue to urban groups: industrialists and their workers who benefit from undiscriminating protectionism; public enterprise managers and labour forces, who also enjoy privileged protection; 'rent-seekers' lobbying for a share in the scarcity premia resulting from import licensing and other discretionary interventions; and so on.

In fact, one of the few reasonably firm generalizations it is possible to report concerning the distributional effects of adjustment programmes is that they are associated with declining real formal-sector wages. In consequence, Pastor (1987) found for Latin American countries that IMF programmes were strongly and significantly associated with declines in labour's share in the functional distribution of income. Some of the country studies in Killick (1995d) were consistent with this (and none contradicted it). Job losses are a serious threat. Reductions in civil service over-manning are often included in IFI programmes. Reduced employment is also likely to result from measures to raise the efficiency of public enterprises, or to privatize them. It may result from reduced protection of local import-substituting industries. People with previously adequate incomes who find their principal source of income destroyed as a result of such unemployment-creating measures are often styled the 'new poor', and these unfortunates are likely to belong chiefly to the urban population. Although it is increasingly common to include 'safety net' provisions in programmes, to mitigate the losses of this class, such measures are often not very effective and many of those at risk (and their families) end up with reduced real incomes.[18]

This anti-urban bias brings governments face-to-face with the realities of 'the classical asymmetry' because the urban groups are liable to be rather well organized – in chambers of commerce, trade unions, within the leaderships of political parties, and so on – and spatially located so as to be able to make a lot of political trouble. Rurally-based beneficiaries from policy reforms rarely have equivalent political weight.

The difficulty of the political management of policy reform is compounded, of course, by the rather weak macroeconomic results of programmes described in Part II. Those who have researched the politics of adjustment are virtually unanimous about one thing: the importance for the political sustainability of the process of being able to offer populations tangible benefits from the change, without inordinate delay. For example, Haggard and Kaufman's comparative analysis of the politics of adjustment concludes, 'all the chapters stress a simple, but crucial point: reforms are unlikely to be sustained unless they generate adequate economic pay-off to secure at least the acquiescence of broad segments of the electorate' (1992: 36). Nelson's path-breaking work on the same topic reaches an identical conclusion:

> continued acquiescence depends on demonstrated results. The general public and even the educated elite in most countries mainly judge the government's economic management by their own economic situations. They cannot be expected to consider whether things would be still worse in the absence of the policies adopted, nor to separate the tangled interactions of announced policies, actual government actions . . . and factors beyond government control. . . . In many countries, continued economic stagnation or decay has destroyed popular confidence in the government's ability to manage the economy, as well as confirmed initial skepticism about the effects of the policies urged by external agencies.
>
> (Nelson, 1989: 7)

(This, it might be added, is why it is so important that there should be an adequate volume of international assistance available in support of adjustment programmes, to ease the transitional dislocations and speed up the delivery of tangible benefits.)

A final generalization, however, is that *large social consequences are the exception rather than the rule*. For example, while the jobs of public sector employees are obviously put at risk by IFI conditionality which stresses the need to reduce the role of the state, reform and retrench the civil service and privatize public enterprises, actual outcomes are rarely draconian. Thus, the World Bank's *Adjustment in Africa* study (1994a: 170) reported that there had been substantial retrenchments in only a few countries.

The same is true with government spending on social services. There is a widespread belief that programmes are associated with particularly heavy cuts in social spending but the evidence shows that such spending is actually one of the more protected categories of expenditure. Although there *have* been serious declines in the quantity and quality of provision in Africa and Latin America, this deterioration appears to be largely attributable to the rising claims of interest payments on the public debt and general conditions of budgetary stringency, than to the specific provisions of adjustment programmes.[19] It is not typically the case that the axe falls most heavily on welfare services. Usually, it is the capital budget which is chiefly at risk. However, the protection is only relative: social spending *is* cut, only less so than certain other categories. Moreover, when expressed in per capita terms, the fall in service provision can be large.

However, it is not clear that the existence of an adjustment programme, *per se*, makes a decisive difference to the pattern of government spending. Harris and Kusi's 1992 study of the effects of IMF programmes showed these to be associated with relative declines in subsidy expenditures but that there was no obvious programme impact on the functional classification of expenditures, by comparison with a control group of non-programme countries, with the shares of health and education largely unaffected. Pradhan and Swaroop (1993) also found that social spending followed similar trends in programme and non-programme countries, in a study which included the effects of World Bank as well as IMF programmes. Stewart (1991) obtained more adverse results for Bank programmes but for an earlier period. Van der Hoeven and Stewart (1993, Table 8) show that, on average, there was a tendency for the share of social expenditures to fall (as proportions of total spending and GDP) among 'intensively adjusting' Latin American countries in 1981–90, by comparison with non-adjusting countries, but that per capita social service expenditures improved among adjusting countries, compared with a 43 per cent decline among non-adjusters.

The severity of the social consequences of conditionality can be approached from a different direction, by examining whether there is any correlation between IFI programmes and political instability. This has mainly been explored in connection with IMF programmes, which have sometimes been alleged to be destabilizing. Here, too, it is difficult to distinguish programme effects from those of the economic crises which often precede the Fund but, after attempting to control for this and other non-programme influences, Sidell (1988) concluded from a large sample of cases that IMF programmes had not significantly increased political instability. He did not even find any correlation with episodes of collective protest. One major limitation of this study, however, was that it related only to 1969–77. A more up-to-date study is available for 1976–85 but confined to sub-Saharan Africa (Moore and Scarritt, 1990). This similarly concluded that Fund programmes had had no significant impact on the nature of African governments.

Does this mean that, despite the asymmetrical incidence of social costs on urban groups, the political management of adjustment is not such a difficult task after all? The evidence could be read that way but this would not accord with common sense. Unfortunately, the evidence is flawed in not being corrected for the degree of programme implementation. In other words, *non-implementation may be a way of managing (or avoiding) the large political risks attendant upon policy reform.* There are many examples of governments which back-track on programme provisions when they run into organized opposition. One of the reasons why public sector job losses tend to be much smaller than predicted is because governments have been particularly reluctant to honour conditions requiring public sector retrenchments and privatizations, as described earlier.

If indeed non-execution of programme conditions is a necessary feature of the political management of policy change, minimizing the destabilization inherent in major policy shifts, we can conclude with a hypothesis, to be examined later. This is to the effect that *political management is crucial to sustained policy reform but conditionality makes such management more difficult, and that the imperatives of political management are a prime reason for generally rather poor implementation.* On this view, governments need latitude to design and manage reforms in ways that will maximize support whereas conditionality is designed to limit governments' freedom of action (and inaction):

> foreign actors should give governments *as much freedom as possible* in choosing stabilization measures, in order to reconcile the various constraints. . . . The political context greatly differs from one country to another, and from one month to the next within a given country; only the authorities of the country concerned can adapt the programme to changing political constraints as the adjustment progresses.
>
> (Haggard *et al.*, 1995: 128; italics in original)

A tension can thus be seen between conditionality and political management. We will take this topic further, particularly in Chapter 6.

VI Conclusions

The story that emerges from this chapter is as follows.

The adjustment programmes of the World Bank and IMF achieve their economic objectives only to a limited degree. They appear to be instrumental in strengthening export and BoP performance but seem to have little impact on inflation; they do not typically make much difference to the pace of economic growth, in either direction; but they are consistently associated with reduced investment levels, which threaten economic progress in the longer term.

The limited revealed power of programmes is not necessarily attributable to any deficiencies of IFI policy conditionality, however. At least three possible lines of explanation suggest themselves: programmes were knocked off track by exogenous factors; the programmes were poorly designed and the policies ill-chosen; the envisaged policy changes were not executed.

Although implementation is difficult to render into reliable statistical indicators, the evidence suggests that implementation is indeed a problem. Probably the most reliable information relating to the World Bank relates to delays in tranche releases (resulting from laggard implementation), showing half of programmes to be seriously delayed. Implementation is a problem for the IMF too, with many programmes breaking down and much delay in execution.

It is not surprising, therefore, that neither organization has been able to show a systematic connection between their own programmes and improvements in economic policies, as demonstrated in recent published evaluations of experiences with the Fund's ESAF facility and the Bank's adjustment programmes in Africa. It would not be possible to predict changes in the quality of countries' economic policies from information about IFI adjustment lending, a conclusion similar to Mosley *et al.*'s (1991a: 299) answer to their own question whether aid confers power on the World Bank to change recipient policies: 'a little, but not as much as the Bank hoped'.

It is similarly not surprising that the revealed leverage of programmes over specific policy instruments is quite weak. It appears that they can make a decisive difference to policy instruments which are suitable for being treated as preconditions, can be readily monitored, and are simple in the sense that they are directly controlled by the government, involve a small number of individuals and agencies, and are not easy to organize against. But the results are more problematical when it comes to more complex structural or institutional measures.

This limited ability of conditionality to bring about policy change is unfortunate, however. The indications are that the approach to policy which they embody does result in improved economic performance, where it is instituted (except, perhaps, in the area of monetary policy). In other words, it does not appear to be the case that adjustment programmes produce weak results because their policy thrust is ill-chosen (although there *is* often plenty of scope for arguing about the design and sequencing of specific measures). We agree with the 1995 judgement of a Bank Working Group, that 'generally adjustment lending has mostly promoted good policies, but got weak program results' (World Bank, 1995d: 1).

The weak implementation of IFI policies is therefore regrettable. Welfare would usually be increased, perhaps transformed in some cases, were programmes a more effective way of improving policies. It is therefore important to discover the reasons for poor execution and we will turn to this in later chapters.

Finally, however, consideration of the social effects of the programmes points us towards a promising line of enquiry: that conditionality may make the crucial task of the political management of policy change more difficult, by constraining governments' freedom of action and increasing the risks associated with such change.

Notes

1 Volume 1 of this two-volume study was issued in a second edition in 1995.
2 The studies referred to here are World Bank, 1988 and 1992a; Corbo and Rojas, 1992; Elbadawi, 1992; Faini and de Melo, 1990; Faini *et al.*, 1991; and Jayarajah and Branson, 1995.
3 See, for example, a devastating critique of Faini *et al.* (1991) by Montiel (1991) in terms of sample-selectivity bias.
4 See Faini, 1994, and sources cited there for econometric evidence on the positive influence of public-sector investment on private investment. See also Hadjimichael *et al.*, 1995, and Hadjimichael and Ghura, 1995, for further confirmation of the positive correlation between public and private investment.

5 See also Conway, 1994, for an investigation which came too late to be included in my survey. His results are similar to those summarized here.

6 A more recent Fund study (Schadler *et al.*, 1995: footnote 10) confirms that repeated recourse to its credits is common. Of the thirty-six countries receiving stand-by or Extended Facility credits during 1988–91, fifteen were repeat users and another six were obtaining Fund credits for the second time in recent years.

7 For a fuller statement of the analysis summarized see Killick, 1995c.

8 Since drafting the above a second, not dissimilar, IMF study by Schadler and associates (1995) has become available, examining the experiences of countries which obtained stand-by or Extended Facility credits during 1988–91. While avoiding some of the weaknesses of the 1993 study, this too avoids any direct tests of the effects of the Fund's credits: 'It must be recognized, however, that without systematic controls for sample selection bias, exogenous influences, and initial conditions, the before–after comparisons reported in this review cannot be interpreted as indicating solely the effect of IMF support' (Schadler and associates, 1995: 4). We have therefore not included this study in our survey of the literature on the effects of IMF programmes.

9 Significantly, the two reviews of this report which I have seen both read it to be about the effectiveness of Bank programmes – see Schatz, 1994, and Rimmer, 1995.

10 Mosley *et al.* (1991a: 301) similarly found that the implementation of price-based policy changes that could be quickly carried out by a few staff in the Ministry of Finance and central bank was relatively good, compared with institutional changes that require widespread assent.

11 The comparable ratio for the real depreciation of the exchange rate was thirty-five out of forty-two.

12 The report cites Jamaica and Malawi as examples of fairly good compliance with conditionality but limited economic results, and Korea, Mauritius and Thailand as successful adjusters with below-average compliance rates.

13 Kirkpatrick and Weiss, 1995, whose investigations are confined to African countries, also found that countries with above-average records on trade liberalization achieved better economic outcomes, by a number of indicators, than countries more reluctant to liberalize. However, they did not find that the connection arose through exchange rate depreciation, which was not systematically associated with improved performance. By elimination, they suggest that the better results may have resulted from the improved availability of imports made available as a result of adjustment measures and the supporting aid.

14 See Hadjimichael *et al.*, 1995, and Ghura, 1995, for recent evidence along these lines for Africa and for references to other studies pointing to positive connections between the quality of economic policies and indicators of economic performance.

15 'In many developing countries . . . the classical asymmetry between concentrated losers and diffuse gainers is particularly marked . . . crucial sectors that might constitute the core of reform coalitions, such as small peasants and landless laborers, and non-traditional export interests, are less well organized and must overcome significant barriers to collective action in order to be politically effective' (Haggard and Kaufman, 1992: 19).

16 There is a large literature on what has come to be known as 'the costs of adjustment'. This mainly relates to the impact of programmes on poverty, employment and the distribution of income. No attempt is made to systematically survey the results of this literature here. Our focus is the narrower one of programmes' social consequences as they are likely to affect political perceptions of the likely risks and gains.

17 It has been argued that these countries' interests would have been better served by a collective debt default, but whether or not that would have been the case, default clearly was not a painless option.

18 See World Bank, 1994a: 170, and the sources cited there.

19 See Killick, 1995d: 312–13, for references to the evidence supporting the statements made here. See also World Bank, 1995c, confirming the relative protection of social spending and suggesting that *well-implemented* adjustment programmes are actually associated with increased per capita social spending.

3

CONDITIONALITY AND ADJUSTMENT IN SOUTH-EAST ASIA AND LATIN AMERICA

Ramani Gunatilaka and Ana Marr

Chapter 2 was taken up with the evidence bearing directly upon the effects of donor conditionality. In this chapter we take a different approach, with a more detailed look at the adjustment experiences of two important regions, examining the role which conditionality (principally of the IFIs) played in those experiences.

There were particular reasons for choosing these regions. There has been remarkably little discussion of adjustment in South-east Asia (SEA), even though it is regarded as possessing very flexible economies, to such an extent that it was necessary in this case to begin by demonstrating that pro-adjustment policies have indeed been a feature of this part of the world. With the notable exception of the Philippines, theirs was a largely silent adjustment. But it was also highly successful. There is thus special interest in learning more about this and, in particular, in investigating what role IFI conditionality played.

Latin America is different. Until the early 1980s, many Latin American countries had inflexible policies and economies, resistant to the new doctrines of adjustment (although Chile was an early exception to this generalization). Over the last decade-and-a-half, however, there has been a major reversal in attitudes to economic management, as well as some recovery in economic fortunes. The IFIs and other donors have been active at various times in most Latin American countries, so the question again arises about the influence of conditionality in these changes.

Part I (by Ana Marr) takes up the South-east Asian story, while Part II (by Ramani Gunatilaka) deals with Latin America. Both of these analyses are summarized from substantially longer papers published as ODI *Working Papers*, as footnoted, and readers seeking fuller substantiation and referencing should consult these. No attempt is made below to provide supporting citations but the bibliography at the end of the book includes a special listing relating to the two regions studied here.

I South-east Asia[1]

I-1 Introduction

Based on the availability of information, five countries were taken to represent this region: South Korea, Indonesia, Malaysia, Thailand and the Philippines. The striking feature shared by the first four of these is that they implemented economic programmes similar to those recommended by the IMF and World Bank. In the Philippines, in contrast, while some earlier attempts were made to adopt more market-oriented policies, vested interest groups and weak political leaderships prevented the government from enforcing adjustment measures until recently.

The extent to which adjustment-type policies were implemented in South-east Asia (SEA) is analysed in the next section and Section I-3 goes on to examine the degree of influence that IFIs had on the adoption of adjustment programmes in SEA, a central point of analysis being whether or not conditionality played a significant role.

The Philippines is different: a country where many highly conditional loans were put in place but over an extended period did not achieve adjustment. Analysis of the Philippines case is undertaken separately in Section I-4. Section I-5 deals with other ways in which IFIs influenced adjustment in SEA, while Section I-6 concludes and summarizes the main findings.

I-2 Implementation of adjustment

Criteria of adjustment

In order to test the extent to which the countries under study could be said to have undertaken adjustment, we identified the most common items in standard structural adjustment-type programmes and used these as criteria for assessing the extent of adjustment in our five countries. The policy elements used as criteria were:

Macroeconomic management:

1   Reduction or avoidance of large fiscal deficits
2   Avoidance of inflationary monetary expansion
3   Maintenance of a competitive and flexible exchange rate

Market friendliness:

4   Dismantling of controls

5   Financial sector liberalization
6   Privatization of state-owned enterprises

Openness:

7   Trade liberalization
8   Export orientation
9   Exchange control liberalization

In this section and the next we focus on South Korea, Indonesia, Malaysia and Thailand. As will be shown, these implemented most of the policies specified by the above criteria. Over their recent histories, these economies have demonstrated an ability to adapt swiftly to new circumstances harming their economies. Following the oil-price shocks of the early 1980s and the subsequent world recession, the foreign debt service of these countries increased and their exports were severely affected. In the face of this, these economies adjusted quickly and, by adopting more stringent economic reforms, offset the economic imbalances revealed by external shocks. The early 1980s also marked a change in the IFIs' lending policies, resulting from the introduction of conditional structural adjustment lending by the World Bank. Most of the conditions stipulated in the IFIs' adjustment credits were along the lines of the measures identified above as our criteria. In this section we will therefore examine the extent to which SEA countries adopted such policies. At a later stage we will try to disentangle the factors behind this change. Was adjustment undertaken as a result of conditionality, or through influence and persuasion, or as a result of the financial support provided?

The initial situation

Although these four countries started with different levels of initial endowments, they shared a common ability to adapt quickly to challenging circumstances and to implement corrective policies. As early as 1962, poorly-endowed **South Korea** made a conscious effort to design a growth strategy based on an aggressive promotion of exports. Although it combined export promotion with a classic protection of domestic markets, the government made clear its intention of achieving international competitiveness and export growth. However, over-protection during the 'Heavy and Chemical Industries' drive of the 1970s began to generate macroeconomic imbalances and inflationary pressures that threatened the country's competitiveness and growth. By 1979 President Park had prepared a comprehensive stabilization programme but political turmoil intervened and Park was assassinated. The second oil-price shock of the early 1980s exacerbated already large imbalances and foreign indebtedness soared. At the peak of the crisis, in 1980, the economy went into recession and inflation rose to nearly 30 per cent, while long-term external indebtedness increased by more than half during 1979–80 alone.

A severe economic crisis in richly-endowed **Indonesia** in the 1960s prompted the adoption of a drastic change in policy and a stabilization programme was put in place as soon as the new administration of President Suharto took power in 1967. This economic programme introduced market-oriented reforms, the exchange rate was devalued and unified, imports were liberalized and foreign investment encouraged, bringing the economy back on track. As Indonesia is an oil-exporting country, the massive increase in the world oil price in 1973–4 boosted Indonesian government revenues, enabling the government to expand public expenditures. Although investment in rural infrastructure, education and health achieved remarkable reductions in poverty in the 1970s, economic policies became progressively more inward-looking and budgetary dependence on oil revenues made Indonesia dangerously vulnerable to oil price movements. This exposure was evident when petroleum prices slid dramatically in the early 1980s, with a subsequent worldwide recession also reducing the demand for Indonesia's traditional exports. As export revenues dwindled the country's current account balance went into the red, deteriorating by 1983 to a critical deficit of 7.4 per cent of GDP.

Malaysia pursued market-oriented policies for the industrial sector between 1957 and 1968 but intervened to promote rural development and provide social and physical infrastructure. Although growth was stable, based largely on primary product exports, the absolute level of poverty was hardly reduced, particularly among ethnic Malays. Racial discontent led to riots in 1969, prompting a radical change in economic management. An emphasis on encouraging greater participation of ethnic Malays in modern economic activities was reflected in the New Economic Policy, initiated in 1971.

The 1972–3 surge in world oil prices helped Malaysia finance public expenditures as export revenues started to swell during the 1970s. The government's expectations of permanent oil price rises that would support an ever-growing economy prompted it to embark on an unprecedented fiscal expansion. This policy generated massive public deficits during the first half of the 1980s. With a peak of 16 per cent of GDP in 1982, the fiscal deficit recorded an annual average of 12 per cent between 1981 and 1984. As oil revenues started to fade, with the drop in world prices in the early 1980s, the government resorted to foreign borrowing, which grew to a peak of 85 per cent of GDP in 1986. This could not save Malaysia from sinking into recession in 1985, however, when its GDP declined by 1 per cent, after delivering average growth of 7 per cent per annum over the previous five years.

Despite a relatively long tradition of macroeconomic conservatism, **Thailand** was hit by the collapse of non-oil commodity prices in 1979–80. During the 1960s and 1970s, Thailand's import-substituting strategy generated economic growth which was largely unaffected by the first oil shock of 1973 because the prices of farm products, which constituted Thailand's major exports, also rose sharply. However, the sudden increase of oil prices in 1979, with the subsequent fall in world agricultural prices, weakened the country's trade balance. This was magnified by the decision to keep the currency (the baht) tied to the dollar, leading to a significant rise in the real effective exchange rate. By the end of 1980 the current account deficit was up to 6 per cent of GDP and growing fiscal deficits pushed the inflation rate to a high point of 20 per cent.

Overall, then, it can be seen that internal macroeconomic imbalances caused by expansionary fiscal policies and dependence on exports of primary products made these four SEA countries vulnerable to sudden changes in international commodity prices. The external shocks in the early 1980s therefore created imbalances requiring major policy changes.

Adjustment policies, early 1980s to early 1990s

Faced with a tangible economic crisis, these countries reacted remarkably quickly and carried out major policy changes. How close were the adjustment policies adopted in the 1980s to our criteria? In what follows, we analyse countries' performances, as summarized in Table 3.1. The discussion follows the order of the policy criteria set out in the table.

Macroeconomic management

All four of the countries under study were remarkably successful in regaining macroeconomic stability from the initial imbalances just described. Governments achieved this by adhering to the policy prescriptions highlighted by our criteria. In particular, they achieved it by reducing budget deficits to levels that could be prudently financed, keeping inflation under control, and by avoiding exchange rate overvaluation. Table 3.1 shows the high level of policy implementation that these four countries achieved in macroeconomic management.

In each case a contractionary fiscal policy was adopted. This was particularly tight in Malaysia, where budget deficits started substantially higher than in the other three cases. Public expenditure was reduced and new sources of tax revenues exploited. As a result, Malaysia's massive fiscal deficit of 16 per cent of GDP in 1982 was reduced to a 7 per cent annual average in 1983–7, falling further after 1988, with surpluses recorded in 1992 and 1993.

Although not at Malaysia's levels, Thailand's fiscal deficit averaged an uncomfortable 5 per cent of GDP during 1980–5. In 1986, the Thai government introduced a substantially tougher tax collection regime and new taxes, such as a value-added tax, to raise revenues. This, in combination with expenditure cuts, brought public accounts under control and the country started

Table 3.1 Criteria of adjustment programmes – level of implementation (position by end of period)

	South Korea 1980–93	Indonesia 1983–92	Malaysia 1985–92	Thailand 1982–93	Philippines 1986–91
Macroeconomic management					
Reduction/avoidance of large fiscal deficits	high	high	high	high	medium
Avoidance of inflationary credit	high	high	high	high	medium
Competitive and flexible exchange rate	high	high	high	high	medium
Market friendliness					
Dismantling of controls	medium	high	high	high	low
Financial sector reform	medium	high	medium	high	low
Privatization	medium	medium	medium	medium	low
Openness					
Trade liberalization	medium	high	medium	medium	low
Export orientation	high	high	high	high	medium
Exchange-control liberalization	high	high	high	high	medium

registering budget surpluses in 1988 (with a 3 per cent average surplus in 1988–92).

Unlike many Latin American economies, the SEA nations did not experience huge inflationary pressures even at times of crisis. South Korea and Thailand had the highest rates but these were still under 30 per cent per annum at their highest. Tight monetary policies were implemented to bring inflation down to manageable levels. As a result, sharp disinflations during the first half of the 1980s reduced inflation in 1984 to 2.3 per cent in South Korea and to 0.9 per cent in Thailand. Since then the annual rates in these countries have remained around 5 per cent and 4 per cent respectively.

All countries under discussion used the exchange rate as an important instrument of adjustment and all depreciated their currencies in the face of current account deficits. Although exchange rates were devalued to restore competitiveness and current account balance, they were never allowed to become hugely overvalued in the first place. Indeed, in contrast to some Latin American countries, these economies depreciated whenever this seemed necessary, and did not attempt to stick to a fixed rate when such a course appeared no longer viable. Indonesia undertook major devaluations in 1983 (28 per cent) and 1986 (31 per cent). South Korea, having attempted to peg its currency to the US dollar, abandoned this tactic and devalued by 20 per cent in 1980. Of all the countries studied here, it was Thailand that held longest to a fixed rate: the baht was pegged at a fixed rate to the dollar from 1954 to 1984, when it was devalued by 14.8 per cent and then floated.

Market friendliness and openness

Although macroeconomic management was successfully undertaken, other measures aimed at achieving market friendliness and openness showed more variable levels of implementation amongst our four economies (see Table 3.1). All of them had high implementation levels of exchange rate liberalization, permitting market forces to take over from the direct regulation of trade and payments, since these countries opted for some type of floating exchange rate during their adjustment periods, as explained above. The policy of maintaining competitive and flexible exchange rates undoubtedly contributed to the promotion of exports, another common characteristic of SEA economic programmes. These countries successfully employed a variety of approaches when attempting to encourage exports – tax concessions, guarantees of credit to exporters, export contests and so on – though all were agreed on the avoidance of an appreciated exchange rate as a fundamental mechanism. Microeconomic incentives were effective but, crucially, they were set against a background of macroeconomic stability. The growth in exports was closely linked to devaluations. South Korea, for example, improved its current account balance in the period 1982–8 as a result of an export growth stimulated by the devaluations of those years, while in Malaysia, in the late 1980s, dramatic export growth went hand-in-hand with a steady depreciation in real exchange rates. Export-oriented industrialization delivered impressive results: by 1993 Malaysia was the nineteenth largest trading nation in the world. The effects on export growth of Thailand's real devaluation in 1984–8 were quite dramatic, although other factors contributed, notably investments in export industries from Japan and Taiwan. Both of Indonesia's devaluations had clear effects on exports of manufactures, particularly that of 1986, with manufacturing increasing its share of export earnings from 43 per cent in 1985 to 80 per cent in 1993.

Further reforms were also undertaken to encourage rapid export growth and maintain a healthy balance of payments. Trade liberalization programmes were implemented with particular vigour in Indonesia from 1986 onwards, applying far-reaching reforms in trade policies, investment licensing and transport. The currency was devalued, trade regulations simplified and tariff cuts delivered, as part of a package of measures designed to boost exports. In Thailand, although trade policy shifted explicitly in the direction of export promotion from 1981, this was not reflected in an extensive trade liberalization. The maximum tariff rate on most products was cut from 100 per cent to

60 per cent in 1982 but this was offset by the imposition of new tariffs on raw materials and intermediate goods, a tactic aimed at increasing budget revenues. In fact, the tariff structure remained broadly unchanged between 1985 and 1989, with effective protection in the mid-1980s remaining high, at 52 per cent of value added, compared with South Korea's at 28 per cent and Malaysia's 23 per cent. In 1990, however, Thailand began to liberalize in earnest, with large tariff reductions on capital goods and, in 1991, on cars and computers. South Korea opted for a more gradual approach, whereby the average tariff rate was reduced from 32 per cent in 1982 to 21 per cent in 1985 and to 7.5 per cent in 1993. Malaysia, too, reduced tariff rates in the mid-to-late-1980s.

Macroeconomic stability and openness to international markets provided the basis for further reforms in the financial sector and the privatization of state enterprises. This was particularly the case in South Korea, where a sequential approach seems to have been important to the successful outcome of adjustment. The programme began with efforts at stabilization that laid the foundation for the subsequent implementation of industrial restructuring and trade liberalization, which in turn facilitated the liberalization of the financial sector. Although a financial reform was initiated in 1981, with the privatization of four major banks, financial liberalization was only really pursued in the later years. Interest rates were deregulated for most money market instruments in 1991 and lending rates were freed in 1993; special credit facilities were still being controlled as of late 1993, however. Indonesia and Thailand achieved more far-reaching financial sector reforms. An extensive financial liberalization was introduced in Indonesia in 1988–92, while Thailand's generally dynamic banks were strengthened by a broad liberalization of interest rates during the early 1990s.

The privatization of state-owned enterprises has been only partially implemented in the four countries under study, with governments either postponing major action for political reasons or reluctantly selling enterprises while retaining some control over them, as in Indonesia and South Korea. Although more extensively implemented, it is far from clear that the Malaysian privatization programme has managed to avoid thereby creating private monopolies in areas such as airlines, water supply, telecommunications and electricity. The political imperative to favour ethnic Malays has undoubtedly been a factor in this incomplete market orientation and may still threaten the effectiveness of privatization. Thailand, even though historically the least interventionist country in this group, has only partially privatized state-controlled enterprises.

Looking at the record overall, as summarized in Table 3.1, we can conclude for South Korea, Indonesia, Malaysia and Thailand that they followed the precepts of orthodox structural adjustment to quite a high degree. While the implementation of 'market-friendly' measures has been variable, even here the trend has undoubtedly been in the orthodox direction, and the score by the other criteria is high. The question arises, then, of the role of the IFIs in these policy moves.

I-3 The role of conditionality

Voluntary adjustment

Virtually all observers are agreed that, in fact, these countries carried out their adjustment programmes without much input from Fund or Bank conditionality. Key reasons for this included a generally strong commitment to conservative macroeconomic policies; a firm determination to adjust when national economies fell into difficulty; and the governments' ability to execute their chosen policy responses. These factors, and the consequent adoption of policies to regain economic stability, reassured creditors and reduced pressures to accept conditional loans linked to unpopular measures imposed in an atmosphere of crisis.

The most remarkable case was that of Malaysia, where major adjustment was accomplished without any resort to conditional or structural adjustment loans. A desire to redress economic imbalances amongst racial groups has been the major characteristic of Malaysian economic policies since the 1969 riots brought to light the extent of Malays' resentment of Chinese dominance of economic life. The oil boom of the 1970s helped maintain an expansionary policy that promoted distributional objectives in favour of previously disadvantaged groups. When commodity prices collapsed in the early 1980s and the subsequent world recession affected Malaysian exports, the sudden loss of foreign reserves and a sharp economic recession in 1985 awakened widespread concern amongst Malaysians about the state of their economy and put the government in a stronger position to push through reform. The IFIs offered a package of conditional loans to accompany their traditional recipe of structural adjustment but the Mahathir administration chose not to formally adopt the package and continued with its own programme.

Indonesia, too, implemented the government's own adjustment policies. These started in 1983, years before conditional loans were negotiated, in response to the economic crisis described earlier. While the government paid careful attention to policy advice from the World Bank, there was no IMF lending during the 1980s, and the first Bank adjustment loan was not made until 1987. It is clear that the Indonesian response to the crisis was voluntary, 'owned' by the government and carried out without direct outside pressure.

South Korea and Thailand, on the other hand, initiated adjustment packages in the context of IMF and World Bank adjustment loans. However, the money came with low levels of conditionality. As early as 1978, President Park of South Korea requested key economic institutions to propose measures to address the country's macroeconomic imbalances. A comprehensive stabilization programme launched in 1979, but interrupted by the assassination of

President Park, was resumed in the following year with financial support from the IFIs. Although four IMF stand-by loans, two Bank SALs and one sectoral adjustment loan (SECAL) were agreed between 1980 and 1990, these were low on specific conditions in view of the government's evident determination and administrative capacity.

Moreover, where the government was unconvinced of the need for a change, conditions were violated with impunity. For example, the government's unwavering financial support for South Korea's automotive industry, despite its commitment under SAL I to defer this support, proved to be successful, inducing the Bank to omit this condition from SAL II. In other fields, however, South Korea surpassed the targets set for it, as in the promotion of energy efficiency. In sum, South Korea clearly demonstrated its commitment to a programme of reform without undue outside pressure.

The level of conditionality that the World Bank imposed on Thailand under SAL I and SAL II in 1982–4 was higher, but still moderate. In the wake of the oil crisis, Thailand's long history of political instability together with substantial economic imbalances reduced the country's international credit rating. The Bank, believing it had a stronger bargaining position, negotiated policies that included various sectoral reforms. Although these loans had the important effect of preserving Thailand's creditworthiness, they did not incorporate measures that the government was not already prepared to undertake. In fact, before any SALs had been awarded, the government had already taken action in the direction of structural adjustment: export taxes on major agricultural products were eliminated or lowered; the baht was devalued; power tariffs and petroleum prices were raised as all subsidies were removed.

Political commitment shifted in favour of reform as a change in Cabinet brought to the Ministry of Finance an orthodox economist who favoured stringent adjustment and proceeded to negotiate an IMF stand-by that was then used as a pretext for the implementation of his austerity programme. It has been claimed that the Fifth Economic and Social Development Plan for 1982–6 contained between a third and more than half of the measures later included in the SAL. Those few provisions which were genuinely conditional were also the least implemented, e.g. tariff rationalization and price increases in water and bus services.

The Bank tried to insist that these and other failures of compliance be addressed during SAL III, but as growth resumed and Thailand gained access to credit from the Tokyo market, the government, now in a stronger bargaining position, abandoned negotiations and the SAL was allowed to lapse. Thailand's reform efforts implemented after the SAL period reveal the government's serious intentions to restructure the economy and its determination to follow its own instincts in applying structural reforms, rather than having them forced upon it.

I-4 *The special case of the Philippines*

Conditionality was attempted far more extensively in the Philippines but, despite this, domestic factors were ultimately more important in determining the shape of economic policies. When Corazon Aquino came to power in 1986, her team of economists favoured the policies approved of by the IFIs and conditionality was therefore superfluous – although, in fact, Aquino was prevented from executing radical economic reforms by the entrenched power of the Marcos-era business elite, as well as some of her own supporters. In turn, Fidel Ramos came to power in 1992 with a determination to implement market-oriented reforms, with considerable success, although the old oligarchy remained and Congress proved an obstacle to tax reform. It is only recently that an important entrepreneurial middle class has been showing signs of development.

The Marcos regime of 1966–86 was characterized by extensive use of patronage, retaining power by developing a network of clients who, on the classic feudal model, delivered political support in return for economic bene-fits. Such a political structure meant that economic decision-making was heavily influenced by vested interests and the possibility of reform was limited. Monetary and fiscal policies were expansionary, directed mainly to the sugar and coconut industries which formed the main base of Marcos' political support. The bestowing of rents was also associated with high tariffs, quotas and subsidized credits, while continuing balance of payments deficits were handled by recourse to IMF stand-by loans. The Fund was generally unsuccessful in enforcing compliance with conditions and failed to achieve a real devaluation, which was evaded by the government, which turned instead to high-cost foreign borrowing. After Marcos imposed martial law in 1972 the economy was managed essentially by presidential decree, and in the 1970s an expanding economy masked the inefficiency and corruption of the system.

The financial pressures of the early 1980s finally forced a reluctant partial shift by the Marcos administration. The World Bank stepped in to ease the economic crisis (two SALs and six SECALs during the 1980s) on condition that Marcos' inner elite was kept in check and the technocrats allowed to gain ascendancy. The first SAL (1980–5) was formulated under strict Bank supervi-sion but, while some of its conditions were carried through (e.g. tariffs were lowered), resistance from Marcos' inner group and generalized corruption weakened implementation. In 1983, over the protests of the Bank, the government actually reimposed a series of tariff controls. With one eye on the elections of 1984, the administration was most reluctant to take tough measures and risk political fallout, manipulating the figures to make the country's balance of payments position seem less perilous than it was. Once this subterfuge was revealed, in December 1983, foreign creditors and finan-cial institutions became much firmer in their dealings with the government and conditionality was tightened, with the IMF demanding policy change prior to the disbursement of funds.

It was not until 1984–5 that external and domestic pressure forced the appointment of an orthodox banker, Jose Fernandez, as Governor of the Central Bank, and a strict monetarist programme was pushed through. While this stabilization programme had some success, it was opposed by the Marcos clique, favouritism and patronage continued to blunt its effectiveness, and the administration continued to resist pressure for far-reaching structural adjustment.

Fernandez was retained as Central Bank Governor by the Corazon Aquino administration which came to power after Marcos was rejected by the electorate in February 1986. Conditionality was relaxed again as the IFIs believed that the new government was willing to take policy initiatives without outside pressure. The new approach to economic policy was contained in the so-called 'Yellow Book', designed by the Philippines Institute of Development Studies, the Planning Ministry and the University of the Philippines, published in May 1986 and forming the basis of the government's development plan for 1987–92. This reflected most of the economic policies that the IFIs had been advocating for years and negotiations were hence far more cordial than previously. The Aquino administration's first IMF stand-by, for instance, was approved almost immediately after submission.

Furthermore, even before the new government opened negotiations with the World Bank, it had already taken important steps, such as abolishing certain agricultural monopolies and export taxes, reforming the tax system and liberalizing import restrictions. The Bank therefore restricted conditionality to a few key issues. Three of these had already featured in the first two SALs – trade liberalization, tax reform and a public investment programme. It should also be noted that the major task of macroeconomic stabilization had been carried out even before Aquino came to power. Despite all this, implementation often fell short of declared commitment (see Table 3.1). Cronyism was not completely rooted out. Indeed, the privatization programme gave Marcos-era interest groups a chance to revive their fortunes and they lobbied energetically. Trade liberalization, demanded as a condition by the Bank, was resisted both by the Filipino business elite and representatives of foreign business, backed by small manufacturers, farmers and workers who had been hit by recession. In addition, a crippling power shortage brought about by drought affected the country badly, while the Gulf crisis, natural disasters and coup attempts also jolted the government.

Aquino was succeeded by Fidel Ramos in 1992, and the economy quickly returned to growth. A corner-stone of Ramos' economic reform programme was the desire to maintain investor and donor confidence; liberalization and privatization were vigorously pursued. His administration has also established an independent central bank; launched a programme to cut import tariffs; and ended monopolies in the telecommunications and airline businesses.

However, there remain problems, such as the survival of the landowning oligarchy and the fragility of an emerging entrepreneurial middle class.

The case of the Philippines hence shows light conditionality during much of the Marcos administration; when conditionality was tightened it still often failed to produce the desired effects, as domestic forces conspired to blunt the effectiveness of policy reform measures, and lack of compliance went unpunished. Conditionality was again light during the Aquino period, as reform was proposed from within the government. However, domestic factors and exogenous shocks again limited the extent of reform. Despite private sector support for its policies, the regime was not immune to distributional pressures and a national consensus was rarely achieved. Under the more resolute Ramos administration more progress was achieved in structural reform, foreign investment was successfully attracted and the agreement reached with the IMF in May 1994 was regarded by the government as an 'exit facility', with further agreements thought unlikely to be necessary.

I-5 Other IFI influences

The influence of the IFIs' financial support

If the lending by the IFIs was generally not linked to policy changes in the SEA countries, their money played a role in easing external resource constraints, mainly by acting as a catalyst for generating financial assistance from other aid donors. This was particularly evident in Indonesia in the mid-1980s, when, with the fall in oil prices and consequent rise in external debt, commercial loans were hard to secure. Amid some anxiety from international credit markets, Indonesian credibility remained unbroken. This was bolstered by annual World Bank bills of health and two trade loans which persuaded Indonesia's major aid donors to provide balance of payments loans and aid flows totalling US$3.7 billion in 1989–91. This enabled the government to continue its programme of deregulation and to restructure its external debt, while maintaining the confidence of private investors.

Thailand's acceptance of SALs in the early 1980s was opportune, given the extent of its economic difficulties and the adverse effect these had on its international credibility. However, almost uniquely, Thailand received an untranched World Bank credit in support of economic reforms that the government had set out in its fiscal plans. The Bank was perhaps prepared to take such a step because of the limited usefulness of tranching as a control mechanism, given Thailand's substantial 'down-payment' of reforms already in place. These appear to have improved Thailand's creditworthiness, which, combined with the renewed growth of the economy from 1986, helped the country regain access to credits from the Tokyo market. This, in turn, allowed its government to decline a third conditional Bank loan, as already noted. Another important financial source for Thailand has been foreign direct investment, particularly from Japan and Taiwan. These capital flows increased from an annual average of US$270 million during 1980–5 to US$2.4 billion in 1990, and largely explain the expansion of Thai manufacturing exports during the late 1980s and early 1990s.

South Korea's creditworthiness in international financial markets was also improved by securing financial backing from the IMF and the World Bank. The two Korean SALs, negotiated in 1982 and 1984, while significant in terms of credibility enhancement, represented only 13 per cent of the country's external financing in 1982–3. Malaysia, on the other hand, avoided conditional loans altogether and opted for greater incentives to attract foreign direct investment, especially for export industries. Its new flexibility had a dramatic effect on foreign direct investment, which jumped from an average of US$300 million a year in 1983–5 to US$2.0 billion in 1988 and US$4.4 billion in 1993.

In the Philippines, by contrast, the IFIs poured in huge amounts of money to support a regime that was sympathetic to America's foreign policy aim of eradicating communism in the region. Marcos' political situation, however, meant that only by conferring economic favours on key supporters could he retain power. Ready access to IMF stand-bys, instead of facilitating economic change, created a classic case of moral hazard whereby funding helped delay action, sinking the Filipino economy into deeper crisis. It was not until 1982, following financial crisis and political turmoil caused by the assassination of Benigno Aquino, that the IMF finally refused a stand-by, whereupon the World Bank instead offered a credit, conditional on policy changes. Domestic political pressures once again proved to be dominant, however, and most of the Bank's conditions slipped. The country's international credibility reached bottom when the Marcos government's deceptive overstatement of the country's foreign reserves was discovered in 1983.

Corazon Aquino and her team of economists came to power with a renewed credibility which was, in part, boosted by large foreign assistance: during her period Aquino received five SECALs and two IMF stand-bys. More crucially, the Philippines regained market credibility due to evidence of the government's own commitment to change. This was the main factor in a large-scale return of flight capital, with between $4 billion and $12 billion returning in 1986–91. Aware of the need for international recognition, the Ramos government, in turn, gave priority to maintaining foreign investor confidence, by opening and liberalizing the economy and providing a more stable political environment.

Policy dialogue and the role of technocrats

Clearly, financial support from the IFIs – although beneficial – does not alone account for the high-performing economies' adoption of adjustment policies. IFI involvement through policy dialogue and the building of technical capabilities seems also to have been effective in the spread of a market-oriented philosophy amongst advisers and members of the civil service in the SEA region (with the Philippines a partial exception). As these people received education at Western universities and went on to occupy influential positions in government in the 1980s, they tended to favour market-friendly policies. Once in government, they engaged in policy dialogue with major donors; given their orthodox leaning, they had few difficulties in arriving at a convergence of objectives with the external agencies. This helped convince sceptics and finally made conditionality redundant.

This said, it must be stressed that the technocrats' first loyalty was always to their governments. Whenever they felt a threat to the nation's sovereignty, negotiations with foreign lenders ceased, as in Thailand's rejection of SAL III in 1984. It seems that the World Bank made too much out of Thailand's small policy slippages during SAL II, so that the conditions in SAL III were perceived as interference. This was particularly unacceptable given Thailand's proven macroeconomic prudence.

In fact, policy advisers in the four reforming SEA nations have a long history of intellectual excellence and immunity to distributional pressures. They are highly regarded by the rest of society and their opinions are respected. South Korea offers the clearest case of this insulation: since 1963, the country's civil service has been transformed into a technocracy based on the Japanese model, by which entrance to the service and promotion within it are on the basis of performance. In addition, a powerful Economic Planning Board was created in 1961 with broad budgetary authority. The indirect nature of the Board's relation to powerful economic groupings (unlike that of the Finance Ministry) gave it the flexibility and autonomy to carry out the stabilization programme of the early 1980s.

Advisers in Indonesia have been an important force since Suharto's accession to power in 1966. Working closely with the donors' Inter-Governmental Group and with IMF assistance, Suharto's US-trained team prepared and carried through a programme of rapid economic stabilization and the government created mechanisms to insulate this team. With neo-classical leanings, they have often been perceived as a force opposed to the 'engineers' controlling other government departments, who have tended to demand expansionary economic policies, with much success during the oil boom years. However, the fall of oil prices in the early 1980s prompted a current account crisis and the economic team regained the upper hand over the 'engineers'. With presidential backing, they were able to push ahead with their plan for contractionary fiscal and monetary policies.

Technocrats in the Philippines during the Marcos era, although leaning towards IFIs' economic philosophy and negotiating agreements with foreign lenders on policy reform, had much less influence than appeared from outside, often finding themselves marginalized from real policy-making. In fact, their presence helped legitimize a corrupted system of economic management over which they had little practical influence. During the Aquino regime, economic decision-making became more technically-oriented, as the government implemented a programme designed by economists from prestigious universities and research institutes, even though the entrenched power of the Marcos-era elite prevented the government from implementing far-reaching economic reforms, as the bureaucracy lacked enough cohesion to over-ride vested interests.

Economic policy-making and interest groups

An insulated and highly educated technocracy has thus been an important factor in the conceptualization of economic policies in the region. However, a more complex task is that of establishing why governments accepted these policies, and were prepared to impose them upon the population even when the political costs of doing so were expected to be large.

Many observers have acknowledged that the SEA countries (again with the Philippines as an exception) basically represent corporatist states in which decision-making has relatively little to do with elected politicians or society at large. In this context, governments developed mechanisms to share information with and win the support of business elites. By setting rapid economic development as the ultimate objective, governments hoped to achieve legitimacy. Strong authoritarian regimes with centralized decision-making, coupled with only weakly-organized disadvantaged groups, allowed governments to push through reforms. Legitimacy was achieved by delivering an economic progress that trickled down to all groups through better education and improved opportunities for employment. A combination of pragmatism, hard-working populations and a culturally inherent sense of communal welfare, as opposed to individualist progress, seems to have contributed to the adoption of policies combining economic growth with equity.

While the Philippines' strong authoritarian neighbours created the foundation for economic development, Marcos personified weak authoritarianism. His heavy reliance on patron–client networks limited his capacity to pursue coherent economic policies and led the country to political and economic crisis. Interference by powerful vested interests proved hard to eliminate even during Aquino's period and by the time she left office the economy was in disarray, land reform was largely abandoned and severe income inequality persisted. Ramos has achieved what seemed impossible under previous regimes and, although the old dynasties still dominate the business sector, they will have to adapt to more competitive and open markets if they are to survive. The distribution of wealth has changed little, however, and the rich families that have dominated politics for hundreds of years remain in place.

1-6 Conclusions on South-east Asia

From the above analysis, it is clear that conditionality played a very limited role in the formulation and implementation of adjustment policies in SEA. While South Korea, Indonesia, Malaysia and Thailand have been successful economic reformers throughout their recent histories, the Philippines has only recently begun adjusting its economy. External shocks in the early 1980s, as they adversely affected economies worldwide, presented the region with a new challenge and in responding to this all SEA governments, with the exception of Malaysia, agreed to SALs at various times during their reform period.

Were these conditional loans instigators of change? Clearly not in Indonesia, where economic adjustment began some four years before policy-based lending began in 1987. Thailand and South Korea signed loan contracts in the midst of economic reforms but, as the governments had demonstrated their own commitment to change, conditionality was low. Where conditionality was more forcefully attempted, implementation fell to poor levels, as with Thailand's reluctance to restructure petroleum product pricing and South Korea's support for its automotive industry. Only in the Philippines did the IMF eventually manage to force a government to undertake action against its will, and then only briefly. Loans to the pre-Aquino Philippines included a large number of policy conditions but for years non-compliance went unpunished and, as IFIs continued providing financial resources, this generated a classic case of moral hazard. The imposition of the stabilization programme of 1985 was the most forceful expression of conditionality in the region but was perhaps poorly timed, since the resulting economic overkill caused subsequent slippages of other loan conditions.

Were these loans a catalyst for assuring financial assistance from other sources? Probably yes, in the initial stages of reform, when the economies were shaky and the governments' international credibility was lower. IFI financial support alone, however, was insufficient to attract foreign investment, as the case of the Philippines clearly indicates. Only when the governments' own commitment to economic reform was evident did investors start to allocate resources. This was the case for all countries, including the Philippines, where the renewed credibility of the Aquino government attracted the return of flight capital. Once these governments embarked on policy adjustment, this created a virtuous circle whereby reforms attracted foreign capital that gave further impetus to reform.

The IFIs also influenced the shape and direction of economic policies through policy dialogue and the building of intellectual capabilities, as most technocrats received education in Western universities and were directly involved in policy-making. This, however, could only lead to implementation if other groups, especially the political leadership, were to accept the same principles. Domestic politics, culture and history are all contributory factors in explaining why these countries adopted reforms when they did, and these seem the most important factors.

II Latin America[2]

There has, since the early 1980s, been a remarkable reversal of attitudes towards economic policies in the Latin American region, with a shift from a *dirigiste* approach suspicious of markets, emphasizing import-substituting industrialization (ISI) and strongly associated with large macroeconomic imbalances, to a far more open and market-oriented stance built upon more prudent macroeconomic management.

The purpose of this section is to identify the causal factors behind this policy transformation and, particularly, to assess the extent to which the conditionality attached to IFI lending may have had an impact in bringing about this change. We also look at other avenues through which the IFIs may have played a catalytic role, i.e. through policy dialogue and the provision of supporting finance. In addition to these external factors, the extent to which the debt crisis may have had a cathartic effect in jolting governments into new policy directions will be assessed. We hypothesize that the internal political environment was a crucial influence on programme implementation and analyse the factors which create a configuration of political forces conducive to reform.

To assess the relative importance of these factors in the reorientation of policy we consider the adjustment experience of six Latin American countries: Argentina, Bolivia, Chile, Colombia, Ecuador and Mexico. The selection of this sample was, by necessity, governed by the availability of already published material. The framework for analysis in the fuller paper from which this account is derived took as its base the possibility of identifying decisive turning points in the adjustment experience of each country. These were then related to the period of IFI involvement in policy-based lending, as well as to the historical record of adjustment in these countries, in order to isolate the catalytic influences on adjustment.

The discussion is organized as follows. Section II-1 provides an account of the policy situation as it stood (in most of the region) at the beginning of the 1980s. Section II-2 summarizes the significant events associated with these turning points. Section II-3 assesses the role of the IFIs in catalysing policy reform, while Section II-4 focuses on other external influences. Internal political factors influencing reform are analysed in Section II-5 and the final section concentrates on the lessons learned.

II-1 *Policies before the turnaround*

The response of major Latin American countries to the destabilizing effects of the Mexican peso crisis of December 1994 revealed the extent to which market-oriented economic policy reforms in Latin America had taken root. No country, not even Mexico, imposed currency controls; none of them gave any serious thought to abandoning economic liberalism; one-time profligate governments showed they had become more circumspect about big foreign borrowing and high public spending. In fact, several governments pushed further ahead with privatization (Mexico, Brazil and Peru), and Argentina's government used the crisis to push through labour market and pension reforms previously held up in Congress (*The Economist*, 20 May 1995).

This sea-change in economic policy-making in these countries is all the more remarkable given the extent to which the statist, inward-oriented development strategy they had been following at least since the Second World War had previously become entrenched. The theoretical foundation for the state-led ISI strategy which all the major Latin American countries followed was provided by the Prebisch–Singer thesis fashionable in the 1950s. This held that primary sector exports from developing countries faced low income and price elasticities of demand, whereas the converse was true for manufactured exports by industrial countries. Consequently, the commodity terms of trade of developing countries were predicted to deteriorate over time *vis-à-vis* imported manufactured goods. It was therefore recommended that developing countries should establish protective trade barriers and import controls, and raise taxes on traditional exports in order to reallocate resources from primary exports towards manufacturing.

These measures were expected to increase export earnings in the long run but, as is now well known, the anti-export bias of the resulting framework of incentives undermined the ISI growth strategy itself: declining export earnings were progressively less able to finance the new industries' needs for imported inputs and machinery. Consequently, economic growth became constrained by foreign exchange bottlenecks. There were attempts at reducing the extreme anti-export bias of the strategy after the mid-1960s in some Latin American countries but these were thrown off course by ill-designed stabilization efforts and ill-advised external borrowing during the late 1970s. Other than in Chile, the ISI policy framework remained in place in the region until the 1980s.

A key feature of the ISI strategy was that it envisaged a predominant role for the state in economic affairs, not only as protector of emerging industries and regulator of investment flows and prices, but as a direct investor in large enterprises subject to major economies of scale. Thus, by the 1980s the state sectors in these countries had expanded considerably. For example, public sector outlays as a percentage of GDP were at a peak of 42 per cent in Argentina by 1981 and 48 per cent in Mexico a year later. And between 1978 and 1980 state enterprises in these two countries were responsible for 20 and 24 per cent respectively of gross domestic investment. In Brazil this proportion was as high as 39 per cent.

Public controls over the banking system – another feature of the *dirigiste* ISI strategy – led to negative real interest rates for depositors (with nominal rates set below the rate of inflation). Although its objective was to induce investments in capital-intensive industries – a crucial phase in the ISI process – in practice the policy created a regime of financial repression. The latter saw a segmented domestic financial market in which some favoured investors obtained (rationed) credits cheaply, while others were driven to expensive kerb markets. The policy also had the unintended effect of encouraging capital-intensive production methods, although what were needed were more labour-intensive choices.

Although many other developing countries followed similar policies at the time, their adoption in Latin America was particularly encouraged by the political economy of the region. Many of the policy actions were not 'mistakes' or technical misjudgements but the result of deeper political instabilities. The economies of Latin America were (as some continue to be) driven by great inequalities of income. These, in turn, generated fierce distributional conflicts, reflected in chronically large budget deficits, as governments bought the support of various highly mobilized groups with subsidies and other redistributive devices. Larrain and Selowsky, for example, show that public investment in Mexico 'followed a general upward trend conforming to the Mexican political cycle' (1991: 285). Current expenditures too were driven at various times by the political exigencies of providing long-term employment in the state sector.

Meanwhile, also for political reasons, governments were unwilling to raise taxes on the rich to finance growing public expenditures. Predictably, by 1982 public sector deficits in Argentina, Mexico and Brazil were unsustainably high – at 14, 17 and 17 per cent of GDP respectively. While deficits had been covered by resort to the foreign loans which were plentiful in the 1970s, when the period of easy credit ended, countries like Mexico, Bolivia and Ecuador took to printing money to cover the deficit. Argentina had been doing this since the 1950s.

Fiscal expansion and other political-economy factors made Latin America prone to persistently high inflation relative to other regions. High and volatile prices in Argentina had clearly been driven by the monetization of the fiscal deficit since 1961. Between 1975 and 1991 its annual rate of inflation always exceeded 100 per cent and the country ended the 1980s with hyperinflation. Bolivia also experienced hyperinflation. This was in 1985 and was also due to expansionary fiscal policies, compounded, in this case, by a wage–price spiral resulting from indexation. Chile too was a chronic-inflation country between 1950 and 1973, when the military took over. Here too the cause was mainly expansionary fiscal policies. In contrast, Mexico was a low-inflation country, except for two populist public sector spending booms in 1973–81 which also generated balance of payments deficits. The fiscal deficits were partly monetized and the exchange rate substantially devalued, and these measures fuelled inflationary pressures.

Brazil, too, had high and variable rates of inflation for much of 1960–89, generally exceeding 20 per cent per annum, rising to over 100 per cent after 1981. While policy-makers consistently followed a demand-expansion policy, Brazilians learned to live with the consequent inflation because adverse effects were reduced by indexation. However, wage indexation fed into wage–price spirals and Brazil too ended the 1980s with hyperinflation. Only Colombia among the major Latin American countries followed a steadily conservative approach to macroeconomic management.

Wage indexation policies and price controls were typical of the measures adopted in the region to deal with chronic inflation. The prices of agricultural staples and energy products, for instance, were controlled in favour of the urban working class, with adverse effects on rural incomes, energy efficiency and the fiscal deficit, as the energy industries were invariably state monopolies. Governments also increasingly relied on chronically over-valued exchange rates to ameliorate the effects of inflation, favouring urban workers and protecting manufacturing at the expense of politically weak agriculture.

This potent combination of macroeconomic instability, accelerating inflation, negative real interest rates and overvalued exchange rates made for capital flight on a massive scale, creating its own constituency of vested interests. This was especially the case in countries which had no capital controls like Argentina, where capital flight as a percentage of external debt was approximately 52 per cent in 1987, and Mexico, where the corresponding figure was 57 per cent. Capital flight in Venezuela that year was an estimated 106 per cent of total external debt. Since much of the reallocation of privately held domestic assets to foreign assets took place during periods when the exchange rate was overvalued and foreign assets were cheap, this ensured investors – invariably members of local elites – windfall returns in domestic currency terms when devaluation eventually occurred.

Such factors rendered these economies highly vulnerable to the three simultaneous external shocks of the early 1980s which heralded the debt crisis: a cut-off in lending, a rise in world interest rates and a fall in most commodity prices. Almost immediately, governments had to start making major net resource transfers abroad in order to maintain external debt servicing, for which they had to slash their non-interest budget deficits or else find alternative sources of finance. While most governments cut public sector investment drastically, these cuts were insufficient to meet the gap. They consequently shifted to domestic money finance with further inflationary consequences. The latter effects, coupled with rising interest rates, undermined the fiscal situation even more, as economies were driven into recession, further contracting the revenue base.

Thus, the turnaround in economic policy which most Latin American governments engineered during the 1980s must be seen in the context of the economic abyss into which their countries had fallen as a result of earlier policies and from which they had to claw their way out. Their reforms were almost invariably accompanied by credit arrangements with the IMF and World Bank. An interesting feature of the attendant donor–borrower relationships in this region was that, at first, the IFIs – especially the IMF – were regarded with hostility by many Latin Americans, who saw them as agents of pro-capitalist Northern industrial interests intent on perpetuating dependency in the South. Credit arrangements with the IFIs and associated conditionalities were seen as the instruments through which such dependency was enforced. But, as with policies in these countries, it is clear that these negative perceptions too have undergone a sea change.

II-2 The turning points

In this section we will provide highly stylized (and inevitably over-simplified) accounts of the policy turning points in each of our sample countries, before then turning to examine the underlying influences.

By early 1989 the **Argentine** economy was in severe crisis. Earlier stabilization attempts by the Alfonsin administration had failed because the government was unable to control the fiscal deficit. This was driven by years of distributional conflict such that each class-based party that came into power sought to strengthen its alliance with particular corporatist entities through redistribution and subsidies. Although the IFIs had been compelled as a result of US pressure to provide financial support to Argentina throughout most of the 1980s, so that a façade of debt repayment could be maintained, a change in US policy in early 1989 facilitated the IFIs' withdrawal from the Argentine scene.

When Carlos Menem won the presidential elections in May 1989 he inherited an insolvent state: external debt was 538 per cent of total exports for that year; between 1989 and 1990 net long-term capital inflows had plummeted from US$4.7 billion to US$1.2 billion. By July 1989 inflation was running at 200 per cent per month. With the economy incapable of generating any surplus to be redistributed, Menem was forced to distance himself from the lobbying of corporatist entities and the populist rhetoric on which he had won power. Instead, he strengthened ties with the private sector and implemented a drastic orthodox stabilization and structural adjustment programme to forestall a total 'meltdown' of the economy.

Bolivia's long-standing debt-service problems assumed crisis proportions with the collapse of tin prices in 1981 and the rise in international interest rates thereafter. These shocks impacted on an economy weakened by a state capitalism which had fallen prey to the distributional conflicts stemming from the country's highly unequal distribution of income. A bloated public sector, coupled with the weak capacity of the state to institute tax rises, had made Bolivia increasingly dependent on 'borrowed money and borrowed time' in order to manage internal distributional conflicts. The first elected government in eighteen years, which came to power in October 1982, failed to deal with the crisis despite several attempts at stabilization.

The Bolivian hyperinflation of 1984–5 – when inflation rocketed from annual rates of several hundred per cent in 1982–3 to 25,000 per cent per annum by 1985 – was the most dramatic symptom of the 1980s crisis. This forced President Siles Zuazo to resign a year early, whereupon Congress elected Victor Paz Estenssoro of the *Movimento Nacionalista Revolucionario* (MNR) in August 1985. Paz's first priority was to resolve the economic crisis. This he proceeded to do by instituting a drastic orthodox stabilization programme, taking his left-wing supporters completely by surprise. Hyperinflation and the collapse of the state mining system forced the veteran political leader into a new pragmatism, and his 'New Economic Policy' rolled back a revolution which he himself had led more than thirty years earlier.

The turning point in **Chile** occurred much earlier than in the rest of the region. The reorientation of policy was born of the severe macroeconomic crisis, political chaos and social anarchy that ended Allende's experiment with socialism. The military coup of September 1973 which overthrew Allende was the watershed in Chilean history. The military project which emerged subsequently was 'a reaction against the heightened level of class conflict during the Allende government, against the existence of a Marxist left in general, and specifically, against the Allende government's efforts to use the state as an agent for social transformation' (Oppenheim, 1993: 117). Thus, the extreme free market economic strategy which the 'Chicago Boys' (Chilean technocrats, many of whom had trained at the University of Chicago) were independently advocating, representing a complete antithesis to Allende's Marxist approach, was eagerly adopted by the military rulers as matching their own socio-political agenda. The economic liberalization programme, implemented gradually at first, was pursued vigorously from 1976 in almost textbook fashion to 'detoxify a state-hobbled economy' (Pinera, 1994: 224).

In **Colombia** the (more partial) turning point in economic policy-making occurred during the last two years of the Barco government, 1989–90, and was largely confined to the liberalization of trade. A World Bank trade policy loan which had been operational since 1986 included conditions on import liberalization, but Colombian technocrats at the time were unconvinced of the need for this and resorted to subterfuge to evade the Bank's stipulations. Their tactics were to transfer to the free import list only items on the restricted list which did not represent a threat to local producers. By 1988 the Bank had discovered the truth about this 'liberalization' and its relations with Colombia deteriorated seriously. Meanwhile, reduced export earnings following adverse price movements increased Colombian dependence on Bank loans and favourable IFI reports to commercial banks, in order that the country could retain international creditworthiness.

By contrast with earlier years, by the late 1980s exporters had become a strong pressure group, and they lobbied for genuine liberalization. Correspondingly, many industrialists producing for the domestic market had begun to realize that the internal market was no longer a dynamic source of growth. In any case, the prevalence of trade in contraband, much of it related to the laundering of cocaine revenues, had made traditional protection ineffective and tainted it with the growing criminalization of Colombian society. These changes in domestic interest group attitudes therefore encouraged the Barco government to implement a gradual reduction in tariff and non-tariff barriers. Liberalization gathered pace after 1991, when the build-up of foreign reserves forced an acceleration of the process to avoid a revaluation of the currency. Trade policy reforms were followed by sweeping reforms in other sectors, notably the labour market, the tax system and the dismantling of foreign exchange controls.

Mismanagement of the oil boom in the 1970s laid the foundation for **Ecuador**'s crisis in the 1980s. Between the 1970s and mid-1980s the government captured 80 per cent of petroleum revenues, which it used to expand the state sector, to invest in an ISI strategy and to subsidize domestic energy, transport and infrastructure. Large public sector deficits were financed by the accumulation of external debt. Meanwhile, non-petroleum export revenues declined, leaving the economy highly vulnerable to the oil price crash of 1981 and the rise in international interest rates. Commercial credits dried up in the subsequent debt crisis.

Successive stabilization attempts by the Hurtado government in 1982 and 1983 were frustrated by opposition from private business (especially from the coastal chambers of production), labour and the general public. The turning point came with the election of Febres Cordero at the general election of August 1984. Febres' election saw former agrarian elites in coastal agro-exporting and banking circles regaining the control that they had lost during the preceding oil boom, which had shifted the balance of economic power from the coast to the sierra. The new government willingly implemented policy reforms which made agricultural exports from the coast more competitive, but resisted implementing other politically contentious reforms. From mid-1986 the opposition came to dominate Congress, making it impossible for Febres' government to pursue interest rate liberalization. By 1987 the combined effect of exogenous shocks, austerity measures and rising inflation generated violent opposition which undermined the authority of the government and resulted in its collapse.

The turning point in **Mexico**'s policy orientation came with the inauguration of Miguel de la Madrid as President in December 1982, four months after a crisis had brought Mexico to within a hair's breadth of defaulting on its external debt. Although negotiations with the commercial banks and the IMF, in a situation of limited access to international credit and the need to reverse capital flight, pointed in the direction of orthodoxy, the decisive impetus came from the challenge to the *Institutional Revolutionary Party* (PRI) from the right-wing *Partido de Accion Nacional* (PAN). The latter was supported by Northern financial–industrial interests, which had emerged as a powerful pressure group arguing for a greater role for the private sector and the rolling back of the state. The PRI's response to this challenge was to 'elect' de la Madrid (a leader of the conservative faction of policy-makers based in the Treasury and Central Bank) as President. Once elected, he edged structuralist economists out and replaced them with more orthodox advisers.

Under de la Madrid, an initially successful orthodox stabilization attempt in 1983–5 was thrown off course by a combination of fiscal expansion and monetary relaxation, an earthquake in September 1985 and falling oil prices in 1986. There followed in 1987 an attempt at heterodox stabilization by means of an 'Economic Solidarity Pact'. Under this, the government engineered a wide-ranging austerity accord with unions and the private sector, involving measures such as the halving of tariffs. It devalued the peso by a fifth and began restructuring the state enterprise sector. Adjustment intensified with Carlos Salinas' 'election' as President in December 1988. Salinas continued the heterodox approach to stabilization but backed it up with stronger efforts at structural adjustment. A new pact was agreed between government, unions, employers and peasant organizations. The structural correlates of the programme, the parameters of which were defined by the National Development Plan, included direct foreign investment reform, financial sector reform, deregulation and public sector restructuring, including a stronger privatization effort.

The region therefore underwent a number of remarkable policy reversals. The next task is to enquire into the mainsprings of these, starting with the influence of conditionality.

II-3 The influence of the IFIs

Conditionality

Table 3.2 summarizes the evidence relating to the questions raised in the introduction. On the crucial question of the role of IFI conditionality, we find little evidence to support the proposition that conditionality was decisive in bringing about policy transformation. In the cases of Argentina and Bolivia it is unambiguously clear that IFI conditionality played no role in inducing policy change because in neither of these countries were Bank or IMF programmes in operation during the turning points. In Argentina, in particular, the IFIs resumed lending well after the government had implemented a range of difficult structural reforms and a drastic stabilization to bring the macroeconomic crisis under control. IFI conditionality similarly did not push the governments of Mexico and Chile in any direction in which they did not want to go.

Although there were two Fund stand-bys operational in Chile from January 1974 to March 1976, whose demand-reduction policies were in keeping with the general reorientation of economic policy, the stand-bys did not envisage

Table 3.2 Influences on policy reform in Latin America

	Argent-ina	Bolivia	Chile	Colom-bia	Ecuador	Mexico
Turning point	1989	1986	1974–6	1989–90	1984–6	1982
Fund programme in operation at turning point?	No	No	Yes	No	Yes	Yes
Bank programme in operation at turning point?	No	No	Yes	Yes	Yes	Yes
Successful reform?	Yes	Yes	Yes	Yes	(N)	(Y)
Change in political leadership?	Yes	Yes	Yes	No	Yes	Yes

Reasons for success/failure in policy reform

External factors

IFI conditionality?	No	(N)	No	(Y)	PV	No
IFI policy dialogue?	No	Yes	No	No	(N)	Yes
Cathartic effect of debt crisis and/or other external shocks?	Yes	Yes	N/A	(N)	(N)	(Y)
Financial support from IFIs?	No	Yes	Yes	(Y)	Yes	Yes
Financial support from other creditors?	N/A	Yes	N/A	Yes	PV	Yes

Domestic factors

Political leadership committed to reform?	Yes	Yes	Yes	Yes	(Y)	Yes
Political consensus for reform?	Yes	Yes	N/A	Yes	PV	Yes
Change in interest group pressures?	Yes	Yes	N/A	Yes	Yes	Yes
Technocrats influential?	Yes	Yes	Yes	Yes	(Y)	Yes

Notes:
Yes = hypothesis satisfied; (Y) = hypothesis satisfied with qualifications; PV = perverse impact; No = hypothesis not satisfied; (N) = hypothesis not satisfied with qualifications; N/A = not applicable.

the range of intense structural reforms which the government actually undertook. At the same time, the sector-specific nature of the Bank's project loans to Chile during this period preclude the possibility that Bank conditionality wielded an economy-wide influence and brought about the policy reorientation. In Mexico, conditionalities attached to a series of Bank SECALs were of the pro forma rather than the hard core type (see Chapter 1 for this distinction), and were consequently well implemented. The Bank was careful not to venture into politically contentious issues.

Only Colombia provides evidence of the influence of conditionality. Even there, however, dependence on World Bank loans in a climate of reduced export earnings was only one among a number of factors favouring reform. We have mentioned that by the late 1980s exporters had become a strong pressure group lobbying for liberalization. Meanwhile, strong economic reasons for trade policy reform had begun to manifest themselves, in order to accelerate economic growth and prevent a revaluation of the currency. It was this *combination* of pressures, not IFI conditionality alone, which induced Colombia's policy transformation.

IFI conditionality in Ecuador had a perverse effect on programme implementation. There, the turning point coincided with some progress in implementing pro forma conditionalities which government elites saw as directly promoting their own interests. Bank insistence on politically costly liberalization of interest rates and establishment of free trade in food crops, triggered the general backsliding which followed. It is, however, likely that IMF conditionality played some part in keeping the Bolivian government on the straight and narrow path of reform during the run-up to the 1989 presidential elections. Even here, however, the government was, in the main, committed to policy change and had already voluntarily undertaken substantial reforms.

A further feature that emerges is the IFIs' reluctance, or inability, to punish the many slippages in programme execution. Even in the apparently strong case of the Bank withdrawing support from Argentina as a result of contravention of macroeconomic policy conditions, in fact this was more to extricate itself from an agreement it had been forced into than to pressure the government to implement the trigger conditions of its trade policy loan. In Ecuador's case, the Bank did not withdraw support despite widespread slippage on conditions, not only because it was sympathetic towards Ecuador following the earthquake but, more significantly, because its country desk was under strong pressure to spend as a result of budgetary imperatives within the Bank.

Policy dialogue

Policy dialogue was an important factor enabling programme implementation in Bolivia and in Mexico. In the latter country, in particular, the success of the dialogue which was maintained between Bank staff and the Mexican technocratic team drew its strength from three critical factors. First, the two groups were highly compatible in terms of training and experience. Mexican leaders and high officials included highly trained economists and others who had been educated in the US and European universities. They thus shared a common background with most Bank staff and the two sides were willing to engage each other as equals in an intellectual interchange. Moreover, the fact that the recent problems of the Mexican economy had been sufficiently unique that Bank staff 'could no more lay claim to superior expertise based on experience than their client' (World Bank, 1994: 44–5) made for a relatively evenly balanced relationship.

Second, the Bank was willing to play by the rules of Mexican political management. As obvious and high profile Bank involvement in policy decisions was regarded by Mexican officials as politically unacceptable, the Bank agreed to provide loan support for adjustment in sub-sector after sub-sector, and in individual industries, instead of attempting to push for a comprehensive SAL. Likewise, the Bank was content to confine its dialogue to areas where advice was acceptable. For this reason, there was at that time no dialogue on social policy topics like population growth and education. The Bank similarly did not press for reforms that were at odds with the government's own programme. Instead, it provided incentives and encouragement to reform-minded elements within government. In this respect, the Bank's background analyses are likely to have been used by Mexican technocrats to push for necessary policy changes.

The Bank's approach in Mexico can be contrasted with that followed in Ecuador, where there was little useful policy dialogue. When the Bank tried to insist on politically unpalatable reforms, the Ecuadorian negotiating team appeared to go along with these but with every intention of fudging implementation. In this case, the record on implementation would probably have been more favourable if the Bank had concentrated on working out a consensus for reform with the Ecuadorians.

Financial support

Access to IFI credit was an important factor in facilitating adjustment by easing the foreign exchange constraint in all the countries in the sample except Argentina. In Ecuador, the financial contribution of an agricultural SECAL was significant in relieving the import constraint and enabling agricultural growth. Likewise in Mexico, financial support provided by the IFIs, and their role in enabling Mexico to reschedule its debt obligations to international commercial banks, provided the government with a breathing space during which reforms could be undertaken. However, it is also likely that the soft budget constraint provided by the IFIs in the early 1990s blunted Mexico's reform effort and contributed to the peso crisis of December 1994.

The evidence also suggests that where financial support was available from other creditors, it was useful in promoting the reform effort only in countries where the government was already convinced of the need for reform, as in Colombia, and in Mexico in the 1980s. In Bolivia, the breathing space that other creditors were forced to provide took the unusual form of a 'consensual default' on commercial debt. But in Ecuador, availability of credit from alternative sources had the negative effect of enabling the government to evade hard core Bank conditionality and go ahead with its own agenda, as exemplified by the Santa Elena irrigation project.

II-4 Other external influences

We find strong evidence from Argentina and Bolivia in support of the proposition that the cathartic effect of the debt crisis and the drying up of international bank credit jolted governments into new policy directions. This was the dominant factor in Argentina's policy transformation. As we have shown, decades of distributional conflict had driven Argentina to bankruptcy. Carlos Menem was forced to align himself with the business community and effect strong stabilization measures backed up by sweeping structural reforms but only when it became evident that no international creditors, not even the IFIs, were willing to lend to Argentina without major policy reversals. In this case, the IFIs' withholding financial assistance until internal conditions were conducive to reform played a pivotal role in bringing about the change.

Similarly, in Bolivia, the hyperinflation of 1985 seems to have been the catalytic factor, in turn triggered by the debt crisis and other external events. These forced Victor Paz to face up to a set of harsh domestic and international realities – particularly the financial limits to state capitalism – with a new pragmatism. Moreover, the Bolivian government was keen to obtain assistance under the Brady Plan and this encouraged them further down the path of reform.

It is also likely that policy-makers in Argentina, Bolivia, Mexico and Colombia were favourably influenced by the demonstrated success of the neo-liberal experiment in Chile, perhaps even by developments in South-east Asia. However, the materials we analysed did not yield specific evidence on this proposition.

II-5 Internal factors influencing policy change

There is overwhelming evidence that a political leadership committed to change is a *sine qua non* of successful reform. In all the countries in the sample, other than Colombia, the reorientation of economic policy coincided with a change in political leadership. This enabled a fresh approach to tackling the economic crisis, with new leaders and technocrats coming to the fore. In some countries, this also signalled a favourable change in the attitudes of special interest groups constituting the support base of the governing party.

Committed political leadership can arise through the necessity to confront harsh economic realities in the face of a severe budget constraint, as with the erstwhile Peronist Carlos Menem and Bolivia's one-time revolutionary, Victor Paz. Alternatively, it can bring into the ascendancy reform-minded leaders leaning towards orthodoxy, like Miguel de la Madrid or the Chilean military junta. Committed political leadership was probably the most important determinant of reform in Chile, where Pinochet's socio-political programme for the total rejection of Allende's Marxist economic model coincided with the thrust of economic orthodoxy.

On the other hand, the commitment of political leaders to reform can depend on changes in interest group pressures. In Colombia, the emergence of exporters as a powerful group lobbying for liberalization, and gradual acceptance by other industrialists that outward-orientation would generate a stronger growth dynamic than producing for the internal market, convinced the Barco administration that trade liberalization could be politically expedient. This point is reinforced by evidence from Ecuador: like Menem and Paz, Presidents Hurtado, Febres and Borja were all convinced of the need for policy change but were none of them able to overcome the adversarial regionalism of Ecuadorian politics to construct a consensus for sustained reform. Some progress was made during Febres' tenure, when the coastal elites who came to power with him saw the advantages of providing incentives to exporters through measures such as exchange rate reform. But the prospect of alienating political support in the sierra if the marketing of food crops was to be liberalized, or interest rates were to be rationalized, made Febres' government reluctant to move on such reforms. In Mexico too, it was the rise of the right-wing PAN, representing Northern industrial interests, which made it politically expedient for the PRI to move towards orthodoxy in economic policy.

The countries in the sample also provide strong evidence for the view that a political consensus for reform is an important determinant of successful programme implementation. While in Mexico the PRI's rightward shift ensured a tacit consensus between itself and its right-wing challengers, an opposition-dominated Congress in Ecuador made it impossible for Febres' government to forge ahead with interest rate reform. In contrast, the rightward shift in the economic policy stance of both Menem and Paz enabled them to command enough congressional support to pass their respective reform packages. Even in Colombia, where politics had traditionally been consensual, VAT reform required a coalition of some Liberals and a faction of the Conservative Party to get it through Congress.

Thus, the extent to which there is a political consensus for reform at the turning point and after is paramount to successful programme implementation in democratic or quasi-democratic political systems (Argentina, Bolivia and Mexico). However, the need for a consensus can be done away with in a strong military dictatorship, whose leaders can afford to wait for the reforms to bear fruit in order that they will be self-sustaining thereafter, as in Chile.

The case studies also show that even in democratic systems political leaders have had to resort to a degree of authoritarianism in order to force reforms past potential losers, such as organized labour. Thus, Menem broke up strikes so that he could implement public enterprise reforms and Paz went further, detaining union leaders and confining numbers of them to remote river ports. Mexico might be thought to have had a natural advantage in this area compared to other governments, as the *modus operandi* of the PRI had always been to internalize and transmute dissent by co-opting labour unions and resorting to electoral fraud when necessary. Nevertheless, even Mexico's leaders were forced to strike a deal with labour through the *Pacto* to compensate workers for harsh stabilization measures. Similar compensatory measures might have raised support for Ecuador's reforms had the government sought it.

Compared with these internal political factors, the evidence further suggests that technocrats have little leverage over policy-making unless they are supported by their political leaders. On the Latin American evidence, technocrats function as facilitators rather than as catalysers in the adjustment process. They provide the expertise for the design of programmes for which the politicians provide leadership. Ecuador in 1984–6 provides a good example of a committed technocratic team making little progress because they lacked support from the political leadership. In some countries the political leaders were themselves economists intellectually convinced of the need for reform, such as Miguel de la Madrid, Carlos Salinas and Cesar Gaviria. In Argentina, Bolivia and Chile, the political leaders, though not economists themselves, were also committed to orthodox reform but depended on their advisers to formulate and implement the reforms. The technocratic elite in these countries shared similar educational and professional backgrounds. Largely educated in free-market economic theory at North American universities, many of them had close links with the IFIs and some had worked in the IMF or in the Bank.

II-6 *Conclusions on Latin America*

Clearly, when there is little congruence between the reform agenda of the government and that envisaged for it by the IFIs, the odds are heavily stacked against donor attempts to induce reforms through financial leverage. On the contrary, IFI involvement in adjustment lending in these situations can provide a recalcitrant government with a degree of financial ease that enables it to put off reforms. Meanwhile, the lending agency concerned almost always suffers a loss of credibility, especially because the IFIs' – particularly the Bank's – record on punishing noncompliance is poor. Donors would therefore be better advised to withhold financial assistance until the drying up of external credit and the subsequent financial crisis forces a government to grasp the nettle of reform for itself, as in Argentina. Alternatively, they should wait until internal political developments create a more favourable environment for change.

By contrast, we have seen that where there is consensus between donors and recipients on the reform agenda, this has made for much better implementation. In this regard, our evidence on the internal factors influencing reform suggests that the degree of congruence between them is determined by a favourable configuration of domestic forces at the time of reform. Domestic factors emerge as the key determinants of successful policy change. Foremost among these is a leadership convinced of the need for change, backed by a political consensus favouring reform.

Further, our evidence shows that policy dialogue with government technocrats and political leaders by IFI staff can play an important role in forging a consensus between them and the government on programme objectives and the reform agenda. Moreover, policy dialogue can contribute to the tailoring of programme objectives to what can be realistically achieved given the configuration of domestic political forces. This would require a greater awareness and monitoring of the internal political situation and technical capacity of borrowing countries than is currently normal in the IFIs, however. The demonstrated success of a limited programme may well generate a consensus and a momentum for more ambitious reforms later on, whereas an over-ambitious programme which ignores the political imperatives is apt to generate a momentum of opposition which can derail the reform effort altogether.

See Regional References at the end of the book for details of the works consulted in the preparation of the above studies.

Notes

1 Based on Ana Marr, 'Conditionality and South-east Asian Adjustment', *ODI Working Paper*, No. 94 (London: ODI), July 1996.
2 This section is based on Ramani Gunatilaka, 'Conditionality and the Political Economy of Policy Reform in Latin America', *ODI Working Paper*, No. 96 (London: ODI), March 1997.

4

THE 'OWNERSHIP' PROBLEM

I Introduction

Chapter 1 concluded that the justification for conditionality stood or fell on its ability to improve policies within recipient countries. The last two chapters, however, have raised doubts about its ability to do so, notwithstanding the widespread use of this modality during the past decade-and-a-half.

Thus, Chapter 2 concluded from a review of evidence from multi-country studies that the adjustment programmes of the World Bank and IMF achieve their objectives only to a rather weak degree, with neither organization able to show a systematic connection between their programmes and movements in economic variables, and with limited revealed leverage over key policy instruments. This result was obtained even though the approach to policy which the IFIs promote does generally result in improved economic performance where it is instituted. This paradox, we suggested, can be substantially explained by the weak extent to which many IFI programmes are implemented. Welfare would most probably be increased, perhaps transformed in some cases, if programmes had greater success in improving policies and it is therefore important to discover the reasons for poor execution.

The regional studies in Chapter 3 raised further doubts about the efficacy of conditionality, for in both South-east Asia and Latin America decisive moves towards improved macro management, and more 'market-friendly', open-economy policies, were shown to owe little to donor conditionality, which either was not an important influence at all or could not achieve reform until domestic conditions became favourable.

It seems, then, that donors have had limited success in using their financial leverage to induce policy reforms, even though many of the recipients have undoubtedly been desperate for the money. Why should this be the case? Is it merely that the leverage has not been wisely applied, so that improved modalities could bring large improvements in outcomes? Or is the problem endemic, so that the whole enterprise is a mistake?

This and the next two chapters take up these questions, attempting to throw light on the reasons for the poor record of policy conditionality. A line of explanation common among donors suggests that failures occur because of weak government 'ownership' of programmes, which is the topic taken up in this chapter. We conclude, however, that, although persuasive, the ownership explanation is limited and superficial. Chapters 5 and 6 therefore extend the debate to examine the implementation problem within an analytical framework derived informally from agency theory. This generates a number of hypotheses about reasons for poor implementation which we test against the evidence in Chapters 5 and 6.

II Meaning and measurement of ownership

It has become common to attribute non-implementation of donor conditions, and disappointing outcomes, to weak government 'ownership' of the measures in question. This makes sense. If a government is alienated from the policy changes it is asked to introduce it is plausible to expect that it will be less than punctilious in executing these stipulations, compared with measures largely designed by the government itself.

But to go beyond what is intuitively plausible, it is necessary to define 'ownership' in some reasonably precise way which can be operationalized in research. This task has been taken furthest in a *World Bank Discussion Paper* by Johnson and Wasty (1993: 2–5). Although they do not offer a generic definition, they identify four dimensions of programme ownership. The first of these is straightforward: the locus of programme initiation, with ownership lowest when it is initiated by the donor agency (the World Bank in their case) despite government disagreement with, and reluctance to implement, some aspects of the programme. By this test, ownership is highest when the government initiates the programme.

Their other three criteria relate to different aspects of what is meant by 'the government'. They distinguish between the intellectual conviction of key policy-makers or ministries (the technocratic dimension) and the demonstrated support of the top leadership (the political dimension). By the former test, ownership is most strongly indicated by 'an observable and detailed consensus among identifiable key ministries/decisionmakers about the nature of the crisis and the necessary remedial actions' (Johnson and Wasty, 1993: 4). Support by the political leadership is most strongly demonstrated by 'specific and dramatic up-front actions'; its absence by uncertainties from the outset about whether the government will act to overcome obstacles to proposed reforms. Their fourth dimension takes up another aspect of the locus of ownership: to the extent that there is government support, how widely is this based? By this test, the strongest indicator of ownership is that the government has launched 'a broad-based public campaign for helping in designing the program and/or to elicit support outside the central government' (Johnson and Wasty, 1993: 5). The weakest level of ownership in this dimension is that 'the government' has not even consulted key executing agencies.

In a different context, Haggard and Kaufman introduce another test: the extent to which a given set of policy reforms becomes 'consolidated', meaning 'not only that policies have persisted over time, but that they have been institutionalized within the policy system' (Haggard and Kaufman, 1992: 7). On their view, consolidation 'involves stabilizing expectations around a new set of incentives and convincing economic agents that they cannot easily be reversed'. This is most likely 'where governments have constructed relatively stable coalitions of political support that encompass major private sector beneficiaries, and have secured at least the acquiescence of the major forces competing within the political system' (1992: 20). Such institutionalization raises the chances that reforms will be persisted with, adding to their credibility.

Note that both these studies agree that ownership in its strongest form requires broadly-based consent. A veteran member of the IMF's staff, Johnson (1994), explores this further, in the context of substantial shortfalls in the implementation of Fund programmes in Africa. In effect, he argues that, although important, it is not enough for governments to own programmes; governments and programmes need to be backed by legitimacy:

> when a government does not have legitimate authority to implement a program, it will also lack political support. In such a situation, the government may find that dependence on other forms of power (force, manipulation, persuasion) or of authority (coercion) will enable it to attain only a rather modest degree of implementation in the face of sabotage, indifference, nonparticipation, and minimum effort and compliance from the general population.
>
> (Johnson, 1994: 406)

(A rather devastating critique of the Fund's programme modalities could be read between the lines of Johnson's article. It could be inferred that the Fund pays far too little attention to these considerations and, indeed, that many of its programmes in Africa are misplaced, but we should not put words into his mouth.)

From the above considerations we can attempt a general ideal-case definition:

> Government ownership is at its strongest when the political leadership and its advisers, with broad support among agencies of state and civil society, decide of their own volition that policy changes are desirable, choose what these changes should be and when they should be introduced, and where these changes become built into parameters of policy and administration which are generally accepted as desirable.

The opposite case is given when reforms are donor-initiated and designed, with little domestic support and few local roots. In such cases we can say the measures are donor-owned. Note that we are here tacitly excluding the not uncommon situation where the design of specific policy measures is donor driven because, *although the government agrees with the desirability of the policy changes in question*, the civil service does not possess the expertise or other resources to allow it to undertake the detailed design. Such a situation occurred in Ghana in the early 1980s, for example. Measures were initially designed by IMF and World Bank staff but ownership could reasonably be described as residing with the government because it fully backed the desirability of the measures and was happy to be able to utilize the expertise of the IFIs.

III The effects of ownership

For each of their dimensions of ownership, Johnson and Wasty defined four levels of intensity, which they then assessed from a pool of eighty-one World Bank adjustment credits in thirty-eight countries approved between 1980 and 1988. They then correlated the resulting ownership ratings with assessments of the success of the programmes in achieving their objectives. They secured impressively strong results, as summarized in Table 4.1.

The first notable feature emerging is that half (40/81) of the programmes were characterized by low or very low government ownership. This gives the lie to Bank claims that it never imposes programmes on unwilling governments. In only a fifth (16/81) of the cases studied was government ownership regarded as very high.

Second, there was a striking positive correlation between ownership and the satisfactoriness of programme outcomes. In statistical terms, Johnson and Wasty (1993: 5) found that ownership was strongly predictive of programme success in three-quarters (73 per cent) of all cases, with outlier results largely

Table 4.1 Correlating programme outcome with borrower ownership

Borrower ownership	Programme outcome				
	Highly satisfactory	*Satisfactory*	*Un- satisfactory*	*Very un- satisfactory*	*Total*
Very high	9	6	0	1	16
High	6	15	2	2	25
Low	4	10	6	3	23
Very low	0	3	7	7	17
Total	19	34	15	13	81

Source: Johnson and Wasty (1993, Table 1).

explicable in terms of the influence of external shocks. Standard tests confirmed the statistical significance of their correlation (Johnson and Wasty, 1993: 23). Of the four separate components of their indicators of ownership, the extent of demonstrated support by a country's political leadership emerged as the most important, and was judged as low or very low in 44 per cent of observations. (Unfortunately, there is no equivalent information for the IMF. However, it is likely that equivalent tests on Fund programmes would yield similar results, not least because many of the Bank programmes analysed by Johnson and Wasty were accompanied by parallel Fund programmes. The IMF's own tendency to attribute non-implementation to 'lack of political will' points in the same direction. That the Fund has been unforthcoming on this subject is not, we suspect, because it thinks ownership is unimportant, but because it has particular difficulties in dealing with this subject.[1])

While Johnson and Wasty have taken rigorous analysis of this elusive topic further than other observers, the thrust of their results is supported by others. A 1991 study of the supervision and monitoring of adjustment programmes by the World Bank's Operations Evaluation Department confirmed the importance of government ownership for programme implementation: 'In the absence of such commitment, intensive supervision aided implementation, but not enough to bring about a significant or sustained adjustment of the economy' (World Bank, 1991: 16). Kahler (1992: 115, Table 2.2) similarly marshals evidence showing a positive (although not perfect) association between government commitment to reform and programme implementation: in nine out of sixteen programmes with high implementation levels there was also strong prior government commitment to reform; in eight of eleven poorly executed programmes there was also low government commitment. The results of Williamson's 1994 thirteen-country study of the political economy of policy reform, although not focused on the concept of ownership, are also consistent with the importance of this variable, pointing strongly to the dominance of domestic political conditions (see Williamson, 1994: 563, Table 1). External aid can be very important but conditionality may be counterproductive: 'A team that does not feel it owns its program is unlikely to pursue it with the enthusiasm and determination that are critical to success, no matter how cleverly or tightly the conditionality terms are defined' (Williamson, 1994: 566).

Findings of the importance of ownership at a more microeconomic level are provided in a study of the liberalization of cereals marketing in African countries (Coulter, 1994), which explains the varied levels of success largely in ownership terms. Marketing liberalization worked best in Mali, where there was a high degree of consensus within the country and with its donors. It worked fairly well in Tanzania, where there was less consensus but the government was willing to allow privatization to occur spontaneously. In Kenya and Malawi the liberalization was insisted upon by the donors in the face of government reluctance and did not realize expected benefits.

Further evidence on the importance of ownership is provided by the research undertaken for the present volume, described in the next chapter, with the results (for Hypothesis number 4) summarized in Table 5.1 and the Master Table (see p. 199). Of our twenty-one countries, there was clear evidence on this in all but one case, and in eighteen of the twenty the extent of ownership, or its absence, was found to have exerted a decisive influence on the degree of programme implementation.

The entries in Row 4 of the Master Table tell an eloquent story. A number of countries in the sample changed during the period studied from weak to vigorous implementation of reforms and in each of these the key was a changed attitude to reform on the part of the political leadership of the day. In Jamaica there was a large contrast between the early and late 1980s. In 1980-3 the adjustment programme was largely donor-designed, with important government reservations, and was crucially undermined by government resistance to the exchange rate reforms stipulated by the IMF. By 1986-8 the situation had changed decisively, with the programme an agreed outcome of extensive policy discussions between the government and the IFIs, resulting in improved execution and economic results. A similar story can be told for the Philippines over roughly the same period: it took a radical change of government (from Marcos to Aquino) for programme execution and results to be reversed from abysmal to satisfactory. Colombia (pre- and post-1989) also conforms to this pattern, as do Argentina (with the advent of the Menem administration as the key factor), Tanzania (with the resignation as head of government of Nyerere as a decisive moment) and Zambia (where the defeat of the Kaunda government was the watershed).

In other cases, ownership was generally strong throughout and so was reform implementation: Chile, Indonesia, Korea, Mexico and Thailand. Chapter 3 discusses most of these cases in more detail. In the case of Thailand, the judgement is offered there that, while local ownership and implementation of the 1982 adjustment package was generally good, 'Those few provisions which were genuinely conditional were also the least implemented'. The opposite conditions applied in another group – steadily reluctant governments, donor-dominated programmes and weak implementation: Guyana, Kenya, Madagascar and Senegal.

The burden of all the evidence surveyed above points overwhelmingly to the crucial importance of ownership. It concurs strongly with the editor's conclusions from a special issue of *World Development* on 'implementing policy change':

> no amount of external donor pressure or resources, by themselves, can produce sustained reform. It takes ownership, both of the policy change to be implemented and of any capacity-building efforts intended to enhance implementation. . . . Unless someone or some group in the country where policy reform is being pursued feels that

the changes are something that they want to see happen, externally initiated change efforts whether at the local or national level are likely to fail. Without policy 'champions' who are willing and able to serve as leaders for change, reform is not possible. *Fundamentally, indigenous leadership is essential for sustainable policy implementation.*

(Brinkerhoff, 1996: 1,396 [emphasis added])

But why should this be so? What is being said here about the ways in which governments work and policies are changed? The weakness of the ownership explanation is that it is *ad hoc*, not set within a theory of government. Is it, as Brinkerhoff suggests, a matter of the personal enthusiasm of the local champions who must implement the reforms? No doubt that is important but the strength of the ownership factor suggests that there must be more to it than that. By itself, the ownership explanation appears superficial.

IV Ownership matters because interests conflict

A major reason why the ownership variable has such a strong explanatory appeal, we suggest, is because underlying it is the more profound matter of the extent of congruence between the interests or objectives of donors and 'recipients', where recipients can be thought of as referring narrowly to the central government (or just to key members of it) or, in the ideal case, extended to include civil society. On this view, when ownership is at its strongest, this is because the government and wider public regard the reforms, and associated timetable of actions, as in their own interests. Ownership is at its weakest when donor objectives dominate and important programme measures are not viewed as in the public (or government's) interest, or (as is common) when the donors push for more rapid action than the government would choose. A government can be said to own a programme when its objectives dominate, and it chooses the means and speed of achieving those objectives.

If ownership has powerful explanatory value but we are right in suggesting that this is often a proxy for conflicts of interest, this implies that such conflicts are common. There may indeed remain clashes in belief systems, even in this era after 'the end of history'. Gordon points to one frequent source of difficulty:

while donors have viewed structural adjustment as a political instrument to radically downsize African states, governments generally have seen it as a means of shoring up the status quo. Given these widely differing perspectives, it is not surprising that adjustment became such a highly contested terrain of public policy.

(Gordon, 1996: 1,529)

However, to assert the frequency of interest conflicts it is not necessary to imply a confrontational view of donor–government relations. While agreeing with Gordon, there nonetheless is today greater global convergence on the desirable strategy of economic policy than has been the case for many years. Flat ideologically-based stand-offs have become rare, as witness the changes in Latin American attitudes towards the IMF recorded in Chapter 3. My study of IMF programmes similarly found adversarial situations to be exceptional, with workmanlike relationships in most cases (Killick, 1995b: 114–15).

Even with shared general attitudes between donors and recipients, however, *conflicts of interest must be expected to be the general case*, for a number of reasons:

1   Donor agencies and recipient governments operate against the background of differing histories, traditions and institutional constraints. These differences will often result in contrasting perceptions of what changes are desirable and feasible, and of how best to achieve them. Indeed, one of the weaknesses of the conditionality of the IFIs, with its broad similarity across countries, is that it tends to be ahistorical, pulling against the path-dependent nature of reform processes at the national level.[2]

2   Relatedly, donors and governments are answerable to, and have to satisfy, radically contrasting constituencies, and their respective remits differ accordingly. Governments have to worry about their electorates, particularly about strategic groups of supporters and 'floaters'. Even unelected governments have to maintain the support of key groups in the army, the trade unions, landowners, the church, etc. On the donor side, to take the specific case of the IFIs, they have to remain within the policy parameters set by their boards. These in turn (particularly in the case of the IMF) are dominated by the governments of the G7 industrial countries, which means that IFI managements and staffs are obliged to try keeping the representatives of these important countries 'on board'. That such different constituencies will result in conflicts over such matters as trade and investment policies is obvious.

3   Besides being answerable to contrasting constituencies, the parties will also be driven in separate directions by the exigencies of maintaining internal political balance. This is most obviously the case with recipient governments. Stability requires the maintenance of a balance within these coalitions of interests and viewpoints, and this necessity tends to turn policy decisions into 'resultants' of complex bargaining processes and trade-offs, rather than 'rational' optimizing choices among alternatives.[3] A large donor agency like the World Bank and (to a lesser extent) the IMF can likewise be viewed as a coalition of departmental and other interests, which also have to be balanced. The specific policy preferences arising from these balancing acts by donors and recipients can hardly be expected to coincide in many cases.

4   There are also moral hazard aspects which can also lead to conflicts. Two versions can be identified:

   a   The government may see it as in its interests to make insincere policy promises in order to secure financial support and may then use this money in order to postpone reform. Such action is liable to create an overt clash with the donor (unless that agency is under pressure to spend its budget regardless). There have been many examples of this, as described in Chapter 6.

   b   Moral hazard is created when one party to a transaction does not bear the full consequences of its actions. One of the long-standing complaints about donor–recipient relationships is that the costs of mistakes fall almost exclusively on recipient governments and peoples. This complaint has particular point in the context of IFI adjustment programmes, where (partly because of the convention of treating the IFIs as 'preferred creditors', meaning that they have first claim on a governments resources to ensure the full servicing of past IFI credits) these institutions are little affected if adjustment costs turn out to be higher than expected.

   This basic asymmetry tends to make governments more risk-averse than IFI lenders and creates sometimes major differences in time horizons, with IFIs able to take a detached view and to emphasize the long-term economic gains of reform, while governments are more preoccupied with identifying the short-term losers and gainers, and with surviving the period of initial pain. Governments therefore tend to take a less sanguine view than donors of the political costs and dangers of policy change.

5   Finally, there is resentment of foreign intervention and of the apparent erosion of national sovereignty that results from conditionality. This set of considerations requires rather fuller discussion, for it is at the heart of why conditionality is often counterproductive.

V National resentment and the erosion of sovereignty[4]

The ability of international agencies or – even worse – other governments to apparently stipulate the key elements of a recipient government's policies is a natural source of resentment, not least because it is an unwanted reminder of the unequal distribution of power around the world, and of the home country's weakness in that distribution. This resentment is apt to be intensified by manifest discrepancies between the actions of donor governments at home and those which they urge upon recipient countries, as demonstrated by donor–government tendencies to urge environmental policies on developing countries, e.g. in the matter of energy pricing, which they are unwilling to apply domestically, or their reluctance to submit themselves to the fiscal-monetary disciplines of the IMF they so readily urge upon others, moving the Fund's official historian to observe:

> there is an understandable perception of asymmetry between developing and industrial country members in that the conditionality applied to the use of the Fund's resources has significantly affected developing members, while surveillance under Article IV . . . seems to have had little practical effect on the large industrial members.
>
> (de Vries, 1987: 284)

Hard core conditionality, as defined in Chapter 1, rests on the presumption either that the donor agency knows better than national policy-makers which policies are good for domestic economic performance or that they have a better judgement of what is politically feasible, even though local officials and politicians ought to have better information about these matters. This presumption of superior knowledge adds to the resentments, which are further fuelled when an agency is inconsistent in its policy stipulations, perhaps as a result of changes in personnel. Past approaches to policy of agencies like the World Bank have been notoriously subject to the vagaries of fashion. The Bank knows best, but *what* it knows best changes over time.

Then there is the sovereignty issue. The debate about conditionality is strewn with allegations of donor-agency erosion of national sovereignty. Is there substance in this complaint or is it mere nationalist rhetoric? The question whether IFI conditionality is inconsistent with national sovereignty is taken up by Zormelo (1996a) in a background paper commissioned for this project.

In broad terms, Zormelo answers in the negative: IFI conditionality does not breach sovereignty, provided only that the agencies remain within the terms of their Articles of Agreement, and that the credit agreements are not coercive and are freely entered into by borrowing governments. Some types of conditionality do come closer to infringing sovereignty than others, including attempts to use it to influence borrowing governments' defence spending, or even to change their systems of government, but even here conditionality can be defended.

Confusion arises, Zormelo suggests, in mistakenly thinking that sovereignty is located in the government of the day, whereas in legal terms it adheres in the institutions of the state, which have a life beyond the transience of particular governments. When it comes to the use of donors' financial leverage to reform systems of governance, he points out that the Universal Declaration of Human Rights states that 'The will of the people shall be the basis of the authority of governments' whereas many of the governments targeted by 'political' conditionality are deficient in authority so derived:

where unaccountable and imposed governments are careless with the use of a country's resources and do not respect the rights of the citizens, and the citizens themselves are clamouring for change, then political conditionalities can be justified if the aim is to correct the situation.

(Zormelo, 1996a: 22)

Zormelo concedes, though, that the use of conditionality related to systems of governance is dangerous territory for the IFIs, whose Articles place restrictions on the extent to which they can discriminate between member countries on political grounds. However, the agencies take some pains to remain within their Articles. It is for this reason that the World Bank makes a distinction between issues of 'governance' (which it has defined as 'the manner in which power is exercised in the management of a country's economic and social resources for development' – World Bank, 1994d: xiv) in which it claims a legitimate interest because the quality of governance affects the productivity with which its credits are employed, and wider issues of human rights observance, democratization and the like, from which it endeavours to steer clear. However, this is probably not a sustainable distinction. For one thing, the conditions identified by the Bank as conducive to 'good governance' can have large implications for the wider system of a country's government, as Nelson and Eglinton argue:

The World Bank defined poor governance narrowly as lack of accountability, transparency, and predictability on the part of politicians and bureaucrats, and the absence of the rule of law. But this definition led inexorably to broader issues. Transparency requires not only open competition for public contracts, but adequate information on government projects and programs, and therefore the freedom of the media. Accountability entails not only effective financial accounting and auditing, but penalties for corrupt or inept politicians. That in turn implies some form of elections and the freedom of association and speech to make such elections meaningful. A predictable rule of law requires an independent and competent judiciary. Thus the notion of improved governance as crucial for economic growth expanded from improved public administration to a series of prescriptions sounding very much like guidelines for pluralist democracy.

(Nelson and Eglinton, 1993: 15)

Second, however, as a historical proposition, it is by no means obvious that such qualities as transparency and accountability are actually associated with the improved utilization of economic resources. Plenty of contrary examples suggest themselves and attempts by academic researchers to 'explain' countries' economic performance by reference to regime types have had little success.[5] Indeed, it is possible that the political changes implicit in the Bank's desire for improved governance in some countries could actually worsen economic policies, e.g. by introducing the demons of the electoral cycle, undermining what the Bank seeks to do in the improvement of policies. Again, examples could be given, of which Kenya has been cited in an earlier chapter.

A second grey area acknowledged by Zormelo, where the practice of conditionality may threaten sovereignty, arises from the unequal treatment of countries in otherwise comparable situations. Various researchers have found substantial inequalities of treatment. I have elsewhere set out evidence on this relating to the IMF, concluding that political lobbying by major shareholder governments had prevented the Fund from observing its principle of uniformity of treatment and, at its worst, had forced it to provide essentially unconditional finance to favoured governments despite proven records of economic mismanagement (Killick, 1995b: 128). Stiles' (1991: 36) study of Fund decision processes similarly concluded that these resulted in specially favourable consideration of large, important countries, in contrast with the routine treatment accorded to small countries.

Similar tendencies exist within the World Bank. Mosley et al.'s study of the Bank's adjustment lending found that 'The poorer the recipient's initial *political* bargaining position . . . the more stringent the conditions imposed on it, regardless of the severity of the level of *economic* mismanagement, as measured by the severity of distortions in individual markets' (1991a: 125). Internal evidence from the Bank confirms inequalities of treatment. Its review of the effectiveness of the monitoring and supervision of adjustment programmes concluded that 'There were wide differences in the way the Bank decided whether the conditions for tranche release were satisfied' (World Bank, 1991: 16). Turkey, the Philippines, Côte d'Ivoire and Jamaica were among the beneficiaries of inconsistent treatment, although no obvious pattern in favour of the large and powerful emerges from the report's full list of examples.

In their wider examination of donor applications of conditionality, Nelson and Eglinton (1993: 82) similarly found large inconsistencies in the treatment of individual countries, a tendency which they regard as having been aggravated by the proliferation of conditionality described in Chapter 1. The fact is that in its more rigorous forms conditionality is something which happens to the governments of poor, weak or desperate countries. This helps explain why such a high proportion of it has become concentrated in sub-Saharan Africa. Large, politically powerful countries can expect to be exempt unless they get into a serious financial crisis. As one donor official put it, 'China is an exception to everything'.

It is perhaps not very important whether jurists would hold that conditionality breaches national sovereignty because it is based on inequalities in negotiating power which lead to large inconsistencies in country treatment, and because, in straying however reluctantly into using their financial leverage to achieve political change, the IFIs have gone beyond the terms of their Articles. What is more pertinent is that populist assertions of national sovereignty in opposition to agencies of international capitalism headquartered in another country's capital can have strong emotive force and undermine the acceptability of policies promoted by those agencies.

We have seen, then, that there are various sources of national resentment of conditionality, resentment that it is not difficult for a domestic opposition to exploit, perhaps inflame. Where it exists, hostility to outside 'interference' can add powerfully to perceptions of differences of interest as between donors and recipients. It can sometimes undermine the prospects of policy reform by creating a generalized suspicion of changes advocated outside, whatever the merits of the proposed reforms. This is another reason for valuing local ownership of reform programmes, and why it is likely to be associated with successful reform.

VI The extent of interest conflicts

There are, then, a number of reasons why donor and recipient interests, objectives and priorities must be expected to differ, and to be perceived to differ, even in the absence of any major disagreement about the desirable general thrust of economy policy. Sometimes the differences will be acute, sometimes minor, but it is rare for donor–recipient interests to completely coincide.

Evidence of the important influence of perceived differences in donor–borrower interests is provided by our country studies. Table 5.1 (Item 3) summarizes the findings relating to the hypothesis that programme implementation is prejudiced when IFI and government objectives differ, creating conflicts of interest. As can be seen, this proposition was consistent with the facts in all the seventeen cases for which there was clear evidence. Where IFI and government objectives were seen as broadly congruent, implementation was good (Gambia, Ghana, Korea, Mexico, Thailand, etc.); where interests were seen as seriously conflicting, execution was generally weak (Jamaica, Kenya, Madagascar, the Philippines, Senegal, etc.). The (post-1991) Indian case is interesting. Here the government's general policy stance was strongly pro-reform but it dragged its feet on the public enterprise reforms pushed by the donors because it feared adverse consequences for employment and its own political standing. Thus, while there was much progress on other fronts, movement in this area was slight.

One possibility here is that conflicts will be minimized – and programme success enhanced – through the development of long-term, trust-enhancing relationships between a donor agency (in the present case, the World Bank) and a recipient government. The evidence for this was also examined in our country survey and is reported as the final hypothesis in Table 5.1 and the Master Table (on p. 199). In fact, Table 5.1 shows that there were rather more situations that were inconsistent with this hypothesis than cases which supported it (nine against six). In fact, this was the second-most-weakly supported of all our hypotheses.

Scrutiny of Hypothesis 15 of the Master Table reveals a wide range of outcomes from long-term relationships – from the Mexican (and perhaps Indian) case where the growing familiarity of the two parties with each other resulted in the emergence of a policy consensus, to the IFIs' nightmare scenario where a government used the knowledge it had acquired through frequent contacts with the Bank the better to deceive it (Colombia, Turkey, perhaps Malawi), or where long-term relationships apparently did little to narrow policy differences between the Bank and government (Kenya, Madagascar, the Philippines, Zambia).

VII Conclusion

To recapitulate, we have seen that there is a substantial accumulation of statistically-based and other evidence showing that the extent of government ownership of reform programmes exerts a decisive influence on their implementation and the results they achieve. We have suggested, however, that the ownership explanation is superficial because it is not set within a framework which explicates *why* ownership should exert so decisive an influence.

While stopping well short of providing a full theoretical framework, we have suggested that what has been called ownership has strong explanatory power because it is a proxy indicator of the extent to which the policy reforms in question are perceived by those who must execute them as being in their own, and their compatriots', interests. Where local ownership is complete, the government is taking the main decisions about what changes should be made and when; local goals and priorities dominate and the motivation for vigorous implementation is strong. When local ownership is lacking, it is the donors' objectives and priorities which dominate, and a gap is created between the interests of the initiators and executors of the reforms. We are thus calling in aid an interest-dominated model of politics.

We have further given reasons for thinking that, even though there is growing convergence around the globe on the desirable content of economic policy, the objectives and interests of donor agencies and of recipient governments can rarely be expected to coincide. The two parties are conditioned by different historical and institutional backgrounds; they are answerable to different constituencies; they each have their own internal management imperatives; there may be differences in attitude to the role of the supporting finance offered by donors (the moral hazard issue); there are asymmetries in the incidence of adjustment costs, including the costs of mistakes, and these lead to differing attitudes to risk and the desirable speed of change; nationalistic resentment of donor 'interference' and of inequities in the treatment of countries is apt to give rise to generalized suspicion of externally-recom-mended policy reforms.

It will be a thesis of the following two chapters that these differences between donors and recipients have the paradoxical effect of simultaneously pushing the donors into the use of conditionality and of undermining its effec-tiveness. Within game-theoretic applications to economics, the model which suggests itself as the most useful for analysing the donor–recipient relation-ship is that presented in agency theory. We therefore proceed next to outline this and its relevance to the conditionality problem, as a preliminary to appli-cation of hypotheses derived from agency theory to the relevant evidence, in the next two chapters.

Notes

1   On this see Killick, 1995b: 152–5.
2   On the influence of path-dependence see Jones in Killick, 1995a, Chapter 4.
3   The idea of policy outcomes as 'resultants' is taken from Allison, 1971: 162.
4   See Nelson and Eglinton, 1993, for a good discussion of this topic, from which I
    have borrowed freely.
5   See Healey and Robinson, 1992, for a useful survey of this literature.

5

THE MODEL, THE RESEARCH, SOME RESULTS

The last chapter criticized the 'ownership' explanation of the weak execution of donor policy conditions on the grounds that it was not set within a model of government. Insofar as there is a model, it appears to refer to the motivations of individual actors in the policy process. When they identify with a measure, regard it as their own, ministers and their officials will be keen to implement it. But when it is perceived as imposed from outside, sulkiness will pervade, there will be resentment, foot-dragging, sabotage and back-sliding.

No doubt such considerations do come into play but this account seems unsatisfactory as a general model. In the late twentieth century we are more accustomed to models based around the self-interest of the actors involved. What is it about weak ownership which might make the key individuals regard it as against their interests to implement the measures at issue? This is a genuine puzzle, for we have given evidence earlier suggesting that well-implemented adjustment programmes bring superior economic results, with presumably beneficial effects on governments' popularity. The approach we adopt here is in a political-economy tradition that has assumed growing influence in economics in recent years (e.g. see Rodrik, 1996b, and the literature surveyed there).

The analytical framework called in aid to answer our puzzle is drawn from agency theory.[1] The purpose of this chapter is to provide an informal sketch of this and its applicability to the conditionality problem, to describe the methods used in assembling evidence, and to begin the task of confronting the hypotheses arising from our application of agency theory with the evidence obtained, examining the extent of interest conflicts between donors and recipients.

I Conditionality as an agency problem

An informal statement of the principal–agent problem[2]

Principal–agent issues arise when the maximization of more than one party's utility requires some form of co-operative action, when the objective functions of these parties differ and when at least one of them has imperfect information about the actions of the other. If, for simplicity, we confine ourselves to only two parties, it may then raise the utility of one party (the 'principal' – P) to contract the other party (the 'agent' – A) to act in ways which promote P's objectives. In this case, the question arises how, with imperfect information, P can satisfy herself that A is carrying out his contractual obligations. This problem becomes more intractable when there is not the one-to-one relationship between A's actions and their outcomes which would permit actions to be inferred from results. There will be an asymmetry of information: in the absence of corrective actions by P, A will always know more about what he has done, and how he has done it, than P.

P can seek to minimize the informational asymmetry by including monitoring and enforcement clauses in the contract. However, the implementation of these will require resources to be used and costs to be incurred, known as agency costs. These can be prohibitive, however. Alternatively, P may enhance the incentives on offer to raise the likelihood that A sees it as in his own interests to implement his contractual commitments. When such a situation is achieved there is said to be 'incentive compatibility'. However, raising the rewards in the presence of imperfect information about A's actions could have the perverse effect of creating a moral hazard, whereby the probability that A will implement is actually reduced by up-front payments to him, so the necessity for monitoring cannot be dispensed with. Another set of costs also enters the frame: the costs (including opportunity costs) that A will incur if he carries out his side of the bargain. Evidently, the larger these costs the greater the compensation needed if incentive compatibility is to be attained.

The principal–agent issue, then, is about incentives: how to design a contract which embodies a structure of rewards and penalties that make it in A's interest to act in ways which further P's utility, and which punishes deviations from that course?[3] The design of such a contract is, however, subject to certain constraints. The most pertinent is A's 'participation constraint': since A incurs costs in executing P's wishes (the time taken, other resources utilized, utility foregone as a result of this activity), the value of the incentives offered must be larger than these costs for A to have an inducement to agree to the contract. Moreover, the relevant cost calculation should be risk-adjusted. In the absence of provisions to insure him against such contingencies, A stands the risk of having his actions knocked off course by events which are beyond his control, thereby forfeiting incentive payments. A will hence tend to be risk-averse and will seek a risk-sharing compact with P, according to which P provides insurance against shocks. Whether a given contract satisfies the participation constraint will thus depend, *inter alia*, on A's perception of the adequacy of the insurance it offers.

Another constraint influencing the incentive system relates to the extent of difference between P and A's objective functions.[4] The larger the differences between them, the larger the inducement that P will have to offer in order to reach agreement with A: A's participation constraint will be larger in this case because he will perceive a greater risk that actions which promote P's objectives will detract from the realization of his own objectives.

Finally, it should be made explicit that the notion of rewards for A's implementation of agreed actions entails that there must be punishments (normally the withholding of present or future rewards) for non-performance. If there were no punishments, it would be in A's interests to take the reward and then renege on his part of the agreement.

Non-implementation as an agency problem

The principal–agent literature does not have a strong empirical orientation. Insofar as it has been applied to real-world issues, these have largely been confined to employer–employee relationships, owner-control of corporate managements, and certain problems in insurance. However, while much of the formal working-out of the theory is irrelevant to the problem on hand, it is fairly clear how arguments about conditionality can be illuminated by treating them as a species of agency problem. The necessary ingredients are present.

First, there are two parties whose objectives can be assumed to differ to greater or lesser extent, for reasons set out in the previous chapter. Moreover, the relationship between donor and recipient has the hierarchical character which is a feature of agency analysis, with the donor seeking to use superior financial resources to induce the recipient government to undertake actions it otherwise would not choose. There is, secondly, imperfect and asymmetrical information, with neither party in full command of the relevant facts, but with the government always in a position to know more than the donor about what it has done and intends to do. Donors expend resources in monitoring and supervising programme execution but they will never secure complete knowledge of the extent of execution. Furthermore, because of ignorance, time-lags, second-order effects, noise in the system and other complexities, it will rarely be feasible to infer actions from results. The action of policy instruments upon an economy is usually too complicated for that.

On this view, then, the donors (including the IFIs) are the principals seeking, through what Chapter 1 called their 'hard core' conditionality, to induce foreign governments (the agents) to undertake certain actions desired by the donors, in return for access to international capital (including, in some cases, debt relief) through a co-operative activity known as policy (or institutional) reform. Adoption of such a perspective points to a number of potentially fruitful lines of questioning. It is from these that many of the hypotheses set out in the Appendix to this chapter have been derived.

Some qualifications

Between them, the issues specified in the Appendix comprehend most of the important questions surrounding the use of donor conditionality. There is, however, a risk of distorting our answers to the implementation problem by trying to force it into a mould for which it is not a perfect fit. The problem fits the principal–agent mould quite well but not like a glove. For example, the frequency and size of natural disasters, terms of trade and other exogenous shocks affect the implementation of conditionality to an extent not fully captured by the earlier reference to insurance and risk-sharing.

Another difficulty in utilizing the categories of principal and agent is that, being concerned with individuals, the parent literature can treat both parties as single optimizing decision units but such treatment is dangerous in the conditionality case. Each donor and recipient government is actually a collectivity, within which there are varying interests, viewpoints and objectives. This fragmentation may sometimes make it misleading to analyse them as single decision units.

On the donor side, take the IMF as an illustration. To the outsider, this looks more like a single decision unit than most donor agencies: it has mechanisms for ensuring that the wider world hears a single Fund point of view, and rather strong internal control mechanisms to reinforce that. Yet, conditioning its negotiating position *vis-à-vis* a member government, various forces will come into play. Some Executive Directors are apt to take a special interest, perhaps seeking to secure a favourable deal for a friendly borrowing government. The IMF's Managing Director may well have one viewpoint, seeing a specific case through the prism of an overall relationship with the Fund's membership, particularly with key shareholders. The Policy Development and Review Department, charged with securing consistency across countries, will have its own view; so will the relevant Geographical Department, which will see any one negotiation in the historical context of its relations with the country and government in question. The Finance Department may well be in on the act, particularly if there is any question about the borrowing government's ability to service past Fund credits. The personality and self-confidence of the Mission Head will also exert an influence. So, even within this monolithic-seeming agency a host of competing influences is at work, affecting its negotiating position and freedom of manoeuvre. *Mutatis mutandis*, this is true of all other donor agencies, particularly the World Bank.

It is even more true of recipient governments, which must almost always be thought of as coalitions, with lesser or greater unity of purpose. One of the specific conditionality problems which arises here is that negotiations usually have to be conducted by some lead ministry, say the Ministry of Finance, which may not, however, be able to deliver on its promises of policy actions, where these have to be implemented by other departments of government. There is also the possibility that reformists within government could harness the desire for a credit to tip the balance of power within government in favour of themselves.

An implication of this line of argument is that particular care has to be taken when considering 'the donor's' or 'the recipient's' objectives. Since both are collectivities, each is apt to pursue multiple objectives which may be contradictory, subject to unresolved tradeoffs, inconsistent over time. By the same token, we need to be wary about treating them as optimizers, both because of their coalitional nature and because of the serious motivational over-simplification involved in treating actors as seeking only to maximize their own utilities.

Lastly, as was pointed out when the above ideas were put to the staffs of the IMF and World Bank, these institutions can from a different perspective be regarded as agents rather than principals. Both have active Executive Boards which take a continuous interest in the institutions' policies and activities. At this level, there is a clear sense in which both institutions are executing the policy wishes of their Boards, the principals (with the Boards having the problem of how to construct incentive systems for managements and staffs which ensure that their wishes are carried out). The considerable extent to which the IFIs' policies are determined by the USA and other G7 governments is well known. There have been notorious occasions on which the Fund or the Bank have been reduced to implementing policies clearly identified with just one or a few major shareholders (see Chapter 6 on Argentina). However, the boot is on the other foot when it comes to relationships at the country-programme level. From the perspective of the borrowing government, it is the IFI which is calling the policy shots. It is with this latter situation with which we are concerned in this book.

II The nature of the evidence

The methods employed and the limitations of the study

Agency theory suggests a number of potentially fruitful lines of enquiry. However, it also poses a research problem because the questions raised are not readily amenable to the economist's standard tools of empirical research. Our response to this difficulty is described below.

Although we also draw upon quantitative evidence where this is available, we rely chiefly on an approach first developed, with somewhat different objectives, in a study of the effects of IMF programmes (see Killick, 1995b, especially pp. 86–7). The approach there was to apply to the results of a large sample of country case studies, drawn from all developing regions, conducted and published by other researchers, a common analytical framework designed to throw light on the issues which were under investigation in that book. This approach worked well and, although largely qualitative, provided evidence consistent with cross-country results obtained independently by others, while offering a richer tableau of information.

The same approach is adopted here, in this case by reference to country experiences with World Bank structural adjustment credits, with the results of other authors' country studies utilized to throw light on the hypotheses set out in the Appendix. There is a bias in the twenty-one countries studied, in that we were confined to those countries for which already published case studies were available, although it is not obvious in what direction this bias might affect our results. Precautions were taken to guard against researcher selection biases within the population of the countries for which a relevant literature was available, as described in the Appendix, although we cannot claim that the chosen countries are a random sample.

A further limitation is imposed by the fact that most of our observations are drawn from World Bank experiences. We need to be cautious in applying the resulting generalizations to the IMF and other agencies. On the other hand, the present writer has already researched the IMF case quite substantially (Killick, 1984a, 1984b, 1995b) and is thus in some position to assess the transferability of results across the two Bretton Woods agencies. We are, in any case, able to present below quite a lot of information relating specifically to the Fund.

As another limitation, we might also refer back to the self-imposed restraint mentioned at the outset that we do not here enter into the debate about the appropriateness of the policy content of the IFIs' programmes. The main defence for this, spelled out in Chapter 2, is that well-implemented programmes do usually bring improved economic performance and that the general weakness of programme results is chiefly a result of incomplete implementation. In their general thrust, the policies seem sound; it is the poor execution we need most to understand. However, it must be admitted that this is not a full defence, for while the general policy thrust of the programmes may be sound, that is by no means to say that all the specific measures they incorporate are well chosen – the devil is usually in the detail. Moreover – and here is a serious shortcoming – whether or not programme specifics are well chosen will affect the likely response of the economy and hence the government's calculations of the benefits to be gained from implementation. Our defence here is that independent assessment of the suitability of the manifold policy provisions in the many programmes in our twenty-one countries was beyond the resources available to us, but readers should remain aware of this limitation in our work.

The task for my colleague, Ramani Gunatilaka, was to go through the materials on the chosen countries (146 different sources were consulted) to see to what extent they threw light on the hypotheses developed for this project. The results obtained will be cited extensively in what follows and in Chapter 6. They are summarized in the Master Table (see p. 199) and Table 5.1 in summary and simplified form. The matrix in the Master Table sets out the chief hypotheses that were examined (a few were dropped from the table because little relevant or reliable evidence could be brought to bear on them – see the Appendix to this chapter) and the countries studied. The entries in the matrix cells attempt, in a highly abbreviated way which inevitably loses much of the richness of the material, to marshal the evidence bearing upon the

Table 5.1 Statistical summary of hypothesis tests in the Master Table (number of

Hypothesis

Relating to participation constraints

1 The probability of implementation is a function of the extent to which governments/ministers/officials perceive the benefits of compliance, in terms of their own objectives, to outweigh the costs

2 Recipients' calculations of costs and benefits will be particularly sensitive to the extent to which programme measures are expected to affect the distribution of income, and to the relative degrees of organization of gainers and losers

3 Programme implementation is prejudiced when the objectives of donors and governments differ, resulting in conflicts of interest

4 Programme 'ownership', an indicator of the extent of interest conflict, will have a decisive influence on programme implementation

5 Implementation will be a function of the reward system through its influence on governments' or ministers' perceptions of likely net costs and benefits

6 Agreeing an IFI adjustment programme, through its pre-commitment effect, raises the credibility of the government's own policies, and private sector responses to these

Relating to rewards and punishments

7 When objectives differ it is not possible to devise an incentive system sufficient to ensure that governments fully promote donors' objectives

8 Noncompliance with the terms of a loan is not effectively punished by reduced access to new credits

9 Programme effectiveness is undermined by political, bureaucratic and financial pressures upon donor agencies to lend

10 The availability of a credit, by easing financial constraints, weakens the incentive to implement reforms (moral hazard)

11 Implementation and programme effectiveness is reduced by the extent to which the donor has multiple, conflicting or unclear objectives, and by the number of other donors applying separate conditionality

12 There is an 'adverse selection' problem, with donors continuing to support poorly performing recipient governments to safeguard past loans and/or to maintain an appearance of success

Other influences on implementation

13 The initial economic and political situation conditions programme implementation

14 Programme implementation is powerfully influenced by exogenous shocks

15 A long relationship between a donor and a government improves programme implementation

---

Notes:
N/A = non applicable
N/EV = little evidence available related to the hypothesis

observations and percentages)

N/A	N/EV	Consistent with hypothesis?				
(1)	(2)	Unclear (3)	No (4)	Yes (5)	(5) as % of (4) + (5) (6)	(5) as % of (3) + (4) + (5) (7)
1	2	1	–	17	100	94
–	3	–	4	14	78	78
2	1	1	–	17	100	94
–	–	1	2	18	90	86
5	2	–	2	12	86	86
2	8	4	7	–	0.00	0.00
4	3	1	–	13	100	93
4	1	4	–	12	100	75
1	9	1	3	7	70	64
–	9	1	2	9	82	75
7	1	1	–	12	100	92
7	4	1	2	7	78	70
–	2	2	–	17	100	89
–	7	–	3	11	79	79
4	1	1	9	6	40	38

hypotheses. Table 5.1 takes the process of digestion further, presenting summary statistics of the extent to which each hypothesis is supported by the evidence. Column (6) of the table is probably the most useful, giving the number of cases in which each hypothesis is borne out by the country evidence, as a percentage of the total number of unambiguous 'Yes' and 'No' entries.

Such summary statistics carry the danger of lending spurious precision to an essentially judgemental approach to hypothesis testing. To some, this methodology will no doubt seem excessively subjective, vulnerable to researcher-bias (although the more usual econometric approach to hypothesis testing is not exactly immune to manipulation). There is a natural tendency to find what one is looking for. Against that, various precautions were taken, not least the presentation of the results prior to publication at a large number of seminars of IFI and other donor officials, as well as of academics and other interested people. Moreover, we have compared our results with independent evidence wherever that has been possible (as with the 'ownership' issue discussed in Chapter 4, where our results were seen as strongly consistent with the work of Johnson and Wasty). Our results agreed well with such evidence; there were few surprises.

Our best chance of convincing readers that we have done our human best to avoid bias is transparency: to present as much of the evidence as possible so that they may form their own assessments. Readers should therefore test the judgements offered in the Master Table against their own knowledge of any specific cases, and also to consult the Appendix on the methods employed. We stand or fall by the objectivity we have been able to achieve.

The appropriateness of an agency approach

While it is right to remain cautious in interpreting our results, our confidence in the validity of the results that emerge is increased by the fact that the principal–agent line of enquiry described above appears to fit the facts rather well. As can be seen from Table 5.1, most of our hypotheses received quite high levels of confirmation. Virtually all the results had the 'right' sign. The basic premise of the agency approach is that outcomes are a result of calculations by governments and their officials of whether implementation will be in their own interests. The results in Hypothesis 1 of the Master Table and Table 5.1 provide rather strong confirmation of the appropriateness of this (not particularly controversial) premise. Thus, from Table 5.1 Hypothesis 1 it can be seen that we obtained clear evidence on this from seventeen out of a possible maximum of twenty-one observations and that in all the seventeen cases the probability that programme measures would be implemented appeared to be a function of the extent to which the government and its officials perceived this to be in their own interests.

This is perhaps most clearly illustrated by those of our countries where attitudes to adjustment measures have changed radically. Governments which have displayed hostility to proposals for policy reforms are apt to lose office, or to change tack, when a deteriorating economy means that the costs of change no longer outweigh the benefits. All former bets are off in an economic crisis; actions that had been anathema begin to take on previously unsuspected attractions. In Argentina, for example, the Alfonsin government backed away from executing key stabilization measures and concomitant structural reforms when, in 1986–7, it found the proposed measures being attacked in the run-up to an election by the opposition leader (ironically, Carlos Menem) and even by the governing Radical Party's own presidential candidate (Erro, 1993: 153–4). The calculation changed radically, however, when on winning the election Menem discovered the extent of economic crisis he had inherited. Grasping that it would no longer be possible to run the political system by the time-honoured method of buying support from the trade unions and other corporatist entities, and in denial of his own Peronist rhetoric, he saw that economic reform was essential for political success.

Several of our other countries offer variations on this theme: Jamaica, Tanzania, Uganda. In Ghana too the depth of the economic crisis in 1982 made it possible to persuade a populist leader (Rawlings) that a turnaround in policy that contradicted all his instincts was inescapable if economic and political disaster was to be avoided (Callaghy, 1990: 275). Economic crisis, in this case triggered by a famine and the withdrawal of economic support by the USSR, occasioned a comparable reversal in Madagascar in 1987–8, from barely-concealed obstruction of adjustment reforms to acceptance (if still grudging) of the need for action (Hewitt, 1992; Pryor, 1990).[5]

Again, the Philippines, until the last few crisis months of the Marcos government, had a long record of resisting measures pushed by the IFIs which threatened the regime's power base or economic rents. When in 1986 the Aquino administration was elected to power it was able to take a markedly different view of where its interests lay because a number of the measures promoted by the Washington institutions had the effect of striking at the privileges and power of its opponents, the old pro-Marcos elite. Such measures were promptly introduced, while there was much foot-dragging on others which did not so happily coincide with political expediency (Mosley, 1991: 62). Finally we might mention The Gambia, where the government decided to implement a reform programme only because it seemed to offer the lesser political threat when compared with the danger that continued inaction would have dire economic consequences and provide Senegal with an excuse for annexing the country (Radelet, 1992: 1,095–6).

We should also remember one of the conclusions of Marr's survey of South-east Asian experiences, summarized in Chapter 3 (p. 69): that compliance with such conditionality as the IFIs attempted in those countries was high only when governments regarded implementation to be in their own interests, and that it was violated when the governments were unconvinced of the need for change. At a different level, confirmation of governments' use of judgements about their self-interests comes from a World Bank study of 'the economics and politics of government ownership'. This included research to identify the circumstances in which aid donors might use their resources to promote the reform and/or privatization of public enterprises to best effect. Top of a list of three circumstances which it concluded should exist before donor influence was likely to be effective was that 'Reform must be politically desirable – the benefits to the leadership and its constituencies must outweigh the costs' (World Bank, 1995b: 175).

We should next get beyond this perhaps rather banal level of generalization to unpack in more detail the elements that are likely to go into governments' judgements about the net benefits of implementing donor conditionality. In line with the agency theory framework, we look at various aspects of governments' participation constraints before proceeding, in Chapter 6, to examine the incentives that donors can offer to overcome these constraints.

III Participation constraints

Conflicting objectives

In plainer language, a government's participation constraints can be thought of as a measure of the extent of its aversion to actions stipulated as conditions in return for a loan. They thus reflect the extent to which 'the government' (or, more likely, key actors within it) sees its objectives and interests as being in conflict with those of the donor in question. We have already covered some of this ground, in Chapter 4's treatment of the 'ownership' issue. We saw there, from our own and other evidence, a strong positive association between the extent of government ownership and programme implementation.

In large measure, the degree of government ownership reflects the extent to which its own objectives dominate those of the conditionality-imposing donors. Further evidence on this factor, as it relates to World Bank structural adjustment programmes, is provided in Hypothesis 3 of the Master Table and Table 5.1 (results which are closely correlated with the ownership results in Hypothesis 4). Programme implementation was found to be a function of the extent of difference or convergence of government and Bank objectives in all seventeen of the countries for which we had clear evidence on this topic.

Given the evidence presented in Chapter 4, it will perhaps suffice here to provide a few additional examples. In a few cases, Bank and government goals were rather starkly opposed. Thus in Kenya, the Bank's attempts to reduce state interventionism and promote liberalization have tended to conflict with the imperatives of a clientelist, ethnically-based political system, where the ruling elite relies for maintaining itself in power on the use of public resources and patronage to reward supporters and buy off putative opponents (Mosley, 1991: 290). The liberalization of maize marketing and privatization of public enterprises are two areas where this conflict has been particularly sharp. The

Bank, together with the IMF and other donors, have for long been insisting on progress in these areas, but with scant success because of government reluctance to forgo the patronage and rents generated by these state interventions (Ryan, 1996).

Other countries illustrate a less severe form of a similar problem: selective implementation according to the extent to which various adjustment measures are, or are not, congruent with government objectives. In India privatization was a sticking point, mainly because of the likely loss of jobs among an organized and vocal class of urban workers (Manor, 1993: 6), even though in other respects there was after 1991 a high degree of agreement between the economic policy goals of the Rao government and the World Bank. In Colombia, the reduction of protection was a sticky area through much of the 1980s, with cosmetic liberalization of goods that were little imported but reluctance to reduce the privileges of a politically influential industrial sector, until the emergence of an export lobby as an important counterweight to the import-substituters induced the government to move closer to what the Bank desired (Urrutia, 1994: 292).

Similarly, in Jamaica under successive governments there was a long history of highly selective implementation of reforms determined by political calculations, with many examples of foot-dragging or back-sliding, until the later 1980s when the Bank and other donors adopted a 'soft underbelly' approach which concentrated on supporting measures which the government itself favoured (Harrigan, 1991: 350). In Thailand, according to a well-researched examination of adjustment in the 1980s, compliance was least on those measures which were pressed most stridently by the Bank. The Thai authorities retained throughout a clear view of the measures that were compatible with their restructuring objectives and politely but firmly resisted any external advice which did not fit (Sahasakul et al., 1991: 103, 113). Then there is Senegal. Reviewing the record of the 1980s, Berg et al. pithily summarize it in these words:

> Weak implementation derives in part from the Senegalese unwillingness to apply policies they felt compelled to agree to in formal policy loan documents . . . lack of conviction or outright opposition to specific reforms could be translated into non-implementation because of the permissive environment prevailing in Senegal. . . . When faced with the domestic political risks of imposing an unpopular reform . . . the authorities have been inclined to risk donor wrath arising from violation of conditionality.
>
> (Berg et al., 1990: 109)

Selective implementation, according to governments' own priorities, gives rise to a major difficulty in economy-wide adjustment programmes: that they are (or should be) designed as packages, with individual measures intended to reinforce each other. Cherry-picking leads to an incoherence which can under-mine even those measures which are undertaken. We came across this problem during our researches in Kenya, where a senior World Bank official identified the *partiality* of reform measures as one of the principal sources of weaknesses in that country's adjustment efforts: there had been appreciable liberalization in parts of the economy but the economic response had been weak, especially from private investors, because much interventionism remained in other areas of economic life and because of uncertainties about the ruling elite's respect of property rights.

The costs of implementation

When weighing whether it is likely to be in its interests to implement a given package of measures a government needs to consider various potential costs.

Distributional costs

A recent study of the politics of adjustment concluded that government actions 'which may appear to indicate bad faith . . . or economic irra-tionality . . . are determined by anticipation of social reactions' (Haggard *et al.*, 1995: 117). One of our hypotheses anticipated a similar feature: that government calculations of costs and benefits are particularly sensitive to the likely effect of reform measures on the distribution of income, and to the rela-tive levels of social organization of gainers and losers. Our results on this are summarized in Table 5.1, Hypothesis 2, where it will be seen that the hypoth-esis was confirmed in fourteen out of eighteen observations.

These fourteen cases identify a variety of groups as carrying particular weight in government calculations, as indicated in the equivalent entries in the Master Table. We have just mentioned the influence of import-substi-tuting and then export-oriented industrialists in Colombia. The military is another group which may be of particular importance, as in Thailand and Uganda. The public sector itself – the civil service, teachers, employees and managers of public enterprises – often has special influence. This was the case in Senegal, where in 1989 a teachers' strike led the government to renege on public sector salary commitments (Berg *et al.*, 1990: 176–8), and in Ghana, India, Kenya, Madagascar and Zambia where public sector opposition stalled the implementation of privatization.

Often this sensitivity to public sector workers is extended to a general concern with organized groups within the urban economy. Besides examples already cited, Zambia – the most urbanized country in Africa – provides a prime case. One of the most fundamental reasons for the failure of successive attempts at adjustment conditionality in the 1980s was that it attacked the heart of the Kaunda government's urban political base without creating an alternative constituency in favour of reform (Hawkins, 1991: 845). Highly visible and damaging riots in the Copperbelt and Lusaka over a 120 per cent increase in staple food prices in December 1986 caused the President to lose his nerve and reverse the liberalization. Strikes by public sector workers caused the adjustment programme to be abandoned altogether in the following year (Callaghy, 1990: 296).

The government of Thailand also proved resistant to measures urged by the World Bank in the earlier 1980s which would have reduced the welfare of influential – largely urban-based – groups by raising the prices of petrol, public transport, electricity and water (Sahasakul *et al.*, 1991: 103). A not dissimilar situation prevailed in Jamaica during the mid-1980s, when the Seaga government sought to avoid devaluation and other measures that would have hit unionized labour hard by instead pursuing a stringent monetary policy. Similar concerns prompted the government to renege on Bank conditions in 1986–8 by reintroducing subsidies on basic imports (Harrigan, 1991: 338).

However, a pro-urban bias is not an invariable rule. One, admittedly rather insignificant, exception is provided by The Gambia. There in the later 1980s the main political base of the ruling party was in the rural areas and this benefited from adjustment measures, such as suspension of the export tax, liberalization of the rice trade and increases in the groundnut price. The chief opposition to the government was in the towns and it was there that most of the 'adjustment costs' were concentrated (Radelet, 1992: 1095). Kenya also provides a partial exception to the pro-city rule, for there ethnic concerns dominate and a large proportion of the Moi government's supporters dwell in rural areas. The Philippines, too, is an exception, where rural landlords exerted powerful political influence for many years.

A more firmly-based generalization is that the distributional concerns just discussed rarely work in favour of the poor and often work against them. This stems from the combination of the facts (a) that a large majority of the poor in developing countries lives in rural areas and (b) that they are rarely well organized and therefore usually do not exercise the political clout which their numbers might suggest. Of our twenty-one case studies, only in Indonesia was much sensitivity shown to the interests of the poor, *per se*, and even there the government demonstrated a willingness to increase their hardships, e.g. by reducing subsidies on fuel and rice, when the government deemed it necessary (Thorbecke, 1992: 43–4, 55).

The significance of the Indonesian case is that it is one of the four countries whose governments demonstrated an ability to override special interest concerns. All four – Chile under Pinochet (1973–89); Indonesia to the present time; South Korea until the early 1990s; and Malawi until 1994 – were ruled by regimes that were authoritarian, strong (the two attributes do not necessarily go together) and often repressive. It is therefore not surprising that they were less influenced by distributional considerations when deciding whether or not to comply with adjustment conditionality. The idea that it takes a repressive regime to implement an adjustment programme is by now discredited,[6] but the four countries just mentioned do point to a certain advantage that such regimes possess when undertaking economic reforms, just as we shall later point to difficulties created for such reforms by the shift towards more democratic governments in various parts of the developing world. Authoritarianism is neither necessary nor sufficient – but it may help.

Transactions costs

While discussing the costs that governments will weigh in the balance when deciding whether to proceed with a policy change we ought also to consider the transactions costs and, in particular, the capabilities of the public administration to execute agreed-upon measures. Unfortunately, we have little hard evidence to offer. We sought during our case study work to collect information on these aspects but with few results. We can therefore do no better than offer a few generalizations which are either uncontroversial or are consistent with our own background understanding.

a   *Implementation capabilities often are very limited*, especially in the poorer developing countries. In sub-Saharan Africa, for example, many public workers receive abysmally inadequate remuneration, resulting in migration of the most capable to the private sector or abroad, and low motivation among those left behind, leading to corruption, moonlighting and other debilitating practices (Klitgaard, 1989). The ostensible costs to government of rectifying such situations are large, e.g. in terms of the direct budgetary costs of bringing civil service pay and conditions up to sensible standards, or the other types of cost that would be involved in accepting even larger numbers of foreign technical assistance personnel. Meantime, Fund and, particularly, Bank conditionality appears to take little or no cognisance of governments' limited capacities to simultaneously undertake a multiplicity of policy changes. Within the IFIs, little effort appears to have gone into the tailoring of policy stipulations to government administrative constraints, to avoid requirements for complex actions by public administrations in no condition to carry them through.

b   *These limitations are much aggravated by the explosion of conditionality* described in Chapter 1. It was shown there that the average number of policy conditions contained in an adjustment programme has been increasing, that the number of donors using conditionality has been rising, and that the range of policy matters on which conditionality is applied has widened over time. We cited a Bank estimate that the average number of policy stipulations in its own adjustment credits in 1989–91 was fifty-six. Governments are often incapable of carrying out the full range of their paper commitments, or could do so only by incurring exorbitant transactions costs. That this point may not have been fully grasped by the Bank (and perhaps other donor agencies) is indicated by evidence that the number of conditions per programme is inversely correlated with state capabilities and the country's previous track record with programme implementation (World Bank, 1995a: 129). To seek to compensate for weak capabilities by *increasing* the number of conditions is a peculiar way of proceeding and surely doomed to failure.

c   *The proliferation of conditionality is only part of a wider trend*, particularly as it relates to creditor responses to the 1982 debt crisis, which has had the effect of imposing even larger transactions costs upon debtor governments and which are part of the context in which implementation capabilities must be viewed. In 1993 I examined this in connection with the situation of indebted African countries, concluding that past approaches to debt and adjustment issues

> have been seriously sub-optimal. The information, opportunity and other economic costs of negotiations are large. A rough esti- mate of the number of negotiations in 1980–92 approaches 8,000. Probably the chief costs involved are the opportunity costs resulting from the large demands placed by multiple and complex negotiations upon the key cadres of officials dealing with the design and management of economic policy. There are also substantial information costs, although these have dimin- ished over time and much of the information secured as a result is of genuine value. There are also financial costs arising from various delays; and investor risks arising from uncertainties generated by frequent policy changes, incomplete implementa- tion and doubts about the political sustainability of adjustment.
>
> (Killick, 1993a: 1)

Up-dating the estimate of the number of negotiations to 1996 would probably bring the total of negotiations to over 10,000.

d   Nevertheless, *it is easy to exaggerate the extent to which implementation capabil- ities act as the* binding *constraint.* This judgement is based on observation of widely differing implementation records among countries that might be expected to have similar capabilities – say Kenya and Malawi, or Tanzania and Uganda. Perhaps this is a topic on which it is useful to invoke the hoary concept of 'political will'. It is *that* which is most likely to be the binding constraint. As the saying goes, where there's a will there's a way. However, this must be immediately qualified by acknowledging the need to distinguish between easy measures (e.g. changes in administered prices) and difficult ones (e.g. reform of the banking system). For the latter there may indeed be major limitations on what can be done, even when the will is there.

The influence of long-term relationships

The literature on agency theory suggests that the incentive problem will be reduced when there is a long-term relationship between the two parties. In the context of donor–recipient relations, this might be expected to hold by inducing a convergence of the goals of the two parties, increasing local owner-ship and lowering government resistance to measures favoured by donors. Convergence might be expected to come about through growing under-standing of each other's goals, viewpoints and constraints; and through a building-up of trust, with a consequentially greater willingness of each party to compromise with the other. This tendency might be reinforced by raising the government's concern to maintain its reputation for trustworthiness and consistency.

The Master Table (Hypothesis 15) includes a number of cases which appear to fit this pattern. Mexico perhaps provides the classic example and one that is unusually well documented, in a World Bank study of its relations with Mexico in 1948–92 (World Bank, 1994c). This shows how gradually there was built up within Mexico a corps of policy advisers who had similar training and attitudes as their Bank counterparts, and were their equals in professional competence. It shows too how the Bank gradually learned to be sensitive to local political realities and not to push for reforms at odds with the govern-ment's own priorities, recognizing there was little it could achieve through financial leverage alone. As suggested in Chapter 3, it is likely that the exis-tence of such a relationship contributed to the eventual adoption of major reforms after 1983. Ghana and Uganda also provide positive examples, albeit on the basis of less protracted contacts with the IFIs. In both cases improving understanding between the government and the Bank led to substantial convergence and the building of trust between them, increasing government ownership and desire to implement, while at the same time reducing the extent to which the Bank felt it necessary to insist on rigorous and wide-ranging conditionality. In Jamaica, too, there were benefits from long association, particularly in an improved IFI understanding of the country's politics, leading them to adopt the 'soft under-belly' approach described earlier.

However, these cases were the exception. Hypothesis 15 of Table 5.1 shows that out of fifteen observations, we found that in only six cases did the exis-tence of a long-term relationship with the Bank appear to be associated with improved programme execution, with nine contrary observations. In fact, this was the least well supported of our hypotheses.

A 'long and close' relationship (Stallings, 1990: 158), in contrast with the country's often troubled relationship with the IMF, did not, for instance, deter the Colombian government from deceiving the Bank in 1985 about the extent of trade liberalization (see Chapter 3). It did not prevent a near break-down in relations with the government of Kenya by the mid-1990s

(Ryan, 1996), nor persistent non-implementation by the government of Senegal. In the Philippines, a long history of dealings with the Marcos regime did not lead to convergence or concern with reputational considerations; it took a political revolution before the Bank had a government with which it could do serious business. Something similar could be said of Tanzania, with the resignation of President Nyerere in 1985 as the watershed; and of Zambia, with the defeat of President Kaunda's government in 1991 as the break-point. Sometimes familiarity breeds contempt – or a greater expertise in deception. Thus, it has been said of Turkey that its long relationship with the IFIs allowed the government to develop institutional mechanisms for circumventing conditionality, particularly in the area of trade liberalization in the earlier 1980s (Kirkpatrick and Onis, 1991: 27–8; Foroutan, 1991: 449).

On closer examination, such apparently perverse results are perhaps not surprising. We need first to consider the *quality* of the relationship in this context. On the one hand, it can mean the development of linkages of the type described for Mexico, where indeed the relationship was conducive to positive outcomes. But, against this, it is all too easy to infer a 'relationship' from the necessity of a country to keep going back to the IFIs for assistance, with a long succession of programmes taken as evidence, or of the IFIs to keep lending in order to avoid arrears on past credits. The quality of the relationship in this case may be poor, with a succession of new programmes indicating consistently weak policies, continuing government–IFI disagreements and failed programmes. Madagascar (until recently) fits this description, as do Kenya, Senegal, the Philippines and Zambia during the relevant parts of their recent economic histories.

There is also the question, *relations at what level?* There is an ever-present danger that visiting missions from the IFIs will derive from contacts with their *technocratic* opposite numbers in the civil service the belief that there is also a meeting of minds at the *political* level and that genuine conversion is occurring. The development of relationships at the technocratic level may be sufficient in situations where expert advisers do exert a decisive influence, as they have at various times in such countries as Chile, Ghana, Indonesia and Mexico. But such a situation is not the rule. Technocrats are frequently marginalized or are merely one voice among many in the policy process. Sometimes, they are used to provide a cloak of respectability, to deceive donor agencies into believing there is greater agreement than actually exists. The Marcos administration in the Philippines was well known for use of this tactic; it has also been used by the Moi administration in Kenya and, outside our sample, by the Mobutu government in Zaire (Kahler, 1992: 128). As Kahler remarks, establishing good relations with the technocrats alone is unlikely to be enough for *sustained* reform; it will usually be essential to reach the political leadership as well. We might here recall Haggard and Kaufman's (1992: 7) concept of the 'consolidation' of reforms, referring to a situation where reforms become institutionalized within a political system. The IFIs are not necessarily well placed to build up close relations at that level, although much may depend on whether they have resident representatives in place who can attempt this task. Bilateral donors ought to be better placed, through their diplomatic representatives.

Another aspect of the locus of the relationship has to do with the impermanence of governments. A long-lasting record of dealings with a *country* may not betoken very much if that country has been subject to political instability and discontinuity among key policy-makers. It happens that most of our twenty-one countries have been marked by an unusual degree of political continuity, so they do not well illustrate this point. In fact, they illustrate a very different fact: that whether continuity of government is good for the implementation of reforms depends on the nature of the government that is enjoying this continuity. We have already cited several cases where political *change* was necessary for policy reform: in much of Latin America in the early 1980s, in Tanzania, in Zambia, and so on.

In short, we can see that the grounds for hypothesizing that long-term relationships will be favourable to implementation are weaker than appeared at first sight. Indeed, the expected 'sign' of the relationship is quite ambiguous. It all depends. . . . It is easy to point to a Mexican-style relationship as favourable because it results in a two-way convergence that penetrates quite deeply into the political process. But such an outcome is not easily achieved and is not signified merely by a long history of lending to a given country. From within the World Bank, Johnson and Wasty (1993: 10) have observed this, finding that 'the frequency and amount of government–Bank interaction is neither a necessary nor a sufficient guarantee for borrower ownership'.

Does conditionality raise policy credibility?

Chapter 1's statement of the arguments for conditionality included the suggestion that it can provide a 'technology of commitment', with donor agencies acting as 'external agencies of restraint'. On this view, acceptance of conditionality allows a government to surrender some discretionary powers in order to commit itself to pursue a certain set of policies for some time into the future, thereby increasing public (particularly investor) confidence that the policies will not be reversed. When this occurs, it can be expected to lower governments' participation constraints because the enhanced credibility of their policies will improve their ability to achieve their own objectives and thus bring them benefits.

The importance of policy credibility is much emphasized in modern policy theory, particularly for measures which could easily be reversed or which require the long-term commitment of large resources.[7] There are historical examples of external agencies being utilized to enhance credibility. Chapter 1 has already cited Santaella's (1993) example of the positive credibility effects of League of Nations stabilization programmes in the 1920s. Root (1989) similarly concludes from his studies of early-modern Europe that governments successfully used consortia of external creditors to signal an intention to honour their obligations and by so doing raised their creditworthiness.

Some, however, are sceptical about the ability of donor conditionality to act as a guarantor of time consistency. Collier (1995: 555), for example, argues that it gets in the way of reputation-building because outsiders are unable to distinguish between voluntary and enforced policy actions – between policies which are locally-owned and those which are not (and are hence more apt to be reversed). Clearly, ownership is crucial for policy credibility. If, as suggested in Chapter 4, conditionality undermines ownership then it will also reduce the credibility of the measures in question. Furthermore, the practice of conditionality may increase uncertainties about the time consistency of policies in situations where there are significant disagreements, or tensions, among the conditions presented by different external agencies, and where governments are seen as having access to alternative sources of finance, weakening their necessity to adhere to any one agency's stipulations.

Turning to the evidence, our cases contained no support for the proposition that agreeing an IFI programme raises the credibility of a government's policies, as is shown in Table 5.1, Hypothesis 6. However, this proved a difficult hypothesis on which to obtain evidence. We only have clear indications for seven countries but in none of those was the hypothesis supported.

Among our cases, the Ugandan is perhaps the most interesting. Programmes with the IFIs were in force from the inception of the Museveni regime in 1986 and, despite weak ownership, the implementation record was good. Investors nonetheless held back until well into the 1990s because of fears that reforms might be reversed and from a lack of confidence about property rights, particularly among potential Asian investors who had been expelled from the country in the early 1970s. By the later 1990s, however, confidence was building and investment was booming – not because of a belief in the IFIs' policies (which had been a constant for a decade) but because of the government's (and the President's) demonstrated steady commitment to the policy course it had chosen.

There are other examples. Investors held back in Ghana too, despite strong ownership and a generally good implementation record, because of a mistrust of the Head of State's populist instincts and his revealed suspicion of private enterprise. They also held back in Guyana because of the government's continued avowed commitment to a co-operative socialist ideology and its lack of enthusiasm for private participation in manufacturing (Harrigan, 1991), although this reticence was not surprising because programme implementation was often poor. Kenya and Zambia are other countries where a succession of IFI programmes has apparently done little for policy credibility, but these too are cases marked by poor implementation records.

What these examples suggest is that investors' assessments of the risks of policy reversal are based overwhelmingly on their assessment of the domestic political situation, and of the persuasiveness of governments in presenting their policies. Investors are apparently not inclined to treat the IFIs' *imprimatur* as providing a sufficient predictor of time consistency. Other of our cases appear to bear this out, this time in a positive direction. Successive governments in Chile have a demonstrated record of providing a favourable, dependable policy environment for private investment and have been rewarded with high rates of investment. Although their track records are not yet so firmly established, the governments of Argentina and Mexico have also been able to reap the benefits of increased policy credibility. The same is true (with the past exception of the Philippines) of the South-east Asian countries surveyed in Chapter 3. In all these cases, however, investor judgements appear overwhelmingly based on assessments of domestic politics, with the existence or otherwise of IFI programmes seemingly irrelevant. Governments' highly variable record on programme implementation points to relative unconcern about the effects of their actions on their relations with the IFIs, presumably because they judge that there are few extra gains to be had from building up strong relations.[8]

There was some support among our case countries for the view that conflicting conditionalities, not least the tensions between the policy requirements of macro stabilization (IMF) and of 'structural' measures (World Bank), could undermine policy credibility. It was recorded that disagreements between the Fund and Bank added to uncertainties about policies in Jamaica in the mid-1980s; other inconsistencies in the policy intentions of these two agencies were recorded in several of our other countries – see the Master Table, Hypothesis 11. Finally, Thailand provides an interesting case whereby independently established policy credibility was a means of *avoiding* donor conditionality. By the mid-1980s the policy reputation of the Thai government was such that when the Bank sought to insist on unwanted actions the government was able to let the programme lapse and instead obtain credit from the Tokyo capital market (Dixon, 1996: 1,011).

The tentative rejection on our evidence of the hypothesis that IFI programmes raise policy credibility is consistent with the results of other studies of this topic. Three sources can be cited. First, econometric tests in Mosley *et al.*'s (1991a: 221–2) study of the effects of Bank adjustment programmes found no evidence that these were associated with increased inflows of private capital, a result consistent with unchanged credibility. Second, an examination by Conway (1994: 386) of the effects of IMF programmes in 1976–86 found no evidence of positive reputational effects, although he could only test this for a small sample. Finally, tests for the influence of IMF interventions on policy credibility by Ball and Rausser (1995: 906) not only did not find any positive association but actually found some weak evidence to the contrary: the IMF as undermining policy credibility.

Why the IFI conditionality might so signally fail to provide a serviceable technology of precommitment will become clearer as this chapter unfolds. Two reasons have already been suggested: tensions between conditionality and the all-important ownership factor; and inconsistencies between the policy stipulations of the two Washington institutions (and perhaps other donors too), raising uncertainties. We can also signal a consideration taken up in Chapter 6: that IFI conditionality cannot be expected to have much credibility effect unless these agencies can demonstrate a willingness to punish non-compliance and to stay away from governments that are not serious about policy reform.

The influence of shocks

No account of factors bearing upon governments' perceptions of the gains and losses likely to result from the implementation of conditions would be complete without reference to the large revealed capacity of exogenous shocks to influence the course of events.

Shocks can have impact in opposite directions. On the one hand, studies have found that adverse terms of trade movements, financial shocks (such as unexpected changes in world interest rates, or in access to world capital markets) and natural disasters have all been responsible for slippages in programme implementation. For example, examination of the causes of IMF programme break-downs (Killick, 1995b, Table 3.5 and *passim*) found a statistically significant association between programme completion and commodity terms of trade experiences, with non-completers having much worse relative price experiences. This was consistent with the notion that some programmes were abandoned by governments because of the unexpected difficulties they found themselves in, for which supporting evidence was presented (Killick, 1995b: 109–11). Among our present sample of countries, Malawi provides an illustration. Drought in the southern half of the country and an influx of 700,000 refugees from Mozambique contributed to a food crisis in 1986, necessitating large maize imports, and these developments, combined with a failure of Bank policies on agriculture, prompted the Ministry of Agriculture to execute a U-turn on price and fertilizer subsidy policies in direct violation of SAL conditionality (Harrigan, 1991: 223–34).

The other side of that coin is that favourable turns of event can ease implementation by lowering the expected costs of policy actions (see the Master Table, Hypothesis 14). The Gambia's adoption of a reform programme in 1985–6 coincided with the ending of a drought, good rainfall and a fall in the world price of rice, all combining to counteract the price-raising effects of a major devaluation and to reduce hardships that otherwise would have resulted, making it easier for the government to press ahead with the programme (Radelet, 1992: 1,096). Similarly in Jamaica, the progress of reforms during 1986–8 was enhanced by a fall in world oil prices, the buoyancy of tourism from the USA and dramatic improvements in world bauxite and alumina prices (although the impact of Hurricane Gilbert in October 1988 contributed to a slower pace of reform thereafter) (Harrigan, 1991: 353 and *passim*).

Favourable shocks sometimes cause slippage, however. If, through an unforeseen improvement in export prices or a particularly favourable harvest at home, the economic crisis is eased, governments' cost–benefit calculations may cease to point in favour of pushing ahead with reforms and the programme may be abandoned. Among our survey countries, examples include Colombia, which used rising world coffee prices in the mid-1980s to resist Bank pressure for import liberalization; and Kenya, whose government used the same coffee boom to postpone reforms.

Again, negative shocks can have a favourable influence on the execution of reforms, by inducing or worsening economic crises which induce governments to see it as in their interests to act, just as the Colombians and Kenyans had to act when coffee prices returned to more normal levels. A combination of drought, forest fires and the sudden expulsion of large numbers of its citizens living in Nigeria all contributed to the dire situation which induced Ghana's government to reverse its economic policies in 1982–3. And while our country survey does not provide many other illustrations, earlier work on the adoption of IMF programmes stressed this tendency:

> we are struck by the frequency with which natural disasters are an important, sometimes dominant, factor in decisions to adopt an IMF programme. The drought in Bangladesh has just been mentioned; droughts also had a major influence in The Gambia, Tanzania and Ghana, where they led to forest fires and extensive agricultural damage. Severe hurricanes were important causes of the crises in both Dominica and the Dominican Republic.
>
> (Killick, 1995b: 91)

What this variety of experience suggests is that it is not external shocks, *per se*, which are the decisive factor but rather the ways in which policy-makers respond to them. Shocks are not a large influence lying outside our analysis but rather are an additional reason for analysing why governments act – or fail to act – as they do. On this we are in agreement with the conclusion of Little *et al.*:

> the size of external shocks seems to have little bearing on subsequent economic difficulties: some countries adjusted well to large shocks, others adjusted poorly to small ones. Indeed, countries that experienced positive shocks, through mishandling, sometimes performed worse than countries which experienced negative shocks. Thus, although it is appropriate to point to disturbances emanating from the world economy as the source of difficulty, countries cannot avoid

responsibility for coping with those disturbances badly, since others coped well.

(Little et al., 1993: 394)

To sum up, the evidence suggests that implementation of specific measures is poor when there is a clash in donor and government objectives; that differing objectives are fairly common; that in their assessment of the political pros and cons of executing a measure governments are likely to be particularly influenced by its probable distributional effects and how this is likely to impact upon organized opposition; that conditionality can involve governments in substantial transactions costs, magnified by the increased linkage of aid to policy reforms; that governments cannot usually, as a countervailing benefit, count on agreement to IFI-sponsored measures to significantly enhance the credibility of its policies in the eyes of private agents; and that natural disasters and other shocks can impact heavily upon calculations, although the direction of this impact could be in either direction.

Overall, it appears that governments' participation constraints are often quite high, so the next issue to explore is whether conditionality-applying agencies are able to put in place an 'incentive compatible' reward system sufficient to compensate for the costs which governments expect to incur if they carry out donors' policy stipulations. We take this up in Chapter 6.

APPENDIX: THE SELECTION PROCEDURES FOR THE COUNTRY SAMPLE

We followed the following sequence:

1 Executing a trawl of the literature available at the ODI library on the adjustment experiences of all developing countries which received adjustment loans from the World Bank from 1980 onwards.
2 Categorizing the countries as 'Probables', 'Possibles', 'Doubtful' and 'Out' according to the quantity, quality and relevance to the current study of available country materials.
3 Pilot-testing the framework of hypotheses for organizing and analysing the materials in the country studies on three of the 'Probable' countries, namely Senegal, Turkey and the Philippines.
4 Attempting to up-grade as many 'Possible' countries to the 'Probable' category by searching for additional materials available at other libraries.
5 Categorizing the expanded list of 'Probable' countries (other than those on which pilot tests were performed) according to income as in the *World Development Report 1993.* Two of these countries – The Gambia and Guyana – were not classified in the Bank Report. However, UNDP's *Human Development Report 1993* calculates per capita GNP of these two countries, locating both of them clearly in the lower-middle-income category. The outcome was that of our eventual total of 21 countries, 10 were low-income, 8 lower-middle- and 3 upper-middle-income countries.
6 Selecting a stratified sample from the population of 'Probable' countries as follows:
   Writing the names of the twenty-one 'Probables' on slips of paper which were then put into a box. Shuffling them and drawing each slip out while noting the order in which each country was drawn.
7 Noting the income category of each country thus drawn and proceeding to analyse each country in the order drawn out but according to the ratio 3 : 2 : 1 in terms of income category.
8 The countries were drawn in the following order:

1	Colombia	8	Tanzania	15	Kenya
2	Malawi	9	Madagascar	16	Guyana
3	Zambia	10	Uganda	17	Thailand
4	Jamaica	11	India	18	Ecuador
5	Chile	12	Ghana	19	Côte d'Ivoire
6	Argentina	13	South Korea	20	Indonesia
7	Mexico	14	The Gambia	21	Nigeria

9 Observing the 3 : 2 : 1 ratio, the order in which the analyses should be done was determined as:

1	Malawi	8	Uganda	15	Indonesia
2	Zambia	9	India	16	Guyana
3	Tanzania	10	Chile	17	Thailand
4	Colombia	11	The Gambia	18	South Korea
5	Jamaica	12	Mexico	19	Nigeria
6	Argentina	13	Ghana	20	Ecuador
7	Madagascar	14	Kenya	21	Côte d'Ivoire

In the event, time permitted the analysis to be taken through to No. 18 (S. Korea), to which should be added the initial 'pilot' countries of the Philippines, Senegal and Turkey. It was not possible to include Nigeria, Ecuador or Côte d'Ivoire.

Framework of hypotheses for country survey

a Relating to participation constraints

1 The extent to which governments and/or ministers and/or officials perceive the (risk-adjusted) benefits of compliance, in terms of their own objectives, to outweigh the costs.
2 Recipients' calculations of costs and benefits will be particularly sensitive to the extent to which programme measures are expected to affect the distribution of income, and to the relative degrees of organization of gainers and losers.
3 Programme implementation is prejudiced when the objectives of donors and governments differ, resulting in conflicts of interest.
4 Programme 'ownership', i.e. the extent to which the proposed measures are perceived as government-designed or donor-imposed, will have a decisive influence on programme implementation.
5 Implementation will be a function of the reward system, i.e. the size and concessionality of supporting credits and any associated debt relief and capital inflows, through its influence on governments' or ministers' perceptions of likely net costs and benefits.
6 Agreeing an adjustment programme with the Fund and/or Bank, through its pre-commitment effect, raises the credibility of the government's own policies and therefore enhances private sector responses to these.

b Relating to rewards and punishments

7   When objectives differ, it is not possible to devise an incentive system sufficient to ensure that governments fully promote donors' objectives.

8   Noncompliance with the terms of a loan is not effectively punished by reduced access to new credits.

9   Programme effectiveness is undermined by political, bureaucratic and financial pressures upon donor agencies to lend, including attempts by major shareholder countries to influence decisions in favour of (or against) specific borrower countries.

10 The availability of a credit, by easing financial constraints, has weakened the incentive to implement reforms.

11 Implementation and programme effectiveness is reduced by the extent to which a donor has multiple, conflicting or unclear objectives, and by the number of donors applying separate conditionality.

12 There is an 'adverse selection' problem, with donors continuing to support poorly performing recipient governments in order to safeguard past investments and/or credibility, i.e. to avoid default or arrears; and to maintain an appearance of success.

c Other influences on implementation

13 The initial economic and political situation conditions programme implementation, including the influence of historical and institutional constraints, and the severity of the economic crisis.

14 Programme implementation and effectiveness will also be powerfully influenced by shocks and other unforeseen developments.

15 A long relationship between a donor and a government improves programme implementation and results.

The following hypotheses were also investigated but are not recorded above, nor in the Master Table and Table 5.1. They were dropped because the country survey did not yield relevant evidence in more than a small number of cases. NB, they were *not* dropped because the evidence was inconsistent with the hypothesis in question.

*   Pro-reform elements within the government have used the IFIs' advice and money to strengthen their position *vis-à-vis* conservative elements. This has been decisive in tipping the balance of power in favour of reformers.

*   The ability of programmes to achieve their objectives is influenced by the overall design of the adjustment programme in terms of its appropriate-

ness, internal consistency and sequencing of interrelated programme elements.

- The tranching of credit releases and the other modalities of conditionality have not created an incentive structure tending to maximize programme implementation.
- Large-country borrowers and others in a strong bargaining position are less likely to implement conditionality.
- Donor agencies have imperfect information about the actions of implementing governments, giving rise to substantial potential enforcement costs. Programme implementation will be influenced by resource and other constraints influencing the costs to conditionality-stipulating agencies of overcoming informational asymmetries and of monitoring government execution. These constraints include the adequacy of agency staffing and knowledge.
- A limited degree of donor influence over key policy variables is an important reason for programme shortfalls.
- Effectiveness will be undermined by pressures by donor managements or Boards on their staff to insist on tough-seeming but unrealistic conditionality.
- The ability of programmes to achieve their objectives will be influenced by the feasibility of specifying policy changes as preconditions, to be undertaken prior to approval of the financial support. Conversely, the feasibility of the government merely simulating compliance will have a negative influence on effectiveness.

Notes

1   See Mosley, 1992, for a rather different application of game theory to the conditionality problem, from which I have learnt much. See also Murshed and Sen, 1995, for a formal theoretical application of agency theory to donor–recipient relations.

2   For an excellent succinct survey of this literature see Stiglitz, 1987. Varian, 1993, Chapter 25, provides a formal textbook treatment.

3   See Bird (forthcoming) for an approach to the implementation question which is similar to ours, although it does not formally make use of agency theory. He comes to similar conclusions about the limitations of conditionality.

4   I have not seen this aspect discussed in the agency theory literature, but it seems intuitively obvious that incentives will have to be the larger, the greater is the disagreement between A's goals and P's. This is best thought of as being subsumed in the participation constraint: when their goals differ markedly, A will (in terms of utility forgone) stand to incur large costs, necessitating larger incentive payments to make participation worth his while.

5   Hewitt (1992: 87) quotes a 1986 speech by President Didier Ratsiraka that liberalization measures 'had been pressed upon him by his advisors and that he had never really been in favour of liberalisation'.

6   The empirical literature on this is surveyed in Healey and Robinson, 1992: 117–21.
7   The World Bank's (1995b: 176) study of public enterprises stresses the importance of this in connection with enterprise reform and privatization: 'promises that the leadership makes to compensate losers and protect investors' property rights must be believable'.
8   The unimportance of reputational considerations in Kenya is demonstrated by the typical sequence that the government will first agree to undertake a certain policy reform and then, when the moment for action finally arrives, decide whether or not to implement it. This is probably typical of the situation in quite a number of other countries too.

6

REWARDS, PUNISHMENTS
AND THE INFLUENCE OF
NATIONAL POLITICS

Chapter 5 has led us to expect donor and recipient objectives to differ and that recipient governments will therefore often be reluctant to execute some of the donors' policy stipulations. Given such 'participation constraints', the question we turn to now is whether donors are able to put in place a system of rewards sufficient to overcome this constraint.

I Rewards and punishments

The adequacy of the reward system

The agency framework predicts that the implementation of policy conditions will be sensitive to the adequacy of the incentives offered, relative to governments' participation constraints. When this was formulated as a hypothesis and tested against our country evidence, we obtained substantial validation, as can be seen from Hypothesis 5 of the Master Table and Table 5.1, with twelve out of fourteen observations consistent with the hypothesis.

This is not surprising because, as described in Chapter 1, the IFIs (and to some extent other donor agencies) have developed a number of devices for maximizing the leverage afforded by their financial power. These include the near-universal application of *tranching*, i.e. releasing assistance in instalments subject to satisfactory performance on programme execution; the use of *preconditions* ('prior actions'), whereby certain policy changes must be undertaken before a loan or grant will even be approved; and *cross-conditionality*, whereby access to one source of assistance will also be determined by observance of conditions attached to another source of finance. The most important examples of the latter are the common requirement that access to a World Bank adjustment credit is contingent upon satisfactory observance of the terms of an IMF programme (or other IMF approval of a government's macroeconomic policies). Similar cross-conditionality is attached to access to debt relief.

Quite apart from this type of leveraging, the absolute value of IFI credits is not negligible. Investigation of the scale of IMF loans in 1979–89 showed that the annualized flow from the average credit was equivalent to about a tenth of recipient countries' imports, nearly a quarter of their current account deficit and nearly 30 per cent of their overall deficit (Killick, 1995b: 65). An illustrative calculation for a small random sample of World Bank structural adjustment credits indicated these to be typically only a third as large: equivalent, in annualized terms, to about 3 per cent of imports and 10 per cent of countries' current account deficits.[1] Nevertheless, the indicated scale of support is substantial and to it, at least according to the IFIs, may be added the additional support that may be attracted from other sources – the so-called 'catalytic effect'. The survey of Latin American experiences in Chapter 3 also brought out the valuable contribution made by the IFIs' credits in a number of countries.

However – and this is the main message that our evidence conveys – *when objectives differ the incentive system is generally inadequate to ensure that governments will implement policy conditions.* On this, see Hypothesis 7 of the tables, with Table 5.1 showing that all twelve of the observations on this topic pointed to this conclusion. Various types of situations can be delineated here.

a   *Programmes may be under-funded* relative to the scale of the problems addressed and this leads to poor implementation. The study of the IMF just cited found precisely such an association, with poorly-implemented programmes associated with much smaller credits relative to imports and other balance of payments indicators (Killick, 1995b: 65). As concerns the World Bank, from within our present data pool, Zambia in the latter 1980s is a well-known case, with a programme both seriously under-funded and weakly executed, a situation aggravated by the country's large debt-servicing obligations to the IFIs (Fardi, 1991: 351). Guyana's situation in the same period was much the same, combining a seriously under-funded programme with weak implementation (Harrigan, 1991: 386). The situation in Argentina in the late 1980s, with respect to a Bank trade policy credit, also fitted this description, particularly in the absence of a supporting IMF programme and Paris Club debt relief (Tussie and Botzman, 1990). It has to be said, however, that in all three cases it is doubtful whether larger financial support, within the realm of what might have been feasible, would have made a decisive difference to policy execution. In each case the governments perceived high political risks from carrying out programme provisions, so their participation constraints were high.

b   *Catalytic effects*, whereby reaching an agreement with an IFI induces additional capital inflows from other sources, *are undependable*, and governments know this to be so. Although our country survey did not yield evidence on the existence of catalytic effects, it is worth recalling the conclusion of the survey of South-east Asian experiences in Chapter 3, that IFI support did help attract additional finance from other sources (e.g. for Thailand) but that this was not enough by itself: 'Only when the governments' own commitment to economic reform was evident did investors start to allocate resources' (p. 69).

As regards *private* capital movements, independent sources support this proposition. In the case of IMF programmes, there is a literature. Killick (1995b: 71) surveys this and adds additional evidence, concluding that, although there are specific examples of positive effects, there are negative examples too and that, overall, adoption of IMF programmes is not associated with any significant change in private flows. There is no equivalent evidence relating to Bank SAPs, except that of Mosley *et al.*, already reported, which indicated that implementation of Bank programmes made no difference to private investment inflows: '*as a rule*, and with distinctive exceptions such as Turkey, Bank adjustment loans have failed to have this catalytic effect' (1991a: 229). Rodrik (1996a: 183–7) tested for catalytic effects on various types of private capital flows in 1970–93 for a sample of developing countries, and found that IMF credits had no significant effect, while 'other multilateral' lending (of which the World Bank must have been a substantial part) tended actually to have a *deterrent* effect on private inflows. Bird and Rowlands (forthcoming) also undertake econometric tests for the catalytic effects of IMF programmes, on a panel data set of ninety developing countries for the period 1974–89, and their results too do not support the existence of a general positive catalytic effect, with outcomes that vary across time and location.

The above tests ought, in principle, to pick up any return of *flight capital*. The attraction back home of this type of capital is one of the potential benefits of a Fund or Bank agreement but not one, so far as it is caught by the data, which appears large, or dependable, in practice – although it is possible that having a programme in place does at least staunch the outflow.

As regards *public* capital flows, decisions on which are not primarily determined by market considerations, there is some evidence of a catalytic effect, as donor governments use their aid (and perhaps export credit) allocations to support IFI programmes. Killick (1995b: 71) found some general positive effect on public flows, with some bilateral aid being triggered by agreement with the Fund. Bird and Rowlands also found a significant correlation between IMF programmes and public capital flows, but only for 1973–81 and with some indications of a negative association in 1982–9.

The absence of evidence of any strong positive catalytic effect is actually not surprising, given the result reported earlier that IFI programmes do not raise the credibility of government policies. So far as private flows are concerned, it would be as a result of enhanced investor confidence that additional inflows might be attracted. Gordon (1992: 38), writing from the perspective of a senior USAID official, makes this connection: 'conditionality has lost credence with global financial markets and has not had the "catalytic" role . . . that it was designed to have'.

The account of the experiences of South-east Asian countries in Chapter 3 is instructive in this context. This reports a positive association of IFI programmes with enhanced private inflows in Indonesia, South Korea and Thailand, but that these were all cases whose governments had already demonstrated a determination to pursue prudent and market-friendly policies. By contrast, large-scale IFI support for the Philippines made no impact on foreign investors until eventually a government came to power with a demonstrated commitment to economic liberalization.

In short, investment decisions are based on judgements about the quality of *government* policy-making, for which the existence of an IFI programme is not taken as an adequate proxy. Within the same region, Malaysia has benefited from much increased inward investment even though it has never accepted an IFI adjustment credit – because its government has convinced investors of its commitment to maintaining a good investment climate.

c   Another type of situation arises when *the government perceives political costs or risks to be too great, even though substantial finance is on offer*. A number of examples of this are identified in the Master Table (Hypothesis 7). Thus, in Argentina in 1989 implementation of macroeconomic stabilization measures under a Bank trade policy credit urgently required a devaluation and increasing utility charges, neither of which was the Alfonsin regime prepared to undertake during the run-up to a presidential election. When the political survival of the government was at stake, there was little the Bank could do to induce the implementation of its programme conditions (Tussie and Botzman, 1990: 400). Similarly in Uganda, despite intense donor support of a stabilization attempt in the early 1980s, when political expediency suggested otherwise the Obote regime abandoned stabilization (Loxley, 1989: 77–8). The case of Zambia in 1986 has already been cited, where the government quickly reneged on Fund–Bank adjustment programmes when powerful opposition emerged in the Copperbelt.

The potential political costs of complying with conditionality are, of course, a function of the stringency and scope of the measures in question. The wider the scope, the larger the number of interest groups that will be affected. This rather obvious point is worth making (i) because of the trend towards the proliferation of conditionality, tending to raise potential political costs and thus reduce implementation, and (ii) because it shows the futility of donors' trying to raise the conditionality stakes as a way of obtaining action.

d   Another situation in which the government has little incentive to accept unwanted policy stipulations is *where it is not reliant on obtaining the money on offer*, either because of access to alternative sources of external finance (see the Master Table, Hypothesis 10) or because of the strength of the domestic economy. A number of our countries have fitted this description at various times: Argentina, Mexico, Senegal and South Korea. Turkey provides another case, whose geopolitical importance, and the access to resources which came with that, put it in a position of being able to choose the measures it would carry through (Kirkpatrick and Onis, 1991: 33 and *passim*). We have already cited the Thai case, where a good past record with adjustment measures so raised its creditworthiness in global capital markets that it could afford to turn its back on the Bank when the latter sought to insist on measures with which the government disagreed. Malawi also provides a neat illustration, with compliance with Bank conditionality under her 2nd and 3rd adjustment credits a function of the supply of alternative sources of aid: there was improved compliance under the second programme following a decline in bilateral aid; and reduced compliance under a third credit in the later 1980s coincident with improved availability of bilateral aid (Harrigan, 1991: 253–6).

A last type of situation reducing the incentive to implement is where *the government has little fear of retribution if it does not execute inconvenient measures*. In such situations the expected political costs of given measures may not be excessive but the government judges it can avoid implementation without much loss of financial support.

This then brings us to the issue of the punishment of non-compliance with policy stipulations.

Is non-implementation penalized?

That governments which wilfully fail to honour their policy commitments should as a result be penalized is fundamental to any adequate incentive system. For if obligations can be flouted with impunity governments will soon learn that they can take the money with minimal policy movement, that the political burdens of conditionality are more apparent than real. Of course, they know that the IFIs and other donors possess the potential sanction of withholding their aid. That is why adjustment aid is usually tranched, so that the unspent balance of a credit can be withheld in the event of unsatisfactory policy delivery. Even in the absence of tranching, donors may penalize bad faith by declining new aid. The modalities for punishment are in place, but are they exercised?

On the face of it, the answer is affirmative, for we reported in Chapter 2 that a high proportion of IMF programmes are discontinued, often as a result of 'noncompliance' (to use the IFIs' term) and that World Bank structural adjustment programmes typically take about twice as long as intended because of delayed tranche releases, again because of unsatisfactory progress on the policy front. Against that, however, there are strong indications that non-implementation is rarely punished effectively. There is substantial evidence from a variety of observers as well as from our own study.

To take the latter first, Table 5.1, Hypothesis 8, summarizes the results of asking for our twenty-one countries to what extent implementation deficiencies were effectively punished. We obtained twelve observations and *in all twelve cases there was an absence of effective punishment*. Some examples follow.

Argentina

In 1987–8 the government did not meet the conditions for the release of the second tranche of an agricultural adjustment credit. It failed to institute a federal land tax and to liberalize the importation of tractors and machinery. However, as credits from commercial banks were linked to Bank disbursements, pressure arose to release the tranche. Eventually, the Bank's management recommended a waiver of conditionality to the Board which the latter approved after much acrimonious debate (World Bank, 1993b: vi–viii). An apparently stronger case of punishment occurred a year later when release of the second tranche of a trade policy loan was made contingent on satisfactory implementation of a macroeconomic programme. The government was unable to meet the macro targets and the Bank refused to disburse the second tranche. However, in this case it is evident that the Bank 'punished' Argentina because it was looking for a way out of a programme it had been forced into (mainly by American pressure) in the first place (Tussie and Botzman, 1990: 403 and *passim*).

Jamaica

In the early 1980s the Bank was well aware that the government had complied with the conditions of successive SALs in formal terms only. The government was actually unwilling to implement an adequate stabilization package in relation both to the balance of payments and fiscal management. Despite its own assessment of a mere 40 per cent compliance with critical policy stipulations, the Bank went ahead with further adjustment loans. In fact, tranches of all three SALs were released despite poor macroeconomic performance (Harrigan, 1991: 323).

Kenya

In the candid words of the World Bank (1991: 20), 'there was a lack of commitment and . . . poor progress achieved in previous SALs, and . . . numerous delays encountered in preparation, appraisal, negotiation and signing of these loans. However, the Bank went ahead with lending anyway. The resulting progress with implementation was unsatisfactory.' Mosley (1991: 287) claims that the overall picture 'is one of slippage in all areas' but that this went unpunished. Although release of a SAL second tranche was delayed by nine months because of failure to decontrol maize marketing, the disbursement was finally authorized on the strength of a government undertaking to speedily decontrol maize. Subsequent lack of progress on this issue prompted the Bank to terminate the SAL process but this turned out to be only a 'token slap on the wrist', for soon after the Bank added US$20 million to a line of credit in favour of the Agricultural Finance Corporation. Indeed, except for a few years in the early 1990s (when bilateral donors organized an aid boycott pending progress on movement towards multi-party democracy), Kenya's record exemplified how a well-placed and determined government could flout policy commitments with minimal consequences for aid receipts.

Madagascar

Here was a country, *par excellence*, which ought not to have been in a position to 'get away with it': it had a leftist government with which most donor governments were out of sympathy, no powerful friends at court, and scant economic or geopolitical significance. And yet the Bank continued to release tranches and agree new credits even though its own Performance Audit Report stated that there had been little compliance with conditions. Seven government projects to which the Bank had objected were proceeded with notwithstanding; a promised programme for promoting private sector participation in agricultural marketing was never prepared; a commitment to prepare an action plan on local government finances met a similar fate (World Bank, 1994e: xviii–xix). But the money kept coming in.

Senegal

A similar case to Kenya's, with continuing large-scale inflows of assistance despite a highly imperfect record of compliance. The government well knew that its international supporters – France, the EC and the USA – would take a very dim view of aid slowdowns, with the consequence that

> When faced with the domestic political risks of imposing an unpopular reform . . . the authorities have been inclined to risk donor wrath arising from violation of conditionality. It has certainly proved the appropriate course: sanctions are rare or nonexistent and aid flows mount.
>
> (Berg *et al.*, 1990: 109)

Turkey

Here too the Bank tolerated much slippage in meeting SAL conditions (Kirkpatrick and Onis, 1991, *passim*). Conditions were waived in a number of instances, apparently because of the Bank's perception of the need to maintain quick-dispersing balance of payments support. The rapidity with which the Bank came up with new loans (there were five SALs in as many years) and tranche releases convinced the Turkish authorities that they could push for rapid growth on the expectation that any resulting budgetary overruns would go unpunished. Reports prepared by Bank staff in support of further SALs merely approved past performance as showing 'satisfactory progress' or ignored slippages in meeting targets. For instance, tranches of the first SAL were released without full compliance with conditionality and with poor macroeconomic performance because of concerns that delays would jeopardize an IMF stabilization programme. In the case of the fifth SAL, in 1984, negoti-ations for a Fund stand-by programme were postponed as Turkey's monetary and fiscal policies were not consistent with achieving internal and external balance, but the Bank decided to proceed with a tranche release despite uncer-tainty about the soundness of macroeconomic policies (the Fund stand-by never materialized and the macroeconomic situation deteriorated).

Zambia

This was another country which persistently reneged on agreements with the IFIs during most of the 1980s but which continued to secure large-scale support. In the case of the Bank, the second tranche of all three sectoral loans between 1984 and 1986 were released despite much slippage in implementa-tion, leading a staff member to conclude that 'In retrospect it appears that the World Bank may have gone too far in accommodating Zambia with the maximum amount of resources available' (Fardi, 1991: 345).

Finally from our own research results, we should recall the conclusion from the survey of the four South-east Asian 'reforming country' experiences in Chapter 3 (p. 69) that compliance with the few policy stipulations made by the IFIs was high only when governments regarded the actions as beneficial. When they were unconvinced of the need for action conditionality was violated, *invariably with impunity*.

The results of others' research reinforces the finding of an absence of effec-tive sanctions. Gordon (1992: 37) cites an unpublished PhD thesis by Gates studying the World Bank and USAID which 'found minimal risks for recipi-ents despite non-compliance'. Taking a slightly different approach, Nelson (1990: 19) studied thirty-six adjustment episodes in thirteen developing countries and concluded that financial support for these countries bore no consistent relationship to the extent of reform implementation. Some reformist governments received only moderate financial support; and some that received much support did little by way of structural reforms. Guillaumont and Guillaumont's study of adjustment in the African,

Caribbean and Pacific (ACP) developing countries associated with the European Union found that incomplete implementation of reforms

> has at times been reinforced by the moderate nature of the effective sanctions imposed, i.e. the continuation of aid when the prescribed conditions were not really met. Such has been the attitude of some international institutions, based on a bureaucratic logic of success, whereby conditions are often feigned as met when they have not actually been so.
>
> (Guillaumont and Guillaumont, 1994: 85)

That leniency in the face of non-implementation is not a phenomenon restricted to policy-related lending is indicated by the highly-influential 'Wapenhans Report' of a World Bank Task Force on the quality of its *project* lending:

> Noncompliance remains a serious problem. . . . The Bank, in response to noncompliance, can suspend the right of the Borrower to make withdrawals, or can . . . cancel the undisbursed balance of the loan; but these remedies are rarely exercised. Usually, staff and managers respond to noncompliance by ignoring it, waiving it, or occasionally taking informal steps to deal with it. . . . The high incidence of noncompliance undermines the Bank's credibility. It also indicates inadequate concern about the instruments of governance and a lack of realism at the time of negotiation. If staff and managers are prepared to tolerate high levels of continuous non-compliance, the question arises as to whether such covenants should be included in the first place.
>
> (World Bank, 1992b: 22)

Berg *et al.* (1990: 224) similarly write of 'the reluctance of the international community, including the Bank and the IMF, to stop aid flows to needy countries except in cases of flagrant, repeated and unrepentant nonperformance, which occurs rarely'. Another international donor affected by the same reluctance appears to be the European Community, for, according to its own Court of Auditors:

> Conditions for the release of funds are often still so general that it is not possible to make any objective assessment of their implementation. . . . It is consequently always possible to release funds whatever the scale of the measures actually taken in the recipient country. . . . For special conditions, funds were unblocked by the [European] Commission even though the conditions had not been fully complied with. . . . Mid-Term reviews . . . before the next tranche is

released . . . often contain evasive conclusions that do not result in
clear recommendations.

(European Commission Court of Auditors, 1994, paras. 15.83–5)

There are very few exceptions to the general finding of an absence of effective punishment (although the *financial* misdemeanour of slipping into arrears
in the servicing of past IFI loans is met with large sanctions, as explained
later). It seems that the appearance of punishment conveyed by programme
cancellations (in the case of the IMF) or delays in releasing tranche payments
(the Bank's preferred sanction) is misleading because the costs to a government of waiting out a tranche delay are not usually great and new credits can
usually be negotiated. Mosley *et al.* (1991a: 166–70) do find some evidence
that delinquent governments are less likely to be granted a subsequent credit
by the Bank but report that at the time of their study there appeared to have
been only two cases in which a second credit tranche had not been released due
to non-implementation. They cite a number of examples (Ecuador, Guyana,
Bolivia, Kenya) where tranches had eventually been handed over even though
almost none of the associated conditions had been satisfied, and provide an
amusing account of the rituals which the Bank goes through in order to
convince itself that a tranche may be released.

It is possible that the experiences of the past may not provide a good guide
to the future because aid budgets are shrinking and donors are looking to be
more selective in the governments they support. This factor became evident in
our research in Kenya in late 1995. There was an apparently greater willingness by donors to use the Moi government's poor track record to reduce aid to
that country. However, the incentive to reform created by this greater willingness to cut was flawed because, with reduced total aid budgets, *there was no
realistic possibility that, once cut, the aid would be restored to former levels.* While the
government might, in retrospect, be seen as having erred by giving donors a
reason for reducing allocations, it did not then have an incentive to mend its
ways because the cuts were irreversible. Indeed, by that time aid to Kenya had
been sufficiently reduced that the government had found ways of living
without that support and donors had even less potential leverage than before.

Conditionality and moral hazard

We can at this point return to the suggestion in Chapter 1 (p. 13) that one of
the justifications for conditionality is that it acts as a safeguard against the
danger that governments will use aid money in order to defer necessary policy
changes, and that it serves as a substitute for the loan collateral that commercial lenders would require. It is fairly evident from the last few pages that
conditionality cannot be depended on to fulfil this purpose. Our own country
survey showed a tendency for access to finance to weaken the incentive for
policy action – see the Master Table and Table 5.1, Hypothesis 10, showing

this tendency in nine of the eleven available observations. Among our countries, governments which, at one time or another, used aid resources in order to defer action included Argentina, Jamaica, Kenya, Madagascar, Mexico, the Philippines, Senegal, Tanzania, Turkey, Zambia – even Thailand! Berg *et al.* (1990: 217) put it nicely of Senegal: 'Senegalese authorities have become habituated to solving problems of resource scarcity more by looking for money from donors than by making hard choices.'

To go beyond single-country illustrations, this topic has been most comprehensively examined in a study of IMF programmes by Santaella (1992). On the premise that, in the absence of moral hazard, there would be a positive association between Fund lending and policy performance he tested for correlation between these two variables. Contrary to the hypothesis, he found a generally *negative* association between increases in Fund lending and compliance with its conditionality. He also found that larger programmes were more likely to break down or to require easing of policy conditions (waivers) to keep them in place. These results, he concluded, were consistent with the existence of moral hazard: governments are able 'to engage in "opportunistic behavior" and avoid undertaking adjustment while still using IMF credit . . . the Fund has not been able to enforce its programs. They are not binding commitments' (1992: 89). Although he regards his evidence as suggestive rather than conclusive, he concludes that it indicates 'the presence of a deep problem in the compliance with IMF programs' (Santaella, 1992: 123).

The World Bank (1994a, Table A29) provides an illuminating matrix for African countries during the 1980s, relating trends in the quality of macroeconomic policy with changes in 'net external transfers' (aid). This reveals that while eight (53 per cent) out of fifteen countries classified as having improved their policies received *reduced* aid receipts, only three (27 per cent) out of eleven countries with deteriorating policies had suffered this fate. De Vylder (1994) observes a similar tendency and comments with some outrage on a 'pronounced tendency to reward bad performance with increased flows of aid and loans, and to punish successful policies' (de Vylder, 1994: 3).

> A country which prudently manages its external sector will soon realise that the IFIs and the donor community breathe a sigh of relief – one problem country less! – and rush to mop up arrears from a disaster case instead . . . the marginal rate of tax on 'good behaviour' can be very high.
>
> (de Vylder, 1994: 22)

The danger of moral hazard in such a situation is obvious.

II Why does delinquency go unpunished?

So long as non-implementation incurs little risk of retribution, conditionality clearly cannot serve as a substitute for loan collateral, nor as an assurance against moral hazard. But since the lenders have the means at their disposal for applying sanctions, why are these not more rigorously applied? There are both external and internal forces at work. Underlying them all are the multiple objectives of donor governments and agencies. Were they all willing to give economic efficiency and development overriding priority it would be more feasible to enforce conditionality but foreign policy, security, commercial, financial and institutional objectives rule out any such single-mindedness.

External factors

If we confine ourselves to the international agencies, there are often considerable external pressures upon them to maintain the flow of financial support to favoured countries, undermining the credibility of threats of sanctions in the event of non-implementation. Often this pressure comes from their own shareholders. Successive American and French administrations have had special reputations for the vigour with which they support developing country governments with which they have close relationships. The situation of the IMF is already quite well documented. Thus, of seventeen developing countries examined by Killick:

> at least a third have secured favourable programmes because of special relationships with major shareholder countries. Indeed, a third is probably an underestimate because our sample almost certainly includes other examples which were not documented but which are widely regarded as having been the beneficiaries of this type of influence. . . . Among those who know the Fund well there are disagreements about the extent and effects of political interference in country programme decisions. . . . Nonetheless, it is undoubtedly a real problem and, for our sample at least, *it provides among the strongest explanations for ineffective programmes*. . . . In its more extreme forms it amounts to an unconditional provision of finance for governments with proven records of macroeconomic mismanagement. As such, it contradicts all that the IMF is supposed to stand for, and undermines its legitimacy in other countries whose governments resent the more favourable treatment received by others and which are tempted to try to secure by stealth an equality of treatment they are unable to negotiate formally.
>
> (Killick, 1995b: 119)

What of the World Bank? In the country studies undertaken for this study we sought evidence on this topic, with results summarized in Table 5.1, Hypothesis 9. Out of the eleven countries to which the question was applicable and for which there was evidence, we found important external pressures in six.

Argentina provides a well-documented case (Tussie and Botzman, 1990: 397–402). Having itself earlier been pressured to maintain support for the Alfonsin administration, which was unwilling or unable to take the steps necessary to stabilize the macroeconomic situation, the IMF in the latter part of 1988 refused to finance another largely bogus stabilization programme. Fearful of the consequences of this for its attempts to manage the Latin American debt situation and protect the financial standing of American banks, the Reagan administration applied intense pressure for the Bank to waive its usual criteria and effectively take over the role of the Fund in this case. Given the large importance of the USA as a shareholder, the Bank very reluctantly complied, although it took care to leave itself an exit route should it become politically possible to follow it. In the event, there was a change of American policy, introduced by the new Bush administration in early 1989, following which the Bank withdrew its support, citing noncompliance with policy conditions, but this was an option it was only free to exercise as a result of the change in American policy.

We have already noted Turkey's ability to apparently flout the Bank's conditionality without financial penalty. Particularly in the 1980s, that country occupied a strategically crucial position, as a Muslim country straddling Asia and Europe, as the south-eastern pillar of NATO, and as a source of large-scale emigration, particularly to West Germany. At various times, this resulted in large pressures on the Fund and/or Bank to provide financial support despite weak policies. Jamaica, Kenya and Senegal were among other countries that could usually count on the USA and other powerful friends at court because of their perceived strategic importance in the 1980s, just as the Marcos government in the Philippines had little to fear so long as it could retain the support of successive American administrations (which, however, it eventually lost as domestic opposition grew). Mosley *et al.* (1991a: 128) likewise note that, while it did not necessarily result in an initially less rigorous package of conditionality from the Bank, the support of the USA resulted in 'a more forgiving treatment of slippage on conditions'.

Sometimes the pressure can come from another international agency. Both the Bank and the IMF are likely to take an active interest in the scale of each other's support for a country in which both have adjustment programmes. Whichever is the first to establish a programme is likely to wish that the other should provide as much credit as possible – or at least as much as was assumed when the first of the programmes was written. This generally translates into the Fund leaning on the Bank, irrespective of progress on policy implementation. The Bank itself (1991: 28) has reported such pressure, citing the instances of Senegal and Turkey.

From our own sample, Guyana illustrates a variation on this theme, again with unfortunate results. In 1982 a Bank appraisal mission recommended that the disbursal of the second tranche of a SAP should only occur when a Fund programme had been put back on track. However, Fund staff reversed the direction of this proposed cross-conditionality by insisting on continuation of the Bank programme as a precondition of its own loan. When negotiations with the Fund collapsed, other donors also expressed unwillingness to commit resources to Guyana, leaving the Bank in the unenviable position of having to continue with a hopelessly under-funded SAP (Harrigan, 1991: 382).

The Paris Club – the agency for dealing with requests for debt relief on official loans, mainly by OECD countries – is another source of pressure. It has the rule that it will not agree to a debt relief arrangement unless the debtor-government has an IMF agreement in place. However, creditors are often anxious, for their own reasons, to provide relief for specific debtor countries and hence put pressure on the Fund to agree new programmes, or to pretend that existing programmes are on track, even when the Fund's staff does not believe in the adequacy of the government's macroeconomic policies.

Sometimes multiple sources of pressure come together to create an irresistible force. Such was the case with the SAPs agreed with nine Francophone African countries in connection with the devaluation of the Communauté Financière d'Afrique (CFA) franc in January 1994. That devaluation – the first change against the French franc since 1948 – was the culmination of massive efforts by the IFIs and various donor governments, in opposition for most of the time to the Franc Zone governments and France. When agreement was finally secured on this change, the Bank came under such pressure that its normal safeguards went out of the window, resulting in credits disbursed 100 per cent up-front and approved even though the lender's own assessment of the borrowing governments' ownership of the programmes was generally negative (World Bank, 1995a: 125).

At a slightly different level of explanation, implementation of any one donor's conditions may be undermined because of inconsistencies, or tensions, with the objectives of other agencies. There has, for instance, been tension in certain countries between the policy recommendations of the Fund, with its stress on macro stabilization, and the Bank, which concentrates on strengthening the productive and institutional structures. In broad terms, the Bank's objectives point towards higher levels of government service provisions and capital formation, while the Fund's preoccupation is with reducing budget deficits and hence with keeping all forms of state spending under strict control. For similar reasons, there may also be disagreements about taxation (e.g. of exports), and about the desirable extent of demand deflation. And quite often the Bank's concern to stimulate supply responses makes it favour larger devaluations than the Fund, which may be worried about the inflationary consequences of large changes.

As indicated in the Master Table, Hypothesis 11, our country cases point to examples of this kind, although only in a few of the countries studied. In Ghana there were occasionally severe inter-IFI disputes over fiscal policy and import levels, with the Bank urging a larger public investment programme than the Fund believed to be consistent with macroeconomic balance (Martin, 1993: 158). Again, devaluation in Ghana pushed up the cost of debt service and other foreign denominated payments in the budget and helped breach Fund expenditure ceilings in 1986. The Bank suggested compromises but in general the Fund was not agreeable and its view prevailed (*ibid.*).

There were tensions too in Jamaica in the mid-1980s, where inconsistency between the Fund's stabilization programme and the Bank's trade and liberalization policies led to the 1983–5 SAL programme being undermined by the monetary policy encouraged by the Fund. Growth was held back by inappropriately severe monetary policies, causing high interest rates and exchange rate uncertainty, jeopardizing the response of the private sector (Harrigan, 1991: 322).

Political conditionality is too recent a phenomenon to have entered much into the literature reviewed for our country survey. However, the situation of Kenya in the mid-1990s well illustrated the tensions that were liable to arise between this and the implementation of IFI conditionality directed at economic policies. While some aspects of 'political' conditionality were regarded as congruent with what donors were seeking to achieve through economic conditions – such as measures to improve accountability, control corruption and strengthen property rights – the introduction of political dimensions complicated the (already difficult) task of securing compliance with economic policy requirements. The Kenyan government had interpreted donor stipulations in the early 1990s for the restoration of multi-party democracy as implying a relegation of economic policy requirements, so when (if only in form, not in spirit) the government duly introduced democratic procedures it expected aid flows to be fully restored. When this did not transpire, because of continuing deficiencies in economic policies, the government was very aggrieved and relations with donors were seriously impaired.

The IFIs seek to safeguard against such a situation by avoiding overtly 'political' conditionality but the Kenyan case showed the difficulties of holding this line. In late 1995 an IMF mission went to Nairobi to negotiate a new ESAF programme. However, although it was reasonably satisfied with economic policies, it had to say to the government that unless certain more 'political' conditions being urged by bilateral donors were also met (relating to the persecution of senior personalities thought to have been engaging in large-scale financial irregularities) any economic programme it put before the Board would not receive the necessary support. In this way the agenda of bilateral donors was forced upon the IMF. Not the least of the difficulties with this is that it introduces an additional source of inconsistency in conditionality, depending on the constancy of the bilateral donors and their ability to hold a united front. (A sad postscript to this case: the Kenyan government did eventually give assurances that those responsible would be brought before the courts; the donors called off their aid boycott; a new Fund ESAF credit was duly approved . . . and those responsible for misuse of $400 million of public resources, although they were charged, were freed by the court on a technicality. It seems there is simply no way for outside agencies to enforce their will on a recalcitrant government if it is sufficiently confident and unscrupulous.)

Political conditionality creates the further complication that democracy tends to weaken fiscal policy by introducing an electoral cycle. This was evident in Kenya. It is well documented in Ghana, too, where domestic and external pressures for democratization in the early 1990s contributed seriously to a weakening of fiscal discipline which from the middle of the decade threatened the economic gains achieved in the 1980s (CEPA, 1996).

Internal pressures

Besides these external forces, there is a potentially large array of internal pressures – financial, economic and institutional – undermining the enforcement of IFI conditionality and preventing the punishment of noncompliers.

Adverse selection and the debt problem

To begin with financial factors, there is an ever-present danger of what we can loosely call adverse selection: that the IFIs will feel they must continue lending to poorly-performing countries in order to protect their past investments, to avoid the danger of these countries falling into arrears or defaulting altogether. The risks to multilateral lenders have been minimized by giving them 'preferred creditor' status, meaning that the servicing of their credits has first claim on a country's resources, but this has not prevented some countries from falling seriously into arrears.[2] When they do so this has drastic consequences for the arrears countries, for they become ineligible for any new multilateral credits and may well also suffer losses of bilateral aid as well. Their arrears also weaken the IFIs' balance sheets in some degree. The lending institutions therefore try very hard to prevent borrowing governments from falling into arrears.

The logic of this is that the IFIs can find themselves making new loans on these *financial* grounds, in which case they are in little position to enforce any conditionality which may nominally be attached. Writing from the perspective of the experiences of USAID, Gordon has put the point well: 'Once would-be promoters of reform develop large stakes as creditors in a situation in which repayment is problematical, their reform goals are in danger of becoming subordinated to their creditor interests' (1992: 36).[3]

In recent years this danger has become greater, as obligations to IFIs have assumed a growing proportion of the total external indebtedness of low-income countries. As of 1994, multilateral debt constituted 28 per cent of low-income countries' total external debt stocks and a full 51 per cent of their total debt-servicing payments. The equivalent figures for 1980 were 22 per cent and 20 per cent.[4] Although in 1996 the IFIs entered into an initiative for providing relief to highly indebted poor countries in respect of the servicing of their multilateral debts (the 'HIPC Initiative'), the main way in which the IFIs could respond to the growing debt-servicing difficulties of some of their clients remained the *refinancing* of past credits, maintaining a sufficient flow of new lending to ensure that they could continue to service past credits.

Lending driven by such motivations undermines the credibility of IFI policy conditionality, for a borrowing government will be aware that IFIs' anxiety that it should remain current will allow it to renege on policy commitments with minimal risk of financial penalties. The IFIs deny that lending decisions are determined by such considerations but this denial is short on credibility. Indeed, Fund–Bank debt projections show that new flows *must* be skewed in favour of those with large multilateral debts for the outcome to remain manageable. The extent to which lending is biased by debt considerations is difficult to measure. However, a simple test of the hypothesis that existing multilateral debt servicing drives IFI lending, presented in Figure 6.1, while open to more than one interpretation, is suggestive. In statistical terms, the fit was good and highly significant.[5] More sophisticated econometric testing by Knight and Santaella (1994) similarly found, for the IMF, that prior lending was one of the most powerful and significant of their explanatory variables, where new Fund lending was the dependent variable. The weak responses of many countries to the adjustment programmes of the IFIs, shown in Chapter 2, increases the likelihood that new lending will become driven in this way.

Mosley *et al.* (1991a, Table 5.7 and *passim*) provide evidence along similar lines, suggesting that non-implementation by countries in which the World Bank has already a large financial investment is more likely to go unpunished than in countries where the sunk investment is small. We should add that the investment in question may not always be financial. It may be reputational, where the IFIs have invested so much credibility in the success of a government's adjustment efforts that they have a strong aversion to allowing these efforts to be seen to fail. In such situations the balance of bargaining power shifts from lender to borrower, and here again it will be difficult for the former to enforce any conditionality.

Our country survey tested for the presence of an adverse selection problem, with the results summarized in Hypothesis 12 of the Master Table and Table 5.1. In seven out of ten countries to which the question was applicable and for which there was evidence, there were indications that this was a factor at work. Ghana provided an example of a country where reputational considerations seemed strong, and it was with this case in mind that the responsible World Bank Vice-President stated that if programmes like the Ghanaian one

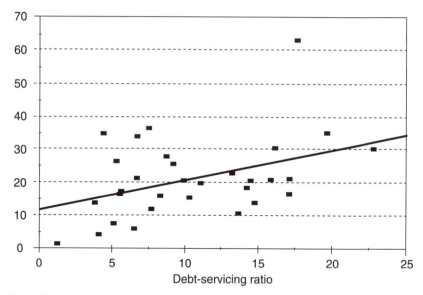

Figure 6.1 Does multilateral indebtedness drive multilateral lending?

Source: Data calculated from IMF–World Bank joint paper on 'Issues and Developments in Multilateral Debt . . . ', 30 March 1995, Table A5.

Note: Observations are average values for 1984–94, expressed as ratios to exports of goods and services, for thirty-two heavily indebted poor countries. Three outlier values are excluded.

failed, it would signify 'a failure of our approach to the economy, a failure of our institutions, a failure of our political will. . . . So we have a very, very big stake in this' (quoted by Callaghy in Nelson, 1990: 283). The position of Tanzania in the early 1990s was similar (Gibbon and Raikes, 1995). Glowing IFI reports on progress there and much less glowing results elsewhere in Africa resulted in Tanzania at that time being seen as a better prospect than many other African countries. Maintenance of this interpretation involved the IFIs in talking the achievements up and the problems down, however. By 1993–5 the indecision, aid dependence and corruption of the government were becoming increasingly hard for donors to ignore, but the IFIs, having invested heavily in the success of their Tanzanian programmes, maintained a public optimism until events unravelled in 1994–5.

Kenya is another country where adverse selection has clearly been at work at various times, as are Zambia and Senegal. On the latter, Berg *et al.* (1990: 220, 224) report on the donors' desire to keep disbursements flowing. In the face of noncompliance with policy conditions they accept cosmetic measures or half-steps so as to retain at least the appearance that the programme remains on track. As regards Zambia, a 1996 unpublished in-house evaluation concluded that both the IMF and World Bank had clearly given that government favourable treatment because of the extent of their pre-existing financial exposure to the country, with both organizations allowing programmes to continue despite numerous and repeated failures of implementation. As the report states, the government came to take it for granted that conditions would be waived, eroding the credibility of performance criteria and other policy stipulations.

Hurry-up lending

Financial motivations may undermine the enforcement of conditionality in another way. Vaubel (1996: 204 and *passim*) asserts that the rhythm of IFI lending is influenced by their own fund-raising strategies, with an acceleration of lending towards the end of a given period of funding, in order that they may demonstrate to their shareholders a 'need' for enhanced funding during the succeeding period. His econometric tests support the existence of such a cycle. Borrowing governments are in relatively strong bargaining positions in the sensitive part of the cycle: in the knowledge that the IFIs will be anxious to keep disbursing, they may see that they are under even less threat of punishment than usual in the event of policy slippages.

Avoiding economic destabilization

It was shown earlier (p. 130) that IFI credits can be quite substantial relative to balance of payments flows. The same is true relative to investment, government revenues and other macroeconomic aggregates. Therefore, penalizing noncompliance by withholding tranche releases could have a seriously destabilizing macroeconomic impact. To withhold money could, indeed, be self-defeating, for the resulting economic disruptions would risk further weakening the viability of the programme and reduce the political feasibility of unpopular policy actions. IFI staffs are well aware of this and this adds to their inclination to find ways of avoiding interruptions to agreed credits. One of the problems here is that it is the *gross* flows provided by a credit which are at risk, whereas the borrowing country is still obliged to service past credits from the same lender – which takes us back to the multilateral debt problem just mentioned.[6] Unfortunately, this was not among the issues explored by our country survey so we have no country illustrations to offer. But it is clear from discussions with IFI and other donor staffs that this factor is a major deterrent to the punishment of non-implementation.

A further, related, deterrent arises from the Bank's practice of attaching macroeconomic conditions (or cross-conditionality with IMF programmes) to sectoral loans. The situation can easily arise in which a sectoral programme is proceeding well but the government falls down on the macro front. Bank staff are then faced with the dilemma that to punish noncompliance at the macro level could derail a good sectoral programme. We found this in connection with an educational adjustment programme in Ghana, where delays in tranche releases on macroeconomic grounds had a seriously disruptive effect on the educational programme. The temptation must be strong in such situations to find ways of overlooking the government's macroeconomic transgressions.

Institutional factors

We commented earlier on the tensions between implementation and the explosion of conditionality, even granting that not all conditions are treated as of equal importance. The problem of the proliferation of conditions is well known within the Bank, has been identified in a succession of its own evaluations of experiences with adjustment lending, and has been addressed at the highest levels within the institution. And yet proliferation persists, suggesting it to be deeply rooted in the Bank's institutional culture.

Part of the problem arises from the tensions between using lending to leverage policy reforms and using it as a way of coping with the multilateral debt problem, as described above. At one level, the Bank's staff identify a financing need which takes cognisance of debt-related flows and therefore points to the desirability of larger credits than could be strictly justified in terms of supporting policy changes. But above them is the Bank's Executive Board, which looks for a link between the size of the recommended credit and the amount of associated policy reform. Board members tend to ask, 'What new policy changes are we getting for our money?' In anticipation of this, the staff load more conditionality into a programme than they would otherwise choose.

The Bank's internal structure – and its sheer size – aggravates the problem, however, for it results in a large number of departments and individuals who need to be consulted about a given programme, all of whom are tempted to add their own favoured measures. The result has been called a 'christmas tree' effect. The load on the tree can only be reduced at the cost of getting into a fight with, perhaps offending, some other department or colleague. The easy way out is to leave it there. Our case study on Kenya revealed an example of this (Ryan, 1995). A conscious joint effort was made in the late 1980s by Kenyan officials and Bank staff to keep the number of conditions in an agricultural adjustment programme to a minimum of essential measures. Once the draft agreement went to Washington, however, the Bank was unable to keep to its side of the bargain. The christmas tree effect took hold and conditions multiplied. This effect has been aggravated by the expansion of the mandate given to the IFIs – particularly the Bank – e.g. in the areas of environmental protection, poverty reduction and improving the position of women.

There is a problem too with *staff incentives*. The Bank's 'Wapenhans Report' on the quality of its project portfolio cited earlier writes (1992b: 17–18) of a pervasive 'pressure to lend'. Recruitment, promotion and career development practices place a premium on 'conceptual and planning' work, as against practical management and the monitoring of implementation. The staff perceive that exposure to appraisal and lending work (preferably for adjustment operations) is the most favourable for career enhancement: 'Higher visibility attaches to achievement in loan processing than in project performance management' and this reinforces an already-existing preference for 'conceptual and planning' work. There is usually a separation between those responsible for negotiating the terms of a loan agreement and those who must oversee its execution, and this can induce unrealism at the design phase. A mission chief may expect to earn kudos for coming back with a tough-looking document bristling with policy stipulations. Whether these are capable of implementation may be a less influential consideration. There is hence a 'culture of commitment', in which staff are judged more by the new projects for which they have won approval and have funds committed than for the quality and outcomes of these projects. These judgements related to the World Bank but we are assured from within that staff incentive structures operate in the same direction in the IMF.

Budgetary systems also contribute to the 'pressures to lend'. Virtually all such systems relate one year's allocation for a department to expenditures in the immediately preceding period, with any unspent balances being lost rather than carried forward. This is so in the Bank, as well as in a good many bilateral donors. It is an approach which creates a powerful incentive for department chiefs to defend their budgets by making sure that the highest possible proportion of allocated monies is actually spent. A desk officer who threatens this tactic by recommending a tranche delay is unlikely to get many thanks. Again, the easy way out is to let noncompliance pass.

The Bank's management took a number of measures in response to the Wapenhans Report and avers that corrective measures have since been taken. How effective these have been is open to doubt, however, for an interesting recent study by Wade still finds, in connection with environmentally-sensitive projects, that 'task managers feel under strong pressure to meet their lending targets and to set higher targets, and . . . have a short tolerance for doing things that may make the project fall behind schedule' (1997: 32).

Asymmetrical information and enforcement costs

The notion of asymmetrical information is central to principal–agent theory, for if principals have perfect (therefore costless) information about the actions of agents the difficulty of structuring incentives to ensure compliance with the principals' objectives is much reduced. In the context of this volume, the donors' difficulties arise from the complexities of the task of monitoring the policy actions of the government and the fact that most of the information needed to gauge the actions of the government is itself mediated through agencies of the state (Kahler, 1992: 120). Moreover, the complexities have been greatly increased by the growing number and range of policy conditions and by the tendency for these to reach into institutional and other 'structural' policies which create particularly formidable informational requirements. It is easy enough to monitor whether a government has increased the producer price for coffee farmers, much harder to judge the adequacy of measures to improve extension services for the same farmers. The IFIs, and a good many other aid donors, make matters more difficult for themselves by insisting on a centralized mode of operations (although the Bank is moving towards decentralization). Even if they also maintain permanent local offices, centring most important powers in headquarters increases the difficulties of making well-informed decisions.

In such situations, an agency which is serious about monitoring and enforcing its conditionality must accept the necessity of incurring potentially large costs to secure the information necessary for the task – as well as accepting the inevitability that the government will always be ahead of it in this game. In practice, the actual donor resources expended on this task are quite limited; it seems they have settled for the inevitability of ignorance. As Gordon (1992: 37) has observed, the other biases against punishing noncompliance are 'reinforced by the difficulty of monitoring compliance and by the bureaucratic incentives within donor agencies', which result in allocating resources for monitoring which 'are minuscule compared to the task involved'.

The IFIs take monitoring the most seriously but even they find themselves able to devote only limited staff time to this task (a fact also related to the issue of staff incentives just discussed). To cite a World Bank report on this topic:

> In the past staffing problems sometimes weakened the effectiveness of supervision missions. These problems included lack of continuity of staff, absence of needed sector specialists in supervision missions, and insufficient coordination with other staff performing related work. Occasionally the staff indicated that career incentives did not encourage careful supervision relative to other activities. . . . Compliance with the current Supervision Guidelines . . . is uneven. Of the 15 operations explicitly examined for compliance, only 3 were found to have followed closely the Guidelines and reporting requirements. In about half of the cases the macroeconomic conditions were not systematically monitored.
>
> (World Bank, 1991: v–vi)

The result of such weaknesses, particularly for the more complex types of policy action, is ignorance about what is going on – an ignorance which a so-minded government can enhance and exploit – and a sense, noted by Nelson and Eglinton (1993: 79), 'of being asked to spread energy too thinly across too wide a range of goals and requirements'.

Until the 1980s, the IMF's response to this problem was to severely limit the range of its conditionality to a restricted number of easily-monitored macroeconomic variables, such as the exchange rate, the growth of domestic credit and new external borrowing. The force of events has pushed it away from this tradition, however, so that the range of its conditionality is today typically much wider. *In any case*, its traditional solution was largely illusory, for the variables which it monitored most closely – its 'performance criteria' – were never satisfactory proxies for the quality of macroeconomic management by the governments to which it was lending.[7] Santaella has put the point well:

> the performance criteria employed by an IMF program are far from being perfect indicators of the adjustment effort carried out by the recipient government. The targeted variables are subject to a great deal of interference stemming from shocks that are exogenous to the adjustment itself. . . . The sole existence of exogenous interference on the adjustment process will intrude with the Fund's ability to disentangle the authorities' performance from the effects of random shocks. For all practical purposes the actual adjustment effort undertaken by the government is *unobservable, or at least non-verifiable*. . . . In spite of the close surveillance of resident representatives, the IMF cannot monitor perfectly the performance of the adjusting government. . . . Therefore, governments do not have the motivation neither to carry out the adjustment in full nor to comply with the targets specified in the original program.
>
> (Santaella, 1992: 99–100 [emphasis added])

In short – and this applies to all conditionality-applying agencies – information on compliance is intrinsically imperfect. This makes it all the harder to punish non-implementation and, indeed, to reward compliance. Any act of reward or punishment stands the risk of being misjudged because based on imperfect knowledge. Especially when combined with the pressures to spend already described, the inevitable consequence is to bias agencies against punishment.

III The dominance of domestic politics

A recapitulation

It is time now to pull some of the threads together. Although we have been through a multitude of differing considerations and a mass of evidence, the overall message which emerges is simple: *domestic political calculations dominate decisions about economic policy changes and donor agencies are relatively powerless in the face of this*. The information presented shows that governments behave as if their actions are the result of calculations of the likely costs and benefits of implementing donor policy stipulations. They act when they perceive it to be in their interests – but these perceptions, in turn, reflect the historical and institutional context in which they are located, the specifics of the political systems in which they operate, and the quality of their leaderships. Their calculations will be particularly sensitive to the extent to which a given package of measures is likely to affect the distribution of income (particularly the incomes of supporters and opponents) and of the ability of losers to make political trouble through collective action. We are reminded here of the suggestion in Chapter 2, that conditionality is apt to make the political tasks of managing policy change more difficult by limiting governments' freedom of manoeuvre.

The centrality of domestic politics is also borne out by the earlier discussion of the influence of adverse shocks on implementation. Reactions varied greatly. In some cases an adverse turn of events increased governments' resolve to act; in others such resolve evaporated. Similarly with favourable shocks – they could be treated as an excuse for deferring action, or as facilitating reform. All depended on the perceptions of the government and on the quality of its leadership.

Governments' calculations of the desirability of implementing a measure are liable to change over time as circumstances change, so political considerations will largely determine the *timing* of measures, although these in turn will be influenced by the contemporary state of the economy. Politics are similarly likely to exert a decisive influence on *which* of the measures being pushed by donor agencies will actually be undertaken, a selection, we suggested, which will be strongly influenced by the extent of congruence between the objectives of the government and of the conditionality-applying agency. Selectivity in implementation is, however, liable to seriously undermine the coherence of reform packages.

In a sense, a finding that governments act from self-interest indicates an opportunity for donors to set in place a system of rewards that will induce governments to undertake the measures favoured by donor agencies in their 'hard core' conditionality. We suggested in Chapter 1 that, in essence, that is what conditionality is about: the linking of actions to financial support. What we have shown, however, is that donors have not actually put a sufficient incentive system in place. This is partly because of limitations on their own resources, the relative weakness of 'catalytic' effects, and the varying extent to which governments are reliant on their assistance anyway. But, above all, the incentive system has failed because donor agencies have proved unwilling or unable to punish noncompliers in a consistent and enduring way by withholding future aid. As we have seen, the reasons for this are many and several of them are deep-rooted, leaving little room for optimism that this situation could be easily improved.

If among the twenty-one countries we have examined for this study there is a single example which encapsulates the summary just presented it is the Philippines, as briefly summarized in Chapter 3 and in Marr (1996). There the nature of successive regimes determined the complexion of economic policies and, despite many interventions, the IFIs and other donors were unable to exert more than a peripheral influence. The Marcos regime of 1966–86 was characterized by cronyism, patronage and 'weak authoritarianism'. Economic decision-making was heavily influenced by vested interests which successfully resisted reform. In almost every year after 1962 the country received loans from the IMF and World Bank, who, however, were generally unsuccessful in enforcing compliance with their policy stipulations. While the IFIs trusted the capabilities of technocrats, these had much less influence within the administration than appeared from outside, often being marginalized in policy-making. Meantime, the assistance flowed in.

In the end it was economic crisis, not donor pressure, which forced some action on the Marcos government. But it was too little too late and the regime was swept away – as a result of mounting *internal* opposition. The Aquino government which succeeded Marcos was more favourable to reform, seeing certain changes as in its own interests. However, despite private sector support for its adjustment programme, the Aquino regime was also much influenced by interest groups and a national consensus was rarely achieved, so reform remained only partial, again despite the urgings of the IFIs and others. It took the election of the Ramos administration in 1992 to bring a decisive break with the policies of the past. The donor agencies were present throughout this 20-year period but it was the unfolding domestic political drama which provided the key that unlocked the door to reform. Indeed, by their support of Marcos the donors had helped to sustain a regime with no serious intentions of reforming its policies.

Other evidence on the influence of national politics

Our finding of the dominance of domestic political factors is actually not surprising, for others who have studied the politics of policy reform have come to similar conclusions. We have five such studies to cite and will take them in order of publication.[8]

Nelson (ed.) (1990) is based on case studies encompassing thirteen developing countries and concludes (p. 330) that 'Broadly, external agencies were less important than domestic political forces in determining the timing and scope of adjustment decisions'. There had been a lot of pressure from the IFIs and other donor agencies in various of the countries studied but 'the degree to which such pressures actually induced decisions that would not otherwise have been taken varied greatly'. Conditionality and other external pressures do not help much in explaining these variations in government responses. Haggard and Kaufman (1992: 9) similarly observe that the wide range of country responses to common international pressures suggests that it is likely to be more fruitful to concentrate on domestic, rather than external, explanations.)

Bates and Krueger (eds) (1993) study the interaction of political and economic factors in episodes of policy reform, basing themselves on eight country studies. They asked their country authors to examine the role of the IFIs in each country but the concluding chapter has nothing to say about the IFIs. Evidently these did not emerge as important players. Instead, the conclusions are overwhelmingly about the influence of domestic politics on the introduction and sustenance of economic reforms, the editors' last words (p. 467) being that 'The major conclusion . . . is that creation of new structures and institutions lies close to the core of the politics of economic policy reform'.

Williamson (ed.) (1994) is similarly based on a case-study approach, in this case a mix of thirteen industrial and developing countries. Its study of factors conducive to the introduction of economic reforms (Table 1, p. 563) overwhelmingly emphasizes such factors as the coherence of the government's economic team, the solidity of the government's political base, the quality of its leadership, and the comprehensiveness of its programme. Foreign aid monies were important in only five of the thirteen cases and conditionality *per se* scarcely features in the discussion (although Williamson does emphasize the importance of the IFIs' intellectual influences (pp. 565–6), a topic we return to in the next chapter).

Haggard, Lafay and Morrisson's (1995) study of the political feasibility of adjustment policies, is another which finds it unnecessary to say much about the influence of conditionality. However, they do examine the role of the donors through a number of brief case studies, concluding that 'The analysis . . . confirms the importance of domestic political alignments. . . . If a government is unwilling to undertake reform . . . the external agencies can accomplish very little by continuing to lend' (p. 76).

Finally, we should recall the results of the research underlying the World Bank's *Bureaucrats in Business* (1995b: 17, 259–61). This sought to identify the circumstances in which aid donors could best promote the reform and/or privatization of public enterprises. The three circumstances which it found should exist before donor influence was likely to be effective all referred to domestic political conditions: (i) that public enterprise reform must be seen by a government to be in its interests, because the benefits to the leadership and its constituents would outweigh the costs; (ii) that reform must be viewed as politically feasible, with the government able to enact the required legislation and overcome opposition; and (iii) that the reforms must be credible, the government's promises must be believed. Between the lines, the authors suggest that conditionality will not get far without the satisfaction of these political desiderata.

We have just mentioned Williamson's identification of the political characteristics most favourable to reform. From within the World Bank, Elbadawi *et al.* (1992: 3 and *passim*) add a further suggestion (probably related to Williamson's identification of the soundness of the government's political base). They studied the factors which influenced governments' decisions to adopt Bank adjustment programmes and found a very strong positive relationship between such decisions and political stability, again implicitly emphasizing the dominance of domestic factors. The relative technocratic competence of the public administration is a further factor, mentioned by a number of observers, with low competence reducing the probability of reform (e.g. Haggard and Kaufman, 1992: 21). Various of our country cases support that proposition: Ghana, Guyana, Senegal, Tanzania and Uganda – all less-developed countries, of course, and all but one in Africa.

Our studies add success in building a national consensus in favour of change as a potentially potent factor, reducing opposition, improving politicians' benefit–cost calculations and increasing the autonomy of policy-makers. Colombia's strong tradition of consensus-building, albeit within a restricted social group, proved positive in this way. The existence of an external threat can be potent in mobilizing an internal consensus, as it did in The Gambia, where the danger of annexation by surrounding Senegal concentrated Gambians' minds on the necessity for economic change.

The unity of the government team is mentioned by Williamson as a factor strengthening the position of governments in designing and implementing reforms. Where this is combined with a good technocratic ability, as in Mexico, for instance, donor agencies are liable to find it particularly unpromising to attempt to impose policy stipulations (as discussed earlier). However, the opposite situation of a fragmented government may be unfriendly territory for them too, a point illustrated by Kenya (Ryan, 1996). If conditionality is to work it requires that there is a collective entity, 'the government', with which donors can enter into meaningful covenants. This breaks down in the absence of collective responsibility or when there is deliberate duplicity, and there have been examples of both in Kenya. Various donor agencies complained in Nairobi about the difficulties of knowing how 'the government's' position on an issue could be ascertained, or who spoke for it. All had learned that it was no good just speaking to a Principal Secretary, or even an individual Minister, but none was clear what best to do instead – a situation, we suppose, to which 'the government' was not averse.

In emphasizing the supremacy of domestic political influences we are implicitly drawing attention to the powerful influence of history and institutions. Ranis and Mahmoud conclude their major study of *The Political Economy of Development Policy Change* as follows: 'In summary, our findings suggest that the determinants of the long-run patterns of policy evolution are intimately linked to economic systems' initial conditions' (1992: 223). This is close to the conclusion of Bates and Krueger already quoted, about the core importance of the 'creation of new structures and institutions' (1993: 467). A critique of conditionality could be written along the lines that it is unable to deal adequately with the fact of path dependence and, in practice if not in principle, is unable to cope with the widely differing traditions and institutional infrastructures of the countries in which it is applied. Conditionality is profoundly ahistorical.

The more standardized the donor approach to the design of reform programmes, the less well is it able to cope with the variety of countries' historical influences. The IFIs reject the common criticism that they apply a standardized approach across countries and point to independent evidence that there is a lot of tailoring to country circumstances. But this is a constrained flexibility: programmes have more in common with each other than the extent of their differences. Peer pressures, intense work-loads, the desire to treat member countries equally and the desire to apply lessons learned in other countries – all these push IFI field staff in the direction of standardization. Moreover their natural technocratic orientation and the often rather rapid turnover of staff in any one post reduce their sensitivity to individual country traditions, institutional particularities and political sensitivities, and result in agencies with short institutional memories.

Does conditionality tip the balance?

A last-ditch defence of conditionality can be offered. This tacitly accepts the dominance of domestic politics but asserts that conditionality provides a means whereby donors can strengthen the position of reformers within governments, and can tip the balance in favour of change. The then World Bank Vice-President responsible for the Bank's operations in Africa asserted this position: [9]

> We're under tremendous pressure from our stockholders, from the development community, from the NGOs . . . to impose conditionality. At the same time . . . we don't impose a lot of conditionality. In a reform situation, you typically do not have a consensus at the beginning. It's always a tiny minority that starts a reform process. So what we do is basically provide the ammunition and support for that tiny minority.

A Bank report on its experiences with forestry projects reports similarly that policy conditions

> are most likely to have a positive effect when internal advocates of policy reforms face difficult political or other constraints to their introduction, and can benefit from the influence that the Bank can apply through policy dialogue, research studies, and lending conditions.
>
> (World Bank, 1994c: 18)

156

Note, however, that this claims an only modest role for conditionality *per se*.

The work of Joan Nelson on the politics of policy reform provides independent support, concluding from her studies that 'Conditions are likely to have the greatest influence in countries where reformist groups within the government are neither in control nor marginal'. If they are in control conditionality is unnecessary; if they are marginal conditionality 'may prompt the motions of compliance but is not likely to generate lasting reform' (Nelson and Eglinton, 1993: 70–1).

But how often are the knife-edge situations favourable to effective intervention most likely to arise? Our own country studies drew a blank on this. That we were able to find little or no evidence bearing upon this question itself suggests that they may be rather rare occurrences. The nearest we came to 'evidence' was when during interview the Bank's Resident Representative in one of the larger African countries asked despairingly, 'What is the point in supporting the reformers within government if they remain a minority and over time are unable to induce the government to act?' To do so is a recipe for the waste of public money. We are reminded also of the exploitation of donors' desire to support reformists by governments (the Philippines and Kenya were cited) who deliberately fielded reform-minded, but politically impotent, technocrats to negotiate with the donors and of a conclusion from the regional studies in Chapter 3, that technocrats have little leverage over policy-making unless they are supported by their political leaders.

Nelson's empirical work indicates that knife-edge situations are rather rare.[10] Only three or four episodes were identified in her study in which conditionality was able to tip the balance – the Philippines in late 1984, the Dominican Republic also in 1984, Zambia in 1985 and possibly Ghana in 1982–3. Even in these cases the record with implementation was decidedly mixed, and those episodes led on to sustained reform only in Ghana.

We also need to ask what political resources the IFIs and other agencies can bring to bear in such situations. How might the policy influence of actors with donor support be strengthened within a national government? It is, after all, easy to imagine situations in which association with outside agencies regarded as bringing undue pressure to bear on internal matters might be a liability rather than an asset.

Of course, one thing they can offer is money. A minister or official can argue that 'if you agree to do such-and-such I can deliver you a credit of $X million'. In times of acute need, that can be persuasive and ability to deliver the money can add to the individual's (or the team's) standing. But this brings us back to the whole question of the adequacy of the reward system. As we saw earlier, the money may be seen as not enough, or not to outweigh the risks. Above all, many governments have learned that they can get the money without, in substance, doing many of the things the donors lay down, i.e. that there is a minimal danger of effective punishment for noncompliance. *Attempting to use conditionality to boost reformers without withholding finance when the reformers'*

157

arguments do not prevail is self-defeating. The reformers are left high and dry, their position weakened, not strengthened.

Another resource which the IFIs can offer reformists is the provision of 'scapegoat services', allowing a government to attempt to deflect the odium resulting from unpopular policy measures which it knows to be necessary onto the foreign devils in Washington. If successful, the political costs to government will be reduced, participation constraints lowered and the likelihood of effective action increased.

Here again, no systematic evidence is available, although there is no doubt that the IMF, in particular, has been used as a scapegoat by a good number of governments. Our country researches turned up only two instances. In Thailand, in the early 1980s, export taxes on major agricultural exports were eliminated or lowered, the baht devalued, and subsidies removed on power and petroleum, all in the context of an IMF stand-by programme. But this loan, rather than imposing these actions, was used by the government as the pretext for the implementation of an austerity programme of its own devising. When it became clear that the economy had been left dangerously exposed by expansionary policies in the early 1980s, a change in Cabinet was prompted and a group of orthodox technocrats gained power. The new head of the Ministry of Finance favoured a stringent stabilization programme and negotiated an IMF loan as a way of justifying the need for adopting such a programme (Christensen *et al.*, 1993: 29).

Our other example is provided by Kenya but draws attention to the ambiguity of scapegoat services as a way of supporting pro-reformists. Writing as someone who was for many years a senior Treasury official, Ryan (1995: 19) reports that the position of technicians was strengthened in Kenya by being able to say of some reform that it was part of an IFI agreement but only by *'making it sound as though it were part of something that is imposed'* (emphasis added). This form of scapegoating is different from the Thai example, providing a way for officials to pretend that they are not reformers but that a policy change is necessary because of the economic powers of the IFIs. It is difficult to imagine that this usage is favourable to the sustained improvement of economic policies, however, as the record of Kenya attests.

While scapegoating *can* be politically useful to pro-reform governments in particular situations, in general Gordon (1992: 44) is probably right to suggest that the extent to which a government scapegoats donors is a negative indicator of its commitment to change, the very opposite of ownership. It is also a tactic apt to back-fire because it creates an image of a weak government knuckling under to outside pressure, thus eroding its domestic support and providing the opposition with a stick with which to beat it.

Overall, then, a defence of conditionality in terms of its ability to tip the political balance in favour of reform bears limited weight. While it has the merit of recognizing the necessity for donors to work through domestic political processes and while there are undoubtedly situations where it can indeed make the crucial difference, such situations appear rather occasional and its potentials for achieving results this way are limited by the tendency for noncompliance to go unpunished. And to the extent that scapegoating results in passing the buck to the IFIs, with its implication of governmental disavowal of the desirability of the changes, it could have thoroughly negative effects on policies in the longer term.

We have come to the end of two rather dense chapters. The reader doubtless needs a summing up. Chapter 7 attempts to pull the strands together and then considers what alternatives donors might have to the use of conditionality.

Notes

1 Based on a random sample of ten adjustment credits to developing countries, taking the most recent credit (all occurring between 1989 and 1992) detailed in World Bank (1992b: 72–6). Annualized credit values were taken; the current account data excluded official grant flows. The figures reported in the text are unweighted means. The weighted equivalents were much lower – 1.0 per cent and 4.6 per cent respectively – but were dominated by a single case (Mexico). The other nine countries were Bangladesh, Burundi, Costa Rica, Kenya, Senegal, Sri Lanka, Tanzania, Togo and Uganda.
2 According to the 1996 *Annual Reports* of the two organizations, as of April 1996 six countries were overdue on payments to the IMF by more than six months to an amount of $3.2 billion, and the equivalent statistics for the World Bank, as at June 1996, were six countries and $1.9 billion respectively.
3 See also Brown, 1992, for a more extended argument along these lines, made with reference to the involvement of the IMF in debt-relief schemes.
4 Calculated from the World Bank's *World Debt Tables, 1994–95*: 221–7.
5 Excluding three outlier values (Guinea-Bissau, São Tomé and Principe and Uganda), the regression was based on average values for 1984–94, with gross multilateral lending as the dependent variable (y) and multilateral debt servicing as the explanatory variable (x), with both expressed as ratios of exports of goods and services. The result was as follows:

$$y = 11.589 + 0.925x \qquad n = 32$$
$$(t = 2.5) \qquad \bar{r}^2 = 0.36$$

The t value is significant at the 99 per cent level.
6 I am indebted for this point to Paul Collier.
7 The unsatisfactory – 'indefensible' – nature of the performance criteria is argued in detail in Killick, 1995b, Chapter 4. The changing nature of the Fund's conditionality is traced in the same volume, pp. 22–34.
8 Additionally, a study by Aslund *et al.* (1996) attributes the widely varying speeds with which formerly centrally-planned countries have made the transition to market-based systems to domestic political forces, even though the advice of the IFIs has been similar in all cases.
9 Kim Jaycox in an interview in *Africa Recovery*, April–September, 1994, p. 9.
10 See Nelson, 1990, whose results on this aspect are summarized by Kahler, 1992: 98.

7

ALTERNATIVES TO CONDITIONALITY

I A paradox revisited

We started with a paradox. There is abundant evidence from around the world that, by most indicators, a policy strategy which maintains macroeconomic stability, that works through and strengthens markets and which is designed to take maximum advantage of international trade and capital movements, yields superior economic results when compared with feasible alternatives. And yet the adjustment programmes of the IFIs, enshrining precisely such a strategy, apparently produce limited results. How is this puzzle to be explained?

Of course, the IFIs and many of their shareholder governments are inclined to deny the premise and claim good results, but the evidence surveyed in Chapter 2 suggests they are wrong. It is concluded there that, while the programmes of the IMF and World Bank are generally associated with improved export performance and balances of payments, they are not typically linked with any improvement in inflation or economic growth and appear to result in substantially lower investment levels, threatening economic progress in the longer term.

We suggested three possible lines of explanation: that the programmes contain poorly chosen policies; that they are knocked off course by exogenous shocks; and, that they are undermined by weak implementation. The first of these possibilities has not been much discussed in this study since the paradox we start with asserts that, in their broad thrust, the policies are appropriate. It is true, however, that the devil is in the detail: it may be that programme results have been undermined by inapt policy specifics, even though the general direction is sound. Much of the controversy about adjustment is on this subject of programme design.[1] Of course, a finding of persistent and pervasive low-quality programmes would itself raise serious questions about the IFIs' approach. However, Chapter 2 points us in a different direction, drawing attention to the positive link between programme implementation and the results achieved. The general tendency for well-executed programmes to result in improved economic results does not suggest that the problem generally lies with ill-chosen measures.

Poor implementation of agreed measures hence looks a more likely explanation of weak outcomes, not least because of the wide-ranging, integrated nature of many adjustment programmes and the unpredictabilities created, therefore, by partial implementation. We showed that there was much evidence of weak implementation of hard core conditionality, manifested by programme break-downs (a particularly large problem for the IMF), programmes which take far longer than originally planned, and a lot of pretending that conditions have been met when the reality is otherwise. In consequence, neither the Fund nor the World Bank had been able to demonstrate convincing connections between their programmes and the policy reforms necessary to achieve the targeted improvements in economic performance. They had not been able to exert the leverage over policy specifics which they sought and which their conditionality was supposed to ensure. The reader is reminded of the discussion centred around Table 2.6, showing the persistence of poor macroeconomic policies in many African countries despite a multitude of Bank and Fund programmes, which appeared impotent even to prevent policy deteriorations. Perhaps this is unfair on the IFIs because of the special difficulties of operating in Africa? Perhaps, but among developing countries a large share of IFI programmes is in Africa, and it is this region that has been subjected to particularly intense hard core policy conditionality.

As reiterated below, much of the implementation problem arises from the imperatives of domestic politics. This factor places in perspective the second possible reason for weak programme results mentioned earlier: the influence of exogenous shocks. Quite apart from the existence of favourable shocks as well as adverse ones, we showed in Chapter 6 that governments' reactions to unforeseen events varied greatly. Sometimes an adverse turn of events hardened governments' determination to act; others used it as a reason for back-tracking. Similarly, favourable shocks may be treated as allowing action to be delayed, or as facilitating intended reforms. While shocks can cause genuine difficulties, it is the government's response to these which holds the key.

So poor programme execution emerges as the crucial element to explain. Financial leverage is supposed to ensure implementation, which is why we have been concentrating on the practice of IFI conditionality. Why is this failing to deliver the goods? And can its weaknesses be rectified? Part II attempts to pull together the evidence and analysis of earlier chapters, and this is followed in Part III by consideration of the pros and cons of an alternative model of donor–recipient relations. Part III also includes a postscript on the potentialities of political conditionality.

II The failure of conditionality

Criteria and assessment

To establish criteria by which to assess its effectiveness, we can return to the case made out in Chapter 1 in justification of conditionality. This was shown to stand or fall on the ability of conditionality to bring about improved economic policies in recipient countries. To the extent that it is able to achieve this, it will further the developmental, balance of payments and efficiency objectives of the IFIs and other aid donors, given the strong connections between the quality of countries' policies and the performance of their economies.[2] By this criterion, then, conditionality is to be understood as providing an assurance of *effective aid*. By a similar logic, however, it can also be seen as *reducing the demand for aid*, for the better is the quality of policies in developing countries, the less assistance will they need and the more quickly will they graduate from reliance on aid. Conditionality can further be seen as acting for IFI lenders as *a substitute for the collateral* which commercial lenders would normally seek, because better policies should increase countries' debt-servicing capacities and reduce the danger that they may be forced to default or seek debt relief. By the same token, it should safeguard against *moral hazard*, meaning, in this context, the danger that the finance provided will allow governments to defer unpopular but necessary policy changes, providing them with a breathing space during which 'something might turn up'.

Chapter 1 also outlined a couple of more specific arguments in justification of conditionality. First, the support and money of donor agencies may be used as a political resource by reformers and this may *tip the balance in favour of change* within a government, when reformers and their opponents are evenly balanced. Conditionality can strengthen the hands of those within government who support the approach to policy favoured by the donor community. Conditionality can lastly be argued to raise the quality of domestic economic policies by *inducing greater consistency over time*. This is important where a government's policies lack credibility and/or are capable of easy reversal. Investors and others may suspect the government's sincerity or its staying-power, fearing that today's policy signals will be reversed sooner rather than later. In such situations, government measures will be rendered less effective because of countervailing public responses. Donor conditionality may help solve this problem. It arises because the public sees its government as having discretionary power to change course at any time and fears it will use that power. The programmes of the IFIs can be seen as providing governments with a credible 'pre-commitment technology', with the IFIs acting as tacit guarantors that agreed policies will be implemented and adhered to consistently over a period of years.

There is a final element in the arguments deployed in Chapter 1 which we should recall here: that the IFIs' supposedly superior ability to exercise conditionality acts as *a justification for continued multilateral lending* in a world of globalized private capital markets. Being less overtly political in their lending decisions, the IFIs are likely to be better at enforcing conditionality than bilateral aid donors and they are also in a better position than private lenders. They are thus the most promising agencies for improving the quality, and time-consistency, of policies within borrowing countries.

The crucial question to ask of conditionality, then, is: *does it result in the execution of improved economic policies?* To the extent that it does, it can be expected to raise the effectiveness of, and/or reduce the demand for, aid; act as a substitute for collateral; and safeguard against moral hazard. Two subsidiary questions are, does conditionality tip the balance of power in favour of reformers?; and does it offer a credible pre-commitment technology?

As a way into such questions, we argued in Chapter 4 that conditionality can be seen as a principal–agent issue. This views the essence of the matter as the ability of donors to create an incentive system sufficient to induce recipient governments to implement policy reforms they otherwise would not undertake, or would undertake only more gradually. Viewed thus, the problem breaks down into an examination of: (1) governments' likely *participation constraints*, particularly sensitive to the extent of differences between donor and recipient objectives and priorities; (2) *the financial incentives* on offer, including: (3) the *threat of withdrawal* of support in the event of non-implementation.

Confronted with the evidence in Chapters 5 and 6, the agency approach appears to fit the facts quite well. Most of our hypotheses received quite high levels of confirmation, as summarized in Table 5.1. The basic premise of the agency approach is that outcomes are a result of calculations by governments and their officials about whether implementation will be in their own interests or not. The results provide rather strong confirmation of the appropriateness of this. There is clear evidence in a high proportion of the twenty-one countries studied in Chapter 5 that the probability that agreed World Bank programme measures will be implemented is a function of the extent to which the government and its officials perceive this to be in their own interests. A similar conclusion emerged from the two regional studies in Chapter 3. Thus, of South-east Asian experiences it was concluded that compliance with such conditionality as the IFIs attempted was high only when governments regarded implementation to be in their own interests, and that conditionality was violated when the governments were unconvinced of the benefits of change. Similarly for Latin America, IFI conditionality could achieve little so long as governments remained unconvinced that they would benefit by introducing the reforms urged upon them. It typically took an economic crisis and associated political changes to tip the cost–benefit calculus in favour of decisive policy change.

Examination of governments' participation constraints – the extent of their aversion to giving effect to the IFIs' hard core policy conditions – suggests that these are often quite high, notwithstanding the greater degree of international agreement that has emerged about the desirable direction of policy. The evidence in Chapter 5 suggests that implementation of measures is poor when there is a clash between donor and government objectives; that, in varying degrees, differing objectives are common; that in their assessment of the political pros and cons of executing a measure, governments are likely to be particularly influenced by its probable distributional effects and how these will impact upon organized opposition; and that conditionality can involve governments in substantial transactions costs.

The frequency of differences in objectives is why government 'ownership' of programmes emerges, in Chapter 4, as an important determinant of programme implementation and, therefore, of the economic results achieved. It is found that the objectives and interests of donor agencies and recipient governments rarely coincide. Given the typical existence of substantial participation constraints, the crucial question is whether donor agencies have been able to put in place an 'incentive compatible' reward system sufficient to compensate for governments' aversions to carrying out donors' hard core policy stipulations. The evidence of our twenty-one-country survey – and of Chapter 3's regional studies – points to an unambiguously negative answer: when objectives differ the incentive system is generally inadequate to ensure implementation.

Incentives may be inadequate for a variety of reasons. Programmes may be under-funded, with the evidence suggesting this to be associated with poor implementation. Further, and notwithstanding frequent claims to the contrary, catalytic effects (whereby reaching an agreement with an IFI induces additional capital inflows from other sources) were found often to be small and/or undependable, particularly in the case of private capital movements. Although some did benefit from induced inward investments (Chapter 3 mentions South Korea and Thailand), others appeared to gain little or not at all. This is actually not surprising, given that IFI programmes are found not to raise the credibility of government policies. Markets' investment decisions are based on judgements about the quality of government policies for which the existence of an IFI programme is evidently not an adequate proxy. There are, however, more indications of a positive response of public capital (chiefly aid) to IFI programmes, which can be important for the poorer countries, although even here the evidence is not strong. Another situation in which the government has little incentive to accept unwanted policy stipulations is where it is not heavily reliant on obtaining the money on offer, because of access to alternative sources of finance or because the domestic economy is strong.

A further, and surely fatal, defect of the incentives offered by donors is that governments often see that they have little to fear if they do not keep their side of the policy-for-money bargain. Chapter 6 found 'an overwhelming body of evidence' that non-implementation is rarely punished effectively. Our country survey threw up many illustrations of this, as did Chapter 3's South-east Asian and Latin American studies. We were able, additionally, to cite independent studies arriving at the same conclusion. It seems that the appearance of punishment conveyed by programme cancellations (in the case of the IMF) or delays in withholding tranche payments (the Bank's preferred sanction) is misleading because the costs to a government of waiting out a tranche delay are usually not great and new credits can generally be negotiated.

Stated baldly, then, our conclusion is that *in the general case, conditionality is not an effective means of improving economic policies in recipient countries. The incentive system, most notably the absence of a credible threat of punishment of non-implementation, is usually inadequate in the face of differences between donors and governments about objectives and priorities, and other factors contributing to governments' participation constraints.* Since we have argued that the justification for conditionality stands or falls on its ability to improve policies in recipient countries, its apparent failure to pass this test is rather devastating. While there is no quarrel with the principle of conditionality, its general failure to achieve donor objectives leaves it naked, without *practical* justification.

What, now, of our findings as they bear on the subsidiary tests of the effectiveness of conditionality: its ability to provide an external agency of pre-commitment and to tip the domestic balance of power in favour of reformers?

As regards pre-commitment, our Chapter 5 cases contained no support for the proposition that agreeing an IFI programme raises the credibility of a government's policies. Whilst this proved a difficult hypothesis on which to obtain evidence, with clear indications for only seven countries, in none of these did there appear to have been a credibility effect. Chapter 3 finds broadly the same situation, although it does mention Thailand and South Korea as countries where IFI agreements may have enhanced credibility. Overall, it appears that investors' assessments of the risks of policy reversal are based on their own judgements about the domestic political scene and that only rather exceptionally do they treat the IFIs' 'seal of approval' as providing a reliable predictor of time consistency (hence the absence of strong catalytic effects already noted). Independent studies provide additional evidence for this conclusion.

This outcome is no surprise. Markets and investors cannot be expected to pay much heed to the signing of IFI adjustment agreements if they have learned by experience that government ownership of such programmes may be slight and actual implementation often leaves much to be desired. In particular, IFI conditionality cannot be expected to have much of a credibility effect unless these agencies can demonstrate a willingness to punish noncompliance and to stay away from governments that are not serious about policy reform. Efficient markets will not treat the signing of agreements, *per se*, as seriously constraining governments' discretionary powers.

Can the case for conditionality be rescued by an observed ability to tip the balance of power in favour of those within government favouring better policies? Our country studies drew a blank on the frequency with which knife-edge situations favourable to effective intervention are most likely to arise, suggesting that they are rather rare occurrences. Research by Nelson was cited indicating that knife-edge situations are indeed rather rare, identifying only three or four episodes in which conditionality was able to tip the balance. Overall, Chapter 6 concludes that a defence of conditionality in terms of an ability to tip the balance bears limited weight. In a supportive political environment the existence within a government of a capable team of technocrats to design and oversee reforms can be hugely productive, but Chapter 3's summary of Latin American experiences draws attention to the limitations of donor support for reform-minded advisers: 'Compared with . . . internal political factors, the evidence suggests that technocrats have little leverage over policy-making unless they are supported by their political leaders . . . technocrats function as facilitators rather than as catalysers in the adjustment process.' The same chapter's discussion of the South-east Asian case, while stressing the large influence of economic advisers in the adoption of adjustment policies, further points out that 'the technocrats' first loyalty has always been to their governments'. Had that been in question they would doubtless have been much less influential.

While the 'tipping the balance' argument has the merit of recognizing the necessity for donors to work through domestic political processes and while there are undoubtedly situations where their aid can indeed make a crucial difference, such situations appear occasional. Here too the effectiveness of conditionality is crucially undermined by the tendency for noncompliance to go unpunished: to try to use conditionality to boost reformers without withholding finance when the reformers do not prevail is self-defeating.

A number of consequences flow from these rather negative findings. If our results are accepted, it follows that conditionality does not fulfil its promise of greater aid effectiveness. On the contrary, we will argue shortly that over-reliance on conditionality by the IFIs has resulted in considerable waste of public resources. By the same token, but subject to an important qualification, it also follows that conditionality does not achieve desired reductions in the demand for aid nor act as a substitute for borrower collateral by raising their future debt-servicing capacities. The qualification is with respect to the established association (set out in Chapter 2) of IFI (mainly IMF) adjustment programmes with depreciated exchange rates, leading to strengthened export and balance of payments outcomes. Doubtless many devaluations have been the direct result of conditionality, so to the extent that demand for aid and ability to service debts are driven by foreign exchange availabilities, this is an important exception to our generally weak results.

However, it cannot be said overall that IFI conditionality is likely to have done much for recipient self-reliance or creditworthiness, for while the worst of the debt problems of Latin American and other middle-income indebted countries appear to be over – a development shown in Chapter 3 to owe little to IFI conditionality – the end of the debt problems of low-income countries – most of which have been subjected to large doses of IFI-inspired policy stipulations – remains elusive. Far from conditionality providing an assurance of borrowers' future ability to repay the IFIs' credits, the continuing severity of the financial problems of low-income countries forced the IMF and World Bank in 1996 to accept that there is a problem of *multilateral* indebtedness and that their past credits can no longer be exempted from debt relief, leading to the 'HIPC Initiative' of that year. That such additional help should be necessary is itself an admission that past highly conditional adjustment programmes have brought scant results. Finally and unsurprisingly, we must recall the earlier evidence showing that conditionality cannot be depended on to safeguard against the danger that borrowers will use aid money in order to defer policy changes.

There are exceptions to these adverse conclusions. It is not our position that conditionality is always and everywhere impotent, although it is rather astonishing that our work has (despite a special search for good news) turned up so few positive examples, given the intensity with which we studied the topic and the number of episodes examined. A case of unconscious bias perhaps? Nevertheless, we did in Chapter 2 identify a small family of instruments with characteristics which made them particularly suitable for use in conditionality and for which there was evidence of substantial implementation. The exchange rate, mentioned above in connection with positive balance of payments outcomes, was among these, as were certain other price-based measures, such as interest rates and public enterprise pricing. Overall, however, the record of conditionality is bleak. And to the extent that it rests upon an assertion of a superior ability to enforce conditionality, the intellectual case for continued IFI lending looks shaky.

The sanctions analogy

In assessing the conditionality record, an analogy suggests itself with the case of economic sanctions. Here, too, external agencies (foreign governments in the sanctions case) seek to construct an incentive system that will induce a target government to do something that it otherwise would not do. There are important differences between sanctions and conditionality, of course. Sanctions are essentially punitive, relying upon inflicting economic and other damage on the target country if it does not comply with the wishes of the sanctions-imposing governments. The potential scale of punishment is often large, affecting a wide range of trade and capital transactions, the movement of people, access to foreign technology and so on. The incentive system is thus prospectively far more potent than in the case of aid conditionality. Against this, sanctions give rise to much larger difficulties of policing and of the maintenance of international solidarity, with major incentives for evasion. Military and foreign-policy considerations are far more important, as are inter-state rivalries. The analogy is hence not exact, but it is close enough to be illuminating.

What, in that case, is the record with sanctions? The most definitive study of this is by Hufbauer *et al.* (1990), who examine the lessons to be drawn from a study of 116 episodes of the use of sanctions. Their main findings relevant to our interests can be summarized as follows:

- Among the various possible objectives of sanctions, the most difficult to fulfil was to induce a target government to take a certain line of action.
- Overall, Hufbauer *et al.* found a 34 per cent success rate, with 33 per cent success when sanctions were intended to achieve 'modest' policy changes, falling to 25 per cent when 'major' policy changes were intended (1990: 93, Table 5.1).
- Success was a function of the incentive system: sanctions 'that inflict heavy costs on the target country are generally successful' (1990: 101). This is suggestive for the case of conditionality, given our finding of weak punishment of noncompliance.
- 'Although it is not true that sanctions "never work", they are of limited utility in achieving foreign policy goals that depend on compelling the target country to take actions it stoutly resists' (1990: 92). They are more likely to be effective when the target country is small and/or policy goals are modest.
- In sanctions-imposing countries 'Policymakers often have inflated expectations of what sanctions can accomplish . . . at most there is a weak correlation between economic deprivation and political willingness to change' (1990: 94).

There are some strong resonances here, not least policy-makers' unrealistic expectations – a stricture which applies particularly, in the conditionality case, to the Boards of the IFIs.

The costs of failure

The general failure of conditionality to provide an effective modality for the improvement of economic policies in aid-receiving countries has important consequences. Most notably, *over-reliance on conditionality has led to major misallocations of resources and large-scale waste of public monies.* Conditionality – governments' willingness to sign policy-for-money agreements – has been used (alongside formal access criteria) as the overriding criterion in the IMF's lending decisions. The same is true of the World Bank's 'structural adjustment' lending. Although the bulk of the Bank's lending has continued to be project-based, rather than policy-related, we are here talking of large sums of money. Table 1.2 shows that in the first half of the 1990s the IFIs alone were devoting over $9 billion per annum to adjustment lending, to which must be added large amounts of additional money from bilateral aid agencies. A total of around $15 billion per annum might be a reasonable estimate.[3] As was shown in Chapter 1, bilateral donors have come to rely more upon conditionality as an allocative device, often 'piggy-backing' on the policy stipulations of the IFIs but also making their own contributions to the conditionality explosion, particularly in laying down political stipulations.

The basic rationale for backing policy reforms with aid is that the money reinforces the reforms – cushioning adjustment costs, making it easier for losers to be compensated, for the vulnerable to be protected, for economic benefits to be generated without too inordinate a delay and for the process of reform to be sustained over time. *Where governments desire reform*, our evidence confirms that supporting finance can indeed play these roles. This comes out most clearly in Chapter 3's South-east Asian and Latin American surveys. Williamson's study of the political economy of policy reform (1994: 566–7) agrees on the potential importance of aid for the success of reform programmes, citing the examples of Korea, Indonesia, Chile and others. What our studies also show, however, is that over-reliance on conditionality resulted in the provision of much finance to governments that were actually not serious about reform or were unable to deliver it. That was money wasted. To this must be added the strong tendency already mentioned for access to finance to weaken the incentive for policy action by creating a soft budget constraint.

Misplaced confidence in what conditionality can achieve has hence resulted in the waste of much money. The list of specific examples that can be drawn from the cases studied in this volume is long – Argentina until 1989; The Gambia until mid-1980s; Jamaica until the early 1980s; Kenya most of the time; Madagascar until the late 1980s; the Philippines until the mid-1980s; Senegal most of the time; Tanzania until the mid-1980s and in the 1990s; Turkey at various times; Zambia most of the time. Others could easily be added during all or part of their recent economic histories: Brazil, Mexico, Nicaragua, Egypt, Sudan, Zaire . . . and so on.

Indeed, the process may well have actually biased aid allocations in favour of governments with poor policy records. Aid allocated to countries with low-quality policy environments is being poured into a bottomless pit. The governments of these countries need lots of money! By contrast, governments which pursue sensible and prudent policies, even though they could put aid to better use, can get by with less. So conditionality results in a shift of resources in favour of poorly-performing governments, with correspondingly less available for the others.

In support of this proposition, we can re-visit Table 2.6 showing, for African countries, an association of Bank adjustment programmes with countries adjudged by the Bank itself to have deteriorating macroeconomic policies. It is worth repeating de Vylder on this, observing a 'pronounced tendency to reward bad performance with increased flows of aid and loans, and to punish successful policies' (1994: 3).

> A country which prudently manages its external sector will soon realise that the IFIs and the donor community breathe a sigh of relief – one problem country less! – and rush to mop up arrears from a disaster case instead . . . the marginal rate of tax on 'good behaviour' can be very high.
>
> (de Vylder, 1994: 22)

A further cost of conditionality, we suggest, is that it distorts the nature of the discourse between the IFIs and borrowing governments, generating resentment, sometimes diverting discussions from the most important issues and putting them in a less constructive setting (Chapter 4). I have been struck by this factor in my researches on IMF policies in developing countries, with conditionality negotiations often degenerating into wrangles about numbers, about whether the credit ceiling should be X million or Y million. Not for the first time, Berg *et al.*'s study of adjustment in Senegal yields an apt quote :

> policy-based lending [by the Bank to Senegal] combined the worst of all worlds. It is full of explicit conditionality, which is almost never seriously invoked. The conditionality dominates the dialogue, reducing the opportunity for uncontentious and open exchange of ideas and true joint problem solving.
>
> (Berg *et al.*, 1990: 227)

To the extent that conditionality has to be taken seriously by governments, it may also, as is suggested towards the end of Chapter 2, make the political management of policy change more difficult, by reducing governments' degrees of freedom, their ability to manoeuvre.

Another way of looking at the consequences of the failure of conditionality is to ask, who gains and who loses from its present heavy use?

The gainers   The most obvious gainers are governments which are reluctant to go far with policy reform but which learn to play the conditionality game successfully, maximizing the amount of adjustment aid received while minimizing unwanted policy actions. Other gainers include staff members of the IFIs, whose careers are enhanced by their 'success' in negotiating new agreements, and conditionality-applying donor agencies (most notably the IMF and the adjustment-lending parts of the World Bank) which are able to offer the modalities of conditionality in justification of their lending and of their need for new infusions of public capital.

The losers   If we assume a fixed total sum of aid, those who would otherwise receive larger shares of this – those pursuing efficient policies according to the story above – are unambiguous losers. If we drop the assumption of a fixed sum of aid, the taxpayers of donor countries are the losers, forgoing income with no compensating gains in terms of the promotion of development or relief of poverty in a high proportion of borrower countries. It could also be argued – although the argument would have to be made carefully – that the peoples of the governments who play the conditionality game successfully are also losers, for they are likely to be saddled with inefficient policies for longer and they, or their children, will eventually have to repay the credits to which the conditions were notionally linked.

The undesirability of such a combination of gainers and losers needs no elaboration. Or perhaps it does, if we consider its geographical implications, for there is little doubt that the conditionality game has been associated with a reallocation of aid to sub-Saharan Africa at the expense of southern and other parts of Asia. This shows up, for example, in the way the allocation of the World Bank's highly concessional IDA resources has been manipulated in favour of Africa, most notably at the expense of China and India. For all Africa's huge problems and acute needs, it is difficult to justify such a manipulation in terms of poverty reduction, or of aid effectiveness considered more generally.

The costs, then, are large. What, in that case, are the possibilities for raising the effectiveness of conditionality and reducing the costs?

The possibilities of doing better

Seen in the context of our principal–agent framework, this question can be rephrased by asking about the likelihood that in future the IFIs and other conditionality-imposing agencies will introduce effective, incentive-compatible policy-for-money contracts. To assess that requires taking a view of the possibilities of (1) reducing recipient participation constraints and (2) strengthening the structure of rewards and punishments.

As regards participation constraints, we suggested in Chapter 5 that to a substantial extent the degree of a government's aversion to, or acceptance of, a donor's policy stipulations will be determined by the extent to which the objectives of the two parties agree. The fact that there is today less argument about the desirable content of policy strategy than there was in the 1960s and 1970s is a favourable factor. Major IFI–government ideological clashes are largely a thing of the past, even large disagreements about the directions in which policy ought to be moving. However, we stressed in Chapter 4 that this leaves much scope for differences in the two parties' objectives and for conflicts of interest: they are conditioned by different historical and institutional backgrounds; they are answerable to different constituencies; they each have their own internal management imperatives; there may be differences in attitude to the role of the supporting finance offered by donors (the moral hazard issue); there are asymmetries in the incidence of adjustment costs, including the costs of mistakes, and these lead to differing attitudes to risk and to the desirable speed of change; nationalistic resentment of donor 'interference' and of favouritism in the treatment of countries is apt to give rise to generalized suspicion of externally-recommended policy reforms.

Our country survey attested to the frequency with which differences of interest occurred and the negative effects of these on conditionality implementation. It was precisely because of the strength of these considerations that we could show in Chapter 4 the large importance of 'ownership' as a determinant of implementation, and why the evidence in Chapter 6 showed domestic political forces normally carry the day in decisions about economic policy. We also drew attention to other sources of differences between donor and recipient, most notably the transactions costs associated with the use of conditionality. We further brought out at a number of points how donor–recipient interest differences have been aggravated by the proliferation of conditionality since the early 1980s, demonstrated in Chapter 1. Nelson and Eglinton's study of conditionality summarizes the point well:

> As the sheer burden of analysis and management increases, donors are likely to become still less willing to take the additional time and effort needed to listen carefully to recipient perspectives and to persuade the relevant host-government officials and agencies that the required reforms are appropriate. For their part, over-burdened recipient officials will become still less capable of effectively presenting recipient country views to donors and developing a consensus within their own governments. Multiple conditionality is also likely to intensify nationalist resentments over intrusive outside pressures, especially when those pressures extend to highly sensitive topics previously regarded as strictly internal affairs.
>
> (Nelson and Eglinton, 1993: 99)

Here, perhaps, there is scope for improvement. If not between them then at least within donor agencies, it ought to be possible to curb the tendency for the number and range of policy stipulations to increase. The IFIs are the main culprits here: surely their managements could demand a reversal of this self-defeating trend? Maybe, but the record is discouraging. The World Bank's very first evaluation of experiences with structural adjustment programmes urged the Bank to 'avoid the temptation of the early SALs to load the operations with a multitude of complex conditions which could not realistically be expected to be implemented fully' and to concentrate on a limited number of high-priority and feasible measures (World Bank, 1986: viii). Successive Bank evaluations have repeated the same message and the most senior levels of the Bank's management have addressed the problem. But the steamroller trundles on, with some programmes in the mid-1990s containing more than a hundred separate policy stipulations. Pressures from the Board and the internal politics of the Bank creating this absurd situation have proved too powerful for its management to overcome, and in recent years these have been powerfully reinforced by the campaigns of special interest groups wishing conditionality to be extended yet further, to protection of the poor, of women, of human rights, of the environment, and so on.

Much the same, if on a smaller scale, can be said of the IMF. We showed that with the Fund too there has been a major proliferation, despite explicit Board decisions that the number of the Fund's stipulations should be limited (Killick, 1995b: 22–7, 35). Given the tenacity with which it has clung to its traditional policy conditions, the only way in which the Fund has been able to accommodate new, more 'structural', variables has been to add them on, creating a ratchet effect. Here too it is difficult to be optimistic about the prospects for effective action to reverse this proliferation, particularly since that might call into question some of the most deeply-entrenched features of the Fund's programmes.

The point about these various sources of interest differences, then, is that they are either intrinsic to the situation or have proved intractable in the face of past attempts to address them. Participation constraints must therefore be expected to remain substantial. Perhaps instead a more incentive-compatible reward structure could be put in place, sufficient to overcome the constraints? Here too it is hard to be optimistic. If we look first at the absolute size of the financial inducements that the IFIs and other donors can offer, the trend is in the opposite direction, with global aid in decline.[4] The tendency in recent years has been to try to use conditionality as a *substitute* for aid, although we have shown that this has rarely succeeded.

The difficulties of securing a higher level of funding in support of adjustment programmes are illustrated by the squeeze which the World Bank has been experiencing on the size of resources which some donor countries (and particularly the US Congress) are willing to make available for its soft-aid IDA window, which is facing an uncertain future at the time of writing (Sanford, 1997). It is illustrated, too, by the extreme difficulty which has been experienced in extracting resources for more adequate debt relief for poor countries. The tendency here, and more generally, is for some bilateral agencies to try to protect their bilateral, government-to-government, programmes by resisting larger allocations for multilateral use. The IMF is a partial exception, however, for its Board has agreed to turn the soft-window ESAF, hitherto 'temporary', into an enlarged and permanent facility.

Overall, though, any substantial increase in the amount of finance which the IFIs and others will be able to offer in support of conditionality-based lending appears unlikely. It is possible, of course, that the growing scarcity of public resources for this purpose might be compensated by increased private flows, i.e. that programmes' catalytic effects might become more potent in the future, given the rapid relative growth of international private capital movements. However, we have shown in Chapter 6 that the weak observed catalytic effects on private capital flows have been a rational response by the markets to the failure of conditionality to provide a credible external pre-commitment mechanism. The markets hence make up their minds on the basis of their own judgements about the quality of a country's policies and are not willing to take the signing of a money-for-policy agreement as an adequate indication of a government's seriousness. In short, *the weakness of catalytic effects is a consequence of the shortcomings of conditionality and is therefore unlikely to change until conditionality can be made more effective or something better put in its place.* But, to strike a more positive note, were effective remedial action to be taken, this would likely be additionally blessed by favourable responses by private capital.

These are all major considerations but of probably even greater importance for the construction of an incentive-compatible incentive system is the feasibility of instituting a credible threat of punishment of non-implementation of conditions. To give a brief restatement of the reasons why punishment has been the exception rather than the rule, set out at length in Chapter 6, the withdrawal of finance from non-implementing governments is difficult because:

- Donor governments have historical, foreign-policy, security, investment and trading reasons for supporting particular borrowing governments, and use their aid, and their influence within the IFIs, to secure lenient treatment for favoured governments. The instruments of donor co-ordination are only exceptionally strong enough to maintain solidarity in the face of conflicting donor interests.

- In specific cases, the World Bank and (particularly) the IMF have strong institutional interests to exert pressure on the other to keep its programme in place.

- The logic of what we have loosely called adverse selection, and of the re-financing approach to poor countries' multilateral debts, conflicts strongly with the withholding of funds from various (often poorly-performing) governments.

- It is, in any case, difficult for international agencies to act against governments which are among their own shareholders and are represented on their Boards.

- Punishment of noncompliers entails reductions in the volume of IFI lending (at least in the short run), which may be interpreted by major shareholder governments as weakening the IFIs' case for additional resources.

- Withdrawal of support is liable to have destabilizing macroeconomic effects in penalized countries, further worsening their economic situations.

- IFI staff incentive systems continue to create pressures to lend, with a lesser concern for the consequences of that lending. Both staff members and the agencies for which they work see a large volume of lending (or giving, as the case may be) as legitimizing their work. Budgetary systems reinforce the pro-lending culture within the Bank.

- Because information on compliance is intrinsically incomplete, the risk that punishment will be ill-judged because based on imperfect understanding further erodes the will to act.

What is the likelihood that this array of obstacles could be overcome in future? There are points of light in the gloom. The ending of the Cold War has reduced the geopolitical motivations for the USA and other major donor governments to prop up poorly-performing governments (as some have already found to their cost). The 'HIPC Initiative' for debt relief adopted in 1996 has the potential to reduce the extent to which debt policies undermine the plausibility of IFI threats of punishment. It ought, in principle, to be possible to address the pro-lending biases of staff appraisal and budgetary systems (the Bank is, in fact, seeking to correct the former), although the difficulties of achieving this are large.

Some of the other factors are intractable, however: agencies' difficulties in punishing their own shareholders; the debilitating effects of multiple donor objectives; the destabilizing macro effects of a withdrawal of expected finance; the problem of asymmetrical information. Overall, the wide range of obstacles and the extent to which they go deep into institutional cultures discourage optimism about the likelihood of fundamental improvement.

Conclusion on conditionality

Let us step back for a moment and reconsider the evidential basis for the rather strong conclusions summarized here. Is the evidence in Chapters 3 to 6 (much of which is summarized in the Master Table) good enough to instill confidence in the results? It must be admitted that the evidence is unlikely to satisfy the purist. For the most part, it is country-based, qualitative and unamenable to accepted techniques of quantitative testing. While it would not be fair to describe it as anecdotal, since we have sought to be systematic and have examined a large number of cases, it sometimes comes uncomfortably close to that and is more qualitative and judgemental than would be ideal. Against that, wherever possible we have tested our evidence against the results of other researchers who have found quantitative ways into some of the issues under investigation, and have found a high degree of congruence between our results and theirs. Readers who have had the patience to go through all the evidence presented in earlier chapters may feel that the sheer cumulative effect of this is persuasive.

Confidence in the conclusions arrived at is increased by the general absence of strong defenders of conditionality among the many IFI and other officials spoken to in the course of this research and in seminar presentations of our results. There was, in fact, much receptiveness to the conclusions presented. Concerning conditionality, a good deal of scepticism, in some cases cynicism, was expressed. Some agencies had already reached conclusions similar to ours and were moving away from reliance on conditionality (only the European Commission appeared to be moving the other way) and there was a good deal of soul-searching within parts of the World Bank. The main exception to the general erosion of faith was at the more senior levels of the IMF, where few doubts were expressed. The Fund has vast experience in this area and its views must be taken seriously. But it is also the agency with the largest investment of credibility in conditionality, so it has a large institutional self-interest in defending present practices. At the best of times, the Fund is not well known as a self-critical organization, and its culture does not encourage the expression of doubts to outsiders.

Overall, then, and with such humility as we can muster, the conclusions we arrive at are that conditionality has generally failed to achieve its objectives and therefore lacks practical justification; that over-reliance on this ineffective modality has wasted much money; and that the obstacles to adequate improvement are probably too indissoluble to be overcome. Recipients' participation constraints are often substantial, with domestic politics dominating decisions about the implementation of policy changes, while the incentive system offered by donors is rarely compatible with inducing recipients to execute hard core conditionality. There are exceptions to these generalizations but not too many. The difficulties of improvement are such that the creation of an incentive-compatible reward system seems improbable.

At the same time, the premise upon which conditionality rests – that the quality of a country's economic policy has a decisive influence on the performance of its economy and, therefore, on the effectiveness of the foreign aid which it receives – remains unchallenged. If conditionality is not an effective means of bringing about sustained improvements in policy, what are the aid agencies to do? What alternative approaches might be developed?

III Alternatives to conditionality

The search for an alternative

There has, in fact, been a good deal of casting around for alternative models of donor–recipient relationships, although these are often dressed up in the language of conditionality, perhaps in the hope of making them more acceptable to donor governments.

Guillaumont and Guillaumont (1994: 90), for example, refer to a 'conditionality crisis' and advocate a switch to what they call 'programme conditionality'. Under this, all countries wishing to receive adjustment aid would submit a plan of economic policy for the following year, on the basis of which donors would make their lending or giving decisions. There would subsequently be an *ex post* evaluation of performance under this plan, on the basis of which (plus, presumably, a new policy plan for the following year) donors would decide new allocations for the following year, and so on.

Others have advocated a switch from the present *ex ante* conditionality to 'positive conditionality', by which is meant the use of donor money to actively support changes within recipient countries, such as use of aid for the promotion of good government or environmental protection. Within the World Bank, a major report on long-term development in Africa advocated placing aid on 'parallel tracks', with programme and project aid being based on past performance in the implementation of governments' own programmes (World Bank, 1989b: 14). Within the Bank there has been a good deal of discussion of the desirability of shifting in favour of greater use of '*ex post* conditionality', implementing the 'parallel tracks' approach.

A related but more radical idea, first put forward by Norwegian Foreign Minister Thorvald Stoltenberg in 1989, is for the expression of aid relationships in the form of formal *development contracts* embodying reciprocal donor and recipient obligations.[5] It would be for recipient governments to design the policy content of these contracts. They would formally commit themselves to these actions in return for donor commitments for agreed levels of aid over a number of years, including compensatory and contingency mechanisms to ensure that policy reforms were not blown off course by external shocks. Most versions of this idea envisage a movement away from IFI leadership of the process, with agreements perhaps supervised by a jointly-appointed 'Development Commission'.

The most significant thing about the ideas just described is that they all imply dissatisfaction with present relationships and all embody the idea of 'ownership', of aid in support of policies devised by recipient governments. Happily, the lessons to be learned from the evidence presented in this study are not all negative. There are some constructive pointers as well. Overwhelmingly the most important of these is the superiority of results obtained from government-initiated measures, with donors influencing the course of events through their intellectual contributions and practical help. This emerges most clearly from the regional studies in Chapter 3 and it is worth repeating the relevant conclusions here.

> Thus, of *South-east Asia*: the IFIs also influenced the shape and direction of economic policies through policy dialogue and the building of intellectual capabilities, as most technocrats received education in Western universities and were directly involved in policy-making. This, however, could only lead to implementation if other groups, especially the political leadership, were to accept the same principles. Domestic politics, culture and history are all contributory factors in explaining why these countries adopted reforms when they did, and these seem the most important factors.

> And on *Latin America*: our evidence shows that policy dialogue with government technocrats and political leaders by IFI staff can play an important role in forging a consensus between them and the government on programme objectives and the reform agenda. Moreover, policy dialogue can contribute to the tailoring of programme objectives to what can be realistically achieved given the configuration of domestic political forces. This would require a greater awareness and monitoring of the internal political situation and technical capacity

of borrowing countries than is currently normal in the IFIs, however. The demonstrated success of a limited programme may well generate a consensus and a momentum for more ambitious reforms later on, whereas an over-ambitious programme which ignores the political imperatives is apt to generate a momentum of opposition which can derail the reform effort altogether.

The principles of an alternative model

Any new model should build upon these lessons, with the implication that 'policy dialogue' should be largely de-linked from negotiations about specific grants or loans. The model that emerges from this study rests upon four principles: ownership, selectivity, support and dialogue.

Ownership

There is little need to elaborate on this. Essentially, it asks the IFIs and other donors to take their own rhetoric about the importance of ownership and the non-coercive nature of conditionality more seriously. The principle of ownership should be vigorously applied at least to programme ('adjustment') aid, although there would be a case for extending it to project aid, on the grounds that the developmental value of individual projects is likely to be strongly influenced by the appropriateness of the wider policy environment. Only emergency humanitarian aid falls clearly outside this principle, although even here the frequency with which countries need this type of help, e.g. to manage food shortages, is itself likely to depend on the quality of policies.

However, as was shown in Chapter 4, ownership is a rather elusive concept. It is natural to think of 'the government' as the desirable locus of ownership but we pointed out that what constitutes – and who can commit – 'the government' is by no means always clear, especially where the principle of collective responsibility is not firmly established. It is often inappropriate to assume that the Ministry of Finance, or any other single department, is in a position to commit the government as a whole. Realization of this has led the Bank, at least, to try to widen its range of interlocutors within government. The strongest form of local ownership is where there has been created a consensus in favour of the policy changes in question, so that they become built into the political fabric. This, in turn, presupposes a political culture of participation and consensus building that is absent in many countries. These complications throw up difficult judgements about the *degree* of local ownership, and borderline cases where there is a proper tendency for donors to give governments the benefit of the doubt. There is no getting away from the necessity for such judgements but, in making them, it would help donor agencies if they were to develop systematic and objective indicators of ownership, and we return to this topic shortly.

Selectivity[6]

The principle that programme aid should be limited to countries with governments that have adopted for themselves the type of policy strategy mentioned at the opening of this chapter implies that there will be fewer governments eligible for such assistance than hitherto, since we have shown that ownership has often been weak in the past. We might recall here Johnson and Wasty's (1993) evidence that programme ownership was rated as low or very low in half of the cases they examined.

Another way of putting this point, then, is to say that donor agencies should become a good deal more discriminating about the governments they are willing to support with programme assistance, which relies essentially on the confidence of the donor agency about the seriousness of recipient governments in the pursuit of efficient, pro-development policies. Greater selectivity should reduce the waste of aid monies associated with past over-reliance on conditionality. It should therefore raise the effectiveness of the assistance provided, diminishing the moral hazard problem, helping to offset the declining total volume of aid with higher productivity and acting as a rationing device which discriminates efficiently in favour of governments that will employ the resources within a supportive policy environment.

The greater concentration of aid on governments with a demonstrated commitment to the pursuit of sound policies could, over time, have the further benefit of raising the credibility of the programmes with which it is associated. This would give them a precommitment value which we have shown is not a normal characteristic of present-day IFI programmes, thereby encouraging larger responses by foreign private investors, inducing the catalytic effects which have often been absent in the past. Lastly, greater discrimination – including stronger determination to stay away from poorly-performing governments – would increase the potential of aid to strengthen the position of reformers within governments, which has been undermined in the past because governments have learned that adjustment aid is unlikely to be withdrawn for long if reforms are not undertaken.

Past experience does not provide too many examples of what we have in mind. However, the Latin America section of Chapter 3 does present the case of Argentina, arguing (with Erro, 1993) that it was the withdrawal of external support in 1989 which induced the newly-elected President Carlos Menem to turn his back on many of his electoral promises and allies to begin the turnaround of policies which during the 1990s began to reverse that country's long-term economic decline. IFI adjustment lending to Argentina did not resume until 1991, well after the reforms were initiated,[7] and this assistance has since been associated with a high degree of success.

Also consistent with the approach advocated here, the Bank now makes a systematic attempt to relate its soft IDA lending to country policy and poverty-reduction indicators, although insufficient information is available to

179

permit its methods to be assessed. For 1994–6 a strong positive correlation is reported (World Bank, 1997: 55–8) between assessment of country performance and IDA lending, with the top 20 per cent performers receiving 31 per cent of commitments against only 2 per cent for the bottom-performing fifth (although there was less clear evidence of correlation among the 'middle' 60 per cent). The Bank rightly points out that lending cannot be wholly determined by past performance, however: it needs the flexibility to be able to respond to exceptional financing needs, e.g. for post-war reconstruction or debt work-outs, or where a new government comes to power.

An implication of greater selectivity is that donors in general, and the IFIs in particular, should not take on responsibilities upon which they cannot deliver. Their staffs often speak as if it is the IFIs which are responsible for policies in borrowing countries, as well as for filling their financing gaps. This is to accept a degree of responsibility which is beyond the capabilities of the donor agencies, ignoring the severe constraints on what they can achieve, and is subversive of the government ownership which is at the heart of effective policies. Policies are a responsibility of domestic governments, including the management of macro balances to avoid unbridgeable financing gaps. If a government chooses to neglect these responsibilities, that is bad news for its people but it cannot be compensated for by conditionality. Aside from the provision of humanitarian relief, the only sensible course for donors in the face of a government's persistent economic mismanagement is to stay away and concentrate their resources on countries that can put the aid to good use.

Of course, a lot of questions are pre-judged in an advocacy of concentrating aid on governments with sound policies. What is meant by 'sound' and who decides? The issue of the desirable content of policies is outside the compass of this volume[8] but, in general outline, there is among practitioners a good degree of consensus about this. There are no large disagreements about what stabilizes an economy and what propels it forward, particularly where progress has hitherto been held back by dysfunctional policies. But, as observed earlier, the devil is in the detail; about the specifics, and about questions of timing and sequencing, there remains much scope for disagreement. An important corollary, then, of withdrawing from hard core conditionality and reliance instead on overall judgements about governments' intentions is that donor agencies, specifically the IMF and World Bank, must be willing to take a more eclectic view of what constitutes an acceptable programme.

Support

Our evidence showed the value of financial aid in support of well-conceived programmes – permitting quicker results, cushioning the shocks, easing the political management of change – and it also showed that programmes were sometimes undermined by inadequate support. Not the least of the advantages of the greater selectivity advocated here is that it would allow a concentration of scarce resources on countries offering the most welcoming policy environments.

One of the quandaries in which World Bank (and perhaps IMF) staff have found themselves is that there is often a mis-match between the size of a country's prospective financing gap and the range of policy reforms which it is sensible to stipulate. The Bank's Executive Board looks for a linkage between the size of credit proposed and the amount of policy change that credit will 'buy'. When countries face large financing needs, this is one of the reasons why adjustment programmes become over-loaded with specific policy stipulations – so much so that a former Bank chief economist for Africa pleaded in 1995, in a widely-distributed memo, for 'gap-filling without shame', de-linking the quantities of conditionality and finance.

There are two important ways in which well-established modalities of financial support should be augmented. One is for the greater provision of *contingency financing*. As shown earlier, many reform efforts are deflected by unforeseeable shocks. Over the last three decades the world has turned its back on the international provision of such assistance, with the IMF's contingency financing facility being turned, in effect, into a minor source of supplementary financing for high-conditionality programmes. Access to this should be liberalized once more. The Bank too should be free to increase its lending to governments which find their programmes in difficulties through no fault of their own.

A second additional avenue of support is *debt relief* for governments which have opted for serious programmes of policy reform. The debt question is large and complex.[9] As it relates to low-income countries, past responses have represented a slow and grudging coming-to-terms by creditors with the debilitating effects of large debt overhangs and debtors' severely limited prospective debt-servicing capacities. The HIPC Initiative agreed in 1996 represented, on paper, a substantial advance but at the time of writing only limited progress has been made in applying the improved terms offered by this scheme. In the context of this volume, and without wishing to get into the complexities, there are a few obvious points to be made:

a   There is no logical distinction between decisions about debt relief and about other forms of financial assistance. Such decisions should thus be taken in the context of donors' overall country aid strategies.

b   Debt relief to governments pursuing weak or inappropriate policies leads to a waste of resources, no less than other forms of aid to such governments. Creditor governments have been right, therefore, to insist on a case-by-case approach, even though this has led them too into an ineffective over-reliance on conditionality.

c   Governments with large financing gaps but a demonstrated seriousness in the pursuit of sound economic policies should not additionally have to wrestle with large debt-related obligations. They should be provided with quicker and more generous debt forgiveness and relief than has hitherto been available from the Paris Club, the IFIs and certain other creditors.

The support so far discussed has been financial but there is also technical assistance (TA). This provision of expertise, education and training has long featured prominently in the aid policies of most bilateral donors and has grown in importance for the IFIs, but there is now disillusionment about this too. Berg (1993) has chronicled the change from an earlier benign approval of TA to increasing doubts and criticisms, because it did not appear to be fostering greater self-reliance in recipient countries: 'Despite thirty years of a heavy technical assistance presence and much training, local institutions remain weak and this type of assistance persists' (Berg, 1993: 244).

The possibility of using TA fruitfully is important to the argument we are making here because, without it, there is no ready answer to the accusation that greater selectivity in aid would disadvantage governments with weak public administrations, little expertise and, therefore, limited capabilities for preparing and executing convincing policy programmes (although we suggested in Chapter 6 that it is easy to exaggerate the problem of limited capabilities, and that much can be achieved on quite slender organizational resources if the political will is there). Such governments should be sharply differentiated from those whose policies are simply ill-chosen. It is the latter who should be discriminated against in the distribution of aid.

Fortunately, by no means all the evidence on TA is negative. Hildebrand and Grindle (1994) undertook a comparative study of donor efforts at local capacity-building in six developing countries and found that TA was often valuable. It had provided much useful training, had strengthened links between incentives and performance, and had been associated with innovative approaches to the solution of public problems. Once again, however, owner-ship appeared to hold the key. Berg found that this was often weak: 'Its donor-driven character . . . has led to excessive use [of TA], inefficient alloca-tion, weak local ownership, and hence limited commitment' (1993: 246). Hildebrand and Grindle stress the same factor but more positively: the most positive results they found occurred when a clear need had been articulated by local policy-makers, programme managers and other stake-holders.

One of the most abiding difficulties here is that the provision of TA personnel is often unwanted, just another aspect of donor conditionality. Governments frequently regard the foreign 'experts' working within their departments as, at best, serving two masters – themselves and those who have provided them – and they are justified in taking that view. Here again, there is a strong case for de-linking aid from conditionality, and for the IFIs and others to be willing to participate in recruitment mechanisms which would reassure governments about the independence of the expertise provided.

Dialogue

The two extracts from Chapter 3 repeated a few pages ago make the essential case for a switch from conditionality to dialogue: dialogue works better. It is possible to see adjustment in both South-east Asia and Latin America as success stories for the IFIs. But it is a success flowing from the intellectual influence of the Fund and Bank, and from their contacts over a long period with personnel who emerged at the political and technical levels as crucial agents of change.

The model we are advocating here might be labelled 'the Mexican model', for the brief account in Chapter 3 shows how in that country the Bank staff came to terms with their limited leverage over policies and the likelihood that insisting on the use of conditionality would merely create friction. Instead, they chose the route of dialogue, being willing to accept programmes and measures which fell short of what they would have preferred in the belief that the government's intentions were sound. In consequence, Bank staff have exerted long-term influence over adjustment policies in Mexico and enjoyed constructive relationships. Pondering what general lessons might be learned from this experience, a Bank study of its long-term relations with Mexico concluded:

> While it may be true that the Bank has to be involved in financing a sector in order to get a seat at the policy table, the Bank should not use lending for leverage in policy decision-making. The experience is that clients will avoid Bank financing if the Bank tries to use lending for leverage where there is sensitivity concerning Bank involvement in policymaking. Lending matched with supporting ESW [analytical work] and low-key advice given early in the decision process in the context of informal interchanges are to be preferred to resorting to conditionality.
>
> (World Bank, 1994c: 148)

The task, then, is for the agencies to reorient themselves to concentrate on the exercise of influence, and to maximize the number of entry points through which that might be exerted. As will be shown shortly, they already have a number of such possibilities.

Some specifics

The next step is to offer some elaboration of the general principles just outlined.

Identifying ownership

The point was made earlier that if agencies are to concentrate more aid on governments that are serious about maintaining sound policies they need to develop objective indicators of ownership (and, by implication, expertise in that area). The World Bank has, in fact, recently undertaken precisely such an exercise which illustrates our point very well.

Bureaucrats in Business (World Bank, 1995b) is concerned with the performance and reform of state-owned enterprises. As reported in Chapter 6, its conclusions are close to those arrived at here: that there is little that conditionality by itself can do, that ownership and domestic politics are all-important, and that certain preconditions must be satisfied for effective enterprise reform. This raised the question of how to identify situations in which the conditions for successful enterprise reform are satisfied. Its authors therefore undertook research to identify predictive indicators. We will return to the specifics of this shortly but the points to be made here are that an international organization has shown: (a) it recognises the need to adapt in these directions; (b) that it has been able to do *and publish* politically sensitive analysis without major repercussions; (c) that it is feasible to identify indicators with predictive power; but (d) that these are highly specific to the policy segment with which they were concerned.[10]

Point (d) means that, when we consider the range of economic policies, there is a potentially large number of specific indicators that might be deployed. However, there is a more broad-brush approach to the prediction of government ownership, which is to *use past performance as a predictor of the future*. This was mentioned earlier as '*ex post* conditionality': the provision of support to governments with proven policy records. This is sometimes discussed in terms of 'rewarding good behaviour' but that is a wrong way to think of it. Governments have a *duty* to pursue policies that will promote the welfare of their peoples. Their reward for doing so is improved economic performance and, presumably, greater political popularity. It is part of the argument made earlier that it is governments, not aid agencies, which are responsible for the quality of policies. It is not for the agencies to 'reward' governments for doing what they ought to do.

What they can do, though, is to assist governments to go further down the paths of virtue, using past progress as an earnest of continuing serious intent. There are problems about too heavy a reliance on the predictive value of past performance, of course, mainly arising from the impermanence of political life. Governments come and go. They also sometimes change course in mid-term, for good or ill. The concept of government ownership is difficult to apply when there is serious political instability. Johnson and Wasty's (1993: 7) research revealed that virtually all cases of high government ownership occurred in a stable political environment and Elbadawi *et al.*'s (1992) study of adjustment programmes in Africa found a strong positive association between adoption of a programme and political stability in the preceding years.

What, then, to do in countries plagued by chronic political instability? In the worst cases, it is probably an illusion to think there is anything at all to be done through programme aid. In the absence of a tolerably settled government, or when the very institutions of state are under threat, the prerequisites for effective programme aid are not met and the most that donors can do is to respond to humanitarian needs until stability is restored. It is in less extreme situations that the value of having indicators of government commitment would be of greatest value. At the political level, these should be sensitive enough to differentiate between situations where a government is making a tactical retreat from a reform the better to manage opposition to it and cases where the government has lost heart and abandoned the endeavour altogether. Indicators of ownership should also provide evidence on the extent to which stake-holders have been consulted about the reforms in question, and the extent to which the changes have broad-based support.[11] Rather closely related is the notion of 'consolidation' mentioned in Chapter 4, i.e. the extent to which reforms become part of a policy consensus within the political system and thus become institutionalized.

Another test suggests itself: the government's willingness to prepare its own policy document formally requesting finance in support of reforms (the 'Letter of Development Policy' in the terminology of the Bank, the 'Letter of Intent' in the case of the IMF). Such willingness appears a basic requirement but it is one whose observance is startlingly rare. The Fund, as described in Chapter 1, usually insists on drafting the letter in Washington and this is surprisingly common practice within the Bank as well. Here, however, the distinction between willingness and ability is crucial. Governments that lack the technical capability should be provided with expertise, *if they ask for it*. But donors should steer clear of governments which have the capability but such weak commitment to reform that they cannot put a persuasive request together.

So far as economic indicators are concerned, there is a wide range of potential candidates. But given the centrality of fiscal policy both for macroeconomic stability and for the quality of the government's own spending programmes, budgetary indicators nominate themselves as belonging very high on the list.

Finally, as a further illustration of the type of thing we have in mind, we can revert to the indicators of whether a country is ready to reform its state enterprises developed in *Bureaucrats in Business* (World Bank, 1995b: 234–6):

1   One broad criterion was whether reform had come to be regarded as *politically desirable* by the government. A possible indicator of this was found to be whether there had been a change in a regime or coalition, but only if the new grouping did not depend too heavily on state enterprises that its survival would be threatened by reform. Detailed analyses of election results (where they exist) could yield evidence on this, as also data on the extent of over-staffing in the enterprises. Even when this test was not passed, evidence that the emergence of an economic crisis was revealing the unviability of the *status quo*, could also be revealing.

2   A second general criterion was that proposed enterprise reforms should be *politically feasible*, which is seen as having two elements: the extent of control which reformers have over the policy-making process, i.e. over the legislature, the bureaucracy and other levels and agencies of government; and their ability to overcome resistance, e.g. by compensating losers or because of the strength of their political base.

3   The *credibility* of the process was identified as a final criterion for public enterprise reform, disaggregated by the Bank into the reputation of the government for keeping its promises (e.g. in fiscal and trade policy areas); the existence of legal and/or political constraints on policy reversals; and the extent of any international constraints, e.g. as constituted by treaty obligations or by membership of regional or other groupings.

The specifics here are of less relevance for our purposes than the demonstration that an agency like the Bank is free to do this type of analysis and was able to develop various reasonably precise indicators. Not only that but it was able to apply these to specific countries[12] and to publish the (not always favourable) results (see World Bank, 1995b, Chapter 4).

Maximizing influence

We have stressed that donors' main impact on policy reform has been through their influence on the intellectual climate within which governments undertake policy analysis and on specific individuals who rise to prominence, as politicians or advisers. Of course, the IFIs and other donors are only one set of influences among a number and the 'influencing' business is a rather haphazard one: many seeds may be broadcast but only a few will take root, perhaps in largely unpredictable times and places.

But no growth can occur unless seeds are sown and donors can contribute by offering training, by staff exchanges and through their publications. Both the Fund and Bank have specialized training wings, aimed specifically at policy-makers within developing (and now former centrally-planned) countries, and most bilateral donors finance training in their own countries. There is no reason to doubt that these efforts have made considerable contributions over the years. So too have the substantial numbers of former members of the staffs of the IFIs who have returned to prominent positions within their own countries imbued with the philosophies of the organizations from whence they have come.

The influence of the IFIs' publications programmes is elusive but large. This is, perhaps, most true of the Bank, if only because of the Fund's narrower, more specialized focus. It is no exaggeration to say that since the early 1980s the Bank has become the single most important influence on thinking about development policy. Its annual *World Development Report* has been the flagship, augmented by its journals, numerous other reports and a large and widely distributed series of *Working Papers*. By virtue of the superior resources devoted to these publications, and their high general quality, they have had an enormous impact on development economics and upon the thinking of large numbers of people working within governments.

These important but more or less indirect means of exerting influence can be reinforced by more targeted activities directed at influencing specific governments. Donors already have a number of such openings but are not necessarily making the best use of these. A high proportion, for example, peri-odically prepare country aid strategy papers. Sometimes, however, these are seen as agency papers, not necessarily involving much consultation with the government of the country in question. Only exceptionally is there a serious attempt at consensus-building. The World Bank, for example, prepares peri-odic Country Assistance Strategy papers but, although authors are required to consult with the government, these are regarded as staff documents (which eventually go to the Board) and are not used as instruments for intellectual bridge-building. The same is true, more understandably, of the Country Economic Memoranda prepared periodically by the Bank. The IMF has its own ready-made instrument in the form of its Article IV consultations with governments concerning macroeconomic policy. This is a valuable instrument which has undoubtedly helped to increase mutual understanding, although the Fund's institutional culture does not always encourage the degree of give-and-take necessary for creating genuine consensus between its staff and government officials.

Another instrument that has become important within the Bank's opera-tions in low-income countries is the Public Expenditure Review. These are tending to become approximately annual and typically include a review of the overall budget situation augmented by some more specialized studies. The nature of these enforces close co-operation between Bank staff (or consultants) and officials of the Ministry of Finance and there have been a few cases where initiation of these has been gradually transferred from the Bank to the govern-ment. But they remain rather closely oriented to the Bank's operational needs and have not been designed as a vehicle for consensus-building.

Rather more so, and of growing importance, are the 'sector investment programmes' (SIPs) now being promoted by the Bank and other donors. These are to some extent a response to the past failings of conditionality, an attempt to find a new vehicle for government–donor co-operation, linking sector strategies with government budgeting and donor commitments (Harrold *et al.*, 1995; Jones, 1997). So long as the Bank and other donors can resist any inclinations to wish SIPs upon unconvinced governments, and are patient enough to wait until genuinely joint exercises are feasible, here too is a promising avenue for the exercise of policy influence. Some are already devoting more advisory and other resources to joint preparatory project and sectoral studies.

A final point of influence to be mentioned is the analytical papers which provide the intellectual background to specific policy reforms recommended by a given donor – what the Bank calls its Economic and Sector Work. Various writers are agreed on the importance of this, as necessary to ensuring that policy recommendations are well grounded and as a vehicle for intellectual persuasion. Here again, however, this is too often undertaken by agency staff, or consultants engaged for the purpose, with little genuine involvement of local counterparts. In defence, the agencies point to the, no doubt real, difficulties of achieving partnership. The argument of this chapter is that, in that case, it is better to hold off until genuine partnership becomes possible.

There are other points of entry too. Donors do not lack opportunities for regular policy dialogue. But only rarely have these been conceived within a consensus-building framework – a necessarily slow and uncertain process. Too often they have been undermined by the urge to spend characteristic of the aid industry.

A residual role for conditionality?

In the scheme of things advocated in this chapter, does there remain a role for conditionality? We should here revert to the distinction introduced in Chapter 1 between 'pro forma' and 'hard core' conditionality (while recognizing that in practice these tend to shade into each other). Pro forma conditionality was described as policy commitments written into aid agreements for the convenience of both parties. These are consensual, included in order to set out systematically and clearly a mutually-agreed package of measures, codifying what should be done and in what sequence; serving as a kind of institutionalized memory against the possibility of changes among key ministers, officials, perhaps even the government itself; providing a vehicle through which the agencies can undertake their programme lending, and for persuading the managements and/or Boards of aid agencies of the adequacy of the policy programme. Hard core conditionality, by contrast, was seen as coercive: actions, or promises of actions, made only at the insistence of the lender or giver, measures that would not otherwise be undertaken, promised involuntarily by governments in urgent need of money.

The thrust of our argument, then, is the desirability of a major shift (at least in the IFIs, which make the most use of conditionality) from the hard core to the pro forma variety. The question may well be asked: why, in that case, bother with the modalities of conditionality at all? The answer is that, for reasons just suggested, these may make life easier for both parties, may smooth the path for policy reform, make it more orderly, more assured.

There is also the special case of scapegoating, discussed in Chapter 6. This involves a species of pro forma conditionality, since both parties are agreed on the necessity for certain policy changes but the government finds it politic to publicly pretend otherwise in order to shift the blame onto the donors. If indeed such a pretence eases the political management of change, it seems reasonable for the donors to be willing to go along with it. But it is a usage to be treated with great caution. For scapegoating requires a government to tacitly confess that it has bowed to the will of foreigners, contrary to its perception of the public interest – a double-edged way of avoiding unpopularity! Moreover, the implied rejection of the desirability of the reforms may be detrimental to the longer-term political sustainability of the process.

But what of hard core conditionality? Are we advocating its complete abandonment? Nearly but not quite. The most favourable situation, where the borderline between the hard core and pro forma forms is particularly obscure, is where there are good reasons for believing that conditionality may tip the balance of power within a government in favour of the reformers. Along these lines, Nelson and Eglinton conclude from their study that 'Conditions are likely to have the greatest influence in countries where reformist groups within the government are neither in control nor marginal' (1993: 70–1). Where they are in control, conditions are redundant, and when they are marginal, conditionality 'may prompt the motions of compliance but is not likely to generate lasting reform'. Unfortunately, as described earlier, when we examined the evidence, we were unable to find more than a few instances where conditionality had tipped the balance in favour of change, although this is a difficult question on which to obtain evidence and knife-edge situations may be more common than our studies revealed.

What about other types of situation? What about the use of hard core conditionality when governments are faced with such a severe financial crisis that they regard themselves as having no alternative to 'taking the medicine' in order to get the money? The general answer to this is clear from our evidence: that while economic crisis may indeed force governments into some short-term measures, these are likely to be reversed, or in other ways undermined, as soon as financial stringency eases. However, our country evidence does yield a few instances where a government whose hands were forced by economic crisis subsequently came to believe in the intrinsic merits of the course it had embarked upon, and stayed with it. Ghana post-1982 seems to fit the bill best. With qualifications, Uganda post-1992 also comes into this category.[13] The argument could be made that such success stories cannot be predicted in advance and, therefore, that it is worth taking some failures in order to secure the successes.

On closer examination, however, the Ghana case is better regarded as illustrating a situation where conditionality tipped the balance in favour of reform. There was by 1982 a strong reform-oriented group within the administration, opposed by radical revolutionaries and, in some degree, by the Head of Government, Flt-Lt Rawlings. An acute economic crisis in 1980–2, the drying up of alternative sources of credit and the availability of the conditional finance of the IFIs permitted the reformists to convince Rawlings of the need to act. Although there remained considerable radical opposition (which subsequently self-destructed) to policies of 'structural adjustment', there was a considerable degree of government ownership of the general thrust of the programme from the beginning (although many of the specific measures were designed by Fund and Bank staff).

It is possible to take a different tack and argue that many of the difficulties with conditionality have arisen because the applying agencies have not paid enough attention to the special characteristics of policy instruments that are amenable to successful use in this way. In Chapter 2 three key determinants of the extent of leverage were identified: (1) the *simplicity* of the policy instrument in question (determined by the extent of direct control exerted over it by the government, the number of individuals and agencies through which a change had to be negotiated and effectuated, and the strength of those opposed to change); (2) the ease with which it could be *monitored*; and (3) its amenability to *treatment as a precondition*.[14] A currency devaluation is a classic example of a policy change which meets these criteria and we suggested that it was no accident that it was with this that the IMF had had most success in its programmes. Other price-based instruments also possess some of these characteristics, whereas policies requiring institutional changes rarely do.

A use of hard core conditionality which was stripped down to the much narrower range of policies passing these tests could therefore be defended. This would have the advantage of reducing the amount of change required to the cultures of the IFIs and others, but the disadvantage that it would leave these agencies in a policy-imposing mind-set, with the danger of a gradual but inexorable restoration of full-blown conditionality.

Our general conclusion, then, is that continued use of pro forma conditionality should be retained as useful, if not hugely important, but that donors should be extremely reluctant to use the hard core variety, except, perhaps, in the case of measures that can be incorporated as prior actions, or where there are specific grounds for believing that levying policy conditions will tip the domestic political balance in favour of change.

Changing donor practices

The suggestions made already would imply substantial changes in donor practices. Others can be added, addressed principally to the tasks of promoting consensus-building and greater selectivity in the governments supported.

Greater *decentralization* of responsibilities within agencies is one option. The aid business, by and large, is highly centralized. Although most agencies maintain local offices, substantive powers are usually retained by head office. This is notoriously true of the Fund, with decision-making firmly retained in Washington, but it is also the case with most bilateral donors. There have, however, been moves towards decentralization within the Bank (the Fund seems immune to such possibilities, for no obvious reason) and a few bilateral donors, e.g. the UK's Department for International Development, have gone some distance in this direction. On this, we agree with the argument made in a report on the future of multilateral development banks (MDBs):

> One means of striking the right balance between national ownership and the active involvement of MDBs is to have effective field offices. Where strong field offices exist and operational responsibilities have been delegated to them, they facilitate the day-to-day conduct of business, ensure on-the-spot assessments of country needs, tailor technical solutions to local realities, and support in-country coordination of development assistance.
>
> (Development Committee, 1996: iv)

Through the cultivation of personal contacts and more intimate understanding of local goals and constraints, field offices are more likely to exert influence and avoid the imposition of inappropriate headquarters-designed conditions. However, there is a down-side: the danger that in consequence of their superior local knowledge, and their close contacts with local policy-makers, field offices may 'go native', becoming advocates of 'their' countries, making selectivity and objectively-based decisions harder rather than easier. Schemes of decentralization should therefore safeguard against this.

A second type of reform within donor agencies involves addressing the *incentive systems* which at present give rise to unselective pro-spending biases. We treated these briefly in Chapter 6, citing an internal Bank report's finding of a pervasive 'pressure to lend' and 'culture of commitment', with recruitment, promotion and career-development practices placing a premium on 'conceptual and planning' work, as against practical management and the monitoring of implementation. Similar incentive distortions exist within the IMF and bilateral agencies. While we can offer no expertise in the design of staff assessments and incentives, it surely ought to be possible to design systems which avoid such biases.

Chapter 6 also mentioned the perverse influence of the Bank's (but not the IMF's) *budgetary systems* which relate one year's allocation for a department to expenditures in the immediately preceding period, with any unspent balances reverting to general resources. This creates a powerful incentive for each department to make sure it spends its budget and tells powerfully against selectivity. Systems based on more or less rigid country allocations similarly create biases against selectivity, which requires the flexibility to switch resources across countries. Here, too, it ought surely to be possible to devise more efficient alternatives, as is suggested by changes introduced into their budgetary systems by the Finnish and Norwegian aid administrations to facilitate greater flexibility across countries, e.g. by allocating more money on a regional basis.

Some difficulties

The change of direction advocated here would, of course, have its difficulties. There would obviously be geopolitical resistances to a more discriminating approach. Favourite sons would be threatened; trading and investment ties would be invoked; so would foreign policy and security considerations – all in favour of continuing the pretence of conditional aid to anti-reform governments. Public opinion might also be mobilized. Undoubtedly one of the strong impulses behind the growth in certain forms of conditionality since the early 1980s has been a public desire to 'do something' – about protecting the environment, enhancing the position of women, improving the observance of human rights and so on. We have already pointed out that a consequence of a more discriminating provision of programme (and perhaps project) aid would almost certainly be that significantly less would go to sub-Saharan Africa and that could be politically difficult to sell.

But to set against these obstacles are some favourable factors. The end of the Cold War has already been mentioned, reducing the strength of security-cum-foreign-policy motivations for distorting aid allocation decisions. The move towards freer trade embodied in the outcome of the 'Uruguay Round' negotiations and the creation of the World Trade Organization may signal a reduced pressure to use of aid for protectionist purposes. The emergence of generally tighter aid budgets in recent years is also likely to incline donor governments to place higher priority on aid effectiveness and, therefore, greater selectivity. During field work for this project in Kenya in late 1995 a number of donor representatives contrasted the present search for savings with earlier periods when there were large pressures to spend.

Another factor tending to undermine the rationale for IFI and other public-agency conditionality in the more advanced developing countries is what might be described as the *privatization of punishment*. If official aid agencies are reluctant to punish, private capital markets are not! Mexico discovered this to its cost in late 1994, even if its punishment was only partly justified. Of course, there are real questions about the efficiency with which capital markets perform – the dangers of poorly-informed herd behaviour, of myopia, of destabilizing speculation – but there is little doubt that governments whose countries receive substantial inflows of foreign capital, or aspire to do so, are constrained in the extent to which they can mismanage their economies without suffering sharp losses of foreign capital. Even where (as in much of Africa) private foreign portfolio capital is not a major factor, the great difficulties which governments experience in enforcing exchange controls mean that they must have regard to the danger of sparking a flight of capital out of the country. Governments are more constrained than they used to be and, in consequence, there would be less need for conditionality even if it were effective.

Another earlier caution should also be repeated: taking the primacy of government ownership seriously imposes on donors (particularly the IFIs) an obligation to take a longer-term and more eclectic view of what constitutes an acceptable government programme, a willingness to view these in the round and not to nit-pick about details, an acceptance that programmes will often fall some way short what donors regard as ideal. Second-best programmes are a necessary price to pay for local ownership, and for affording governments the leeway they will need for the political management of policy change. If donor agencies are not willing to change attitudes in these ways, the consequence will probably be the old conditionality through the back door, with governments whose programmes are rejected forced to ask the agencies what they have to do in order to gain acceptance.

This tendency towards hidden conditionality is probably the largest practical obstacle that the reorientation of donor practices advocated here would face. Take the case of a government with a poor past record which is in financial difficulties and looking for IFI support. The Fund and/or Bank enter into discussions with it and, having assessed the policies it intends to pursue, decide that these do not form a reasonable basis for programme support. The government could then reasonably ask what it has to do additionally, or differently, in order to secure approval. If the IFIs spell out their answers in detail, it might be difficult to differentiate the answers from old-style conditionality.

This is a real difficulty. However, the scenario described does have the large merit of leaving it as the responsibility of government to design the reform package and of avoiding the 'christmas tree' cascading of stipulations which often marks the present situation. Also, the nature of the government–donor dialogue would be different, less confrontational, less at risk in being diverted into haggling over numbers or stand-offs over second-order specifics. The dangers of conditionality-through-the-back-door could be further reduced by spelling out the rules of the game clearly, fully and publicly, defining the nature of the policy framework which IFIs and other donors would be looking for in their programme lending. Governments would then have a fairly clear idea of the changes that would be looked for *as, indeed, they already do*; there is no great mystery about the types of policies favoured by the IFIs.

The danger described would also be less to the extent that past policy performance is used as a predictor of the future. But what of a newly-arrived government? Here donors should surely be inclined to give it the benefit of the doubt. What about the more difficult case of an established government with a poor track record which promises to do better in future? There is no simple way out of this dilemma. Whether or not to provide support is necessarily a matter of fine judgement. However, the dilemma could be reduced by (a) reducing the agency pressures to spend which have so often prejudiced past decisions and (b) stating *and demonstrating* that the consequences for governments which avoidably fail to live up to their promises will be serious, with the threshold for subsequent re-entry raised significantly.[15]

When considering the transition to a more discriminating approach, it would also be crucially important to bear in mind the distinction made earlier between governments that are unwilling to pursue sensible policies and those that lack the expertise and technical skills necessary for the preparation of an adequate programme. It is the former regimes that should be avoided. The latter should be given all possible assistance to raise their competence, providing they ask for it, with a view to reaching a situation where programme aid makes sense. However, we should remember that *conditionality is part of the capacity problem*, because its proliferation has added greatly to the pressures on the limited policy-making resources of the weaker administrations, subtracting from their ability to devote time to their countries' own policy needs.

It is also clear that there should be a reasonable period of transition from the present donor policies to the exercise of greater selectivity. Recipient governments should be given reasonable notice, to give the tardy among them time to 'get their act together'. At the same time, the transition should be announced and managed in such a way as to leave at-risk recipients in no doubt that the donor agencies are serious, and that the financial consequences of not responding will be serious.

How realistic is it to look for such changes? The impression gained during the course of this project is that the thrust of what we are advocating is pushing at an open door among various bilateral donors and important parts of the World Bank. Many of their staff have to live and work with the problems described in earlier chapters. They know conditionality does not work well and that change is necessary. The IMF remains a depressing exception, although its staff too lives with the deficiencies of conditionality and there must be many closet reformers within it hoping for change. Conditionality is so central to the Fund's lending operations that to withdraw from it in the way advocated here could be seen as striking at its *raison d'être*, even though we see it rather as a way of raising the Fund's policy effectiveness. The other major sources of resistance are in the Treasuries and Central Banks of major donor countries, many of which retain an abiding belief in conditionality. Thus, for example, they insist that access to the IMF's ESAF window should be subject to 'especially vigorous' conditionality, and that debt relief should similarly be subject to rigorous IMF-style conditionality. Perhaps the evidence marshalled in this book will help to weaken such misplaced faith.

A postscript on political conditionality

This study has confined itself to conditionality relating to economic policies. However, Chapter 1 noted the growth of 'political' conditionality in recent years, particularly among bilateral donors. This includes conditions relating to 'good governance', the observance of human rights and the rule of law, and the introduction or strengthening of multi-party democracy. The question arises, what light does our work throw on the likely effectiveness of political conditionality? A few comments can be offered.[16]

1   There can be substantial tensions in the simultaneous pursuit of economic and political conditionality. This was brought out in Chapter 6's discussion of reasons why delinquency in the observance of economic policy stipulations often goes unpunished. We cited the Kenyan case where the government felt that, having introduced multi-party elections as demanded by the donor community, the requirements of economic conditionality should be eased. We also mentioned both Kenya and Ghana as examples where a donor-supported push to democratize had led to an electorally-driven weakening of fiscal control with consequential macroeconomic destabilization.

2   We further used the Kenyan case to illustrate how, despite their best endeavours to avoid it, the IFIs inevitably get caught up in the exercise of political conditionality, jeopardizing their intended even-handedness across regimes, and with it their perceived legitimacy.

3   The democracy-promoting version of conditionality throws up a type of internal tension, if not contradiction, for which there is no exact parallel in the economic policy area. Democratization is about accountability but this will be undermined if policies are dictated from outside. As Guillaumont and Guillaumont (1994: 95) put it: 'It is difficult for countries which adopt democratic institutions to have their economic policy . . . entirely decided during negotiations with representatives of international institutions and lenders.'

4   The logic of the principal–agent framework adopted above evokes considerable scepticism about the likely efficacy of the political type. By definition, government participation constraints are bound to be high because it is in the nature of the case that the donors are seeking to pressure undemocratic governments to open themselves up to competition, with the possibility – often probability – of electoral defeat. Given this, the reward system is most unlikely to be adequate. Again, there are likely to be difficulties over more-than-temporary punishment of recalcitrant undemocratic regimes (again illustrated by the Kenyan case). There are likely to be inconsistencies both across countries and over time, induced by the mixed motives of donors and the difficulties of sustaining a united front among them. As with economic stipulations, probably the greatest potential of political conditionality arises in situations where there is already a large *internal* pressure for democratization, so that external leverage might tip the balance in favour of reform.

5   As with economic conditionality, there is much scope for fudging democratic requirements and governments will soon learn to manipulate these. Kenya again illustrates this, with the KANU government introducing the formalities of multi-party democracy while ruthlessly exploiting its powers of incumbency to ensure electoral outcomes in its favour.

So, without questioning the objectives of those who would deploy political conditionality, it is difficult not to be sceptical. There are parallels in this case with the more general use of economic sanctions, the effects of which, we have already seen (pp. 167–8), tend to be quite weak. The conclusion of Sørensen's survey on this topic is also chastening:

> The message emerging from these contributions is that political conditionality will never be a magical solution to the problems of creating sustained democratic progress in developing countries. It may have a minor role to play in specific situations where leaders abuse political and other human rights, provided the country in question is susceptible to donor pressure and provided donors are willing to apply pressure in a consistent manner.
>
> (Sørensen, 1993: 5)

Unfortunately, because of conflicts of interests and objectives among them, donors tend actually to be inconsistent in this area.

In short, then, believers in reform should no more place great faith in the potency of political stipulations than they should in the economic variety. There probably are situations where donor pressure can be effective, e.g. in dealing with the most egregious civil rights offenders, or in preventing specific threats to established democratic rights (as, arguably, in Peru in 1992 and Guatemala in 1993). But external sanctions will very rarely be sufficient in themselves; they are only likely to be effective when reinforcing powerful internal forces.

Notes

1 For the author's own contribution to this discussion see Killick, 1993b, on the design of structural adjustment programmes and 1995b (especially Chapter 4) on the IMF's programmes.

2 Throughout this chapter it will be convenient to treat, and describe, the IMF as an aid donor agency. Strictly speaking, it is not that. Indeed, it stoutly resists the idea that it is a development agency. However, the differences between it and straightforward aid agencies have become smaller, as it has widened its policy concerned, lengthened the term of much of its lending and introduced the SAF and ESAF facilities offering credits on notably 'soft' terms, particularly in terms of the interest rate payable. In any case, our treatment here of the IMF as an aid agency is one of convenience only and is not intended to pre-judge the wider discussion of the essential nature of the Fund.

3 OECD data (1996, Tables 12 and 26) classify 12 per cent of total DAC country commitments as 'programme assistance' in 1992–3 (latest available), against total commitments of nearly $66 billion in 1993, implying a figure for programme aid of c. $8 billion. A high but unknown proportion of this would have been conditional. The total of $15 billion in the text assumes that $6 billion of the $8 billion was conditional.

4 According to OECD data, there was a 15 per cent decline in the real value of total aid flows in 1991–5: aid as a percentage of GNP fell from 0.34 in 1992 to 0.27 in

1995, and two-thirds of the DAC donor countries cut their aid programmes during 1995 alone (OECD, 1996).

5 On this elusive subject see Jayawardena, 1993, on which I have drawn for this paragraph.

6 On this topic see Nelson, 1996.

7 However, the IMF did approve a new stand-by credit in late 1989 and in correspondence have pointed out that 'Argentina was eligible to purchase [i.e. utilize the credit] on two occasions in 1990', although it chose not to take advantage of this possibility.

8 For the writer's own contributions to the substantive policy debate see Killick, 1993b, about the design of structural adjustment packages and 1995b (especially Chapter 4) on the design of stabilization programmes.

9 Good factual and analytical coverage of the debt problem is provided in Volume 1 of the World Bank's annual *Global Development Finance* report (formerly *World Debt Tables*). UNCTAD's annual *Trade and Development Report* provides a different perspective.

10 See also World Bank, 1997, Box 4.1, for a brief description of the system of performance indicators that it has developed to guide its IDA lending.

11 Johnson and Wasty (1993: 8) singled out the extent of support for reform of key pressure groups, or the absence of opposition from them, as perhaps the single most important element of ownership.

12 Egypt, Ghana, the Philippines, India, Senegal and Turkey.

13 It is tempting to add Argentina post-1989, where economic crisis prompted the beginning of a reform process (see earlier and Chapter 3). But the IFIs stayed away in this case and conditionality was not a factor. If anything, the Argentinian experience rather points away from use of hard core conditionality.

14 See also Nelson and Eglinton (1993: 69) for a similar view. See also Morrissey, 1995, for an interesting exploration of the types of policies that might best be chosen in the trade and tax reform areas depending on differing levels of political commitment and institutional capacity.

15 Indeed, such a process was actually proposed by the Bank in a report on its adjustment lending in Africa (World Bank, 1995d: 3).

16 For a valuable in-depth treatment of this topic see Nelson and Eglinton, 1992.

BIBLIOGRAPHY

Works cited in the main text

Allison, G.T. (1971) *Essence of Decision: Explaining the Cuban Missile Crisis*, Boston, MA: Little, Brown & Co.

Aslund, A., P. Boone and S. Johnson (1996) 'How to Stabilise', *Brookings Papers on Economic Activity No. 1*, Washington, DC: Brookings Institution.

Ball, R. and G. Rausser (1995) 'Governance Structures and the Durability of Economic Reforms: Evidence from Inflation Stabilization', *World Development* 23(6), June.

Bates, R.H. and A.O. Krueger (eds) (1993) *Political and Economic Interactions in Economic Policy Reform*, Oxford: Blackwell.

Berg, E.J. (1993) *Rethinking Technical Cooperation*, Bethesda, MD: Development Alternatives Inc.

Berg, E. and Associates (1990) *Adjustment Postponed: Economic Policy Reform in Senegal in the 1980s*, Bethesda, MD: Development Alternatives Inc., October.

Bird, G. (forthcoming) 'The Effectiveness of Conditionality and the Political Economy of Policy Reform: Is it Simply a Matter of Political Will?', *Journal of Policy Reform*.

Bird, G. and D. Rowlands (forthcoming) 'The Catalytic Effect of Lending by the International Financial Institutions', *World Economy*.

Bleaney, M.F. (1996) 'Macroeconomic Stability, Investment and Growth in Developing Countries', *Journal of Development Economics* 48(2), March.

Bouton, L., C. Jones and M. Kiguel (1994) 'Macroeconomic Reform and Growth in Africa: *Adjustment in Africa* Revisited', *World Bank Policy Research Working Paper*, No. WPS 1,394, Washington, DC: World Bank, December.

Brinkerhoff, D.W. (1996) 'Process Perspectives on Policy Change: Highlighting Implementation', in D.W. Brinkerhoff (ed.) 'Implementing policy change', special issue of *World Development* 24(9), September.

Brown, R. (1992) 'The IMF and Paris Club Rescheduling: A Conflicting Role?', *Journal of International Development* 4(3), May–June.

Burnside, C. and D. Dollar (1997) 'Aid, Policies and Growth', *Policy Research Working Paper 1,777*, Washington, DC: World Bank, June.

Callaghy, T.M. (1990) 'Lost Between State and Market: The Politics of Economic Adjustment in Ghana, Zambia and Nigeria', in J.M. Nelson (ed.).

Callaghy, T.M. and J. Ravenhill (eds) (1993) *Hemmed In: Responses to Africa's Economic Decline*, New York: Columbia University Press.

Campbell, B.K. and J. Loxley (eds) (1989) *Structural Adjustment in Africa*, Basingstoke and London: Macmillan.

Centre for Policy Analysis (CEPA) (1996) *Macroeconomic Review and Outlook, 1996*, Accra: CEPA.

Christensen, S., D. Dollar, A. Siamwalla and P. Vichyanond (1993) *Thailand: The Institutional and Political Underpinnings of Growth*, Washington, DC: World Bank.

Collier, P. (1995) 'The Marginalization of Africa', *International Labour Review* 134(4–5).

Collier, P., P. Guillaumont, S. Guillaumont and J.W. Gunning (1997) 'Redesigning Conditionality', *World Development* 25(9), September.

Conway, P. (1994) 'IMF Lending Programs: Participation and Impact', *Journal of Development Economics* 45(2), December.

Corbo, V. and P. Rojas (1992) 'World Bank-supported Adjustment Programs: Country Performance and Effectiveness', in V. Corbo *et al.* (eds), Chapter 3.

Corbo, V., S. Fischer and S.B. Webb (eds) (1992) *Adjustment Lending Revisited*, Washington, DC: World Bank.

Coulter, J. (1994) 'Liberalization of Cereals Marketing in Sub-Saharan Africa: Lessons from Experience', *Marketing Series No. 9*, Chatham, UK: Natural Resources Institute.

Development Committee (1996) *Serving a Changing World: Report of the Task Force on Multilateral Development Banks*, Washington, DC: Development Committee (c/o World Bank), March.

Dixon, C. (1996) 'Thailand: Economy', *Regional Surveys of the World: Far East* (27th edn), London: Europa Publications.

Duncan, A. and J. Howell (eds) (1992) *Structural Adjustment and the African Farmer*, London and Portsmouth: Overseas Development Institute and James Currey.

Easterly, W., M. Kremer, L. Pritchett and L. Summers (1993) 'Good Policy or Good Luck? Country Growth Performance and Temporary Shocks', *Journal of Monetary Economics* December.

Edwards, S. (1989) 'The IMF and the Developing Countries: A Critical Evaluation', Carnegie-Rochester Conference Series on Public Policy No. 31, Amsterdam: North-Holland.

Elbadawi, I.A. (1992) 'Have World Bank-supported Adjustment Programs Improved Economic Performance in Sub-Saharan Africa?', *World Bank Working Paper*, No. WPS 1,001, Washington, DC: World Bank, October.

Elbadawi, I.A., D. Ghura and G. Uwujaren (1992) 'Why Structural Adjustment has not Succeeded in Africa', *World Bank Working Paper*, No. WPS 1,000, Washington, DC: World Bank, October.

Erro, D.G. (1993) *Resolving the Argentine Paradox: Politics and Development, 1966–1992*, Boulder, CO and London: Lynne Rienner.

European Commission Court of Auditors (1994) *Report for 1993*, Brussels: European Commission, November.

Faini, R. (1994) 'Public and Private Investment in Africa: Crowding Out or Crowding In?', in P. Guillaumont and S. Guillaumont (eds).

Faini, R. and J. de Melo (1990) 'Adjustment, Investment and the Real Exchange Rate in Developing Countries', *World Bank Working Paper*, No. WPS 473, Washington, DC: World Bank, August.

Faini, R., J. de Melo, A. Senhadji-Semlali and J. Stanton (1991) 'Macro Performance under Structural Adjustment', in V. Thomas *et al.* (eds) (See also comment by P. Montiel in the same volume.)

Fardi, M. (1991) 'Zambia: Reform and Reversal', in V. Thomas *et al.* (eds).

Foroutan, F. (1991) 'Turkey: Structural Transformation and the Threat to Sustainability', in V. Thomas *et al.* (eds).

Ghura, D. (1995) 'Macro Policies, External Forces, and Economic Growth in Sub-Saharan Africa', *Economic Development and Cultural Change* 43(4), July.

Gibbon, P. and P. Raikes (April 1995) *Structural Adjustment in Tanzania, 1986–94*, Copenhagen: Centre for Development Research.

Goldsmith, A.A. (1988) 'Policy Dialogue, Conditionality, and Agricultural Development: Implications of India's Green Revolution', *Journal of Developing Areas* 22, January.

Gordon, D.F. (1992) 'Conditionality in Policy-based Lending in Africa: USAID Experience', in P. Mosley (ed.) *Development Finance and Policy Reform*, London: Macmillan.

Gordon, D.F. (1996) 'Sustaining Economic Reform under Political Liberalization in Africa: Issues and Implications', *World Development* 24(9), September.

Guillaumont, P. and S. Guillaumont (eds) (1994) *Adjustment and Development: The Experience of the ACP Countries*, Paris: Economica.

Gunatilaka, R. (1997) 'Conditionality and the Political Economy of Policy Reform in Latin America', *ODI Working Paper*, No. 96, London: Overseas Development Institute, March.

Hadjimichael, M.T. and D. Ghura (1995) 'Public Policies and Private Savings and Investment in Sub-Saharan Africa: An Empirical Investigation', *Working Paper*, No. WP/95/19, Washington, DC: International Monetary Fund, February.

Hadjimichael, M.T., D. Ghura, M. Mühleisen, R. Nord and E. Murat Ucer (1995) 'Sub-Saharan Africa: Growth, Saving, and Investment, 1986–93', *Occasional Paper*, No. 118, Washington, DC: International Monetary Fund.

Haggard, S. and R.R. Kaufman (eds) (1992) *The Politics of Economic Adjustment*, Princeton, NJ: Princeton University Press.

Haggard, S. and S.B. Webb (eds) (1994) *Voting for Reform*, New York: Oxford University Press for the World Bank.

Haggard, S., J.-D. Lafay and C. Morrisson (1995) *Political Feasibility of Adjustment in Developing Countries*, Paris: OECD Development Centre.

Harrigan, J. (1991) 'Malawi', 'Jamaica' and 'Guyana', in P. Mosley *et al.* (1991b).

Harris, G. and N. Kusi (1992) 'The Impact of the IMF on Government Expenditures: A Study of African LDCs', *Journal of International Development* 4(1), January.

Harrold, P. and Associates (1995) 'The Broad Sector Approach to Investment Lending: Sector Investment Programs', *Discussion Paper*, No. 302, Washington: World Bank.

Hawkins, J.J. Jr (1991) 'Understanding the Failure of IMF Reform: The Zambian Case', *World Development* 19(7), July.

Healey, J.M. and M. Robinson (1992) *Democracy, Political Change and Economic Policy: Sub-Saharan Africa in Comparative Perspective*, London: Overseas Development Institute.

Hewitt, A. (1992) 'Madagascar', in A. Duncan and J. Howell (eds).

Hewitt, A. and T. Killick (1996) 'Bilateral Aid Conditionality: A First View', in O. Stokke (ed.) *Foreign Aid Towards the Year 2000*, London: Frank Cass.

Hildebrand, M.E. and M.S. Grindle (1994) *Building Sustainable Capacity: Challenges for the Public Sector*, Cambridge, MA: Harvard Institute for International Development.

Hoeven, R. van der and F. Stewart (1993) *Social Development during Periods of Structural Adjustment in Latin America*, ILO Interdepartmental Project on Structural Adjustment, *Occasional Paper*, No. 18, Geneva: International Labour Organization, December.

Hopkins, R., A. Powell, A. Roy and C.L. Gilbert (1997) 'The World Bank and Conditionality', *Journal of International Development* 9(4), June.

Hufbauer, G.C., J.J. Schott and K.A. Elliott (1990) *Economic Sanctions Reconsidered* (2nd edn), Washington, DC: Institute for International Economics.

Inter-American Development Bank (1995) *Economic and Social Progress in Latin America: Overcoming Volatility*, Baltimore, MD: Johns Hopkins University Press (for IADB).

International Monetary Fund (1994) *Annual Report 1994*.

Isham, J. and D. Kaufmann (1995) 'The Forgotten Rationale for Policy Reform: The Productivity of Investment Projects', *World Bank Policy Research Working Paper*, No. 1,549, Washington, DC: World Bank, November.

Jayarajah, C. and W. Branson (1995) *Structural and Sectoral Adjustment: World Bank Experience, 1980–92*, Washington, DC: World Bank, Operations Evaluation Department.

Jayawardena, L. (1993) *The Potential of Development Contracts*, Helsinki: UNU-WIDER.

Johnson, J.H. and S.S. Wasty (1993) 'Borrower Ownership of Adjustment Programs and the Political Economy of Reform', *World Bank Discussion Paper*, No. 199, Washington, DC: World Bank.

Johnson, O.E.G. (1994) 'Managing Adjustment Costs, Political Authority, and the Implementation of Adjustment Programs, with Special Reference to African Countries', *World Development* 22(3), March.

Jones, S.P. (1997) 'Sector Investment Programs in Africa: Issues and Experiences', Washington, DC: World Bank Technical Paper, 374, August.

Kahler, M. (1992) 'External Influence, Conditionality, and the Politics of Adjustment', in S. Haggard and R.R. Kaufman (eds).

Kekic, L. (1995) 'The IMF and Eastern Europe', *Economies in Transition*, London: Economist Intelligence Unit, 3rd Quarter 1995.

Khan, M.S. (1990) 'The Macroeconomic Effects of Fund-supported Adjustment Programs', *IMF Staff Papers* 37(2), June.

Kierzkowski, H. (1987) 'Recent Advances in International Trade Theory: A Selective Survey', *Oxford Review of Economic Policy* 3(1), Spring.

Killick, T. (ed.) (1984a) *The Quest for Economic Stabilisation: The IMF and the Third World*, London: Gower Publishing Company and Overseas Development Institute.

Killick, T. (ed.) (1984b) *The IMF and Stabilisation: Developing Country Experiences*, London: Overseas Development Institute and Gower.

Killick, T. (1993a) 'Enhancing the Cost-effectiveness of Africa's Negotiations with its Creditors', in UNCTAD, *International Monetary and Financial Issues for the 1990s*, Vol. III, New York: United Nations Conference on Trade and Development.

Killick, T. (1993b) *The Adaptive Economy: Adjustment Policies in Small, Low-income Countries*, Washington, DC, and London: World Bank and Overseas Development Institute.

Killick, T. (ed.) (1995a) *The Flexible Economy: Causes and Consequences of the Adaptability of National Economies*, London and New York: Routledge and Overseas Development Institute.

Killick, T. (1995b) *IMF Programmes in Developing Countries: Design and Impact*, London and New York: Routledge, and Overseas Development Institute.

Killick, T. (1995c) 'Can the IMF Help Low-income Countries? Experiences with its Structural Adjustment Facilities' (review article), *World Economy* 18(4), July.

Killick, T. (1995d) 'Structural Adjustment and Poverty: An Interpretative Survey', *Development and Change* 26(2), April.

Kirkpatrick, C. and Z. Onis (1991) 'Turkey', in P. Mosley *et al.* (1991b).

Kirkpatrick, C. and J. Weiss (1995) 'Trade Policy Reforms and Performance in Africa in the 1980s', *Journal of Modern African Studies* 33(2), June.

Klitgaard, R. (1989) 'Incentive Myopia', *World Development* 17(4), April.

Knight, M. and J.A. Santaella (1994) 'Economic Determinants of Fund Financial Arrangements', *IMF Working Paper*, No. WP/94/36, Washington, DC: International Monetary Fund, March.

Krueger, A.O. (1987) 'The Importance of Economic Policy in Development: Contrasts between Korea and Turkey', in H. Kierzkowski (ed.) *Protection and Competition in International Trade*, Oxford: Basil Blackwell.

Krueger, A.O., C. Michalopoulos and V.W. Ruttan (1989) *Aid and Development*, Baltimore, MD: Johns Hopkins University Press.

Larrain, F. and M. Selowsky (eds) (1991) *The Public Sector and the Latin American Crisis*, San Francisco, CA: International Center for Economic Growth.

Little, I.M.D., R. Cooper, W.M. Corden and S. Rajapatirana (1993) *Boom, Crisis and Adjustment: The Macroeconomic Experience of Developing Countries*, New York and Oxford: Oxford University Press for the World Bank.

Loxley, J. (1989) 'The IMF, the World Bank and Reconstruction in Uganda', in B.K. Campbell and J. Loxley (eds).

Manor, J. (1993) 'The Political Sustainability of Economic Liberalization in India', Brighton: Institute of Development Studies (mimeo).

Marr, A. (1996) 'Conditionality and South-east Asian Adjustment', *ODI Working Paper*, No. 94, London: Overseas Development Institute, July.

Martin, M. (1993) 'Neither Phoenix nor Icarus: Negotiating Economic Reform in Ghana and Zambia', in T.M. Callaghy and J. Ravenhill (eds).

Mistry, P.S. (1994) *Multilateral Debt: An Emerging Crisis?*, The Hague: FONDAD, February.

Montiel, P. (1991) 'Comment' in V. Thomas *et al.* (eds).

Moore, W.H. and J.R. Scarritt (1990) 'IMF Conditionality and Polity Characteristics in Black Africa: An Exploratory Analysis', *Africa Today* 37(4).

Morrissey, O. (1995) 'Political Commitment, Institutional Capacity and Tax Policy Reform in Tanzania', *World Development* 23(4), April.

Mosley, P. (1991) 'The Philippines', 'Kenya' and 'Ecuador', in P. Mosley *et al.* (1991b).

Mosley, P. (1992) 'A Theory of Conditionality', in P. Mosley (ed.) *Development Finance and Policy Reform*, London and New York: Macmillan and St Martin's Press.

Mosley, P., J. Harrigan and J. Toye (1991a) *Aid and Power: The World Bank and Policy-based Lending*, Vol. 1, London: Routledge. (A 2nd edn was published in 1995.)

Mosley, P., J. Harrigan and J. Toye (1991b) *Aid and Power: The World Bank and Policy-based Lending*, Vol. 2, *Case Studies*, London: Routledge.

Mosley, P., T. Subasat and J. Weeks (1995) 'Assessing "Adjustment in Africa"', *World Development* 23(9), September.

Murshed, S.M. and S. Sen (1995) 'Aid Conditionality and Military Expenditure Reduction in Developing Countries: Models of Asymmetric Information', *Economic Journal* 105(429): 498–509, March.

Nelson, J.M. (ed.) (1989) *Fragile Coalitions: The Politics of Economic Adjustment*, New Brunswick, NJ: Overseas Development Council and Transaction Books.

Nelson, J.M. (ed.) (1990) *Economic Crisis and Policy Choice: The Politics of Adjustment in the Third World*, Princeton, NJ: Princeton University Press.

Nelson, J.M. (1996) 'Promoting Policy Reforms: The Twilight of Conditionality?', *World Development* 24(9): 1,551–9, September.

Nelson, J.M. with S.J. Eglinton (1992) *Encouraging Democracy: What Role for Conditional Aid?*, Washington, DC: Overseas Development Council.

Nelson, J.M. and S.J. Eglinton (1993) *Global Goals, Contentious Means: Issues of Multiple Aid Conditionality*, Washington, DC: Overseas Development Council.

Ohlin, G. (1970) 'The Evolution of Aid Doctrine', in J. Bhagwati and R. Eckhaus (eds) *Foreign Aid*, Harmondsworth: Penguin Books.

Oppenheim, L.H. (1993) *Politics in Chile: Democracy, Authoritarianism, and the Search for Development*, Boulder, CO: Westview Press.

Organization for Economic Co-operation and Development (OECD) (1996) *Development Co-operation, 1995*, Paris: OECD.

Oyejide, A., B. Ndulu and J.W. Gunning (eds) (1997) 'Editors' Introduction and Overview', in *Regional Integration and Trade Liberalization in Sub-Saharan Africa; Vol. 2: Country Case Studies*, London and Basingstoke: Macmillan.

Pastor, M. Jr (1987) 'The Effects of IMF Programs in the Third World: Debate and Evidence from Latin America', *World Development* 15(2), February.

Pinera, J. (1994) 'Chile', in J. Williamson (ed.) *The Political Economy of Policy Reform*, Washington, DC: Institute of International Economics.

Polak, J.J. (1991) *The Changing Nature of IMF Conditionality*, Essays in International Finance, No. 84, September, Princeton, NJ: Princeton University Press.

Pradhan, S. and V. Swaroop (1993) 'Public Spending and Adjustment', *Finance and Development* 30(3), September.

Pryor, F.L. (1990) *The Political Economy of Poverty, Equity and Growth: Malawi and Madagascar*, Washington, DC: World Bank.

Psacharopoulos, G. *et al.* (1992) 'Poverty and Income Distribution in Latin America: The Story of the 1980s', Latin American and Caribbean Technical Department, *Regional Studies Programme*, Report No. 27, Washington, DC: World Bank, December.

Radelet, S. (1992) 'Reform without Revolt: The Political-economy of Economic Reform in The Gambia', *World Development* 20(8), August.

Ranis, G. and S.A. Mahmoud (1992) *The Political Economy of Development Policy Change*, Cambridge, MA and Oxford: Blackwell.

Reynolds, L.G. (1985) *Economic Growth in the Third World, 1850–1980*, New Haven, CT and London: Yale University Press.

Riddell, R.C. (1987) *Foreign Aid Reconsidered*, London: James Currey and Overseas Development Institute.

Rimmer, D. (1995) 'Adjustment Blues' (review article), *African Affairs* 94(374), January.

Rodrik, D. (1996a) 'Why is there Multilateral Lending?', in M. Bruno and B. Pleskovic (eds) *Annual Bank Conference on Development Economics, 1995*, Washington, DC: World Bank.

Rodrik, D. (1996b) 'Understanding Economic Policy Reform', *Journal of Economic Literature* XXXIV, March.

Root, H. (1989) 'Tying the King's Hands: Credible Commitment and Royal Fiscal Policy during the Old Regime', *Rationality and Society* 1: 240–50, October.

Ryan, T.C.I. (1995) 'The Design and Implementation of High-impact Adjustment Lending', a report for the Africa Region of the World Bank, Nairobi, July (mimeo).

Ryan, T.C.I. (1996) 'Does Conditionality Matter? The Kenya Case', London: Overseas Development Institute (mimeo).

Sachs, J.D. (1989) 'Conditionality, Debt Relief, and the Developing Country Debt Crisis', in J.D. Sachs (ed.) *Developing Country Debt and Economic Performance*, Vol. 1, Chicago, IL: University of Chicago Press.

Sahasakul, C., N. Thongpakde and K. Kraisoraphong (1991) 'Thailand', in P. Mosley *et al.* (1991b).

Sanford, J. (1997) 'Alternative Ways to Fund the International Development Association (IDA)', *World Development* 25(3), March.

Santaella, J.A. (1992) 'IMF Programs: Inducing Adjustment or Opportunistic Behavior?', Chapter 4 in *Stablization Programs, Credibility and External Enforcement*, University of California, Los Angeles, PhD Dissertation, June.

Santaella, J.A. (1993) 'Stabilization Programs and External Enforcement: Experience from the 1920s', *IMF Staff Papers* 40(3), September.

Schadler, S., A. Bennett, M. Carkovic, L. Dicks-Mireaux, M. Mecagni, J.H.J. Morsink and M.A. Savastano (1995) 'IMF Conditionality: Experience Under Stand-By and Extended Arrangements', *IMF Occasional Paper*, No. 128, Washington, DC: World Bank, September.

Schadler, S., F. Rozwadowski, S. Tiwari and D.O. Robinson (1993) 'Economic Adjustment in Low-income Countries: Experience under the Enhanced Structural Adjustment Facility', *Occasional Paper*, No. 106, Washington, DC: International Monetary Fund, September.

Schatz, S.P. (1994) 'Structural Adjustment in Africa: A Failing Grade So Far', *Journal of Modern African Studies* 32(4).

Sidell, S.R. (1988) *The IMF and Third World Instability: Is There a Connection?*, Basingstoke: Macmillan.

Sørensen, G. (1993) 'Editor's Introduction', to Special Issue on Political Conditionality, *European Journal of Development Research* 5(1), June.

Stewart, F. (1991) 'The Many Faces of Adjustment', *World Development* 19(12), December.

Stiglitz, J.E. (1987) 'Principal and Agent', in J. Eatwell, M. Milgate and P. Newman (eds) *New Palgrave Dictionary of Economics*, London: Macmillan Press, pp. 966–72.

Stiles, K.W. (1991) *Negotiating Debt: The IMF Lending Process*, Boulder, CO: Westview Press.

Thomas, V., A. Chhibber, M. Dailami and J. de Melo (eds) (1991) *Restructuring Economies in Distress: Policy Reform and the World Bank*, Oxford and New York: Oxford University Press for World Bank.

Thorbecke, E. (1992) *Adjustment and Equity in Indonesia*, Paris: OECD Development Centre Studies.

Toye, J. and C. Jackson (1996) 'Public Expenditure Policy and Poverty Reduction: Has the World Bank got it Right?', *IDS Bulletin* 27(1), January.

Tussie, D. and M. Botzman (1990) 'Sweet Entanglement: Argentina and the World Bank 1985–9', *Development Policy Review* 8(4): 391–409, December.

Urrutia, M. (1994) 'Colombia', in J. Williamson (ed.) *The Political Economy of Policy Reform*, Washington, DC: Institute for International Economics.

Varian, H.R. (1993) *Intermediate Microeconomics* (3rd edn), London: W.W. Norton, .

Vaubel, R. (1996) 'Bureaucracy at the IMF and the World Bank: A Comparison of the Evidence', *World Economy* 19(2), March.

Vries, M.G. de (1987) *Balance of Payments Adjustment, 1945 to 1986: The IMF Experience*, Washington, DC: International Monetary Fund.

Vylder, S. de (1994) 'Why Deficits Grow: A Critical Discussion of the Impact of Structural Adjustment Lending on the External Account in Low-income Countries', paper presented at Colloquium on New Directions in Development Economics, Stockholm: SAREC.

Wade, R. (1997), 'Development and Environment: Marital Difficulties at the World Bank', *Global Economic Institutions Working Paper* No. 29, London: Centre for Economic Policy Research, July.

Walters, Sir A. (1994) 'Do We Need the IMF and the World Bank?', *Current Controversies* No. 10, London: Institute of Economic Affairs.

White, H. (1997) 'The Economic and Social Impact of Adjustment in Africa: Further Empirical Analysis', *Working Paper No. 245*, The Hague: Institute of Social Studies, April.

Williamson, J. (ed.) (1994) *The Political Economy of Policy Reform*, Washington, DC: Institute for International Economics.

World Bank (1986) *Structural Adjustment Lending: A First Review of Experience*, Washington, DC: International Bank for Reconstruction and Development, September.

World Bank (1988) *Adjustment Lending: An Evaluation of Ten Years of Experience*, Washington, DC: World Bank.

World Bank (1989a) *Annual Review of Evaluation Results*, Operations Evaluation Department Report No. 8,164, Washington, DC: World Bank, October.

World Bank (1989b) *Sub-Saharan Africa: From Crisis to Sustainable Growth*, Washington, DC: World Bank.

World Bank (1990) *Adjustment Lending Policies for Sustainable Growth*, Policy and Research Series No. 14, Washington, DC: World Bank, September.

World Bank (1991) *Effectiveness of SAL Supervision and Monitoring*, Operations Evaluation Department Report No. 9,711, Washington, DC: World Bank, June.

World Bank (1992a) *The Third Report on Adjustment Lending: Private and Public Resources for Growth*, Washington, DC: World Bank.

World Bank (1992b) *Effective Implementation: Key to Development Impact* ('Wapenhans Report'), Portfolio Management Task Force, Washington, DC: World Bank.

World Bank (1993a) *The East Asian Miracle: Economic Growth and Public Policy*, New York: Oxford University Press.

World Bank (1993b) *Performance Audit Report: Argentina – Agricultural Sector Loan*, Operations Evaluation Department Report No. 11,925, Washington, DC: World Bank.

World Bank (1994a) *Adjustment in Africa: Reforms, Results and the Road Ahead*, New York, NY: Oxford University Press for the World Bank.

World Bank (1994b) *Conditional Lending Experience in World Bank-financed Forestry Projects*, Operations Evaluation Department Report No. 13,820, Washington, DC: World Bank, December.

World Bank (1994c) *Study of Bank/Mexico Relations, 1948–1992*, Operations Evaluation Department Report No. 12,923, Washington, DC: World Bank, April.

World Bank (1994d) *Governance: The World Bank's Experience*, Washington, DC: World Bank, May.

World Bank (1994e) *Performance Audit Report: Madagascar – Agricultural Sector Adjustment Credit*, Operations Evaluation Department Report No. 13,081, Washington, DC: World Bank, 23 May.

World Bank (1995a) *Annual Report on Portfolio Performance, FY 1994*, Vol. III, Washington, DC: World Bank, March.

World Bank (1995b) *Bureaucrats in Business*, Oxford and New York: Oxford University Press.

World Bank (1995c) *The Social Impact of Adjustment Operations: An Overview*, Operations Evaluation Department Report No. 14,776, Washington, DC: World Bank, June.

World Bank (1995d) 'Higher Impact Adjustment Lending', Report of a Working Group to SPA Plenary, Washington, DC: World Bank, October.

World Bank (1997) *IDA in Action, 1993–1996: The Pursuit of Sustained Poverty Reduction*, Washington, DC: World Bank.

Zormelo, D. (1996a) 'Is Aid Conditionality Consistent with National Sovereignty?', *ODI Working Paper*, No. 95, London: Overseas Development Institute, November.

Zormelo, D. (1996b) 'The Implementation of World Bank/IMF Conditionalities: A Case Study of Ghana', London: Overseas Development Institute, April (submitted).

Chapter 3 regional references

The following are selected key works consulted in the preparation of the regional studies summarized in Chapter 3. Complete lists of all works consulted are provided in Gunatilaka (1997) and Marr (1996).

Latin America

General

Balassa, B., G.M. Bueno, P.-P. Kuczynski and M.H. Simonsen (1986) *Toward Renewed Economic Growth in Latin America*, Washington, DC: Institute for International Economics.

Corbo, V. (1994) 'Economic Policies and Performance in Latin America', in E. Grilli and D. Salvatore (eds) *Handbook of Comparative Economic Policies*, Vol. 4, *Economic Development*, Westport, CT: Greenwood Press.

International Monetary Fund (1992) *International Financial Statistics* Yearbook, Vol. XLV, Washington, DC: International Monetary Fund.

Larrain, F. and M. Selowsky (eds) (1991) *The Public Sector and the Latin American Crisis*, San Francisco, CA: International Center for Economic Growth.

Little, I.M.D., R.N. Cooper, W.M. Corden and S. Rajapatirana (1993) *Boom, Crisis and Adjustment: The Macroeconomic Experience of Developing Countries*, Oxford: Oxford University Press for the World Bank.

McKinnon, R.I. (1973) *Money and Capital in Economic Development*, Washington, DC: Brookings Institution.

Pastor, M. Jr (1990) 'Capital Flight from Latin America', *World Development* 18(1): 1–18, January.

Prebisch, R. (1959) 'International Trade and Payments in an Era of Coexistence: Commercial Policy in the Underdeveloped Countries', *American Economic Review*, Papers and Proceedings, 251–73.

Sachs, J. (ed.) (1989) *Developing Country Debt and the World Economy*, Chicago, IL: University of Chicago Press.

Wiarda, H.J. and H.F. Kline (1990) *Latin American Politics and Development* (3rd edn), Boulder, CO: Westview Press.

Williamson, J. (ed.) (1994) *The Political Economy of Policy Reform*, Washington, DC: Institute of International Economics.

Argentina

Erro, D.G. (1993) *Resolving the Argentine Paradox: Politics and Development 1966–1992*, Boulder, CO and London: Lynne Rienner Publishers Inc.

Snow, P.G. and G.W. Wynia (1990) 'Argentina: Politics in a Conflict Society', in H.J. Wiarda and H.F. Kline, *Latin American Politics and Development* (3rd edn), Boulder, CO: Westview Press.

Tussie, D. and M. Botzman (1990) 'Sweet Entanglement: Argentina and the World Bank 1985–9', *Development Policy Review* 8(4): 391–409, December.

Bolivia

Gamarra, E.A. and J.M. Malloy (1990) 'Bolivia', in H.J. Wiarda and H.F. Kline, *Latin American Politics and Development* (3rd edn), Boulder, CO: Westview Press.

Klein, H.S. (1992) *Bolivia, The Evolution of a Multi-ethnic Society* (2nd edn), New York: Oxford University Press.

Sachs, J. and J.A. Morales (eds) (1988) *Bolivia 1952–1986*, International Centre for Economic Growth, Country Studies No. 6, California: ICS Press.

Chile

Moran, C. (1991) 'Chile: Economic Crisis and Recovery', in V. Thomas *et al.* (eds) *Restructuring Economies in Distress: Policy Reform and the World Bank*, Oxford and New York: Oxford University Press for the World Bank.

Oppenheim, L.H. (1993) *Politics in Chile: Democracy, Authoritarianism, and the Search for Development*, Boulder, CO: Westview Press.

Pinera, J. (1994) 'Chile', in J. Williamson (ed.) *The Political Economy of Policy Reform*, Washington, DC: Institute of International Economics.

Stallings, B. (1990) 'Politics and Economic Crisis: A Comparative Study of Chile, Peru and Colombia', in J.M. Nelson (ed.) *Economic Crisis and Policy Choice: The Politics of Adjustment in the Third World*, Princeton, NJ: Princeton University Press.

Colombia

Stallings, B. (1990) 'Politics and Economic Crisis: A Comparative Study of Chile, Peru and Colombia', in J.M. Nelson (ed.) *Economic Crisis and Policy Choice: The Politics of Adjustment in the Third World*, Princeton, NJ: Princeton University Press,

Urrutia, M. (1994) 'Colombia', in J. Williamson (ed.) *The Political Economy of Policy Reform*, Washington, DC: Institute of International Economics.

Ecuador

De Janvry, A., A. Graham, E. Sadoulet, R. Espinel, W. Spurrier, H.-P. Nissen and F. Welsch (1994) *The Political Feasibility of Adjustment in Ecuador and Venezuela*, Paris: OECD.

Mosley, P. (1991) 'Ecuador', in P. Mosley *et al.* *Aid and Power: The World Bank and Policy-based Lending*, Vol. 2, *Case Studies*, London: Routledge.

Mexico

Kaufman, R.R. (1990) 'Stabilization and Adjustment in Argentina, Brazil, and Mexico', in J.M. Nelson (ed.) *Economic Crisis and Policy Choice: The Politics of Adjustment in the Third World*, Princeton, NJ: Princeton University Press.

Nash, J. (1991) 'Mexico: Adjustment and Stabilization', in V. Thomas *et al.* (eds) *Restructuring Economies in Distress: Policy Reform and the World Bank*, Oxford and New York: Oxford University Press for the World Bank.

World Bank (1994) *OED Study of Bank/Mexico Relations, 1948–1992*, Operations Evaluation Department Report No. 12,923, Washington, DC: World Bank.

South-east Asia

South Korea

Byung Sun Choi (1991) 'The Structure of Economic Policy-making Institutions in Korea and the Strategy Role of the Economic Planning Board', in G. Caidau and Bun Woong Kim (eds) *A Dragon's Progress: Development and Administration in Korea*, Hartford CT: Kumarian Press.

Lee-Jay Cho and Yoon Hyung Kim (1991) 'Political, Economic and Social Developments in the 1980s', in Lee-Jay Cho and Yoon Hyung Kim (eds) *Economic Development in the Republic of Korea: A Policy Perspective*, an East–West Center Book, Hawaii: University of Hawaii Press.

Chung, J. (1996) 'The Republic of Korea: Economy', *Regional Surveys of the World: Far East* (27th edn), London: Europa Publications.

Haggard, S., R.N. Cooper, S. Collins, B. Kim and C. Ro (1994) *Macroeconomic Policy and Adjustment in Korea, 1970–1990*, Cambridge, MA: Harvard Institute for International Development/Korean Development Institute.

Kim, K. and D. Leipziger (1993) *Korea: A Case of Government-Led Development*, Washington, DC: World Bank.

Mansoor, Dailami (1991) 'Korea: Successful Adjustment', in V. Thomas *et al.* (eds) *Restructuring Economies in Distress: Policy Reform and the World Bank*, Oxford and New York: Oxford University Press.

Westphal, L. (1991) 'Comments', in V. Thomas *et al.* (eds) *Restructuring Economies in Distress: Policy Reform and the World Bank*, Oxford and New York: Oxford University Press.

Indonesia

Ahmed, S. (1991) 'Indonesia: Stabilization and Structural Change', in V. Thomas *et al.* (eds) *Restructuring Economies in Distress: Policy Reform and the World Bank*, Oxford and New York: Oxford University Press.

Azis, I.J. (1994) 'Indonesia', in J. Williamson (ed.) *The Political Economy of Policy Reform*, Washington, DC: Institute of International Economics.

Battacharya, A. and M. Pangestu (1993) *Indonesia: Development Transformation and Public Policy*, Washington, DC: World Bank.

Cribb, R. (1996) 'Indonesia: History', *Regional Surveys of the World: Far East* (27th edn), London: Europa Publications.

Hill, H. (1995) 'Indonesia: From "Chronic Dropout" to "Miracle"?', *Journal of International Development* 7(5), September–October.

Robison, R. (1988) 'Resisting Structural Adjustment: Conflict over Industry Policy in Indonesia', in J. Carlsson and T. Shaw (eds) *Newly Industrializing Countries and the Political Economy of South-South Relations*, Macmillan International Political Economy Series, London: Macmillan.

Sadiq, A. (1991) 'Indonesia: Stabilization and Structural Change', in V. Thomas *et al.* (eds) *Restructuring Economies in Distress: Policy Reform and the World Bank*, Oxford and New York: Oxford University Press.

Thorbecke, E. (1992) *Adjustment and Equity in Indonesia*, Paris: OECD.

Wing Thye Woo, B. Glassburner and A. Nasution (1994) *Macroeconomic Policies, Crises and Long-term Growth in Indonesia, 1965–90*, World Bank Comparative Macroeconomic Studies, Washington, DC: World Bank.

Malaysia

Bruton, H. (1992) *The Political Economy of Poverty, Equity, and Growth – Sri Lanka and Malaysia*, Washington, DC: World Bank.

Demery, D. and L. Demery (1992) *Adjustment and Equity in Malaysia*, Paris: OECD.

Moore, S. (1996) 'Malaysia: Economy', *Regional Surveys of the World: Far East* (27th edn), London: Europa Publications.

Salleh, M. and S.D. Meyanathan (1993) *Malaysia: Growth, Equity and Structural Adjustment*, Washington, DC: World Bank.

Thailand

Christensen, S., D. Dollar, A. Siamwalla and P. Vichyanond (1993) *Thailand: The Institutional and Political Underpinnings of Growth*, Washington, DC: World Bank.

Dixon, C. (1996) 'Thailand: Economy', *Regional Surveys of the World: Far East* (27th edn), London: Europa Publications.

Doner, R. and A. Laothamatas (1994) 'Thailand: Economic and Political Gradualism', in S. Haggard and S. Webb, *Voting for Reform: Democracy, Political Liberalization and Economic Adjustment*, Washington, DC: World Bank.

Sahasakul, C., N. Thongpakde and K. Kraisoraphong (1991) 'Thailand', in P. Mosley et al. *Aid and Power: The World Bank and Policy-based Lending*, Vol. 2, London: Routledge.

The Philippines

Dohner, R. and S. Haggard (1994) *The Political Feasibility of Adjustment in the Philippines*, Paris: OECD.

Haggard, S. (1990) 'The Political Economy of the Philippine Debt Crisis', in J. Nelson (ed.) *Economic Crisis and Policy Change; The Politics of Adjustment in the Third World*, Princeton, NJ: Princeton University Press.

Hodgkinson, E. (1996) 'The Philippines: Economy', *Regional Surveys of the World: Far East* (27th edn), London: Europa Publications.

Malaluan, N.A. (1994) 'Philippines 2000 and the Politics of Reform', *Kasarinlan: Philippines Quarterly of Third World Studies* 9(2–3): 37–53.

Morisawa, K. (1993) 'The Political Economy of the Privatization and Liberalization Program under Aquino Government: The Problems and Prospects', *Osaka City University Economic Review* 28(1).

Mosley, P. (1991) 'The Philippines', in P. Mosley et al. *Aid and Power: The World Bank and Policy-based Lending* Vol. 2, London: Routledge.

INDEX

accountability 4, 95, 143, 195

ACP countries 136–7

adjustment, structural 2, 4, 5, 10, 15, 19–100, 105, 108–27, 132–8, 154–8 *passim*, 160–1, 165, 177–86, 189–90, 199; in Latin America 53, 70–84, 163, 169; in South-east Asia 53, 57–70, 109, 132, 136, 163, 169; *see also* breakdowns; costs; implementation; ownership

administrative capacity 2, 14, 84, 114–15, 177, 182, 194

adverse selection 126, 144–7, 174

advice/advisers 11, 67–8, 116, 166; *see also* technocrats

Africa 5, 6, 12, 15, 17n2, 18n5, 24, 28–9, 34–8, 45, 47–9 *passim*, 87, 89, 96, 114, 115, 139, 146, 155, 161, 169, 171, 176, 184, 192; *see also* *individual countries*

agency theory 99–104, 108–23, 129, 163

agriculture 2, 3, 7, 41, 45, 73, 76, 80, 121

Alfonsin, President/regime 74, 109, 132, 141

Allende, President/regime 75, 82

Aquino, Benigno 66; Corazon, President/regime 63–9 *passim*, 90, 109, 153

Argentina 70–4, 77–83 *passim*, 90, 109, 120, 130–4 *passim*, 139, 141, 169, 179, 197n7,13, 198–9

arrears, debt servicing 13, 126, 144, 145

Asia 171; South 6, 171; South-east 17, 53–70, 81, 109, 120, 130, 132, 136,

163, 166, 169, 177, 183; *see also* *individual countries*

asymmetry, classical 43, 46, 51n15; informational 101, 102, 149- 51, 175

automotive industry 62, 69

authoritarianism 68, 83, 113–14, 153

balance of payments 19, 25–7 *passim*, 32, 40, 42, 49, 59, 63, 65, 134, 136, 147, 160, 166, 167; *see also* deficits

Ball, R. 120

banks/banking 2, 60, 71–2, 115, 134; multilateral development 191

Bangladesh 122

Barco, President/regime 75–6, 82

bargaining power 96, 127, 145, 147

Bates, R.H. 154, 155

benchmark criteria 7, 31

Benin 37

Berg, E. 28, 40, 111, 112, 135, 137, 139, 146, 170, 182

Bird, G. 127n3, 131

Bleaney, M.F. 14

Bolivia 70, 72, 74–5, 77–9, 81–3 *passim*, 138

Borja, President 82

borrowing, non-concessional 7, 63, 72, 147, 151

Botzman, M. 130, 132, 134, 141

Bouton, L. 34–6, 42, 43

Brady Plan 81

Branson, W. 23–5 *passim*, 39, 41, 42

Brazil 71–3 *passim*, 169

breakdowns, programme 117, 121–2, 133, 135, 161, 164

Brinkerhoff, D.W. 90–1

Burkina Faso 37
Burnside, C. 13–14, 36, 38
Burundi 37

Callaghy, T.M. 109, 113, 146
Cameroon 37
cancellation, of programmes 138, 164
capacity building 177, 182, 194, 196–9 *passim*
capital 12, 164, 173, 174, 192; flight 66, 69, 73, 76, 131, 192; flows 71, 74, 120, 130–2, 164, 173, 192; formation 14, 22, 24, 39; markets 12, 17, 121, 162, 192
Caribbean 46
'catalytic' effect 70, 81, 130–2, 152, 164, 165, 173, 179
Central African Republic 37
CEPA (Centre for Policy Analysis) 144
CFA franc 142
Chile 53, 70, 72, 77–9, 81–3 *passim*, 90, 113, 117, 120, 169, 199
China/Chinese 61, 96, 171
Christensen, S. 158
civil service 41, 44, 46, 47, 67, 88, 112
cocaine 76
coffee 122, 150
Cold War 3, 174, 192
collateral 12, 138, 140, 162, 163, 166
Collier, P. 15, 119
Colombia 29, 70, 73, 75–6, 78, 79, 81, 82, 90, 98, 111, 112, 116, 122, 155, 199
commitment, policy 7–8, 15, 62, 66, 69, 78–82 *passim*, 89, 118, 131, 149, 158, 185; 'technology' 15, 118
communism 3, 45, 66
competitiveness 55, 58
conditionality 1–52, 77–9, 81, 85, 92–6, 102–4, 109–27, 133–51, 156–8, 188–90, 194–6, 199; alternatives to 17, 176–96; compliance/non-compliance with 27–38, 109–23, 129–39, 144–51, 163, 165, 174; enforcement of 9, 13, 17, 101, 144, 150; failure of 161–76; hard core 11, 27, 94, 161, 163, 164, 188–90; in Latin America 77–9, 81, 85; legitimation of 12–17, 85; modalities 6–9, 170, 188; political 4, 9, 143–4, 194–6; pro forma 9–11, 27, 79, 188, 190; in

South-east Asia 61–70, 85; *see also* effectiveness
Congo 37
consistency, policy 15, 119, 162
consolidation, reform 87, 117–18
consultation 9, 11, 86, 187
contingency financing 181
contraband 76
Conway, P. 39, 40, 42, 120
Corbo, V. 21, 22, 24
corruption 3, 63, 114, 143, 146
costs, of adjustment 2, 15, 43, 48, 51n16, 93, 98, 112–15, 169, 171; agency 101, 150; of conditionality failure 168–71; distributional 112–14; enforcement 150; transaction 114–15, 123, 164, 172
Côte d'Ivoire 13n5, 37, 45, 96
Coulter, J. 89
credibility 15, 65, 66, 69, 83, 118–21, 123, 125, 131, 145, 147, 154, 162, 164, 165, 179, 186
credit 1, 7, 31, 40, 44, 59, 72, 151
creditors, preferred 12, 93, 144
creditworthiness 62, 65, 66, 76, 132–3, 166
cronyism 63, 64, 153
cross-conditionality 8–9, 39, 129, 142, 147
culture 68, 69, 177, 178, 191

deadlines 29, 31
debt 12, 33, 45, 55, 56, 65, 70, 73, 74, 76, 81, 115, 141, 144–5, 148, 166, 174, 181; refinancing 145, 174; relief 9, 130, 142, 145, 162, 167, 173, 175, 181–2, 194; rescheduling 80; service 9, 13, 47, 55, 73, 74, 130, 143, 145, 162, 166, 181
decentralization 190–1
deception 28–9, 98, 116–17, 137
default 12, 52n17, 76, 81, 126, 144, 162
deficits, balance of payments 32, 56–8 *passim*, 63, 72; budgetary 1, 31, 33, 39, 41, 42, 54, 57, 58, 72–6 *passim*, 142
deflation 142
delinquency 140–51, 195
demand, for aid 162, 163, 166
democracy/democratization 4, 9, 95, 143, 144, 194, 195

dependency 74
depreciation, currency 58, 59
deregulation 77
destabilization 48, 70, 147–8, 174, 195
devaluation 6, 39, 40, 42, 44, 56, 58, 59, 62, 63, 72, 73, 77, 113, 121, 132, 142, 143, 158, 166, 190
development 13, 16; Committee 191; Commission 177; contracts 177
'dialogue' 11, 66–70, 78–80, 84, 177, 178, 183, 193
disasters 103, 121–3 *passim*
disinflation 58
Dixon, C. 120
Dollar, D. 14, 36, 38
Dominica 122
Dominican Republic 122, 157
donor–recipient relations 3–4, 9–12, 74, 83–8, 91–9, 102–4, 110, 116–18, 126–7, 140, 141, 143, 152–8, 174–80, 186–96 *passim; see also* dialogue; interest conflicts; penalties; rewards
drought 64, 121, 122

Easterly, W. 14
Economist, The 71
Ecuador 70, 72, 76, 79–83 *passim*, 138
education 3, 25, 40, 48, 56, 68, 80, 148, 182
Edwards, S. 31
effectiveness, of adjustment 19–27, 126; of aid 13–14, 162, 163, 166, 171, 176, 179, 192; of conditionality 17, 19–52, 156–9, 165–7, 189
Eglinton, S.J. 17n3, 95, 96, 151, 157, 172, 189
Egypt 169
EIU 31
Elbadawi, I.A. 22–4 *passim*, 155, 184
elites 47, 63, 64, 68, 73, 76, 82, 110, 112
emigration 141
employment 46–8 *passim*, 51n16, 68, 72, 97
energy 3, 73, 76, 93
environment 2, 3, 93, 148, 176, 192; policy 13–14, 27, 31, 36–7, 84, 119–20, 169, 178, 181
Erro, D.G. 109, 179
Europe 16, 119; Eastern 3, 31, 45
European Union 5, 135, 137–8, 175

exchange controls 58, 71, 192; rate 1, 6, 13, 39, 41, 42, 51n11,13, 54–9 *passim*, 72, 73, 82, 90, 143, 151, 166, 167
expenditure, public 1, 7, 39–40, 47–8, 52n19, 56, 57, 72, 142, 143, 187; military 3, 94
exports 13, 22–4 *passim*, 27, 32, 42, 43, 49, 55–9 *passim*, 66, 71, 76, 79, 111, 160, 166; promotion 44, 55, 59; taxes 62, 64, 71, 113, 142, 158
extension 150

Faini, R. 22, 24, 25, 39
Fardi, M. 130, 136
Febres Cordero, President/regime 76, 82
Fernandez, José 64
fertilizers 45, 121
Finland 191
financial sector, reform of 2, 7, 55, 58, 60, 77
fiscal policy 13, 32–3, 42, 57, 63, 67, 72, 143, 185, 186
flexibility 8, 66, 67, 156, 180, 191
foreign exchange 71, 76, 80, 166
foreign policy interests 3, 12, 66, 140, 167, 168, 174, 192
Foroutan, F. 117
France 5, 135, 140, 142

G7 governments 92, 104
Gabon 37
Gambia, The 37, 97, 109, 113, 121, 122, 155, 169, 199
Gaviria, Cesar, President 83
Germany 5, 141
Ghana 18n5, 37, 45, 88, 97, 109, 112, 116, 117, 119, 122, 143–8 *passim*, 155, 157, 189–90, 195, 199
Gibbon, P. 146
Goldsmith, A.A. 17n3
Gordon, D.F. 91, 92, 131–2, 136, 144, 150, 158
governance 4, 9, 94–6, 176, 194
Grindle, M.S. 182
groundnuts 113
growth, economic 13–14, 22, 24–7 *passim*, 33, 41–3 *passim*, 49, 55–7 *passim*, 68, 71, 160
Guatemala 196

Guillaumont, P. and S. 28–9, 136, 176, 195
Gunatilaka, Ramani 70–84, 105
Guyana 90, 119, 130, 138, 142, 155, 199

Hadjimichael, M.P. 13–14
Haggard, S. 38, 46–7, 49, 87, 112, 117–18, 153–5 *passim*
Harrigan, Jane 21, 111, 113, 119, 121, 122, 130, 133, 134, 142, 143
Harris, G. 47–8
Harrold, P. 187
Hawkins, J.J. Jr 112
health 40, 48, 56
Hewitt, A. 9, 109
Hildebrand, M.E. 182
HIPC initiative 145, 167, 175, 181
historical factors 69, 92, 98, 156, 174, 177
Hoeven, R. van der 48
Hopkins, R. 17
Hufbauer, G.C. 167, 168
Hurtado, President/regime 76, 82

IDA 171, 173, 179–80
IMF 1–2, 4–6, 8, 9, 13, 16, 17, 19, 20, 23, 92, 94, 96, 103–5 *passim*, 122, 129–30, 149, 151, 158, 166–8, 175–6, 186, 187, 190, 191, 194, 196n2; and adjustment 4, 25–8, 30–4, 39–43 *passim*, 46–9, 61, 63, 66, 77, 85, 87, 89, 120, 130, 131, 139–43 *passim*, 147, 160, 161, 170–3, 180–1, 185–7 *passim*, 190, 193–4; ESAF 4, 7, 25, 26, 31–4, 49, 51n6,8, 143, 144, 173, 194, 196n2; stand-bys 4, 7, 31, 51n6,8, 62–6 *passim*, 77, 136, 158; and World Bank 120, 142, 143, 174
implementation, of SAPs 19, 27–38, 41–3, 48–50, 54–61, 69, 79–85 *passim*, 89, 90, 97, 100, 103, 105, 110–27 *passim*, 127n3, 130, 160, 161, 165, 171–2; *see also* non-implementation
imports 26, 28–9, 34, 45, 51n13, 71, 113, 121, 143; 'strangulation' 26; substitution 44, 46, 56, 70, 111, 112
incentives 1, 13, 59, 101, 116, 126,

127n4, 129–33 *passim*, 152, 163–7 *passim*, 176, 191; compatibility 101, 123, 164
income 26, 43, 46, 68, 72, 73; distribution 51n16, 72, 74, 112, 125, 152
India 17n3, 97, 98, 111, 112, 171, 199
Indonesia 54, 56, 58–61 *passim*, 65, 67, 69, 90, 113, 117, 132, 169, 199
industrialization 59; ISI 70–2, 76
industry 3, 44, 46, 56; Heavy and Chemical drive 55
inflation 22, 24, 26, 27, 41, 49, 55–8, 72–6 *passim*, 160; hyper 72, 73, 75, 81
infrastructure 25, 56, 76
instability, political 48, 62, 72, 118, 184–5
institutions 25, 92, 98, 148–9; reform 40, 190
insurance 101–3 *passim*
interest conflicts 91–3, 97–8, 100, 164, 171–3
interest groups 54, 68, 76, 78, 81, 82, 132, 153, 172
interest rates 2, 32, 39, 60, 72–6 *passim*, 79, 82, 121, 143, 167
investment 14, 24–7 *passim*, 49, 50n4, 64, 71–3 *passim*, 143, 145, 147, 160; foreign 13, 15, 16, 56, 59, 65–6, 69, 77, 119–20, 131–2, 164, 179; SIPs 187
Isham, J. 14

Jackson, C. 40
Jamaica 51n12, 90, 96, 97, 109, 111, 113, 116, 120–2 *passim*, 134, 139, 141, 143, 169, 199
Japan 5, 59, 66, 67
Jayarajah, C. 23–5 *passim*, 39, 41, 42
Johnson, J.H. 10, 86, 88–9, 108, 118, 179, 184
Johnson, O.E.G. 87
Jones, S. 187

Kahler, M. 10, 89, 117, 150
Kaufman, R.R. 46–7, 87, 117–18, 153–5 *passim*
Kaufmann, D. 14
Kaunda, President/regime 90, 112–13, 117

Kekic, L. 31
Kennedy, President 17n3
Kenya 10, 18n5, 29, 37, 89, 90, 96–8, 110–13 *passim*, 117, 119, 122, 128n8, 134–5, 138–9, 141, 143–4, 146, 148, 155, 157, 158, 169, 192, 195, 199
Khan, M.S. 19
Killick, T. 1, 8, 9, 19, 20, 23, 25, 30, 39, 40, 42–4 *passim*, 46, 92, 96, 104, 105, 115, 121, 122, 130, 131, 140, 172
Kirkpatrick, C. 117, 133, 135
Klitgaard, R. 114
Knight, M. 145
Korea, South 18n5, 51n12, 54–62 *passim*, 66, 67, 69, 90, 97, 113, 132, 133, 164, 165, 169, 199
Krueger, A.O. 13, 18n5, 154, 155
Kusi, N. 47–8

labour 46, 76, 83, 113
Lafay, S.-J. 154
land reform 68
landless 44, 45
Larrain, F. 72
Latin America 6, 12, 17, 45–8 *passim*, 53, 70–84, 92, 118, 130, 141, 163, 166, 169, 177–8, 183; *see also individual countries*
law, rule of 4, 95, 194
leadership, political 54, 69, 78, 81–91 *passim*, 152, 154, 155, 177
League of Nations 16, 119
legitimacy, government 68, 87
letters of intent/development policy 8, 9, 11, 185
leverage, financial 7, 8, 10, 38–41, 50, 83, 85, 94, 97, 116, 129, 148, 161, 183, 190
liberalization 75, 112, 132, 143; exchange 32, 58, 59; financial sector 32, 55, 60, 76, 79; market 9, 89; trade 1, 2 , 7, 28–9, 32, 40, 42, 44, 51n13, 55–60 *passim*, 64, 75–6, 79, 82, 111, 113, 116, 117, 127, 134
Little, I.M.D. 122–3
Loxley, J. 132

Madagascar 37, 90, 97, 98, 109, 112, 117, 135, 139, 169, 199

Madrid, Miguel de la, President/regime 76–7, 82, 83
Mahathir, Mohamed 61
Mahmoud, S.A. 155–6
maize 110, 121, 135
Malawi 37, 51n12, 89, 98, 113, 121, 133, 199
Malaysia 54, 56, 57, 59–61 *passim*, 66, 69, 132
Mali 37, 89
Manor, J. 111
manufacturing 59, 71, 73, 119
Marcos, Ferdinand, President/regime 63–8 *passim*, 90, 109, 117, 141, 153
marketing 41, 89, 110, 135; boards 32
markets 1–2, 9, 43, 72, 162, 173; friendliness 54–5, 59–61, 67
Marr, Ana 53–70, 109
Martin, M. 143
Master Table 90, 97–8, 105–8 *passim*, 112, 116, 120, 121, 126, 129, 133, 142–3, 145, 175, 199
Mauritania 37
Mauritius 51n12
Melo, J. de 25
Menem, Carlos, President/regime 74, 81–3 *passim*, 90, 109, 179
Mexico 38, 70–3, 76–83 *passim*, 90, 97, 98, 116, 117, 120, 133, 139, 155, 169, 183, 192, 199
mining 3, 75
Moi, President/regime 10, 117, 138
monetary policy 13, 43, 50, 58, 63–4, 67, 113, 143
monitoring 9, 38, 96, 101, 149–51 *passim*, 177, 190
monopolies 60, 64, 73
moral hazard 13, 38, 66, 69, 93, 98, 101, 138–9, 162, 163, 171, 179
Moore, W.H. 48
Morocco 45
Morrisson, C. 154
Mosley, P. 12, 19, 21, 22, 24, 29, 41, 42, 50, 96, 109, 110, 120, 127n1, 131, 134–5, 138, 141, 145
Mozambique 37, 121
Museveni, President/regime 119

NATO 141
Nelson, J.M. 17n3, 47, 95, 96, 136–7, 146, 150–1, 153, 157, 165, 172, 189

Netherlands 5
Nicaragua 169
Niger 37
Nigeria 37
non-implementation, of SAPs 48, 86, 89, 102, 111, 117, 133–51, 163–5 *passim*, 168, 174
Norway 191
Nyerere, President 90, 117

objectives, donor 10, 12, 91, 97, 98, 101–3, 110, 116, 123, 125, 129, 130, 140, 142, 163–5 *passim*, 171, 175, 196; recipient 91, 97, 98, 101–4 *passim*, 110, 111, 116, 123, 125, 129, 130, 163–5 *passim*, 171
Obote, Milton, President/regime 132
OECD 9, 142
oil 61, 67, 76; prices 55–7 *passim*, 62, 65, 67, 69, 76, 77, 121
Onis, Z. 117, 133, 135
openness 55, 58, 59, 61
Oppenheim, L.H. 75
'ownership', of SAPs 10, 11, 17, 86–100, 110, 116, 119, 121, 125, 142, 158, 164, 165, 171, 177–86, 190–3 *passim*
Oyejide, A. 40

Paris Club 9, 130, 142, 182
Park, President/regime 55, 61–2
participation constraints 101, 110–23, 125, 129, 130, 158, 163–5 *passim*, 171, 173, 176, 195
Pastor, M. Jr 46
path dependence 92, 156
patron–client networks 68
patronage 63, 64, 110–11, 153
Paz Estenssoro, Victor, President/regime 75, 81–3 *passim*
penalties/punishment 8, 16, 101, 102, 106–7, 121, 126, 133–8, 151, 152, 157, 164–8 *passim*, 171, 174, 192, 195
performance criteria/indicators 5, 7, 8, 21–6, 30–2, 151
Peru 71, 196
petroleum products 2, 56, 62, 76
Philippines 53, 54, 63–9 *passim*, 90, 96–8 *passim*, 109, 113, 117, 120, 132, 139, 141, 153, 157, 169, 199

Pinera, J. 75
Pinochet, President/regime 82, 113
Polak, J.J. 1, 5
political: factors 12, 14–16, 43–50, 55, 60, 63, 66, 68, 70, 72, 80–100 *passim*, 113, 116, 118–20, 132, 143–4, 151–8, 161, 166, 172, 176–8, 184–6, 194–6; will 89, 115; *see also* governance
poverty 3, 44–6 *passim*, 51n16, 56, 113; reduction 2, 56, 148, 171, 179
Pradhan, S. 48
Prebisch–Singer thesis 71
preconditions/prior actions 6–7, 10, 11, 27, 38, 39, 50, 127, 129, 184, 190
prices 39, 45, 51n10, 62, 72, 113, 115, 167, 190; commodity 56, 57, 61, 62, 73, 74, 121–2; producer 2, 32, 57, 150
principal–agent framework 17, 100–3, 108, 149, 163, 171, 195
private sector 1, 2, 40, 65, 74, 76, 77, 87, 119, 143, 153
privatization 2, 7, 9, 28, 29, 40, 44, 46–8 *passim*, 55, 58, 60, 64, 71, 77, 110–12 *passim*, 128n7, 154; of punishment 192
protectionism 46, 55, 60, 71, 76, 111, 192
Pryor, F.L. 109
Psacharopoulos, G. 46
public enterprises 2, 7, 28, 39, 46, 47, 55, 60, 71, 77, 83, 97, 110, 112, 128n7, 154, 167, 184–6 *passim*

quantitative restrictions 28
quotas 63

racial factors 56, 60, 61, 113
Radelet, S. 109, 113, 121
Raikes, P. 146
Ramos, Fidel, President/regime 63, 64, 68, 153
Ranis, G. 155–6
Raussen, G. 120
Rawlings, President/regime 109, 189
recession 27, 55, 56, 61, 73
recipient governments 13–16, 92–100, 103, 110–23, 151–8 *passim*; *see also* donor–recipient relations; political factors; resentment

refinancing 145, 174
reform/reformers 2, 13–16 *passim*, 32, 35, 38, 40, 43, 48–9, 60, 64, 84, 87, 97–9 *passim*, 117–18, 190; *see also* adjustment
rents/rent seeking 46, 63, 111
repayment, of loans 12–13, 16, 74, 144, 166, 170
repression 113–14; financial 72
reputation 16, 116, 117, 119, 120, 128n8, 145
resentment/resistance 93–100 *passim*, 116, 170–2 *passim*
reserves, foreign exchange 7, 42, 61, 66
restructuring 2, 34, 60, 77, 111
retrenchment 47, 48
revenue 1, 56, 57, 60, 73, 76, 147
review clauses/missions 8
rewards 11, 15, 101, 102, 106–7, 123, 125–33 *passim*, 151, 152, 157, 164, 171, 173, 176, 195
Reynolds, L.G. 14
rice 113, 121
rights, civil 10, 196; human 4, 9, 94–5, 192, 194, 196; property 112, 119, 143
riots 56, 61
risks 48, 50, 98, 101–3 *passim*, 144, 165, 171
Rodrik, D. 17, 100, 131
Rojas, P. 21, 22, 24
Root, H. 119
Rowlands, D. 131
Rwanda 37
Ryan, T.C.J. 111, 117, 148, 155, 158

Sachs, J.D. 17
safety-net provisions 46
Sahasakul, C. 111, 113
salaries 112, 114
Salinas, Carlos, President/regime 77, 83
Sanford, J. 173
sanctions 11, 133, 135–7 *passim*, 140, 167–8, 196
Santaella, J.A. 16, 118–19, 139, 145, 151
savings 22, 24–5
scapegoats 16, 158–9, 188–9
Scarritt, J.R. 48
Schadler, S. 31–4
Schatz, S.P. 41

security interests 3, 12, 140, 141, 174, 192
selectivity 179–80, 182, 190–2 *passim*, 194
Selowsky, M. 72
Senegal 28, 37, 38, 90, 97, 109, 111, 112, 117, 133, 135, 139, 141, 146, 155, 169, 170, 199
sequencing, of reform 50, 180
shocks, external 14, 28, 49, 55, 57, 65, 69, 73, 74, 76, 89, 103, 121–3, 126, 151, 152, 160, 161, 177, 181.
Sidell, R.R. 48
Sierra Leone 29, 36
Siles Zuazo, President 75
simplicity 38–9, 50, 190
slippage 29, 30, 32, 39, 67, 69, 79, 121, 122, 135–6, 141, 147
social factors 43–50 *passim*; services 44, 47–8, 52n19
Sorensen, G. 196
sovereignty 93–7
stabilization 26, 49, 55, 56, 60–4 *passim*, 67, 69, 71, 74–7 *passim*, 81, 109, 119, 120, 132, 134, 136, 141, 143, 158
Stallings, B. 116
state, role of 47, 71
Stewart, F. 48
Stiles, K.W. 96
stipulations 10–12, 14, 31, 114, 164, 172, 193, 195; *see also* conditionality
Stoltenberg, Thorwald 177
strikes 83, 112–13
subsidies 2, 6, 13, 44, 47, 62, 63, 72, 74, 76, 113, 121, 158
Sudan 169
Suharto, President/regime 56, 67
Swaroop, V. 48

Taiwan 59, 66
Tanzania 18n5, 37, 45, 89, 90, 109, 117, 118, 122, 139, 145, 155, 169, 199
tariffs 59–60, 62–4 *passim*, 76, 77
taxation 2, 6, 44, 57, 63, 64, 72, 74, 76, 134; concessions 59; export 62, 64, 71, 113, 142, 158; VAT 57, 82
teachers 112
technical assistance 182
technocrats 66–9 *passim*, 75, 79–84

passim, 86, 117, 153, 155, 157, 158, 166, 177; 'Chicago Boys' 75
tests 20, 23, 25–6, 41, 51n8, 175
Thailand 51n12, 54, 56–62, 65–9 *passim*, 90, 97, 111–13 *passim*, 120, 132, 133, 139, 158, 164, 165, 199
Thorbecke, E. 113
timing, of reform 152, 180
Togo 37
Toye, J. 21, 40
trade 12, 13, 25, 57, 59, 192; liberalization 1, 2, 7, 28–9, 32, 40, 42, 44, 51n13, 55–60 *passim*, 64, 75–6, 79, 82, 111, 113, 116, 117, 122, 134; terms of 14, 34, 71, 103, 121
trade unions 46, 77, 83, 109
training 80, 116, 182, 186
tranching 7, 10, 29–30, 49, 65, 96, 127, 129, 133, 134, 136, 138, 164
'transition' economies 31
transparency 4, 95
transport 59, 76
treatment, of beneficiaries 96–8, 140, 141, 171, 174
trigger criteria 7, 8, 10, 11, 27, 30–1, 79
Turkey 18n5, 38, 96, 98, 117, 131, 133, 135–6, 139, 141, 169, 199
Tussie, D. 130, 132, 134, 141

Uganda 2, 37, 109, 112, 116, 119, 132, 155, 189, 199
underfunding, programme 130, 164
unemployed 44, 45
United Kingdom 5; DFID 190
United States 5, 17n3, 66, 74, 104, 135, 140, 141, 173, 175; USAID 9, 17n3, 136, 144
urban population 45–6, 48, 112–13
Urrutia, M. 29, 111
Uruguay Round 192
USSR 109; former 3

Vaubel, R. 147

Venezuela 73
Vries, M.G. de 94
Vylder, S. de 139, 169

Wade, R. 149
wages 44, 46, 72, 73, 114
waivers 8, 28, 134, 136, 139, 141
Walters, Sir A. 17
Wasty, S.S. 10, 86, 88–9, 108, 118, 179, 184
Webb, S.B. 38
welfare 44, 45, 47, 50, 68, 85
White, H. 41
Williamson, J. 89, 154, 155, 169
withdrawal/withholding, of aid 81, 133, 147, 163, 164, 174, 175, 179
Wolfensohn, James 17n2
women 3, 148, 192
World Bank 1, 4–10 *passim*, 14, 17, 17n2, 18n4, 19, 92, 94–8, 103–5 *passim*, 120, 129, 130, 147–50 *passim*, 154–5, 166–7, 175–91 *passim*, 194; and adjustment 21–30, 34–42, 48–50, 61–7 *passim*, 79–80, 85, 88–9, 96, 104–5, 110–17, 120, 131, 134–5, 139–43, 145, 147, 156, 160–1, 168, 172, 179–87 *passim*, 193–4, SALs 2, 4, 7, 9, 52, 62–9 *passim*, 80, 130, 131, 134–6, 168, 172, SECALs 2, 62, 63, 66, 79, 80, 136; and IMF 120, 142, 143, 174; Operations Evaluation Department 39–40, 89; Performance Audit Report 135; Wapenhans Report 137, 148–9; *World Development Report* 186
World Development 90–1
World Trade Organization 192

Zaire 117, 169
Zambia 36, 37, 90, 98, 112–13, 117–19 *passim*, 130, 132, 136, 139, 146–7, 157, 169, 199
Zimbabwe 37
Zormelo, D. 94–6 *passim*

The 'water controversy' concerns one of the central c
that water is not an element but rather a compound. T D0153546
discovery was contentious in the 1780s and has occ.
century historians. The matter is tied up with the larger issues of the so-called
Chemical Revolution of the late eighteenth century. A case can be made for James
Watt or Henry Cavendish or Antoine Lavoisier as having priority in the discovery,
depending upon precisely what the discovery is taken to consist in; however,
neither the protagonists themselves in the 1780s nor modern historians qualify as
those most fervently interested in the affair. In fact, the controversy attracted most
attention in early Victorian Britain some fifty to seventy years after the actual work
of Watt, Cavendish and Lavoisier.

The central historical question to which the book addresses itself is why the
priority claims of long-dead natural philosophers so preoccupied a wide range of
people in the later period. The answer to the question lies in understanding the
enormous symbolic importance of James Watt and Henry Cavendish in nineteenth-
century science and society. More than credit for a particular discovery was at stake
here. When we examine the various agendas of the participants in the Victorian
phase of the water controversy we find it driven by filial loyalty and nationalism
but also, most importantly, by ideological struggles about the nature of science and
its relation to technological invention and innovation in British society.

At a more general, theoretical, level this study also provides important insights
into conceptions of the nature of discovery as they are debated by modern historians,
philosophers and sociologists of science.

About the Author

David Philip Miller is Senior Lecturer, School of History and Philosophy of
Science, University of New South Wales, Australia.

Science, Technology and Culture, 1700–1945

Series Editors

David M. Knight
University of Durham

and

Trevor H. Levere
University of Toronto

This new series focuses on the social, cultural, industrial and economic contexts of science and technology from the 'scientific revolution' up to the Second World War. Economic historians now cover the relations of science to technology and industrial application, while social and cultural historians have similarly recognized the realms of science and technology and, indeed, that these have helped to define culture and society. Through the agricultural and industrial revolutions of the eighteenth century, the coffee-house culture of the Enlightenment, the spread of museums, botanic gardens and expositions in the nineteenth century, to the Franco-Prussian War of 1870, seen as a victory for German science, this process has gathered momentum; while in the twentieth century the dependence of society, in both war and peace alike, on science and technology is evident. This series will provide an outlet for studies that address issues of the interaction of science, technology and culture in the period from 1700 to 1945, at the same time as including new research within the field of the history of science itself that embraces these perspectives.

Also in this series

Hewett Cottrell Watson:
Victorian Plant Ecologist and Evolutionist
Frank N. Egerton

Chemical Structure, Spatial Arrangement:
The Early History of Stereochemistry, 1874–1914
Peter J. Ramberg

British University Observatories, c. 1820–1939
Roger Hutchins

Phrenology and the Origins of Victorian Scientific Naturalism
John van Wyhe

Science, Technology and Culture, 1700–1945

DISCOVERING WATER

For Margaret

Discovering Water

James Watt, Henry Cavendish and the
Nineteenth-Century 'Water Controversy'

DAVID PHILIP MILLER
University of New South Wales, Australia

Routledge
Taylor & Francis Group

LONDON AND NEW YORK

First published 2004 by Ashgate Publishing

2 Park Square, Milton Park, Abingdon, Oxon OX14 4RN
711 Third Avenue, New York, NY 10017, USA

Routledge is an imprint of the Taylor & Francis Group, an informa business

First issued in paperback 2017

British Library Cataloguing in Publication Data
Miller, David Philip
   Discovering water: James Watt, Henry Cavendish and the
   nineteenth-century 'Water Controversy'. – (Science,
   Technology and culture, 1700–1945)
   1. Watt, James, 1736–1819–Contributions in the chemical
   analysis of water 2. Cavendish, Henry, 1731–1810–
   Contributions of the chemical analysis of water 3. Science–
   Philosophy–History–19th century 4. Discoveries in
   Science–Great Britain–History–18th century
   5. Discoveries in science–Great Britain–History–19th
   century 6. Water–Composition
   I. Title
   509.4'1'09034

US Library of Congress Cataloging-in-Publication Data
Miller, David Philip.
   Discovering water: James Watt, Henry Cavendish, and the nineteenth-century 'Water
   Controversy'/David Philip Miller.
      p. cm. – (Science, technology and culture, 1700–1945)
   Includes bibliographical references and index (alk. paper).
   1. Water–Composition. 2. Watt, James, 1736–1819. 3. Cavendish, Henry, 1731–1810.
   I. Title. II. Series.

QD142.M55 2003
546'22'09–dc21   2003056077

ISBN 978-0-7546-3177-4 (hbk)
ISBN 978-1-138-25845-7 (pbk)

Typeset by Manton Typesetters, Louth, Lincolnshire, UK

Contents

List of Figures and Tables   ix

Preface and Acknowledgements   xi

Abbreviations used in Footnotes   xiii

1   Introduction   1

2   The Nature of Discovery: The Attributional Model   11

3   The Beginnings of a Dispute and its Interpretation   27

4   Attributional Survey: Phase One, 1784–1830   59

5   Keeping Account: James Watt Jr and the Filial Project   83

6   The French Connection: Arago Re-opens the Controversy   105

7   Managing the Symbols of Victorian Science: 'Gentlemen of Science' and the Water Controversy   129

8   The Advocates of Watt: Brougham, Jeffrey and Muirhead   169

9   The Defence of Cavendish: Character, Precision and Discipline   193

10   The Controversy Joined, 1840–60   215

11   Still Waters: Attributional Survey, 1830–1900   253

12   Conclusions   279

Appendix: Attributional Survey Database   285

Bibliography   289

Index   307

List of Figures and Tables

Figures

5.1 James Watt Jr. Portrait by L. de Longastre.   87
      Reproduced by permission of Julian Gibson-Watt. Reprinted by
      permission of Oxford University Press from Henry W. Dickinson
      and Rhys Jenkins, *James Watt and the Steam Engine*, Oxford, The
      Clarendon Press, 1927
6.1 François Arago. Lithograph by Delpach.   108
      Reproduced by permission of Trinity College Cambridge
7.1 The Reverend William Vernon Harcourt. Plaster Bust by Matthew
      Noble.   130
      National Portrait Gallery, London
7.2 The Reverend William Whewell. Lithograph by Eddis.   146
      Reproduced by permission of Trinity College Cambridge
7.3 Dr David Brewster.   165
      Photograph reproduced by permission of Special Collections,
      Edinburgh University Library
8.1 Henry, Lord Brougham. Portrait by S. Gambardella.   171
      Reproduced by permission of the Treasurer and Masters of the Bench
      of Lincoln's Inn
9.1 Professor George Wilson.   207
      Photograph reproduced by permission of Special Collections,
      Edinburgh University Library
11.1 Attributions of the discovery of the composition of water in a sample
      of chemistry textbooks, 1840–99   273

Table

11.1 Comparison of articles in editions of *Chambers's Encyclopaedia*   263

Preface and Acknowledgements

It must have been about 1963 that I blew myself up trying to make water. Being a nerd just as it was ceasing to be fashionable, I'd persuaded my father to buy me not just a chemistry set but a batch of high-class chemical apparatus from the local 'swap shop'. I'd read about hydrogen and how it burned in air with a blue flame to produce water. Synthesizing water appealed to me and I duly produced hydrogen, using zinc and sulphuric acid, in a small flask with a beautiful, delicate spout. After what I took to be a suitable interval to make sure that all air had been driven from the flask so that it was full of hydrogen, I struck a match and lit the emerging gas … The fact that I survived the explosion was quite remarkable, as the apparatus distributed itself to all corners of the room without any of it connecting with me. My schoolmasters subsequently advised that I should be a chemist. Fortunately I didn't listen to them and now, many years later, I find myself wrestling again with the composition of water but from a safe, historical point of view.

I was embarked all those years ago on a childhood journey of discovery, but I knew that I was not the discoverer. My chemistry books told me that. I had acquired a small library of the kind of texts you could find on the bottom shelf in second-hand book stores, some of which I still have, books by people with quaint-sounding names like Holmyard and Lowry. One of these was Lowry's *Historical Introduction to Chemistry* in the 1926 reprint. This, like many books of its genre and period, told me in no uncertain terms that 'Cavendish (1781) prepares water by burning inflammable air with common air'.[1] I, like generations of schoolchildren, grew up knowing that this discovery belonged to, the mysteriously 'Honourable', Henry Cavendish.

We will see in these pages that the schoolchildren of the twentieth century were the recipients of a sanitized story about the discovery of the composition of water. It was a surprise to me later to learn that there had been a controversy about that question and that another childhood acquaintance from a different field, the 'engineer' James Watt, at one stage was championed as the discoverer. The closure of the water controversy was a complex, protracted business. One could argue, in fact, that it is still not entirely closed at least so far as historians are concerned. I hope in this book to throw some light on why kids like me learned what we did about the composition of water. I hope also to throw some light on the nature of scientific discovery and on Victorian scientific culture.

I owe debts to many people who have helped me in the eighteen months or so during which this book has been researched and written. The hard work of my

---

[1] T.M. Lowry, *Historical Introduction to Chemistry* 1926, p. 113. The first edition was 1915.

colleagues in the School of History and Philosophy of Science made it possible for me to be away on leave for a whole year once the kindness of the university itself had granted me that leave and supported it financially. Miranda Chan of the School provided indispensable help in making it all happen. During time spent researching in the UK I was privileged to hold a Visiting Research Fellowship at the Institute for Advanced Studies in the Humanities at the University of Edinburgh. At the Institute, the Director, Professor John Frow, and Mrs Anthea Taylor helped to make my stay a most pleasant and productive one. During my time in Sydney the Unit for History and Philosophy of Science at Sydney University kindly hosted me as a Visiting Fellow. At another stage, the Science Studies Unit at the University of Edinburgh made me welcome, for which I am most thankful. David and Celia Bloor, Ivan Crozier, Patricia Fara, Jim Endersby, Malcolm Nicolson and Rona Ferguson, Jeffrey Sturchio and Carole Tansley were generous in making an itinerant researcher feel at home, as, in a rather different way, were my parents Albert and Dorothy, my sister Shirley and the boys, Albert and Eleanor Emmett, and the Hughes family. Seminars at the universities of Aberdeen, Cambridge and Sydney helped me to hone my ideas, as did colleagues in Taiwan during a visit to their National Conference in the History of Science. Thanks to Professor Fu Daiwie for that opportunity.

A historian inevitably makes himself a serial pest in any number of libraries. I owe particular thanks to Peter Asplin and colleagues in Special Collections at the University of Glasgow Library, to Sheila Noble and all the other staff in Special Collections, the University of Edinburgh Library, to Norman Reid at the University of St Andrews Library, to staff at the National Library of Scotland who aided and abetted my study of a bewildering battery of chemistry texts and much else besides, and to staff at the British Library. Joanna Best and others at the Wren Library, Trinity College Cambridge were most helpful, as were staff at the Royal College of Surgeons (Edinburgh) and, not least, in the Interlibrary Loans Section of the Library of the University of New South Wales.

For permission to quote from material in their care, I am grateful to: Birmingham City Archives; Cambridge University Library; Special Collections, Glasgow University Library; Special Collections, Edinburgh University Library; St Andrews University Library; University College London Library; Trinity College Cambridge, the British Library, and the National Library of Scotland.

Apart from my general debt to the scholars whose work I have used, I owe particular scholarly and personal debts to Jack Morrell, John Schuster, David Oldroyd, Rod Home, Simon Schaffer and Richard Yeo. Thank you, gentlemen. Friends in the water at Bondi, Cranbrook and the Des Renford Aquatic Centre helped to keep me fresh and, reasonably, fit. Having the blowtorch of Australian scepticism applied to the belly of a project like this one is a sobering experience! It has made me, as my Bondi mates would say, 'as dry as a Pommie's towel'. Finally, special thanks to my wife Margaret for her constant, loving, help and support, in this as in all else. Our children, Kylie and Tom, have shown a suitably vague but cheerful interest in my obsession while providing me with many other reasons, in the water and out, for being proud of them.

Sydney
New South Wales
April 2003

Abbreviations used in Footnotes

Watt Papers	Boulton and Watt Collection and Muirhead Collection, Birmingham Central Library
Watt Papers (Doldowlod)	The Papers of James Watt and his Family (formerly held at Doldowlod House), Birmingham Central Library
Muirhead Papers	James Patrick Muirhead Papers, Special Collections, Glasgow University Library
Brougham Papers	Papers of Henry Brougham, Lord Brougham and Vaux, University College London Library
Whewell Papers	Papers of the Reverend William Whewell, Trinity College Library, Cambridge
Forbes Papers	Papers of James David Forbes, University of St Andrews Library

Chapter 1

Introduction

Initial Orientations

Being first in science is important, as it is in geographical discovery. Entering virgin territory geographically or conceptually is a privilege that few of us will experience. 'Proudly to have thought where none have thought before' might be the scientist's Star Trek experience. However, merely thinking and discovering are a world apart, as we shall see. Discovery is a social as well as an intellectual process. It is, we will argue, a property ascribed to certain intellectual, and practical, processes rather than inherent in them.

This book concerns discovering water, specifically discovering that water is not an element, as had been thought from ancient Greek times until the eighteenth century, but rather a compound. To be able to claim that momentous discovery would be a precious thing. It is perhaps understandable that there was a contest, a priority dispute. What is surprising is how long that dispute lasted and the variety of people drawn into the lists. The contest endured for at least seventy years, from the 1780s into the 1850s. Those in the running to be credited with the discovery were the dour Scottish engineer and improver of the steam engine, James Watt, the aristocratic and eccentric natural philosopher, Henry Cavendish, and the French chemist, tax farmer and victim of the revolutionary guillotine, Antoine Laurent Lavoisier. They took relatively little part in open priority dispute themselves. It was in the 1830s through to the 1850s, when the original protagonists were long dead, that the 'water controversy', or the 'water question' as it was often called, reached its highest intensity. I am interested to understand why this was so.

It will be useful to establish some basic features of the controversy's chronology and *dramatis personae*. The water question reached its peak in the aftermath of the 1839 meeting of the British Association for the Advancement of Science in Birmingham. That meeting was a small one because it was held amidst Chartist agitation. Those who attended were deliberately marking the relationship between science and industrialization. The Association had met since its founding in 1831 in major academic venues, regional centres and commercial ports, but this was a highly symbolic meeting in a primarily manufacturing town. The President-elect of the Association at Birmingham was the Reverend William Vernon Harcourt, the Oxford-educated son of the Archbishop of York. Harcourt had been one of the founders of the Association in 1831 at its first, York, meeting.

On the evening of Monday, 26 August 1839, Harcourt delivered a discourse to the Association's General Meeting in Birmingham Town Hall. Touching on a variety of topics, Harcourt addressed himself to the water question. Specifically, he took issue with claims published by the Perpetual Secretary of the French Académie des Sciences, François Arago, shortly before, in his long-delayed *Eloge de James*

1

Watt. Arago, aided in production of the *Eloge* by Watt's son, James Watt Jr, and by the prominent lawyer and politician, Henry, Lord Brougham, had made strong claims that Harcourt took issue with.[1] Arago claimed priority in the discovery of the compound nature of water for James Watt. Even more contentiously, he claimed to show, with the aid of Brougham's investigations, that the other British claimant to the honour, Henry Cavendish, had taken Watt's ideas as his own. Harcourt defended Cavendish's claim to priority and rebuked those who cast aspersions on his honesty. Although Harcourt tried to give due recognition to Watt's steam-engine improvements, the reception of his 'Address' was mixed. Many were aghast that Harcourt should take this occasion to launch what they construed as an attack upon a local hero who symbolized for many that union of science and industrial development that the Birmingham meeting was supposed to celebrate.

The 1840s saw a spate of publications on the water question as Harcourt and his supporters among the 'Gentlemen of Science' of the Association squared off against Arago, Brougham, James Watt Jr and Watt's relative and recruit as family historian, James Patrick Muirhead. Pamphlets and books became the occasion for long essays in the various reviews through which so much intellectual debate in early Victorian Britain took place. In 1851, a Scottish chemical lecturer, Dr George Wilson, published his *Life of the Honourable Henry Cavendish*. A peculiar biography, this work was largely devoted to a thorough dissection of the water question and the literature that it had generated up to that point. In the following decades an orthodoxy emerged that gave the palm to Cavendish.

A similar sort of orthodoxy had emerged in the period between the 1780s and the publication of Arago's *Eloge*. The dispute between the protagonists themselves had been brief and mild compared with what was to come later. The term 'water controversy' was not employed in the 1780s, but the question of the discovery of the composition of water was of great moment. Many people perceived it as a key event in the battle between the supporters and opponents of the chemistry of phlogiston. Precisely what happened during the combustion of inflammable air was in dispute. The answer that was eventually accepted and became part of the new system and language of chemistry associated with the name of Lavoisier, was, of course, that 'hydrogen' burned with 'oxygen' to produce water as a compound of those two gases. Lavoisier's claim to the discovery was challenged, especially in Britain by supporters of Cavendish. Watt, too, was sometimes given credit for having important ideas on the subject. On the whole, however, by the 1790s Cavendish was regarded as the discoverer, in Britain at least.

Returning to the rationale for this study, it might be considered that the second phase of the water controversy is a peculiar topic for book-length examination. Even the first phase has not received substantial modern treatment, being very briefly dealt with, for example, in Jan Golinski's excellent study of the public culture of chemistry during the relevant period.[2] This itself is perhaps an indication that historians have thought the water question to be somehow unworthy of treatment, as a 'storm in a teacup'.

---

[1] Throughout, 'Watt' refers to the famous engineer, 'Watt Jr' to his son James.

[2] Jan Golinski, *Science as Public Culture. Chemistry and Enlightenment in Britain, 1760–1820*, 1992, pp. 133–37.

The fact that Watt and Cavendish themselves remained rather cool about the issue, at least in public, means that the second phase of the controversy is easily seen as a minor imbroglio driven by Watt Jr's filial concerns, Scottish nationalism, and Arago's and Brougham's political agendas. This perspective is doubly attractive if one is convinced, as most modern historians appear to be, of the solidity of Cavendish's claim and the tenuousness of Watt's. The recent biographers of Cavendish, Jungnickel and McCormmach, were wary of the controversy because in their view (which has much going for it) the historical picture of Cavendish has been severely distorted by the undue attention given to the water controversy.[3] Although Wilson's biography vindicated Cavendish's claim, it neglected to develop many other aspects of his life and in some ways painted a rather jaundiced picture of the man. Having discussed the first phase of the controversy, Jungnickel and McCormmach offer the following observation:

> A second water controversy arose long after the participants in the first were dead. It was prompted by the Secretary of the French Academy D.F.J. Arago, who in his *éloge* of Watt asserted that Priestley was the first person to prove that air could be converted into water and that Watt was the first person to understand it. The consequent furor initiated by Harcourt's presidential address at the British Association meeting in 1839 was sustained by a passion of another kind, nationalism. Since the revived controversy was the occasion for Cavendish's unpublished scientific work to begin to be made public, it had that value if perhaps no other.[4]

Clearly, in writing this book I am asserting that, on the contrary, the water controversy is a worthy and a useful topic. I am also arguing that there was much more driving it than competing nationalisms pitching the Scot versus the Englishman. At the simplest level, the sheer 'air time' that the controversy received, especially in its second, Victorian, phase, makes it worthy of study. We need to be curious about what our forebears found important about this issue, however trite it may seem to us now. More technically, study of the water controversy usefully documents an example of a long-delayed priority dispute. Robert Merton argued many years ago that priority disputes in science are a vital element in understanding the nature of science and of the scientific community. Priority disputes were particularly revealing, Merton suggested, when they were conducted not by the immediate claimants to priority but by others who, apparently, had little to gain personally from the settlement of the controversy. Merton's contention was that such priority disputes are important because they reveal the normative structure of science and how it drives the scientific community.[5]

I share Merton's view that such episodes are revealing, but my account of why they are so differs markedly from his. My account is based in a philosophy and

---

[3] Christa Jungnickel and Russell McCormmach, *Cavendish. The Experimental Life*, 1999, pp. 10–14. Although I disagree with the authors on the importance and character of the second phase of the water controversy, I have benefited enormously from their work.

[4] Ibid., p. 380.

[5] See Robert K. Merton, *The Sociology of Science. Theoretical and Empirical Investigations*, 1973, pp. 291–93. Merton, though finding the water controversy important and revealing, nevertheless described it as 'the most tedious and sectarian' on the calendar of eighteenth-century disputes! (p. 288).

sociology of science that rejects the kind of universal normative explanation of scientific action that animates Merton's scheme and gives his approach much in common as an explanatory strategy with universalist philosophies of science. The water controversy is not in my view a secure basis for discerning how scientific communities in general operate. It can be used, as I use it, to support what is called a 'finitist' account of scientific practice and to illustrate a specific view of scientific discovery.[6]

Far from being merely an object lesson in the pernicious influence of nationalism in science, the controversy is a window onto the cultural politics of early Victorian science. The fact that the controversy loomed large for many members of the early Victorian scientific community, the way that they divided up on it, and how they argued their cases are all indicative of deep currents and major emergent structures in early Victorian culture. These features of the controversy feed into larger debates about the nature of science, about the relationship between science and technology and economic transformation, about the appropriate organization of scientific activity, and so on. This is why, in my view, the water controversy is worth studying.

James Watt (1736–1819) and Henry Cavendish (1731–1810) were iconic figures in Victorian culture.[7] Though their significances were many and varied, as a first approximation Watt represented a close liaison between science and technology, one, moreover, unmediated by a university-trained scientific élite. Watt's accomplishments demonstrated that it was possible for the intelligent autodidact to rise to great things, including, perhaps, philosophical insight and scientific discovery. Men such as Watt combined science and action to promote industrial development. Many members of the industrial middle class regarded them as scientific heroes to be revered and emulated.

On the other hand, the emergent, university-trained, and increasingly specialized scientific élite considered too much popular adulation for Watt as 'philosopher' or 'scientist' to be dangerous. As that élite sought to negotiate their relationship with governments and wider publics, they were cautious about portraying too close a link between science and practical utility. They needed support for sustained trains of research aimed primarily at understanding the natural world. Only if such support was forthcoming would the real benefits of utility eventually flow, they argued. This was an argument on the basis of 'ultimate utility' but also on civilizational grounds. For the scientific élite Cavendish was a more apposite icon

---

[6] The single best critique of Merton along these lines is Michael Mulkay, 'Interpretation and the use of rules: The case of the norms of science', *Transactions of the New York Academy of Sciences*, Series 2, **9**, 1980, 111–25. On 'finitism' see Barry Barnes, David Bloor and John Henry, *Scientific Knowledge. A Sociological Analysis*, 1996, pp. 54–80.

[7] There is an enormous literature on James Watt, but the interested reader might usefully enter it via two recent publications: the first volume of a major new biography, Richard L. Hills, *James Watt. Volume 1: His Time in Scotland, 1736–1774*, 2002, and a delightful introductory essay by Ben Marsden, *Watt's Perfect Engine. Steam and the Age of Invention*, 2002, which is reliable and has an excellent section on Watt's reputation and iconic status. Christine MacLeod is undertaking an important study of Watt's nineteenth-century reputation, especially among the industrial classes, as part of her book in progress entitled *Heroes of Invention: Celebrating the industrial culture of nineteenth-century Britain*.

than Watt. Cavendish represented in their estimation a person who pursued a methodical, cautious, sustained train of research. This research was of the highest quality and driven by curiosity alone. The highest standard was reached precisely because the research was pursued in this manner. Ultimately, much rested upon the outcome of the contest between these competing icons and ideologies: relations between science and government; the organization and hierarchy of science education; and the organization of scientific institutions. In this sense, as a historian, to enter the water controversy and merely seek to arbitrate it is in my view to miss the point.

A key feature of this book is that I do not seek to resolve the water controversy. In terms of modern controversy studies I seek a 'symmetrical' approach. I aim to understand and explain the stances taken and arguments involved, not judging their relative value. Given that the modern scientific, and historical, consensus is that Cavendish discovered the compound nature of water, many readers will find a symmetrical approach disturbing. This is because when credit has already been distributed, to pursue a symmetrical approach is automatically to challenge the *status quo*.[8] I give the case of Watt and his supporters more credit than most people would consider they deserve. I do this not by explicitly siding with the Watt camp but just by taking them seriously. This approach, however, offers advantages to historical understanding.

Suppose that my stance were more of a 'realist' one – that there were a *correct* answer to the question 'Who discovered the composition of water?' Suppose that I then set out to ascertain that correct answer through historical research devoted entirely to the actions of the original protagonists in the 1780s. Where would this place me in relation to the Victorian water controversy? I would end up throwing my weight on one side of the balance, the side that was right (or most right) in my view. Their understanding, in so far as it coincided with mine, would require no further explanation. They would have simply got the history right. My task in that situation would be to explain why those who got the history 'wrong' were diverted from the truth. The problem with this, of course, is that my historical research into what happened in the 1780s cannot stand outside the controversy itself. I will bring philosophical conceptions to the task that will align me in the controversy. In particular, I will have to bring to the task conceptions of what it means to discover something. If my conceptions coincide, let us say, with those maintained by the supporters of Cavendish, then it is not surprising that I end up sharing their view of the identity of the discoverer. My task, then, is not only to describe the competing discovery accounts offered by the supporters of Watt and Cavendish, but also to bring out the underlying, competing, criteria of what constitutes discovery. This allows me to build plausible connections between substantive positions taken in the priority dispute, different stipulations about what the criteria of discovery should be, and the interests that sustained them. In this way the nature, course and

---

[8] For the original statement of the principle of symmetry see David Bloor, *Knowledge and Social Imagery*, 1976. A relevant exchange on symmetry, neutrality and capture of the analyst occurs in Pam Scott et al., 'Captives of controversy: The myth of the neutral social researcher in contemporary scientific controversies', *Science, Technology & Human Values*, **15**, 1990, 474–94, the response by Harry Collins, idem, **16**, 1991, 249–51 and the rejoinder, idem, **16**, 1991, 252–55.

significance of the water controversy in early Victorian scientific culture can be better understood. This understanding does not depend on resolving the original controversy and, I argue, is best served by not attempting such a resolution.

The Structure of the Story

The theoretical stances that inform my approach are delineated in Chapter 2 and are based in the sociology of scientific knowledge (SSK). Underlying the work of the 'Edinburgh School' in SSK and of my own approach is a 'finitist' account of knowledge and meaning. This is a quite general account applicable to the terms of scientific discourse, including such concepts as 'scientific discovery'. Finitism radically contextualizes those terms. When applied to the notion of 'discovery', finitism leads us to an 'attributional' model of the process. This model was admirably developed by Augustine Brannigan many years ago in a way that has yet to be significantly improved upon. Work from within the Edinburgh School, notably by Barry Barnes, made clear the links between finitism and the attributional model.[9] This chapter also describes the rhetorical analysis of discovery accounts, which, according to some, should supplant SSK-based accounts. I argue that, on the contrary, these rhetorical approaches are a useful supplement to the attributional model based in finitism, not a viable substitute for it, at least if our aim is historical explanation. Although in some senses distracting from the historical narrative, much of which can be read without serious concern for these deeper philosophical questions, Chapter 2 underpins both the general approach taken and the detailed historiography pursued.

One consequence of my SSK-based approach is that Chapter 3, dealing with the period in the 1780s when the original scientific, or natural philosophical, work was done, has self-imposed limitations. For reasons already given, this chapter cannot be, and does not attempt to be, an account of who *really* discovered the composition of water. The aim is rather to survey those 'happenings' that became the subject of controversy. Maintaining neutrality in doing this is a strain. For I can no more excise myself from existing cultures of interpretation than could the historical actors whom I study. I can, however, highlight pivotal points about which the Victorian water controversy was to turn. Apart from telling the 'story of water' in the 1780s in this way, this chapter also surveys the historiography of the Chemical Revolution, the part played in it by the discovery of the composition of water and seeks to contextualize the chemical investigations of Watt and Cavendish.

Chapter 4 provides the first of two 'attributional surveys'. Finitism leads us to the view that meaning is a matter of usage. So too is the attribution of discovery. The attributions made by protagonists in the controversy are really only the tip of an iceberg. The rest of the iceberg is composed of a myriad of attributions made during the course of everyday activities and other exchanges. The water controversy, the nature of water, the work of Watt, Cavendish and Lavoisier are all topics that were (and are) dealt with in various types of surviving literature. Among the least

---

[9] See Augustine Brannigan, *The Social Basis of Scientific Discoveries*, 1981 and Barry Barnes, *T.S. Kuhn and Social Science*, 1982, pp. 41–45, 94–101.

diffuse of these, and therefore reasonably accessible, are accounts that appeared in encyclopaedias, dictionaries and textbooks. These reached a far wider audience than the documents of explicit controversy. They were also, of necessity, constrained to be brief and to distil the outcomes of more complex accounts.[10] Any act designed to change meaning, and to change minds, faces the constraints of prior structured belief. Chapter 4 is an attempt to characterize the prior structured belief that was faced by those in the Watt camp who sought to re-open the 'water controversy' in the 1830s.

Most prominent within that camp was the great engineer's son, James Watt Jr. Chapter 5 is the first of the central sequence of chapters (Chapters 5–9) analysing the involvement of various individuals and groups in the controversy and it deals with the younger Watt. Some have considered that the Victorian water controversy requires little explanation other than the impetus given to it by filial piety. It is certainly true that the controversy was kicked along by what I call the 'filial project', with its various textual, monumental and other commemorations of Watt. I examine Watt Jr's own life and preoccupations. Watt Jr was certainly very jealous of his father's reputation and he sought to propagate a particular image of his father. Watt Jr's approach to the water controversy was shaped by his intensely empirical mindset that was reflected in his accounting practices within business. Keeping account, for Watt Jr, whether in matters of business or reputation, was an enduring feature of Enlightenment rationalism. We will see that his approach to discovery is assimilable to one of the major stances identified in Chapter 2, and yet the origins of that approach in his case were clearly culturally specific. Although Watt Jr's push was primarily filial, he did have views about scientific and business development and so participated in the wider ideological uses that the industrial middle class made of his father's reputation.

Watt Jr's written contributions to the water controversy were not substantial. However, he was constantly behind the scenes of others' efforts. This was so in the case of François Arago, whose key role in the controversy is the focus of Chapter 6. A later Secretary of the Académie des Sciences, Berthelot, was to take a nationalistic line in the late nineteenth century in reclaiming the discovery of the composition of water for Lavoisier.[11] Arago's nationalism did not take that form. He relegated Lavoisier to the background, as did most participants in the Victorian water controversy, and considered the rival claims of Watt and Cavendish. Though heavily prompted by both Watt Jr and Lord Brougham, Arago had his own reasons for wishing to laud Watt and to cast his vote against Cavendish. I argue that these reasons had to do with Arago's radical political stance regarding both French industrial development and the conduct of the Académie des Sciences. Arago found the example of Watt useful in arguing for closer linkages between the science of the Académie and technology for industrial and commercial development. Also, Cavendish's sometimes non-communicative behaviour and his reputation as a strangely aloof character did not endear him to Arago, who was engaged in a

---

[10] In the terms developed by Latour and Woolgar, such accounts are obliged to drop modalities and to become more 'fact-like'. See Latour and Woolgar, *Laboratory Life: The Social Construction of Scientific Facts*, 1979, pp. 75–86.

[11] M. Berthelot, *La Révolution Chimique, Lavoisier*, 1902 (first edition 1890), pp. 109–33.

campaign to open the communications of the Académie to greater public scrutiny. So we see once again the varied interests behind attempts to revive the claims of Watt. Arago's scientific credibility was most important to the Watt cause.

Science in Britain was undergoing a major organizational and leadership transformation in the 1830s as Arago prepared, delivered and published his *Eloge de James Watt*. Whilst the reform movement in the Royal Society of London had formally failed when John Herschel was defeated for the Presidency by the Duke of Sussex in November 1830, in practice a new leadership was emerging. This leadership transcended the old, paternalistic and aristocratic structures of the 'Banksian Learned Empire'. A key development was the founding of the British Association for the Advancement of Science (BAAS) in 1831. Although initially the product of a provincial thrust, the BAAS was rapidly suborned by a university and metropolitan élite, Morrell and Thackray's 'Gentlemen of Science'.[12] These developments provide the crucial context for the phase of the water controversy recounted in Chapter 7. This phase turns on Harcourt's 'Address' to the 1839 Meeting of the Association in Birmingham.

Harcourt's 'Address' is interesting not only for its explicit contribution to the controversy but also for the kind of argument that is made in it. In its published version, at least, this 'Address' took the sophistication of the discussion of discovery to a new level. The defence of Cavendish's claim is mounted via the other main vehicle discussed in Chapter 2, a heuristic argument that involves inferring Cavendish's claim to the discovery from a close examination of the train of research in which he was involved. This was the approach to be taken by most of those involved with the leadership of the Association.

Not all the prominent scientists in Britain, however, were entirely enthusiastic about the BAAS and its conduct. John Herschel was rather lukewarm about it. Charles Babbage and David Brewster were at times openly hostile. A key target of this hostility was William Whewell. We see in Chapter 7 that Whewell was very much behind the scenes as Harcourt developed his arguments. The water question had entered an ideological maelstrom of competing ideas about the nature of science, how it should be supported, conducted and organized, and how it should relate to the industrial arts, or as we would say, 'technology'. Whewell was at the centre of this debate, as was his chief critic David Brewster. Brewster's involvement in the water question is also a primary concern of this chapter.

In Chapter 8 we return to the Watt camp and examine the 'advocates of Watt' – Henry Brougham, Francis Jeffrey and James Patrick Muirhead. These gentlemen, Scottish lawyers all, took the Watt camp's fight into the 1840s and beyond, as Watt Jr's health began to fail before his death in 1848. Brougham had long been involved with the making of Watt's reputation. This chimed in well with his efforts to promote Mechanics' Institutes, adult education and 'Useful Knowledge'. In the 1830s and 1840s the former Lord Chancellor was something of a loose cannon in scientific affairs as well as in politics. We trace his relations with the emergent scientific élite as another stimulus to Brougham's heterodox views. Brougham's old friend, co-founder of the *Edinburgh Review* and fellow judge, Francis Jeffrey

---

[12] Jack Morrell and Arnold Thackray, *Gentlemen of Science: Early Years of the British Association for the Advancement of Science*, 1981.

had long remained very much on the periphery of the water question, even though he had been as proud a custodian as any of James Watt's reputation. Jeffrey was drawn into the water question via the affairs of the *Edinburgh Review* and ended up writing one of the most detailed pro-Watt articles for that *Review* in 1848. We will see that Jeffrey and Brougham together pursued an empirical account of discovery, strongly reminiscent of legal pleading in its reliance on the evidence of circumstance. Muirhead completes the trio of lawyers. As the person anointed by Watt Jr to pursue family history and the fight for his father's reputation, Muirhead devoted considerable time and effort to the publication of Watt's *Correspondence* on the water question. His arguments are analysed also for their strategies. The way in which the advocates of Watt cast their arguments was intended to make the water question analogous to a legal issue and not a scientific one. As outsiders to the emergent scientific community, it was clear to them, as to others, that if the issue were fought on scientific terms, then their credibility would be hard to sustain.

We then turn to those who carried forward the Cavendish cause. The character of Cavendish – what our controversialists called the personal and the scientific character of the man – was a potent ideological resource. We examine the general ideological importance of Cavendish to the 'Gentlemen of Science' of the British Association. Cavendish was in many ways a 'live' force in the science of the 1840s, especially with regard to his reputation for precision. This was a value at a premium in early Victorian scientific culture. For the first time in the 1840s it becomes possible to speak of an organized discipline of chemistry. However, chemistry was regarded by many as only just emerging into full scientific status. Identification with the scientific style of Cavendish was useful to the chemists in the quest to gain, and retain, that status. Certainly from this number emerged the most important chemical writer on the water question, Dr George Wilson. We examine Wilson's involvement in the controversy and his arguments (in *The Life of the Honourable Henry Cavendish*) for awarding the discovery to Cavendish. Like Harcourt, Wilson pursued elaborate hermeneutic arguments often involving complex chemical knowledge.

Having laid out the argumentative strategies and the driving interests of the various individuals and groups involved in the controversy, Chapter 10 shifts into a diachronic account of the interactions involved in the controversy during the key decades of the 1840s and 1850s. The focus here is upon evolving mutual perceptions and changing stances.

By the 1850s, the controversy had reached a turning point. It was clear that the efforts on behalf of Watt had largely failed among scientific specialists. The 'closure' of the dispute, however, though dependent primarily on such expert opinion, was ultimately an attributional matter. In the final substantive chapter before the conclusion, I present a second attributional survey, looking once again at the way in which Watt, Cavendish and the water question were dealt with in encyclopaedias and textbooks, this time in the mid- to late nineteenth century. The 'knowledge' that Cavendish was the discoverer of the composition of water was established among scientists, students and the wider reading public through these processes. The threads are pulled together and conclusions are drawn in the final chapter. By this time, it is hoped, the water question's importance to early Victorian scientific culture will be apparent and a fillip will have been given to attributional approaches to the understanding of scientific discovery.

Chapter 2

The Nature of Discovery: The Attributional Model

The making of discoveries is what science is all about, the stuff of the scientific career and of scientific reputation. Stories about science told at every level, from the most austere philosophical accounts to the heroic tales recounted in the recent 'Sobel Effect' literature, turn around the notion of scientific discovery.[1] The aim of this chapter is to discuss various understandings of scientific discovery and the approach to be taken in this book.

Discoveries as Found Objects or as Ideas Successfully Passing Philosophical Tests

Virtually all accounts of scientific discovery (and of discovery in general) treat it as a process of revelation. We discover 'things', and those things, whether objects or processes, are taken to subsist in nature independently of our knowledge of them. Discoveries are, I suggest, usually conceptualized as objects in a landscape. The landscape pre-exists and human scientific activity either enables us to uncover (literally *dis*cover) objects in that landscape or it does not. Treating discoveries as found objects is, of course, to adopt an essentially realist view of the relationship between the meanings of science and the external world. In so far as realist epistemologies are qualified or dropped, then rationalist views usually take over. Correspondence notions of truth, of the match between scientific discovery and found objects, tend to be abandoned in favour of more tenuous notions of coherence. On this view, the landscape of possible discoveries does not directly determine our uncovering of them, but it does still constrain decisively what we can say about nature and in that sense limits the discoveries that are available to be made.

Philosophical approaches to discovery have divided on the question of the existence of a 'logic of scientific discovery'. Inductivist philosophies have generally been happy to treat their versions of scientific method as providing such a logic. Modern approaches that claim to achieve machine-based discovery are the most radical versions of inductivism in this connection. The family of hypotheticalist philosophies, such as falsificationism, are built upon a distinction between a 'context of discovery' and a 'context of justification'. Despite his talk of 'the logic' of

---

[1] See Thomas Nickles, 'Discovery', in R. Olby et al. (eds), *Companion to the History of Modern Science*, 1990, pp. 148–65 and David Philip Miller, 'The Sobel effect', *Metascience*, 11, 2002, 185–200.

scientific discovery, Karl Popper remained adamant that the processes of discovery, in the sense of the psychological processes enacted by the discoverer, are inaccessible to logical inquiry and essentially ineffable. This logical inaccessibility of the processes producing discoveries does not signify much, in Popper's scheme, because until the ideas thrown up by scientists have negotiated the context of justification they cannot be dignified with the title 'discovery' anyway. For Popper, then, to have made a discovery is to have propounded a theory that has survived attempted falsification at some level. As Popper himself put it, in this way we may discover who has made a discovery.[2] Hypotheticalism, then, rejects the idea of a logic of discovery, leaving the process whereby theories are arrived at as the province of the 'irrational', that is, the psychological, sociological or historical. Such philosophies do, however, typically provide criteria of 'scientificity' which a new theory, or idea, or experimental finding has to meet in order that it be recognized as a 'discovery'.

We can usefully tag this set of approaches in their entirety as philosophical models of scientific discovery. There are as many of these models as there are candidate philosophies of science. These models represent a significant departure from the found objects view of discovery although those who adhere to such philosophical models usually, and reasonably, adopt realist language about discoveries in situations where the philosophical filter is considered to have done its work effectively. Proponents of philosophical models do vary, however, in the degree to which they insist upon a *logical* account of discovery. Covering law-style accounts of scientific explanation or even just 'good reasons' for holding scientific beliefs provide alternative philosophical stances. Much historical work on scientific discovery from within 'internalist' traditions in the history of science has been conducted on the basis of these looser constructions of the philosophical basis of sound science. Nevertheless that historical work does retain a philosophical criterion of 'scientificity' as part of its own structure.

Discoveries as Sociological Process: The Attributional Model

However they may vary, philosophical models of discovery rely for their credibility upon the perceived strength of the philosophical account of scientificity upon which they are based. In rejecting the possibility of scientific method, or at the least radically contextualizing it, the sociology of scientific knowledge has therefore provided a rather different, and sometimes quite contrary, set of conceptions of scientific discovery and what it means to study it historically.

Thomas Kuhn heralded the appearance of *The Structure of Scientific Revolutions* with a famous article on discovery in which he argued that there are two classes of discovery.[3] One class is predictable and relatively easy to specify in terms of who did what, when and where. The other class he regards as impossible to specify in those terms. The two types of discovery occur respectively, of course, in what Kuhn was to call 'normal science' and 'revolutionary science'. The consequences of Kuhn's analysis of scientific process for ideas about discovery depend ultimately

---

[2] Karl Popper, *The Logic of Scientific Discovery*, 1959, p. 31.

[3] T.S. Kuhn, 'Historical structure of scientific discovery', *Science*, **136**, 1962, 760–64.

upon the interpretation of Kuhn that is adopted. A very influential interpretation is that which takes the seeds of conventionalism in Kuhn and drives them towards a full-blown constructivism so far as scientific knowledge, and the terms used to describe that knowledge (including 'discovery'), are concerned. Two key authors in this process have been Augustine Brannigan and Barry Barnes, who have developed the attributional model of scientific discovery.

Barnes arrives at the attributional model of discovery as a particular outcome of the general philosophy of 'finitism' which he sees Kuhn as having pioneered in relation to science. The problem with Kuhn, however, was that, having perceived the non-viability of a rule-governed account of science during major intellectual transformations (paradigm shifts), he retained such an account in normal science. Whereas some scholars sought to repair Kuhn's irrationalism by painting his revolutionary science as normal, others sought to enshrine his constructivism by painting his normal science as revolutionary. This is what Barnes does by placing finitism at the centre of *all* scientific activity. Finitism is an understanding of concepts and concept application and use that derives ultimately from Wittgensteinian ideas about meaning and rules. It is a quite general set of propositions that applies to all concepts, be they everyday, scientific or metascientific ones such as 'experiment', 'discovery' and so on. The easiest way to depict finitism is by reference to its opposite, 'extensional semantics'. According to 'extensional semantics' concepts have predefined extension: all things in the universe are either 'A' or 'not A'. The concept A has a predetermined set of things in it. We may have identified some of them correctly, but not others. Any new instance is placed into the appropriate category according to a determinative set of rules. Philosophical models of discovery essentially provide a set of putative rules according to which instances of scientific activity can be securely identified as obeying or not obeying those rules, and therefore as 'discoveries' or 'not discoveries'.[4]

Finitism treats concepts, on the contrary, as the ongoing product of contingent judgements of similarity and difference. No set of determinative rules is available. Any rule that we may try to use to make establishment of similarity and difference a logical matter, or something that any reasonable person would *have* to admit, is liable to break down, especially if there are incentives for some people to interpret that rule differently. Philosophical criteria are interpretable in divergent and yet still legitimate ways, and so no set of rules as advocated and applied by historical actors can be determinative in identifying one activity rather than another as a 'discovery' while there are people determined to disagree. Any set of criteria used by historians to identify discoveries will be subject to the same limitation.

Barnes uses the example of the discovery of Neptune to illustrate some of these points about the nature of discovery. In the mid-1840s there was great excitement when Adams in Britain and Leverrier in France both claimed discovery of a new planet. Calculations had been made of an orbit for an undiscovered planet x that would produce the known perturbations in the orbits of the known planets. Then observers located the object in the sky. Although there were disputes in Europe about who should get the credit (Adams or Leverrier), there was consensus that one

---

[4] Barry Barnes, *T.S. Kuhn and Social Science*, 1982, pp. 41–45. Augustine Brannigan, *The Social Basis of Scientific Discoveries*, 1981 arrives at a similar position via ethnomethodological precepts.

of them had made the discovery. From the United States, however, came dissenting voices. It was claimed that there was a discrepancy between the predicted orbit and the observed orbit of the optical object. Therefore, the Americans claimed, Adams and Leverrier had actually predicted a *different* planet from the one that was discovered with the telescope. There was an unwillingness to accept this in Europe, it being argued that there would inevitably be some margin of error, some difference between the prediction and the observation. The key question was: what divergence between them was acceptable? Where do we draw the line between a discrepancy so large that it invalidates the putative discovery and one that is within acceptable limits? In the end this was a matter of judgement, and the question was resolved by who could make their judgement stick within the community.[5]

The point is that Adams's and Leverrier's activity represents something that may be placed in the category 'discovery' or 'not discovery'. A judgement has to be made about whether this instance is the same as, or different from, other instances already classified as discoveries. If there is incentive to do so, then any particular judgement can be challenged quite logically; that is, the challenge can be made out as compliant with a given set of rules. Another point to note is that the discovery and the criteria by which it is judged to be a discovery become 'true' together.

In the case of the water controversy there were a number of accounts of what the discovery consisted of. These might be listed crudely as follows:

1 Obtaining water in an apparatus after the explosion of a gaseous mixture (that we now know to have involved a combination of hydrogen and oxygen rather than a condensation of moisture from the gases but that the historical actors didn't so explain)
2 Obtaining water and explaining its production as the result of a chemical combination of two gases
3 Obtaining water and explaining it as the product of the combination of inflammable air and dephlogisticated air, or, obtaining water and explaining it as the product of the combination of inflammable air and dephlogisticated air involving 'elementary' heat
4 Obtaining water and explaining it as the product of the combination of hydrogen and oxygen
5 Obtaining water and explaining it as the product of the combination of hydrogen and oxygen and showing how that reaction related to the whole series of cognate reactions in the New Chemistry of Lavoisier.

The list could be lengthened in various ways by imposing other criteria, for example by saying of (2), (3), (4) and (5) that they must be part of a sequence of demonstrative, quantitative experiments. Depending upon how the discovery was defined, and how the criteria for counting as a discovery were set up, cases could be made for a variety of individuals as the 'true' discoverer.

The controversy over priority of discovery thus involves a number of individuals and groups trying to make the case for their version of the discovery, their criteria of

discovery and their discoverer. They make attributions and promote criteria according to their interests and objectives. Eventually some attributions win out and the nature of the discovery and the identity of the discoverer are established as a consensus within the community. In achieving that consensus the history and character of the discovery are typically recast in ways that depict it as an event at which the discoverer was uniquely present. Rhetorical accounts of discovery come to appear non-rhetorical. An event is 'naturalized' and a discoverer reified.[6] This, then, is the attributional model of discovery. It is a controversial model, first, for all those who believe in the possibility of some objective basis for scientific knowledge and who adopt extensional semantics as their theory of how concepts relate to the world. It is also a controversial model for those who feel that, rather than going too far, it does not go far enough in treating discoveries as literary and rhetorical accomplishments.

The most radical account of scientific discoveries within the field of science studies has been that offered by discourse analysis on the one hand and by actor-network theory on the other. Both these approaches challenge the conventional sociology of knowledge by claiming to undermine the sociologists' use of realist sociological categories such as 'interest', or indeed 'society'. They claim to take us back to statements 'pure and simple' or to networks of associations that avoid the reifications of traditional sociological categories and even the presumptions of distinctions between human and non-human actors. On this view, attributional approaches to discovery such as mine are contradictory because they relativize the concept of discovery but then rely on realist sociological language to explain why certain attributions stick and others do not. Such critics say that all we can have are discovery accounts. The analyst's task is to show how those accounts are 'accomplished'.[7]

This last approach involves, in my view, pseudo-empiricism, claiming to be able to access discovery accounts somehow free of context. It involves either abdicating the task of explanation or, in so far as explanations are pursued, smuggling sociological terms in via the back door again.[8] But it can be a useful corrective to over-eager generalization. We need to be reminded of individuals and 'contexts' in continual movement. If scepticism about sociological categories is applied for its own sake, however, the possibilities of historical explanation seem to dissolve before our eyes.

There is, however, another sense in which the discourse analysis approach is useful. It draws our attention to the structures of argument involved in attributional

---

[6] For a pioneering case study of these processes see Augustine Brannigan, 'The reification of Mendel', *Social Studies of Science*, **9**, 1979, 423–54.

[7] See as key documents in this tradition: Steve Woolgar, 'Discovery: Logic and sequence in a scientific text', in K. Knorr, R. Krohn and R. Whitley (eds), *The Social Process of Scientific Investigation*, 1980, pp. 239–68; G. Nigel Gilbert and Michael Mulkay, *Opening Pandora's Box: A Sociological Analysis of Scientists' Discourse*, 1984; Bruno Latour, 'Give me a laboratory and I will raise the world', in K. Knorr-Cetina and Michael Mulkay (eds), *Science Observed*, 1983, pp. 141–70; Bruno Latour, *Science in Action: How to Follow Scientists and Engineers through Society*, 1987.

[8] For critiques along these lines see Steven Shapin, 'Talking History: Reflections on discourse analysis', *Isis*, **75**, 1984, 125–28 and also Simon Schaffer, 'The eighteenth Brumaire of Bruno Latour', *Studies in the History and Philosophy of Science*, **22**, 1991, 174–92.

processes. These structures need to be examined in any worthwhile account of scientific discovery. When Nickles complains that 'social critics' have reduced the topic of discovery to 'vanishing point', he should be taken as meaning that 'discovery' as traditionally understood is no longer examinable.[9] Barnes does at one point suggest that the term be removed from the lexicon: 'To speak of "discovery" is to abet a form of collective self-forgetfulness, harmless, even "functional", in science itself, but disastrous if the aim is to study science.'[10] However, the work of Brannigan and Barnes does not mean that discovery ceases to be interesting; attention merely shifts to understanding the processes of attribution. Structures of argument in the making of attributions by different groups, processes whereby discovery events are naturalized and discoverers reified, and historical variations in what Brannigan calls the 'grammar' of discovery, become the focus of attention.

One danger of a sociological approach to discovery lies in a lack of historical sensitivity in the face of the interests involved. The play of interests occurs within a cultural field that shapes and constrains the freedom of interested parties to pursue their goals. In other words, structure exists as well as agency. Simon Schaffer's discussion of discovery accounts in the late eighteenth and early nineteenth centuries makes some important points in this regard. During that period the view of heroic authors of scientific discovery was in the ascendant. Lengthy historical processes that produced objects labelled discoveries were rewritten to represent discovery as an 'individual moment with an individual author'.[11] Whilst, importantly, these discovery stories were designed to support particular sets of technical practices associated with the nominated discoverers, they also served more general ideological functions. Among those functions was the legitimation of a more specialized research community defined against the more open forums of eighteenth-century natural philosophy. The issue of who could legitimately participate in scientific discourse was being negotiated. So was the closely related issue of who could legitimately write the history of scientific discovery.

Deploying the Attributional Model: The Case of the Water Controversy

The general claim made by advocates of the attributional model of discovery is that discoveries are not to be found. They are not to be found in the heads of individuals or in the state of preparedness of a culture. I would claim, however, contra the discourse analysts and the actor-network theorists, that discoveries can be found in a culture being more or less successfully attributed to particular individuals.

An attributional study of the water controversy involves, therefore, a number of elements. First it involves identifying the texts in which attributions are made. Second we must clarify the tactics and strategies used by those making the attributions. Third we seek to explain why the varied attributions were made and why and how particular tactics and strategies were used in trying to make them

[9] Nickles, 'Discovery', p. 164.

[10] Barnes, *T.S. Kuhn and Social Science*, p. 45.

[11] Simon Schaffer, 'Scientific discoveries and the end of natural philosophy', *Social Studies of Science*, **16**, 1986, 397.

stick. My basic assumption is that attributions are 'interested'. They are made as they are because there is some perceived advantage to be gained in so doing. The interests concerned may be of a technical kind. As Schaffer puts it, arguing for a particular discovery account may be driven by the concern to 'fix' certain technical practices. At other times wider interests may be involved in attributions of discovery. The wider issues might be more general questions of scientific style in which individual discoverers come to symbolize the disciplinary enterprise or, indeed, science as a whole but with particular institutional characteristics. Ultimately, then, attributions can be understood by referring them to causes in the cultural context. By approaching them in this way we learn about the process of discovery itself and we also learn about the culture whose attributions we are studying – in the case of the water controversy, early Victorian scientific culture.

I now want to distinguish major strategies of attribution in the nineteenth-century water controversy and also to indicate a range of forums within which attributional processes took place. I then go on to suggest how we can relate these strategies and forums to the characteristics of the opposing groups.

Strategies of Attribution

Let me deal with strategies first. Gross has suggested that there are a number of basic argumentative strategies available in a situation where priority to a discovery is contested.[12] In following one strategy, supporters of a candidate-discoverer challenge the 'sameness' of the respective discoveries of the two, or more, candidates. It can be argued that the apparent sameness of the discovery claims is illusory. The favoured candidate is depicted as putting forward a genuine, correct, or 'the best' knowledge claim whilst the others are painted as being wide of the mark in some way. If such a case can be argued convincingly, then questions of priority, in a temporal sense, become irrelevant. We might call this the 'argument from difference'. The fact that someone comes up with the wrong finding before your candidate signifies nothing if your candidate has the right one. A second approach is to assert the identity or 'essential similarity' of the discovery statements of the rival candidates, to say that they had the same idea, but to argue that one of them had temporal priority. We will call this the 'argument from synonymity and priority'. A third approach is to contend over matters of 'right method'. In fact this might, depending on circumstances, be treated as a separate approach or seen as an aspect of the 'sameness' or 'difference' of competing candidate discoveries.[13]

I will demonstrate that the Watt/Cavendish case did involve a cleavage along just these lines. Generally, Watt's supporters contended that the claims to discovery put forward by Watt and Cavendish were essentially the same. Their man deserved credit, they argued, by virtue of his priority. He had *the* idea (singular) first. The contest becomes a circumstantial one. *What* was claimed was not at issue but *when*

---

[12] Alan G. Gross, 'Do disputes over priority tell us anything about science?', *Science in Context*, **11**, 1998, 169–70.

[13] On the uses of method see John Schuster and Richard Yeo (eds), *The Politics and Rhetoric of Scientific Method*, 1986.

it was said, or stated, was argued about. Watt's camp, then, wanted to play the game of circumstantial evidence. The Cavendish camp would also play that game up to a point. But they did not regard it as their strongest suit. Rather, they tried to show that questions of timing were otiose because the supposed discovery that Watt announced was in fact a farrago of nonsense. Watt's announcement may have been first, but it was just plain wrong, it lay outside the line of development of the New Chemistry and therefore it could not be identified as a discovery.

Let me give some examples to illustrate these strategic and tactical variations by examining briefly how claims were made for the essential similarity or difference of the discovery statements of Cavendish and Watt.[14] This clearly involved definition of what constituted the discovery. Here are some statements on this issue from key texts.

James Patrick Muirhead asked the question this way:

> [W]ho first explained the real cause of the formation of the water, by drawing and stating the conclusion that water is composed of two gases, which unite in the process of their combustion, or explosion ... Who was in point of fact the first to make public that theory, after having formed it altogether independently of the idea of others[?][15]

Muirhead's framing of the question in this way assumed and sought to enforce the essential similarity of Watt's and Cavendish's statements. What we are directed to look for are statements saying that 'water is composed of two gases ...'. At this level, Watt and Cavendish can be seen as stating the same thing even though they apparently differed on what those gases were. Muirhead is claiming that their statements are similar *enough* to be treated as identical. Muirhead is playing down the importance of the issue of the exact identity of the gases, a point that his opponents regarded as much more important. Indeed one of the grounds used by those arguing for Cavendish was that Watt laboured under misapprehensions about the nature of the gases involved. Making that point, or indeed arguing against it, involved entering quite deeply into the chemistry, a route that Muirhead wanted to avoid. If Muirhead could gain acceptance of his account of what the essence of the discovery was, then he could concentrate on the circumstantial evidence concerning *when* the two candidate discoverers first made their ideas public. He argued that Cavendish did not provide conclusions from his experiments until July 1784 whereas Watt had made his idea known much sooner. As Muirhead put it at one point, 'the question has become one of evidence much more than chemistry'.[16] The question did not just 'become' one of evidence. It was a matter of conscious and strenuous effort by Muirhead and his allies to portray the question in that way and to keep the controversy focused on that approach.

A second kind of statement came from William Vernon Harcourt and William Whewell. In the published version of his Presidential Address to the British

---

[14] These examples involve me in making statements out of context. I do this only in order to illustrate my point concretely. The statements are thoroughly contextualized in later sections of the book.

[15] J.P. Muirhead (ed.), *The Correspondence of the late James Watt on his Discovery of the Theory of the Composition of Water*, 1846, p. xxxiv.

[16] Muirhead (ed.), *Correspondence*, pp. cxvii–cxviii.

Association for the Advancement of Science at Birmingham in 1839, Harcourt stated:

> Whilst the views of Cavendish are shown by the internal evidence of the experiments themselves ... to have been from the first precise and philosophical, those of ... Watt were ... vague and wavering to a degree scarcely comprehensible to those who have not studied the ideas prevalent at that period of chemical history.[17]

According to Harcourt, then, far from the views of Watt and Cavendish being essentially similar, as Muirhead claimed, they were completely different. Watt's statement was 'vague and wavering', Cavendish's was 'precise and philosophical'. This was partly to do with Watt's ideas about what the gases were, but it was more to do with the claimed inadequacies of his conception of the role of heat in the composition of water and his failure to quantify. Whewell put this clearly in a private letter of support written to Harcourt:

> Your case, as you first put it, remains to my mind quite unshaken. But perhaps you may be wishing to know how the subject presents itself to my mind, looking at it rather with reference to the general course of the history of Science than to any special evidence of dates and the like ...
> I think your remark is quite decisive – that Watt's views are utterly damaged by involving a composition of ponderable and imponderable elements. This of itself was enough to show that he did not consider elementary composition with the rigour and distinctness which the discovery of the synthesis and analysis of bodies at that time required ... [Watt's hypothesis] was by its very terms unsuited to the step which science then had to take.[18]

This last statement by Whewell quite explicitly placed Watt outside what he considered to be the line of progress in science. As we will see, Whewell and other members of the Cavendish camp had a quite exclusive self-conception as arbiters of the history of science. Because this statement was made in a private letter, its attributional significance is much reduced (its persuasiveness was directed at Harcourt only and he was already converted!). Of more significance was what Whewell had to say in his *History of the Inductive Sciences*. In the second edition Whewell gave the credit to Cavendish and made no mention of Watt at all. In the third edition he repudiated 'recent attempts to deprive Cavendish of the credit of his discovery of the composition of water, and to transfer it to Watt ...Watt not only did not anticipate, but did not fully appreciate the discovery of Cavendish and Lavoisier ...'.[19]

Let me give a final example of how members of the Cavendish camp sought to open up chemical differences, that is, to stress the differences between the discovery statements of Watt and Cavendish. This comes from George Wilson, the author of *The Life of the Honble Henry Cavendish*, published in 1851. This is a severe and

---

[17] William Vernon Harcourt, 'Address', *Report of the Ninth Meeting of the British Association for the Advancement of Science held at Birmingham in August 1839*, 1840, p. 23.

[18] Whewell to Harcourt, 11 February 1840, in *The Harcourt Papers*, vol. 14, pp. 105–106.

[19] William Whewell, *History of the Inductive Sciences. From the Earliest to the Present Time*, third edn, 1857, vol. 3, pp. 111–12.

complex book. Wilson himself, quite a witty man, once described it as a 'very dry book despite the amount of water in it'. Most of it consists of a study of the water controversy. It is also a paradoxical work combining as it does some very sophisticated historical analysis and some very crude presentist historiography.

In the same vein as Harcourt but in much more detail, Wilson claimed to show that Priestley's experiments, upon which Watt relied in drawing his conclusions, used charcoal in preparing his inflammable air. This could not have produced the pure mixture of gases in the correct ratio to leave only water on combustion. Therefore, in so far as Watt's inferences were correct, they *could not have been properly drawn* from Priestley's experiments. Thus either we say that Watt drew his inferences from Cavendish's experiments as imperfectly transmitted via Priestley's attempt to replicate them, or we cut Watt's inferences adrift from a sound experimental basis altogether and they become groundless, if inspired, speculations. Either way, the idea that Watt inferred a theory of the composition of water by a sound method is made to look suspect and Cavendish is left as the only candidate in the field.

Wilson believed that the issue of discovery could and should be decided on his knowledge of the true state of affairs. And that true state of affairs centred most clearly on the sustained experimental programme of Cavendish, his careful, judicious and accurate method of working:

> Had [Cavendish] never experimented, or had he never reported his results to Priestley, there is no reason to suppose that Watt would have conjectured, even remotely, that water is a compound of oxygen and inflammable air. *He was not on the track of such a discovery.* His speculations on the convertibility of steam into a permanent gas by the change of all its latent into sensible heat, did not point in that, but in exactly the opposite direction. He was following Priestley in all his devious wanderings, and going astray along with him ... when Priestley's repetition of Cavendish's experiments (in which all that was true and significant was Cavendish's) arrested him in his mistaken course, and enabled him to approximate to the true theory of the composition of water.[20]

It is important here to recall Wilson's and Harcourt's overall conception of what the discovery of the composition of water consisted in and what its significance was. That significance was not confined to showing that water is a compound rather than an element. It involved the typification of a whole class of chemical reactions and therefore the establishment of the basis of modern chemical practice. On this conception, the discovery could only be properly found in the wider context of a disciplined and sustained programme of research of the kind, and the range, pursued by Cavendish and not so readily attributable to Watt. Wilson's whole account of the controversy was predicated on a concern to assert the standards of modern chemical discipline that Cavendish was taken to prefigure. 'Discovery' is treated within that disciplinary framework and in the end Cavendish and Watt are judged against it.

Here, then, are some examples of different attributional strategies. Throughout my analysis of the water controversy I will be concerned to identify and interpret the attributional strategies employed by different individuals and groupings. I will

---

[20] George Wilson, *The Life of the Honourable Henry Cavendish*, 1851, p. 437. (My italics.)

also be concerned with the context of these strategies in relation to the forums in which they were deployed and the interests that they served. We can now examine the question of attributional forums.

Forums of Attribution

Attributional processes occur in a variety of forums. The most obvious place to look for attributions (and in many controversy studies the only place investigated) is in texts making explicit contributions to the 'controversy itself'. So, for example, François Arago's *Eloge de James Watt* is recognized by everybody as a central document in the water controversy. In his *Eloge* Arago attributed the discovery of the composition of water to James Watt. Depending upon how the *Eloge* was published, it would have a certain readership. (Initially published in French, it would have had a limited British readership if it had not been translated into English. In fact it was translated twice into English, published twice as a pamphlet and also in the *Edinburgh New Philosophical Journal*.) Accounts of such central publications in newspapers, in the weekly and monthly press, and in the reviews reached much wider audiences still. So did articles in encyclopaedias on 'chemistry', 'water', 'James Watt', 'Henry Cavendish' and so on. In these texts, too, statements were made about who discovered the compound nature of water. Generally, these statements were simpler than those in the central documents of the controversy. Other important sorts of texts were delivered lectures or circulated lecture notes and also chemistry textbooks. The latter might employ a historical method of presentation or they might lard an analytical approach with the odd bit of historical 'colour'. Such texts were presumably important in so far as they would help to shape the next generation of expert opinion. The problem with texts, of course, is that it is notoriously difficult, perhaps impossible, to determine what readers took away from them (if anything). That attributions of particular sorts were made can be established. How they related to opinion within various communities is very uncertain.

Any form of human communication is potentially a vehicle of attribution: inscriptions on monuments; conversations with 'informed' individuals. Conversations have, of course, disappeared into the ether and are not to be captured. Interestingly, Watt Jr did once suggest to Henry Brougham that he include reference in the inscription for a monument to Watt's discovery of the composition of water. Writing claims in stone may have much to recommend it, but in terms of potential audience paper is far more effective.

So forums of attribution are numerous. Are they all as important as each other? One distinction we might be tempted to make is that between forums for 'expert' opinion and those for 'popular' opinion. We tend to think that forums in which expert opinion is established are more important (in the sense of authoritative) than those in which popular opinion is formed. Controversy studies have often distinguished, following Harry Collins,[21] between a 'core set' and the rest. The

---

[21] Harry Collins, *Changing Order. Replication and Induction in Scientific Practice*, 1985, pp. 142–48.

'core set' is that grouping whose decisions on a matter tend to be decisive because they are recognized as the key authorities, as the best-informed judges of the science in question and so on. Perhaps it does not matter what readers of popular, ephemeral literature imbibed by way of attributions on such questions. In so far as participants in the controversy have influence over what happens in various forums, then they can, of course, seek to shape processes of attribution. However, any easy distinction between 'expert' and 'popular' forums will be avoided since the boundary line was under negotiation during the period we are concerned with. Such distinctions are not timeless nor are they uniquely specifiable. Where the line is to be drawn tends, in fact, to become part of the controversy.[22] In this study, for example, the status of encyclopaedias as expert or popular forums is varied, ambiguous and changing and the contending parties are engaged in a mutual questioning and claiming of expertise. It is in any case arguable that the more popular forums, with their practical demands for simplification and brevity, are in fact crucial to the naturalizing of discoveries and the reification of discoverers.

Strategy and Structure

The argumentative strategies and forums used by participants in controversies are not randomly distributed. There is usually a discernible relationship between the strategies adopted, the forums employed, the characteristics of the strategists, and the structural features of the situation that the groups find themselves in.

It has struck me, for example, that the Watt camp had certain collective characteristics that would predispose them towards the argument from circumstantial evidence to temporal priority (the argument of synonymity and priority). By the Watt camp I mean primarily James Watt Jr, Henry Brougham, Francis Jeffrey, James Patrick Muirhead and François Arago. I suggest that all these characters were 'outsiders' so far as British science, let alone chemistry, was concerned in the 1830s to 1850s when the controversy was at its height. I believe that the argument from circumstantial evidence for temporal priority was primarily an outsiders' argument in this case.

In thumbnail-sketch terms we can say that Jeffrey was a literary critic, known as the founder and long-term editor of the *Edinburgh Review*. He was also a prominent advocate and a judge. Before he became Watt Jr's eyes and hands, James Patrick Muirhead was an Oxford-trained lawyer with antiquarian and Scottish historical interests. Brougham at one time or another might have claimed scientific insider status: in the 1790s, while still a student at Edinburgh University, Brougham published work on optics in the *Philosophical Transactions of the Royal Society of London*. In his old age in the 1850s Brougham returned to optics as a supporter of Sir David Brewster's rearguard action for the corpuscular theory of light against the

---

[22] See Stephen Hilgartner, 'The dominant view of popularization: Conceptual problems, political uses', *Social Studies of Science*, **20**, 1990, 519–39, also Anne Secord, 'Science in the pub: Artisan botanists in early nineteenth-century Lancashire', *History of Science*, **32**, 1994, 269–315 and Bernadette Bensaude-Vincent, 'A genealogy of the increasing gap between science and the public', *Public Understanding of Science*, **10**, 2001, 99–113.

undulatory orthodoxy of the scientific establishment within the Royal Society and the British Association. In between Brougham was a successful and celebrated lawyer, the defender of Queen Caroline, Lord Chancellor in Lord Grey's reform government, and a major problem for his own party, the Whigs. Watt Jr might have claimed some general scientific credentials during his youth, during his revolutionary days in France and also in connection with experiments on steam navigation. But he certainly did not claim such expertise by the 1830s and 1840s. Arago is more problematic for my argument in the sense that he was obviously a very prominent scientist as Perpetual Secretary of the Académie des Sciences. However, his reputation was primarily as an astronomer. And that reputation was not impeccable because his judgement was seen by many as compromised by nationalistic fervour, radical political views and a consequent belief in promoting the openness of scientific institutions to an inappropriate extent.

The case of Arago raises a general point about the scientific credentials of all these Watt supporters. Those credentials had to be negotiated in context. It would be *possible* to argue for the scientific understanding brought to their work by all of these characters. Even J.P. Muirhead at one point claimed to have a technical understanding of the chemistry involved in the water controversy second to none. Having read much of his correspondence and seen how, privately, he took on the arguments of some of the expert chemists on the Cavendish side, I would have to agree with him. Muirhead could have made claims to expertise and held his own in substantive chemical argument and interpretation, if he and his allies had chosen to do so. He did not so choose. Brougham at times *did* choose to claim expertise. His self-diagnosed omniscience was hard to control. His allies winced and feared for their cause when Brougham put his scientific, or worse his chemical, hat on. Arago's *prima facie* scientific credibility could be, and was, readily challenged by his opponents in the water controversy.

So, remembering always this point about the negotiated character of expertise, we can say, however, that generally speaking the Watt camp did not build their case on knowledge of chemistry (of the 1840s or the 1780s). They spent little time discussing the meanings, and the rival merits, of Watt's and Cavendish's discovery statements. Their professional expertise lay, if anywhere, in the law, in argument about evidence. Understandably, then, their focus was upon the circumstantial evidence of temporal priority. They insisted that the key issue at stake in the controversy was more akin to a legal than to a scientific one, and that the ability to judge such matters was not confined to scientific specialists. This was put plainly by Francis Jeffrey to George Wilson: 'I know I am but a child in your mind in any question of chemistry and I have nothing but my poor Logic to combat your Science with. But ... I have taken up a strong impression that the question we have to consider is much more a question of logic than of science ...'.[23] When Watt Jr selected Muirhead to undertake the editing of his father's correspondence on the water question, he expressed the view that 'As a question of evidence, this falls peculiarly within the sphere of your pursuits.'[24] In arguing their case on the basis of

---

[23] Francis Jeffrey to George Wilson, n.d. [1847], Special Collections, Edinburgh University Library Dk. 623/1/37.

[24] Muirhead (ed.), *Correspondence*, 1846, p. ii.

circumstantial evidence the Watt camp were confident that they could carry 'public' opinion with them. Muirhead and Watt Jr relied heavily on distributing free copies of the *Correspondence* when it was published in 1846. As responses came back from those receiving complimentary copies, Muirhead expressed confidence that they were winning the battle:

> The feeling has been so uniform in all the letters I have recd from <u>unscientific</u> readers that I am certain a very strong impression has been produced as to your father's priority. This is a great point, and may help to reconcile us to any rubs that may come from the <u>doctissimi</u> – Forbes and all his Company![25]

These 'unscientific' readers also often used legal analogies when writing about the priority dispute. Thus, Gilbert Hamilton wrote to Muirhead: 'I can only hold such sentiments as a Juror may draw from the evidence before him & I do believe no felon was ever hanged on surer testimony.'[26] The legitimacy of non-expert judgement was at stake here. If the discovery can be attributed on the basis of circumstantial evidence, then 'everyman' is a legitimate judge of the scientific priority dispute, just as 'everyman' is a legitimate juror under the law. Cavendish's supporters were to challenge all these interlinked positions.

We have seen something of the basic attributional strategy of the Cavendish camp in the brief extracts from the writings of Harcourt, Whewell and Wilson. Who were the members of this camp? They were members of the scientific élite of Oxford, Cambridge, London and Edinburgh. They were prominent among the leadership of the British Association and the 'rising stars' of the Royal Society of London. Besides Harcourt and Whewell we might mention George Peacock, prominent mathematical reformer, Trinity College man and Dean of Ely; George Airy, Astronomer Royal; James David Forbes, Professor of Natural Philosophy at the University of Edinburgh. These were joined by members of the chemical community such as Professor Thomas Graham. Graham was a Scot, trained under Thomas Thomson, who took the chair of Chemistry at University College London. In the 1840s Graham was President of the newly founded Chemical Society of London and also of the 'Cavendish Society', a chemical publishing society that published, among other works, Wilson's *Life of Cavendish*.

Although members of this grouping were collectively, if haltingly, approaching occupational professionalism, they were decisively status professionals. That is, they were making a strong bid to control the conduct of esoteric science as pursued by disciplined, trained research scientists. They were fighting at a number of boundaries: with advocates of 'fringe sciences' such as phrenology; with the 'social scientists' and statisticians; and, very significantly for us, with 'practical' scientists and engineers. These sorts of struggles were common in the nineteenth century. The Cavendish camp was engaged in what Tom Gieryn has called 'boundary work'.[27] Cavendish was a symbol of precise, disinterested, sustained

---

25 Muirhead to Watt Jr, 23 December 1846, Muirhead Papers, MS GEN 1354/1081.

26 Gilbert Hamilton to J.P. Muirhead, 5 January 1847, Muirhead Papers, MS GEN 1354/161.

27 See, for example, Thomas F. Gieryn, 'Boundary-work and the demarcation of science from non-science: Strains and interests in professional ideologies of scientists', *American Sociological Review*,

research, a symbol in the self-image of his advocates and supporters. Watt symbolized the autodidact, scientist-engineer, vital to the welfare of the country but not, so far as members of the Cavendish camp were concerned, to be confused with the 'real' scientists. The élite chemists saw their science as overshadowed by its reputation for coarse practicality and in need of academic respectability. Identification with the likes of Cavendish, and gaining the approval of the Cambridge men, were important aspects of that campaign for respectability. These are some of the aspects of professional vested interests that rendered the Cavendish/Watt issue important in early Victorian Britain and that will be explored further.

The control of interpretation of the history of science was also of vital importance to the Cavendish camp. Whewell's *History of the Inductive Sciences* was a key document in this control. It was not a personal project on Whewell's part but a communal one in which his inner circle advised him on the winnowings, selections, inclusions and exclusions that should in their view be made in the historical account, especially with regard to recent scientific work. There was an attempt to assert that only those in command of the science were in a position to arbitrate on matters of scientific discovery. The water controversy clearly involved the assertion of this principle, and it was reflected in the attributional strategy pursued by Whewell and others of the Cavendish camp, against the legalistic, everyman-his-own-judge, approach of Watt's supporters. The 1840s and 1850s were, I think, the key decades during which this ascendancy of expertise was secured. By the 1850s and 1860s not only the major societies and their publications were controlled by the pro-Cavendish élite, but also key vehicles of scientific popularization and historical memory. This control was not complete, however. Other literary areas were not so controlled and there we find for many years examples of attributions to Watt. We will see such examples in textbooks, popular encyclopaedias and in what might be called a nationalistic Scottish literature.

Earlier historians of the water controversy have tended to focus on resolving for themselves the question of who *really* discovered the composition of water. They have invariably adopted one perspective or another and come out in favour of the obvious candidate. If they have treated the matter as essentially one of circumstantial evidence, then they have followed the Watt camp. If they have engaged with the minutiae of the chemistry promulgated by Watt and Cavendish to distinguish between their conceptions and render the temporal dimension irrelevant, then, they have tended to find in Cavendish's favour, or perhaps in Lavoisier's. In my study I have sought to avoid this. The key to understanding the 'victory' of Cavendish lies not in what he really did in the 1780s, even presuming that that reality could be unearthed in some non-committal way. Rather the key lies in what was done by assorted participants in the second phase of the controversy in the 1830s through the 1850s and during subsequent textual attributions. 'Discovery' is a designation or status accomplished through attributional processes. It is not enough, as Schaffer has argued, to deconstruct heroic discovery stories. We need to understand the functions

---

48, 1983, 781–95 on John Tyndall. In the United States, the case of Thomas Edison's relations with the scientific community is an instructive one. See David A. Hounshell, 'Edison and the pure science ideal in 19th-century America', *Science*, **207**, 8 February 1980, 612–16.

of such mythical accounts within the communities that produce them.[28] The task of the historian, in my view, is to try to understand and explain the variety of attributions made, the strategies employed in making them, and why and how some won out over others. We thus need to establish the competing versions of the idea of 'discovery' being promoted by the opposing sides, at a time when that idea was in the midst of a major cultural transition.

---

[28] Simon Schaffer, 'Making up Discovery', in Margaret Boden (ed.), *Dimensions of Creativity*, 1994, p. 18. In so far as myths serve functions for communities, the deconstruction of the myth of the heroic individual discoverer is often done in the name of collectivist views of the nature of science. For an interesting recent case study see Abigail O'Sullivan, 'Henry Dale's Nobel Prize Winning "Discovery"', *Minerva*, **39**, 2001, 409–24.

Chapter 3

The Beginnings of a Dispute and its Interpretation

Introduction

It is impossible to simply state the facts concerning the eighteenth-century research relevant to the discovery of the composition of water. However, some such attempt must be made so that various occurrences are made familiar for the purposes of interpretative discussion. As we will see, not the least of the artificialities in recounting research on the composition of water is that most of the work was directed at other objectives at the time. Only in retrospect did the various activities appear as a coherent, linear progress towards a discovery. Only in retrospect did that discovery come to have an important place in the larger transformation in thought and practice that came to be known as the Chemical Revolution.

Having outlined the major events leading to the 'discovery' and also the first-phase controversy over that discovery (in so far as there was one in the late eighteenth century), we will then sketch the historiography of the Chemical Revolution. Depending upon the historiographical position that is adopted concerning that larger transformation, the character and significance of the discovery of the compound nature of water changes. We will also pursue a deeper contextual account of the work of both James Watt and of Henry Cavendish on water. This is in order to show how far the conceptions of each investigator departed from those subsequently, and most commonly, attributed to them by various parties within the historiography of the Chemical Revolution. Once this is accomplished, we are well placed to pursue the arguments and attributional strategies of the succeeding decades.

The Story of Water

In recounting the story of water in the 1780s my aim is to set out the key events and processes that, by common consent of nineteenth- and twentieth-century historians, constituted the basic framework of investigations into the nature of water. Once again, it is not my intention to try to resolve the controversy in this, its first, phase. Nor is it my intention to tell the fullest story possible. For that, Partington remains an indispensable source.[1]

The story begins conventionally with experiments by various investigators that involved the explosion of inflammable air with either common air or dephlogisticated

---

[1] J.R. Partington, *A History of Chemistry*, vol. 3, 1962, pp. 325–62, 436–57.

air. Joseph Priestley was among the first when, in 1775, he noted that the explosion was much louder when dephlogisticated air was used than when common air was employed. The scientific interest at this point lay in the strength of gaseous explosions. Volta introduced another dimension to such experiments when, in 1776–1777, he developed the technique of firing gaseous mixtures in closed vessels using an electric spark to ignite them. Volta invented a eudiometer to prosecute such experiments and to measure the volume changes of the different airs when such explosions occurred. The itinerant lecturer in natural philosophy, John Warltire, a friend and correspondent of Joseph Priestley, was also firing explosive mixtures. It appears from his correspondence with Priestley that they conducted firings in glass vessels and observed the deposition of moisture on the inside of the vessel, though this was mentioned only with regard to explosions of inflammable and common air. Priestley's account of this in his *Experiments and Observations*[2] recounts Warltire's belief that the appearance of the moisture confirmed a long-held view that common air, when phlogisticated, 'deposits its moisture'. The belief was that the moisture was present in the gaseous mixture and deposited (not produced) by the explosion. This observation, though clearly of interest, was made almost in passing. Priestley returned immediately to the issues of the violence of the explosion and the unfavourable comparison between the firing of inflammable air and of gunpowder. Warltire apparently conducted these experiments with a view to determining the change in weight after the explosion. He claimed to find a loss of weight.

Henry Cavendish began a celebrated series of experiments in 1781 upon which his claims to the discovery were to be based. These, it was contended, were the experiments eventually published as 'Experiments on Air' in the *Philosophical Transactions* in 1784 and 1785. Cavendish's announced aim was to study the 'phlogistication' of common air, a process well known to diminish the volume of the air.[3] He was concerned to find out what became of the air that was 'lost or condensed'. Thus phlogistication by explosion with inflammable air was only one of a number of processes that Cavendish was concerned with. (The others were calcination of metals, the burning of sulphur and phosphorus, the mixture of common air with nitrous air, respiration of animals, and the action of an electric spark.)

When it came to the explosion with inflammable air, Cavendish acknowledged Warltire's experiment but, unlike him, did not record a significant loss of weight. Cavendish was still guided in his measurements by his eudiometric experiments published earlier, in 1783. That is, he was concerned with the diminution of the common air by phlogistication. He measured the point at which complete phlogistication (or maximum diminution) occurred as being 423 measures of inflammable air to 1000 measures of common air. When a mixture with these proportions was exploded, 'almost all the inflammable air, and about one-fifth of the common air, lose their elasticity, and are condensed into the dew which lines the glass'.[4] Cavendish then devised an apparatus to burn together larger quantities of inflammable air and common air in order to obtain a more substantial quantity of

---

[2] Joseph Priestley, *Experiments and Observations*, vol. 2, 1781, pp. 395–98.

[3] Henry Cavendish, 'Experiments on air', *Philosophical Transactions*, **74**, 1784, 119–53.

[4] Ibid., p. 128.

the 'dew'. By various tests he found the dew to be plain water. The phrase he used was that the inflammable air and about one-fifth of the common air 'are turned into pure water'. Our natural assumption would be that Cavendish meant that the gases had formed water as a compound. However, Cavendish did not say that, and, as we will see upon examining this point in more detail, there are good reasons for thinking that at this stage Cavendish's explanation for what was going on here invoked a condensation, not a compounding process.

Cavendish's next series of experiments involved exploding various mixtures of inflammable and dephlogisticated airs. He found that when mixed in the proportion very close to 2 to 1, these airs were converted into the same weight of water; that is, the weight of the airs before the explosion was equal to the weight of water present after it. However, and this too was of great consequence, Cavendish found the liquid to be acid to the taste and identified a small quantity of 'nitrous acid' in the water. He eventually explained this fact in the paper published in 1785.[5]

It is important to remember that, although Cavendish conducted these experiments from 1781, they were not published until 1784. When Cavendish commenced his experiments, Watt was returning to some of his earlier investigations with steam. He was in regular contact with Joseph Priestley, Joseph Black and others on chemical matters. As we will see in more detail later, Watt had formed a view about the possible conversion of water into air if it were heated. In late 1782 Priestley reported an experiment using an earthenware retort in which it seemed that precisely this did happen; that is, water was converted into air. The experiment was, however, subsequently explained in another way and the effect discredited. This did not undermine Watt's faith in his theory. In early 1783 Priestley learned of Cavendish's experiment in which dephlogisticated air and inflammable air were exploded by the electric spark, producing a deposit of water of equal weight. Priestley determined to repeat this experiment, which he claimed to have done. He was not entirely happy with his weighings but stated that he 'always found, as nearly as I could judge, the weight of the decomposed air in the moisture acquired by the paper'.[6]

Much was to hang on this experiment during the second phase of the water controversy. The reason is as follows. Priestley's ostensible repetition of Cavendish's experiment was subsequently judged not to be so in a crucial respect. In order to make sure that his inflammable air was dry (and thus not contaminated with the very substance whose production was at issue) Priestley produced it by heating charcoal in an earthenware retort. For the same reason, he also produced his dephlogisticated air by heating nitre. Priestley regarded these measures as improvements upon Cavendish's experiments but not interfering with the essential similarity of the two sets of experiments. From the vantage point of post-Lavoisian chemistry the mixture of gases so generated (hydrogen, carbon monoxide, oxygen and nitrogen) could not physically have produced the same result as Cavendish's experiment did. Whether his ostensible reliance on Priestley's retrospectively flawed experiment fatally wounded Watt's claim to discovery, or was irrelevant to it, was to be a matter of heated debate, becoming known as 'the charcoal argument'.

---

[5] Cavendish, 'Experiments on air', *Philosophical Transactions*, **75**, 1785, 372–84.

[6] *Philosophical Transactions*, **73**, 1783, 398–434, at p. 414.

For now, we need simply to note that, on learning from Priestley of this experiment (or via Priestley of Cavendish's experiment) Watt was moved to venture the hypothesis that 'water is composed of dephlogisticated and inflammable air, or phlogiston, deprived of part of their latent heat'. This view, expressed in a letter to Joseph Black of 21 April 1783, was repeated in much this form in letters to Gilbert Hamilton and J.A. De Luc at about the same time.[7] Watt set out to formally communicate his ideas by writing a letter to Priestley on 26 April 1783 that was intended to be read to the Royal Society of London, along with Priestley's account of his experiments. However, on 29 April Priestley informed Watt about the problem with the earthenware retort experiments, in which water was ostensibly converted into air. Watt decided to withdraw his letter and asked that it not be communicated to the Royal Society at that point. The letter had been sent to London, however, and was seen by a number of people in scientific circles there.

As Watt's communication lay in abeyance, other developments were in train involving Lavoisier. On 24 June 1783, Lavoisier and Laplace performed an experiment burning inflammable and dephlogisticated air in a closed glass vessel and obtained a quantity of water. This was a rather hasty effort and not characterized by the careful quantification usually associated with the work of these natural philosophers. A brief account of this experiment was published in December 1783.[8] Quickly and efficiently, Lavoisier and his collaborators went on to devise and prosecute quantitative experiments culminating in the famous and masterly experiment in which water was decomposed and then synthesized.[9]

Stimulated by Lavoisier's rapid moves, Cavendish had his first paper recounting his experiments on air read at the Royal Society on 15 January 1784. It was at this juncture that seeds of conflict between Watt and Cavendish were sown. Watt was preoccupied with steam engine troubles but on 1 March 1784 his friend De Luc, having obtained a copy of Cavendish's paper, wrote to Watt that: 'In short, he [Cavendish] expounds and proves your system, word for word, and says nothing of you.'[10] De Luc encouraged Watt (as Sir Joseph Banks had done previously) to submit to the Royal Society his original letter to Priestley and a new one written to De Luc which would then be read to a meeting of the Society. De Luc also advised Watt to be cautious and not cause jealousy that might jeopardize his fortunes with steam projects. Watt's reply to De Luc was a peculiar mixture of defiance and diffidence and is worth quoting at length:

> On the slight glance I have been able to give your extract of the paper [Cavendish's], I think his theory very different from mine; which of the two is right I cannot say; his is more likely to be so, as he has made many more experiments, and, consequently has more facts to argue upon.

---

[7] Watt to Black, 21 April 1783, printed in E. Robinson and D. McKie (eds), *Partners in Science*, 1970, pp. 124–27, at p. 126. For the letters to Hamilton and De Luc see J.P. Muirhead (ed.), *Correspondence*, 1846, pp. 20–21.

[8] *Obs. Phys.*, **23**, 1783, 452–55.

[9] For accounts of this see: Henry Guerlac, 'Chemistry as a branch of physics: Laplace's collaboration with Lavoisier', *Historical Studies in the Physical Sciences*, **7**, 1976, 205–16; Robert J. Morris, 'Lavoisier and the caloric theory', *The British Journal for the History of Science*, **6**, 1972, 1–38.

[10] Muirhead (ed.), *Correspondence*, pp. 43–44.

I by no means wish to make any illiberal attack on Mr. C. It is <u>barely</u> possible he may have heard nothing of my theory; but as the Frenchman said when he found a man in bed with his wife, '<u>I suspect something</u>'.

As to what you say of making myself 'des jaloux', that idea would weigh little; for, were I convinced I had had foul play, if I did not assert my right, it would either be from a contempt of the modicum of reputation which could result from such a theory; from the conviction in my own mind that I was their superior; or from an indolence, that makes it easier to me to bear wrongs, than to seek redress. In point of interest, in so far as connected with money, that would be no bar; for, though I am dependent on the favour of the public, I am not on Mr. C. or his friends; and could despise the united power of <u>the illustrious house of Cavendish</u>, as Mr Fox calls them.[11]

Watt resolved to have his letters on water read at the Royal Society. In London the following week he saw Sir Joseph Banks and, with De Luc's assistance, resubmitted his original letter to Priestley and a new letter to De Luc. Watt explained to Banks his reasons for withdrawing the paper originally. Watt was anxious that Banks not think 'his own [Banks's] honour a little called into question', nor did Watt want Banks to feel, as he evidently did, that the withdrawal was a slight upon the Royal Society.[12] This was a time when 'dissensions' racked the Society, and in this politically charged atmosphere significance was easily read into actions. One dimension of that dispute concerned Banks's supposed mistreatment of certain classes of person, especially provincial dissenters. On the occasion of one rejection of such a character for the Fellowship, Joseph Priestley threatened no longer to publish his writings through the Royal Society. It appears that Banks may have thought that Watt, who after all was closely associated with Priestley, had withdrawn his paper as a political act. McCormmach has suggested that the reading of Cavendish's 'Experiments on Air' on 15 January 1784 was a 'power move'. The previous three meetings of the Society had been disrupted by political debate and criticism of Banks and his conduct of the institution. Among the charges made by the opposition was that under Banks the Royal Society had become scientifically feeble compared with Newton's day. The reading of Cavendish's highly significant 'Experiments on Air' would have been a very useful retort to such claims.[13] The fact that Cavendish was one of Banks's most valued advisers and supporters at this time also fits the picture, as does the fact that when Paul Maty, one of Banks's chief critics, resigned the post of Secretary to the Royal Society, Charles Blagden assumed the position. Blagden was also Cavendish's assistant, and his behaviour in the water controversy was to be a major issue, as we shall see in a moment.

Further evidence that the water question became entangled at least a little with the wider politics of the Royal Society is provided by the fact that Maty, as editor of *A New Review*, ensured that only the part volume of the *Philosophical Transactions* containing Watt's paper (part 2) was reviewed in his journal. The other part volume

---

[11] Watt to De Luc, 6 March 1784, in Muirhead (ed.), *Correspondence*, 1846, pp. 47–49.

[12] Watt to De Luc, 12 April 1784 in Muirhead (ed.), *Correspondence*, 1846, p. 51.

[13] Russell McCormmach, 'Henry Cavendish on the Proper Method of Rectifying Abuses', in Elizabeth Garber (ed.), *Beyond History of Science. Essays in Honor of Robert E. Schofield*, 1990, p. 43. On the dissensions see also John L. Heilbron, 'A mathematicians' mutiny with morals', in Paul Horwich (ed.), *World Changes: Thomas Kuhn and the nature of science*, 1993, pp. 81–129.

containing Cavendish's paper was studiously ignored.[14] Although Watt was personally unwilling to become a *cause célèbre* in the Royal Society dissensions, others would have been happy to make him so. For later writers on the water question, this institutional dimension remained open as an issue to pursue. In the 1840s David Brewster was to seize it.

Returning now to Watt in the process of resubmitting his paper, we find him anxious to avoid suspicion that he had been making a political point, since Banks had 'always behaved in a friendly manner towards us'.[15] Characteristically Watt adopted a deferential manner, asking, among other things, that the Society excuse the defects of his style, 'which must naturally be concluded to savour more of the mechanic than of the philosopher'.[16] Watt's paper was read to the Society in late April and early May, spanning more than one meeting. Banks courteously reported the approbation it had received. Watt's deference masked resentments that spilled over when he wrote to friends outside official Royal Society circles. To Mr Fry in Bristol Watt reported that his papers had been read, and he promised to send copies if they were printed.

> But I have had the honour, like other great men, to have had my ideas pirated. Soon after I wrote my first paper on the subject, Dr Blagden explained my theory to M. Lavoisier at Paris; and soon after that, M. Lavoisier invented it himself and read a paper on the subject to the Royal Academy of Sciences. Since that, Mr Cavendish has read a paper to the Royal Society on the same idea, without making the least mention of me. The one is a French Financier; and the other a member of the illustrious house of Cavendish, worth above £100,000, and does not spend £1000 per year. Rich men may do mean actions. May you and I always persevere in our integrity, and despise such doings.[17]

The Royal Society's Committee of Papers ordered the printing of Watt's paper and Watt then negotiated with Blagden exactly how the two letters (to Priestley and to De Luc) would be published. Watt, like Cavendish earlier, made changes along the way.[18] A device was settled upon that avoided repetition but made clear the early date at which Watt had developed his key ideas.[19] By this time, however, the hope that his paper might appear in the same half-volume as Cavendish's 'Experiments

---

[14] See *A New Review*, **7**, 1785, 106–10. The review, almost certainly by Maty himself, strenuously defended Watt's 'hypothetical' contribution in a way that suggests that the hypothetical character of Watt's paper was a matter for comment and criticism at the time.

[15] Watt to De Luc, 12 April 1784 in Muirhead (ed.), *Correspondence*, 1846, p. 51. The 'us' here is probably Boulton and Watt.

[16] Watt to Banks, 12 April 1784, in ibid., p. 53. Such diffidence invited the response 'no, you are a philosopher'! As I have argued, it was important to Watt to be thought of as such. See David Philip Miller, '"Puffing Jamie"', *History of Science*, **38**, 2000, 5–7.

[17] Watt to Mr Fry, 15 May 1784, in Muirhead (ed.), *Correspondence*, 1846, p. 61. As Muirhead notes, Watt probably meant to indicate Cavendish's worth as £1,000,000, which would have been more accurate.

[18] The changes made in Cavendish's paper, including interpolations by Blagden, were to become part of the controversy and charge of conspiracy and fraud.

[19] See Blagden to Watt and Watt to Blagden, 27 May 1784 in Muirhead (ed.), *Correspondence*, 1846, pp. 62–65.

on Air' was forlorn. It ended up being published in the subsequent half-volume. Beyond this the controversy between Cavendish and Watt seems to have created little stir. Watt certainly remained suspicious of what had gone on, especially with regard to various misdatings of documents, but if we are to believe the recollections of his son, no lasting antagonism existed towards Cavendish. When Watt was elected a Fellow of the Royal Society in 1785 he met Cavendish on friendly terms, and they remained on such terms until Cavendish's death.[20]

Watt took little or no part in the extended public debates between the supporters of phlogiston and the antiphlogistians led by Lavoisier. As Lavoisier and his colleagues realized the importance of the water question to the completion of the new chemistry of combustion, calcination and respiration, they performed more demonstrative experiments. Whether or not we as historians regard these moves by Lavoisier as the true clinching of the real composition of water or as an exercise in engrossment of the discoveries of others, they did generate the latter sorts of concerns in Britain. Blagden had visited Paris in June 1783. He was later to claim in a letter that was published in Crell's *Chemische Annalen* in 1786 that the experiment of 24 June, at which he was present, had been performed some days after he (Blagden) had informed Lavoisier and others of the work of Cavendish and Watt.[21] Efforts were made in Britain to resist not only the substantive case of the antiphlogistians but also the tendency of Lavoisier and his followers to gather more and more credit for the transformation of chemistry. However, British chemists, one by one, with the enduring exception of Joseph Priestley, acceded to the abandonment of phlogiston. Even as they did this, there was widespread uneasiness about the totalizing quality of Lavoisier's new chemistry, its new language and its seamless systemic quality. The adoption of the Lavoisian system remained equivocal. We will see in Chapter 4 that this equivocation allowed the survival for a time of what we might call 'hybrid' characterizations of the synthesis of water, hybrid in the sense that they often involved the unconscious marrying of older ideas with a Lavoisian gloss.

For the moment enough has been given of the story of water in the 1780s to gain our bearings in the second phase of the water controversy. Of course, getting those bearings also requires us to come to terms with the wider chemical context within which the water story was played out. For modern historians, and for the protagonists in the controversy in the mid-nineteenth century, the story of water was part of a major scientific transformation, a Chemical Revolution. It is to interpretations of that Revolution that we now turn.

---

[20] In 1786, for example, Watt discussed with De Luc the misdatings of the preprints that Cavendish circulated and of his own letter to De Luc in the *Philosophical Transactions*. The former stated that Cavendish's paper was read in January 1783 (rather than 1784) and the latter was dated in April 1784 (rather than 1783). On Watt's relations with Cavendish see 'Letter from James Watt Esq. To the Editor', in Muirhead (ed.), *Correspondence*, p. iv.

[21] *Chemische Annalen*, 1786, 58–61. A translation of this letter is printed in Muirhead (ed.), *Correspondence*, pp. 71–74. For a rejection of such charges see Berthelot, *La Révolution Chimique, Lavoisier*, 1902 and for a gentle prosecution of them see T.E. Thorpe, 'Presidential Address, Section B', *Report of the Sixtieth Meeting of the British Association*, 1891, 761–71.

The 'Chemical Revolution' and its Historiography

The discovery of the composition of water cannot be addressed without coming to terms with the history of the 'Chemical Revolution'. Indeed, the understanding of the meaning of that discovery, its significance and even its existence as an event, depend upon what position one takes in the historiography of the Chemical Revolution. As I have tried to stress, my subject-matter is not the discovery of the composition of water 'itself' but rather nineteenth-century debates in Britain about that discovery. (Of course, if the attributional model of discovery is taken seriously, then the distinction between the discovery 'itself' and later debates about it is purely chronological rather than substantial.) It might be said that my concern is not with the history of the Chemical Revolution but with the history of ideas about that Revolution, or, put another way, with the history of histories of the Chemical Revolution. The disputants in the nineteenth-century water controversy were, effectively, arguing about the history of the Chemical Revolution and about the place of particular individuals within it. One way of reading this book (though frankly not the major intention in writing it) is as a contribution to the history of the concept of a late-eighteenth-century revolution in chemistry. That concept has had a career, and the origins and development of that career can be a matter of study in their own right.

John McEvoy and others have examined the career of the concept of the 'Chemical Revolution'.[22] McEvoy delineates a number of phases in the historiography in concentrating on the differences between what he calls the 'positivist-whig' interpretation on the one hand, and the 'postpositivist' on the other.

The 'positivist-whig' historiography, which McEvoy sees as dominating from the mid-nineteenth to the mid-twentieth century, was manifest in the well-known writings of historians such as Herbert Butterfield, Charles C. Gillispie, Robert Multhauf, James R. Partington, Douglas McKie and Maurice Crosland. This historiography has a number of features. It is progressivist in that it sees the Chemical Revolution as an episode in the emergence of a scientific approach to nature from a pre-scientific age in which phlogiston theory dominated. It is objectivist, though McEvoy does not use this term. Whether the objectivism was based in inductivism, falsificationism or conventionalism, the triumph of oxygen theory over phlogiston theory was regarded as sealed by the method of science. It is Manichean, treating the Chemical Revolution as a story of the victory of the forces

---

[22] John G. McEvoy, 'Positivism, Whiggism, and the Chemical Revolution: A study in the historiography of chemistry', *History of Science*, **35**, 1997, 1–33. See also John G. McEvoy, 'The Chemical Revolution in context', *The Eighteenth Century: Theory and Interpretation*, **33**, 1992, 198–216; Rachel Laudan, 'Histories of the sciences and their uses: A review to 1913', *History of Science*, **31**, 1993, 1–34; Bernadette Bensaude-Vincent, 'A founder myth in the history of science? – The Lavoisier case', in Loren Graham, Wolf Lepenies and Peter Weingart (eds), *Functions and Uses of Disciplinary Histories*, 1983, pp. 53–78; idem, *Lavoisier: Mémoires d'une révolution*, 1993, pp. 343–418; Arthur Donovan, 'The Chemical Revolution revisited', in Stephen H. Cutliffe, *Science and Technology in the Eighteenth Century: Essays of the Lawrence Henry Gipson Institute for Eighteenth Century Studies*, 1984, pp. 1–15. Also see the essays in Arthur Donovan (ed.), *The Chemical Revolution: Essays in Reinterpretation*, in *Osiris*, **4**, 1988, 5–231.

of light over those of darkness. In this connection the contest was usually set up as one between Lavoisier and Priestley, the former as the 'genius' in touch with the truths of nature, the latter as diverted from the true scientific path by his character and his religious and political obsessions. The positivist-whig historiography depicted scientific change as involving 'cognitive inversion' and as proceeding via 'crucial experiments' (of which Lavoisier's analysis and synthesis of water was one) and via 'eureka moments' of discovery. Another feature of this historiography was its emphasis upon the quantitative character of the new chemistry as a distinguishing feature of its scientificity when compared with the qualitative approach of phlogiston theorists. A strong founder myth pervades the literature of this historiographical tradition, especially, but not exclusively, among French scholars, as Lavoisier was painted as the founding father of modern chemistry. A variant on the founder myth, and one of much importance in our story, is that which placed Lavoisier under the guiding shadow of Newton. According to this 'Anglo-Saxon' view, the history of modern chemistry was to be found in a lineage that incorporated Joseph Black, Henry Cavendish and Lavoisier as well as Boyle, Newton and Dalton. Indeed, some chemist–historians of the later nineteenth century in Britain were to argue for Cavendish as the founder of modern chemistry. Some modern historians of science and the participants in the nineteenth-century water controversy shared the positivist approach.

The postpositivist approach has involved a challenge to the various features of the positivist historiography. Black and white became shades of grey. Scientific virtues were found in phlogiston theory in that it played a productive role in the development of pneumatic chemistry, the chemistry of airs. There was no necessary antipathy between chemistry pursued via phlogiston theory and a quantitative approach. Generally, the phlogiston theory and its associated practices were granted much greater integrity as a viable system of thought. This was a way of thinking about scientific paradigms that many of us learned from Kuhn. Lavoisier did not loom so large in this postpostivist historiography. The historical reputation of others was resuscitated, notably, of course, that of Priestley: 'Priestley functioned in the Chemical Revolution not as a dogmatic and entrenched defender of the phlogiston theory but as a source of much-needed criticism of Lavoisier and his supporters.'[23] The stark contrast between the rational, clear-sighted Lavoisier and his confused, benighted opponents is muted at the least. Along with epistemological views that problematized objectivism and sought to contextualize scientific change came the notion that Priestley's theological and political views and activities should no longer be seen as leading him astray scientifically. Rather they should be seen as shaping what was regarded increasingly as a legitimate set of scientific commitments and beliefs. The suspicion within this approach of the notion of 'crucial experiment' and the contention that experiments could only be crucial relative to a particular theoretical framework complicated the process of conceptual change. (This may explain, incidentally, the otherwise surprising lack of attention by historians in recent decades to the discovery of the composition of water.) As the Manichean conception of the Chemical Revolution has been superseded by an ecumenical one,

---

[23] McEvoy, 'Positivism, Whiggism', p. 23.

the urge among historians to participate in fights over scientific priority has come to seem increasingly pointless (though still hard to avoid).

Postpositivist accounts have, however, usually sought some refuge in other notions of objectivism. It is well known that Kuhn sought some sort of rationality in processes of theory change by appealing to such notions as simplicity. Alan Musgrave's account of the Chemical Revolution tried to fit it to the philosophy of Imre Lakatos, arguing that phlogiston theory and oxygen theory were, respectively, 'declining' and 'progressive' research programmes in the period 1770 to 1785.[24] Musgrave's approach remains objectivist in presuming that the identification of a programme of research as progressive or otherwise is something that can be done objectively, can be done by us now and was done by the protagonists in the late 1780s. As Musgrave might jokingly say, the protagonists eventually all read Lakatos, except Priestley, of course. Rejecting the timeless objectivity of the inductivists' crucial experiments, Musgrave substitutes a different form of objectivism based in the rationality of research programmes. The interpretation of the experiments on water is, on this view, either smoothly progressive, as with oxygen theory, or backward looking and regressive, as when Cavendish reverted to phlogiston as imponderable in the 1784 phlogiston theory deployed to account for the experiments in which water was produced.[25] Finding various 'external' explanations of theory change to be inadequate, Musgrave triumphantly offers us the rational choice of a progressive programme of research. The problem, of course, is that logic does not constrain judgements of what is progressive and what is not. Interpretative flexibility remains and the reasons why actors choose to pursue divergent interpretations still require explanation.

Postpositivist approaches have themselves come under criticism on a number of counts from sociological and so-called 'postmodernist' perspectives. Constructivist and postmodernist perspectives treat scientific change as a thoroughly constructed process that cannot be explained by appeal to reality or rationality as usually conceived. Notions of reality and rationality always require thorough contextual interpretation. The interpretative flexibility in both experimental set-ups and in any set of rules of method for conducting and interpreting them is never exhausted. We then look to other processes to curtail that interpretative flexibility. In the sociology of scientific knowledge, professional vested interests and/or wider social interests are invoked as explanations for the acceptance of certain interpretations rather than others, interpretations that eventually become routine, 'natural' and 'true'.[26] In actor-network theory, an attempt is made at a neutral, monistic account of the solidification of certain interpretations rather than others.[27]

---

[24] Alan Musgrave, 'Why did oxygen supplant phlogiston? Research programmes in the Chemical Revolution', in Colin Howson (ed.), *Method and Appraisal in the Physical Sciences. The Critical Background to Modern Science, 1800–1905*, 1976, pp. 181–209.

[25] Ibid., pp. 204–205.

[26] See Barry Barnes, David Bloor and John Henry, *Scientific Knowledge. A Sociological Analysis*, 1996.

[27] The central text is Bruno Latour, *Science in Action: How to Follow Scientists and Engineers through Society*, 1987. For important critiques see Steven Shapin, 'Following scientists around', *Social Studies of Science*, **18**, 1988, 533–50 and Simon Schaffer, 'The eighteenth Brumaire of Bruno Latour', *Studies in the History and Philosophy of Science*, **22**, 1991, 174–92.

As attention has been directed to the problem of interpretative closure, mechanisms involved in that process have come under greater scrutiny. The meeting of experimental, literary and social practices has become a focus of inquiry. Since the issue of language was so clearly announced as such by participants in the Chemical Revolution, it has naturally become an important focus for analysing such processes. From this perspective, the experiments on the composition of water become a key site where the linguistic and experimental practices of the new chemistry are woven together. The efforts of the French to effect this 'linguistic' revolution were still resisted to some extent by British investigators, even as they accepted what they took to be the major import of the Lavoisian scheme.[28]

With such constructivist approaches, the historiography of the Chemical Revolution links up conceptually with the attributional model of discovery as discussed in Chapter 2. Key discoveries in the Chemical Revolution become attached to Lavoisier through an active rhetorical process in which Lavoisier himself and his colleagues were directly involved as part and parcel of their scientific investigations. That rhetorical process then also 'spilled out' into secondary accounts of various sorts that were also of great importance to the attributional process.

In the case of Lavoisier, Bernadette Bensaude-Vincent's explorations of the founder myth and its construction provide a telling example of the way in which the detailed attributional processes of working science link up to the wider politics of reputation and scientific symbolism. Bensaude-Vincent shows that nineteenth-century French chemists paid inordinate attention to the history of their field and constructed a founder myth around the figure of Lavoisier.[29] Even before this, Lavoisier depicted himself as the progenitor of not just a revolution in chemistry but a *foundation* of the field. Lavoisier's studied neglect of history and the work of others in the *Traité élémentaire de chimie* was part of his claim to a radical innovation having no continuities with past work in the field. The founder myth also claimed for Lavoisier's system the status of template for the whole future development of chemistry. Even after Humphry Davy's discovery that acids need not contain oxygen and the rise of atomic theory seemed to challenge such a claim, French chemists, led by J.B. Dumas, preserved the Lavoisian founder myth.

In the nineteenth century, significant impetus was given to this myth making by international politics, especially the relations of France and Germany:

> [Lavoisier] seems to have become the emblem of French power, so that all the nationalist militancy stirred up between France and Prussia due to the politics of the day focused on his person. So it was that the legend of a chemist became one of the stakes in a complex game of political rivalry.[30]

---

[28] For a key text see: Steven Shapin, 'Pump and Circumstance: Boyle's literary technology', *Social Studies of Science*, **14**, 1984, 481–520 and on this intersection in late eighteenth-century chemistry see Wilda Anderson, *Between the Library and the Laboratory. The Language of Chemistry in Eighteenth-Century France*, 1984; Lissa Roberts, 'A Word and the World: The significance of naming the calorimeter', *Isis*, **82**, 1991, 198–222; Jan Golinski, 'The Chemical Revolution and the politics of language', *The Eighteenth Century*, **33**, 1992, 238–51.

[29] Bensaude-Vincent, 'A founder myth in the history of sciences?', pp. 53–78.

[30] Ibid., p. 65.

Bensaude-Vincent recalls Wurtz's famous statement in 1869 on the eve of the Franco-Prussian War that 'La chimie est une science française: elle fut constituée par Lavoisier, d'immortelle mémoire.'[31] The responses from the German side represented shots in an ongoing propaganda war set against the reascendency of German chemistry in the 1850s, especially in the organic field.

There are a number of ways that the British arguments about Watt and Cavendish relate to these continental battles over the reputation of Lavoisier. First, although Lavoisier's system was fairly quickly adopted in Britain, the origins of the new chemistry were disputed. In particular, the importance of the British pneumatic tradition leading from Hales and Black through Priestley and Cavendish was asserted. British discussions of the discovery of the composition of water were overshadowed by what most took to be the engrossing tendencies of the French chemists with their state-sponsored New Chemistry and new nomenclature.[32] Cavendish and Blagden had to take steps in 1785 to assert Cavendish's priority over Lavoisier in the water experiments. British chemical texts of various sorts in the late eighteenth and early nineteenth centuries were routinely in the business of asserting Cavendish's claims against the ever-engrossing efforts of the French. As Lavoisier's accomplishment, and even the new nomenclature, were accepted, the British remained resistant to the idea that a Chemical Revolution had been effected in the sense that the French claimed.[33] The texts examined in Chapter 4 as an attributional survey have this as a constant backdrop. The British attempts to put forward Cavendish as their own candidate as the 'founding father' of chemistry would have created pressure against any claims that reduced Cavendish's reputation in any way. Hence came, perhaps, one source of pressure to neglect the claims of Watt to honours in the discovery of the composition of water, to leave them on one side, to contest them if raised. We will see also that British chemical texts of the later nineteenth century were still actively engaged in this struggle. By that time, although the defence of Cavendish's claims was still solid, there was a significant minority who even on the water question sided with Lavoisier as contests over methodology and pedagogy cut across entrenched nationalistic habits. As McEvoy noted, British historians of the late nineteenth and early twentieth centuries also participated in seeking to substitute an Anglo-Saxon 'positivist-whig' story for that promulgated by the French.

A second way in which the 'geopolitics' of Lavoisier's reputation is relevant to our story is through the involvement of a number of continental chemists in the Cavendish/Watt contest. Arago, though not a chemist, was clearly a major player.

---

[31] Ibid. The statement was made in C.A. Wurtz, *Dictionnaire de chimie pure et appliquée*, 1869, p. 1. For detailed discussions see Alan J. Rocke, 'Pride and Prejudice in chemistry: Chauvinism and the pursuit of science', *Bulletin of the History of Chemistry*, **13–14**, 1992–93, 29–40 and idem, *Nationalizing Science. Adolph Wurtz and the Battle for French Chemistry*, 2001.

[32] It is worth remembering here the discussions in Britain at this time of the issue of publication, the balance between public and private interests and how they were best served, a debate in which Watt participated informally. (See Jan Golinski, *Science as Public Culture: Chemistry and Enlightenment in Britain, 1760–1820*, 1992, pp. 41–44 and also Bensaude-Vincent, *Lavoisier*, p. 93).

[33] See David Knight, 'Revolutions in Science', in W.R. Shea (ed.), *Revolutions in Science. Their Meaning and Relevance*, 1988, pp. 50–51, 63.

J.B. Dumas, the French chemist who contributed so substantially to the Lavoisier founder myth, also participated and, interestingly, was claimed as a supporter by the Watt camp. A number of continental chemists and chemist–historians were courted by the Watt camp and expressed support for at least some recognition of Watt's claim. Although it takes us beyond the scope of the present work, and requires further investigation, it does seem likely that the decision to support Watt against Cavendish in the water question may have been the product of careful calculation by those chemists. In so far as Cavendish was put forward by many members of the British scientific élite as their candidate, against Lavoisier, for the title of 'founding father' of chemistry, then one can see why someone like Dumas might be happy for some of Cavendish's credit to be 'siphoned off', as it were, to an unthreatening figure like Watt. There may have been an element of this too with Arago, although we will see that he had other reasons for wanting to elevate Watt. It is possible also that German chemists and chemist–historians could have supported Watt in the belief that expanding the cast of characters with a claim to the discovery of the composition of water would, rather than elevate Lavoisier, act to bring him and his advocates closer to earth.

Although these aspects of the international politics of chemical mythology are not dealt with systematically in what follows, they do need to be borne in mind as a set of considerations possibly reinforcing, or cutting across, the domestic interest politics of chemical reputation that is investigated and emphasized. Now let us narrow our considerations from the broad historiography of the Chemical Revolution and chemical mythology to consider the place of the water experiments in chemical histories.

The Composition of Water in Histories of the Chemical Revolution

Charles Gillispie provides a classic example of the positivist treatment of the discovery of the composition of water in the Chemical Revolution. Gillispie argues that Lavoisier's work before 1783 was breaking loose from the chemistry of principles but carried with it, in the claim that oxygen is the acidifying principle, 'a diminishing residue of these old notions'.[34] Lavoisier had asked what is produced when hydrogen burns but he had found no product. At this point Gillispie introduced the English chemists to the scene. Priestley is depicted as mentioning the production of dew on the explosion of inflammable air with common air. However, Priestley was trying to determine the weight of heat. Cavendish repeated the experiment, made some measurements of how much of the air disappeared, and established that pure water was the product.

> In England James Watt ... in France Gaspard Monge ... made the same discovery, independently, almost simultaneously, and in the case of Monge with no less clarity. Once again, therefore, the interesting question is not who made water, but who understood what had happened? For though the composition of water was the last of the great discoveries of the English pneumatic school, Cavendish interpreted his results as the

[34] Charles C. Gillispie, *The Edge of Objectivity*, 1960, p. 227.

condensation of water, not its synthesis. Indeed, the light weight of hydrogen encouraged certain of the English chemists, militant in their last ditch, to identify it for a time with phlogiston itself.[35]

The implication is that the English school discovered water only in the sense of stumbling across it materially. Stumbling is probably the right word since Watt is not granted the clarity that Monge (or Cavendish) is allowed. Whilst the English exploited the possibilities in this outcome for defending phlogiston, Lavoisier

> seized upon Cavendish's results as upon a piece of tactical fortune. Lavoisier ... instantly saw water, seemingly the simplest of substances and classically the most intuitive of elements, rather as the oxide of that gas which is – to anticipate the rest of nomenclature – hydrogenerative. (Ibid., p. 228)

There followed Lavoisier's experiments before the Académie, the announcement of the results and, in due course, the experiment in analysis. Gillispie notes that Lavoisier made 'very fleeting mention of Cavendish', leaving the reader to suppose that this was the natural extension of Lavoisier's earlier work with hydrogen. Such a reader, he says, 'would be right, in principle if not in fact'.

> For this dramatic demonstration that water is an oxide, though not a 'crucial experiment' in the Baconian sense, was nevertheless decisive historically in the campaign to exorcise phlogiston in favor of a positive concept of combustion as that chemical reaction in which oxygen combines.[36]

Lavoisier's frontal attack on phlogiston 'made of chemistry a modern science', in the sense that it became a quantitative science: 'Henceforth, the chemist weighs amounts. He does not distil out principles.' Gillispie acknowledges that some historians do not see such a clear rupture, especially where Lavoisier's treatment of heat was concerned. Lavoisier's use of caloric (a subtle, elastic fluid and thus imponderable and all-permeating) means, according to Maurice Daumas,[37] that Lavoisier had not completely broken with the old system of 'principles'. Yet, Gillispie maintained, although Lavoisier uses the notion of caloric, he does not do so chemically: 'For caloric does not act as a chemical agent. It is excluded, absolutely excluded from the practice of chemistry, by the most elementary consideration of method.' Because heat (like light) is not confined within the boundaries of experiment, it cannot enter into the weighing of masses which has now become the essence of the science of chemistry. According to Gillispie, caloric 'entered permissively rather than constitutively into the structure of theory. Caloric disappeared from science in the nineteenth century. Nevertheless, the theory of oxidation, and by extension the conception of chemical reaction, remain what they were left by Lavoisier, and not by Priestley.' Gillispie's sleight of hand here is to treat caloric as an erroneous optional extra, only loosely tied to the core of Lavoisier's chemistry, which can be, and was, removed over time with *no change* in the central

---

[35] Ibid., p. 228.

[36] Ibid., p. 229.

[37] Maurice Daumas, *Lavoisier, théoricien et expérimentateur*, 1955.

theory. This is to translate the nineteenth-century meanings of the theory of oxidation back into the 1780s, rather than to inquire, as Daumas does, of the ways in which Lavoisier remained a man of the eighteenth century.[38]

Among those of more recent authors, Arthur Donovan's portrait of Lavoisier offers a concise account of the great Frenchman's development of the new theory of combustion. Donovan sees the 'Memoir on heat' produced with Laplace and read to the Académie in June 1783 as 'the final stone in the arch formed by Lavoisier's interrelated theories of acidification, calcination, combustion and respiration'. The composition of water then takes its place: 'Lavoisier then adorned this arch with his dramatic announcement that water, long thought to be an element, is in fact a compound formed by the combination of the two gases.'[39] What Donovan describes as Lavoisier's 'demonstration' of the compound nature of water conforms, he tells us, 'to the well-established pattern of British discovery and French explanation', a pattern transformed into a theme in modern historiography by Henry Guerlac.[40] All along, as Lavoisier had developed his other theories, Priestley had been characterized by Lavoisier as a most valuable experimentalist but lacking system and discipline. Donovan seems to share this view of Priestley, describing him as engaged in the 'apparently aimless ransacking of nature', and as 'prolific, chatty, and unsystematic'.[41] It is in this sense that Lavoisier is seen as giving theoretical coherence to the rather chaotic experimental discoveries of the British. It is acknowledged that when Lavoisier turned again to the burning together of hydrogen and oxygen, the experiment performed on 24 June 1783, much had already been achieved on the other side of the English Channel. Priestley had already reported finding water and Blagden had brought to Paris the news of Cavendish's quantitative finding that the weight of the water produced was the same as the weight of the gases burned. However, the complex, large-scale experiment that Lavoisier performed completed the construction of his 'comprehensive new theory'. Even as Lavoisier proceeded smoothly to this climax, 'false leads and confusion' were evident in Britain as Priestley created havoc with his claim to have converted water into a new kind of air by intense heat with quicklime. Watt and other of Priestley's friends are mentioned here as among those led astray, even as Priestley also announced his repetition of Cavendish's experiment of turning air into water. Priestley's retraction of his interpretation of the earlier experiment added to the confusion.[42] The impression we get is that the experiment performed in Paris on 24 June 1783 saw Lavoisier rise magisterially above those confusions (and above Cavendish's interpretative reticence) and show how the compound nature of water fit into the grand theoretical edifice that was now all but complete. Donovan does not explicitly award Lavoisier the *discovery* of the compound nature of water. Rather he writes of Lavoisier's *demonstration* of the fact, capped, of course, by the 1784 analysis and synthesis experiment. Donovan implicitly treats discovery as an empirical matter and reserves the term

---

[38] Gillispie, *Edge of Objectivity*, pp. 235–37.

[39] Arthur Donovan, *Antoine Lavoisier. Science, Administration, and Revolution*, 1993, pp. 153–54.

[40] Ibid., p. 154; Guerlac, 'Chemistry as a Branch of Physics', 193–276.

[41] Donovan, *Lavoisier*, pp. 139, 140.

[42] Ibid., p. 155.

'demonstration' for discoveries interpreted 'correctly'. This is a common and understandable approach in histories written from a French vantage point. Such a perspective has little or no place for Watt as someone who at best was a speculator hanging off Priestley's fraying coat tails.

A number of writers have addressed more directly the work done by Watt and Cavendish on the composition of water in the 1780s, have sought to interpret it, and to assess its significance for the resolution of the water controversy. Most of these writers have seen their historical task to be the resolution of the water question. In pursuing that objective they have inevitably read the work of Watt and Cavendish against the knowledge of what the composition of water came to mean in the years following Watt's and Cavendish's work. Broadly speaking, they have read it by reference to the impending Chemical Revolution.

One of the most comprehensive and accomplished treatments of the discovery of the compound nature of water is that provided by J.R. Partington in his multi-volume *A History of Chemistry* and also in an earlier monograph on *The Composition of Water*.[43] In his treatment of Cavendish, Partington takes us way beyond the simplistic accounts of most positivist-whig history. Partington finds Cavendish as a chemist 'a remarkably accurate experimenter' but 'lacking in ability to draw far-reaching generalisations from his results, which Lavoisier and Dalton possessed in a pre-eminent degree'.[44] Cavendish, Partington tells us, was the first to discover (in 1781) the experimental fact that 'hydrogen and oxygen gases (called by any names we wish), mixed in proper proportions (practically 2 vols to 1), can be completely converted into *their own weight* of water'.[45] Partington notes that we would expect Cavendish to conclude from this that the water had been produced from the gases and was a compound of them. But, he says, we need to appreciate that Cavendish remained under the influence of phlogiston theory. Partington explains Cavendish's meaning thus:

> He seems to have represented his results as follows. Let ϕ stand for phlogiston. Inflammable air is (water + ϕ), dephlogisticated air is (water − ϕ). When the two gases combine the reaction is:
>
> $$(\text{water} + \phi) + (\text{water} - \phi) = 2 \text{ water}$$
>
> The water pre-exists in both gases, and is deposited as a result of a redistribution of phlogiston. Cavendish's explanation is quite consistent with the view that water is an element.[46]

Partington recognized that this explanation on Cavendish's part is akin to the explanations given by others, though with the differences being crucial in some cases. This *sort* of deconstruction of Cavendish as discoverer of the compound nature of water had been engaged in by Berzelius, and by B. Paul in the nineteenth

---

[43] Partington, *History of Chemistry*, vols 3 and 4, 1962, 1964; idem, *The Composition of Water*, 1928.

[44] Partington, *History of Chemistry*, vol. 3, p. 312.

[45] Ibid., p. 332.

[46] Ibid., p. 334.

century.[47] George Wilson's deconstruction differed crucially in attributing to Cavendish the belief that hydrogen was phlogiston, in which case one quantity of water *was produced*, and the other set free, from the gases. Since on this view at least some of the water was produced, Wilson felt that this was a basis for attributing the discovery of the compound nature of water to Cavendish. Partington, however, disagreed since, he contended, Cavendish had dropped the idea that inflammable air was phlogiston, an idea he had entertained back in 1766. For Cavendish in 1784, phlogiston was, once again, imponderable. This being so, the above characterization of the reactions that he envisaged must hold, and we must acknowledge that in 1784 Cavendish still considered water to be an element. He was aware, as Partington tells us, that Lavoisier had an alternative explanation not involving phlogiston at all in which the gases united to form water as a compound. But Cavendish rejected this while still recognizing that experimentally the two explanations were difficult to distinguish.

Partington's treatment of Watt is also extensive and detailed. The overall impression, however, is of Watt's unfortunate reliance upon Priestley's confused, and confusing, experimental work, his lack of an experimental base of his own, and his long-continuing belief in the presence of water in all sorts of air.[48]

Partington provides us with a full account of the water controversy, but he is happy to take his conclusion from the work of Hermann Kopp, the German chemist and historian of chemistry:

> Kopp concluded that: 'Cavendish was the first to establish the fact from which the knowledge of the composition of water proceeded' but did not state the components of water; Watt 'first concluded from these facts that water is a compound, but without reaching a true knowledge of the components'; Lavoisier, from the same facts 'and with the recognition of the compound nature of water, first gave the correct determination and the exact statement of the components'. I think that this is the correct view.[49]

Partington thus divides the credit, or perhaps invites the reader to decide which is the most important contribution (the most important dimension of discovery) and to allocate credit accordingly. Partington expressed no preference himself. However, in his earlier discussion of these matters he was less generous to Watt's confusions and saw Lavoisier's first publication on the question in 1783 as 'simply a deduction' from Cavendish's experiments, seeming to elevate the importance of the latter.[50] He also placed the water controversy in a longer narrative, including earlier ideas about water and subsequent attempts to determine its composition ever more

---

[47] Ibid., pp. 334–35. J.J. Berzelius, *Traité de Chimie*, 1845, vol. 1, p. 354; B.H. Paul, 'Gas', in Henry Watts, *A Dictionary of Chemistry*, vol. 2, 1864, 773–82.

[48] Partington, *History of Chemistry*, vol. 3, pp. 345–62. Watt's continuing 'erroneous' beliefs about water and airs are located in a letter to Black in 1788, and in Watt's contribution to the pamphlet (with Thomas Beddoes), *Considerations on the Medicinal use and on the Production of Factitious Airs*, 1794–1795, p. 114.

[49] Partington, *History of Chemistry*, vol. 3, p. 359. Kopp's major treatment of the question is 'Die Entdeckung der Zusammensetzung des Wassers', in H. Kopp, *Beiträge zur Geschichte der Chemie*, Drittes Stück, 1875, pp. 237–310.

[50] Partington, *Composition of Water*, 1928, pp. 31 (Watt's confusion), 36 (on Lavoisier).

accurately. The overall story he described as 'an account of the experimental investigations leading to our present very exact knowledge of the composition of water'.[51] Partington, I think, admired the great experimentalist Cavendish and wished that he had been a little more prone to adventurous interpretation of results.

Partington takes us a considerable distance into a contextualized account of Cavendish's, and Watt's, understanding of the nature of water. However, another notable feature of Partington's account is that his treatment of the water controversy is profoundly ahistorical. He acknowledges no phases in it, only the search for the facts about it pursued by many people over a period close to 200 years. Thus, in relation to particular points of interpretation, he gathered opinions and arguments from the 1780s, the 1840s and beyond. He himself debated with De Luc, with Wilson, Berzelius, Muirhead, Brougham, Arago, and so on. It is in this sense that I say that his account is ahistorical. Its ready deployment of chemical truths against which to judge participants' work is another feature that places Partington's account within the positivist-whig tradition identified by McEvoy. This despite the fact that Partington provides in many respects one of the most detailed and nuanced contextualizations available of the work of Watt and Cavendish on water. Although he is not one-eyed about Cavendish, Partington is very much in the interpretative tradition that descended from the writings of members of the Cavendish camp such as Harcourt, Whewell and Wilson. This is so because his primary concern is to discern the *meanings* of the contributions of the historical actors. There have, however, also been writings in the empirical tradition descended from the Watt camp's approach.

Sidney M. Edelstein provided a classical example of this in a paper published in 1948. Decisively titled, 'Priestley settles the Water Controversy', this paper claimed that a letter that Edelstein had recently acquired settled the major scientific controversy.[52] Edelstein assumed throughout his account that the ideas of Watt and Cavendish about water were essentially the same. The question was treated as being about who knew what when. Specifically, Edelstein contended that the whole business could be reduced to the question of whether Cavendish's communications to Priestley about his experiments also included *conclusions*. Both George Wilson and members of the Watt camp used arguments concerning this matter. Wilson contended that conclusions must have been communicated, and that Priestley was a pivotal figure because he would have known this. Muirhead argued, equally vehemently, that no such communication of conclusions took place, because there were no conclusions to be communicated.

Edelstein's Priestley letter, dated 14 December 1783, was addressed to Sir Joseph Banks, President of the Royal Society. It was in response to a communication from Banks regarding a paper by Lavoisier, evidently on water. Priestley wrote:

> Mr. Watt is the person who is properly concerned in this business. For the idea of water consisting of pure air and phlogiston was his, I believe, before I knew him; and you will find it in the letter which he addressed to me, which was delivered along with the last paper which I sent to The Royal Society, but which he afterwards withdrew.

---

[51] Ibid., p. vii.

[52] Sidney M. Edelstein, 'Priestley settles the Water Controversy', *Chymia*, **1**, 1948, 123–37.

This letter he now wishes to put into the hands of Mr. De Luc, who will make some use of it. You will oblige us both, therefore, if you will give orders to have this letter delivered to Mr. De Luc, who will wait upon you for the purpose.[53]

Edelstein drew his conclusion from what this letter failed to say. Since water was mentioned as Watt's business, but no mention was made of Cavendish, Edelstein concluded that: 'No theory had been presented by Cavendish to Priestley, and apparently not to Sir Joseph Banks, on the composition of water before December 14, 1783.'[54] This conclusion becomes part of a chain of circumstantially based reasoning that, by placing Watt's theory as no later than April 1783, gave him priority. The claim that both Muirhead and Wilson had effectively nominated Priestley as the person best placed to arbitrate the question gives additional force to Edelstein's case.

I am not concerned to argue with Edelstein over this, although it should be noted that other interpretations are possible, notably that Priestley, far from just conveying his knowledge to Banks, was already making an interested *claim* for his friend Watt in the face of competition from other quarters. That might be why he does not mention Cavendish. Another point to note is that this exchange between Banks and Priestley occurred during the Royal Society dissensions of 1783–84, which, as we have seen, involved culturally based oppositions of which Cavendish and Watt were in many ways symbolic. So what Priestley said might well have been a claim prompted by these underlying tensions. However, the main point to be made at this stage about Edelstein's argument is that it is classically empirical in character. In complete contrast to Partington, the *meaning* of Cavendish's and Watt's conclusions scarcely enters the question at all for Edelstein. Everything is made to depend on who said what and when. It is simply assumed that if Watt's temporal priority can be established then his theory passes muster as the discovery.

Another historian who entered the fray in a broadly similar manner was Robert E. Schofield, well known for his work on the Lunar Society of Birmingham, which gave an unaccustomed prominence to the activities of provincial scientists and industrialists in the Industrial Revolution. In his work on the history of chemistry, Schofield can be seen in one sense as part of the postpositivist thrust. He resuscitated the reputation of Priestley as an important contributor to the Chemical Revolution rather than seeing him as just the reactionary face of the recalcitrant phlogistonists. Given this, it is understandable, perhaps, that Schofield also engaged in reviving Watt's claims to the discovery of the composition of water. The way that he did so, however, smacks more of the positivist concern with priority than the postpositivist project.

In a paper published in 1964 Schofield provided more epistolary evidence in the Watt cause.[55] He noted that Edelstein's publication had not induced any change in Partington's account and that general histories of science by A. Rupert Hall and others had been published in the interim which discussed the discovery of the compound nature of water without mentioning Watt at all. Edelstein's optimism

---

[53] Ibid., p. 123.

[54] Ibid., p. 137.

[55] Robert E. Schofield, 'Still more on the Water Controversy', *Chymia*, **9**, 1964, 71–76.

about resolving the controversy had been misplaced, Schofield said: 'opinion still favors the claims of Cavendish and it has become obvious that the introduction of new evidence is unlikely to settle a controversy that primarily feeds on conflicting interpretation'.[56] Nevertheless, in the hopes of restoring Watt 'to the status of an independent proposer' of the theory, Schofield presented two further letters, this time from Priestley to J.A. De Luc.

The first letter, dated 13 December 1783, was undoubtedly the letter to De Luc that enclosed the letter to Banks dated 14 December 1783 that was published by Edelstein. Priestley's letter to De Luc again stated that the idea about water now advanced by Lavoisier had occurred to Watt 'a long time ago'. The second letter, dated 27 December 1783, also contained Priestley's testimony on priority: 'In my opinion Mr. Watt first entertained the idea you mention, and the experiment of Mr. Cavendish proved the justness of it, tho Mr. Cavendish had not that idea himself.'[57] The second letter also makes it clear, according to Schofield, that in arriving at his theory Watt relied on Cavendish's experiments, not on Priestley's. This is important because it is agreed that Priestley's so-called repetition of Cavendish's experiment on exploding inflammable and dephlogisticated airs involved an important difference. Priestley obtained his 'inflammable air' from charcoal, not from zinc. This we now know (as did participants in the second phase of the controversy) meant that Priestley's experiment could not have produced the 'right' result quantitatively. Thus Watt relied upon Cavendish's experiments, and, using them, arrived at the 'right' theory before Cavendish.

Schofield presented these letters as cutting past 'the irrelevancies which have persistently crept into the argument'. These irrelevancies he identified as: 'the personality of De Luc, Watt's failure to accept the theory of oxidation (Cavendish did not accept it either), the tragi-comedy of misdatings and interpolations'. Schofield wanted to leave aside 'useless and invidious remarks' about the character of Cavendish, Blagden and Watt, and the 'heated tones and recriminations of nineteenth century controversialists'.[58] In short, Schofield would have us put aside the substance of the whole second phase of the controversy as lost in irrelevancies. His conclusion is worth quoting at length:

> Cavendish caught the possible significance of some casual experiments made by Priestley and Warltire and instituted a series of experiments which might naturally lead him to a conclusion about the composition of water. Before he had arrived at that conclusion, however, or at least before he was sure enough to mention it, he reported on his experiments to Priestley. Priestley, attempting to adapt these experiments to a different purpose, reported them and reported the results to Watt, who then gave the experiment an interpretation, at least as unambiguous as that later published by Cavendish, stating the composite nature of water. This interpretation was formally written before the date of any written statement by Cavendish, but not, apparently, before a Cavendish interpretation

---

[56] Ibid., p. 71.

[57] Ibid., p. 74. 'The idea' here refers to Watt's early notion that water could be converted into air by long-continued heating. The Cavendish camp treated the incorrectness of this idea as a disqualification. Schofield comments: 'That the idea is incorrect is less important than the predisposition it would provide for Watt's interpretation of Cavendish's experiment' (p. 75).

[58] Ibid., p. 75.

was known to Charles Blagden. Watt's paper was withdrawn from publication when it became incongruous to the Priestley paper it had been written to accompany; Watt did not attempt to publish his claim until after Lavoisier's announcement of 'his' experiments and conclusions, evidently based on Blagden's report of Cavendish's work. When Watt learned of Lavoisier's papers, he attempted to establish his priority, but was then forestalled by the reading of the paper by Cavendish.[59]

This is an entirely plausible conclusion as to what occurred in 1783–84. If I were in the business of seeking to resolve the controversy, I would probably adopt something like this. But I do not seek resolution. What is notable about Schofield's account is that, like Edelstein's and like the account favoured by the Watt camp in the nineteenth century, it is a circumstantial one. Although Schofield takes more notice than Edelstein of matters of meaning, he still sidesteps them, as in the matter of Watt's early, but 'erroneous' theory and on the charcoal issue. His account is empirical in its primary reliance on testimony concerning timing and in its dismissal of rhetorical processes as irrelevant, useless and invidious.

It must be remembered, however, that although Schofield and Edelstein do battle with Partington and others on the water question, all share a similar perspective on the Chemical Revolution. The fight is worth fighting, precisely because of the perceived centrality of the discovery of the composition of water to the story of that Revolution.

It is perhaps stating the obvious to say that neither Watt nor Cavendish knew what was around the corner as they prosecuted their work on water. We need to try to recover what it was that they thought they were doing at that moment and then to see how they responded to later events, especially the articulation of the New Chemistry by Lavoisier. The protagonists themselves, and other chemists, had to decide in the later 1780s and 1790s how the work of Watt and Cavendish fit into the evolving story. The original impetus to, and meaning of, their work was transformed through this process of reinterpretation. The positivist-whig historiography was at work even then, assimilating Cavendish to the progressive story of chemistry and sidelining Watt. Fortunately, scholars examining the work of Watt's chemical mentor, Joseph Black,[60] and Watt's own work within the tradition that Black led, have given us many of the materials necessary to reconstruct the deeper chemical context of Watt's claims on the composition of water. Others, notably Jungnickel and McCormmach, have provided similar insights into Cavendish. It is to these that we now turn.

---

[59] Ibid., pp. 75–76.

[60] Joseph Black (1728–1799) was Professor at Glasgow from 1756 and at Edinburgh from 1766. He and Watt worked together in Black's laboratory at the University of Glasgow, and maintained a correspondence for the rest of Black's life. See Eric Robinson and Douglas McKie (eds), *Partners in Science. Letters of James Watt and Joseph Black*, 1970.

James Watt, Joseph Black and the Scottish Tradition

Watt was working in a line of inquiry that did not relate directly to the problem of the chemical composition of water as we understand that problem, or, indeed, as the generations subsequent to Watt came to understand it. The issue of the nature of water was encompassed in Watt's intellectual universe, as in Joseph Black's, by the problem of heat. The composition of water was conceived as the reverse of what we would call decomposition, but what Black and Watt called 'inflammation'. This, as taught for many years in Black's lectures and set out, for example, in the 1797 edition of the *Encyclopaedia Britannica*, was one of a number of effects of heat.

The laboratory of Black and Watt, at Glasgow, was concerned in various ways with the heating of water, and especially with what we would call changes of state. The composition and decomposition of water was a part of this problematic for Black and Watt since it involved (in the changing of water into air and air into water) the same sorts of processes. Although history has separated Watt's work on the composition of water, on the one hand, and his experiments on steam in relation to his engine improvements on the other, there was an essential continuity between them. I suggest that Watt himself, and his friends and associates, made no such distinction.[61] Students at the University of Edinburgh attending Black's lectures and those of his successor, Thomas Charles Hope, also had some exposure to these continuities in the way Hope lectured about the 'experiments of Dr. Watt'. Within that Scottish tradition, at least, Watt was a chemist, not just because of his work with chlorine bleaching and alkali manufacture[62] but because of his work with Black, and on his own account, on heat.

Joseph Black's definition of chemistry in his early Edinburgh lectures was 'the Study of the effects of Heat & Mixture on Bodies and Mixtures of Bodies, with a view to the improvement of our knowledge'.[63] The topic of heat always began, and

---

[61] Much attention has been lavished, of course, on the relationship between Black's discovery of latent heat and Watt's improvements of the steam engine. Robison's writings on this question, though unreliable, have been enormously influential historiographically. (See Donald Cardwell, *From Watt to Clausius: the rise of thermodynamics in the early industrial age*, 1971, pp. 41–42.) Watt himself denied this connection in the sense that he repudiated the suggestion that he had been a pupil of Black. Watt did not deny, however, that the issue of latent heat and his steam-engine work were substantively related. In denying the specific indebtedness to Black, Watt, and his son after him, sought to make the great engineer's work completely *sui generis*. (See Chapter 5 below.) Hence my suggestion that in understanding Watt's intellectual world, his views on heat, his work on steam, and his ideas about the composition of water are best seen as all of a piece.

[62] Later accounts of Watt tend to neatly divide his mechanical and his chemical exploits, and exemplify the latter by reference to chlorine bleaching and alkali manufacture. See, for example, A.E. Musson and Eric Robinson, *Science and Technology in the Industrial Revolution*, 1969, chs 8 and 10. Richard L. Hills, *James Watt. Volume 1: His time in Scotland, 1736–1774*, 2002 seems to maintain this distinction and makes little connection between Watt's work on heat with Black and his chemical interests. Watt is treated primarily as a 'chemical engineer' in his work on bleaching, alkali and for the Delftfield Pottery (pp. 143–79 and 303–11).

[63] Lecture, 17 November 1766, in Blagden MS 'Notes of Dr Black's Lectures', 1766–67, Wellcome Institute for History of Medicine, as quoted in Henry Guerlac, 'Joseph Black's Work on Heat', in A.D.C. Simpson (ed.), *Joseph Black 1728–1799. A Commemorative Symposium*, 1982, p. 13.

took up a substantial portion of, Black's lecture courses in chemistry. Black's first chemistry lectures were delivered in Glasgow in 1757–58, and his association with James Watt dates from this time also. By the mid-1760s John Robison had joined the circle and Black was delivering lectures that the best of his students perceived to be highly original, especially in regard to Black's discovery of what came to be known as 'latent heat'.

Black's work on heat had a number of roots. It was partly inspired by William Cullen's experiments on evaporative cooling and partly by meditations on processes of freezing. Simple facts, such as the longevity of snowfalls upon the ground even when the temperature rose above freezing, convinced Black that processes of freezing and vaporization involved large quantities of heat well beyond those that ought to be required according to prevailing ideas. His first major experiments on raising the temperature of water and ice were conducted in 1761, and a year later he performed experiments on vaporization. From these experiments, values were obtained for the quantity of heat required for (what would later be called latent heat of) fusion and vaporization.

Watt became involved in this work first through his famous efforts with the model of a Newcomen Engine undertaken as part of his duties as instrument maker to the University of Glasgow. In the winter, spring and summer of 1764 Watt performed a series of experiments on steam. He was able to show that steam could heat about six times its own weight of water to boiling point. In the working of the Newcomen Engine this manifested itself in the large quantities of cold water necessary to condense the steam in the cylinder. When this result was mentioned to Black, and Watt learned of the idea of latent heat, he realized that this explained the phenomenon of the steam engine. Watt's crucial move to the separate condenser, which he made in 1765, was inspired by these experiments. Black and Robison were to claim that Black's work was Watt's inspiration, but the engineer himself denied that this was the case, maintaining that he arrived at the idea independently of learning about Black's notion of latent heat.[64] Watt, however, did not deny his general debt to Black.

It is true, and most important to our current concerns, that from 1764 Watt's work on heat was undertaken as part of Black's tradition of work.[65] Black benefited from Watt's experimental acumen and skill. Watt surely benefited as Black and his students turned at least some of their experiments in directions suggested by, and relevant to the task of, improving the steam engine. Black drew an explicit connection between accurate determination of the latent heat of steam and the measurement of how well fuel was being used. Watt drew inspiration from work on the lowering of the latent heat of vaporization in situations of reduced pressure in pursuing plans to save fuel by operating at such reduced pressures, but his experiments showed the ultimate futility of any such scheme. The experimental work on determination of specific heats undertaken at Glasgow before Black's departure for Edinburgh in 1766 was closely connected with Watt's search for metals and alloys that would enable a cylinder to be made that absorbed less heat.

---

[64] See Arthur Donovan, *Philosophical Chemistry in the Scottish Enlightenment. The Doctrines and Discoveries of William Cullen and Joseph Black*, 1975, esp. pp. 250–64.

[65] The following relies heavily on Guerlac, 'Joseph Black's work on heat', pp. 13–22.

All this is by way of enabling us to comprehend properly the roots and the character of Watt's chemical work. For him, as for his collaborator Black, the phenomena of heat were central to *chemical* processes. The focus upon steam and upon processes of its vaporization and condensation significantly shaped the ideas that Watt brought to the chemistry of airs. In so far as this connection can be made, Watt's 'speculation' on the composition of water in 1783 can itself be placed in a tradition of work. This opens the possibility that it was not a 'random' speculation or an inspired hunch without any sustained bases, as the anti-Watt, pro-Cavendish camp sought to portray it. There was, then, a coherent basis on which Watt's claim *could have been defended*. That it was not seriously defended during the first phase of the controversy was probably due to the fact that most British chemists, including, crucially, Black himself (and Thomas Charles Hope, his successor at Edinburgh), acceded quite quickly to the New Chemistry of Lavoisier, as can be seen in the shifts taking place in the lectures at Edinburgh.[66] Watt's achievements were lauded in those lectures. His experiments on steam and vaporization survived intact. However, his contribution to pneumatic chemistry paled, and was then excised unnoticed, as the all-powerful Lavoisian scheme came to dominate.

One of the few authors to set Watt's chemical work into a carefully observed context was David R. Dyck.[67] Dyck set himself the task of examining the relationships between conceptions of heat and chemistry during the eighteenth century. He makes a number of very important points about Watt's work on steam and water.

First Dyck reminds us that Watt's understanding of, and explanation of, the composition of water involved an integral role in the chemical process for latent heat. In this Watt went beyond Black's own work, since Black did not really attempt an integration of his physical work on heat and other aspects of his chemistry. The two sat side by side. They were conceptually linked for Black, but he did not actively mobilize the heat concepts to solve chemical problems as conventionally recognized. However, Watt, and other of Black's students and followers (such as Crawford, Cleghorn and Irvine, who were active in the development of ideas about heat) brought them together. Second, Watt's explanation of the composition of water had also grown out of ideas about the relationships of water, air and fire that existed in older traditions and works. He long believed that if water could be heated enough, it would change not just into steam but ultimately into air.

Watt's work on the composition of water thus was part of a 'Scottish School' of chemical work deriving from, but also in some ways departing from, the work of Black. That strand, and its distinctiveness, have been virtually lost sight of because of the readiness and near-totality with which Lavoisier's interpretation was adopted in Britain and, most importantly, because of the way chemists and commentators

---

[66] On the Scottish response to Lavoisier see Arthur Donovan, 'The new nomenclature among the Scots: Assessing novel chemical claims in a culture under strain', in Bernadette Bensaude-Vincent and Ferdinando Abbri (eds), *Lavoisier in European Context. Negotiating a New Language for Chemistry*, 1995, pp. 113–21. On Black see also C.E. Perrin, 'A reluctant catalyst: Joseph Black and the Edinburgh reception of Lavoisier's Chemistry', *Ambix*, **29**, 1982, 141–76.

[67] David Ralph Dyck, 'The nature of heat and its relationship to chemistry in the eighteenth century', unpublished PhD thesis, University of Wisconsin, 1967.

retrospectively assimilated Black's work, seen as a *physical* account of heat, to the new system. Once that had been done, Watt's integration of Black's heat theory into chemical processes began to look like a backward step, if it was recognized at all. Those taking Watt's chemical statements seriously in the second phase of the water controversy inevitably found them archaic and outlandish in the way that they incorporated latent heat into the chemical process proper. Whewell put it clearly when he said:

> Watt's views are utterly damaged by involving a composition of ponderable and imponderable elements. This of itself was enough to show that he did not consider elementary composition with the rigour and distinctness which the discovery of the synthesis and analysis of bodies at that time required.[68]

In this way it was much easier to ignore the discredited tradition within which Watt worked and to sideline him as merely engaged in speculative inference on the basis of the experiments of others when he ventured his views about the nature of water.

The view that if only steam could be heated enough then it would be converted into air, just as water if heated enough was converted into steam, was an idea with a history, and in its general form Watt could have acquired it from Eller,[69] who suggested that water is converted into air by combination with elementary fire. The early decades of Watt's interest in chemistry and heat (the 1760s and 1770s) saw a proliferation of ideas about entities actively involved in chemical reactions including not only phlogiston but also heat (fire) and light.[70] Watt characterized his long-held views on the relations of water and air in a letter to Matthew Boulton in 1782:

> You may remember that I have often said that if water could be heated red-hot or something more, it would probably be converted into some kind of air, because steam would in that case have lost all its latent heat, and that it would have been turned solely into sensible heat, and probably a total change of the nature of the fluid would ensue.[71]

Watt believed when he wrote this letter that Priestley had performed an experiment that proved that this change did indeed happen.

Watt expressed the same idea in a letter to Black at the same time.[72] The context in which he did so is important. Watt had been advised by De Luc of the latter's intention to write something on heat. De Luc was seeking information from Black, and Watt believed that De Luc would try to do justice to Black's claims to the discovery of latent heat. Watt explained to Black that he would provide De Luc with an account of his own work. This would be difficult because Watt sometimes found it hard to distinguish between 'the suggestions of my own mind' and 'what I

---

[68] Whewell to Harcourt, 11 February 1840, in *The Harcourt Papers*, vol. xiv, pp. 105–106.

[69] Johann Theodor Eller, *Physikalisch-Chymisch-Medicinische Abhandlungen aus den Gedenkschriften der König*, 1764.

[70] See Hélène Metzger, *Newton, Stahl, Boerhaave et la Doctrine Chimique*, 1930.

[71] Quoted in J.P. Muirhead, *The Origin and Progress of the Mechanical Inventions of James Watt*, 3 vols, 1854, vol. 2, p. 167.

[72] James Watt to Joseph Black, 13 December 1782, transcribed in Eric Robinson and Douglas McKie (eds), *Partners in Science. Letters of James Watt and Joseph Black*, 1970, pp. 117–19.

have learnt from you'.[73] Watt then explained what experimental results he considered to be his own, the theoretical ideas that had grown out of them, and how Priestley had provided experimental support:

> What I mean to tell him that I think my own, is the trying the experiment on the latent heat *in vacuo* and the finding it to be greater than under the pressure of the Atmosphere – The expts to ascertain the different degrees of heat at which water boils under different pressures – the expansion which steam in its perfect state receives from heat and the experiments on the bulk of water when converted into steam together with a theory which I have devised which accounts for the boiling heats of the water not following a Geometrical progression, and showing that as steam parts with its latent heat as it acquires sensible heat or is more compressed, that when it arrives at a certain point it will have no latent heat and may under proper compression be an elastic fluid nearly as specifically heavy as water and at which point I conceive it will again change its state and become something else than steam or water. My Opinion has been that it would then become air, which many things had led me to conclude and which is confirmed by an experiment which Dr Priestley made the other day in his usual way of Groping about … [74]

Watt also recounted this phase in his intellectual history in his 'Thoughts on the Constituent Parts of Water' as published in the *Philosophical Transactions*, which, of course, took the form of a letter to De Luc dated 26 November 1783.[75] He explains how he reached the view that steam might be changed directly into air if only enough heat were supplied to it:

> This opinion arose from a discovery that the latent heat contained in steam diminished in proportion as the sensible heat of the water from which it was produced increased; or, in other words, that the latent heat of steam was less when it was produced under a greater pressure, or in a more dense state, and greater when it was produced under a less pressure, or in a less dense state; which led me to conclude, that when a very great degree of heat was necessary for the production of steam, the latent heat would be wholly changed into sensible heat; and that, in such cases, the steam itself might suffer some remarkable change.[76]

The point of Watt's paper in the *Philosophical Transactions* was, of course, that he now abandoned this opinion for the theory that became his claim to the discovery

---

[73] Ibid.

[74] Ibid., at pp. 117–18. The account continues by describing Priestley's experiment: 'as he had succeeded in turning the acid into air by heat only, he wanted to try what water would become in like circumstances. He under saturated some very caustic lime with an ounce of Water, and subjected it to a white heat in an earthen retort, he fixed a Balloon between the receiver and the retort, No water or *moisture* came over but a quantity of Air = in weight to water viz. 200oz measures, a very small part of wch was fixt air and the rest —of the nature of Atmospheric air but rather more Phlogisticated, he has repeated the experiment with the same results … '.

[75] James Watt, 'Thoughts on the constituent parts of water and of dephlogisticated air; with an account of some experiments on that subject. In a letter from Mr. James Watt, Engineer, to Mr. De Luc, F.R.S.', *Philosophical Transactions*, **74**, 1784, 329–53.

[76] Ibid., p. 335.

of the composition of water. What must be noticed, however, is that Watt's thinking and ideas about the relations of water and air go back some way; that, primed probably by ideas on water/air conversion by earlier authors, he had been entertaining such ideas for some time during his experiments on steam. It can also be seen that whilst his abandonment of his earlier views was a significant break, there were also deep continuities, especially in the centrality of heat to the chemical process that he envisaged.

As Dyck argues, Watt's distinctive chemical explanation in his work on the composition of water (as well as the distinctiveness of that by Crawford, Cleghorn and Irvine) was effectively submerged by the assimilation of Black's work to the Lavoisian system in the 1780s and 1790s. Watt had taken up and pursued some of the possibilities that Black's doctrines offered for explanation of chemical change in terms of latent heat, possibilities that Black himself had not pursued. Once those doctrines were subsumed into another system, Watt's work would come to seem peculiar and misdirected if examined in detail. Even by the late 1780s and 1790s this process was well under way. There were some 'lags', however, where assimilation into the Lavoisian system was resisted and where something of the Scottish tradition in its unassimilated form can be seen. Articles in the third edition (1797) of the *Encyclopaedia Britannica* written by John Robison are an important example. As is well known, Robison, for political reasons, resisted the lure of system that he and others saw as characteristic of French chemistry.[77] We will see in the next chapter how Robison's articles, fiercely defensive of the empirical approach that he attributed to Black, preserved as if in amber some of the meanings and understandings of the unassimilated Black tradition, not least of these the language of the transformation of water into air by the application of heat.

Watt himself did not participate in the public discussions concerning water or in the public debate between supporters and opponents of phlogiston during the later 1780s and the 1790s. This lack of an ongoing presence in the debates may explain why Watt's claim to discovery was largely overlooked, even by students taught by Black and Hope in Edinburgh during that period.[78] Watt had other preoccupations and these, together with his well-known diffidence, may explain his lack of continuing involvement.

There were, however, two contexts in which Watt did return publicly to the chemistry of airs. The first was in his cooperation with Thomas Beddoes and the latter's Pneumatic Institution. Watt's interest in the medical uses of airs had been prompted in part by the illness of his daughter Jessie, who died in June 1794. In a joint publication with Beddoes, issued first in 1794–95, there is a letter by Watt, dated 2 September 1794, in which he makes the statement that 'no species of artificial air is obtained except water is obviously present, or that there is reason to suspect it may be contained as an element, or part of one of the substances

---

[77] See Donovan, 'New nomenclature', pp. 119–20 and J.B. Morrell, 'Professors Robison and Playfair and the *Theophobia Gallica*: Natural philosophy, religion and politics in Edinburgh, 1789–1815', *Notes and Records of the Royal Society of London*, **26**, 1971, 43–63.

[78] See James Kendall, 'The first chemical society, the first chemical journal, and the Chemical Revolution', *Proceedings of the Royal Society of Edinburgh*, **63A**, 1952, 346–58, 385–400. The issue of the Edinburgh 'neglect' of Watt's claim is discussed in the attributional context in Chapter 4.

concerned ... '.[79] This is redolent still of supposedly superseded ideas that water is contained in gases. In the 1796 edition Watt described a pneumatic apparatus of his own design for producing factitious airs in quantity. He also described the preparation of 'Inflammable or Hydrogene Airs'. In this category Watt included gases made from zinc and iron by the action of water, from charcoal heated to redness, and water (producing what he calls 'heavy inflammable air') and also gases produced by heating animal substances (what Watt calls 'animal inflammable air').[80] As Partington notes, Watt seems at this time, over a decade after such gases were carefully distinguished in the work of Cavendish and Lavoisier, to have still regarded them all as varieties of one kind of inflammable air. This also suggests that Watt long continued to think of generic airs distinguished by their combinations with elementary heat. Humphry Davy reported from conversations that he had with Watt and Keir in 1799 that they were both still phlogistians, this at a time when the recalcitrant Priestley, in American exile, is usually considered the last bastion.[81] The second, more remote, context in which Watt revisited his views on water occurred during his editing in 1814 of his friend Robison's *Encyclopaedia Britannica* articles on 'Steam' and 'The Steam-Engine' for republication. The significance of this production lies mainly elsewhere in that it is direct testimony from Watt about his route to his steam-engine improvements. However, his revision also contains an account of his experiments on steam and those of his associates. Here Watt finally laid to rest the notion that if all the latent heat of steam could be converted to sensible heat, then the steam would become air. His later experiments on steam showed that the grounds on which he saw the possibility of this interconvertibility of latent and sensible heat were unfounded. Watt's recognition of this constituted his final discarding of the central pillar upon which his views on water had been built. It appears likely that Watt saw himself as a chemical interloper who lacked the experimental wherewithal to continue involvement in the strenuous battles of the 1780s and 1790s.

It should be noted that the second phase of the water controversy in the 1830s to 1850s (and indeed the attributional processes operating between the two phases) involved at various levels the suppression, or selective highlighting, of the contextual account of Watt's ideas on water that we have painted here. The Watt camp, whose members argued their case primarily using an empirical model of discovery (that of synonymity and priority), sought therefore to minimize the difference between the conceptions of the composition of water held by Watt, Cavendish and Lavoisier. They sought to treat the ideas of Watt and Cavendish, in particular, as essentially the same. They were aided in this by the processes that encouraged assimilation of Black's work, and that of his followers, to the same intellectual universe as the

---

[79] Thomas Beddoes, *Considerations on the Medicinal Use and on the Production of Factitious Airs*, 1794–95, Part II, pp. 19–22, at p. 20. On Watt's work with Beddoes see Dorothy A. Stansfield and Ronald G. Stansfield, 'Dr. Thomas Beddoes and James Watt: Preparatory work 1794–96 for the Bristol Pneumatic Institute', *Medical History*, **30**, 1986, 276–302.

[80] Beddoes, *Considerations on the Medicinal Use and on the Production of Factitious Airs*, 3rd edn, enlarged, 1796, pp. 212–15.

[81] Humphry Davy to Davies Gilbert, 22 February 1799, cited in A. Clow and N.L. Clow, *The Chemical Revolution*, 1992 [1952], p. 496.

progenitors and supporters of the New Chemistry. In so far as this assimilation was achieved, it became possible to argue the circumstantial case for priority in terms of dates. Cavendish supporters, on the other hand, had every incentive to reveal the *dissimilarities* between Watt's work and conceptual universe and those of Cavendish and Lavoisier. Hence the emphasis in Harcourt's, Whewell's and Peacock's writings, for example, upon Watt as unaligned with the directions in which the science of chemistry 'had' to progress. Their attempts to restore Watt to his intellectual context were not inspired primarily by a search for good historical practice but by the need to place him outside the main line of development of chemistry as a realm of investigation.

Cavendish's Route to Water

The historical accounts of Cavendish's work on water which came down to modern historians from the water controversy tended to assimilate Cavendish to the Lavoisian Revolution in chemistry. Recent scholarship, however, has begun to thoroughly recontextualize it. The recent biographers of Cavendish, Jungnickel and McCormmach have made important contributions in this regard.

We have already seen to some extent, in Partington's account of Cavendish, the contextualization of his experimental work on water. It is very doubtful that Cavendish considered that water was not an element during the course of his experimental work. His basic idea was that water 'condensed' during the explosion of the mixed gases rather than being formed. Only in later years was his experimental work extracted from this theoretical context and placed into another (Lavoisier's) in which water is, indeed, formed as a compound. Similarly Cavendish considered his 'Experiments on Air' as providing a key element in the defence of phlogiston theory against the antiphlogistians, and many did see it this way.

There is, however, another sense in which Cavendish's work requires contextualization. This has to do with the aims of his research. Once we place the 'Experiments on Air' in a longer train of inquiry we begin to see what it was that Cavendish considered himself to be doing. Cavendish's interest lay, as he announced at the beginning of the first paper, in the various ways in which common air was phlogisticated. Such phlogistication was the consumption of 'good' air. Activities such as breathing common air, burning things in it, and processes such as putrefaction of animal or vegetable material, were all ways of phlogisticating the air.

Joseph Priestley had done important work on the goodness of air. In a paper published in 1772[82] he reviewed the field of pneumatic chemistry, announced the discovery of a new kind of air (nitrous air) and showed how the latter could be used as a measure of the goodness of common air. Nitrous air phlogisticated common air when mixed with it and Priestley developed this into a test of goodness using a device known as a 'eudiometer' to measure the diminution of the common air. The design of new, improved eudiometers and their use to measure the goodness of the

---

[82] Joseph Priestley, 'Observations on different kinds of air', *Philosophical Transactions*, **62**, 1772, 147–264.

air in various places and conditions became a popular area of inquiry, and an area of strong medical interest, in the late 1770s and early 1780s.[83]

Before the appearance of his first paper on 'Experiments on Airs' in 1784, Cavendish had published in the *Philosophical Transactions* an account of a new eudiometer and its use in measuring the goodness of air. He reported numerous trials of samples of air taken in London and Kensington in a range of weathers and at different times of day. From these he concluded that the degree of phlogistication of the air did not vary between places or times. On the basis of these measurements he also arrived at a figure that we can interpret as a measure of the concentration of oxygen in the atmosphere. Much has been made of the accuracy of Cavendish's figure of 20.83 per cent.[84]

Now we can see the 'Experiments on Air' in a new light. As Jungnickel and McCormmach put it:

> We might expect that just as he [Cavendish] and Black had replaced the ancient element air with distinct gases, he would show that the ancient element water was a combination of gases, but that is not what he thought he did. He did not bring into question the elemental notion of water, even as his experiments laid the factual basis for our modern understanding of water as a chemical combination of gases. His way of referring to water was ambiguous as to its elemental or compound nature ... [85]

Cavendish's eudiometry experiments were the most important of a range of inspirations for his inquiry into the modes of phlogistication of common air, of which the explosion of air with inflammable air by an electric spark in a closed glass vessel was one. Cavendish was in fact critical of medical eudiometry and his intervention is usually seen as important in the demise of that tradition. His 'Experiments on Air' involved a shift of eudiometric devices from the medical context to the investigation of combustion.[86] The production of dew had been observed by Warltire and Priestley, whose work Cavendish was repeating. However, Cavendish went further. His observation was that the dew condensed out of the inflammable air and approximately a one-fifth part of the common air. This was not the *production* of water but more like its release. When dephlogisticated air (which Cavendish regarded as water deprived of its phlogiston) was exploded with inflammable air (which he considered to be either pure phlogiston, or more likely, water united to phlogiston), the deprivation and surfeit of phlogiston effectively cancelled each other out to produce pure water. The elemental character of water was unchallenged in this process

We can see, then, that there was considerable retrospective reorientation involved in locating Cavendish in a single progressive line as part of the 'logic' of the Chemical Revolution. Some of this reorientation occurred thanks to Cavendish

---

[83] On the medical and social reform context of eudiometry see Simon Schaffer, 'Measuring virtue: Eudiometry, enlightenment and pneumatic medicine', in Andrew Cunningham and Roger French (eds), *The medical enlightenment of the eighteenth century*, 1990, pp. 281–318.

[84] Christa Jungnickel and Russell McCormmach, *Cavendish*, 1999, pp. 357–59.

[85] Ibid., pp. 362–63.

[86] Schaffer, 'Measuring virtue', pp. 312–13.

himself during his ongoing participation in chemical debate; some was accomplished on his behalf by Blagden. The rest can be located in attributional processes during the later eighteenth and very early nineteenth centuries. By the time of the second phase of the controversy there was little attempt, even by the Watt camp, to restore Cavendish's work to its original context. The closest that participants came to this was to reassert (as did David Brewster, for example) that there was no essential difference in the extent to which both Watt and Cavendish were in the thrall of phlogiston theory.

Conclusion

We have been concerned in this chapter with the 'action' in the 1780s concerning understandings of the nature of water. That action became, of course, the central focus of the second phase of the water controversy. It has, in more recent times, been incorporated into historical writing on the first phase of the water controversy and, more broadly, on the Chemical Revolution.

The significance attributed to various pieces of the action depends upon historiographical assumptions (positivist-whig, postpositivist, 'postmodern') and, more specifically, upon the model of discovery adopted. The confident stipulations of the positivist-whig approach read backwards from the rights and wrongs of the New Chemistry in its mature formulations and find matches or mismatches in the case of the work of Lavoisier, Cavendish and Watt. Whilst the work of Lavoisier and Cavendish has been readily assimilable to the mainline story of the Chemical Revolution and the place of understandings of water in that story, Watt has been marginalized. Watt is dismissed as engaged in ungrounded speculation or as having ideas rooted in 'failed' traditions. Postpositivist and postmodern historiographies avoid such confident stipulations, although they tend to persist in telling the mainline story in a different way. Lavoisier, and Cavendish to a lesser extent, are still the focus but their relative standing as discoverers emerges not from the inherent validity of their ideas, but from sociological and rhetorical processes. There has been no serious attempt to reinsert Watt into the picture. Whilst this would be possible, it is not my aim here to do more than hint at the possibility. The fact remains that Watt was written out of the picture. In the next chapter I exhibit some of the processes whereby this came about in the years before the attempt to revive his claim.

Chapter 4

Attributional Survey:
Phase One, 1784–1830

When the theory of the composition of water was spoken of in the presence of my father, he calmly but uniformly sustained his claim to its discovery; and once, on my hinting that it was passed over by some writers, and not correctly given by others, he observed ... *he should leave posterity to decide.*[1]

Introduction

This chapter reports on the way in which scientific publications of various types discussed, more often merely mentioned, the discovery of the compound nature of water (and who made it) during the period when the controversy proper was quiet. The attributional approach to discovery involves the idea that cumulative usage is just as important, if not more important, than explicit argument in establishing discovery claims. The chapter examines encyclopaedia articles as well as scientific texts, especially, but not solely, chemical ones, and also survey histories and popular representations of the main protagonists. The circumstances of the production of some of these attributions will also be sketched. The survey enables an assessment to be made of the 'gradient' or the distribution of credit for discovery that prevailed when the second phase of the water controversy began.

From the perspective being taken in this book, James Watt's attitude to the issue of credit for discovery of the theory of the composition of water, expressed in the epigram for this chapter, was paradoxical. The son recalls his father wanting to 'leave posterity to decide', and yet being indifferent to what writers were saying about the question. Yet what is posterity if not what writers *in the future* will say? That will surely be conditioned, if not determined, by what writers have said in the interim. Of course, Watt's attitude makes sense if we assume, as is most commonly done, that it is possible for posterity to decide on the 'facts' of the matter independently of what others have said. If the 'truth' is accessible independently, then Watt's attitude is justifiable. We have seen, however, in our discussion of the nature of discovery, that there is much to be said for an attributional model of that process. On that view, the discoverer is the person attributed with the discovery by his/her ongoing community. This, I suppose, is what posterity is. Attributions create the discoverer, and the discovery.

---

[1] 'Letter from James Watt Esq., to the Editor', in James Patrick Muirhead (ed.), *Correspondence of the late James Watt on his discovery of the theory of the composition of water*, 1846, pp. iii–iv.

I have drawn a distinction between a first phase and a second phase of the water controversy. In the first phase the claimants themselves were involved. The second phase, involving various parties arguing on behalf of the long-dead claimants, occurred some fifty to seventy years later. During the interim there were few public signs of the controversy, but this does not mean that nothing was happening. In various more or less public utterances, interpretations were being offered of the meaning of the controversy. This might be done by the author of a dictionary who stated, for example, that Cavendish discovered the composition of water. Such a statement, by what it said and by what it left out, concretized and simplified the historical process in a way that favoured one interpretation and rendered it as 'fact-like'. Numerous statements of that type fed into the perception of the issue within the scientific and wider cultures. Since such processes were occurring between what I have called the phases of the controversy, the controversy is, in a sense, a continuous process. The appearance of phases is created by a hiatus in the explicit declamatory contributions that we normally associate with controversy.

Attributional processes between the 1780s and the 1830s are important because, as I will argue here, they seemed to place Cavendish in a stronger position than Watt by the later period. In the second phase of explicit controversy the supporters of Watt started from a difficult, but perhaps not impossible, position. We will see that the pattern of attributions had created what we might call an interpretative gradient in the culture that made arguing the case for Watt an uphill battle.

Although the water controversy as such was relatively quiet during this interim period, other issues concerning the history of chemistry were, of course, much in agitation. Even as the victory of the antiphlogistians was substantially conceded in Britain and elsewhere, the significance of the New Chemistry and its origins were still debated. As David Knight,[2] among others, has shown, practitioners and writers of chemistry during the French wars and beyond betrayed little sense of any revolutionary change in the field, let alone of a recent *foundation* of it. They sought to distance their subject from revolutionary implications (whether associated with the French or with Joseph Priestley) and to demonstrate that it was not a French science. The latter demonstration involved competition in research, certainly, and the accomplishments of Humphry Davy and of John Dalton conspicuously contradicted key aspects of the Lavoisian system, namely, that oxygen was the sole acidic principle and that the chemistry of atoms was useless metaphysics. The demonstration also involved writing the history of the developments in the New Chemistry in a way that downplayed the system-building of the French and emphasized the virtues of inductive inference and avoidance of speculation. Alternative lineages for the development of the science made much play of the contributions of Joseph Black and Henry Cavendish, in particular. Their research could be shown to have many of the virtues claimed exclusively by the more rabid Lavoisians, including great precision and quantification, as well as some, like caution, that had somehow been overlooked by others. It must be remembered as we proceed that the texts that we examine below were almost invariably engaged in these sorts of ideological battles.

---

[2] David Knight, 'Revolutions in science: Chemistry and the Romantic reaction to science', in W.R. Shea (ed.), *Revolutions in Science. Their Meaning and Relevance*, 1988, pp. 49–69.

In studying processes of attribution we rely necessarily upon the examination of relevant texts, in this case treatises on chemistry, dictionaries of arts and sciences and, importantly, encyclopaedias. These texts relate somewhat differently to different audiences. There is, for example, the audience of active chemists, what Harry Collins calls the 'core set'.[3] The members of the core set are significant because they are recognized 'experts' in the area. Their attributions will carry particular weight and may even settle a controversy if others bow to their verdict. However, the literature relevant to opinion formation among the core set, and expressing their views, was broader in the early nineteenth century than it would be now. Thus expert chemists would both write for and read major encyclopaedias of the period.[4] Encyclopaedias were not purely popular publications. Understandings beyond the core set, however, are also important when people struggle not just over scientific credit but also over iconic status in the culture. So representations in the more popular literature also need to be considered.

Whilst published texts are the most central materials to be surveyed from an attributional perspective, other documents can be informative. The informal communication system is known to be as important as the formal one in the development of scientific opinion. The content of chemical lectures is of obvious interest here. What were students of chemistry, such as the numerous medical students taught chemistry at the University of Edinburgh, told about the composition and decomposition of water during their lectures? Monuments provide a further possible 'text'. It appears, for example, that Watt Jr came close at one point to commemorating his father's 'discovery' in the inscription upon the monumental statue created to Watt's memory in Westminster Abbey.[5] In that way an attribution might be literally 'carved in stone'. Such processes are, however, rare, and their permanence perhaps more than balanced by their immobility, and therefore inaccessibility to large audiences. The disappearance of lectures into the ether, except in private students' notes, also limits their circulation. Hence the power of the *printed* word.

Chemical Treatises and Texts

Systematic treatises and texts of chemistry began to proliferate in the late eighteenth century, variously reporting and summarizing research in the field and increasingly offering systematic surveys of it for students at all levels.

First there were texts through which the merits or otherwise of the New Chemistry were debated. Among these were the translations of foreign texts such as Fourcroy's

---

[3] Harry Collins, *Changing Order*, 1985, pp. 142–48.

[4] See Richard Yeo, *Encyclopaedic Visions: Scientific Dictionaries and Enlightenment Culture*, 2001, especially ch. 10.

[5] Thus amidst negotiations with Henry, Lord Brougham, about the wording of the inscription for the Westminster monument Watt Jr was looking at his father's composition of water papers. At one stage he asked Brougham: 'I know not whether it would be proper in the Inscription to allude to this, certainly the most important theory of the later half of the last century ... '. See James Watt Jr to Henry Brougham, 27 October 1834, Brougham Papers, 27, 514. In the end no mention was made of this in the inscription.

Elements of Natural History and of Chemistry. In the text itself there is little reference to the 'water question' but, not surprisingly, a very French-centred exposition of the New Chemistry. William Nicholson's 'Preface' to his translation of Fourcroy in 1788 tried to make it clear that while the French systematized the findings concerning the composition and decomposition of water, the British philosophers had been instrumental in generating those findings and had not gained enough credit. Nicholson's main concern was to restore the credit that he considered due to Cavendish. He believed that historical mistakes had been made, caused by 'the want of a speedy and faithful communication of philosophical discoveries between Great Britain and the Continent, together with the unprincipled conduct of such persons as are daily employed in endeavouring to appropriate to themselves the discoveries of others'. Watt came in for mention, much as in Nicholson's *Dictionary of Chemistry* discussed in detail below.[6]

When he came to the specific issue of the discovery of the composition of water, Nicholson began with Macquer's experiment in 1776 in which inflammable air was burned in a bottle and a white china saucer placed over the flame was moistened. The fluid appeared to Macquer to be pure water, but no tests were done. Then Nicholson reported the experiments of Lavoisier and Macquer of 1777, and then those of Warltire before April 1781, and of Priestley.

> It was in the summer of the year 1781, that Mr Henry Cavendish was busied in examining what becomes of the air lost by phlogistication, and made those valuable experiments which were read before the Royal Society on the 15th of January, 1784 ... This great philosopher, who may be considered as the true discoverer of the composition of water, appears to think, with Mr Watt, that in those experiments of Dr Priestley's, in which the vitriolic and nitrous acids seemed to be converted into dephlogisticated air, the acids served only to decompose the water by depriving it of its phlogistic part; but he thinks it unnecessary to include the consideration of elementary heat as Mr Watt does, because, in his opinion it is more likely that there is no such thing and that the bringing the consideration forward in every chemical experiment, in which increase or diminution of heat takes place, might occasion more trouble and perplexity than it is worth.[7]

Returning to his chronology, Nicholson noted that Watt interpreted Warltire's and Priestley's experiments differently:

> [He] inferred from these experiments, that water is a compound of the burned airs, which have given out their latent heat of combustion; and communicated his sentiments to Dr. Priestley in a letter, dated April 26, 1783, and he concludes, that in every case wherein dephlogisticated air was produced, water has been decomposed, by the use of some substance which had a stronger attraction to its phlogiston than is possessed by the dephlogisticated air, which is therefore set at liberty. He repeated some experiments particularly with a view to decide this point, and in several of them the quantity of

---

[6] A.F. Fourcroy, *Elements of Natural History and of Chemistry ... Translated into English, with Occasional Notes, and an Historical Preface by the Translator*, 1788, pp. iii–iv. Not the least of Fourcroy's sins was his award of the understanding of heat to Wilcke, Irvine, Crawford, Kirwan, Lavoisier and De la Place. Nicholson's translation added a note: 'Dr. Black of Edinburgh is indubitably the father of the modern doctrine of heat' (p. 116).

[7] Ibid., pp. xi–xii.

dephlogisticated air added to the acid which came over, greatly exceeded the original weight of acid employed. He dissolved magnesia, calcareous earth, and minium respectively in pale nitrous acid, and on distilling to dryness, found nearly the whole of the nitrous acid in the retort, highly phlogisticated. From common nitre the dephlogisticated air was sixteen times the weight of the nitrous acid which was missing. Mr Watt has therefore a claim to the merit of a discoverer with regard to the composition of water, and has the advantage of priority in the discovery of its decomposition.[8]

Nicholson's account of Watt's work is notable for a number of things. Whilst he gave priority to Cavendish so far as the composition of water was concerned, he did give extensive attention to Watt. He presented Watt as an independent, but not the first, discoverer of the composition of water and gave him priority in discovery of the decomposition of water.

Another translation of the fifth edition of Fourcroy was published in Edinburgh in 1800 with notes by John Thomson, Surgeon.[9] Thomson too was anxious to assert Cavendish's claims against those assumed by Fourcroy for the French philosophers.[10] He did so by pointing to Cavendish's experiments of 1781, to Lavoisier's expectation of the production of an acid rather than pure water on the combustion of hydrogen and oxygen, and to the fact that Lavoisier's famous experiment of June 1783 was professedly indebted to Cavendish's prior work. Watt received a minor mention later in the story: 'It is but justice to add, that the same inference, respecting the decomposition of water, had been made by Mr Watt, and communicated by him in a letter to Dr Priestley, dated April 26 1783.' It is odd that Watt is not credited with *anything* so far as the composition of water is concerned, only with the inference regarding decomposition.

Among a number of important manuals of chemistry published in the nineteenth century was that produced by William Thomas Brande of the Royal Institution.[11] The 'Historical Sketch of the Origin and Progress of Chemical Philosophy' that Brande provided as a Preface to that work traced the origins of chemistry as a science to Boyle, Hooke and Mayow in the seventeenth century. Knight is right when he states that 'the reader would come away with no feeling of an eighteenth-century Chemical Revolution except for the new vocabulary; and with the idea that the honest endeavours of Englishmen and others had been unfairly eclipsed'.[12] Brande dealt with the composition of water in words very close to those deployed in *The London Encyclopaedia* discussed below. Once again we have a publication casually mentioning Watt's inference but focusing upon Cavendish's 'masterly manner'. This statement was to change significantly, especially in the 1841 edition of the work.

---

[8] Ibid., pp. xiii–xiv.

[9] A.F. Fourcroy, *Elements of Chemistry and Natural History To Which is Prefixed the Philosophy of Chemistry, 5th edition with notes. By John Thomson, Surgeon, Edinburgh*, 3 vols, 1800. Thomson rose from assistant apothecary at the Edinburgh Royal Infirmary in 1790 to the position of surgeon there a decade later, and Professor of Surgery to the College of Surgeons of Edinburgh in 1805 and the Professorship of Military Surgery a year later at the University of Edinburgh. In 1799–1800 he taught a chemistry class in Edinburgh. His translation of Fourcroy went to five editions (*DNB*).

[10] He does this in note 'q', on pp. 237–44.

[11] William Thomas Brande, *A Manual of Chemistry*, second edn, 3 vols, 1821.

[12] Knight, 'Revolutions in Science', p. 63.

Another writer who gave some attention to Watt was John Murray M.D. (died 1820) whose *Elements of Chemistry* and *System of Chemistry* went through a number of editions. After Murray's death in 1820 these were edited by his son, also, rather confusingly, John Murray. Murray Senior's first statement on the water question came in the first edition of his *Elements of Chemistry*, published in two volumes in 1802. Under the heading 'Water' we find this:

> The idea of the composition of water seems to have occurred about the same time to Mr. Watt and Mr. Cavendish; the former inferring it from some experiments in which it was decomposed; the latter, from finding that when oxygen and hydrogen gases are fired together, water is the only sensible product. The latter experiment was soon after performed on a large scale with the greatest accuracy by Lavoisier and the French chemists, with the same result.[13]

Murray goes on to explain that besides its intrinsic importance, this discovery also had an 'adventitious consequence' at the time in the debate between the supporters and opponents of phlogiston. This attribution is interesting first because it appears to divide the credit equally, even mentioning Watt first. It also, like many of these early attributions, emphasized that Watt's idea came from decomposition experiments rather than from Priestley's composition experiments.

Murray's *A System of Chemistry*, which had reached its fourth edition by 1819, offered a similar, though more extended, story. First we are told that it was concluded 'nearly about the same time, by Watt and Cavendish, that water is a compound, formed from the combination of the base of this inflammable air with oxygen'.[14] Then in a later section we are given a more detailed account. The conclusion, we are told, was drawn 'nearly at the same time by Watt and by Cavendish', their memoirs being published in the same volume of the *Philosophical Transactions*. Watt was now depicted as relying upon Priestley's decomposition *and* composition experiments in drawing his inference. Cavendish was differentiated and elevated somewhat. In his case the compound nature of water 'was established, on evidence still more decisive', and Cavendish sorted out the problem of the production of acid during the combustion of hydrogen.[15] Thus, in this more discursive account in *A System*, Watt was still given considerable credit, and still mentioned before Cavendish, but the latter's efforts were depicted as more decisive and sustained.

Meanwhile *Elements of Chemistry* was going through its own sequence of editions. An advertisement at the front of the fifth edition of 1822 carried the, not quite impartial, statement that the work had 'so long been considered as standard by the Public'.[16] This fifth edition had been revised by John Murray, the younger, and we do find some significant alterations so far as 'water' is concerned that bring Cavendish to the fore. In a move increasingly typical of the genre, 'the facts' were given first:

> When hydrogen gas is burnt, an operation in which oxygen is combined with it, water is formed, and is the only sensible product; and when water is acted on by substances

---

13 John Murray M.D., *Elements of Chemistry in Two Volumes*, 1802, vol. 1, p. 244.
14 John Murray, *A System of Chemistry*, fourth edn, 1819, p. 98.
15 Ibid., pp. 111–13.
16 Murray, *Elements of Chemistry in Two Volumes*, revised by John Murray, 1822, p. iv.

capable of attracting oxygen, these are oxidated, the water disappears, and hydrogen gas is evolved. From these facts, the conclusion was drawn by Cavendish and Watt, that water is a compound of hydrogen and oxygen; and the experiment, of forming water by burning hydrogen gas, was executed by the former philosopher on a considerable scale, and its composition clearly demonstrated.[17]

This statement elevated and differentiated Cavendish further. He was now placed before Watt as the first mentioned. Whilst they both drew conclusions from the facts, Cavendish 'clearly demonstrated' the composition. This is also a good example of how texts reinterpreted the work of Cavendish and Watt within the framework of the New Chemistry. Taken literally as an account of what they did, this statement is hopelessly inaccurate, whiggish and positivistic. Yet as a text it undoubtedly works. Murray's texts did carry Watt's claim into the 1820s and beyond and were noted by James Watt Jr and Muirhead to counter the view that the consensus had been entirely for Cavendish. Nevertheless we can detect in these works and their ongoing revisions what we might call an 'attributional drift' in favour of Cavendish.

There were texts in this early period, however, that did not mention Watt at all. Given its lack of scope for extensive exposition, it is perhaps unsurprising that Jane Marcet's *Conversations on Chemistry* was one of these. Yet Mrs Marcet did manage to mention Cavendish. The work was, of course, a very elementary one and it was intended particularly for a female readership. Material was presented in conversational style (being considered as more accessible to women in that form), the conversation occurring between Caroline, Emily and the Governess, Mrs B. Conversation VII is on hydrogen and explores the properties of the gas, including its combustion to form water. Then Mrs B informs the girls:

> The composition of water was demonstrated about the same period, both by Mr. Cavendish, in this country, and by the celebrated French chemist Lavoisier. The latter invented a very perfect and ingenious apparatus to perform, with great accuracy, and upon a larger scale, the formation of water by the combination of oxygen and hydrogen gases.[18]

So Watt has disappeared, Cavendish and Lavoisier do the demonstrating, and Lavoisier provides the large-scale proof. Though clearly not a serious chemical text, Marcet's *Conversations*, which went through numerous editions and was not restricted in use to female students, should not be underestimated for its opinion-making potential among non-specialist audiences.

The same can be said for Samuel Parkes's *The Chemical Catechism*. This, like Marcet's *Conversations*, was first published in 1806 and went through numerous editions. Its dogmatic form of presentation, however, did not lend itself to ready revision and it accumulated in later editions a cumbrous set of notes. In the section 'Of Water', the catechism asks: 'how is it known that water is a compound substance?'

---

[17] Ibid., p. 305.

[18] [Jane Marcet], *Conversations on Chemistry; in which the Elements of that Science are Familiarly Explained and Illustrated by Experiments*, 2 vols, 1817. This was the fifth edition. A reader of the copy that I consulted (held in Special Collections, Edinburgh University Library) had written in the margin at this point, by way of correction: 'After Mr Cavendish had discovered water to be the product Lavoisier <u>enlarged</u> upon it, or extended the expt'.

The answer given is an experimental one, but a note informs us that 'This [the compound nature of water] was discovered by Mr. Cavendish in 1781. Dr. Priestley had previously combined the two gases by combustion; but Mr. Cavendish was the first who drew the proper conclusion from the Doctor's experiment.'[19]

One might be forgiven at this stage for thinking that 'serious' texts tended to mention Watt whilst less serious, or more elementary, ones did not. However, this view cannot be sustained, as the Aikins' *Dictionary of Chemistry and Mineralogy* illustrates. Published in 1807, in two substantial volumes, this was a major work of reference in its time. The compilers explained in their prefatory remarks that they had been forced to leave much out. This included everything relating to geology, to the applications of chemistry to medicine, 'and to the History of science, except to reclaim the merit of discovery in a few disputed instances for those to whom it appeared to be justly due'.[20] If we take this literally to mean that historical material was *only* included when merit was being redistributed, then we have to take the authors' tribute to Cavendish, and omission of any reference to Watt, as an instance of their doing justice in the case of the composition of water.

Under the entry for hydrogen gas the Aikins informed us that 'it is unquestionably owing chiefly to the valuable researches of Mr. Cavendish that the production of water and the combustion of inflammable air have been proved to be constantly concomitant'.[21] In the entry for 'Water', the discussion of the composition of water first mentioned Macquer, Warltire and Priestley before giving details of Cavendish's experiments and telling us that Cavendish drew the conclusion that water was composed of oxygen and hydrogen. There followed an account of the experiments of Lavoisier and Laplace, of Le Fevre de Gineau and of Vauquelin, Fourcroy and Seguin. Finally, Priestley's rearguard action was discussed and dismissed. The Aikins concluded that the experiments on this question of the composition of water 'have been performed with such particular care by the most accurate and intelligent chemists of the age, that no fact in the whole circle of chemical science is more satisfactorily demonstrated'.[22] Clearly, though, in the Aikins' view, Watt had no share in this. Their omission of any mention of him in a detailed discussion, in such a substantial work of reference, could not fail to have some ongoing attributional effects.

Finally, let us examine one of the most important chemical works of the early nineteenth century, Humphry Davy's *Elements of Chemical Philosophy*, published in 1812. The work begins with a historical view of the progress of chemistry. In this Cavendish loomed large alongside Lavoisier. Except for Cavendish, Davy declared, there was no one who could be compared with Lavoisier 'for precision of logic, extent of view, and sagacity of induction'. Cavendish himself was noted for his wide and minute knowledge of Natural Philosophy, and

---

19 Samuel Parkes, *The Chemical Catechism*, eighteenth edn, 1818. On Parkes's and Marcet's works see David Knight, 'Accomplishment or dogma: Chemistry in the introductory works of Jane Marcet and Samuel Parkes', *Ambix*, **33**, 1986, 94–98.

20 A. and C.R. Aikin, *A Dictionary of Chemistry and Mineralogy*, 2 vols, 1807, p. vi.

21 Ibid., vol. 1, p. 556.

22 Ibid., vol. 2, p. 474. The article 'Water' covers pages 470–86 and the discussion of the composition of water is on pp. 472–74.

he carried into his chemical researches a delicacy and precision, which have never been exceeded: possessing depth and extent of mathematical knowledge, he reasoned with the caution of a geometer upon the results of his experiments: it may be said of him, what, perhaps, can scarcely be said of any other person, that whatever he accomplished, was perfect at the moment of production. His processes were all of a finished nature; executed by the hand of a master, they required no correction; the accuracy and beauty of his earliest labours even, have remained unimpaired amidst the progress of discovery, and their merits have been illustrated by discussion, and exalted by time.[23]

Davy noted that Cavendish continued to adhere to the doctrine of phlogiston. However, the implication was that his masterly works transcended adherence to that erroneous philosophy, so that the doctrine of Lavoisier 'soon after it was framed, received some important confirmations from the two grand discoveries of Cavendish, respecting the composition of water, and nitric acid'.[24] Davy in this way assimilated Cavendish to the New Chemistry of Lavoisier, attributed to him the discovery of the composition of water, and made no mention whatever of James Watt.[25] There was a real sense in which Davy's painstaking experiments in the electrolysis of water were his tribute to Cavendish's style and precision.[26] Within the chemical community itself, and among the wide circle of Davy's fashionable admirers garnered through his Royal Institution lectures, the treatment of the water question in this influential work would have been an important resource. We will see that Watt Jr was to take some trouble in the 1820s to try to change Davy's mind.

Dictionaries and Encyclopaedias

The 1797 third edition of the *Encyclopaedia Britannica* included in the article 'Water' an extended 'Historical Account of the Discovery of the Composition of Water',[27] followed by a description of a series of experiments presented as 'Proofs of the Composition of Water'. The historical section acknowledged immediately that there was an issue of attribution:

> The history of this curious and interesting discovery we shall trace back with as much precision and impartiality as possible to the first hints that were thrown out upon the subject, and endeavour at the same time to assign to all who have contributed to the discovery the merit to which they are respectively intitled.[28]

---

[23] Humphry Davy, *Elements of Chemical Philosophy*, 1812, pp. 37, 42. It is hard not to see in these remarks, also, a comparison between the durability of Cavendish's work and the undermining of aspects of Lavoisier's that Davy was engaged in.

[24] Ibid., pp. 43–44.

[25] Watt is mentioned in Davy's *Elements* but solely in relation to his investigations of latent heat and their connection with his improvements of the steam engine (pp. 86–87).

[26] Partington, *History of Chemistry*, vol. 4, 1964, pp. 41–42 and Colin A. Russell, 'The electrochemical theory of Sir Humphry Davy', *Annals of Science*, **15**, 1959, 1–25; **19**, 1963, 255–71.

[27] *Encyclopaedia Britannica*, third edition, vol. 18, 1797, pp. 807–808.

[28] Ibid., p. 807.

Warltire's work of 1781 was recounted, as was Cavendish's experimental work of the same year which was represented as a repetition of Warltire's experiment, occurring after the publication of Priestley's account of Warltire's work in the fifth volume of his *Experiments and Observations* in 1781. We are told, following Cavendish's own account in the *Philosophical Transactions* for 1784, that 'Mr Cavendish concluded, that when inflammable and common air are exploded in a proper proportion, almost all the inflammable air, and near one-fifth of the common air, lose their elasticity, and are condensed into dew; which, when examined is found to be water'.[29] Dealt with next were Priestley's experiments that were undertaken after Cavendish had informed the Reverend of his experiments. What Priestley did, and why he did it, was expressed in an interesting fashion:

> Having formerly observed several remarkable changes in fluid substances, in consequence of long exposure to heat in glass vessels hermetically sealed, Dr Priestley formed a design of exposing all kinds of solid substances to great heats in close vessels. As many substances consist of parts so volatile as to fly off before attaining any considerable degree of heat in the usual pressure of the atmosphere, he imagined that if the same substances were compelled to bear great heats under a greater pressure, they might assume new forms, and undergo remarkable changes.[30]

These, then, were the experiments that were drawn to Watt's attention and stimulated his exertions on the composition of water question. It is noteworthy that both Priestley's and Watt's trajectory into that question focused upon the role of heat in relation to major changes in form. In Watt's case he was clearly still thinking very much within the tradition established (with Watt's help) twenty years earlier by his friend Joseph Black. Watt's initial response to Priestley was to mention 'a similar idea of his, that it might be possible to convert water or steam into permanent air'. The author of the article then reports from Watt's account of his theory as published in the *Philosophical Transactions* in 1784. The centrality of heat is once again apparent. Watt had long held the belief that 'air was a modification of water'. This belief, we are told, 'arose from a discovery; that the latent heat contained in steam diminished in proportion as the sensible heat of the water from which it was produced increased. In other words the denser the steam was, the less latent heat it contained.' Watt is quoted at length on the deflagration of inflammable and dephlogisticated air:

> These two kinds of air unite with violence, they become red hot, and upon cooling totally disappear. When the vessel is cooled, a quantity of water is found in it equal to the weight of the air employed. The water is then the only remaining product of the process; and water, light, and heat are all the products ... Are we then not authorised to conclude; that water is composed of dephlogisticated air and phlogiston deprived of part of their latent or elementary heat; that dephlogisticated or pure air is composed of water deprived of its phlogiston and united to elementary heat and light; and that the latter are contained in it in a latent state, so as not to be sensible to the thermometer or to the eye; and if light be only a modification of heat, or a circumstance attending it, or a component part of the

---

[29] Ibid.
[30] Ibid.

inflammable air, then pure or dephlogisticated air is composed of water deprived of its phlogiston and united to elementary heat.[31]

The author of the article 'Water' had already expressed the view that Watt's theory had been demonstrated to be true. Returning to this, he anticipated the objection that some would deny this because Watt employed the term 'phlogiston', 'a word which is now exploded from philosophy as the name of an imaginary substance'. The author met this anticipated objection by observing that Watt used the word 'as synonymous with inflammable air'.

What I find particularly interesting and revealing about the quotation from Watt, the anticipated difficulty, and the response to that difficulty, is that Watt's treatment of the role of heat and light in the process was not considered remarkable or problematic. It was noted that Cavendish continued to differ from Watt on the role of heat since Cavendish did not believe that there was such a thing as elementary heat. However, this was not seen as a problem in accrediting Watt's theory. The presentation was quite comfortable in leaving Watt's theory firmly, if implicitly, in the Black chemical tradition. Thus the chemical/material nature of heat, or otherwise, was not selected as a major issue in evaluating the worth of theories.

The section concluded with an allocation of credit in the discovery. Watt 'was the first person who formed the true theory'. Importantly, however, his theory was not a speculation quickly perceived in a eureka-like experience. Watt had suspected something of the sort for many years, believing that 'if the latent heat of steam could be wholly converted into sensible heat by a great increase of heat, the steam might suffer some remarkable change, such as into permanent air'.[32] The author made the point that Watt was prepared and primed, this being evident from the speed with which he formed the theory on hearing of the experiment from Priestley. Cavendish, independently of Watt, made ingenious experiments, 'which led him to conclude, that it was highly probable that water was a composition of air'. Cavendish 'went as far as his experiments would permit him, and he went no further'. The import of this remark was that Cavendish, independently of Watt but subsequent to him, formed the theory and did so on a strong experimental basis of his own, cautious, making. The author treated Priestley as being merely the 'instrument of promoting this discovery'. Priestley was attacked for the vagueness of his ideas and the randomness of his experiments, and his continuing opposition to Lavoisier's chemistry was seen as irrational. The author (almost certainly John Robison) expressed himself 'now no longer surprised at the singularity of Dr Priestley's opinions in religion; either at his incredulity in some high things, or at his licentious sentiments in others'.[33] Black was then mentioned, by contrast, as doing the honourable thing in candidly admitting in his lectures the truth of the Lavoisian System. Lavoisier, to his great credit, 'was the first person who demonstrated the theory, and put it beyond doubt'.

So far as our immediate focus is concerned, then, the third edition of the *Britannica* in its explicit treatment of the history of the theory of the composition of water

---

[31] Ibid., p. 808, quoting from Watt, 'Thoughts on the constituent parts of water', p. 333.

[32] *Encyclopaedia Britannica*, third edn, vol. 18, p. 808.

[33] Ibid., p. 809. This will be recognized, so far as Priestley is concerned, as a typical 'positivist-whig' move to consign Priestley to the sphere of darkness.

offered a nuanced account in which credit was divided in various ways on a variety of criteria. There is no doubt, however, that Watt was attributed with the first statement of the true theory. The *Britannica*, however, was not consistent in its treatment of the issue. Where nuance was not possible, or redundant, Cavendish was credited. Thus in the article 'Steam', amidst further recountings pertaining to material heat and light, we find the bald reference to Cavendish as the discoverer of the chemical composition of water.[34] It seems to me that Cavendish would not recognize his discovery in the account of it given in this article. The account smacks so much of the Black chemical tradition that it is a peculiar attribution indeed.[35]

After the 1797 edition of the *Britannica* the next major vehicle in which material relevant to the water question appeared was the 1801 *Supplement* to the third edition, produced under the editorship of George Gleig. A major contribution to volume one of this *Supplement* was a new article on 'Chemistry' by Thomas Thomson. Thomson noted that, although the article 'Chemistry' in the third edition was written 'only about ten years ago, the language and reasoning of chemistry have been so greatly improved, and the number of facts have accumulated so much, that we find ourselves under the necessity of tracing over again the very elements of the science'.[36] Thomson, in effect, weeded out what he regarded as the archaisms of his predecessor. In the section dealing with the composition of water, Thomson noted that this great discovery 'has contributed more perhaps than any other to the advancement of the science of chemistry, by furnishing a key for the explanation of a prodigious number of phenomena'. His historical account mentioned Scheele (as making the first attempt to discover what was produced in the burning of hydrogen gas), Macquer (1776), Bucquet and Lavoisier (1777). Warltire's experiments of 1781 with Priestley's encouragement and participation are then discussed. We are next told quite straightforwardly that Cavendish, from his experiments conducted in 1781, 'concluded that water was a compound – Mr Cavendish must therefore be considered as the real discoverer of the composition of water'.

> He [Cavendish] was the first who ascertained that water was produced by firing oxygen and hydrogen gas, and the first that drew the proper conclusion from that fact. Mr Watt, indeed, had also drawn the proper conclusion from the experiments of Dr Priestley and Mr Warltire, and had even performed a number of experiments himself to ascertain that fact, before Mr Cavendish had communicated this; but he [Watt] had been deterred from publishing his theory by some experiments of Dr. Priestley which appeared contrary to it. He has therefore a claim to the merit of the discovery; a claim, however, which does

---

34 'Steam', *Encyclopaedia Britannica*, third edn, 1797, vol. 18, pp. 733–43, at p. 737. The relevant section states: 'in vital or atmospheric air there is not only a prodigious quantity of fire which is not in the vapour of water, but … it also contains light, or the cause of light, in a combined state. This is fully evinced by the great discovery of Mr Cavendish of the composition of water. Here we are taught that water (and consequently its vapour) consists of air from which the light and greatest part of the fire have been separated.'

35 Those places in Black's lectures, as edited by Robison, where Cavendish is credited with the discovery were gladly noted by the Cavendish camp or 'kept quiet' by the Watt supporters.

36 'Chemistry', *Supplement to the Encyclopaedia Britannica*, 1801, 2 vols, vol. 1, p. 212.

not affect Mr Cavendish, who knew nothing of the theory and experiments of that ingenious philosopher.[37]

The primary credit was given to Cavendish, but Watt was also admitted to have 'a claim'. That claim was treated, however, as quite independent of Cavendish's. The suggestion appears to be that the discoveries were quite separate and equivalent, though Cavendish was treated as the incumbent and Watt as the 'other claimant'. The account proceeded to a discussion of Lavoisier's work and hence to 'proofs' of the composition.

The 1810, fourth, edition of the *Britannica* retained in many respects the article 'Chemistry' as set out by Thomson. However, the section dealing with the composition of water had undergone a crucial change.[38] Significantly, I think, the 'Proof of the Composition of Water' was now presented *before* the 'History of the Discovery'. This was part of a general tendency to supersede historical by analytical accounts of the science. Rather than the chief facts of the science being conveyed historically, they were now presented in a more analytical or demonstrative fashion. The proofs consisted largely of a recounting of Lavoisier's experiments. It was then observed that, while Lavoisier provided the final confirmation of the component parts of water, that knowledge was 'indebted for its origin and progress, chiefly, if not entirely to the English philosophers'.[39]

The brief historical account is presented in a way less concerned with, and less certain as to, priority. Of Cavendish's experiments as made in 1781 Thomson says they were 'undoubtedly conclusive with regard to the composition of water'. Watt still featured; he was described as appearing to 'entertain the same ideas' on the subject. The quotation from the key letter to Priestley was given and Thomson commented: 'Thus it appears that Mr Watt had a just view of the composition of water, and of the nature of the process by which its component parts pass to a liquid state from that of an elastic fluid.'[40] Thomson's focus, more so than in 1801, was upon how the *fact* was eventually established beyond doubt. Thomson's account, as we have seen, appeared in a number of publications from the 1801 supplement to the *Britannica* onwards, including his *History of the Royal Society*, which still mentioned Watt. By 1830 in his *History of Chemistry*, short, rather pat accounts were no longer mentioning Watt and making unproblematic attributions to Cavendish. Thomson's 'line' on such matters had become very clearly identifiable to Watt Jr and Muirhead, who were in the habit in the 1830s and 1840s of referring to the 'Thomsonian' approach to the water question.[41]

Returning to the *Britannica*, we note that from the *Supplement* to the fourth, fifth and sixth editions produced from 1815 onwards under the editorship of Macvey Napier, a systematic attempt was made to include biographical accounts of major figures. Thus it was that articles on Cavendish and on Watt were added to those on

---

[37] Ibid., p. 289.

[38] 'Chemistry', *Encyclopaedia Britannica*, fourth edition, 1810, vol. 5, pp. 496–98.

[39] Ibid., p. 497.

[40] Ibid., p. 498.

[41] See, for example, Watt to Muirhead, 10 January 1840, Muirhead Papers, MS GEN 1354/463. Thomas Thomson, *History of the Royal Society*, 1812, p. 471.

'Chemistry' and 'Water' as places where the composition of water might be discussed. The article on Cavendish was contributed by Thomas Young, that on Watt by James Watt Jr, albeit anonymously.[42]

Other encyclopaedias often followed the same basic pattern as had emerged in the later editions of the *Britannica*, mentioning Watt, giving him some credit, but attributing the discovery to Cavendish. The *Encyclopaedia Edinensis*, a compact encyclopaedia in six volumes intended for a popular audience, contrived to do this by awarding Watt the discovery in the biographical article on the great engineer (an article that appears heavily reliant on Watt Jr's memoir in the *Britannica*) but awarding it to Cavendish in the discussion of water in the article 'Chemistry'. Consistency was not always a strong point in encyclopaedias and was probably not helped in the case of the *Edinensis* by the death of the original editor during the course of its production.[43]

The London Encyclopaedia, published in 1829 in twenty-two volumes, described itself as offering a 'popular view of the present state of knowledge'. It dealt in various ways with the composition of water in its entries for 'Water' and for 'Chemistry'. Under 'Water' we are told that Cavendish

> demonstrated about the year 1784, that [water] is composed, in fact, of two distinct aeriform fluids – oxygen and hydrogen; containing eighty-eight parts by weight out of every 100 of the former and twelve of the latter. This was the result of three years of laborious experiments.
>
> The late Mr. Watt, the celebrated improver of the steam-engine, seems to have inferred at the same period (in 1783), independently of Mr Cavendish, that water was a compound body of the kind it has been since proven to be … [44]

Later in the same article, in reference to oxygen it was stated that 'It was reserved for Mr. Cavendish, as we have seen, first to suggest in 1781, and prove beyond dispute in 1784, the important quantum of this vivifying ingredient contained in water.'[45] Once economy of expression was required, the modalities concerning others' contributions were dropped and the 'fact' of Cavendish's discovery simply stated.

The article 'Chemistry' in *The London Encyclopaedia* contained an intermediate statement mentioning both Watt and Cavendish but concentrating upon the latter. We are told that Cavendish's experiments led to the discovery of the composition of water. The production of dew on the combustion of hydrogen had been noticed by a number of people. It was 'referred by Mr. Watt to the production of water in 1783;

---

[42] These are examined below, and the memoir of Watt in the *Britannica* is discussed in detail in Chapter 5.

[43] See *Encyclopaedia Edinensis: or Dictionary of Arts, Sciences and Literature in Six Volumes*, 1827, 'Chemistry', vol. 2, pp. 255–387, at p. 276, 'Watt, James', vol. 6, pp. 638–39, at p. 638. The original editor was Dr James Millar, who survived long enough to write the article 'Chemistry' but not that on 'Watt'.

[44] 'Water' in *The London Encyclopaedia or Universal Dictionary of Science, Art, Literature, and Practical Mechanics, comprising a Popular View of the Present State of Knowledge*, 1829, 22 vols, vol. 22, pp. 565–69, at p. 567.

[45] Ibid., p. 568.

but experimental proofs were still wanting, and they were supplied in a masterly manner by Cavendish in a paper given to the Royal Society in 1784'.[46] Throughout these accounts, then, a consistent impression was given of a qualitative difference between the two researchers. Little emphasis was placed on dates. Indeed, in the 'Chemistry' article, to judge by dates alone, Watt would seem to have priority. But Cavendish's 'masterly manner' was emphasized, in a way reminiscent of Davy's depiction. Generally, whilst Watt 'infers', Cavendish 'proves' and 'demonstrates'. Given the similarities between these articles and the account given in Brande's *Manual of Chemistry*, it appears that Brande was the author. A similar recycling process occurred with the writings of William Nicholson.

As we have seen, Nicholson's first statement was made in his translation of Fourcroy's *Elements of Natural History and of Chemistry*, published in 1788.[47] One of the key objectives of his historical preface was the restoration of credit to Cavendish in the face of French claims. A very similar account was given in Nicholson's *A Dictionary of Chemistry*, published in two volumes in 1795. The most extensive discussion of the composition of water in this work occurred in the article 'Water'.[48] Nicholson made some observations there on the issue of discovery:

> The powers of nature, which are ever the same, and are continually performing their operations before us, whether we understand them or not, often present facts of the utmost value and importance, which we overlook, or regard with indifference. Hence it happens, that when an enlightened observer makes any discovery, it is almost always observed that somebody has seen the fact before him, or given some confused hints respecting its theory. It is evident, however, that the first discoverer, if there be any merit in discovery, is not the man who finds the treasure, and supposes it to be none, but he who is conscious of its value, and applies it to use. On these principles it is, that the claims of the discoverers of the composition of water must be estimated.[49]

Nicholson then presented the 'facts' much as he had done in his translation of Fourcroy. The exploits of Macquer, Bucquet and Lavoisier, Warltire and Priestley were recounted but no 'award' of the title of discoverer made. Cavendish, however, on the strength of his 1781 experiments and the conclusions drawn from them 'may be considered as the true discoverer of the composition of water'.[50] Watt's inferences from Warltire's and Priestley's experiments and his own experiments, to test the proposition that wherever dephlogisticated air is produced water has been decomposed, were also regarded as highly significant. We are told, as we were in Nicholson's edition of Fourcroy, that 'Mr. Watt has therefore a claim to the merit of

---

[46] 'Chemistry', *The London Encyclopaedia*, 1829, vol. 5, pp. 363–560, at p. 369.

[47] A.F. Fourcroy, *Elements of Natural History, and of Chemistry; being the second edition of The Elementary Lectures on those Sciences, first published in 1782. Translated into English. With occasional Notes and an Historical Preface, by the Translator*, 4 vols, 1788. Nicholson's important text, *The First Principles of Chemistry*, 1790 descried the system-building of Lavoisier and the speculations of Priestley.

[48] 'Water', in William Nicholson, *A Dictionary of Chemistry*, 2 vols, 1795, vol. 2, pp. 1013–25.

[49] Ibid., p. 1018.

[50] Ibid., p. 1019.

a discoverer with regard to the composition of water, and has the advantage of priority in the discovery of the decomposition'.

So Nicholson called Cavendish the '*true* discoverer' while describing Watt as '*a* discoverer'. We are left to guess how he saw this distinction following from the principle of attribution that he had enunciated in the beginning. Perhaps Watt was close enough to the 'right answer' (apart from the business about latent heat) to be regarded as 'conscious of the value' of the inferences made from experiments. Operating independently of Cavendish, he was *a* discoverer. Cavendish, though, in getting the 'right' answer and proving it by quantitative experiments, was to be regarded as the *true* discoverer. He, more than anyone, had, according to Nicholson's dictum, found the treasure, was conscious of its value and applied it to use.

Nicholson's text had an interesting fate in the hands of Andrew Ure, who took over the *Dictionary of Chemistry* as it was published in 1821.[51] The entry for 'Water' in Ure's publication was taken, as was much else, largely verbatim, from Nicholson's *Dictionary*. However, there were two crucial differences. First, at the end of the passage dealing with Cavendish's experiments, the sentence describing him as the 'true discoverer' was simply omitted. Although the section providing details of Watt's experiments and describing him as '*a* discoverer' was also omitted, the key words (about Watt inferring that water is a compound) remain.[52] Reading Ure's *Dictionary* one might well conclude that Watt was the first to infer anything about the compound nature of water. Two minor changes transformed a clearly pro-Cavendish statement into a clearly pro-Watt one. In this case we have the word of at least one reader that such was the impression given, the reader being none other than James Watt Jr. In a letter to James Patrick Muirhead, one of a number that discussed the merits or otherwise of various texts relating to his father, Watt Jr expressed his liking for Ure's account: 'Ure's Dictionary of Chemistry, published in 1820, article "Water" ... gives my father all I claim for him, and probably was written before my short life of him was printed in the Encyc. Brit., and is on that account the more valuable.'[53] Exactly why Ure took these steps is not known. Ure's association with the Andersonian Institution, his concern with the practical side of chemistry and his strained relations with Thomas Thomson may all have contributed to his decision to give greater prominence to Watt as discoverer in this rather surreptitious manner.[54]

---

51 Andrew Ure, *Dictionary of Chemistry on the Basis of Mr Nicholson's*, 1821.

52 Ure, *Dictionary of Chemistry*, 'Water', cols 3 and 4 (no pagination).

53 James Watt Jr to J.P. Muirhead, 9 April 1843, Muirhead Papers, MS GEN 1354/643. Watt was actually comparing Ure's account favourably with that given in W.T. Brande's *Manual of Chemistry* at this point. Elsewhere he commented unfavourably on Nicholson. Watt Jr seems not to have realized that Ure's account derived from that of Nicholson. Ure's *Dictionary* was subsequently taken over by Henry Watts's *Dictionary of Chemistry*, which developed yet another interpretation of the water question. See Chapter 11.

54 On Ure see W.V. Farrar, 'Andrew Ure F.R.S., and the philosophy of manufactures', *Notes and Records of the Royal Society of London*, **27**, 1973, 299–324.

Lecture Courses

Lecturing on chemistry became big business from the late eighteenth and early nineteenth centuries. The subject itself became very popular in fashionable circles, as evident, for example, in the lectures of Humphry Davy at the Royal Institution. After the passage of the Apothecaries Act in 1815, chemistry lecture courses proliferated to cater to those seeking to qualify for the medical profession. However, the most important and popular figures in the chemical lecturing stakes were probably the chemists of the Scottish universities, men who passed thousands of students through their lecture halls. Joseph Black, first at Glasgow and then at Edinburgh, was probably the most prominent of these. Doyle calculates that in the 1790s the average attendance at Black's lectures was about 225 and suggests that at Edinburgh from 1766 Black taught about 5000 students. These included numerous individuals subsequently influential in science and medicine. This made Black a significant force in the diffusion of chemical knowledge in the late eighteenth century.[55] The lectures of Black, and his successor as Professor of Chemistry at Edinburgh, Hope, are worth particular attention for two reasons: they are well documented, and they are the place where one would expect Watt to be given his due if he was to be given it anywhere. Here, too, however, we find the credit given to him strictly qualified and quick to fade in the early nineteenth century.

So far as Black's students were concerned, Watt would be known as a chemical collaborator of their great teacher in his research on steam, latent heat and the phenomena of heat more generally. Robison, in his edition of Black's lectures, observed that Watt was from his earliest acquaintance with Black at Glasgow 'a philosopher, in the most exalted sense of the word'. Watt's contributions to Black's researches were 'always recited in the class, with the most cordial acknowledgment of obligation to Mr. Watt'.[56] Black's discussion of the discovery of the composition of water, as rendered in the published version of his lectures, recounted the familiar story of Watt's letter to De Luc of April 1783 on Priestley's experiments, the decision to delay publication of that letter, Cavendish's renewed attention to the problem and his publication of results and conclusions already communicated to Lavoisier.

> although Mr Cavendish is the undoubted author of this decisive experiment, and, with Mr. Watt, is also the author of the important doctrine of the composition of water, Mr Lavoisier has the still greater merit of seeing this proposition *in all its importance*. *This* incited him to undertake these laborious and expensive experiments, which confirmed those of Mr Cavendish beyond a doubt; and he also had the sagacity to perceive *immediately*, that by means of this proposition, he should extricate his great system from difficulties and objections which I think would otherwise have been unsurmountable ... [57]

---

[55] W.P. Doyle, 'Black, Hope and Lavoisier', in A.D.C. Simpson (ed.), *Joseph Black 1728–1799. A Commemorative Symposium*, 1982, p. 43.

[56] *Lectures on the Elements of Chemistry delivered in the University of Edinburgh by the late Joseph Black, M.D ... Now Published from his Manuscripts by John Robison, LLD*, 2 vols, 1803, vol. 1, pp. xliii–xliv.

[57] Ibid., vol. 2, pp. 237–38.

Elsewhere in the lectures, in a more general statement of the generation of the New Chemistry, Black stated that:

> The fundamental experiments were first made, and the leading inferences were first drawn in this country, by Dr Priestley, the Honourable Mr Cavendish, and my friend Mr Watt. But it was chiefly in France that they were repeated, with proper attention to all the circumstances that would affect the result, and this result was made the foundation of a new theory of combustion.[58]

Black was here giving Watt a share with Cavendish in the discovery of the 'doctrine' of the composition of water, seeming to distinguish the discovery of the doctrine from the experimental work that made it possible, as also from the larger theoretical structure that Lavoisier incorporated it into. However, in other parts of the lectures, and in Robison's commentary thereon, different statements appear that baldly attribute the discovery of the composition of water to Cavendish.[59] To read those alone would give a very different impression of the situation. Such statements may not have been intended to exclude Watt, merely doing so by way of a necessary shorthand in discussing such matters.

As Perrin has argued,[60] Black's role in the reception of Lavoisier's Chemistry in Edinburgh was that of a reluctant catalyst. Black early acknowledged Lavoisier's System as superior and yet he had his doubts about the finality of 'the System'. An examination of students' notes of Black's (and Hope's) lectures suggests the possibility that Black had difficulty in incorporating the New Chemistry into his lecture course. Notes survive that were made by a James Scott in the 1785–86 lecture season, when Black was in regular correspondence with Watt and others about the work on the composition of water. However, at those points in the lectures where these findings would logically have been discussed, there is silence.[61] Lecture notes for 1788 indicate that Lecture 69 on 'Inflammable Bodies'

---

[58] Ibid., vol. 1, p. 238.

[59] See, for example, vol. 1, p. lvii, vol. 2, p. 215, vol. 2, p. 737, note 16. It should be remembered that Robison's contributions were coloured very much by his political sentiments. He mistrusted the way that the French, as he saw it, had operated in their chemistry, that is, in concert, authoritatively, with government endorsement and support, to secure the new chemistry as *French* chemistry. Robison's prime concern was to reclaim credit for Cavendish, not to arbitrate between the British claimants. For Robison's sentiments, see vol. 2, p. 217.

[60] C.E. Perrin, 'A reluctant catalyst: Joseph Black and the Edinburgh reception of Lavoisier's Chemistry', *Ambix*, 21, 1982, 141–76.

[61] James Scott, 'Dr Black's Chemestry [sic]', 6 vols, Royal College of Physicians, Edinburgh, MS Black 2 (1)–(6). The notes for Lecture 108, in vol. 6, indicate Black saying, before discussing the physical properties of water, that he would not examine there its chemical properties because 'we considered several when speaking of those bodies of w^c it is the natural menstruum, as the salts and many compounds resulting from the Union of other Bodies wth salts as the Metals, Absorbent Earths and Inflammable Substances'. However, when one turns to the previous lectures dealing with those topics mentioned, there is virtually nothing said about water, or experiments relating to its composition. For example, Lecture 69, on Inflammable Bodies, apparently discussed only sulphur, charcoal, ardent spirits, oils and bitumens, there being no sign of 'Inflammable Air'. It is possible that Black regarded these issues as so fluid, as it were, at the time that he decided that the best policy was to leave the material out altogether. A systematic survey of extant notes on Black's lectures has not been attempted

did now discuss inflammable air. Cavendish's work with it was mentioned, but the key section on the explosion of inflammable air with common air or dephlogisticated air mentioned only Priestley: 'Dr Priestley on mixing the two airs in a close vial, and firing them with the Electric Spark, found that they were both consum'd, nothing remaining but a quantity of water equal in weight to the two airs ... '.[62]

By the mid-1790s, when Black and Hope were lecturing jointly, lecture notes tell a fuller story:

> Dr. Priestley who first tried this experiment [the explosion of hydrogen mixed with oxygen, now so called] having the airs mixed in the same vessels called them his pocket pistols. It was a question of much difficulty to determine what became of the Airs, but it is now proved that the result is Water for this very important & wonderful discovery we are indebted to Mr. Cavendish. Mr. Lavoisier supposed there must be some product like the Sulphuric Acid or the Carbonic Acid but could come to no conclusion on making experiments. He also observed as well as others that the sides of the vessels had dewy drops.
>
> Mr. Cavendish previously passed the different Airs through tubes that should be sure to absorb the moisture, he then exploded them & found that when the due portions were used the result was invariably water perfectly pure ... This was soon afterwards confirmed by the most superb experiments by the French Chemists.[63]

The only mention of Watt in these lectures is as the inventor of a 'convenient portable' apparatus for the production of hydrogen by the decomposition of water by hot iron. He is not mentioned as a contender for the credit of discovery.

The evidence from lecture notes, while ambiguous in helping us trace what Black was saying to his students, does strongly suggest that, even among his Edinburgh friends, Watt's claims to credit were scarcely mentioned whereas those of Cavendish were repeatedly noted. The same pattern emerges from an examination of relevant papers delivered to the Chemical Society founded by Black's students in 1785–86 in Edinburgh and to the longer-lived Natural History Society.[64] A number of dissertations read before the Chemical Society in 1785 dealt with the composition of water and most attributions were to Cavendish, though there are hints that Black and some of the students adhered to Watt's account involving heat without mentioning

---

but rather a sampling made. For details of resources see: William A. Cole, 'Manuscripts of Joseph Black's Lectures on Chemistry', in Simpson (ed.), *Joseph Black 1728–1799*. pp. 53–69.

[62] Anonymous, 'Lecture notes on Joseph Black's Lectures, ca 1788', Edinburgh University Library, Special Collections MS Dc.2.42–43, vol. 2, p. 380. The other mention of the composition of water occurs in the lecture, not numbered, in which analysis of waters was discussed. There we find: 'Lavoisier and some French Chemists suppose that water is composed of Empyreal [another name for Dephlog^d] & Inflammable Air; because upon firing these two airs nothing remains but a small quantity of Water, into which the two airs are changed; and from this Doctrine they are enabled to Explain many phenomena in Chemistry' (vol. 3, p. 320).

[63] Anon., 'Chemistry by Drs Black and Hope', 1796–97, Edinburgh University Library, Special Collections, MS Gen 48D, Section 81.

[64] On these societies see Perrin, 'A Reluctant catalyst', 141–76 and J. Kendall, 'The first chemical society, the first chemical journal and the Chemical Revolution', *Proceedings of the Royal Society of Edinburgh*, **63A**, 1952, 346–58.

Watt's name.[65] Two dissertations are particularly interesting. One by Thomas Beddoes, titled 'An Attempt to Point out some of the Consequences which Flow from Mr. Cavendish's Discovery of the Component Parts of Water', makes the attribution to Cavendish as the title suggests, but also notes that Cavendish's experiments might be explained another way:

> Dr Black seemed to me to hint at such an explanation & undoubtedly if two different hypothesis [*sic*] can be adjusted to any set of appearances, both become uncertain ... Might not the water have been combined with the Airs & so have existed in its proper form[?] If so, it follows that Inflammable & Vital Air differ only in the proportion of their ingredients ...

A second essay, by Mr George Kirkaldie, 'On Dephlogisticated Air', raised the issue of whether earth entered into the composition of dephlogisticated air and pointed to Cavendish's experiments as showing that this is not so: 'for from these it appears, that by uniting with a certain quantity of the principle of Inflammability it may be wholly converted into dew, & surely if it contained any Earth, it would be evident upon such condensation'. Kirkaldie also believed that Cavendish's experiments on water were open to a different interpretation. He argued that:

> something else is necessary to the formation of water from Dephlogisticated & Inflammable Air or pure phlogiston, than their simple mixture, & such I am very much inclined to believe is a quantity of Heat supplied by the Electricity, passing into the Latent state during the formation of the water ... My idea of Dephlogisticated Air then is, that it consists of a watery principal [*sic*] combined with heat & that by the addition of phlogiston to it, agreeable to the opinion of Mr Cavendish, water is formed, which again being deprived of its heat, is converted into Ice. Dephlogisticated Air then seems only to differ from Vapour, in being destitute of phlogiston, as seems Evident f[ro]m the Specific gravity of these two fluids.

These sorts of objections to Cavendish's interpretation of his experiments, coming from within the Black tradition, echo the explanations that Watt himself was offering of the phenomena. Yet, remarkably and mysteriously, these students made no mention of Watt.

We can only guess, in the end, what Black's students took away from his lectures on the specific question of the composition of water. It does appear, however, that Cavendish was treated as the central figure in the work and that the accurate determinations of the French were also acknowledged. The students would undoubtedly have had a concrete impression of Watt as an active and important chemist from the 1760s onwards and that he did 'hover around' the water question. It does appear that Robison's rendition of these affairs in his edited version of Black's lectures and in the *Britannica* gave a more prominent role to Watt than was perceived in Black's and Hope's lectures.

---

65 'Dissertations Read before the Chemical Society Instituted in the beginning of the Year 1785', Edinburgh University Library, Special Collections, MS 2748. There are also a number of interesting papers which discuss the composition of water in 'Papers of the Natural History Society', 15 vols, Edinburgh University Library, Special Collections, Da67NAT (See vol. 2, p. 185ff, vol. 3, p. 180ff, vol. 4, p. 186ff).

The fact that Watt was held out to students as Black's chemical collaborator is perhaps more significant than it might appear. In Black's case the relation with students was regarded as very important. It is well known that Black was very tardy in laying public claim through publication to his own discoveries on heat, in fact he never did so. While there were undoubtedly other reasons for this (Robison describes him as hating authorship), one reason given was the belief that expounding one's discoveries to students was a legitimate, perhaps even sufficient, form of publication.[66] Given the number and quality of Black's students over the years and their ubiquity in British scientific life, this belief probably had some substance. From our immediate point of view it is important to note that what was said about the composition of water in these lectures probably stuck with the auditors and shaped their view of the question in the longer term. Yet Black and his friends did recognize the precariousness of claims based on having expounded discoveries to classes of students. Watt and Robison, among a number of Black's close associates, urged him to publish, recognizing that reputation beyond one's face-to-face circle depended on that.

We must remember, then, that in the late eighteenth and early nineteenth centuries the handling of intellectual property rights was still an ambiguous matter about which many were ambivalent. It was into this climate that Watt's claims regarding the composition of water were launched. It was also in this climate that his decision about whether or not to press his claims (beyond the act of publication in the *Philosophical Transactions*) had to be made. In expressing to his son the view that posterity would decide, he perhaps had in mind not only subsequent readers of the literature but also informal media of communication such as those involving teachers and students.

The successor of Black and Robison in teaching chemistry at Edinburgh University, Thomas Charles Hope taught for Black as the latter's health began to fail in the later 1790s, and continued to do so as Black's successor into the 1840s. His extensive lecture notes, though difficult in many ways to decipher and to date, provide some insights into how Watt was treated before the Edinburgh student audience through the early decades of the nineteenth century.

In a lecture on 'Vapourisation', the fundamentals of which were probably laid in the 1790s but which was continually modified and updated, Watt was identified as among those who had conducted experiments 'to discover the degree of elasticity or Expansive force, which the vapor of water possess when generated at different temperatures'.[67] The others names were Robison, Bettancourt, Dalton, Schmidt, Ure and Sothern [*sic*].[68] In the second part of his lecture material on vaporization Hope stated:

---

[66] See the valuable discussion in Jan Golinski, *Science as Public Culture. Chemistry and Enlightenment in Britain, 1760–1820*, 1992, pp. 11–49. Golinski discusses these issues with reference to William Cullen and Joseph Black and finds them symptomatic of a gradual and halting working through of issues of public and private interest and the role of the professoriate in emergent academic chemistry.

[67] Thomas Charles Hope, Lecture Notes on Chemistry 1790–1842, Edinburgh University Library, Special Collections, Gen. 268–72 at Gen. 268, envelope 31.

[68] The name of Sothern [Southern] is added in pencil, probably later.

Some Exper[t] made by Dr Watt, demonstrate in a manner still more striking ... that Vapor contains a vast store of [latent heat] which becomes apparent at the moment of condensation.

Knowing well that water is converted into Steam at a Temp. much below its usual one, when freed from the pressure of the Atm[osphere] he was in hopes that he would save much fuel, if in those engines & operations, in which the production of Steam is concerned, he caused the formation of it to take place in vacuo.

To submit this to the test of Expt he contrived an App[aratus] & distilled a quantity of water releived [*sic*] from the usual pressure.[69]

In a story familiar from the *Britannica* articles on heat and steam, it is recounted that Watt found that the production of steam at low pressure required the same input of heat the bulk of which reappeared as the latent heat of condensation. Watt, we are told, concluded from these experiments, against his initial expectations and hopes, that 'the same quantity of heat was required to form vapour in vacuo, as under the usual pressure, & that consequently the ... same quantity of fuel would be requisite in both cases; & that there would be no economy in Distilling, or generating vapour in vacuo'.[70] This certainly presents 'Dr Watt' as an exemplary chemist and experimenter in developing the idea, submitting it to the test of experiment, accepting the verdict, and moving on. It was also, presumably, used as a potentially powerful example for the students of the relationship that could subsist between experimental inquiry and practical arts.[71]

Other of Hope's lecture notes pertain directly to the water question. In his 'Old Notes' on 'Hydrogene' and their successive revisions we find a simplification of the discovery story. In the 'Old Notes' the account is very similar to that given in Black's lectures. Of Watt it is noted that 'Mr Watt of Birmingham, at the time that Mr Cavendish was proving by Exp[t] the fact, conjectured that water was actually the product.'[72] Watt's place in this account was small, and his 'conjectural' activity did not rate the same notice as the 'proving' experiments of Cavendish. In later versions of the notes, however, Watt was expunged entirely and the attribution becomes a rather bald statement:

The discovery of this fact [the composition of water] is one of the most curious & important of modern chemistry. It is due to the late Mr Cavendish of Lond[on] a Gent[n] of Noble family & great fortune & a profound Philosopher. This very interesting Discovery was made in the summer of the year 1781.[73]

The fact remains, however, that the documentary evidence that we have concerning the content of lectures on chemical topics in Scotland suggests that some modest

---

[69] Hope, Lecture Notes, envelope 31.

[70] Thomas Charles Hope, Lecture Notes on Chemistry, *c*. 1790–1842, 'Vaporisation, 2[d] Part', Edinburgh University Library, Special Collections, Gen. 268, envelope 32.

[71] Robison had also emphasized this point in his edition of Black's lectures where he repeatedly referred to Watt as the 'pupil' of Black and attributed at least some of the success of Watt's steam-engine innovations to the science he derived collaboratively from Black.

[72] 'Hydrogene N 3[d] Old Notes', Edinburgh University Library, Special Collections, Gen. 271, envelope 147.

[73] 'Hydrogene', Edinburgh University Library, Special Collections, Gen. 271, envelope 148.

early recognition of Watt's contribution to the discovery of the composition of water gave way, under curricular pressure if nothing else, to simpler, less historical expositions that gave the stage solely to Cavendish.[74] Even then, though, Watt's general reputation as a chemist, as a researcher on heat and steam, remained established in the oral university tradition, and through the encyclopaedic one. Many British chemical texts thrust Cavendish forward as the discoverer against the usurping French. Some ignored Watt in the process, but others gave him a joint, more often a subsidiary, role in the discovery. This provided some basis on which an attempt could be made to resurrect Watt's claims, though it was clearly to be an uphill struggle. We now turn to examine those who led that attempt, prominent among whom was a prodigal son.

---

[74] Hope's lecture notes frequently included notes to himself on the need to condense and shorten material. He decided that the number of lectures devoted to heat was far too great given the rather different relation of that topic to the field of chemistry as it had evolved in the years after the adoption of the Lavoisian System. Eventually, heat left the chemical curriculum altogether in the lectures of William Gregory, Professor of Chemistry at the University of Edinburgh. See the text for the course, William Gregory, *Outlines of Chemistry*, 1845, vol. 1.

Keeping Account:
James Watt Jr and the Filial Project

Depend upon it, My Dear Sir, that your appeal to my filial duties is not made in vain. It has been the study and endeavour of my life to cause justice to be done to my father's merits ... [1]

Introduction

There can be little doubt that the 'water controversy' would not have been as significant an issue as it became in early Victorian Britain had it not been for the involvement of James Watt's eldest, and only surviving, son, James Watt Jr. Watt Jr devoted much time to propagating and defending his father's reputation. Apart from being extremely zealous in monitoring, criticizing and shaping writing about his father, Watt Jr also concerned himself with other commemorations, such as various monuments, their inscriptions, and, especially, the Greenock Public Library. Besides written and monumental memorials to the great engineer, the son seems to have regarded the business of Boulton, Watt & Co. as itself a kind of sacred trust. His concern for the economic success of that business and for its reputation was another way in which the son sought to keep the memory of the father alive.

Within the filial project so defined, the 'water controversy' was very important to Watt Jr because he took it as illustrating his father's 'philosophical character', a crucial ingredient of his standing as a public benefactor. Watt Jr's own writing on the water question was not extensive but he was constantly behind the scenes, consulting on, and contributing to, the work of Arago, Brougham and Muirhead. Like those writers, Watt Jr subscribed, I suggest, to an empirical view of the nature of discovery. Watt Jr's attitude in business and in 'literary' controversy was that 'the facts' were the key, and that he had them. He considered his father's claim to priority to be a clear-cut, empirically demonstrable one. The efforts of the supporters of Cavendish to show otherwise were, in his opinion, 'sophistical'.

First let us sketch Watt Jr's early years. From consideration of his family environment, education, early radicalism and prodigal return to his father's business, we can discern many of the roots of the mature man's attitude towards his illustrious father. We can thereby understand his actions in defending and promoting Watt's reputation in general, and his claim to priority in the water controversy in particular.

---

[1] James Watt Jr to François Arago, 29 September 1834, Watt Papers (Doldowlod), W/10.

Watt Jr's Early Years

Watt Jr was born in 1769, the year in which his father obtained the first patent on the condensing steam engine. His youngest years saw the death of his mother (née Margaret Miller) in 1773, the family move to Birmingham in the following year, and the inauguration of his father's partnership with Matthew Boulton. The loss of his mother and a strained relationship with his stepmother (Watt married his second wife, Ann Macgregor, in 1776) may have led to a disproportionate emotional investment in his relationship with his father.[2] The latter's severity towards him might also have contributed to Watt Jr's rebellion and break with his father in 1790 over the son's radical support of the French Revolution.

Eric Robinson[3] and, more recently, Peter Jones[4] have explored the education of the sons of Boulton and Watt, the sons who in their turn were to become business partners. Robinson showed the practicality of the education desired by Boulton and Watt for their sons. There was strong emphasis on modern languages, science and commerce. Watt Jr was first intended as an engineer and was sent by his father to John Wilkinson's Bersham iron works to acquire the skills of machine drawing and carpentry, as well as geometry, arithmetic, algebra and merchant's accounts. The classics could be studied but only in the little time thereafter available. Watt was less indulgent than Boulton of purely literary studies and dourly warned his son off light reading. Robinson describes Watt as a rather 'sour' father.

At the age of fifteen, Watt Jr was sent to Geneva under the eye of Watt's friend J.A. De Luc to attend lectures at the Academy there. His father continued to hector him by letter about rising early for study, economy in expenditure, and seriousness in reading matter. There was a small element of light relief when he was allowed to take fencing lessons in company with Joseph Priestley Jr, who was also in Geneva at the time. In late 1785 young Jimmy moved on his father's instructions to study with the Reverend M. Reinhard at Stadtfeld near Eisenach in Upper Saxony, there to learn German, and thence in 1787 to Freiberg's School of Mines. His return to England in late October 1787 met his father's stern demands that he account for his 'reckless' expenditure while overseas. His father also tackled him about accusations of insubordination to his stepmother. Watt determined that domestic peace and his son's future were best served by apprenticing him in the counting house of Taylor & Maxwell, Manchester fustian makers.

Watt Jr found Manchester an exciting place where he could develop his scientific activities and indulge his radical political enthusiasms. He came under the influence

---

[2] Years later, when Watt Jr was in his mid-60s, he sent to Arago a long extract he had found in his father's journal. This very moving passage, written when Watt was surveying for the Caledonian Canal in 1773, related to the circumstances of his wife's death. Watt Jr sent this to Arago to demonstrate 'the affectionate character of his [Watt's] mind'. It appears that even at this juncture it was important to Watt Jr to demonstrate the depth of his father's sense of bereavement. See James Watt Jr to François Arago, 22 January 1835, Watt Papers (Doldowlod), W/10.

[3] Eric Robinson, 'Training captains of industry: The education of Matthew Robinson Boulton (1770–1842) and the younger James Watt (1769–1848)', *Annals of Science*, **10**, 1954, 301–13.

[4] Peter M. Jones, 'Living the Enlightenment and the French Revolution: James Watt, Matthew Boulton, and their sons', *The Historical Journal*, **42**, 1999, 157–82.

of Thomas Cooper and Thomas Walker, both significant figures in Manchester business and in radical politics, through both the Manchester Literary and Philosophical Society, of which he became Secretary,[5] and the Manchester Constitutional Society, of which he was a founding member in June 1789.

The political rift between father and son widened. Though in many intellectual respects Watt shared the liberal Enlightenment values of his Lunar Society associates, he was more conservative than they.[6] While condemning the 'Church and King' mobs which sacked Priestley's house in Birmingham, he lamented the way that the times were making the Lunar Society meetings more affairs of politics than of philosophy. His son, and young friends, by contrast resigned *en masse* from the Manchester Literary and Philosophical Society when it refused to take a political stance by deciding not to send a message of sympathy to Priestley on the occasion of the Priestley Riots, as the Derby Philosophical Society had done.[7]

When Watt Jr's apprenticeship with Taylor & Maxwell ended he took a position with T. & R. Walker, textile merchandisers, as a commercial representative. The senior partner in this firm, Thomas Walker, was his political associate as well as his employer, and the two certainly saw travel on behalf of the firm and support of liberty as appropriately conjoined concerns.

In March 1792 Watt Jr, Thomas Cooper and John Tuffen landed at Calais and travelled to Paris. Although Watt Jr was representing his firm on business he was also intent upon supporting the cause of liberty in France. In Paris he renewed contacts including many of the leading chemists (de Morveau, Fourcroy, Lavoisier) though the latter were preoccupied with politics. Watt Jr and Cooper presented an address to the Jacobin Club of Paris from the Manchester Constitutional Society. Such fraternal acts of solidarity were commonplace. However, they were noted, and became the subject of a denunciation by Edmund Burke in the House of Commons on 30 April 1792. As Cobbett's *Parliamentary History* reported, Burke stated that:

> There were in this country men who scrupled not to enter into an alliance with a set in France of the worst traitors and regicides that had ever been heard of – the club of the Jacobins. Agents had been sent from this country, to enter into a federation with that iniquitous club, and those agents were men of some consideration in this country; the names he alluded to were Thomas Cooper and James Watt. Here Mr Burke read the

---

[5] At this time Watt Jr was the author of two papers: 'Some account of a mine in which Aërated Barytes is found', *Memoirs of the Literary and Philosophical Society of Manchester*, **3**, 1789, 598–609 and 'On the effects produced by different combinations of the Terra Ponderosa given to Animals', idem, **3**, 1789, 609–18.

[6] Boulton and Watt had to moderate their radical political associations for commercial reasons since, whatever Watt might protest to the contrary, their business and its support (not least through patents) depended upon the political establishment. Only occasionally, when it seemed that that Establishment might fail him through its corrupt character, did Watt sound off against it, and then only in private to his wife. Thus, when it appeared that the House of Commons might pass Hornblower's bill, Watt wrote to Ann Watt: 'A little more of this will make me an enemy of corrpt p^ts [practices] and a democrate if democracy were less evil' (Watt to A. Watt, n.d. [March 1792], as quoted in Jones, 'Living the Enlightenment', p. 170).

[7] Eric Robinson, 'An English Jacobin: James Watt, Junior, 1769–1848', *Cambridge Historical Journal*, **11**, 1954–55, 351.

address presented to the club of the Jacobins by those gentlemen on the 16th of April ... And what did those people do? did they only give their own sentiments? No. By the answer of the Jacobin club, it appeared that those worthies of Manchester undertook– from what authority he knew not– to represent all England.[8]

Through the year 1792, reports of Watt Jr's activities in France caused consternation in the Watt household. Watt was anxious that the failure of reports to distinguish between himself and his son was harming his own reputation and that at a crucial time when parliamentary support for Watt against the Hornblowers on patent questions was vital.[9]

As the Revolution progressed, Watt Jr took a crash course in party division. He gravitated to the Brissotin wing of the Jacobins with their opposition to extra-parliamentary radicalism. Much to Watt's relief, business took his son out of Paris in September 1792 just as the events of the Terror escalated. Watt Jr proceeded via Nantes, Bordeaux, Marseilles, and Leghorn to Naples. However, their correspondence reveals a widening gulf of mutual political incomprehension. His son's continued allegiance to extreme democratic views (as he saw them) brought Watt to the verge of despair and abandonment, even as it became apparent that counter-revolutionary measures in Britain could well make the return of Watt Jr difficult, if not impossible.

Watt Jr considered joining the French army, but even his radical friends advised against that. The imprisonment and execution of many of the Brissotins was a cruel lesson in the realities of the Terror. Then, in October 1793, in the midst of his son's growing crisis of doubt, Watt suddenly softened his approach, advising his son not to give way to a 'fruitless despondence'. He encouraged him to stay abroad and provided him with money. Watt Jr accepted these overtures of goodwill gladly and the tide in their relationship seems to have turned in October and November 1793. Watt Jr appears to have realized his dire situation and welcomed his father's willingness to rescue him despite all their prior disagreements. His half-sister Jessie was dying from consumption at this time and this may have brought the family closer.

The reasons for Watt's change of heart are a matter for speculation. Jones suggests that he may have been alarmed by Watt Jr's melancholia or that he wanted to prevent his son joining radical members of their circle emigrating to the United States. Another possibility, Jones suggests, is that the partners Boulton and Watt were considering retirement and were anxious to settle 'the business on the next generation'.[10] As it turned out, Watt Jr returned to England very quietly early in February 1794, staying at first in London. Then in March he returned to Birmingham, where he lodged with Matthew Boulton. The relationship with his stepmother remained difficult and he agreed with his father not to seek to live under the same roof.

A few months later a new engine-building company was established in which Watt, Watt Jr, Gregory Watt, Matthew Boulton and Matthew Robinson Boulton

---

8 William Cobbett, *The Parliamentary History of England from the Earliest Period to the Year 1803*, vol. 29, 1817, pp. 1317–24, at pp. 1322–3. See also D.V. Erdman, *Commerce des lumières: John Oswald and the British in Paris, 1790–1793*, 1986, pp. 150–55.

9 Jones, 'Living the Enlightenment', p. 172.

10 Ibid., p. 179.

5.1 James Watt Jr

were all partners. Thereafter Watt Jr expended his energies on the family business. It is plausible that Watt Jr's devotion to that business and to his father's reputation drew extra strength from a relationship forged in extreme conflict, subsequent reconciliation and the realization on the son's part of the depth of his often distant and severe father's love for him.

Watt Jr, the Family Business and Intellectual Outlook

The first major assignment undertaken by Robinson Boulton and Watt Jr was to deal with engine pirates, especially in Lancashire. As Musson and Robinson put it, they were the 'generals in charge of the battle against the Manchester pirates' and the young Turks 'organised a complete system of espionage' in detecting pirate engines.[11] Watt, evidently delighted with their efforts, remarked that 'But for the good sense and indefatigable activity of Mr Boulton Junr and my son, we must have succumbed, for want of animal life and Spirits'.[12] Watt was clearly relieved that his errant son's energy and enthusiasm were now directed toward the support and advancement of the family enterprise.

Watt Jr was also intimately involved in the establishment of the Soho Foundry, which opened in January 1796. Boulton and Watt had relied heavily on John Wilkinson for the supply of components for their engines. Wilkinson had turned against them through acts of piracy of his own and there had been problems of supply and quality control with engine parts. These factors, together with the impending expiry of the engine patent in 1800, induced the company to engage more actively in engine manufacture than had previously been the case.

Watt was not a partner in the Soho Foundry, though Watt Jr and Gregory Watt were. In 1800, Watt retired from business entirely. With the death of Gregory Watt in 1804 and of Matthew Boulton in 1809, James Watt Jr and Matthew Robinson Boulton were left as the sole owners of the Soho Engine Manufactory and the Soho Foundry. The nature of the business was changing after the expiry of the Watt patent. The grounds of competition with other engine makers and suppliers changed. Boulton, Watt & Co., Soho undertook a range of initiatives in manufacture, organization and accounting, sales and service and marketing. Although some of these activities engaged Robinson Boulton, it was becoming apparent that Watt Jr was more committed to the business than his partner. Watt Jr's business and accounting skills were applied to an elaborate costing exercise in both the Engine Manufactory and the Foundry in the early nineteenth century. Watt Jr also provided much of the after-sales service to purchasers of the firm's engines.[13] Jennifer Tann observes that from that time, however, Watt Jr 'took the major management decisions in the firm'.[14] In later years Watt Jr was to speak of

---

[11] A.E. Musson and Eric Robinson, *Science and Technology in the Industrial Revolution*, 1969, pp. 413–14.

[12] James Watt to Joseph Black, 1 June 1796, quoted in Eric Robinson and Douglas McKie, *Partners in Science. Letters of James Watt and Joseph Black*, 1970, pp. 224–25.

[13] Jennifer Tann (ed.), *The Selected Papers of Boulton and Watt, Volume 1*, 1981, pp. 233, 276.

[14] Ibid., p. 30.

Robinson Boulton as a sleeping partner. Major initiatives such as a significant move into the manufacture of marine engines lay with Watt Jr.[15] All this encouraged Watt Jr to think of himself as the sole saviour of the company's name and the chief custodian of its reputation.

In his later years Watt Jr reflected on this directly. By the mid-1830s Robinson Boulton, who had long been relatively inactive in the business, decided to retire. Watt Jr resolved to 'take the whole upon myself'. As he explained to François Arago:

> I did hope that a Firm which has now lasted for more than 60 years, might have continued to the end of our respective lives, and I have made great sacrifices of time to the business, which is in a most prosperous state, to obtain that object. But ... I have given way to his wishes. At my period of life, and with a fortune ample to my wants; it may seem to you an Act of folly, that I should continue to expose myself to the exertions which the management of such a business as ours requires, and I might add to its possible vicissitudes; but so it is, that I have an insuperable aversion to desert a concern, founded by my father, and which has contributed not a little to his reputation, and has placed myself in a forward rank among the Manufacturers of this Country. It has been the pride & pleasure of my life to continue & keep up that business ... [16]

It was not until 1840 that Watt Jr became the sole owner of the foundry business on the dissolution of the partnership with Boulton. He quickly involved new partners: Henry Wollaston Blake (a London businessman and banker); and two former employees, James Brown and Gilbert Hamilton.[17] He was pleased with this arrangement, entered into in 1841. The unfortunate nature of his relationship with Robinson Boulton becomes apparent from Watt Jr's comments to Henry Brougham on his former partner's death:

> My early friend and partner for so many years, Mr Boulton, paid the debt of nature on the 18th Inst. ... we have had no intercourse since the dissolution of our partnership, but I have remained upon friendly terms with his family. My resentments will now be buried with him, and I set out tomorrow for Aston hall to render what consolations I can to his family, and to attend his funeral.[18]

---

[15] Ibid., pp. 17–18. Watt Jr pursued experiments on marine engines using the *Caledonia*, a ship purchased specially for the purpose from the steamship pioneer Henry Bell of Glasgow. In October 1817 Watt Jr sailed in the *Caledonia* to Holland and then up the Rhine as far as Coblenz, visiting Antwerp and Rotterdam before returning in the spring of 1818. Then he conducted an extensive series of experiments with the ship on the Thames that informed improvements in the construction and adaptation of marine engines. When he had finished with it, the ship was sold to the Danish government. See Martin Bellamy, 'P.S. *Caledonia*: Denmark's first steamship', *The Mariner's Mirror*, **80**, 1994, 55–58 and James Patrick Muirhead, *The Life of James Watt with Selections from his Correspondence*, 1858, pp. 442–44. See also Watt Jr to John Rennie, 3, 4, 6, 14, 15, 16 October 1817, National Library of Scotland, Rennie Manuscripts, MSS19824, ff. 116–25.

[16] James Watt Jr to François Arago, 8 November 1835, Watt Papers (Doldowlod), W/10.

[17] See W.K.V. Gale, 'Soho Foundry: Some facts and fallacies', *Transactions of the Newcomen Society*, **34**, 1961–62, 83.

[18] James Watt Jr to Henry, Lord Brougham, 21 May 1842, Brougham Papers, 20,148.

As he pondered the past at Robinson Boulton's graveside, Watt Jr probably considered himself as the last man standing among the company of those who had made the name of Watt famous in the land.

Let us now discuss what the educational and early formative experiences of Watt Jr meant for his stance in relation to the water controversy. Perhaps the first point to note is that the education that Watt Jr and the younger Boulton received was one of ardent rationalism and intense practicality. The link between philosophical, manufacturing and commercial concerns was made evident in Matthew Boulton's advice to his son:

> A man will never make a good Chymist unless he acquires dexterity, & neatness in making exp[ts], even down to the pulverising in a Mortar, or blowing the Bellows, distinctness, order, regularity, neatness, & Cleanliness are necessary in the Laboratory, Manufactory, & the Counting house.[19]

These were sound proceedings, as a chemist drew upon the same virtues as informed successful manufacturing and commercial activity. Note also that esoteric knowledge was not particularly stressed, the implication being that someone possessed of the requisite practical skills and virtues gained in successful manufacturing or commerce would be able to deal in chemical matters. We have already observed (in Chapter 3) that the chemical traditions deriving from Joseph Black were fashioned by their adherents in the 1790s and 1800s as very much against the pursuit of systems of chemistry and for a sober experimental approach. This sort of notion informed Watt Jr's picture of his father as a chemist.

Peter Jones makes another interesting observation about Watt Jr and his generation. Their experiences helped to mark out their attitudes from those of their liberal fathers. In particular, there was in the generations after 1792 a weakening of ideals of free trade in knowledge. One sign of this was the decision by Robinson Boulton and Watt Jr to no longer allow visitors to tour the Soho Manufactory. Proprietary interests now decisively outweighed openness of communication: 'A new generation was in charge; one which no longer shared the reflexes of those who came to maturity in the high decades of the Enlightenment.'[20]

In 1841, Watt Jr's coadjutor in the filial project, James Patrick Muirhead, paid a visit to Watt Jr's old friend, the poet William Wordsworth, who recalled their young, radical days in France. As Muirhead reported the conversation with Wordsworth to his mother: 'They [Watt Jr and Wordsworth] thus both began life as ardent (and he adds, thoughtless) radicals, but have both become, in the course of their lives, as all sensible men he thinks have done, good sober-minded *conservatives*.'[21] Wordsworth greatly approved of Sir Robert Peel's administration. Watt Jr certainly shared this view.[22]

---

19 Matthew Boulton to Matthew Robinson Boulton, 19 December 1787, as quoted in Eric Robinson, 'Training captains of industry', p. 309.

20 Peter M. Jones, 'Living the Enlightenment', p. 181.

21 J.P. Muirhead to Mrs Muirhead, 1 September 1841, reproduced in Anon, 'A day with Wordsworth', *Blackwood's Magazine*, **221**, June 1927, 733.

22 See James Watt Jr to Henry, Lord Brougham, 30 March 1842, Brougham Papers, 20,145.

Watt Jr's tough proprietorial approach showed in the way that he ran the business, in his spirited defence of his Radnorshire estates[23] from the encroachments of poachers, and, ironically, railway companies, and, not least, in the way he defended his father's claims to inventive and scientific glory. It showed also in Watt Jr's attitude to various institutional developments. He saw little value, for example, in Mechanics' Institutes. When Brougham tried to interest him in promoting an Institute in Birmingham, Watt Jr declared that he could not help, 'not being a convert to the advantages of the Institutions you recommend'. Watt Jr was happy with the system of training pursued for many years at Boulton, Watt & Co., which had been 'productive at all times of a number of able mechanics, who are now to be found in most parts of the Kingdom'.[24]

Watt Jr and his loyal Soho engineers often exhibited a strong antipathy towards the organized engineering profession. This was linked in Watt Jr's mind to the activities of the 'pirates' who had plagued his father. Stimulated by a strongly negative review of the translation of Arago's *Eloge* in the 'Engineer's Journal' in 1839, Watt Jr recalled that 'there has at all times, within my Memory, been a spirit of jealousy among this class against the whole race of the Soho Engineers, who in return have treated them with due contempt ... '.[25] Watt Jr then provided a very interesting insight into a publication in the *Edinburgh Review* in 1809 ostensibly by John Playfair. He recalled that the engineering opposition

> stirred up Olinthus Gregory a Professor at Woolwich to stand forward as their champion; to claim for them sundry inventions originating with my father or ourselves, & to vituperate others. That roused my choleric and with the assistance of Professor Playfair and the connivance of Jeffrey, I put forth the Olynthiad in the Edinburgh Review ... That proved a settler for some years, and although they revived afterwards, we never troubled ourselves more about them. They are now dazzled & confounded by the excess of praise which Arago has bestowed on my father, and though they cannot contest the truths he brings forward, they employ some pettifogging hireling scribbler to undermine them by sarcasm & insinuation.[26]

Watt Jr doubted the disavowals of any knowledge of the review by James Walker, then President of the Institution of Civil Engineers, or as Watt Jr referred to him,

---

[23] Watt had bought a significant landholding in Wales between the settlements of Rhayader and Builth Wells that included Doldowlod Farm. Watt Jr prided himself upon continuing and advancing the work that his father had begun in improving these estates. He was locked for some years in legal battles with encroachers upon these lands and was also upset by the prospect of railway companies acquiring a right of way through them.

[24] James Watt Jr to Henry Brougham, 17 October 1824, Brougham Papers, 27,390. On training at Soho see also Sidney Pollard, *The Genesis of Modern Management*, 1965, pp. 175–76.

[25] Watt Jr to Muirhead, 3 November 1839, Muirhead Papers, MS GEN 1354/405. The review to which Watt Jr referred was in *The Civil Engineer and Architect's Journal*, **2**, 1839, 399–419. It gave extensive translated extracts from Arago's *Eloge* and substantial commentary of a rather sarcastic nature by the translator. It was very critical of Arago and dismissive of the claims for Watt regarding the composition of water.

[26] Watt Jr to Muirhead, 3 November 1839. The article referred to as 'the Olynthiad' was published as: [John Playfair], 'Account of the steam engine', *Edinburgh Review*, **13**, January 1809, 311–33. Gregory responded in the *Monthly Magazine* (August 1809) and Playfair et al. retorted in *Edinburgh Review*, **15**, October 1809, 245–54.

'Chief of the Mongrel Engineers'. One detects in Watt Jr's perception of the relationship between the Soho Engineers and the organized profession the usual whiff of paranoia. This episode certainly provides further evidence for Hugh Torrens's depiction of Watt Jr and Watt himself as ruthlessly manipulating publications in the cause of Watt's priority.[27]

Watt Jr also strongly disapproved of the way that scientific bodies such as the British Association cavalierly communicated what he regarded as commercially confidential information.[28] It was as if the experience of fighting engine pirates in the immediate aftermath of his reconciliation with his father led him to see pirates everywhere subsequently. This, I believe, gives us some insight into Watt Jr's hypersensitivity where matters of paternal reputation were concerned and, within that, his long-standing preoccupation with credit in the 'water controversy'. If I am right that the psychological springs in these varied contexts were the same, then it is perhaps no surprise that the conceptual structure and method of argument (that of the accountant and legal prosecutor) was also the same in those different contexts.

The Filial Project

In August 1819, James Watt lay dying and the vicissitudes of his final illness were lovingly recorded in correspondence between his son and John Rennie.[29] On the day after his father's death Watt Jr wrote:

> I have indeed lost a father whom I deeply reverenced and dearly loved, and whose affection I enjoyed in return. Long years of intimate communication had sunk the father in the friend, and the loss of such a father and such a friend cannot but leave a void that I must strongly feel ... It remains for me now to pay due honours to his memory ... [30]

There was a great variety of occasions on which Watt Jr actively engaged in the cultivation of his father's reputation or assisted the efforts of others. By the 1840s some of Cavendish's supporters detected the influence of Aston Hall everywhere,

---

[27] See Hugh Torrens, 'Jonathan Hornblower (1753–1815) and the steam engine: A historiographic analysis', in Denis Smith (ed.), *Perceptions of Great Engineers: Fact and Fantasy*, 1994, pp. 26–27.

[28] Watt Jr was not impressed by the exhibition of manufactures at the Birmingham meeting of the BAAS in 1839, that same meeting at which Harcourt assailed his father's scientific reputation. He maintained that such exhibitions were of no use in originating inventions: 'the sooner we resume our ancient habits of privacy and exclusion, particularly with regard to such processes as we may still alone possess, the more it will tend to the advantage of our manufacturing interests. And narrow minded as these opinions my appear to the members of the British Association and to some of our political economists, we hope that our warning voice may not be raised in vain, to prevent a repetition of such suicidal folly.' See Watt Jr, 'Note upon the Meeting of the British Scientific Association at Birmingham', n.d. [early September 1839], as quoted in Jack Morrell and Arnold Thackray, *Gentlemen of Science: Early Years of the British Association for the Advancement of Science*, 1981, p. 264.

[29] National Library of Scotland, Rennie MSS 19824, ff. 132–33, 134–35, 138–39.

[30] Watt Jr to John Rennie, 26 August 1819, National Library of Scotland, Rennie MSS 19824, ff. 153–54. Rather poignantly, this letter was signed for the first time, 'James Watt' rather than 'James Watt Jr'.

monitoring, parrying and seeking to stifle criticism of the 'great steamer'. Watt Jr certainly spent over forty years of his life engaged on the filial project in one form or another. Before his father's death Watt Jr assisted with some of the autobiographical work in which Watt sought to enforce his version of events regarding his major inventions and his relations with Joseph Black. Various incidents in the immediate aftermath of his father's death indicate that the strong urge remained to control what was said about him, particularly so far as priority was concerned but also in regard to Watt's early life and background.

In the *Monthly Magazine* for 1 October 1819 a memoir of James Watt appeared by Mr William Playfair. A substantially different, but identifiably related, memoir appeared in the *New Monthly Magazine* two months later.[31] The proprietors of that last august journal advised readers that, although the memoir appeared in its rival journal first, it had been contracted originally for itself, with Playfair receiving 'a handsome remuneration'. It was further explained that while the memoir was 'in the hands of a friend of the late Mr Watt, for revision, the writer thought proper to dispose of a copy of the same to the old Monthly Magazine'. The editor left the public to 'form their own opinion on the conduct of Mr. Playfair'.[32]

The 'friend' to whom the editor submitted the article was James Watt Jr, who strongly disapproved of it. The version that finally appeared in the *New Monthly Magazine* was altered substantially. Nevertheless, Watt Jr was livid. Playfair himself sent a copy of the memoir to Heathfield *after* it had been published in the *Monthly Magazine*. Even worse, it appears that Playfair concocted a letter to himself from a 'John Smith' offering to withhold from publication certain 'facts' about Watt for a consideration. How the attempted blackmail ended up is unclear.[33] Watt Jr was certainly persuaded of the need to make sure that press accounts of his father were, wherever possible, scrutinized before publication. In an exchange with the publishers of the *Annual Obituary*, whose obituarist had relied on Playfair's memoir, Watt Jr rejected the result entirely and sent a composition of his own.[34]

Watt Jr began to familiarize himself with the papers that his father had left. One of the surprises he found was a bundle of correspondence concerning the water

---

[31] William Playfair, 'The late JAMES WATT, Esq, F.R.S. &c &c', *Monthly Magazine*, 1 October 1819, 230–39; idem, 'Memoir of James Watt Esq. F.R.S.', *New Monthly Magazine*, **12**, December 1819, 576–84. Playfair was a brother (evidently a black sheep) of Professor John Playfair, a long-standing friend of the Watt family.

[32] *New Monthly Magazine*, **12**, December 1819, 576.

[33] See William Playfair to Watt Jr, 12 October 1819, 22 October 1819; H. Colbourn to Watt Jr, 11 September 1819; John Rennie to Watt Jr, 11 September 1819, 25 October 1819, 1 November 1819; Watt Jr to John Rennie, 14 October 1819, all in Watt Papers (Doldowlod), C6/10. This also contains the letter from 'John Smith', dated London, 7 October 1819. The letter retails claims about the manner in which Boulton accumulated and held onto his fortune at the expense of others and accuses Watt of complicity in this. It also remarks on Watt's meanness and claims that 'Murdoch not Watt improved the Engine. As to the Crank it was no Invention at all and the Great Improvement in Execution Mr Watt had nothing to do with.' Other material on the affair includes: Watt Jr to John Rennie, 10 September 1819, 21 October 1819, 28 October 1819, National Library of Scotland, Rennie Papers, 19824, ff. 155–56, 160–61 and 164–65.

[34] See Messrs Longman & Co. to Watt Jr, 21 December 1819 and 4 January 1820; Watt Jr to Messrs Longman & Co., 1 January 1819 [1820]; Watt Papers (Doldowlod), C6/10.

controversy. The normal process of collecting obituaries of his father expanded into critiques of them and a resolution that a proper biography should be undertaken. 'It is my intention', Watt Jr wrote to John Rennie, 'to devote all my spare time to the collecting and arranging materials for a history of my father, as soon as I can set about it.' An early move to engage John Barrow of the Admiralty to write the biography came to nothing.[35]

In 1823 Watt Jr agreed to write an account of his father for the *Supplement* to the fourth, fifth and sixth editions of the *Encyclopaedia Britannica* then being produced under the editorship of Macvey Napier. The *Britannica* had included biographical articles from its second edition but Napier was also adding biographical articles on recent lives.[36] Napier approached Watt Jr in May 1823 to undertake the life of his father at a point when the *Supplement* was almost complete. The entry for 'James Watt' would appear in the final half-volume. The editor made it clear that the article would have to be of four or five pages at most, be confined to 'such particulars as are most useful and proper to be inserted in a work of reference', and would be due in October. Napier explained that he was approaching Watt Jr in order to obtain a definitive account: 'I am the more anxious to get the article from an authentic and authoritative quarter, from having been informed, that some inaccurate allusions to some part of your father's life, in an earlier portion of the work, had given pain ... '.[37] Napier appeared to recognize that with the biography of Watt he was on sensitive territory, being monitored by Watt Jr, so why not approach the possessor of the filial 'eagle eye' directly?

Napier waited six weeks for a diffident reply from Watt Jr, who explained that he had been working on a memoir of his father as a larger project but was constantly diverted by business. Uncertain whether he could supply the article in time, he would do his best to provide a brief statement of Watt's inventions. As to previous errors: 'My father was convinced that no intentional error respecting him was introduced into your publication, and I have always considered myself and the public indebted to it for having called from my father himself that correction & narrative which is given in the republication of Professor Robison's Tracts.' On 1 September a nervous and uncertain Napier wrote to check that he and Watt Jr did in fact have an agreement about the article. He reiterated the shortage of space, the necessity of sticking to the key facts and he also suggested that Watt Jr might make some use of Francis Jeffrey's 'admirable character of your father'.[38] This was a reference to the obituary of Watt written by Jeffrey for *The Scotsman* newspaper. In late October, when the deadline had passed, Napier

---

35 Watt Jr to John Rennie, 14 October 1819, Press Copy, Watt Papers (Doldowlod), C6/10.

36 See Richard Yeo, 'Alphabetical lives: Scientific biography in historical dictionaries and encyclopaedias', in Michael Shortland and Richard Yeo (eds), *Telling Lives in Science: Essays on Scientific Biography*, 1996, pp. 155–61. See also Richard Yeo, *Encyclopaedic Visions: Scientific Dictionaries and Enlightenment Culture*, 2001, pp. 260–64.

37 Macvey Napier to Watt Jr, 9 May 1823, Watt Papers (Doldowlod), C6/10. The inaccuracies referred to were those in the articles on 'Steam' and 'Steam Engine' by John Robison, which had been the subject of significant 'correction' by Watt himself in 1813–14. See Chapter 7 for more details.

38 Watt Jr to Napier, 19 June 1823 and Napier to Watt Jr, 1 September 1823, Watt Papers (Doldowlod), C6/10.

had still received nothing. He could allow another few weeks but must have an assurance that Watt Jr would produce the article. That assurance was finally forthcoming.[39]

Watt Jr eventually sent the memoir of his father to Napier on 22 December 1823, explaining that he had been as brief as possible. He had tried to describe 'the history and nature of his principal Inventions, give little more than an enumeration of the rest, and a short notice of the leading events of his life'.[40] Two days later, on Christmas Eve, Watt Jr forwarded some additions and amendments and yet more on Boxing Day. Napier must have had mixed feelings when Watt Jr helpfully advised that he was having the memoir written out again with the amendments and additions included. Still further revisions followed on New Year's Eve.[41] Amidst this flurry and fuss of amendments Napier praised the article as exactly the sort of account that suited the work in which it was to appear.[42] Perhaps he hoped to stem the flow of additions and amendments from Aston Hall that threatened to continue unabated. These were the last thing Napier needed. He did agree, however, to try to edit other articles down in order to make room for the extended version. Against usual practice, Napier also granted Watt Jr copyright on the piece.

Two other issues were debated in these epistolary exchanges – the question of identifying Watt Jr as the author, and the content of another biographical article in the *Supplement*.[43] Watt Jr wanted to remain anonymous:

> I think it will not answer any good purpose to make it known I am the author. From the space to which I was limited the present memoir necessarily contains many assertions unaccompanied by the proofs, and until I am able to give both together in a longer work, I should wish to withhold my name; as what is said with the intention of doing justice to my father's merits, might be considered in me the result of partiality & prejudice, until it can be substantiated by the original documents.[44]

Napier tried to dissuade the bashful contributor. Named authors were very important to him commercially.[45] He asked why Watt Jr had such scruples: 'It is <u>impossible</u> that you can praise your father too much. Praise from you is not only natural, & graceful, but most proper. You cannot publish an <u>extended</u> memoir without speaking of him as you think right. What objection then, can there be, to do this, in the present short one?'[46] Napier indicated that if anonymity was insisted upon he must be able to say at least that the memoir came from a '<u>near relative</u> of Mr Watt' in order that the authoritative character of the article be

---

[39] Napier to Watt Jr, 26 October 1823 and Watt Jr to Napier, 30 October 1823 (Copy), Watt Papers (Doldowlod), C6/10.

[40] Watt Jr to Napier, 22 December 1823 (Copy), Watt Papers (Doldowlod), C6/10.

[41] Watt Jr to Napier, 24, 26 and 31 December 1823 (Copies), Watt Papers (Doldowlod), C6/10.

[42] Napier to Watt Jr, 26 December 1823, Watt Papers (Doldowlod), C6/10.

[43] Napier to Watt Jr, 3 January 1824, Watt Papers (Doldowlod), C6/10.

[44] Watt Jr to Napier, 31 December 1823 (Copy), Watt Papers (Doldowlod), C6/10.

[45] On the importance of 'names' in marketing the *Britannica* see Yeo, *Encyclopaedic Visions*, pp. 257–59.

[46] Napier to Watt Jr, 3 January 1824, Watt Papers (Doldowlod), C6/10.

appreciated.[47] However, Watt Jr stood firm, asking that any allusion to the author be 'as little definite as possible', if it could not be passed *sub silentio*.[48] Watt Jr's reticence is perhaps best explained by his expectation of a hostile reception from certain quarters to his father's claims to invention and discovery and his anticipation, therefore, that his statements would be regarded, and dismissed, as interested and biased. In those circumstances he wanted to be identified only when he was free to make the best and fullest case, incorporating all available evidence. Such a case would, he hoped, be beyond reproach or challenge. It was to be many years before that case was mounted.

Watt Jr largely had it his way. He substantially exceeded the four or five pages stipulated. The additions were all included. His anonymity was preserved – just. A note at the end of the memoir stated: 'The Editor has received this article from a quarter which entitles him to state, with the utmost confidence, that it contains an accurate and faithful account of Mr Watt. The brilliant eulogium with which it so properly concludes is known to have been written by Mr Jeffrey.'[49]

The other matter negotiated by Napier and Watt Jr at this time confirms the overweening preoccupation with his father's reputation. It concerned an earlier biography in the *Supplement* of John Rennie (1761–1821) by John Barrow. Watt Jr had been presented with a copy of this biography by Rennie's son. Predictably, he took exception to a statement made there about the elder Rennie's position *vis-à-vis* the firm of Boulton & Watt. The article also contained a statement about Boulton and the Mint to which Robinson Boulton took exception. Watt Jr wanted a correction. In fact he wanted the article to be rewritten and he and Robinson Boulton had gathered materials to help Barrow to do that. Napier was aghast at this suggestion. He was quite happy as editor to include a note in the article on Watt correcting the mistakes and observed that the corrections would appear at the same time as the mistakes.[50] Watt Jr refused to back down. He volunteered to make good any financial cost that might be involved in producing a revised life. Robinson Boulton and Watt Jr approached Barrow about it, who took umbrage. He considered that they were 'meddling with things' that did not concern them, and thought Watt Jr 'the most obstinate & wrong-headed man I ever met with – different, very different, in all respects from his father … '. Barrow left it to the Rennies what to do. They decided to comply.[51] One begins to see why, over the years, the dogged insistence of Aston Hall, backed by determination and financial resources, came to be regarded as an almost pathological exhibition of filial piety.

In 1824, Watt Jr was also active in the shadows of the great meeting at the Freemasons' Tavern to open a subscription for a monument to his father. That

---

[47] Ibid.

[48] Watt Jr to Napier, 10 January 1824 (Copy), Watt Papers (Doldowlod), C6/10.

[49] See 'James Watt', *Supplement* to the fourth, fifth and sixth editions of *Encyclopaedia Britannica*, vol. 6, pp. 778–85, at p. 785.

[50] Watt Jr to Napier, 22 and 31 December 1823; Napier to Watt Jr, 26 December 1823 and 3 January 1824, Watt Papers (Doldowlod), C6/10.

[51] John Barrow to George Rennie, 27 November 1823, National Library of Scotland, MSS 19938, ff. 38–39 and ff. 40–41; Barrow to George Rennie, 7 January 1824, Macvey Napier Correspondence, British Library Add. MSS. 34,611, ff. 217–18.

meeting was chaired by Charles Hampden Turner, a family friend, and addressed by numerous luminaries.[52] The massive sculpture by Francis Chantrey that resulted from this process was finally installed in Westminster Abbey in 1834 and provided a fascinating episode in the filial project. Henry Brougham had agreed to write the inscription for this monument, an activity for which he was already quite renowned. He had written an inscription for a statue of Watt given by Watt Jr to Glasgow University.[53] Watt Jr requested a number of changes to Brougham's draft of the Westminster inscription.[54] He silently changed his father's birthdate and age since Brougham, who was not renowned, as we shall see, for attention to detail, had them wrong. Watt Jr wanted the line 'Educated at Glasgow' removed, as untrue:

> He [Watt] has himself stated in his letter to Dr Brewster, prefixed to the latters edition of Dr Robison's Essay on the Steam Engine, that he never attended any lectures at the College of Glasgow, & I have heard him say that the only tuition he received, was at the Grammar School of Greenock.[55]

The most interesting and telling change that Watt Jr requested concerned the line initially rendered by Brougham as 'Happily trained in philosophic research'. The words 'Happily trained', Watt Jr suggested, were inappropriate given the general understanding of training as 'instruction given or directed by others'.

> Upon reading the Memorials of Dr Black & Mr Robison, your Lordship will perceive that when my father first became acquainted with the Professors at Glasgow, in the year 1757, he being then 21, he was already qualified in point of scientific attainments to be their associate, and possessed a knowledge of the arts which they had not. I believe that independent of the tuition of the Grammar school of Greenock, which from ill health he was little able to attend, and a years practice with a Mathematical instrument maker in London, all his knowledge was acquired by his own reading and observations and reflections. It strikes me therefore that for the above two words you might substitute 'early devoted', 'early turned' or 'early applied'.[56]

---

[52] For the speeches made on this occasion see François Arago, *Historical Eloge of James Watt ... Translated ... by James Patrick Muirhead*, 1839, pp. 183–239.

[53] See James Watt Jr to Henry Brougham, 31 March 1833, Brougham Papers, 44,876.

[54] The version that Watt Jr corrected originally read thus: 'Not to perpetuate a name/Which must endure while the peaceful arts flourish/ But to testify/That mankind can distinguish those/Who have best earned their gratitude/The King/With many of the most eminent individuals in the Realm/Raised this monument to/James Watt/LLD FRS/Who by applying with unparalleled success/A great original Genius/Happily trained in Philosophic research/To the improvement of the Steam Engine/Enlarged the resources of his country/Increased the power of man/And exalted himself/To the highest place among the followers of science/And the real benfactors of the world/He was born at Greenock in MDCCXLI/ Educated at Glasgow/Died at Heathfield near Birmingham/MDCCCXIX/Aged/LXXVII'. See James Watt to Henry Brougham, 13 July 1834, and enclosure, Brougham Papers, 27,513.

[55] James Watt to Henry Brougham, 13 July 1834, Brougham Papers, 27,513.

[56] James Watt Jr to Henry Brougham, 14 March 1835, Brougham Papers, 27,743. Brougham agreed to the change though it is hard not to see in his original wording a concern to assimilate Watt to the Mechanics' Institute and SDUK movements with which Brougham was so closely involved. The final version of the inscription read: 'Not to perpetuate a name/Which must endure while the peaceful arts flourish/But to shew/That Mankind have learnt to honour those/Who best deserve their gratitude/The

One of Watt Jr's primary concerns, then, was to get a clear statement depicting his father as an autodidact. It was important that the great engineer's mechanical and philosophical genius be seen as original and native to him.

This was a point that Watt Jr insisted upon on all occasions. Many of Watt Jr's points of correction to Arago's *Eloge* were to concern this same question. The merest whiff of the idea that his father depended on others evoked Watt Jr's protests. For example, the hapless James David Forbes wrote a memoir of John Robison in which he mentioned that Robison had rendered great service to Watt in his lawsuits. On receiving a copy of this document, Watt Jr generally praised it but then rather curtly observed: 'I am not aware upon what grounds you state, in alluding to the mutual friendship which existed between Dr Robison and My Father, that "by far the greatest services" were conferred by the former. And you will oblige me by explaining to what you refer.'[57] Somewhat taken aback, Forbes wrote to Robison's widow: 'Mr Watt, I find, most unexpectedly ... has taken umbrage at the expression used in my Memoir of Sir J. Robison ... intimating that Mr Watt, senior, received great benefits at the hands of Dr Robison; by which I referred chiefly to his support of Mr Watt's Patent Right.'[58]

In responding to Watt Jr, Forbes offered a similar clarification:

> In saying (as I did advisedly) that 'by far the greatest services, in the ordinary acceptation of the terms, were conferred by Dr Robison on Mr Watt', I referred more particularly to Dr Robison's exertions and important evidence on occasion of the Patent Trial, as well as to the valuable articles in the Encyclopaedia Britannica in which Dr Robison preserved so admirable a record of Mr Watt's Discoveries. I have not attempted to decide which of these eminent friends derived most intellectual profit and enjoyment from each others Society,- but by 'services in the ordinary acceptation of the term' I referred to the promotion of Fortune & Fame, in which respects Dr Robison was able to confer a

King/His Ministers and many of the Nobles/And Commoners of the Realm/Raised this monument to/ JAMES WATT/Who directing the force of an original genius/Early exercised in philosophic research/ To the improvement of/The Steam Engine/Enlarged the resources of his country/Increased the power of man/And rose to an eminent place/Among the most illustrious followers of science/And the real benefactors of the World/Born at Greenock MDCCXXXVI/Died at Heathfield in Staffordshire MDCCCXIX'. This statue of Watt, and a photograph of the marble inscription stone, were to be seen in November 2002 at the Scottish National Portrait Gallery in Edinburgh. The statue is on loan to the Gallery for a time before being transferred to its new owner, Heriot-Watt University.

57 James Watt Jr to James David Forbes, 13 March 1846, Forbes Papers, Incoming Letters 1846, no. 22.

58 James D. Forbes to Mrs Robison, 16 March 1846, Forbes Papers, Letterbook IV, p. 93. Mrs Robison's reply, written in a very old, spidery hand, is of interest even though it somewhat misconstrues the nature of Watt Jr's concern: 'I am sorry you have had any Trouble with Mr Watt's supposed offence. I attend'd Mr Robison to London and all was pleasant in the Meeting. If Mr Watt, Junior, had been there Himself, he must have thought so. The scientifick Gentlemen were all interested to convince the least informed of the Jury, that all was compleat, and, perfect, in the patent of Mr Watt, and, even the Judge himself was much pleased, as He said, He was too little of an Artist, to form an opinion of his own. In this simple statement I cannot see any help required or given, except Mr Robison's exertion in complying with Mr Watts wish, He should attend the Tryal: Mr Rs bad health made it difficult (but happily had no bad effect). If you chuse to forward this paper, that I never knew any wish or attempt to detract from his worthy Fathers indisputed Talents & merits In which by personal knowledge has long been esteemed & admired by, R. Robison' (R. Robison to James David Forbes, [?] March 1846, Forbes Papers).

substantial benefit on his friend, which the latter, to the close of his life, gratefully acknowledged.[59]

Watt Jr at this time was deep in a 'campaign', as he called it, defending his father, himself, Brougham and Arago from the strictures of an acerbic article in the *Quarterly Review* written anonymously by George Peacock, one of the more strident of Cavendish's defenders.[60] It seems likely that, being busy defending his father's originality on the water question, Watt Jr had assumed that Forbes (a known associate of the Cavendish camp) was making a parallel attack on the originality of his father's improvements to the steam engine. Robison had been a witness to those improvements and, it was widely known, discussed them with Watt at the time they were first conceived. So it appears that on this occasion, too, Watt Jr, by now close to the end of his life, almost blind, and in very poor health, was still resisting the slightest hint that his father's inventions and discoveries were the product of anything but his native, untutored and unaided genius.

The Water Controversy and the Filial Project

Watt Jr is the 'Mr Gradgrind' of the water controversy. The appeal to the 'facts of the case' came most insistently from him. He believed that establishing the facts would settle the priority issue in the same way that the accounting ledger would settle matters of business. The publication projects, including the article on his father for the *Supplement* to the *Encyclopaedia Britannica* and the publication of the *Correspondence*, were conceived as getting the facts out into the open. Information and advice to Arago during the production of the *Eloge* were cast as getting the facts straight. Watt Jr's anger at the defenders of Cavendish was directed at what he believed was their sophistry in arguing around, and in spite of, the facts. He adopted the same attitude as his father to the idea that posterity could decide on the basis of the facts. Just as his father did not need to be trained to see the facts of chemistry, so, Watt Jr contended, he – and indeed anyone else willing to see – could discern the facts of the priority dispute. In terms of the attributional strategies discussed in Chapter 2, Watt Jr definitely employed synonymity and priority. That is, he assumed that there was no significant difference between the claims made by his father and by Henry Cavendish. The only issue was who got there first. The merits of the ideas promulgated, or their place in a train of research, are of little relevance on this view. Who and when are more important than the details of what. There is a marked similarity between Watt Jr's ideas about how a priority dispute should be adjudged and how a business problem should be solved, or a series of experiments on steamship engines conducted. The rigorous pursuit of the facts by keeping account was the key.

Watt Jr's memoir in the *Supplement* to the *Encyclopaedia Britannica* was his first public statement on the water question. What does he have to say there? First,

---

[59] James David Forbes to James Watt Jr, 17 March 1846, Forbes Papers, Incoming Letters 1846, no. 23.

[60] [George Peacock], 'Arago and Brougham on Black, Cavendish, Priestley and Watt', *Quarterly Review*, **77**, 1845, 105–39.

it should be noted that the article, even when not directly discussing the water controversy, was concerned to assert Watt's credentials as a philosopher. The memoir began with the words 'James Watt, a Philosopher, mechanician and Civil Engineer ... ', sobriquets that were usually reversed in other accounts, if 'philosopher' was used at all.[61] Watt's experimental investigation of the consumption of steam in the model engine at Glasgow University was conducted, we are told, in a 'truly philosophical manner'. Referring to the investigations and inventions involved in developing his rotative engines, the memoir stated: 'we are impressed by a union of philosophical research, of physical skill, and of mechanical ingenuity, which has, we believe, no parallel in modern times'.[62] Thus were the philosophical credentials asserted.

The memoir devoted just over two pages to the water question itself. The claims made are as follows. First, that in early 1783 Watt reached the conclusion from Priestley's experiments that 'water is a compound of dephlogisticated and inflammable airs (as they were then called) deprived of their latent or elementary heat and he was the first to make known this theory', in a letter to Priestley dated 26 April 1783. Second, that the letter circulated in London among members of the Royal Society including Joseph Banks and Charles Blagden, but before the letter was read to the Society Watt asked for a delay in its reading because of 'new experiments' by Priestley. Third, that Watt sent a revised edition of his letter to De Luc on 26 November 1783 which was read to the Royal Society on 29 April 1784 and published in the *Philosophical Transactions* of that year. On 15 January 1784 Cavendish read a paper concerning his experiments which, it is claimed, drew 'the same inference as Mr Watt; with this difference only, that he did not admit elementary heat into his explanation'. It was also claimed that Cavendish knew of Watt's paper when his (C's) paper was read, stated that his experiments were made in 1781 but said nothing about when he formed his conclusions, and stated that a friend of his (Blagden) gave an account of his experiments and the conclusion drawn from them to Lavoisier in the summer of 1783. Finally, the memoir contended that Watt had not heard of Cavendish's experiments when he drew his conclusion.

This represents a brief, clear statement of the empirical position. The documented facts are treated as clear: that Watt first drew the conclusion; that the conclusion did not differ significantly from the conclusion later announced by Cavendish (and therefore was the *same* and not a different, or inferior, or the wrong conclusion). So far as Cavendish is concerned, the facts presented are used to imply that he did not have a conclusion when Watt did, may have arrived at it later and separately, or may have derived it from Watt. In any case, Cavendish did not make any conclusions public before Watt. Even as this story was elaborated during the course of the controversy, the central features of it remained in all the Watt camp's effusions.

---

[61] The British Biographical Archive provides a handy collection of biographies of Watt that can be compared with each other in this regard. See also the discussion of encyclopaedia entries in Chapter 11, and my article '"Puffing Jamie": The commercial and ideological importance of being a "philosopher" in the case of the reputation of James Watt (1736–1819)', *History of Science*, **38**, 2000, 1–24.

[62] See [James Watt Jr], 'Memoir of James Watt', *Supplement* to the fourth, fifth and sixth edition of the *Encyclopaedia Britannica*, vol. 6, p. 781.

A note at the end of the section dealing with the water question referred to the confusion of dates of Watt's letter to De Luc (regarding when it was written and when it was read to the Royal Society), expressing calmly an inability to explain this. It also stated: 'It is also a circumstance not to be passed over, that Mr Cavendish circulated the copies of his paper given him for private distribution with the erroneous date on the fly leaf "read 15th January 1783"!'.[63] These issues were to receive considerable elaboration, especially by Lord Brougham, but the implication of bad faith on Cavendish's part was already there.

Twenty years passed before Watt Jr appeared in print again on the water question. By 1846 when the *Correspondence of the late James Watt on his discovery of the theory of the composition of water* was published, Watt Jr was in poor health and almost blind. Muirhead did the major work of editing and introducing the *Correspondence*. Nevertheless Watt Jr exercised close supervision. He contributed a prefatory letter and this provides our second opportunity to discern Watt Jr's public stance on the water question. In consigning to Muirhead the task of editing and introducing the *Correspondence*, Watt Jr presented the exercise as an evidential one that 'falls peculiarly within the sphere of your pursuits'.[64] Chemical knowledge might be useful, and Watt Jr recalled that he himself was 'tolerably versed in the facts and doctrines of the new system of chemistry, which the able writings and generalization of Lavoisier had caused to be commonly received'.[65] However, the skill of lawyers such as Muirhead (and Brougham) in considering and weighing evidence was, Watt Jr considered, the most important qualification.

Having recounted his consultations about the correspondence with various parties over the years, to which we will turn in a moment, Watt Jr then recalled his memoir in the *Britannica*. He reproduced the text of that section of the memoir which dealt with the water question. He described this text as 'necessarily somewhat imperfect' because 'the whole of the facts since ascertained' were not known to him then.[66] What facts did he mean? He did not notice any correction or addition to the basic elements of the empirical account that we outlined above. What he *did* do, however, was discuss the additional information that Lord Brougham had uncovered about the Cavendish camp's supposed fiddling with documents. He also reported the negative outcome of investigations in the Cavendish papers seeking to find an earlier statement of *conclusions* by Cavendish. The overall message, then, was that the facts regarding priority had long been established, that they were rooted in the public documentary base but decisively confirmed by the private correspondence now published. Watt Jr's own memoir, Arago's *Eloge* and Brougham's account in *Lives of Men of Letters and Science* were all grounded in that documentary base. Harcourt's pronouncements were made in ignorance of it, Watt Jr claimed.

The long hiatus between Watt Jr's literary interventions was not a period of inattention to the water controversy on his part. He recounted in his Preface the original discovery, in August 1819, of the water correspondence bundled among his

---

[63] It appears from the copy of the memoir in the Watt Papers (Doldowlod), 3/26 that the final point about Cavendish circulating erroneously dated 'offprints' was added in the proof stage.

[64] Preface, *Correspondence*, p. ii.

[65] Ibid., p. iii.

[66] Ibid., p. vi.

father's papers. Watt Jr reported being immediately struck that the correspondence contained proofs of his father's claim 'ample, satisfactory, and conclusive'.[67] Nevertheless, he repeatedly sought the opinions of others. Almost immediately Watt Jr showed the papers to John Corrie, then President of the Philosophical Society of Birmingham, whose view of their significance coincided with his own. The next to see the correspondence, or at least extracts from it, in 1820 was Watt Jr's old Manchester friend Dr William Henry, who agreed with his assessment of the import of the materials. Henry saw the original correspondence later, in 1835 and 1836, on visits to Aston Hall. According to Watt Jr, this 'had the natural effect of strengthening the opinion he had formed and expressed in 1820; and upon the latter occasion he mentioned his intention of writing a history of Chemistry, in which he said he should do justice to my father's claims to the priority'.[68] On a visit to Edinburgh not long after his father's death, Watt consulted Drs Hope and Brewster about the correspondence, but they were unable to draw the same conclusions in favour of Watt's priority.

In September 1824, Sir Humphry Davy visited Watt Jr for a few days at Aston Hall and was shown the memoir for the *Britannica* and also the original correspondence on the water question. Watt Jr recalled the occasion thus:

> I directed his attention to what is there said [in the memoir] on my father's claim to the discovery of the theory of the composition of water; but the facts stated appeared to be new to him ... . I mentioned my desire to do justice and inquired if he knew of any papers left by Mr Cavendish from which the date of his conclusions might be ascertained; but he was ignorant of the existence of any such papers. I then laid before him the press copies of my father's letters, and the original ones of his correspondents, which he read over with much interest, and appeared exceedingly struck with their contents. He expressed concern at the effect which their publication must produce (a concern not unnaturally proceeding from his known attachment to Mr Cavendish) and he did not then, or at our subsequent meeting in 1826, endeavour to lessen their force, or to call in question the deductions resulting from their perusal. In the last conversation I had with him here on the subject, he said he thought that my father's theory, admitting the latent heat, would prove correct.[69]

Watt Jr's mention of his 'subsequent meeting' with Davy in 1826 turns out to have been a very interesting occasion. On 30 August 1826 a meeting was held in the Assembly Rooms in Greenock to consider the erection of a monument to the memory of Watt. The local worthies were gathered to consider the appropriate form of commemoration. The meeting was informed that Watt Jr was in town and had expressed his preference for a statue from the chisel of Chantrey. After some discussion, a deputation was sent to bring important guests to the Meeting – Watt Jr, but also Sir Humphry Davy.

The Chairman, Sir M.S. Stewart, spoke first and it became plain that his ear had been bent by Watt Jr about his father's philosophical credentials. In the midst of a long panegyric are these words:

---

67 Ibid., p. iv.

68 Ibid., pp. iv, v and note.

69 Ibid., pp. ix–x.

I speak it under the correction of the high authority near me, that we greatly injure the fame and narrow the reputation of Mr Watt, if we consider him only as a great practical mechanic. I believe him to have been a profound philosopher, and a subtle chemist; and that it was by the aid and complete mastery of these sciences that his penetrating intellect, after years of intense labour, brought to perfection a series of combinations unexampled in the history of the world ... bestowing a new and inexhaustible power upon civilized man.[70]

Watt Jr then rose and, after long preliminaries, announced that he would donate a sum of £2000 to be used in erecting a building for a library in which the statue would be placed. Davy also spoke in rhapsodic terms about Watt and 'the triumph of philosophy, as applied to practical purposes'.[71] The rhetorical force of presenting Davy as convinced by the water correspondence was considerable, not least because Davy's obituary of Cavendish and his *Elements of Chemistry* were major sources of the mythology surrounding that great natural philosopher. Davy's characterizations of Cavendish and his work were already standard reference points.

Arago was the next to be shown the original correspondence at Aston Hall, where he briefly sojourned *en route* to the British Association meeting at Edinburgh in 1834. It was already known that Arago was preparing his *Eloge* of Watt for the Académie des Sciences. We examine the springs of Arago's work and the saga of Watt Jr's exchanges with him in Chapter 6. For the moment we need only note what Watt Jr had to say about Arago and the water correspondence. He stated that during the 1834 visit he asked Arago if he had examined the water question, and that Arago responded positively, saying that he had convinced himself of Watt's priority by examining the available public documents. Watt Jr then showed Arago the correspondence which 'put the seal on his conviction'.[72] Arago asked to use the material and Watt Jr agreed. Watt Jr emphasized that the account of the water question given in the *Eloge* as read to the Institute in December 1834 'experienced no alteration' between then and the publication of the *Eloge* in 1839. The implication once again was that the correspondence provided a kernel of clear and enduring factual information about the water question.

Watt Jr recalled that in the same year as Arago's visit, Lord Brougham was writing the inscription for the monument to Watt in Westminster Abbey. As we have seen, Watt Jr called Brougham's attention to the water question, considering that the inscription might include something about Watt's priority. In the end it did not, but Brougham's perusal of the water correspondence started him upon a train of research. Watt Jr had asked Brougham to examine the available documents 'with the discrimination of a lawyer, and the impartiality of a judge'.[73] This led Brougham to investigations among the Cavendish papers and the archives of the Royal Society

---

[70] 'Report from the Greenock Advertiser, of the Proceedings of a Meeting, held in the Assembly-Rooms, Greenock, for the purpose of deliberating on the erection of a Monument to the Memory of the late James Watt, Esquire', reproduced as an Appendix in George Williamson, *Letters Respecting the Watt Family*, 1840, pp. 50–67, at p. 54.

[71] Ibid., p. 59. Davy had evidently been recruited to the cause.

[72] Ibid., p. x.

[73] Ibid., p. xi.

that produced the story told in his 'Historical Note' appended to Arago's *Eloge*. That 'Historical Note' itself carried further notes upon it by Watt Jr.

We have seen, then, that Watt Jr regarded the water correspondence as irrefutable factual evidence for his father's priority. However, he continually sought reinforcement of that belief by revealing the correspondence to other key individuals. The water controversy assumed such importance in the filial project because it was the issue upon which Watt's claims to philosophical eminence were challenged. They were challenged precisely because they were claims to philosophical status that Watt Jr and others considered crucial in presenting the great engineer as simultaneously the great student of fundamental nature. At stake in the end was the perceived relationship between science and technology.

Conclusion

We will meet Watt Jr many more times in the course of this study. We have seen enough, however, to understand the dimensions of his filial project and how his early life informed and impelled it. We have also seen that Watt Jr's approach to the issue of priority of discovery was an empirical one, itself very much in tune with the pragmatic keeping of account that underlay his important contributions to the business that his father had founded. In this sense, keeping account was a major impetus to the water controversy. This empirical approach was not entirely personal. It drew strength from a philosophical stance that some other parties to the water question shared, including François Arago. Why did this prominent French scientist participate in the water controversy? To that question we now turn.

Chapter 6

The French Connection:
Arago Re-opens the Controversy

Introduction

The *éloge*[1] of James Watt that was delivered to the Académie des Sciences by
François Arago on 8 December 1834 and published nearly five years later is a
fascinating document. It played a key role in the water controversy, setting out in
very stark and challenging terms the case for Watt's priority and accusing Cavendish
and his friends of underhand dealings. Being the occasion for Harcourt's counter-
attack at the meeting of the BAAS in Birmingham in 1839, the *Eloge* became the
hinge about which the controversy turned.

Why did Arago write the *Eloge* of Watt? Why did he make an issue of the water
controversy in the way that he did? In France, Arago's treatment of Watt had major
local implications that were quite different from those driving the controversy in
Britain. I argue that the *Eloge* was one vehicle by which Arago sought to convey
messages about the processes of invention and innovation and their importance in
the industrial and political development of France. I suggest that his account of
Watt also reflected to some extent Arago's concern to remodel and reform the
communication processes of the Académie des Sciences. In addressing historical
issues of discovery, priority and communication Arago intended that morals be
drawn about the best way to organize the Académie's contemporary affairs. It is
indeed ironic that an *Eloge* of a man who died in 1819, that was not begun until
1834, and which had timely publication as one of its subtexts, should have finally
appeared in print in 1839 after the lengthy saga we now examine.

The first manifestation of the *Eloge* was the document prepared by Arago for
delivery at the meeting of the Académie des Sciences in December 1834. This
spoken version was important to Arago because it was delivered directly to a
fashionable and powerful French audience. We can be reasonably sure that this
version concentrated much more than the published one on Arago's 'dissertations'
(as Watt Jr called them) on steam power in France and on open communication in
science. Thus it probably contained less material than later published accounts on
Watt as such and more on the messages that Arago sought to convey through his
account of the life. This document is not available, but we can know something of
its contents from two sources: press reports of the meeting, and exchanges between
Arago and James Watt Jr during the course of preparing the spoken version of the

---

[1] I use *éloge* to refer to the spoken version of Arago's memoir of Watt, and *Eloge* to refer to the
published versions.

éloge. On the way to the British Association meeting in Edinburgh in 1834 Arago met with Watt Jr. During Arago's stay in Britain, and in the months leading up to the delivery of the *éloge* later in the year, they were in regular contact.

When the *éloge* had been delivered, attention turned to its publication. This was to be a long and tortuous process in which Arago again maintained close contact with Watt Jr and also with other interested parties, notably Henry, Lord Brougham. Brougham had long been a defender and promoter of the reputation of James Watt. He was present at the Académie for the delivery of the *éloge* and he was to write crucial material appended to the published version as well as give advice on the larger text. Thus in the late 1830s numerous exchanges about the content of the *Eloge* occurred and we have archival records of James Watt Jr's comments and annotations upon an intermediate version and upon the first proofs of the document. These processes fed into the publication of the *Eloge* in France in 1839.[2]

The *Eloge*, Arago's Career and Concerns

Why did Arago write the *Eloge* of Watt? A straightforward answer might be that it was Arago's job as Perpetual Secretary of the Academy to prepare *éloges* of deceased members (Watt had been elected in 1808). Perhaps in writing about Watt Arago simply did his duty. However, Arago did not write all the *éloges* that were presented to the Academy. He chose those whom he was to write about and his biographers tell us that Arago used the *éloges* to convey messages about his vision of the relationship of science and society in industrialization. Here is John Cawood on the issue:

> Pendant la période où il fut à la fois Secrétaire perpétuel et député, les efforts d'Arago pour démontrer la fonction sociale de la science prirent trois formes essentielles. Dans ses écrits et dans ses discours à l'Académie et à la chambre des députés, tout d'abord, il développa un système général d'idées sur la rôle de la science dans le progrès social. Deuxièmement, il plaida pour que le développement industriel profite de l'application de la technologie. Il se préoccupa, enfin, des problèmes sociaux, éducatifs et politiques posés par le développement industriel. A l'Académie, il exprimait souvent ses idées dans les 'éloges', courtes biographies d'hommes de science distingués, qu'Arago transformait en déclarations générales sur la fonction de la science.[3]

---

[2] The *Eloge* appeared in France as: D.F.J. Arago, 'Eloge historique de James Watt', *Mémoires de l'Académie Royale des Sciences de l'Institut de France*, **17**, 1840, lxi–clxxxviii, having also previously appeared in the *Annuaire du Bureau des Longitudes* for 1839.

[3] John Cawood, 'François Arago, homme de science et homme politique', *La Recherche*, **16**, 1985, 1469. On the *éloges* of Arago see Maurice Crosland, *Science under Control: The French Academy of Sciences 1795–1914*, 1992, pp. 360–61, and on those of Cuvier see Dorinda Outram, 'The language of natural power: The *Eloges* of George Cuvier', *History of Science*, **16**, 1978, 153–78. Translation of quotation: 'During the period when he held the position of perpetual secretary and deputy, Arago's efforts to show the social function of science took three essential forms. In his writings and his speeches at the Academy and at the Chamber of Deputies, from the first, he developed a general system of ideas on the role of science in social progress. Secondly, he argued that industrial development profits from the application of technology. He preoccupied himself, finally, with social, educational and political problems posed by industrial development. At the Academy he often put forward these

Arago praised the ideas of Condorcet that science was the way to the perfectibility of man, that science would dissipate prejudice and moral and intellectual sickness. The ideological benefits of science were complemented by its practical benefits through technology. It was in this connection that Arago discussed the steam engine 'qui, selon lui, avait bénéficié du développement des théories de la chaleur'.[4] His *éloge* of Watt devoted considerable space to an argument about the industrial gains to be had by application of steam power to industry and transportation. Arago's notable advocacy of Watt's priority in discovery of the composition of water was thus part of a larger picture in which he sought to assimilate science, technology and industrial development. Arago's more general political aims of expanding democratic franchise and of bringing education to the workers were readily united into this picture.

Arago was in many respects an heir to the industrializing ideology of J.-A. Chaptal, who sought to advance the French economy by bringing science, engineering, entrepreneurship and a well-educated workforce together.[5] Horn and Jacob find many similarities between the views of Chaptal and Watt and an ongoing circle of mutual admiration including them both, especially via Berthollet. Crosland notes the similarities between the careers of Chaptal and Gay-Lussac, a point that I would echo for Gay-Lussac's good friend and coadjutor Arago. Arago and Chaptal were, of course, both members of the Society of Arcueil, though of different generations.[6] So Arago's views about the relations of science and industry were not unique to him but he was part of a tradition of thought in late eighteenth- and early nineteenth-century France.

In writing *éloges*, Arago was also coming to terms with a long tradition within the Académie. His predecessor, Georges Cuvier, managed a number of tropes in his *éloges*. The tendency of the natural philosopher to solitude and disengagement from the world was emphasized by Cuvier, but he also dealt with the dangers of 'solitude' transforming into 'isolation'. Cuvier's management of images of the natural philosopher was closely dependent upon the positions that he had chosen to take within the changing political climate of French society.[7] Arago faced quite other circumstances and took a very different personal political stance. In fact, Arago led a liberal political faction within the Académie directly opposed to Cuvier's attitudes and policies. The two were in open conflict about public access to the workings of the Académie and also ranged on opposite sides in the Cuvier–Geoffroy debate. Indeed, the latter debate was the occasion for provocative action by Arago, very soon after his 1830 election as Perpetual Secretary, to open the proceedings of the Académie to public scrutiny.[8]

---

ideas in the *éloges*, short biographies of distinguished men of science, which Arago transformed into general declarations on the function of science.'

[4] Cawood, 'François Arago', 1470.

[5] See Jeff Horn and Margaret C. Jacob, 'Jean-Antoine Chaptal and the cultural roots of French industrialization', *Technology and Culture*, **39**, 1998, 671–98.

[6] See Maurice Crosland, *The Society of Arcueil*, 1967, pp. 113–16, 247 and Crosland, *Gay-Lussac, Scientist and Bourgeois*, 1978.

[7] Outram, 'The language of natural power', 153–178.

[8] See Dorinda Outram, *Georges Cuvier*, 1987 and Toby A. Appel, *The Cuvier–Geoffroy Debate. French Biology in the Decades before Darwin*, 1987, pp. 120–21, 160–61.

6.1 François Arago

By 1834 Arago was approaching the height of his powers. As a young man he had risen quickly via the Ecole Polytechnique, a position at the Paris Observatory and election to the Académie des Sciences at the age of twenty-three. Though patronized and befriended by members of the Society of Arcueil, Arago's relationship with many of his colleagues was often tense. For example, he worked closely with J.B. Biot at various times but they were also continually in dispute. Arago's republican views led him into a political career from 1830. Indeed, his scientific and political careers were not really separate since as Perpetual Secretary of the Académie he pursued a political programme involving, among other things, opening up the scientific community to greater public access and the promotion of technological change. To the end of his life Arago continued to bring technological matters before the Académie. In 1852, a year before his death, he exhibited a sample of the new undersea telegraph cable laid, joining England and France.[9] In

his career in the Chamber of Deputies he frequently concerned himself with scientific and technological issues, promoting similar objectives. It is not surprising, then, that Arago, in his *éloges*, was much more anxious to stress the active involvement of scientific figures in practical and political affairs than was Cuvier. Arago also emphasized more than did Cuvier the dangers of solitude translating into isolation for the man of knowledge. For Arago, active communication was vital to the proper pursuit of the life of science.

In entering into issues of discovery and priority as Arago did in the *Eloge* of Watt, he was addressing matters that had been an abiding concern for him throughout his career. His early years as a young researcher in cooperation and competition with Biot had given Arago a strong sense of the importance of guarding and establishing priority. This issue recurred through Arago's career in a variety of connections: the disputes over the wave theory of light; Arago's support for Daguerre as the inventor of 'photography'; his support of Leverrier against the claims of Adams to the discovery of the planet Neptune. The positions on priority and discovery, what they consist in and how they are to be established and accounted for, were thus not something only discussed in the *Eloge* of Watt. They were an ongoing concern. What Arago had to say about Watt was conditioned by his prior writings about discovery and priority as generic issues. A point that emerges in all these examples as dear to Arago's heart (and important to his ideology) is that discovery and priority claims can and should be judged on the basis of *public* statements and claims, and must involve openness of communication. Arago believed that it was the scientist's responsibility to openly communicate findings. Not to do so was, in his view, an abdication of responsibility and a neglect of public duty. In consequence, if findings were not fully and openly communicated there could be no priority or credit claimed for them. This view was allied to Arago's republican doctrine. The founding of the *Comptes rendus* and other steps that Arago took to open up the Académie des Sciences to public scrutiny and to improve its publication practices were closely linked to his ideas about the appropriate mechanisms for crediting discovery and priority. Thus, before and after dealing with Watt, Arago relied heavily on priority of communication as a criterion of discovery.

In taking Daguerre's part against the Englishman W. Henry Fox-Talbot in the case of the discovery of photography, Arago tried to ensure the early communication of Daguerre's process through the Académie with his announcement on 7 January 1839. However, because the French government's pension to Daguerre was not secured until later that year, Arago's announcement on behalf of Daguerre had to be made in 'deliberately vague terms' and not fully published until August 1839.[10] Thus even where direct commercial concerns intruded, open communication should, according to Arago, be pursued as much as possible.

In 1843 Arago remarked on this question again, this time in some observations on the career of William Herschel. Arago was impressed by Herschel's habit of publishing his findings immediately. Herschel was to be contrasted in his openness with the researcher who, 'in love with his discoveries, as the miser is with his

---

[9] See John L. Davis, 'Artisans and savants: The role of the Academy of Sciences in the process of electrical innovation in France, 1850–1880', *Annals of Science*, **55**, 1998, 299.

[10] Crosland, *Science under Control*, p. 255.

treasure, buries them in the ground, takes care even lest his discoveries be suspected, for fear that some other experimenter develops them or applies them. The public owes nothing to someone who has rendered no service to it.'[11] As Crosland observes, Arago's emphasis was upon avoiding priority disputes by clearly dated publication (as in the *Comptes rendus*). Retrospective claims based on testimony could never be authentic in the way that such publicly documented announcements were.[12] Once again, in October 1846, during a speech at the Académie supporting Leverrier against the recently announced, but unpublished, claims of John Couch Adams in the dispute over the discovery of Neptune, Arago invoked the criterion of open communication:

> What! M. Le Verrier has made his research available to the entire scientific world: following the formulae of our learned compatriot, everyone has been able to see the new planet ... and to-day we are called upon to share this glory, so loyally and legitimately acquired, with a young man who has communicated nothing to the public ... [13]

Given this preoccupation with priority through open communication, it is hardly surprising that Arago sided with Watt in the water controversy case. For Arago the emergent characterization of Cavendish as reluctant to publish, and not needful of fame because of his aristocratic and financial status, would automatically incline him against Cavendish's case. The fact that Cuvier had been Cavendish's elogist did not help matters. If Watt could claim priority of communication, then the case was made. Private testimony concerning Cavendish's actions, theories about what he must have thought, or testimonies to his character were beside the point. Also corruption of the communication process of the kind that Arago, and Brougham, claimed had gone on through the wiles of Blagden and Cavendish was anathema. We must not forget, finally, that Arago was likely to welcome the chance to expose, or at least give an airing to, such *'ancien régime'* corruption.

Thus the criteria of discovery that Arago sought to apply in the water controversy emphasized precisely those aspects of scientific communication that he was working hard to facilitate through his role in the scientific community. This provides, then, a major contextual reason why Arago would prefer one sort of accounting of discovery over another. He, along with the rest of the Watt camp, emphasized the importance of the dates of the key documents in the water controversy. The Cavendish camp on the contrary perforce went in for complex hermeneutics, what Watt Jr called 'tedious sophistical declamation upon the merits of ... their theories'.[14]

---

11 *Comptes rendus*, **17**, 1843, 776n, taken from Arago, 'Notice sur la vie et les travaux de William Herschel', *Annuaire du Bureau des Longitudes*, 1842, 462–63, as quoted in Crosland, *Science under Control*, p. 280. Arago, *Biographies of Distinguished Scientific Men*, 1857, 195 remarks on William Herschel's memoirs on Newton's rings that Herschel himself had 'said that it was the only occasion on which he had reason to regret having, according to his constant method, published his labours immediately, as fast as they were performed'.

12 Crosland, *Science under Control*, p. 280.

13 Ibid., p. 372. See also Morton Grosser, *The Discovery of Neptune*, 1962 and Robert W. Smith, 'The Cambridge Network in action: The discovery of Neptune', *Isis*, **80**, 1989, 395–422.

14 Watt Jr, 'Note upon the Presidents discourse at the Birmingham Scientific Meeting, for Eloge p.

We can say that Arago's *Eloge* of Watt had a special significance for him because of the opportunities it offered to develop themes close to his heart and central to his public career as scientist and politician. The time that he devoted to the *Eloge*, the constant delays in order to accommodate Watt Jr (of which more below), are indications of his concern to back his case as authentically and effectively as possible.

Gathering Material for the *Eloge*: Arago and James Watt Jr

In late August and early September 1834 Arago visited Britain to attend the British Association meeting in Edinburgh. Whewell and William Buckland, the geologist and palaeontologist, had tried to persuade Arago to attend the Cambridge gathering of the Association in 1833 but those plans had fallen through. All were delighted when it became clear that Arago would attend in 1834. It was during the course of the 1834 visit that Arago had an important meeting with James Watt Jr preparatory to writing the *éloge* of Watt.

Arago's intention to visit was announced in a rather roundabout fashion. Watt Jr's friend, the sculptor Francis Chantrey, wrote to him on 20 August 1834 enclosing a letter from Joseph Barclay Pentland to the Reverend William Buckland that had been forwarded to him (Chantrey) by Buckland. Pentland had been an intermediary between French and British scientists since his days in the early 1820s as an assistant in Cuvier's laboratory. A former student of Buckland, and the chief intermediary between him and Cuvier in matters palaeontological, by 1834 Pentland appears to have been functioning as Arago's 'minder' in the great astronomer's relations with the British.[15] Pentland's letter announced that he had persuaded Arago to accompany him to the Edinburgh meeting and that Arago wished to visit Buckland in Oxford and Watt Jr in Birmingham.

> Arago intends to visit Birmingham to see your friend Mr Watt, as he proposes to read his Eloge of the Illustrious Inventor of the Steam Engine, at the next Publick meeting of the Institute in November and will be glad to talk over many circumstances with your friend & Mr Bolton, as well as to visit their superb Establishment. Will you therefore write a line to Mr Watt on the subject.[16]

90', Muirhead Papers, MS GEN 1354/296. This note, modified by Muirhead, subsequently appeared in his translation of the *Eloge*, pp. 115–17.

[15] On Pentland see William A.S. Sarjeant and Justin B. Delair, 'An Irish naturalist in Cuvier's laboratory. The letters of Joseph Pentland 1820–1832', *Bulletin of the British Museum of Natural History (Historical Series)*, **6**, 1980, 245–319. Pentland had close relations with the Foreign Office. He undertook diplomatic representative tasks in South America in the later 1830s. Through most of the exchanges that we are concerned with his mail travelled via diplomatic pouches and the Foreign Office. The possibility occurs that Pentland might have been 'keeping an eye' on the situation in France.

[16] J.B. Pentland to William Buckland, 15 August 1834, Watt Papers (Doldowlod), W/12. At this stage Arago planned to read the *éloge* at the November meeting of the Académie but the reading was eventually postponed to December.

Arago's wish to visit the Soho works, and the inclusion of major industrial centres in his itinerary, show that he was anxious to gain more first-hand information about British industrialization. The proposed visit to Soho was a sensitive matter because of problems of industrial espionage. Watt Jr explained that visitors could not be shown around the works for that reason and that the rule was applied without exception.[17] Watt Jr was anxious to spend two days with Arago so as to be able to convey 'all the information he ought to possess respecting the subject of his Eloge'.[18]

In the event Arago was able to spend only one day at Watt Jr's house, Monday, 1 September. As Watt Jr later recalled to George Rennie:

> [Arago] was in such a hurry to get to the Edinburgh Meeting that I could only get him to give me one day, during which I communicated all that time permitted, and above all completely satisfied him by an inspection of my fathers private correspondence that he had had foul play between Cavendish & his friends, with regard to the priority of publication.[19]

There was hope of a second visit from Arago after the Edinburgh meeting but, as Watt Jr recalled, instead of returning to Birmingham, Arago 'spent his time in Dumfriesshire and then hurried to London in bad health'.[20] From London, Arago expressed his regret at not being able to return to Aston Hall. Arago hoped for, and relied upon, Watt Jr's continuing assistance. In particular, he said: 'J'espère que vous voudrez bien remarquer qu'il n'est plus en mon pouvoir de ne pas traiter en détail la question de priorité que la découverte de la composition de l'eau a fait naître, et que vous seul pouvez ma conduire à une solution définitive.'[21] Further, Arago reassured Watt Jr that he would use the correspondence shown to him with 'toute la réserve que le grand nom de Cavendish commande'. It is clear that at this stage there was certainly no intention to inflame matters with the Cavendish family unnecessarily. Arago also advised that he had seen David Brewster, who had said nothing to change the view of the matter.[22]

---

17 Watt Jr to William Buckland, 26 August 1834, Watt Papers (Doldowlod), W/12. Such caution on the part of individual establishments was matched by government measures, though the latter were largely ineffective. See David J. Jeremy, 'Damming the flood: British government efforts to check the outflow of technicians and machinery, 1780–1843', *Business History Review*, **51**, 1977, 1–34.

18 Watt Jr to Chantrey, 22 August 1834; Buckland to Chantrey, 20 August 1834; Watt Jr to Buckland, 26 August 1834, Watt Papers (Doldowlod), W/12.

19 Watt Jr to George Rennie, 24 October 1834, Watt Papers (Doldowlod), W/12. Watt Jr continued: 'Indeed he appeared to have made up his mind upon this subject from the published documents alone, before seeing those I possess, of which I have given him a copy.'

20 Ibid.

21 Arago to Watt Jr, 22 September 1834, Watt Papers (Doldowlod), W/10.

22 Ibid. The reference is to those passages in his correspondence in which Watt wrote defiantly about not being subjugated by the might of the House of Cavendish. Brewster had written the article 'Watt' for his *Edinburgh Encyclopaedia*. Although he quoted there extensively from Watt Jr's account of the water controversy, Brewster also clearly stated his belief that Watt's claim was not strong. See 'James Watt', *The Edinburgh Encyclopaedia*, 18 vols, 1830, vol. 18, pp. 784–87. On Brewster's changing views on the water controversy see below, Chapter 7.

Watt Jr dutifully sent a flurry of documents to London after Arago, some via Peter Ewart, whom Watt Jr had invited to Aston Hall so as to meet Arago on his anticipated return there from Edinburgh. Ewart was one of Watt's few surviving pupils, and Watt Jr was anxious that Arago learn from him about his father's skills as a craftsman. Ewart and Arago did meet and discuss this question in London and as late as 2 October there were plans for Arago to return to Birmingham with Ewart for another meeting with Watt Jr Arago's indisposition prevented this.[23] When it was clear that Arago was not going to visit him again, Watt Jr wrote him a series of long letters (on 3 October, 8 October and 13 October 1834) dealing with various aspects of his father's life. As Watt Jr recalled to George Rennie: '[Arago] has kept me hard at work for several weeks; much of which would have been avoided had he kept his appointment for returning here. But your men of Genius will take their own course, and I am satisfied that neither zeal nor talent will be wanting on his part and I only fear he has allowed himself too little time.'[24]

Watt Jr was particularly anxious that Arago take seriously his father's 'abilities as a draftsman and as a workman'. Ewart testified to these abilities and Watt Jr's effort to bring Ewart and Arago together seems to have been motivated primarily by the desire to convey that message. Watt Jr inundated Arago with drawings made by his father both early and late in his life: 'There was no process, or manipulation of Art, with which he was unacquainted, and for which he did not occasionally practice either to supply his own wants, or to endeavour to perfect them. In fact, this was one of the most distinguishing parts of his character.' Watt Jr went to almost the same lengths to convince Arago of the success that his father had enjoyed as a civil engineer. He devoted one letter (13 October 1834) to recounting the defences that Boulton & Watt made of their patent in which he made some play of the characteristics of the witnesses on either side, his father having scientific support and the opposition supported largely by engine makers. Boulton & Watt's counsel accused the latter, Watt Jr said, of coming to the court 'to prostitute their own ignorance'. When the case was won, we are told, Boulton & Watt showed gentlemanly restraint in recovering the arrears of payments due to them: 'To those who had continued to pay, they made large and liberal allowances, and they exacted far short of their dues from their opponents.'[25]

The Construction of the *Eloge*

The *éloge* as read in early December 1834 remains something of a mystery. I have not found the copied manuscript version promised to James Watt Jr shortly after the reading. But we can make an educated guess as to its content in various ways. We know something of what was added to the *éloge* later, and so by a process of subtraction from the published version we can mock up the orally delivered one. We know what Watt Jr had supplied to Arago in 1834 in his letters and by way of

---

[23] See Ewart to Watt Jr, 2 October 1834, Watt Papers, W/10 and Watt to Arago, [3 October] 1834, Watt Papers, WP/10.

[24] Watt Jr to Rennie, 24 October 1834, Watt Papers, W/12.

[25] Watt Jr to Arago, 3 October? 1834, Watt Papers, WP/10.

other documents. The *éloge* was also reviewed quite extensively in the French press, there being accounts in the following: *Courier Français*, *Journal de Commerce*, *Gazette de France*, *Journal de Paris*, *Journal des Débats* and *Temps*.[26] These accounts are of some assistance. Pentland's letters tell us that the *éloge* as read was watered down in technical detail because of the popular nature of the audience. Arago stated that he wanted to include more material on the water controversy in the published version because some of the Academicians were not convinced of Watt's priority on the strength of what he had said.

From these sources we can conclude that the *éloge* of Watt was transformed while it was 'in press'. It was in such a state for a very long time, much longer than was initially intended. Correspondence from Pentland in the aftermath of the reading discussed publication as a matter of months or up to a year away. The *éloge* was repeatedly described as 'in press' in correspondence over ensuing years. Many reasons might be invoked for this long delay. In one sense it was an institutional habit – the Académie was noted for tardiness in the publication of its *Memoirs*. However, Arago was trying to address that problem. Another reason for the delay was the pressure of business for Arago during these years in all his roles within the Académie and in the Chamber of Deputies, as also in metropolitan Paris politics. Watt Jr was also preoccupied at various times with his business affairs, the retirement of his partner, Matthew Robinson Boulton, and eventually extracting himself from the business. Land disputes on his Radnorshire estates distracted Watt Jr, as did the threatened intrusion of railway projects upon them. However, at least some of the delay must be attributed to the perceived necessity (variously on Arago's part and on that of Watt Jr and Brougham) for wholesale changes and additions to the text.

The reaction of the French public press and from within the Académie prompted Arago to try to shore up some of his arguments. Beyond this, however, Arago had promised to consult Watt Jr before publishing anything. Brougham also was treated as a trusted adviser. This meant that between 1834 and 1839 there was much epistolary to-and-fro. More than this, on at least two occasions Watt Jr visited Paris primarily for interviews and negotiations with Arago about the *Eloge*.

Once it became clear that Arago would not visit Aston Hall again before returning to Paris, Watt Jr set about transcribing documents and sending them to him. The first batch, sent with Peter Ewart, included: transcripts of correspondence relating to the decomposition of water together with a translation of Blagden's paper in Crell's *Annals* of 1786; Watt's specifications for a range of mechanical inventions; two manuscript volumes of Watt's reports as a civil engineer; Dr Henry's letter of 8 June 1820; Hatchette's 'Notice des Travaux de Mr Watt' of 11 August 1819; and two portraits of Watt, one for Arago and the other for Pentland.[27] Shortly afterwards, Watt Jr sent the first of a sequence of long letters to Arago concerning Watt. At this stage, too, the agreement seems to have been struck that Watt Jr would see the *Eloge*

---

[26] This according to the reports of J.B. Pentland, who was monitoring the French press and promised to send Watt Jr copies of mentions of the *éloge*.

[27] 'List of Documents sent by Mr Ewart to Mr Arago', 1 October 1834, Watt Papers (Doldowlod), W/10. The transcripts of the water controversy correspondence were annotated as to be left with Arago. The rest of the material, apart from the portraits, was presumably to be returned. The list was signed by Ewart and so perhaps functioned as a receipt.

before it was printed. The rationale was that Arago, working necessarily from imperfect sources, would fall into errors of omission and commission that Watt Jr, with his superior documentary base, would be in a position to correct.[28]

For material relating to 'the leading events of my father's life' Watt Jr pointed Arago to his own short memoir in the *Supplement* to the *Encyclopaedia Britannica* and to Dr Robison's essay on steam and steam engines with Watt's own notes thereon. Watt Jr wrote proudly of his father's abilities as a draftsman and workman, a point that he was anxious to make. He also conveyed the admiration that Rennie, Telford and Smeaton had had for his father's work as a civil engineer. Arago was referred to Robison's edition of Joseph Black's lectures for material on how Watt had conducted experiments supporting Black's development of the Theory of Latent Heat.[29]

On 8 October Watt Jr sent to Arago a list of English publications in which the water question was treated, pronouncing on the value of each one. Watt Jr singled out particularly the *Encyclopaedia Britannica* article 'Water' (in what he wrongly identified as the '1st edn 1797') as a 'very elaborate & well written article [which] states the claims of Mr Watt, Cavendish, Priestley & Lavoisier fairly giving Mr Watt the merit of the discovery of the Theory'.[30] There followed on 13 October a long letter from Watt Jr, already referred to, recounting Boulton & Watt's court battles. Watt also sent the Minutes of the Committee of the House of Commons, and a printed pamphlet of the arguments of the judges in the Common Pleas and Kings Bench containing the Patent of 1769, the Act of Parliament in 1775 and other material.[31]

These seem to have been the main communications before the initial composition and reading of the *éloge*, Arago saying, via Pentland, that he had documents enough.[32] Arago, of course, had other sources. Leonard Horner had promised him information on the numbers of steam engines employed in factories in Britain. John Taylor was obtaining similar information about the mines of Cornwall. Arago had visited key sites in Greenock, Watt's birthplace, and had met several friends of Watt who had given recollections of the great man. Chantrey gave advice on Watt's statue-copying machine and Faraday on the machinery for producing medals and coins that Watt had developed.[33] On this basis, and with whatever other sources he had available to him locally, Arago, who by his own testimony had not written a line of the *éloge* as of the end of September 1834, composed the piece delivered to the Académie on 8 December.

Watt Jr's access to, and therefore response to, the *éloge* as delivered was delayed. He received from Pentland copies of newspaper reports and summaries. Arago was intent upon beefing up the section on the water question. As Pentland reported, Arago wanted

---

[28] Watt Jr to Arago, 3 October?, 1834, Watt Papers, WP/10.

[29] Ibid.

[30] Watt Jr to Arago, 8 October 1834, Watt Papers (Doldowlod) W/10.

[31] Watt Jr reports having done this in Watt Jr to Peter Ewart, 24 October 1834, Watt Papers (Doldowlod), W/12.

[32] Reported in ibid.

[33] Arago to Watt Jr, 30 September 1834, Watt Papers (Doldowlod), W/10.

to show the world the importance of this early part of Mr Watt's Scientifick Career and to prove on the authority of Priestley & others (wch he had neglected to do before ye publick reading of his Eloge) that your father preceded Cavendish & Lavoisier by several months in one of the most important discoveries of modern Chemistry.[34]

In the New Year 1835 Pentland was still promising Watt Jr a copy of the *éloge* soon, even as he explained how Arago's other engagements were delaying the revisions. Pentland did, however, send Watt Jr an extract 'drawn up at my suggestion, & under my eyes' from Arago's manuscript. He requested that Watt Jr send it to Professor Jameson of Edinburgh 'for his Journal'.[35] This was a reference to Robert Jameson, editor of the *Edinburgh New Philosophical Journal* in which Arago had already published a number of his *éloges*.

Watt Jr's watchful and critical eye went to work immediately. He found the newspaper reports of the *éloge* 'full of mistakes and blunders of all kinds'. The abstract of the memoir made by Pentland contained 'several erroneous statements which I am sure Mr Arago will thank me for pointing out and be glad to have the opportunity of correcting ... '.[36] Watt Jr decided not to send the abstract to Jameson, 'as I am sure you will agree with me that nothing ought to appear in print, particularly in this country, in Mr Arago's name, until it has attained the utmost degree of accuracy'.[37] Watt Jr hoped that Arago would accompany Pentland to the Dublin meeting of the British Association in June 1835 and visit him on the way so that he could go through the *éloge* with Arago with all the sources before him. There was little hope of this, however, since Arago intended to visit his native town, Perpignan, on an electioneering tour.[38]

Watt Jr's liking for authentic documents was satisfied by a key acquisition that he quickly passed on to Arago. This was a memorandum sent to Watt Jr by his cousin Miss Jane Campbell, who in 1798 had taken down from her mother's dictation an account of Watt's early years. Miss Campbell's mother, Mrs Marion Campbell, was the great engineer's first cousin, a daughter of his mother's brother, Mr Muirhead. The cousins had spent much time together in their youth and on that basis Mrs Campbell had recorded her recollections. Watt Jr's advice to Arago was to 'obliterate what you have already written of this period of my father's life, and to subscribe, if you please, this entire narrative in its place'.[39] Arago acceded to Watt Jr's wishes, though he was unable to see any material difference between

---

[34] J.B. Pentland to J. Watt Jr, [15?] December 1834, Watt Papers (Doldowlod), W/10.

[35] J.B. Pentland to Watt Jr, 3 January [1835], Watt Papers (Doldowlod), W/10.

[36] Watt Jr to Pentland, 19 January 1835, Watt Papers (Doldowlod), W/10.

[37] Ibid.

[38] Ibid and J.B. Pentland to Watt Jr, 23 January 1835, Watt Papers (Doldowlod), W/10.

[39] Watt Jr to Arago, 22 January 1835, Watt Papers (Doldowlod), W/10. See Eric Robinson, 'James Watt and the tea kettle. A myth justified', *History Today*, 6, April 1956, 261–65. Robinson here misidentifies the document that Arago used. It was not Dr Gibson's letter but the memorandum discussed here. This document, via the account of it given in the *Eloge*, became the basis for two nineteenth-century paintings: Robert W. Buss, *Watt's First Experiment with Steam*, exhibited at the Royal Academy of Arts in 1845, and engraved by James Scott; and the better-known painting by Marcus Stone, *Watt discovering the Condensation of Steam*, 1863. See David Philip Miller, 'True Myths: James Watt's Kettle, his Condenser and his Chemistry', *History of Science*, forthcoming.

Mrs Campbell's account and what he had already written based on the testimony of others.[40]

The delay in getting a copy of the *éloge* to Watt Jr continued despite repeated promises. Pentland, in trying to explain Arago's dilatoriness, invoked his election to the Corporation of Paris and his work for the Chamber of Deputies, but also Arago's character as a person 'who with little natural order, is suddenly launched in a life of business, and of a business to which he has never been accustomed'.[41] Finally the promised copy of the *éloge* arrived at Aston Hall sometime in early June 1835, having been sent by Pentland with a letter of 6 June.[42] From that date the reasons, and apologies, for delay were issued from Birmingham rather than Paris.

By August, according to Pentland, Arago was 'extremely anxious' to hear from Watt Jr and was taking silence as displeasure. Watt Jr for his part offered the illness and death of a friend and relative, Dr Gibson, as the reason for not yet having given Arago's memoir more than a 'cursory perusal'.[43] Watt Jr planned to visit Paris later in the year with the specific and sole object of seeing Arago about the memoir. Pentland presented the matter as urgent: the time for printing the memoirs of the Institute was at hand, but Arago had promised not to publish until Watt Jr had had his say on the manuscript. In November 1835 Watt Jr explained his continuing failure to respond. His business partner, Matthew Robinson Boulton, was finally retiring and Watt Jr had decided to take the whole business upon himself.[44]

Watt Jr was very pleased with Arago's account of the water question. There were still errors to deal with, again especially in relation to Watt's early years. Watt Jr reiterated that he wanted Arago to 'adopt implicitly the narrative of Mrs Campbell' in preference to other 'traditionary stories'. However, beyond this no comprehensive response was forthcoming.[45] The next year Watt Jr was still promising to devote himself to the memoir, but Arago had ceased to communicate with him. Watt Jr now pleaded lawsuits against encroachers upon his Radnorshire estates as the excuse for literary inactivity. He asked if Arago could defer publication until spring, and pledged once more to give Arago his remarks by that time or else to deliver them personally to Paris.[46]

Watt Jr was in Paris by 21 March 1837 and over the next few weeks met Arago a number of times about the memoir. We have from that time a set of notes on the

---

[40] Arago to Watt Jr, 16 February 1835, Watt Papers (Doldowlod), W/10.

[41] Pentland to Watt Jr, 17 April 1835, Watt Papers (Doldowlod), W/10.

[42] Pentland to Watt Jr, 6 June 1835; Watt Jr to Pentland, 14 June 1835, Watt Papers (Doldowlod), W/10.

[43] Pentland to Watt Jr, 13 August 1835; Watt Jr to Pentland, 29 August 1835, Watt Papers (Doldowlod), W/10.

[44] Watt Jr to Arago, 8 November 1835, W/10. Watt Jr did not become the sole owner of the business until a deed of dissolution of the co-partnership on 1 October 1840. On his partner's retirement and the rearrangement of the business see W.K.V. Gale, 'Soho Foundry: Some facts and fallacies', *Transactions of the Newcomen Society*, **34**, 1961–62, 83 and Robert B. Williams, 'Accounting for management as an expression of eighteenth century rationalism: Two case studies', unpublished PhD thesis, University of Wollongong, 1995, pp. 334–35.

[45] Watt Jr to Pentland, 8 November 1835, Watt Papers (Doldowlod), W/10.

[46] Watt Jr to Pentland, 30 December 1836, Watt Papers (Doldowlod), W/10.

memoir by Watt Jr.[47] They reveal that he was still preoccupied with family history, pointing out that Watt's father was not a shipbuilder, as Arago apparently had it, but a ships' chandler, general merchant and local worthy of Greenock. Watt Jr referred Arago yet again to the memorandum of Mrs Campbell for authentic information about Watt's early years. From Watt's letters to his father the story of the London 'apprenticeship' period was outlined. Watt Jr, in the notes, also argued Savery's position in the history of steam as the first to construct a steam engine and to apply it to practical purposes. On Papin, however, Watt Jr was almost silent. Given the contentiousness of Arago's claims for Papin, it seems that Watt Jr may have been diplomatically avoiding a fight when he stated simply that he offered 'no remarks upon Papin's contrivances as I have not been able to procure the books referred to, & have not entered into any examination of the evidence'.[48]

Watt Jr offered comments and information on a range of other topics that need not detain us beyond listing them.[49] Also buried in the notes is an interesting observation by Watt Jr on Edmund Burke's opposition to the 1775 Patent Extension Bill. Arago had sought to make political capital out of this supposed opposition. It was useful to Arago to depict conservative forces opposing technological ventures that subsequently turned out to be of enormous national economic value. Presenting Burke's opposition in this light would, he probably hoped, show up those of the legitimist party in France who opposed the encouragement of new technologies. Watt Jr's advice on what Burke's opposition signified would not have been welcome since it implied that the opposition was merely the outcome of attempted service to a constituent: 'Mr Burke opposed the bill at the instance of a Mr Gainsborough who claimed some similar invention. He did so as a matter of routine, usual between members and their constituents.'[50] Watt Jr subsequently observed that whilst he had been able to persuade Arago to tone down his remarks on Burke, he had not been successful in removing them altogether along with the political message: 'I could not get him to omit the part about Burke, although Brougham had also remonstrated upon it; but he has much altered it, and paid him some high comp[ts]; as I said to him "couronnant de fleurs sa victime avant de l'immoler".' [51]

---

[47] 'Notes upon Mr Arago's Memoir of Mr Watt. Paris April 1837', Watt Papers (Doldowlod), G/19.

[48] Ibid.

[49] These included: Matthew Boulton's status as a manufacturer and his relationship with Watt; those who assisted Watt in obtaining prolongation of the 1775 Patent; the fact that Boulton & Watt in their early days did not manufacture many of the parts for their steam engines; the witnesses who testified for Watt at various legal proceedings; Watt's involvement in improvements of his estates in Wales; his work on apparatus for Thomas Beddoes's pneumatic medicine ventures; the commemoration of Watt at Greenock by public subscription and by donation from Watt Jr to build a public library; the unfulfilled intention of government to recognize Watt's distinction by a peerage.

[50] Ibid. Watt Jr's observation is corroborated by Burke's correspondence: Edmund Burke to Richard Champion, 28 December 1775, in George H. Guttridge (ed.), *The Correspondence of Edmund Burke*, vol. III, 1961, pp. 239–41 and Edmund Burke to Robert Smith, 6 April 1775 in R.B. McDowell and John A. Woods (eds), *The Correspondence of Edmund Burke*, vol. IX, 1970, pp. 406–408, at p. 407. Here Burke presents himself as the good local member simply doing the bidding of his Bristol constituents in relaying their opposition to Boulton & Watt's application.

[51] J. Watt Jr to M.R. Boulton, 2 May 1839, Watt Papers (Doldowlod), W/10.

Watt Jr not only advised Arago to pay floral tribute to Burke before immolating him, but he also suggested that he add some remarks about changes to the patent law promoted by Lord Brougham. These changes were suggested on the first proofs of the *Eloge*. The final result read as follows. Referring to those who opposed the Boulton & Watt application for an extension of their patent, Arago stated:

> I was curious to learn to what class of society those members of Parliament belonged ... who refused to the man of genius a small fraction of that wealth which he was about to create. Conceive my surprise, when I learned that at their head stood the celebrated Burke! Is it then the fact, that a man may be given to profound thought, may possess extensive knowledge and sterling honesty, be pre-eminently endowed with oratorical talents to move and carry along with him political assemblies, and yet be wanting in plain common sense? Since the important and wise improvements which Lord Brougham has introduced into the law of patents, inventors will not be subjected to that long series of annoyances to which Mr Watt was exposed.[52]

Thus Arago did take Watt Jr's advice up to a point, but the possibility of a stab at Burke was too tempting. We would be safe in assuming, I think, that Burke had been immolated in the original delivery of the *éloge* before the Académie in 1834 without the benefit of floral tribute. That would have been the opportunity that Arago needed. He could afford to compromise somewhat with the cultural requirements of Watt Jr and Brougham in their judgement of the best way to position the great engineer in the political climate of Britain in the late 1830s. We can consider more fully now the next stage, the production and correction of the first proofs of the *Eloge*.

After his return from Paris in the spring of 1837, Watt Jr wrote to Arago thanking him for his 'great civilities and attentions' during the visit. He was glad particularly for Arago's 'ready compliance with my wishes of rendering your eloge conformable to the facts supplied by me of the personal history of my father'.[53] Further additions to the *Eloge* were, however, afoot. As Watt Jr reported, Lord Brougham had completed his researches among the Cavendish papers and written his 'Historical Note' on Watt's claims to 'the first invention of the theory of the decomposition of Water'. Watt Jr had met with Brougham about the Note and they went together to the Royal Society where they inspected Cavendish's original manuscript of 'Experiments on air' and the interpolations that it contained, clearly in Blagden's hand. These interpolations appeared to show that Cavendish's paper had been surreptitiously altered in important ways to make it appear that he had clear priority over Watt.[54] Brougham had entrusted his memoir to Watt Jr for comments before it was forwarded to Arago. It appears to have already been agreed that Brougham's memoir would be appended to the *Eloge* as published. Watt Jr looked forward to the proof sheets.[55] Almost a year later, in April 1838, he was still waiting.

---

[52] The passage as translated in *Life of James Watt by M. Arago*, 1839, p. 55.

[53] Watt Jr to Arago, 5 June 1837, Press Copy, Watt Papers (Doldowlod), W/10.

[54] On these alterations see Henry Brougham, 'Historical note on the discovery of the theory of the composition of water', in François Arago, *Historical Eloge of James Watt ... Translated ... by James Patrick Muirhead*, 1839, pp. 157–73.

[55] Watt Jr to Arago, 5 June 1837, Press Copy, Watt Papers (Doldowlod), W/10.

Finally, on 17 March 1839, Arago wrote to Watt Jr enclosing the first dozen sheets of the proofs with a promise of the rest to follow shortly and the request that Watt Jr return them as soon as possible.[56] Watt Jr's immediate response was favourable and he was gratified that Arago had incorporated the information about his father's personal history. However, it appeared to him that Arago had 'probably mislaid and forgotten' the 'additional Memorandums' that Watt Jr had left with Arago in Paris in 1837. Watt Jr repeated his view that incorporation of these suggested changes was necessary 'to make it altogether agreeable to my father's surviving friends and the descendants of those who are dead'.[57]

Watt Jr intended to return to Paris with the corrected proofs in order to provide Arago personally 'such further explanations and corroborative proofs as I am now able to furnish from other and unforeseen sources'. Watt Jr had other reasons for the journey. He was suffering from a complaint in his legs that had confined him to the house since the beginning of the year. He hoped that the journey would improve his condition.[58] A few days later correspondence with Pentland reveals that the latter was back on the scene after his absence in South America. Watt Jr looked forward to seeing Pentland again and asked him to keep Arago 'in humour until he sees me'.[59]

Some time before 19 April Watt Jr received the remaining proofs, for he wrote to Pentland that day thanking him for them and advising his intention to leave for Paris on the following Sunday, expecting to arrive four to six days later.[60] We learn from Pentland that he had persuaded Arago to wait. Pentland was anxious to see Watt Jr there because Brougham was still in Paris. The noble Lord had been giving notes about Watt to Arago 'which I should be anxious you shd see before they are printed since I am one of those who presumes to doubt his Ldp's infallibility in Science as in Politics'.[61]

Watt Jr arrived in Paris on the Saturday and had a meeting with Arago the following Monday. On the Wednesday Watt Jr's party and Pentland breakfasted with Arago at the Observatory and then Watt Jr and Arago retired for three or four hours' work. Arago adopted almost every one of Watt Jr's suggestions. It was at this point that the final struggle over the references to Burke occurred. Watt Jr confided to M.R. Boulton that other of Arago's 'dissertations I judged it useless to attempt to get him to suppress or abridge'.[62] A week later we get a glimpse of Watt Jr's still ongoing discussions with Arago, this time concerning Arkwright, his fortune and the development of spinning machinery. They were evidently extracting what they

---

[56] Arago to Watt Jr, 17 March 1839, Watt Papers (Doldowlod), W/10.

[57] Watt Jr to Arago, 4 April 1839, Watt Papers (Doldowlod), W/10.

[58] Ibid. Watt Jr advised that if the second batch of proofs had not arrived in the course of the next fortnight he would begin his journey then, meeting with Lord Brougham on his way through London.

[59] Watt Jr to Pentland, 9 April 1839; Pentland to Watt Jr, 4 April [1839], Watt Papers (Doldowlod), W/10. Pentland's letter conveyed Arago's anxiety to publish almost immediately.

[60] Watt Jr to Pentland, 19 April 1839, Watt Papers (Doldowlod), W/10. It is interesting to note that Watt Jr intended to stay again at Maurice's Hotel and that he required accommodation for himself, a friend and servants.

[61] Pentland to Watt Jr, 16 April 1839, Watt Papers (Doldowlod), W/10.

[62] Watt Jr to M.R. Boulton, 2 May 1839, Watt Papers (Doldowlod), W/10.

could from 'Mr Baines' Book' of value to Arago's account. Watt Jr was also proffering more information about his father's later years and his investment in the estate on the banks of the River Wye in Wales. Watt had engaged in various improvements to the estate in which his son had followed him.[63] More meetings occurred with Watt Jr having a seemingly endless fund of changes to suggest. Finally, he advised Arago that he had 'exhausted all I have to say', and showed that he had a sense of humour:

> I will not answer that if I should remain here a month longer, fresh matter may not occur to me. I therefore beg to suggest your adopting the expedient proposed respecting a Gentleman we talked about yesterday and applying forthwith to Louis Philippe for an order for my banishment from Paris.[64]

Even as the final printing proceeded, Watt Jr was sending corrections. But by mid-June all was over and attention was shifting to despatch of early copies of the *Eloge* to those who should have them.[65] The long saga of the production of the French version of the *Eloge* was at an end.

What were the key changes made in the *Eloge* over the years? One of the most important from our point of view was the addition of Brougham's 'Historical Note' on the water question as an appendix. Arago's account of the water controversy, although beefed up from the version read to the Académie, still used very little primary information. He quoted one or two key passages but did not exploit the Watt correspondence significantly. The inclusion of Brougham's note rectified that situation and arguably changed the status of the whole document to make it much more substantially about the water question. Also significant were the changes to the account of Watt's family background and circumstances. Initially Arago had made Watt's family origins out to be more humble than they in fact were, perhaps because it fitted his purposes that Watt's rise to eminence be as steep as possible. Thus Arago was concerned 'to show in what a humble condition projects were elaborated, which were destined to raise the British nation to an unheard of height of power'.[66] Watt Jr was anxious to correct this.

Another notable feature of the exchanges is that Watt Jr constantly sought to insert material concerning his father's craft skills and civil engineering work in a way that shows pride in his father's versatility. But Arago resisted changes of this

---

[63] Watt Jr to Arago, 8 May 1839, Watt Papers (Doldowlod), W/10. 'Mr Baines' book' was Edward Baines, *History of the Cotton Manufacture in Great Britain*, 1835. It is notable that in retailing the story of the Wye estate, Watt Jr was anxious to assimilate the activities and taste of his father and himself. This reinforces again the sense we have of Watt Jr's almost obsessive concern to identify with (and mimic) his father.

[64] Watt Jr to Arago, 28 May 1839, Watt Papers (Doldowlod), W/10.

[65] Watt Jr to Arago, 31 May 1839, 4 June 1839, Watt Papers (Doldowlod), W/10. See document 'Distribution of Copies of Mr Arago's Eloge. June & July 1839' preserved in Watt Papers (Doldowlod), W/10.

[66] Arago, *Historical Eloge of James Watt*, p. 2. It is interesting to compare Cuvier's account of Cavendish in his *éloge* as overcoming the potential obstacle of his wealth in order to do great scientific work. (See Georges Cuvier, 'Henry Cavendish', as reproduced in Eduard Farber (ed.), *Great Chemists*, 1961, pp. 229–38, at p. 229.)

sort. He was much more inclined to see the civil engineering work in particular as having been a waste of Watt's time when he could and should have been pursuing his steam-engine improvements. There are perhaps echoes here of cultural differences concerning the merits or otherwise of specialization.

There were some tensions over Arago's 'steam nationalism', particularly unresolved disagreements about French contributions to the development of the steam engine and the credit due to Papin. We have also seen that Watt Jr had tried to persuade Arago to remove some remarks about Edmund Burke. He failed in this but did have them toned down. In the end Watt Jr was prepared to allow Arago some of his political points. He did not even try to change various sections of the *Eloge* in which Arago pursued matters important to him but tangential to the life of Watt. This was notably true of Arago's long excursus on the social effects of the steam engine and on the question of machinery and the working class.

Apart from these areas of substantive change, the long negotiation between Watt Jr and Arago about the *Eloge* reveals much about their respective characters and perspectives. It confirms our view of Watt Jr as remarkably determined and dogged in pursuit of his filial objectives and willing to go to almost any lengths to achieve them. It also supports our view of him as adopting a strongly empirical perspective on the questions at issue. Arago is revealed as overworked, given to procrastination, but also capable of long bouts of determined work exhibiting rhetorical flourish and strong ideological purpose.

British Versions of the *Eloge*

The translation of the *Eloge* into English had interested Arago from the beginning. In 1834 he hoped that the *Edinburgh New Philosophical Journal* (*ENPJ*) would publish a translation. It did do so, but not until October 1839.[67] The editor of that journal, Robert Jameson, noted the 'considerable delay' that had occurred in printing 'the most important *Eloge* ever written by Arago'.[68] The *ENPJ* had a tradition of publishing *éloges* delivered to the Académie des Sciences, including those of Volta, Young and Fourier by Arago himself.[69] For reasons explained elsewhere,[70] two English versions of the *Eloge* appeared very quickly; the first with various appendices and notes was published by Jameson, and the second with a somewhat different but overlapping suite of appendices and additional notes by Muirhead.

---

[67] The *ENPJ* translation (**27**, October 1839, 221–91) was the same text as was published separately as a pamphlet in Edinburgh. The *Journal* also split off and printed 'On Machinery Considered in Relation to the Prosperity of the Working Classes' by M. Arago (297–310). It also printed Brougham's 'Historical Account' (316–24). The final inclusion was 'Additional Notes' on Arago's Memoir by J.P. Muirhead (310–15). This last item, however, was not published in the Edinburgh pamphlet edition of the *Eloge* because of a falling out between Muirhead and Jameson, on which see Chapter 8.

[68] *ENPJ*, **27**, October 1839, 221n.

[69] See Arago, 'Historical Eloge of Alexander Volta', *ENPJ*, **16**, January 1834, 1–33; 'Biographical Memoir of Thomas Young', *ENPJ*, **20**, 1836, 213–40; 'Historical Eloge of J. Fourier', *ENPJ*, **26**, 1839, 1–24, 217–44.

[70] See Chapter 8, below.

These translations of the *Eloge* exhibit at least one major structural difference from the original French publication. One of Arago's 'dissertations', the long section on machinery and the working class that had appeared in the main text of the French version, after the account of the steam engine, was removed from the body of the *Eloge* and appended as a 'Dissertation on Machinery and the Working Class'. Muirhead stated that the change was made in order to give the recounting of the life of Watt greater continuity.[71] There were, however, other reasons. Muirhead and Arago had a different agenda. Arago's political purposes were served by making the machinery question central to the piece. His objectives, after all, had to do with encouraging industrial development in France. These were tangential concerns in the filial project of Watt Jr. Indeed, they were unnecessarily distracting and vexatious in a work designed to commemorate Watt himself. Muirhead provided significant annotations and notes to his translation of Arago's *Eloge*. They confirm the aspects of the *Eloge* that remained of concern to him and to Watt Jr.

In considering the wider reaction to the *Eloge* in Britain in the 1840s and beyond, we inevitably enter into the water controversy itself. The account of Watt was evaluated against Arago's reputation in Britain and in its turn shaped that reputation. So it is important at this point to indicate how Arago was thought of in Britain.

Arago was well known in Britain by the time of the publication of his *Eloge* of Watt. He had visited in 1816 and 1819 on scientific business connected with measurements of the arc of the meridian. He had been awarded the Copley Medal of the Royal Society of London in 1825 and other honours. Arago's researches and his methodology were among those most attractive to key members of the reform group in the Royal Society such as Babbage and Herschel in their quest to raise 'mathematical physics' to a new height in Britain.[72] There was great interest in snaring Arago for the Cambridge meeting of the British Association in 1833, disappointment when he failed to appear, and a proportionate sense of triumph when he did attend the 1834 meeting in Edinburgh. Arago was a key figure in the 'magnetic crusade' of the British Association and a promoter, indeed originator, of that type of 'Humboldtian science'. As Perpetual Secretary of the French Académie, he long remained a vital bridge between British and French science as also in his capacity as editor (with Gay-Lussac) of the *Annales de Chemie et Physique*.

Arago came to be regarded as a larger-than-life character. The brilliant scientist was a stirring and invigorating personal presence who left long-lasting impressions. He was, in short, charismatic.[73] He was also often difficult and disagreeable.

---

[71] See 'Preface', Arago, *Historical Eloge of James Watt*, 1839, p. viii.

[72] Maurice Crosland and Crosbie W. Smith, 'The transmission of physics from France to Britain, 1800–1840', *Historical Studies in the Physical Sciences*, **9**, 1978, 1–61; David Philip Miller, 'The revival of the physical sciences in Britain, 1815–1840', *Osiris*, new series, **2**, 1986, 107–34.

[73] John Hope to J.D. Forbes, 20 August 1834, Forbes Papers, Incoming Letters, 1834, no. 26. Hope wanted to offer Arago hospitality during the Edinburgh BAAS meeting because of Arago's kindness to him some twenty years before. An observer of Arago in action in the Chamber of Deputies offered the following description: 'The very moment he enters on his subject he concentrates on himself the eyes and the attention of all. He takes science as it were in his hands: he strips it of its asperities and its technical forms, and he renders it so clear, that the most ignorant are astonished, as they are charmed at

Beneath his dealings with James Watt Jr, which remained friendly throughout, one senses a care on Watt Jr's part to humour Arago and not to push him too far or too hard. Thus, for example, Watt Jr allowed Arago his 'extended dissertations' in the *Eloge*, presumably thinking it unproductive to risk standing up to the great man once too often. When Arago was crossed so decisively by Harcourt, the reports were that Arago was 'very violent' and out to 'pulverise' the unfortunate cleric. Murchison, without reason for exhibiting bravado on Arago's behalf, expected Arago's 'thunder and lightning' to come down on Harcourt's head.[74] Under a thin cloak of anonymity, George Peacock said this of Arago:

> when M. Arago foregoes the high position which the scientific world has assigned to him, and consents, from an unhappy ambition, to put forward views on subjects connected with scientific history which may startle by their novelty or singularity, or gratify a feeling of national vanity ... it becomes a public and imperative duty to withstand him.[75]

Arago's stance in the mid-1840s in the controversy over the discovery of Neptune did not win him friends in Britain. All would admit that, by the criteria of priority of discovery that emphasized public communication, Leverrier had published his calculation of the new planet's orbit first. On the basis of Leverrier's predictions, Galle had been the first to 'find' the new planet in the night sky in late September 1846. In this sense Arago's championing of Leverrier was entirely reasonable, especially given Arago's long-standing endorsement of public communication as the real test of discovery. What angered John Couch Adams's supporters was what they saw as Arago's inflexibility and the arrogance and nationalist fervour, with which he pressed Leverrier's, and entirely dismissed Adams's, claims.

After Arago's death in 1853 there was great interest in Britain in his works. Many were translated into English. An evaluation of these works in the *Edinburgh Review* in October 1856 by Baden Powell summarized many of the views of Arago that had circulated in the British scientific community in his lifetime.[76] The impression conveyed there was of a supremely confident young man whose rise had been extremely rapid. Arago had made the most of his opportunities and used colourfully elaborated accounts of his adventures to build mystique. His involvement in politics and, in particular, his 'extreme Republican' views were lamented.[77]

---

the ease with which they understand its mysteries. There is something perfectly lucid in his demonstrations. His manner is so expressive that light seems to issue from his eyes, from his lips, from his very fingers ... When he is as it were face to face with science, he looks into its very depths, draws forth its inmost secrets, and displays all its wonders; he invests his admiration of it with the most magnificent language, his expressions become more and more ardent, his style more coloured, and his eloquence is equal to the grandeur of his subject.' (See *Edinburgh Review*, October 1856, p. 314.)

[74] Roderick Murchison to William Vernon Harcourt, 28 December 1839, in Jack Morrell and Arnold Thackray (eds), *Gentlemen of Science: Early Correspondence of the British Association for the Advancement of Science*, 1984, pp. 328–29.

[75] [George Peacock], 'Arago and Brougham on Black, Cavendish, Priestley and Watt', *Quarterly Review*, **77**, 1845, 139.

[76] Baden Powell, 'The life and works of Francis Arago', *Edinburgh Review*, **104**, October 1856, 301–37.

[77] Ibid., p. 308.

Although Arago's 'ardent temperament' did have its sweet side, Powell regretfully concluded that Arago's 'moral qualities were not altogether marked by the same elevation as his intellectual faculties':

> In some instances we fear, even those discussions properly belonging to science were not uninfluenced by unworthy and ungenerous passions. His views of the scientific claims of other philosophers, of the priority of discoveries, and similar questions, were too often dictated by prejudice or partiality, party spirit, or national jealousy; while his personal demeanour towards his contemporaries, and especially his subordinates, was frequently offensive from an arrogant, overbearing spirit, displayed both in the affairs of the Academy of Sciences, and the management of the Observatory, as well as in other cases to which his influence extended, so as to obtain for him the sobriquet of the 'Napoleon of Science'.[78]

In this neat fashion common British attitudes to French science and politics were encapsulated in the evaluation of Arago.

Even an admirer like John Herschel was, by the 1850s, very wary of what he regarded as the great Frenchman's slapdash popular writings. Herschel found some of the contents of Arago's popular lectures 'astounding' and hoped that 'for the credit of A's memory' W.H. Smyth and his colleagues, who were engaged in translating Arago, had 'used the pruning hook' more than other translators. Herschel found many things in Arago's publications 'utterly subversive of all rational principle and unworthy of the merest Tyro'.[79] Among a number of the Cambridge group there was a similar tone of exasperation over a talent carelessly, erratically and irascibly applied as one meets in discussions of Arago's coadjutors in the Watt case, Charles Babbage and Henry Brougham. Of course we need to remember that Herschel and others of the Cambridge group were not disinterested parties so far as Arago's reputation and character were concerned, since they had tangled rather strenuously in the dispute over the discovery of Neptune in 1846. In that dispute the Cambridge group had their own political agenda, though it was pursued with a little more reserve than Arago displayed in his histrionics before the Académie. Whilst the Cambridge group were divided on the Watt case, it would be fair to say that attitudes towards Arago hardened after the Neptune controversy. The kind of assessment of him offered by Powell became commonplace after that time.[80] Shortly after Arago's death, Alexander von Humboldt complained at the 'infamous manner' in which the *Quarterly Review* had treated his great friend and attributed the treatment to 'party spirit'.[81]

Smyth et al. heavily annotated their translations of Arago's works, including the *Eloge* of Watt, in order to correct perceived partialities and errors in Arago's

---

[78] Ibid., p. 311.

[79] J.F.W. Herschel to W.H. Smyth, 8 November 1857 and Herschel to R. Grant, 21 March 1858, Royal Society, Herschel Papers.

[80] Another dimension of antagonism toward Arago related to Arago's treatment of Thomas Young and his French competitor on the Rosetta stone decipherment. Arago ventured into this in his *éloge* of Young. Smyth et al. comment on this in a footnote in *Biographies of Distinguished Scientific Men*.

[81] A. von Humboldt to Varhagen von Ense, 12 December 1853 in *Letters of Alexander von Humboldt, written between the years 1827 and 1858 to Varhagen von Ense*, 1860, p. 217.

accounts.[82] With regard to his biographical writings in particular, Arago was recognized as having great talent. His extensive breadth of knowledge of scientific fields was combined with a 'singularly happy style of lucid eloquence in expounding and illustrating' his subjects' lives and works. This talent was, however, used with partisan intent. British readers would be aware in particular of Arago's nationalistic efforts on behalf of Daguerre and of Leverrier and of his *Eloge* of Watt. Even the latter, although praising Watt and, it was thought, exaggerating his claims against Cavendish for ideological reasons, sought to elevate French achievements in steam-engine development beyond their rightful place.[83]

So by 1857, when the annotated version of the *Eloge* appeared in the translation of Arago's *Biographies of Distinguished Scientific Men*, the reading public were already well prepared to treat it as an untrustworthy and ideologically driven document. Arago's contentious text was effectively enveloped by the explosion of anodyne mid-Victorian biographical writing. Smiles's *Lives of Boulton and Watt* deliberately contrasted itself with the combative style of Arago's and Muirhead's contentious writing.

Conclusion

Arago's *Eloge* of Watt was a complex document in both origin and argument. Arago was certainly driven to undertake it by, and realized through it, a range of ideological objectives as part of his involvement in the politics of French science, technology and industrial development. For these purposes Arago was intent upon assimilating Watt the philosopher and Watt the engineer. However, the *Eloge* was also driven by a nationalism that considered it vital to assert France's role in the development of industrial technology, a role that Arago was arguing should be resumed and extended. Arago's related struggle to open up the Académie to the wider world involved him in seeking to open up its communications. This was linked in a number of his *éloges*, including that of Watt, with the individual's willingness to communicate. Arago used the case of Cavendish as a symbol of non-communication and its consquences.

Arago's decision to seek information and advice from Watt Jr inevitably made him hostage in some degree to the filial project. Watt Jr had some impact upon the characterization of his father in the *Eloge* as an autodidact. He and Brougham between them certainly gave a prominence to the water controversy, and the 'crime

---

[82] François Arago, *Biographies of Distinguished Scientific Men, translated by W.H. Smyth, Baden Powell and Robert Grant*, 1857. Smyth et al. state at the point where Arago's *Eloge* deals with the misdating of Cavendish's reprints: 'Our author must have been excited here, for he thinks that not only the high-minded Cavendish and Blagden, but even the printers of the papers, were in a conspiracy against Watt; and, though he calls God to witness that he means nothing against their probity, he makes a very bold insinuation that they were leagued against truth' (p. 573). At another point in the treatment of the water question, drawing a direct contrast with Arago's work, they refer to Harcourt's 1839 'Address' as 'alike free from reckless assertion, and that hot nationality which warps judgment' (p. 575).

[83] Baden Powell, 'The life and works of Francis Arago', 312.

of Cavendish', that it might not otherwise have had. Watt Jr acknowledged, however, that there were limits to his capacity to divert Arago from some of his key ideological objectives in writing the *Eloge*, especially that of associating the forces of conservatism with wrong-headed opposition to technological development. Arago's nationalism, his ready assimilation of science and technology, his attack upon the iconic Cavendish and, it must be said, the association of these actions in the minds of his critics with his ardent republicanism, set up a clash with those who sought to manage the symbols of early Victorian science in Britain.

Chapter 7

Managing the Symbols of Victorian Science: 'Gentlemen of Science' and the Water Controversy

Introduction

The water controversy was given life in its second phase when Arago and Brougham's challenge was taken up by the Reverend William Vernon Harcourt in his Presidential Address to the Birmingham meeting of the British Association for the Advancement of Science in August 1839. Sir David Brewster tackled the issue also, and in distinctive style. He was to be one of the few major figures to actually change his mind publicly about the water question. In this chapter we examine the substance of Harcourt's 'Address' and also Brewster's writings and conversion, placing them in the context of the British Association's early years and the 'boundary work' engaged in by its leaders. The basic form and internal workings of British science were being negotiated during these years under the growing dominance of metropolitan, Cambridge and Oxford savants. They did not go unchallenged, however. Brewster's struggles with the Cambridge élite in particular intersected substantially with the water controversy and profoundly shaped his, and their, stance within it.

Harcourt Intervenes

William Vernon Harcourt (1789–1871) was the son of the Archbishop of York. He graduated in classics from Christ Church Oxford in 1811, but while at the university, he had developed scientific interests, particularly in geology and chemistry. He pursued a clerical career, was instrumental in founding the Yorkshire Philosophical Society in 1822 and was part of the provincial thrust behind the establishment of the British Association in 1831.[1] By the time we encounter him, Harcourt, in alliance with some members of the Cambridge group, had quickly become one of the chief orchestrators of the Association.

In his extended published response to Arago, which appeared in 1840, Harcourt claimed to show decisively that the credit for the discovery of the compound nature

---

[1] On Harcourt see *DNB* and Jack Morrell and Arnold Thackray, *Gentlemen of Science: Early Years of the British Association for the Advancement of Science*, 1981, pp. 535–36.

7.1   The Reverend William Vernon Harcourt

of water lay with Henry Cavendish.[2] Harcourt's case in support of Cavendish rested on what he called 'three positions' that are worth quoting at length:

---

[2] 'Address by the Rev. W. Vernon Harcourt', *Report of the Ninth Meeting of the British Association for the Advancement of Science held at Birmingham in August 1839*, 1840, pp. 3–69. Importantly, Harcourt, Whewell and Peacock regarded Harcourt's work as exhibiting sound historical practice compared with the slipshod efforts of Arago and Brougham. For a forceful statement of this position see: [George Peacock], 'Arago and Brougham on Black, Cavendish, Priestley and Watt', *Quarterly Review*, **77**, 1845, 105–39.

(1)   The experiments which Cavendish made in the summer of 1781 not only necessarily involved the *notion* (which is the claim set up for Watt), but substantially established the *fact* (which is the claim set up for Priestley) of the composition of water.

(2)   The experiment which Priestley made in April 1783, *for the professed purpose of verifying the fact of the conversion of air into water, communicated to him by Cavendish*, added nothing to the proofs which Cavendish had already obtained of it nearly two years before.

(3)   Whilst the views of Cavendish are shown by the internal evidence of the experiments themselves, and the train of reasoning which they imply, to have been from the first precise and philosophical, those of Priestley and Watt were always, as regards the former, and till after the publication of Cavendish's and Lavoisier's papers, as regards the latter, vague and wavering to a degree scarcely comprehensible to those who have not studied the ideas prevalent at that period of chemical history.[3]

Thus at least part of Harcourt's case rested upon the claim that Cavendish engaged in a superior, more precise and philosophical approach to a train of research. Priestley and Watt, by comparison, appeared to Harcourt to be 'vague and wavering'.[4] Harcourt acknowledged that the well-versed historian of chemistry might empathize with Priestley and Watt's indecision and confusion given the ideas then prevalent. It was precisely Cavendish's ability to operate within the prevailing theoretical framework without being under its thrall that distinguished him as the superior investigator and hence strengthened his claim to priority.

Elsewhere in his Address Harcourt reinforced these contrasting pictures of Watt and Cavendish as experimentalists and philosophers. Because his ideas about the composition of water were closely bound up with phlogiston theory, Watt was guilty of 'loose reasoning', as were some of the best chemists of the day. Cavendish, on the other hand, steadily moved from 'truth to truth, on every point on which experiments afforded ground for reasoning, unfettered by the complexity of the phlogistic theory'.[5] Cavendish 'alone seemed to understand, as it became a disciple of the school of Newton, the true use of a hypothesis: he valued neither system otherwise than as an expression of facts, or as a guide to future inquiry'.[6] It was not that Cavendish rejected phlogiston theory when he was doing the work on water but rather, Harcourt claimed, that his experiments were effectively independent of theory in the sense that their value was not dependent on particular theoretical presuppositions. Harcourt quoted Humphry Davy on Cavendish's 'finished' technique. Cavendish, according to Davy, 'combined the greatest depth of

---

[3] 'Address by the Rev. W. Vernon Harcourt', p. 23.

[4] George Peacock, Dean of Ely, and another of the Cambridge clerisy, was to echo Harcourt's case in perhaps even more unflattering terms some years later. Peacock described the theory of the composition of water as proposed by Watt as 'unprofitable and worthless', and Watt's paper in the *Philosophical Transactions* as 'singularly obscure'. According to Peacock, Priestley's experiments, upon which Watt reasoned, were the product of a mind 'not disciplined to the habits of correct inductive reasoning'. Cavendish's memoir, on the other hand, was a model of precision and intelligibility, to be expected from one 'trained in the best and most rigorous school of inductive philosophy'. (See Peacock, 'Arago and Brougham', pp. 114, 131, 133.)

[5] 'Address by the Rev. W. Vernon Harcourt', p. 10.

[6] Ibid.

mathematical knowledge with delicacy and precision' in experimental work. Cavendish's 'processes were all of a finished nature; executed by the hand of a master they required no correction'. Moreover the progress of chemical knowledge had left the 'accuracy' and 'beauty' of Cavendish's work unimpaired. Thus said Davy on Cavendish's death in 1810.[7]

Harcourt argued that because of Cavendish's 'training in the rules of demonstration' and his superior clarity of thought, to him 'hypothetical thoughts and expressions were no stumbling block'.

> If the question then be, who reformed the expressions and logic of chemistry, or who furnished the simple terms in which we now state the elements of water? the answer is, Lavoisier; but if it be, who discovered and unfolded the most important facts on which that reformation relied? who detected and proved the composition of water, and deduced the train of corollaries which flowed from it? the answer is Cavendish. The discovery was not one of those which was within every man's reach, especially in an age of loose experiment and inconclusive reasoning: it was one which could never have been made, but by a strict appreciation of quantities, and a careful elimination of the sources of error …[8]

So, to recapitulate: Harcourt's case for Cavendish was not based just on the contention that he was first to perform certain experiments or to entertain the notion of the compound nature of water (although Harcourt does claim this), but also that Cavendish's claim lay in the nature and quality of his chain of reasoning upon carefully and precisely conducted experiments. Harcourt's definition of the nature and significance of the discovery was such that it closely matched the traits claimed for Cavendish. Thus, Harcourt asked rhetorically what gave importance to the discovery of the composition of water in the history of science? The answer: 'Not merely, as has been too popularly stated, that it banished water from among the elements, but that whilst it accounted for an infinite number of phenomena, it introduced into chemistry distinctness of thought and accuracy of reasoning, and led to the general prevalence of a sounder logic.'[9]

---

[7] 'Address by the Rev. W. Vernon Harcourt', p. 7; Humphry Davy, *The Collected Works of Sir Humphry Davy, Bart. LL.D. F.R.S. Edited by his Brother John Davy, M.D. F.R.S.*, 9 vols, 1839, vol. 7, pp. 127–28. Davy's own views on the discovery of the composition of water, as expressed in 1806, and John Davy's commentary thereon, are set out on 130–39. Davy repeated these views in his influential *Elements of Chemical Philosophy*, 1812, p. 37. Watt Jr claimed that Humphry Davy changed his mind on seeing the relevant private correspondence in 1820 and 1826. See Chapter 5 above.

[8] 'Address by the Rev. W. Vernon Harcourt', pp. 12–13.

[9] Ibid., p. 8. George Wilson, the other chief writer for Cavendish, makes a very similar point: 'It is not easy to convey to the general reader, a just conception of the importance which men of science attach to the discovery of the composition of water. It is not merely that a body reputed from the earliest ages an element, has been shown to consist of two altogether dissimilar invisible gases. Hydrogen represents in its properties and relations all the metals and metallic substances in nature: oxygen all the non-metallic ones. Water, which is the union of the two, typifies the constitution of every compound body. All the refined and subtle speculations of the present day concerning the composition of complex substances, are but expansions of the idea which Cavendish's exposition of the nature of water first made familiar to men.' George Wilson, 'Lives of Men of Letters and Science who Flourished in the Time of George III by Henry, Lord Brougham', *British Quarterly Review*, **2**, 1845, 245–46.

Harcourt can be interpreted here as adopting a 'paradigm-dependent' notion of discovery. This may seem odd, because Harcourt was arguing for Cavendish's relative independence from the phlogistic paradigm. But in fact Harcourt was making the attribution of discovery to Cavendish dependent upon Cavendish having prosecuted an exemplary form of disciplined experimental practice. Harcourt emphasized the relationship between credit for discovery and traditions of scientific practice. Harcourt's specific contention was that Cavendish had some claim to have initiated the reformation of chemistry with this work and exhibited exemplary practices. The image of Watt conveyed by Harcourt, by contrast, was of an unsystematic interloper stumbling out of his depth, albeit inventively. In this, Harcourt claimed, Watt had much in common with Priestley, who 'deserves to be admired not more for his inventive fertility and indefatigable industry in experiment, than for the honest candour with which he related every fortuitous success and extraneous hint, and the liberal profusion with which he scattered his gold abroad for public use, as fast as he drew it from the mine'.[10] Priestley exhibited, in other words, a lack of caution, deliberation and discrimination.

It was the approach to scientific investigation, the quantitative skills, the cautious but rigorous reasoning upon experiments which Harcourt praised in Cavendish (and found lacking in Watt) and which he made a criterion for the attribution of discovery. These characteristics were precisely those on which the clerical wing of the Cambridge group among the Gentlemen of Science of the British Association relied in claiming their place as overseers of the scientific enterprise in early Victorian Britain. As previously noted, the conceptions of discovery being rehearsed in the water controversy were part of a larger contest about the nature of discovery, discoverers and originality in innovation. This larger contest incorporated other important controversies in which many of the same groups and individuals were involved. Alignments in the water controversy closely paralleled those in debates about the morality and genius of scientific discoverers, the life and conduct of Sir Isaac Newton, and the patent controversies considering the originality of patentees and whether and how they were to be rewarded.[11]

---

[10] 'Address by the Rev. W. Vernon Harcourt', p. 15. The implied contrast here is with Cavendish's famous shyness and unwillingness to publish or part with his work. For the standard Mertonian view of this issue in science communication which, incidentally, relies on the example of Cavendish, see Merton's essay on 'Priorities in scientific discovery', Robert K. Merton, *The Sociology of Science. Theoretical and Empirical Investigations*, 1973, pp. 286–324. On the negotiation of 'communalism' see Michael Mulkay, 'Interpretation and the use of rules: The case of the norms of science', *Transactions of the New York Academy of Sciences*, Series 2, **39**, 1980, 119–23.

[11] Among key writings on these controversies see Richard Yeo, *Defining Science: William Whewell, Natural Knowledge, and Public Debate in Early Victorian Britain*, 1993; idem, 'An Idol of the Marketplace: Baconianism in nineteenth-century Britain, 1830–1917', *History of Science*, **23**, 1985, 251–98; idem, 'Genius, method and morality: Images of Newton in Britain, 1760–1860', *Science in Context*, **2**, 1988, 257–84; Paul Theerman, 'Unaccustomed role: The scientist as historical biographer – Two nineteenth-century portrayals of Newton', *Biography*, **8**, 1985, 145–62. And on the patent controversy and Watt see: Christine MacLeod, 'Concepts of invention and the patent controversy in Britain', in Robert Fox (ed.), *Technological Change. Methods and Themes in the History of Technology*, 1996, pp. 137–53; idem, 'James Watt, heroic invention and the idea of the Industrial Revolution', in Maxine Berg and Kristine Bruland (eds), *Technological Revolutions in Europe. Historical Perspectives*,

Having seen the outlines of Harcourt's substantive published argument concerning priority, we now have to inquire after the circumstances that caused him to enter the fray at all. Can we discover why Harcourt chose to respond to Arago's *Eloge*? We need to backtrack a little to examine, first of all, the proximate circumstances of Harcourt's intervention. The version of Harcourt's Address to the British Association, upon which the above analysis relies, was published in 1840. What was actually delivered at the Birmingham meeting was a much rougher, undeveloped argument. In the interval between the meeting and the publication of the Address, there was significant discussion between Harcourt and his associates about the content and argumentative strategy of the piece.

From newspaper reports and an account in *The Athenaeum*, as well as private remarks of those present, we can tentatively reconstruct the Address as delivered. Harcourt himself stated that it was composed quickly with only limited materials available to him: 'When I wrote my answer to Arago I had only a fortnight to prepare it, & nothing but the publications of Priestley Cavendish & Watt before me.' Muirhead learned from discussions with Professor Edward Forbes, who was present at the occasion, that there was 'hardly any evidence' in Harcourt's speech. It had concentrated on the argument from Cavendish's general character.[12]

As reported by *The Athenaeum*, a report that Harcourt acknowledged as the most accurate one available in the press, the Address certainly began its examination of the water question by concentrating on character. Having set out Arago's claims against Cavendish, Harcourt quoted Davy's panegyric on the great natural philosopher's indifference to fame and his love of truth and knowledge. Then, however, he did make a version of the argument that we see in the published version about the different theoretical universes of Watt and Cavendish, how Watt's ideas were 'infected' by phlogiston theory whilst Cavendish's cleverly remained unfettered by it. Harcourt then elaborated on what he took to be some of the weaknesses of Watt's paper and the strengths of Cavendish's. Thus, whatever one thinks of Harcourt's argument, it is not just from character.

When we turn to local press reports of the speech, *Aris's Birmingham Gazette* gave only a few lines to that part dealing with the water question:

> On this subject [the history of the steam engine] he quoted the history of Watt, as referred to in the memoir by Arago, whose zeal however went too far when he imprinted honours upon him which belonged to the brow of Cavendish. The true merits of the latter were scarcely known to fame; for with all his proficiency in knowledge he was diffident in bringing forward his discoveries, and fearful of the voice of reputation.[13]

The *Gazette* had decided not to burden its readers with any notice of the complex arguments that Harcourt, according to *The Athenaeum*, had indeed offered. The

---

1998, pp. 96–116; David Philip Miller, '"Puffing Jamie": The commercial and ideological importance of being a "philosopher" in the case of the reputation of James Watt (1736–1819)', *History of Science*, **38**, 2000, 1–24.

[12] Harcourt to Forbes, 11 January 1840, Forbes Correspondence, Incoming 1840, Item 2; J.P. Muirhead to James Watt, 14 October 1839, Muirhead Papers, MS GEN 1354/365.

[13] *Aris's Gazette*, 2 September 1839.

Birmingham Journal, the other major local newspaper of the time, reported rather differently. Although it too concentrated upon Harcourt's remarks about Cavendish's character, it then acknowledged that Harcourt had delivered an 'elaborate dissertation' and reported his comparison of Cavendish's judicious use of hypothesis with that made by others. We are then told that 'this part of the address, which occupied some time, was received with marked applause'.[14] All in all it appears that Harcourt's Address as delivered to the General Meeting was not limited to arguments from Cavendish's character.

When Muirhead said that it *was* so limited, and that there was 'hardly any evidence' in it, he was referring to the fact that Harcourt did not provide *circumstantial* evidence to contradict Arago (and Brougham) on the question of the priority of publication or the accusation of fraud.[15] For Muirhead and other members of the Watt camp, who assumed that Watt's and Cavendish's discoveries were essentially the same, such circumstantial evidence was the only kind of evidence that mattered. Thus Muirhead regarded Harcourt's evidence for the chemical and methodological differences between the two protagonists as no evidence at all.

In the aftermath of the meeting, the correspondence back and forth between Harcourt's friends in the British Association evinced a general acknowledgement that Harcourt had much work to do in developing a published version of his response to Arago's *Eloge*. The Wattites' discussions of Harcourt's spoken address indicated that they considered that he had shot from the hip without a defensible case and that some of the wiser of Harcourt's friends were realizing that he had got himself in a scrape. Watt Jr had learned from some of those present that the address 'did not gain applause, nor give satisfaction'. (The *Birmingham Journal*, on the contrary, reported regular, bracketed, 'Cheers' in its account, though it also, paradoxically, recorded that the meeting offered 'no accommodation for reporters'!) Watt Jr also understood that 'but for the decorum due to his [Harcourt's] rank & station there, some of the parties present would actually have hissed'.[16] If Harcourt persisted, he would be either readily 'skewered' by Watt Jr, or broken by Brougham like a 'butterfly on the wheel'.[17] Failing this, or perhaps in addition for good measure, 'the unfortunate aristocratic Canon of York, the worthy founder of the British Association, will be pulverized' by Arago.[18]

The stir created by Harcourt's Address among those he called the 'Wattites' was reported by the geologist Roderick Murchison:

> The bold shot which you fired at Birmingham in re 'Cavendish versus Watt' was, as you might indeed have anticipated, sure to bring down Arago's thunder and lightning on your head. In the meantime Watt himself [that is, James Watt Jr] is much *up*, and with all his

---

[14] *Birmingham Journal*, 31 August 1839.

[15] This is confirmed by Muirhead's response to Harcourt in a note in his translation of Arago's *Eloge*. See François Arago, *Historical Eloge of James Watt ... Translated ... by James Patrick Muirhead*, 1839, pp. 114–16, note.

[16] Watt Jr to Muirhead, 28 September 1839, Muirhead Papers, MS GEN 1374/333.

[17] Muirhead to Watt Jr, 10 and 12 September 1839, Muirhead Papers, MS GEN 1374/310 and 311.

[18] Watt Jr to Muirhead, 22 October 1839, Muirhead Papers, MS GEN 1374/379. The words are J.B. Pentland's, quoting his friend Arago, and quoted to Muirhead in this letter by Watt Jr.

friends, or rather they for him, have prepared a refutation of what they consider your misprision of the great steamer.[19]

The refutation in question was Muirhead's translation of Arago's *Eloge* with its notes and annotations.[20] Murchison, having learned that Arago and Brougham were also at work on a response, had consulted the naturalist Robert Brown. Brown had been librarian to Banks and close in other respects to Cavendish, and he was certain that Arago was wrong and that Harcourt was 'essentially correct'. Murchison noted that others were becoming involved: 'Just before I left town new actors appeared on the stage. Watt [Junior] is you must know a great friend of Chantrey, and I found from the latter that all the Wattites (Babbage included) had taken up your discourse as a downright *attack* upon their hero.' Murchison reported further that:

> Chantrey's house was to be the scene of a Watt conclave on the day of which I speak and Babbage was one of the 'priés'. What transpired at the dinner of course I know not. You are perhaps aware that Babbage and Arago run in the same curricle in science, politics and their views of human nature.[21]

This last observation was a revealing one. Watt had come to symbolize the industrial temper and became a hero to those who most wholeheartedly embraced industrial progress. We have seen already the ideological work that Arago sought to do with his account of Watt. Brougham, too, actively deployed Watt in arguing for the necessity and viability of the education of working men, in whose ranks he rather artfully included the great engineer. Babbage, and also John Herschel, from their young Cambridge days pursued an industrial philosophy of mind. We know of Babbage's admiration of Watt and that he regularly sent his works (such as *On the Economy of Machinery and Manufactures*) to Watt Jr.[22] Ashworth suggests that Babbage and Herschel saw themselves as the 'philosophical equivalents of great industrialists such as James Watt, Matthew Boulton, and William Strutt'.[23] In this they had many affinities with Arago and ever fewer with their former Cambridge allies among the Gentlemen of Science. We know that Babbage's admiration for Watt, and what he was taken to represent, continued and it is no surprise to find him among the 'Wattites' in the aftermath of Harcourt's Birmingham Address. Babbage had long fought for the Birmingham meeting of the BAAS as recognition of the

---

[19] Roderick Murchison to William Harcourt, 28 December 1839 in Jack Morrell and Arnold Thackray (eds), *Gentlemen of Science. Early Correspondence of the British Association for the Advancement of Science*, 1984, pp. 328–29. The following draws on Miller, '"Puffing Jamie"', 14–17. On Robert Brown's activities regarding the water controversy see Chapter 10, below.

[20] Arago, *Historical Eloge of James Watt.*

[21] Murchison to Harcourt, 28 December 1839, in Morrell and Thackray (eds), *Gentlemen of Science. Early Correspondence*, p. 329.

[22] See the acknowledgments of receipt of these works in Watt Jr to Babbage, 25 February 1828 and 29 July 1832. British Library, Add. MSS 37184, f. 110 and 37187, f. 54. James Watt Jr also signed *The Times* declaration in favour of Herschel for the Presidency of the Royal Society in 1830 at Babbage's instigation. See Watt Jr to Babbage, 29 November 1830, British Library Add. MSS 37,185, f. 360.

[23] William J. Ashworth, 'Memory, efficiency, and symbolic analysis: Charles Babbage, John Herschel, and the industrial mind', *Isis*, **87**, 1996, 629.

importance of industrial Britain to scientific endeavour. He had in fact resigned from the Council of the organization in late 1838 after a row with Murchison about the appointments of President and Vice-President for the Birmingham meeting. Watt Jr also had concerns about the Association's antics in Birmingham. He considered its public display of achievements in the industrial arts to be 'suicidal folly' so far as protecting Britain's industrial interests was concerned. Given all this, to have Harcourt devalue the achievements of Watt, the home-town hero, was just too much for Babbage and the 'Wattites' to bear. For others, though, Watt had come to symbolize the worship of industrial mechanism at the expense of all else. William Whewell was among those in the clerical wing of the Cambridge group who regarded this as dangerous for society and for science.[24] It was from this quarter that the strongest support for Harcourt came.

The 'Gentlemen of Science' and the Cultural Politics of Science

The 1839 arguments over Watt were skirmishes in an ongoing battle. To understand its roots we need to be aware of some of the deeper background of the cultural politics of science in early nineteenth-century Britain. Those years were tempestuous and eventful ones for British science. They had seen attempts at wholesale, and considerable *de facto*, reform of the Royal Society of London. The policies of Banks's Presidency to preserve what I have called a 'Banksian Learned Empire' had continued to give men of learning from across a broad spectrum of the upper ranks a significant role in the Society. This intellectually inclusive, but socially exclusive, strategy came under attack from scientific devotees who sought greater control over their own affairs and reforms that would render the Society more clearly and exclusively scientific. This process was well under way long before the 'official' reforms of the late 1840s.[25] The same reformist groupings engaged in institutional innovation themselves of both a specialist variety (the Astronomical, Geological and, later, Chemical Societies, for example) and in the entirely novel form of the British Association. The vigour of new provincial scientific organizations in the late eighteenth century had continued into the nineteenth century. Significant regional and local groups of practitioners of science emerged and even larger groups of followers of science provided a willing and supportive audience for

---

[24] On the troubles surrounding the Birmingham meeting see Morrell and Thackray, *Gentlemen of Science: Early Years*, pp. 251–52, 264 and Morrell and Thackray (eds), *Gentlemen of Science. Early Correspondence*, pp. 276–88.

[25] For the 'Banksian Learned Empire' and the reactive reform movement see David Philip Miller, 'The Royal Society of London 1800–1835: A study in the cultural politics of scientific organization', unpublished PhD Dissertation, University of Pennsylvania, 1981. On the reforms of the 1840s see: Roy MacLeod, 'Whigs and Savants: Reflections on the reform movement in the Royal Society, 1830–1848', in Ian Inkster and Jack Morrell (eds), *Metropolis and Province. Science in British Culture 1780–1850*, 1983, pp. 55–90; Iwan Rhys Morus, 'The politics of power: Reform and regulation in the work of William Robert Grove', unpublished PhD thesis, University of Cambridge; Iwan Rhys Morus, 'Correlation and control: William Robert Grove and the construction of a new philosophy of scientific reform', *Studies in History and Philosophy of Science*, **22**, 1991, 589–621.

formal educational lectures, rational entertainments, local scientific meetings, and for the visits of the travelling scientific circus that the British Association became. Greater reliance upon technology and scientific approaches in industry and commerce, as well as in agriculture, facilitated the growth of various cadres of scientific and technical specialists, while educational institutions and new publications catered to their needs also. The 'scientific community' rapidly became more diverse and differentiated. Looked at from the perspective of emergent scientific élites, there was much vitality but a problem of control within a burgeoning system. The British Association became a particularly important vehicle for the exercise of such control. As Morrell and Thackray[26] amply demonstrated, there were divergent plans for the new Association in the beginning, but quite quickly it came to be dominated by an élite group of 'Gentlemen of Science'. While working hard to promote scientific research and a positive evaluation of science in society, this group was also engaged in an effort to control burgeoning scientific activity. They sought to define science's relations with other institutions (its boundaries) in a way that promoted their own version of the scientific future and their own scientific interests.

Although its inadequacies are apparent, the term 'Cambridge Network', coined by Susan Cannon to describe a particular grouping within British science at this time, is a useful place to start in depicting the Gentlemen of Science. Cannon used the term to refer to a constellation of individuals variously associated with Cambridge University and devoted to science, who exhibited a range of characteristics such as broad church sensibilities and an interest in scientific and educational reform. An early node of this network was the 'Analytical Society' in which the young Charles Babbage, John Herschel and George Peacock played a leading part. Their programme of modernization of the teaching and use of mathematics at the university, and more widely, subsequently attracted people like William Whewell and George Biddell Airy.[27]

The careers of the members of the Cambridge Network were diverse, however. Whewell and Peacock took religious orders and built their careers at the university, holding a range of professorships and college positions. Whewell rose, in 1841, on Robert Peel's nomination, to the Mastership of Trinity College, rightly considered as one of the most powerful positions in the country.[28] Peacock, under different

---

26 Morrell and Thackray, *Gentlemen of Science: Early Years.*

27 On the Cambridge Network see Walter Faye Cannon, 'Scientists and Broad Churchmen: An early Victorian Intellectual Network', *Journal of British Studies*, **4**, 1964, 65–88 and an elaborated version of that paper in Susan Faye Cannon, *Science in Culture: The Early Victorian Period*, 1978, pp. 29–71. On the Analytical Society see Philip C. Enros, 'The Analytical Society (1812–1813): Precursor of the renewal of Cambridge mathematics', *Historia Mathematica*, **10**, 1983, 24–47. Other important insights into this grouping are provided by the writings of William J. Ashworth and Timothy Alborn.

28 On Whewell see Richard Yeo, *Defining Science*, 1993 and Menachem Fisch and Simon Schaffer (eds), *William Whewell: A Composite Portrait*, 1991. Thinking of the sources of Whewell's power, I noted in the Whewell Correspondence that a number of individuals who were involved in the water controversy in some way corresponded with Whewell about their sons' admission and attendance at Trinity or another Cambridge College. See, for example, Harcourt to Whewell, 29 January [1846], Whewell Papers, Trinity College Cambridge, Add. Ms.a.205¹³⁶(1–2) regarding his second son going to Trinity; Macvey Napier to Whewell, 19 January [1836?], Add. Ms.a.210¹¹ regarding his son Alexander

political circumstances, might have sought and obtained that position, but the Deanery of Ely offered some compensation. George Airy held successively the Lucasian and Plumian Professorships at Cambridge until his departure for Greenwich Observatory and the Astronomer Royalship in 1835. He held that position for almost fifty years and transformed it into the apex of one of the great scientific bureaucracies of the nineteenth century.[29] Babbage and Herschel took rather different trajectories, thanks largely to their independent financial means. Although at various times they sought, or were importuned to take, university professorships, they ended up retaining the gentlemanly independence to be active in metropolitan scientific institutions and to pursue their trains of research. Babbage was happier venting his misery and frustration on official bodies than in serving them.[30] It is perhaps significant that those members of the Cambridge Network who retained strong career connections with Cambridge University (that is, Whewell, Peacock and Airy) were the most conspicuous supporters of Cavendish in the water controversy. Babbage, though not making it one of his major causes, does appear to have sided with the Watt camp. Herschel, characteristically reserved and anxious to avoid controversy, made noises sympathetic to both Cavendish and Watt. He was certainly more prepared than the Trinity Men were to grant Watt some degree of credit in the affair.[31]

The limitations of the term 'Cambridge Network' appear not just because, over time, there were splits of various sorts between its putative members, but also

who was studying divinity at Trinity; Earl of Burlington to Whewell, 5 and 9 November 1850, Add. Ms.c.88[23–24] on looking after his son Spencer Compton, Lord Cavendish.

[29] On Airy see Robert W. Smith, 'A national observatory transformed: Greenwich in the 19th century', *Journal for the History of Astronomy*, **45**, 1991, 5–20 and Allan Chapman, 'Science and the public good: George Biddell Airy (1801–92) and the concept of a scientific civil servant', in N.A. Rupke (ed.), *Science, Politics and the Public Good: Essays in honour of Margaret Gowing*, 1988, pp. 36–62. On Peacock see M.J. Durand, 'Le Travail mathématique de George Peacock (1791–1858)', *Sciences et Techniques en Perspective*, **11**, 1986–87, 91–151.

[30] On Herschel and Babbage see Gunther Buttmann, *The Shadow of the Telescope. A Biography of John Herschel*, 1970; H.W. Buxton, *Memoir of the Life and Labours of the Late Charles Babbage*, ed. Anthony Hyman, 1988; Simon Schaffer, 'Babbage's Intelligence: Calculating Engines and the Factory System', *Critical Inquiry*, **21**, 1994, 203–27; William J. Ashworth, 'Memory, efficiency and symbolic analysis: Charles Babbage, John Herschel, and the industrial mind', *Isis*, **87**, 1996, 629–53.

[31] Muirhead to Brougham, 18 February 1848, Brougham Papers, 23,380 reported that Herschel, in the wake of Jeffrey's article, 'while he gives Lavoisier the greatest credit, says that Watt is clearly titled to the credit of the first <u>subjective</u> discov[y] and that Cavendish made the first <u>objective</u> discov[y]'. Earlier, in thanking Muirhead for a complimentary copy of the *Correspondence*, Herschel had written a long letter explaining his understanding of the controversy. There he confessed that it was hard to judge the controversy because 'I had been so completely accustomed (with the generality of readers) to look upon Cavendish as the discoverer of the composition of water'. Herschel also noted 'the almost impossibility of placing one's self back in time & knowledge, and bringing one's ideas into that state of confusion in which it must have presented itself to the other Chemists of that day'. After a long disquisition, Herschel divided the 'discovery of the fact' between Cavendish (the Lion's share), Priestley, Warltire and Macquer, while he gave the interpretation to Lavoisier, 'Watt not being however entirely excluded'. (Herschel to Muirhead, 12 March 1847, copy of draft, Herschel Papers, Royal Society of London, vol. 22, 47.3.12.1–6. It is not clear that this letter was ever sent to Muirhead.)

because the political formations of the élite of British science soon transcended the Cambridge group. To be sure, some members of that élite were students of the Cambridge men, or admirers of them, James David Forbes in Edinburgh being a prominent example. Others, however, came from analogous positions at Oxford University (Baden Powell, William Buckland), or from the ranks of metropolitan savants, like the mathematical practitioner, insurance expert and astronomical dogsbody Francis Baily.

The British Association became a key forum in which the 'Gentlemen of Science' worked out their role within the burgeoning scientific enterprise in Britain. There were significant differences of opinion about what the role of the Association should be. The Association began as a provincial initiative and the more radical reformers, like Babbage and Brewster, had very definite ideas about what it should do, envisaging in particular a very active lobbying of government for financial support of science and its practitioners. Initiatives such as the reform of the patent laws were seen by Babbage and Brewster as a suitable cause for the Association to pursue. Babbage was very keen to involve the industrial areas of the country centrally in the Association's affairs and meetings.

These early plans were moderated and modified by an alliance of Oxbridge clerics and some of the original provincial founders, notably Harcourt and John Phillips. In the 1830s, under this control, the Association did lobby government, but primarily for assistance with international collaborative scientific projects. There were some serious reservations about involving government directly or substantially in scientific activity. The gentlemanly voluntarists saw little need for the government to provide employment for devotees of science. There was, after all, great pride in the British voluntarist tradition and what it had achieved, together with considerable suspicion of the centralized French system that intruded the distractions and distortions of party politics into many scientific lives. By the 1840s and 1850s, the career of Arago had for many become an object lesson in the dangers of such patterns of institutional development. Others, however, including Babbage and Brewster, held up the French system as a model of best practice in many respects and lamented the inadequacies of British organizations.

Those who gained control of the Association sought to support the research of individuals, but they did so from the funds of the Association itself. By gathering subscriptions and running meetings at a profit, the Association generated funds that were disbursed to worthy projects. In this way supporters of science around the country who attended the Association's annual meetings were harnessed to finance the research of the scientific élite of the organization. Money was allocated to sections of the Association and drawn to cover expenses incurred by those charged with projects selected for support. The whole process was overseen by a Committee of Recommendations dominated by the 'Gentlemen of Science'. Between 1833 and 1844, according to Morrell and Thackray, well over £20,000 was allocated to the sections in total for support of research. Of this, almost 60 per cent went to Section A (Mathematical and Physical Sciences). Other well-supported sections were Section C (Geology) and Section G (Mechanical Science), both of which received over £3000, or more than 10 per cent of the total allocation. These amounts were, however, not all spent. Over that period only about £12,000 was drawn. Of that sum, almost half went to the top seven recipients and 90 per cent of the money

spent was expended by Sections A, C and G.[32] Some members of the inner circle were beneficiaries of these expenditures: Baily headed the list of grantees, Whewell was third and Harcourt was in the top ten. But generally the projects were defensible, and defended, as involving large-scale data gathering and dealing with topics of great communal interest and importance. As Morrell and Thackray put it, the structure of governance of this research support was 'another device by which the inner cabinet of the Association controlled the General Committee on such important matters as nurturing chosen careers, reinforcing approved ideologies of science, and promoting preferred sorts of scientific work'.[33]

Medical areas, social science and statistics fared poorly in obtaining research support. Care was taken to circumscribe such troublesome areas and they received limited attention. Those seeking the kind of scientific affirmation that it could give continually troubled the Association. The phrenologists dogged the Association's steps for many years on an imitative peripatetic route but were kept at bay. However, the boundary-management that concerns us most centrally in our story is that relating to science and technology or 'Art'.

The Association's section on Mechanical Sciences was established in 1836 as Section G. In line with the attitudes towards the relations of science and the practical arts evinced by Whewell, the constitution and conduct of Section G affirmed the ultimate superiority of the mathematical and physical sciences to engineering practice. The role of the Association was as a scientific arbiter supposedly above the rough and tumble of the invention business. This stance emerged in part from the Association's decision not to follow David Brewster's early suggestion that the Association lobby for patent law reform. What Morrell and Thackray describe as the 'consolidation' phase of the Association's early history in which it visited Oxford, Cambridge, Edinburgh and Dublin put the mechanical arts at a low priority. Various planned initiatives foundered in these early years, including one for Watt Jr to prepare a report on the law of resistance of water to bodies in motion, especially steam-driven vessels.[34] In the mid-1830s, however, a group interested in engineering affairs emerged and the Association's controlling group were ready to deal with issues of the relationship of science to technological progress:

> The assumption of the Association's apologists was that theory and practice were sharply distinct yet connected in certain significant ways. It was true that the mechanical arts often marched independently of mechanical science. But the best route to true, enduring, and satisfactory practice depended on theory ... Theory that was encoded and manipulated via abstract symbols took precedence. Mechanical *science*, transmissible by symbolic language, and not the mechanical *arts*, transmitted by personal demonstration, was to be increasingly professed within the Association.[35]

The banner of 'mechanical *science*' could attract the interest of various groupings. Manufacturers found scientific ratification of their activities; engineers detected a

---

[32] Morrell and Thackray, *Gentlemen of Science: Early Years*, p. 317.

[33] Ibid., pp. 309–10.

[34] Ibid., p. 258. (The suggestion regarding Watt Jr is in Harcourt to Whewell, 20 July 1832, Whewell Papers, W.P.a.205[126].)

[35] Morrell and Thackray, *Gentlemen of Science: Early Years*, pp. 259–60.

basis for their claimed higher status 'as mediators between the natural philosopher and the working mechanic'.[36] Morrell and Thackray show that Section G operated with personnel and structures that clearly placed practical men (engineers) under the control and effective supervision of the university teachers who commanded mechanical science. Officers of the Institution of Civil Engineers such as James Walker and, especially, Thomas Webster were involved with Section G. Walker, who was President of the Institution between 1837 and 1845, was a Vice-President of Section G in 1840. Webster, who was employed by the Institution, served as the Section's Secretary for a number of years. Academic engineers or people with strong scientific backgrounds were more conspicuous in the President's chair and among the Vice-Presidents of the Section.

The engineers were by no means totally subordinated. Sometimes they criticized the work of Section G as impractical. Walker's Presidential speech to the Institution of Civil Engineers in 1841 evinced concerns about the development of academic engineering and the production of too many theoretically qualified engineers whose knowledge exceeded, and levels of practical skill fell short of, the requirements of the job market.[37] Nevertheless the perceived value of cooperation with the Association must have outweighed such concerns. The engineers' position within the Association strengthened in the late 1840s and beyond, though it was not until 1861 that William Fairbairn became the first engineer to assume the Presidency.[38]

The élite dominated engineering within the Association by virtue of their superior command of mathematics and physical science. A number of Cambridge men were so involved. Charles Babbage's engineering interests are well known. William Whewell produced a well-timed text in 1841, *The Mechanics of Engineering. Intended for Use in Universities, and in Colleges of Engineers*. Whewell explained that the work was intended not only to help the education of professional engineers but also to contribute to a liberal education:

> If the common Problems of Engineering were to form part of our general teaching in Mechanics, this science also might become a permanent possession of liberally educated minds. Every roof, frame, bridge, oblique arch, machine, steam-engine, locomotive carriage, might be looked upon as a case to which every well-educated man ought to be able to apply definite and certain principles in order to judge of its structure and working.[39]

The tenor was clearly that the custodians of mechanics had a deal to teach both engineers and the liberally educated gentleman. Moreover the latter, when in command of the principles of mechanics, would be in a position to judge the work of the former.

---

36 Ibid., pp. 260–61.

37 See James Walker in *Proceedings of Institution of Civil Engineers*, 1841, 25–26, as quoted and discussed in R.A. Buchanan, *The Engineers. A History of the Engineering Profession in Britain, 1750–1914*, 1989, pp. 164–65.

38 Crosbie Smith, *The Science of Energy. A Cultural History of Energy Physics in Victorian Britain*, 1998, pp. 140–49 makes the important point that the leadership of the Association was in fact changing with a new generation of more entrepreneurial energy physicists and engineers.

39 William Whewell, *The Mechanics of Engineering. Intended for Use in Universities, and in Colleges of Engineers*, 1841, p. v.

George Airy was notable for a deep and lifelong interest and involvement in engineering problems. As Lucasian, and then Plumian, Professor at Cambridge in the late 1820s and early 1830s, Airy lectured about, among other things, bridges, trusses, toothed wheels, wedges, screws, pulleys, the theory of roofs, arches, domes and groins. During his long tenure as Astronomer Royal, Airy was well known for his ingenuity in dealing with engineering problems. He was frequently consulted by engineers, including Stephenson and Brunel, and helped particularly with the Britannia Bridge over the Menai Straits.[40] Elected an Honorary Member of the Institution of Civil Engineers in 1842, Airy agreed to serve on its Premium Committee, helping to set prize questions and assess responses to them. Some of Airy's suggested topics for premiums capture well his, and his associates', ideas about scientific engineering, as well as their conception of the hierarchical relationship between themselves, the scientifically informed engineer and the practical engineer.[41]

Returning now to the British Association and the management of the boundary between science and practice, we can see more clearly the attitudes encapsulated in the superior, controlling stance of the leadership over matters of engineering practice. These attitudes lay behind relations between the Cavendish and Watt camps. We know that an invitation to Watt Jr to report to the Association was contemplated in 1832 and that the suggestion was to be that he report on the law of the resistance of water to bodies in motion with particular reference to steam-driven vessels. It is not clear whether an invitation was ever made or, if made, what the response was. It is hard to avoid the feeling, however, that if the invitation had been made it would probably have brought into stark relief Watt Jr's lack of competence as a scientific

---

[40] See T.J.N. Hilken, *Engineering at Cambridge University 1783–1965*, 1967, pp. 45–50.

[41] See RGO 6/401, ff. 246 and following for correspondence regarding his election and premiums. Among these papers we find one of Airy's suggestions for a premium topic that illustrates his approach well. It was one on steam engines. First he explained the background to the topic: 'I have examined probably hundreds of steam engines, in a cursory way, while they were at work, and have usually found some of the standing adjustments upon which the engineers know nothing or next to nothing. One of these is the state of the condensometer. Not one engine in ten has [this] in order, and not one engineer in ten has any notion of judging of the state of the condensation from the temperature of the discharged water. It is well known that power is lost by condensing too completely, though I believe no rule, theoretical or practical, exists, by which the proper degree of condensation can be ascertained. And even when that is ascertained, as most advantageous for the mechanical power, it may not be free from inconvenience as regards other considerations, thus the only distinct reason that I ever got from an engineer for not condensing more closely was "that would make the engine jump". I would therefore submit whether the following subject is worthy of being proposed for premium: "To ascertain, from theory or from direct experiment, the degree of condensation which is most favourable for the working of a steam engine, as regards the production of mechanical power: to ascertain also whether any inconvenience is actually produced in any other respect by this degree of condensation, and to show how such inconvenience may be removed: and to give simple rules for the temperature of the discharged water or other indication, adapted to the use of engineers, for securing the proper degree of condensation".' This question captures well the assumed relation between the scientific elite (Airy in this case), the scientifically competent engineer and the merely practical engineer. The first could set the question and judge the quality of answers to it, the second could develop solutions to it, the third could, with suitably simplified instructions, implement the fruits of the investigation without understanding it.

engineer as judged by the standards of the early 1830s. Even if Watt Jr had been competent to so report, it is likely that, given his attitude to the Association and its fundamental violation of proprietary interest, and the danger that it posed, as he saw it, to private individual and national trade, he would still have refused to become involved.

One further example captures very well how the issue of the relations between science and practice was linked to the water controversy. This concerns the Association's work on the hot-blast technique of iron production. The interest of key members of the Watt camp with the defence of James Beaumont Neilson's patent on this technique will be discussed further in the chapter on the advocates of Watt. Suffice it now to say that Lord Brougham had drawn up Neilson's patent specification in 1828 and that Muirhead was closely interested in the defence of that patent. Parallels were drawn explicitly at the time between the difficulties that Neilson had and those experienced by James Watt in dealing with people who sought to circumvent their patents. The two men were also compared in terms of their scientific approach to their inventions.

It will be remembered that the Association had avoided direct involvement in the debate on patent law reform and so stood aloof from the kind of battle involved in relation to Neilson's patent on the hot-blast technique. The Association, however, did involve itself with the study of the hot blast in a characteristic fashion. Its stance epitomized the expert arbitrating role that the Association sought to assume in seemingly rising above matters of technological dispute and operating in the 'public' interest.[42]

The initiative to commission a report on the hot-blast technique appears to have originated with Harcourt. Harcourt was a close associate of Earl Fitzwilliam, who had direct iron-smelting interests. At the Dublin meeting of the Association in 1835 the manager of Fitzwilliam's Elsecar works, Henry Hartop, questioned the quality of iron produced using the hot-blast technique. The focus of the Association's inquiries into the technique concerned its efficacy when compared with the traditional cold-blast method. Eaton Hodgkinson and William Fairbairn conducted the inquiry and concluded from an elaborate series of experiments and measurements that, although there was considerable variation in quality in various respects, the energy savings of the hot-blast technique favoured its general adoption.[43] This allowed the maintenance of some distance from the patent disputes then raging. But the Association's intervention would not have pleased the Neilson camp because, despite its overall endorsement of the technique, it documented its lack of uniform efficacy. This could have been taken by Neilson's opponents as ammunition to argue the incompleteness of the specification. Whether it was so used or not does not matter. Neilson's supporters, like Brougham and Muirhead and Watt Jr, would, I suggest, have perceived the intervention by the Association in that way. To them

---

[42] To an extent, then, the gentlemanly ethos of the Association carried on earlier thinking about the 'practical' and the 'philosophical', practical projects being regarded as disinterested and philosophical in so far as they were pursued in the public, rather than particular private, interest. See David Philip Miller, 'The usefulness of natural philosophy', *The British Journal for the History of Science*, **32**, 1997, 185–201.

[43] Morrell and Thackray, *Gentlemen of Science: Early Years*, 497–98.

the scientists would appear to be blundering in on the topic professing 'neutrality' and scientific indifference to proprietary interests and yet, in fact, giving potential comfort to one side of the struggle. The existence of tension between the Watt camp and the self-appointed scientific arbitrators of the Association is not surprising.

The visibility of practical engineering achievement was a fact of life in early Victorian Britain that the leadership of the Association had to deal with. Their concern was to establish a relationship between science and practice that linked science to those achievements but maintained a careful and significant differentiation between them. Mechanical *science* provided the link. The élite's custody of the mathematically and experimentally based research, upon which, they argued, practice must increasingly rely, provided the differentiation.

There were a number of occasions when the ideology of the relations of science and practice was elaborated at length. An early occasion was at the Association's Cambridge meeting in 1833. William Whewell gave an address in which he argued that a clear distinction must be retained between theory and practice. As Richard Yeo has put it, Whewell 'wanted science to be lauded justly for its intellectual value, rather than incorrectly for its useful application'.[44] He described 'Art' (that is, practical industrial application) as the 'comely and busy mother of a daughter of a far loftier and serener beauty', that serener beauty being, of course, the contemplation of scientific truth.[45] Whewell's *History of the Inductive Sciences* (1837) gave only brief and grudging attention to the practical applications of science.

Whewell's general stance on this was relevant to his interventions in the water question. It is no coincidence that Whewell and George Peacock were very supportive of Harcourt's crossing of swords with Arago. The Watt camp seems to have considered that Harcourt had not acted alone in this. Arago, via his conduit Pentland, vented his spleen over Harcourt's attack, noting that Watt's name 'will be green in the memory of the world, when that of the Harcourts, the Whewells, & the Philips his advisers & abettors, will be for ever buried in oblivion'.[46] Muirhead reported to Watt Jr that Harcourt was 'the tool of others, and that he would not have ventured on such an "adventure perilous" on his own responsibility'.[47] There is other evidence supporting the existence of a pro-Cavendish coterie, though prior involvement of others in the decision for Harcourt to speak on the question cannot be proven. Harcourt confided to his wife the day after the Address, that he got through his 'principal work last night very successfully ... and putting aside common compliments, I am glad to find that the Dean of Ely [George Peacock], of whose judgment I have a great opinion, is highly satisfied with me'.[48] William Whewell

---

[44] *Report of the Third Meeting of the British Association for the Advancement of Science held at Cambridge in 1833*, 1834, xxiv–xxv; Yeo, *Defining Science*, pp. 225–26.

[45] *Report of the Third Meeting*, p. xxv. A very useful account of Whewell's views on technology and 'art' is given in Joost Mertens, 'From Tubal Cain to Faraday: William Whewell as a philosopher of technology', *History of Science*, **38**, 2000, 321–42.

[46] J.B. Pentland to Watt Jr, [?] October 1839, as extracted in Watt to Muirhead, 22 October 1839, Muirhead Papers, MS GEN 1354/379.

[47] J.P. Muirhead to James Watt Jr, 10 September 1839, Muirhead Papers, MS GEN 1354/310.

[48] E.W. Harcourt (ed.), *The Harcourt Papers*, 1880–1905, vol. xiv, p. 97.

7.2   The Reverend William Whewell

was also publicly and privately supportive. His private response to Harcourt's Address and the stir that it created is worth quoting at length:

> I see that you are assailed on various sides for what you have said about Watt and Cavendish. I have no doubt that you will be able to defend yourself easily and well; and indeed I hardly see the necessity of adding anything to what you originally stated.
>
> Your case, as you first put it, remains to my mind quite unshaken. But perhaps you may be wishing to know how the subject presents itself to my mind, looking at it rather

with reference to the general course of the history of Science than to any special evidence of dates and the like ...

In the first place I think your remark is quite decisive – that Watt's views are utterly damaged by involving a composition of ponderable and imponderable elements. This of itself was enough to show that he did not consider elementary composition with the rigour and distinctness which the discovery of the synthesis and analysis of bodies at that time required ...

And thus Watt, who at most can only claim the merit of proposing a hypothesis, proposed one which by its very terms was unsuited to the step which science then had to take.[49]

In this way, Whewell came to Harcourt's aid as the latter prepared the written account of the Birmingham Address with which we began. Whewell's public support came, significantly, in his best-known and most influential works, his *History of the Inductive Sciences* and his *Philosophy of the Inductive Sciences*, where the advice that he gave to Harcourt was developed to elevate the Cavendish camp's position to a matter of philosophical principle.

Whewell quickly found a place in his philosophy of science for the issues raised by the water controversy. In *Philosophy of the Inductive Sciences*, first published in 1840, Whewell discussed the application of the 'idea' of substance in chemistry and in the course of this developed a series of maxims. One of these was the 'Maxim respecting Imponderable Elements', that is, concerning those hypothetical fluids that had at one time or another been deployed to explain phenomena such as heat, light, electricity and magnetism.

It is however plain, that so long as these fluids appear to be without weight, they are not elements of bodies in the same sense as those elements of which we have hitherto been speaking. Indeed we may with good reason doubt whether those phenomena depend upon transferable fluids at all ... Consequently the maxim just stated, that in chemical operations nothing is created, nothing annihilated, does not apply to light and heat. They are not <u>things</u> ... In reasoning respecting chemical synthesis and analysis therefore, we shall only make confusion by attempting to include in our conception the light and heat which are produced and destroyed. Such phenomena may be very proper subjects of study, as indeed they undoubtedly are; but they cannot be studied to advantage by considering them as sharing the nature of composition and decomposition.[50]

Given Whewell's argument that the proper pursuit of science involved the measurement of facts with precision, then chemical composition and decomposition must be studied by measuring the weights of the ingredients and compounds. Because there is no measure of any value in relation to heat and light, 'if we attempt to account for these phenomena *on chemical principles*, we introduce, into investigations themselves perfectly precise and mathematically rigorous, another class of reasonings, vague and insecure, of which the only possible effect is to vitiate the whole reasoning, and to make our conclusions inevitably erroneous'.[51]

[49] Whewell to Harcourt, 11 February 1840, in *The Harcourt Papers*, vol. xiv, pp. 105–106.

[50] William Whewell, *The Philosophy of the Inductive Sciences*, 2 vols, 1840, vol. 1, pp. 399–400.

[51] Ibid., p. 400. It will be noticed that Whewell's philosophical principles reflect rather directly in many respects Lavoisier's philosophical–rhetorical grounding of his new chemistry.

This led Whewell to the maxim that 'imponderable fluids *are* not *to be admitted as chemical elements of bodies*'.[52]

Whewell believed, then, that the best practitioners of chemistry, the 'most philosophical chemists', had proceeded according to this maxim. He proceeded to apply it to the controversy over the composition of water. Noting that, after a long period when the discovery was credited to Cavendish and Lavoisier, a claim had been made for James Watt's priority, Whewell quickly dismissed the usual terms of debate over the controversy: 'It is not our purpose here to discuss the various questions which have arisen on this subject respecting priority of publication, and respecting the translation of opinions published at one time into the language of another period.'[53] Quoting Watt's statement of his views, Whewell noted that Watt 'does admit imponderable fluids as chemical elements; and thus shows a great vagueness and confusion in his idea of chemical composition'.[54] According to Whewell, this flaw in Watt's approach meant that Watt did not understand, let alone anticipate, the discovery of Cavendish and Lavoisier. The conclusion drawn by Cavendish, on the other hand, Whewell considered to have contained 'nothing hypothetical or superfluous'. On this ground Whewell agreed with Harcourt's decision in favour of Cavendish. At the same time, he congratulated both Harcourt and himself: 'we may with pleasure recognise, in this enlightened umpire [Harcourt], a due appreciation of the value of the maxim upon which we are now insisting'. Whewell quoted Harcourt's observation that Cavendish had wisely 'pared off' imponderables 'as complicating chemical with physical considerations'.[55] That Harcourt was in accord with Whewell is, of course, hardly surprising since, as we have seen, Whewell had fed that line of argument to Harcourt earlier in the year!

Whewell's is a powerful argument. He took the philosophical high ground, established the right way of proceeding in science and found Cavendish in accord with it. Watt, by contrast, was adjudged out of line. Whewell was very clear about the philosophical test that a passage of scientific activity should pass before it could be regarded as a scientific discovery. This philosophical test drove a wedge between Cavendish and Watt and rendered circumstantial evidence irrelevant to the choice between them. Whewell made this clear in a note added to the discussion of the controversy in the second edition of *The Philosophy of the Inductive Sciences*, published in 1847:

Since the first edition of this work was published, and also since the second edition of the *History of the Inductive Sciences,* Mr. Watt's correspondence bearing upon the question of the Composition of Water has been published by Mr. Muirhead. I do not find, in this publication, any reason for withdrawing what I have stated in the text above: but with reference to the statement in the *History*, it appears that Mr. Cavendish's claim to

---

[52] Ibid.

[53] Ibid., p. 402.

[54] Ibid.

[55] Ibid., p. 403. There were differences, however, between Harcourt and Whewell. Harcourt thought that Whewell gave too much credit to Lavoisier. He believed that the Frenchman's representation of the phenomena had 'the same defect as that of Watt' in giving heat 'a part in the affinities & composition of the gaseous & liquid substances'. In Harcourt's view Cavendish alone avoided this. See Harcourt to Whewell, 16 March [1840], Whewell Papers, Add. Ms.a.205[138(1–2)].

the discovery was not uncontested in his own time. Mr. Watt had looked at the composition of water, as a problem to be solved, perhaps more distinctly than Mr. Cavendish had done; and he conceived himself wronged by Mr. Cavendish's putting forwards his experiment as the first solution of this problem.[56]

Whewell made a minor concession to the Watt camp here. He conceded that Muirhead's publication of Watt's correspondence provided some insight. It showed us, as a purely historical matter, that Cavendish's claim was contested in its own time. It showed us also, perhaps, that Watt had a clearer focus than Cavendish did upon the problem of the nature of water. Finally it enabled us to understand how it was that Watt felt aggrieved by the lack of recognition granted him. However, the concession was only minor, because these historical insights were treated as irrelevant to the task of designating the discoverer. Whewell might acknowledge that at the time (in the 1780s) people had grounds for granting Watt's claim, but now, in the 1840s, with the correct philosophical test of the question available, there could be no doubt that Cavendish was the discoverer and Watt was irretrievably wide of the mark.

While Whewell traced the sources of Cavendish's success to the ability to conform to scientific inquiry pursued via clear and distinct ideas, others had a rather different emphasis. John Herschel, for example, had some well-known differences with Whewell's idealism and was inclined to emphasize the role of experiment. This is revealed not only in his *Preliminary Discourse on the Study of Natural Philosophy* (1830) but also in the way that he dealt with particular instances of discovery.[57] David Gooding has brought to light Herschel's dealings with Michael Faraday on the occasion of Faraday's announcement of his discovery of the relationship between light and electromagnetism – what we know as the 'Faraday Effect'.[58] This occurred in 1845, at a time when the water controversy was very active. Interestingly it involved a relationship between Herschel and Faraday that paralleled in some key respects that often posited between Watt and Cavendish. Basically, Herschel had an anticipatory idea in 1823 and performed an abortive experiment. He did not pursue the phenomenon any further experimentally. Faraday, in a private train of research, came up with the effect. Herschel's response to Faraday's claim was essentially to say that although he had done similar work, he did not claim priority. He acknowledged instead that Faraday had the stronger claim. Herschel summed his reasoning up nicely in a letter with the phrase 'He who proves discovers'. The idea is, then, that a person engaged in a train of research, a person who elaborates the work around a discovery, who performs a proving experiment, has a strong claim to that discovery. By the 1840s this idea had become a kind of informal social rule of what we might call 'priority politics'.

---

56 William Whewell, *The Philosophy of the Inductive Sciences*, 2nd edition, 2 vols, 1847, vol. 1, p. 419n.

57 J.F.W. Herschel, *A Preliminary Discourse on the Study of Natural Philosophy*, 1830 and see Timothy L. Alborn, 'The "End of Natural Philosophy" revisited: Varieties of scientific discovery', *Nuncius: Annali di storia della scienza*, **3**, 1988, 227–50.

58 David Gooding, '"He who proves, discovers": John Herschel, William Pepys and the Faraday Effect', *Notes and Records of the Royal Society of London*, **39**, 1985, 229–44.

Another example, in relation to an observational science, is provided by the attempt of James David Forbes to claim a discovery. In 1847 he reflected upon his own status as a discoverer in glaciology in a letter to his former pupil and friend E. Batten, who seems to have expressed more confidence in Forbes's claim to the discovery than Forbes himself thought warranted:

> You must allow me some voice in deciding whether the glacier question may safely be left to itself. Your repeated assurances that everyone is satisfied are very pleasing, as expressing a sort of public opinion; but I have the very best reasons for knowing that only a small portion of strict men of science, whose opinion must ultimately decide the matter, are convinced, or at least, if convinced have the candour to allow it. Dr Whewell has spoken out manfully in the new edition of his 'Inductive History', and I hope Lyell will do as much, and then we may expect others to follow. But the result of my reading in the history of science is that in questions of mixed evidence like this a man must work it out to the utmost limit he can, if he means that it shall finally be associated with his name, which is my desire …[59]

The young Forbes had been given advice by David Brewster to specialize in a train of research and he had followed that advice.[60] It is perhaps not surprising that, for a generation becoming increasingly specialized in their own careers, which they envisaged in terms of trains of research, this criterion of discovery should be a popular one. Cavendish would be favoured by this criterion much more so than Watt, since the accepted history portrayed Cavendish, unlike Watt, as an ongoing experimental presence in the emergence of the new chemistry. Forbes's judgement of where priority lay in the water controversy also informed his own mode of scientific life as a putative discoverer. Forbes's generation was one that increasingly pursued a single line of research. Forbes did just that, first with studies of heat and then with studies of glaciation. It is little surprise, then, that for that generation Cavendish's sustained researches were admired and seen as a ratification of the modern order. The road to discovery taken by the new generation was predicated on the judgement that in the water controversy Cavendish was the true discoverer.[61]

Although in some respects their own careers informed their notions of discovery, a key strength of the Cavendish camp in the water controversy lay in the capacity to incorporate their case into a general, objectified philosophical outlook upon science that was widely promulgated. Another strength lay in the closely related task of

---

[59] James David Forbes to E. Batten, 10 January 1847, in John Campbell Shairp, Peter Guthrie Tait and A. Adams-Reilly, *Life and Letters of James David Forbes, F.R.S.*, 1873, pp. 180–81.

[60] See Shairp et al., *Life and Letters of James David Forbes*, p. 46–47.

[61] Forbes's and Herschel's views emphasized the hard work done in connection with discovery. For them this aspect of the process of discovery became an important criterion for determining whether and by whom it had been achieved. This contrasted with the emphasis in Whewell's philosophy upon the role of genius and sudden inspiration. Forbes put it this way to Whewell: 'Perhaps there is some fundamental difference between us on the subject of Practical Knowledge … Of the necessity of patient thought to the elaboration of anything of value I am so strongly convinced that I can hardly admit knowledge suddenly acquired to having much intrinsic worth … ' (Forbes to Whewell, 29 October 1848, Whewell Papers, Add. Ms.a.204[84]). On some of these differences in conception of discovery and the role of genius see Patricia Fara, *Newton. The Making of Genius*, 2002, pp. 222–30.

controlling historical interpretation. This was truly a collective task. The initial production and updating of Whewell's *History of the Inductive Sciences* was a collaborative effort in which Whewell consulted widely, particularly on recent science. Whewell and his collaborators served a self-appointed judicial function. Priority in the water question was just one of the numerous issues that Whewell pronounced upon. He was careful to consult and to build up a consensus around his decisions. Whewell was acutely aware that judgements about what to include in the history, and whom to credit with significant discoveries, were very delicate matters.[62]

Forbes faced similar issues of judgement a few years later when he came to write the historical 'Dissertation' for the eighth edition of the *Encyclopaedia Britannica*. In fact, in negotiating the fee for the job with the editor, Dr T.S. Traill, Forbes put a price on the exercise of his judiciousness, explaining that the task was very difficult:

(1) On account of the immensely scattered literature of modern science (2) on account of these contributions not having yet taken a decided rank in the History of Science, so that the compiler must himself give a judicial opinion upon their merits in many cases (3) on account of the obvious delicacy of dealing with contemporary or almost contemporary operations.[63]

Forbes gained a substantial fee, took the task on, and three years later Whewell sympathized with his colleague:

I know that it requires some effort to act in such a case with perfect impartiality, when one knows that what one has to say will disappoint worthy and laborious people: but the feeling of the value of historical truth supports one under such annoyances. I cannot think otherwise than that your book will be well received: though perhaps not by that class of popular readers who have been led to believe that they can judge of scientific discoveries without knowing anything of science: an impression studiously strengthened by various persons, some of whom know no better, and others ought to ...[64]

There can be no clearer claim by Forbes, Whewell and their ilk to the right to arbitrate the history, even the contemporary history, of scientific discovery. Nor could there be any clearer denial of that right to the scientifically uninitiated.[65] Brougham's contributions to debate on the water question had led Harcourt to publicly advise the noble Lord that 'those who have not had leisure to pursue chemical studies to their foundation' should 'leave chemistry and chemists to themselves – at least so far as regards the minutiae of the science, and arbitrations of the rights of discovery ... '.[66] There is no doubt that part of the opposition to the

---

[62] For examples of Whewell's consultations see: Airy to Whewell, 19 June and 16 November 1846 (Whewell Papers, O.15.48[4] and O.15.48[10]); Forbes to Whewell, 24 September, 26 September and 13 October 1846 (Whewell Papers, O.15.48[24–28]).

[63] J.D. Forbes to T.S. Traill, 10 March 1852, Forbes Papers, Incoming Letters 1852, 25a.

[64] Whewell to Forbes, 10 March 1855, Forbes Papers, Incoming Letters 1855, 40a.

[65] For Whewell's campaign against much scientific journalism and its links with his project of linguistic reform, see Simon Schaffer, 'The history and geography of the intellectual world: Whewell's politics of language', in Menachem Fisch and Simon Schaffer (eds), *William Whewell: A Composite Portrait*, 1991, pp. 201–31.

[66] William Vernon Harcourt, 'Letter to Henry Brougham', *Philosophical Magazine*, **28**, 1846, 524.

claims for Watt in the water question was grounded in the view that both Watt himself and his advocates lacked the requisite scientific understanding to be *bona fide* contributors either to scientific discovery or to its historical elucidation. Not only this, but they failed to recognize what Whewell took to be a historic truth, namely that the superseding of natural philosophy by science, of eighteenth-century modes of inquiry by modern ones, was exactly the exclusion of the inexpert from the councils of judgement. Writing about electrical investigations in the eighteenth century Whewell argued that

> A large and popular circle of spectators and amateurs feel themselves nearly upon a level, in the value of their trials and speculations, with more profound thinkers: at a later period, when the subject is become a science, that is a study in which all must be left far behind who do not come to it with disciplined, informed and logical minds, the cultivators are far more few, and the shout of applause less tumultuous and less loud … [67]

The appeal of the British Association to the likes of Whewell was in part that it offered an ideal vehicle through which to manage the relations of experts and the lay public. Harcourt's Address before that body in 1839, then, was not a lone intervention in the history of science. It was written from the perspective of a scientific grouping whose members were heavily engaged in shaping history. They did so partly in the cause of developing a particular set of institutional frameworks and creating science in their own image.

In a real sense, then, Harcourt's 'Address' as published in 1840 was a common effort of Harcourt and his supporters in the months after his Birmingham speech. Supporters were drawn from among those Gentlemen of Science who commanded the affairs of the British Association and, increasingly, the Royal Society during these years, as well as from the Cavendish family itself. The water question was one issue in a much larger ideological struggle about the nature of science, its relations with other major institutions, and its role in society. The extent of this larger struggle can be further appreciated by considering another individual who was heavily involved in the water controversy but also fought numerous other battles with the Association's leadership – Sir David Brewster. His case is instructive not only because he changed sides in the water controversy but also because, unlike the 'foundation' members of the Watt camp, he also fought explicitly, and for many years, over the larger symbols of science.

Brewster's Intervention and Conversion

In the interval between the delivery of Harcourt's address to the Association and its publication another important document appeared. This was the review of Muirhead's translation of Arago's *Eloge* in the *Edinburgh Review* in January 1840.[68] The Watt

---

[67] William Whewell, *History of the Inductive Sciences*, third edn, 1857, vol. 3, p. 16, as quoted in Simon Schaffer, 'Scientific discoveries and the end of natural philosophy', *Social Studies of Science*, **16**, 1986, 407.

[68] David Brewster, 'Life and discoveries of James Watt', *Edinburgh Review*, **70**, 1840, 466–502.

camp had assumed, complacently, that Brougham would be 'their' reviewer in the *Edinburgh* simply by virtue of seigniorage. However, Macvey Napier, the editor, had already assigned the task to David Brewster, though he left Muirhead, Watt Jr and Brougham guessing as to the reviewer's identity. Their concern that the *Edinburgh* might not be automatically supportive increased when, in response to news reports of Harcourt's British Association speech, Brougham tried to insert a critical note into the *Review*. In enclosing the intended note, Brougham suggested that Harcourt had been appealing to 'vulgar national feelings' at the British Association 'running his lengths, and all because Watt was a Scotchman, and Arago is a Frenchman'. Napier refused to publish the note.[69]

Brewster's review perplexed those on both sides of the water question. He argued that the credit should be distributed between Watt and Cavendish, credit for the *theory* going to Watt but credit for the *discovery* to Cavendish. Brewster suspected that his stance would not be popular. His situation between the camps on the substantive question mirrored his situation in life. Brewster was, in many respects, one of the 'Gentlemen of Science' who had founded, and ran, the British Association. He had been, however, a continual thorn in the side of the Cambridge men almost from the beginning and was at loggerheads with them, especially Whewell and Airy, on many fronts. Brewster regarded himself as a friend of Watt and of Scottish philosophers and inventors generally. Yet, on the water question, Brewster had proved a disappointment to the Watt camp. He had been shown Watt's water correspondence but claimed to be unconvinced by it. As editor of the *Edinburgh Encyclopaedia* he reprinted sections of Watt Jr's *Britannica* article on his father but appended a comment expressing scepticism about the claim to the discovery of the composition of water. On the strength of this alone, by the time the controversy was fully joined in 1839–40, Watt Jr regarded Brewster as one of the enemy.

Brewster's involvement, however, took an interesting twist. In 1846 he published his second major contribution to the controversy, this time unequivocally in Watt's favour. Brewster's 'conversion' was a surprise to the Watt camp, and they treated it

---

[69] Brougham to Napier, 22 September 1839, in Macvey Napier Jr (ed.), *Selection from the Correspondence of the late Macvey Napier Esq*, 1879, pp. 300–301. The text of the unpublished note read: 'Want of room compels us to postpone, to our next Number, a notice of a late address, by a worthy and reverend individual, at the Birmingham general meeting for scientific purposes. This address undertakes to decide, and somewhat peremptorily does assume to decide, upon a question of great scientific interest, namely, Mr. Watt's claims to be regarded as the first discoverer of the composition of water, that is (for no one claimed more for him) to have, in point of time, though unknown to Mr. Cavendish, made that important step. M. Arago, in his admirable memoir of Watt, and Lord Brougham in his dissertation, inserted by M. Arago in that memoir, having distinctly stated the evidence, which is that of dates and documents, Mr. Vernon, not satisfied with the scientific powers of one of these academicians, or the powers of the other to deal with evidence, has somewhat dogmatically denied the whole of their inferences, and made an appeal of a somewhat popular cast against the claims of our countryman. The whole case shall be told in our next Number, both from the documents now before the world, and from others, of much importance, to which we have had access. It is enough for us to state at present that Mr. Vernon's whole theory rests on an assumption of fact absolutely groundless, and contrary to all the evidence, namely, that Dr. Priestley did not, until taught by Mr. Cavendish, ascertain that the weight of the water formed by the combination of the two gases is equal to the weight of the gases. This we undertake to prove wholly untrue, from all the evidence published and unpublished.'

with some caution. Cavendish's supporters observed with knowing condescension. All their prejudices about Brewster as fickle, wrong-headed and contrary in all his dealings were confirmed. So, who was David Brewster? What were his arguments on the water question? Why did he take the stances that he did? Why did he change his mind? We will find answers to many of these questions in the ideological struggles of early nineteenth-century British science, scarce one of which did not enjoy the benefit of Brewster's intervention.

Brewster was the son of the headmaster of Jedburgh Grammar School and proceeded to Edinburgh University to study divinity.[70] At Edinburgh he was a contemporary and friend of Henry Brougham, who was to be a lifelong ally, collaborator and patron. Though originally intended for the Church, Brewster did not follow that path, it is said because of a nervousness that interfered with public speaking. This nervousness was often remarked upon and, though not always debilitating – Brewster gave many fine speeches – it does appear to have blighted his later professorial ambitions.

The career upon which Brewster launched himself early in the new century was the exciting but precarious one of a writer and editor. He held no paid appointment of any kind until 1838, when he became Principal of St Andrews, although he did spend time from the mid-1830s as manager of an estate owned by his sister-in-law. He commenced as editor of the *Edinburgh Magazine* and then of the *Scots Magazine* until 1806 or 1807. He then began the task of editing the *Edinburgh Encyclopaedia* for the publisher Blackwood, a job not completed until 1830. Brewster wrote for other reviews, magazines and encyclopaedias and persuaded Constable to support *The Edinburgh Philosophical Journal*, which he edited jointly with Robert Jameson. They had a very tempestuous relationship. Brewster was always an eager and dogged controversialist. By the mid-1820s, the scientific journal was caught in legal wrangles that resulted in a split and various transformations over the years.[71]

Brewster pursued his scientific work alongside this precarious literary career. Beginning in 1806, he had conducted research especially in experimental optics and optical instruments. The years 1810–18 were his most productive period of research. This brought him a strong international reputation as an experimental natural philosopher. He was also the author of a number of patented inventions, including the kaleidoscope. Though very productive scientifically and a talented and entertaining writer with a growing stable of books to his credit, Brewster was, by the late 1820s, an anxious and frustrated man. He saw that to gain financial stability he needed a secure appointment. Professorships eluded him. Their rewards in the Scottish system could be substantial if large numbers of students could be attracted. Those who did succeed, Brewster denigrated, with some justice but equal measure of envy, as showmen who had little time for research or success in it. Though a professorship would be financially desirable, it would interfere with his research. Brewster's ideal would be a position in which an assistant could discharge the lecturing duties. This was the stance that he took when competing for the

[70] On Brewster see Mrs [Margaret Maria Brewster] Gordon, *The Home Life of Sir David Brewster*, 1869.

[71] See W.H. Brock, 'Brewster as a scientific journalist', in A.D. Morrison-Low and J.J.R. Christie (eds), *'Martyr of Science': Sir David Brewster 1781–1868*, 1984, pp. 37–42.

Edinburgh Chair of Natural Philosophy in 1832–33. He was beaten to that post by his young protégé, James David Forbes, whose family influence, Tory politics, considerable promise and testimonials from luminaries of Cambridge gave the Town Council one excuse too many to reject the highly reputable, but nervous and disputatious, Whig, Brewster.

Brewster pursued a number of plots with his old friend Henry, Lord Brougham, who by the early 1830s was the highest legal officer in the land as Lord Chancellor and a man of considerable influence and substantial patronage. Brougham tried to help Brewster (an evangelical Presbyterian) gain ordination and a living in the Church of England, but in the end nothing came of it. A knighthood in 1831 and a government pension of £100 per annum, increased to £300 in 1836, were tangible outcomes of Brougham's patronage but still not the sufficiency that Brewster sought.[72]

There is no need to doubt Brewster's conviction as to the benefit that would flow from his schemes for the reform of scientific institutions despite their links with his personal frustrations.[73] In the late 1820s Brewster became known, alongside Charles Babbage, as a leader of those who argued that science in Britain was in decline. He railed against the government for its failure to honour scientific men, or, more importantly, to create salaried positions for them. He consistently held up the French state's support of science and of scientists as a contrast. Unreformed scientific organizations and the ancient universities were another target because of their failure to promote scientific research more effectively. The patent laws, in Brewster's view, penalized and taxed inventors rather than rewarding and encouraging them.[74]

The idea of creating a new scientific association was designed, in Brewster's mind at least, to address all these issues. The contrast between the body that Brewster envisaged and the one that was created as the BAAS is largely accounted for by the influence of the Cambridge Network, whose clerical members in particular disagreed with Brewster's vision and resented his flailing criticism of their own beliefs and activities. A number of authors have characterized this culture clash, personified in the antagonism between Brewster and Whewell.[75] None has done it so well as John Hedley Brooke. In the course of his examination of the Brewster–Whewell debate on the plurality of worlds, Brooke explored the sources of animosity between them.[76]

---

[72] See Brewster to Brougham, 22 July 1829, 21 January 1832, 9 May 1832, 28 May 1832, in Brougham Papers, 26,609; 26,615; 15,728 and 26,616.

[73] See Steven Shapin, 'Brewster and the Edinburgh career in science', in Morrison-Low and Christie (eds), *'Martyr of Science'*, pp. 17–23, who sees Brewster's campaign to reform British science as deriving from his 'personal predicament, joined to his moral conception of the proper place of science in Christian civilization' (p. 21).

[74] David Brewster, 'The decline of science in England', *Quarterly Review*, **43**, 1830, 305–42.

[75] Morrell and Thackray, *Gentlemen of Science: Early Years*, pp. 345–48.

[76] John Hedley Brooke, 'Natural theology and the plurality of worlds: Observations on the Brewster–Whewell debate', *Annals of Science*, **34**, 1977, 221–86. In relying on Brooke's exemplary depiction of the personal struggle between Whewell and Brewster that was built up through political, methodological and substantive scientific disputes, I acknowledge that Brooke ultimately regards their theological differences as the most fundamental, underlying even their methodological and substantive scientific stances. On Brewster's theological views and involvement in Scottish religious affairs see Paul Baxter,

Brewster and Whewell initially fell out over one of Brewster's contributions to the decline of science debate in the *Quarterly Review*. In this he suggested, tactfully as ever, that there was nobody 'in all the eight universities in Great Britain who is at present known to be engaged in any train of original research'.[77] Brewster had a scheme to divide the richer professorships and employ on the one hand a 'gifted philosopher', who would pursue his research, and on the other a popular lecturer, who would attend to the needs of students. This also caused offence in Cambridge. Whewell remained unconvinced of the declinists' case and therefore, not surprisingly, of their remedies also. One of these was, as we have seen, the new scientific association that Brewster early conceptualized. Whewell and other Cambridge men (with the exception of Babbage) were against joining with an association based on Brewster's ideas: 'I should feel no great wish to rally around Dr. Brewster's standard after he had thought it necessary to promulgate so bad an opinion of us who happen to be professors in universities ... It requires all one's respect for Dr. Brewster's merits to tolerate such bigotry and folly.'[78] When Harcourt steered the Association along lines more congenial to the Cambridge men, Brewster naturally complained at the directions that 'his' Association had taken, and held the 'contingent from Cambridge' explicitly responsible for its waywardness.[79]

By this point it was inevitable that Whewell's *History of the Inductive Sciences* would meet with Brewster's jaundiced eye. He ridiculed Whewell's neglect of the practical achievements of genius, and of Scotsmen.[80] Whewell's project continued in the *Philosophy of the Inductive Sciences* published in 1841, to which Brewster also gave a hostile reception in the pages of the *Edinburgh*. Whewell, in Kantian terms, favoured the prepared mind as the vehicle by which facts 'became the materials of exact knowledge' and, accordingly, declared against the role of chance in discovery. Brewster, closer than Whewell to the empirical view of discovery, cited examples where accident had played a major part, and accused Whewell of having his head in the clouds of an irrational metaphysics and his book of having little relevance to physical science as such.[81] Brewster considered that his own researches had received little recognition in Whewell's *History* or in his *Philosophy*. This hardly surprised him, given the long tussle that he had engaged in with the Cambridge men on the question of theories of light. In 1841, even as he was reviewing the *Philosophy*, Brewster was in dispute over the refusal of the Royal Society to publish one of his optical papers, a rejection in which Airy and Whewell had played a major role.[82]

'Science and belief in Scotland, 1805–1868: The Scottish evangelicals', unpublished PhD thesis, University of Edinburgh, 1985.

[77] Brewster, 'The Decline of Science in England', 326–27.

[78] William Whewell to J.D. Forbes, 14 July 1831, Forbes Papers, Incoming Letters, 1831, no. 25.

[79] David Brewster, 'Report of the first, second and third meeting of the British Association', *Edinburgh Review*, **60** (1835), 363–94, at 374–82.

[80] David Brewster, 'Whewell's *History of the Inductive Sciences*', *Edinburgh Review*, **66**, 1837, 110–51.

[81] David Brewster, 'Whewell's *Philosophy of the Inductive Sciences*', *Edinburgh Review*, **74**, 1842, pp. 266, 292–96.

[82] On this, see G.N. Cantor, 'The reception of the wave theory of light in Britain: A case study illustrating the role of methodology in scientific debate', *Historical Studies in the Physical Sciences*, **6**,

Beyond even this specific point, though, was Brewster's undoubted bitterness that a man such as Whewell should be sitting in judgement upon him. Whewell's magisterial manner and leisured omniscience (in the absence of any particular, original contribution to scientific knowledge) stuck in the hardworking Scotsman's craw. It must have seemed to him the worst manifestation of a process whereby the Cambridge men's supererogatory mathematical theories were treated as if they were immune to his experimental findings. This view was also consonant with Brewster's aversion to the philosophy of Bacon. There were many versions of Baconian philosophy touted in mid-nineteenth-century Britain and they were used as flexible rhetorical resources. Brewster, however, was inclined to reject any of these uses because he considered Bacon's precepts as failing to engage with the material realities of scientific practice. Whewell's announced self-conception as the writer of a modern *Novum Organon* spoke to Brewster of the same problem.[83]

From this ongoing antagonism one would expect that Brewster's inclination in the water controversy would be very much against Cavendish and for the claims of Watt. However, the situation was not so simple. Let us trace the history of Brewster's relations with the Watt camp before turning to an analysis of his major contributions to the debate on the water question.

Brewster and the Filial Project

We have seen that the filial project pursued by Watt Jr was begun by his father in the years before his death. Watt was not averse to making his own contribution to the historical record where it was considered necessary. The way that the response to Olinthus Gregory was arranged through the *Edinburgh Review*, with Watt father and son active behind Playfair as author, indicates their style of intervention. Brewster became involved in another opportunity for the Watts to set 'straight' various matters regarding the steam-engine innovations. This was done in the form of Watt's notes on, and corrections to, the articles 'Steam' and 'Steam-Engines' written by Robison for the third edition of the *Encyclopaedia Britannica*. These notes and corrections were published in 1822 as part of Brewster's edition of John Robison's *A System of Mechanical Philosophy*.[84]

1975, 109–32; idem, *Optics After Newton*, 1983, pp. 175–76. For the scientific collaboration between Brewster and Brougham see Xiang Chen and Peter Barker, 'Cognitive appraisal and power: David Brewster, Henry Brougham, and the tactics of the emission–undulatory controversy during the early 1850s', *Studies in History and Philosophy of Science*, **23**, 1992, 75–101.

[83] On varieties of 'Baconianism' at this time and a persuasive discussion of the uses made of them see Richard Yeo, 'An idol of the marketplace: Baconianism in nineteenth-century Britain', *History of Science*, **23**, 1985, 251–98. Yeo explains, along the lines suggested here, why Brewster's strong emphasis upon experiment and his interest in applied science and technology, which would normally be considered as the hallmarks of someone inclined to identify with Bacon, did not have that association in his case.

[84] John Robison, *A System of Mechanical Philosophy*, 4 vols, 1822. Watt circulated some separate copies of the amended articles and other material earlier: *The Articles on Steam and Steam-Engines, written for the Encyclopaedia Britannica, by the late John Robison ... With Notes and Additions by James Watt ... And a letter on Some Properties of Steam, by the Late John Southern*, 1818.

On Robison's death in 1805 his family had asked John Playfair to write a biography and to edit Robison's *Britannica* articles for separate publication.[85] Playfair completed half the job; the other half was entrusted to Brewster. Although Watt made various statements implying that his work on the two steam-related pieces was a chore,[86] it seems more likely that it was gladly seized as another opportunity to set the historical record 'straight'. Watt Jr and John Southern assisted Watt in the task during 1813–14. Over the next few years until the work was finally published, Brewster, as editor of the overall project, was a presence in the Watt family's literary affairs. He encouraged Watt to clarify his relations with Joseph Black, pointing out that authors were often in the habit of attributing the steam-engine improvements directly to Black's discovery of latent heat. Brewster also sought, and received, advice from Watt about the patenting and manufacture of his invention, the kaleidoscope. Their correspondence at this time reveals a close relationship, the younger man clearly revelling in their kindred scientific and technical interests.[87] During this, the most scientifically productive phase of his life, Brewster appears to have regarded Watt as a friend and fellow discoverer and inventor. One is tempted to say that Brewster identified with the much older man. It was perhaps for this reason that Watt Jr, after his father's death and the 'discovery' of the water correspondence, included Brewster among those whom he consulted about the import of that correspondence. It would not have pleased Watt Jr that Brewster, along with Hope, was unpersuaded of his father's priority.[88]

When, in 1830, Brewster's *Edinburgh Encyclopaedia* reached volume 18, in which the article on James Watt was to appear, he quoted in full the section of Watt Jr's *Britannica* article dealing with the composition of water and including the footnote on confusion of dates. Brewster, however, chose to append some remarks in which he challenged the article's claims on the water question:

---

[85] The following relies on W.A. Smeaton, 'Some comments on James Watt's published account of his work on steam and steam engines', *Notes and Records of the Royal Society of London*, **26**, 1971, 35–42.

[86] See, for example, Watt to Sir Joseph Banks, 1 March 1815, Royal Society Library, BLA.W.17, as printed in Robinson and McKie, *Partners in Science*, pp. 419–21. Watt states: 'at the instigation of my friends, and to my own great annoyance, I spent all my working hours of the winter of 1813 and spring of 1814 in writing a commentary on my Friend Dr. Robison's memoir upon the Steam Engine in the *Encyclopaedia Britannica*, for the use of Dr. Brewster … '.

[87] See Brewster to Watt, 25 August and 10 December 1815, James Watt Papers (Doldowlod), C6/3. Watt and Brewster were both independently involved in the invention of an improved micrometer with a moveable object-glass only to discover that they had both been anticipated by an earlier inventor, De la Hire. This led to an interesting exchange on the nature of discovery. Brewster's view was that 'an invention which is not communicated to the world is considered as not having been made till the time of its publication. This is the doctrine which has, for a long time, been held both with respect to inventions and discoveries; for it is always to be presumed that a person who does not communicate an invention to the public, does not see its full value, and does not consider it of any public utility' (Brewster to Watt, 12 December 1816, Watt Papers (Doldowlod), C6/4). See also J.P. Muirhead, *The Life of James Watt*, 1858, pp. 233–34.

[88] Brewster recalls consultation about the correspondence in 'Observations connected with the Discovery of the Composition of Water', *London, Edinburgh and Dublin Philosophical Magazine*, **27**, 1845, 195–97, and it is recorded by Watt Jr in his prefatory letter to J.P. Muirhead (ed.), *The Correspondence of the late James Watt*, 1846.

We have copied the preceding statement as that of Mr. Watt's friends; but a regard for the reputation of Mr. Cavendish, independent of higher motives, compels us to acknowledge that the statement is partial, and the argument not well founded. We are not able at present to refer to the original documents, but we had occasion some years ago, along with a distinguished chemist, to examine them with minute attention, and it was then our decided conviction, that the merit of the discovery of the composition of water belonged to Mr. Cavendish.[89]

Through the 1830s Brewster retained this view. When Arago attended the Edinburgh meeting of the British Association in 1834, he consulted not only with Watt Jr but also with others, including Brewster, about the *éloge* of Watt that he was preparing. Arago reported his conversation with Brewster succinctly: 'Mr. Brewster que j'ai questionné au sujet de son article Watt de l'Encyclopédie d'Edimburgh, ne m'a rien dit qui puisse infirmer l'opinion que j'ai adoptée.'[90]

In 1839 Brewster was approached by Macvey Napier to review Arago's *Eloge* for the *Edinburgh Review*. As we have seen, the Watt camp had assumed that Brougham would do the job, as had the great man himself. Napier, however, was inclined to resist Brougham's imperious and presumptuous commands.[91] From Napier's point of view, Brewster had become a regular, reliable reviewer on scientific and technical subjects, whose work was often admired. Watt Jr considered Brewster to be 'already compromised by a hasty opinion given some years ago, which would appear to render him an unfit person'. To leave little to chance, Muirhead briefed Jeffrey, who then saw, and wrote to Napier to 'indoctrinate' him. The clear intent was to get at the reviewer through the editor to prevent erroneous views being propagated on the water question.[92]

Brewster took his work on the review very seriously. He spent several days going over the history, and bestowed 'great labour' on it.[93] He was relieved at Napier's favourable response to the completed article: 'I was literally terrified that you would be dissatisfied with the view I had taken of the Water question.' He felt a great sense of responsibility since the more he studied the subject, 'the more I was convinced that, with all my enthusiasm for Watt, both as a friend whom I loved, and as a countryman whom I worshipped, I must take such a view as would not

---

[89] 'Watt, James', *The Edinburgh Encyclopaedia*, 20 vols, 1830, vol. 18, p. 786. (Reprinted by Routledge in 1999 under the editorship of Richard Yeo.)

[90] Arago to James Watt Jr, 22 September 1834, James Watt Papers (Doldowlod), W/10. Watt Jr's annotation on this letter, summarizing its contents, states: 'Has questioned Brewster who gives a lame Acct.'

[91] On Brougham's estrangement from the *Edinburgh Review* under Napier, see Joanne Shattock, *Politics and Reviewers: The* Edinburgh *and the* Quarterly *in the early Victorian Age*, 1989, pp. 34–38.

[92] Watt Jr to Henry Brougham, 17 October 1839, Brougham Papers, 20,133; Muirhead to Watt Jr, 11 October 1839, Muirhead Papers, MS GEN 1354/357. For Jeffrey's intervention see Jeffrey to Napier, 20 October 1839 in Macvey Napier Jr (ed.), *Selection from the Correspondence of the late Macvey Napier*, 1879, pp. 303–5. See also Muirhead to Watt Jr, 24 October 1839 (MS GEN 1354/384) with its advice that Napier, thanks to Jeffrey, will be ascertaining Brewster's intentions in the review and if need be altering them.

[93] Brewster to Napier, 4 November 1839, Napier Papers, British Library Add. MSS 34,621, ff. 470–71 and 10 December 1839, ff. 537–38.

altogether satisfy his unreasonable and uninstructed friends'.[94] Probably feeling the pressure from the Watt camp from behind the scenes, Brewster reported that he had decided to write to Watt Jr asking point blank whether he and his friends considered his father to have 'actually discovered' the composition of water, and if so on what grounds they believed this. Watt Jr's rather terse response was that he claimed for his father 'the <u>theory</u> of the composition of Water' and that the grounds were as stated in the *Supplement* to the *Encyclopaedia Britannica*.[95] Had Watt Jr claimed the *discovery* for his father, Brewster would have given up the article, but 'as the explicit answer ... omits all mention of discovery, and states that he claimed only the <u>theory,</u> I felt myself relieved from embarrassment'. This gave Brewster a way out of his dilemma, which we will analyse in a moment. He was convinced that the scientific credibility of the *Edinburgh Review* was at stake, as well as his own:

> Had the Review contained an article making Watt the discoverer of the composition of Water, and taking that honour from Cavendish, you would have had thundering replies from the Duke of Devonshire and the Earl of Burlington; and I have no doubt that every chemist in Great Britain would have exploded their fulminating powders against the Review. If Mr. Watt is a wise man, he will write no more on the subject. If I had been a lawyer retained by the Cavendishes, I could make out a very good case to show that Watt himself placed no value on his hypothesis, and did not intend that any claim should be set up in his name in relation to the composition of Water.[96]

Brewster clearly considered the matter settled largely in Cavendish's favour, but with the hope that he had said enough about Watt's independent merit to placate Watt's supporters and to salve his own conscience as a friend of Watt. Let us now examine Brewster's argument in the 1840 article.

The article reviewed the three published versions of Arago's *Eloge*. Brewster early asserted Watt's scientific reputation by stating that the 'succession of inventions and discoveries' that constituted his improvement of the steam engine were 'deduced from the most profound chemical knowledge, and applied by the most exquisite mechanical skill'. He then devoted twenty pages to the history of the steam engine, a sketch of Watt's life, his engine improvements and the problems with patents. Brewster lamented, along with Arago, the time that Watt spent as a civil engineer, unable as he was at that time to capitalize on his patent:

> may we not add our astonishment, that civilized states should still persist in shackling, by bad laws, the freedom of inventive genius, and withholding from the best benefactors of their country, those inalienable rights which are conceded to every other member of

---

94 Brewster to Napier, 7 January 1840, Napier Papers, British Library Add. MSS 34,621, ff. 2–4, printed in Macvey Napier Jr, *Selection from the Correspondence of the late Macvey Napier Esq*, 1879, pp. 314–15.

95 Ibid. That this exchange between Brewster and Watt Jr did occur is confirmed by Watt Jr to Muirhead, 7 December 1839, Muirhead Papers, MS GEN 1354/444.

96 Brewster to Napier, 7 January 1840, in Macvey Napier Jr, *Selection from the Correspondence of the late Macvey Napier Esq*, pp. 314–15. The legal case that Brewster hypothesized here would probably have been based on the fact that Watt, when annotating the articles 'Steam' and 'Steam-Engine', did nothing to question the attributions regarding the composition of water that they contained.

the community? Had Mr. Watt been able to communicate his inventions to the public, and yet retain the same right to them that an author does to the productions of his pen ... our country might have stood even higher than she does in the scale of nations.[97]

This is, of course, a direct reference to the debates about patent law reform that Brewster played a part in. He was not impressed by Muirhead's effort to exculpate Edmund Burke's opposition to the 1775 Act that had granted Watt and Boulton an extension of twenty-five years' protection. It will be recalled that Arago had singled out Burke's opposition to this measure for mention. Muirhead had pointed out, by way of excuse, that Burke was merely representing the interests of a constituent. Brewster regarded this as compounding, not excusing, Burke's 'crime'. If Burke had opposed the Act on principle, being against the granting of monopolies, then Brewster could have respected Burke's motive while regretting his ignorance. To oppose it in order 'to gratify the illegal cupidity of one man [the constituent]' Brewster regarded as indefensible. He urged statesmen of the present day to consider the higher good that would flow from proper recognition of 'intellectual rights' and not allow pressure from the selfish motives of immediate political supporters to cloud their judgement.[98]

Turning, finally, to the water controversy, Brewster made clear immediately his desire for compromise. He referred to it as a 'painful controversy' to be approached with delicacy, and he expressed 'an anxiety which we are sure our readers will share, to allay feelings which should never have been roused, and to reconcile interests which in the equipoise of justice are not at variance'.[99] Brewster's argument ran as follows. There is no doubt that on the basis of experiments performed by others Watt arrived at his hypothesis first. Important as this is, Brewster stressed its limitations, which he claimed were acknowledged by Watt himself. Watt never claimed, according to Brewster, to have *discovered* the composition of water. Quoting a passage from Watt's 1784 paper in the *Philosophical Transactions*, Brewster summarized thus:

> Mr Watt speaks of his <u>hypothesis</u> as a plausible conjecture, which might be refuted by subsequent experiments: and as he never wrote another word on the subject, nor made a single experiment after this paper was printed, how is it possible to identify this hypothesis with the discovery of the composition of water?[100]

Brewster interpreted Black in his lectures as agreeing with this, since Black saw Watt as the first to have the idea. However, Brewster remarked that Cavendish was 'the first who gave it solid foundation and credibility'. Brougham too, according to Brewster, avoided using the straightforward term discovery to apply to Watt's actions. In his Appendix to Arago's *Eloge* Brougham consistently referred to Watt's discovery of the *theory* of the composition of water. So, Brewster concluded, Brougham, Black and Watt himself only ever saw Watt as conjecturing or suggesting

---

[97] David Brewster, 'Life and Discoveries of James Watt', *Edinburgh Review*, **70**, 1840, 466, 478.

[98] Ibid., p. 480.

[99] Ibid., p. 488.

[100] Ibid., p. 494.

that water was composed of oxygen and hydrogen. Cavendish, by contrast, 'proved by infallible experiments, that water consisted of oxygen and hydrogen, and therefore discovered its composition'.[101] Arago, however, 'applies the terms *hypothesis*, *theory*, and *discovery*, indiscriminately' and sometimes he gave Watt all the credit; at other times he gave much of it to Priestley.

> In this way the glory of having discovered the composition of water – that is, of having established it as a *physical truth* – is transferred in *small* shares to a joint-stock company, and *not one of these* is given to Mr. Cavendish! Mr. Watt himself speaks of 'his contempt for the modicum of reputation which would result from his own theory'.[102]

Whilst Watt wanted to claim what was due to him, he would have been astonished, Brewster claimed, if the hypothesis had been made to supersede Cavendish's 'grand experimental discovery'. So Brewster found that the merits of Watt and Cavendish were not in collision.

> Mr. Watt will for ever enjoy the honour of that singular sagacity which presented to him the *hypothesis* of the composition of water; and Cavendish will never lose the glory which belongs to him, of having given that hypothesis, whether he was cognisant of it or not, the force and stability of truth.[103]

Brewster, having established this point, moved on to castigate Harcourt for his treatment of the question, and the Council of the British Association more generally. Harcourt did injustice to Watt's genius in a careless way at the most inappropriate of venues. Brewster linked this to the recent efforts of another member of the Council to deprive Black of credit for the discovery of latent heat. (This was a reference to Whewell's *History of the Inductive Sciences* in which he attributed the discovery to De Luc and Wilcke.) Apart from lamenting these injustices, Brewster also disagreed with Harcourt's main argument, that Watt's hypothesis got the true composition of water wrong because 'hydrogen' and 'phlogiston' are not convertible terms. Watt, Brewster said, asserted that they were so convertible. Moreover, Cavendish and Black both considered Watt's hypothesis as a 'true' one. Thus Brewster did take Harcourt to task for the way in which he dealt with Watt's claim. The President's defence of Cavendish, though, Brewster entirely concurred with, and he regretted the imputations with which Arago had stained Cavendish's character.

Brewster's article was an ingenious compromise. It avoided the retrospective imposition of conceptual standards that Harcourt and Whewell relied upon. It maintained that the basic ideas of Cavendish and Watt were the same and acknowledged the circumstantial evidence for Watt's priority with the hypothesis. It used a methodological criterion to attribute discovery proper to Cavendish's sustained and precise experimental treatment.

---

101 Ibid., p. 495.
102 Ibid., p. 496.
103 Ibid.

No article by Brewster would be complete without a coda attacking the British government's inattention to the support of science and invention. The main thrust this time was the failure of the government to honour Watt, either in his lifetime with a peerage, or after his death with a *national* monument. In Brewster's view, the fact that the monuments that had been raised to Watt had relied upon private funding was typical of the voluntarism that plagued the progress of science in Britain.

The response to Brewster's article was ambivalent. Some people in both camps were pleasantly surprised or relieved. Henry Brougham believed that the author was 'quite right except in a few phrases'.[104] Muirhead felt that 'the mountain seems to have brought forth a mouse; but it is perhaps better that the birth should be a creature thus innocuous, than a Minerva armed'. He noted that Brewster was admiring of Watt and Arago, and, if rather too kind to Cavendish, he had at least attacked Harcourt. The water question, Muirhead felt, 'had perhaps been treated quite as well as could have been looked for' from Brewster. On the whole Muirhead considered that:

> We may thank our stars that the erring Knight has struggled through his slough of despond without more floundering; he has acted wisely in taking no notice of his great original lapsus, but the illustration of the joint-stock company, which he applies to Arago, might with a great deal more propriety be used with regard to himself.[105]

Watt Jr, however, considered Brewster to be persevering in error, and on the substantive point Muirhead agreed: 'I never can be persuaded, that the discovery of the *true* theory of the composition of water, is not the discovery of the composition of water; and with all respect for the chemists who seem to think otherwise, I think their doctrine, upon their own shewing, is ludicrous.'[106]

The Cavendish camp exhibited a similar ambivalence. Forbes considered the review fair on the whole. This rather surprised him 'considering the evidences of the authorship and the alliance with Lord Brougham'. Lord Burlington simply noted that the review 'seems to apportion the merit between Cavendish and Watt'.[107] However, the view was also circulating among Cavendish supporters that Brewster was wrong in allocating credit to Watt even for the theory:

> Brewster is quite wrong – that he has confounded an untenable hypothesis which Watt had early formed about the nature of water, (& which he formally gave up on learning Cavendish's exp[s]) with the opinion which he (Watt) formed on becoming acquainted thro' Priestley with Cavendish's Exp[s] – the priority which Brewster claims for Watt is therefore priority in respect to an erroneous hypothesis ...[108]

---

[104] Brougham to Napier, n.d. [January 1840], Napier Papers, British Library Add. MSS 34,621, vol. XI, ff. 5–6.

[105] Muirhead to Watt Jr, 10 January 1840, Muirhead Papers, MS GEN 1354/462. The 'original lapsus' was Brewster's treatment of the water question in his *Edinburgh Encyclopaedia*.

[106] Watt Jr to Muirhead, 10 January 1840, Muirhead Papers, MS GEN 1354/463 and Muirhead to Watt Jr, 24 January 1840, Muirhead Papers, MS GEN 1354/467.

[107] J.D. Forbes to Whewell, 8 February 1840, (Copy), Forbes Papers, Letterbook III, pp. 50–53; Lord Burlington to W.V. Harcourt, 23 January 1840, *Harcourt Papers*, **14**, pp. 99–100.

[108] Edward Sabine to Humphrey Lloyd, 13 January 1840, Royal Society of London, Terrestrial

While on the surface Brewster's compromise position in the water controversy was seen as such, representatives of both camps quickly moved to question the substantive points upon which he based that compromise.

Meanwhile Brewster's battles with the Cambridge men continued. As we have seen, in 1842 the *Edinburgh Review* published Brewster's review of Whewell's *Philosophy of the Inductive Sciences* in which he took issue directly with Whewell's conception of discovery, a conception that had by then been used by Harcourt to buttress his own case for Cavendish. Brewster's emphasis upon the importance of an experimental train of research in securing the discovery for Cavendish (and its absence in work securing only the theory for Watt) might have been reconciled with Herschel's view of discovery, with Forbes's, or even that of Harcourt himself. In practice, however, the wedge was being driven deeper between Brewster and the Cavendish camp. Brewster was outraged at the short shrift given to his own work by Whewell and at the treatment he received from Airy and Whewell over his optical papers submitted to the Royal Society of London. This at least was how Brewster represented the case to his friend Brougham:

> I am very anxious to have your Lordship's advice respecting some very harsh treatment which I have received from the Council of the Royal Society of London ... The Council have lately rejected an original and valuable Paper, without assigning any reason, and refusing to mention the name of the Reporter on whose authority this was done. The truth is this Paper contains results and views hostile to the Undulatory Theory which seems now to be the Creed of the Society, I believe <u>Airy</u> is the person who has reported on my Paper, & who has done this entirely from personal feelings ... The Royal Society needs Reform, as it is in the hands of a Cambridge Faction hostile to all Scotchmen.[109]

As we will see in a moment, when Brewster ceased to sit on the fence on the water question he also implicitly linked his own fate at the hands of the Royal Society establishment of the 1840s with what he took to be Watt's fate at the hands of its counterpart in the 1780s.

Brewster changed his stance on the water question in an article published in the *North British Review* in 1846.[110] The immediate occasion for the review was the appearance, under Muirhead's editorship, of the Watt *Correspondence* on the water question. The review also encompassed Muirhead's translation of Arago's *Eloge*, Harcourt's published 'Address' to the British Association, Brougham's lives of Watt and Cavendish, and Harcourt's letter to Brougham on his lives of Black, Watt and Cavendish.

The overall structure of the argument is ingenious, if a trifle disingenuous. Brewster, who was writing anonymously, named Drs Brewster and Hope as among those whom Watt Jr consulted shortly after his father's death about the

---

Magnetism Papers, Vol. 1, MS119, letter 84. The view expressed was that of Robert Brown as reported by Sabine.

[109] David Brewster to Henry Brougham, 14 December 1841, Brougham Papers, 26,624. Brewster subsequently described this as 'a case of persecution, arising as I am convinced, from the conduct of Airy & probably of Whewell' (Brewster to Brougham, 23 December 1841, 26,625).

[110] [David Brewster], 'Watt and Cavendish – Controversy respecting the composition of water', *North British Review*, **6**, 1846, 473–508.

7.3   Dr David Brewster

water question, 'but these gentlemen not having seen the correspondence and judging only from the previously published documents, did not entertain the same opinion of the case as Mr Corrie and Dr Henry'.[111] The point being made is that Brewster and Hope did not believe in Watt's priority at that stage. (The claim might be seen as disingenuous because in his *Edinburgh Encyclopaedia* in 1830 Brewster contradicted Watt Jr's account in the *Britannica* ostensibly on the basis

---

[111] Ibid., pp. 475–76.

of having made a detailed examination 'some years ago' of the original documents.[112]) In his 1846 article Brewster presented himself as having been only recently convinced by the evidence in the *Correspondence* which took the reader behind the published documents. On this basis, Brewster unambiguously awarded the discovery to Watt.

Brewster, again not entirely consistently, adopted several of the argumentative strategies of the Watt camp. Thus the review was littered with judicial allusions. The reader was advised that the 'rules of evidence' are the same 'in the forum of science as well as that of law and justice', and at various stages Brewster described evidence as admissible or not. Muirhead's statement assigning the discovery to Watt by analogy with Godson on patents was cited with approval. Brewster also appealed to 'the jury of our readers' and referred to the 'ultimate decision of the public' as if everyman was a qualified judge of the matter.[113] However, Brewster also made an argument from expertise:

> We have ever thought that it is only a scientific man that can judge aright in a controversy, and that it is only an original inquirer who has anticipated others in discovery, and been himself anticipated, who can deal justly and tenderly with the great questions which involve the reputation of a philosopher, and affect the glory of his country.

We can take this as a statement that only those already 'blooded' in the matter of priority disputes, as victors and as victims, should exercise any judicial function in relation to them. It is hard not to see again a specific barb directed at Whewell and his ilk. Sounding uncannily like Robert Merton, Brewster continued:

> Such a man has a personal interest in the honest adjudication of scientific disputes. The case which he tries may be his own … An alien in the republic of letters cannot administer its laws. A pleader without its vernacular tongue cannot cross-question its witnesses. Hence do we exclude ourselves and all our anonymous craft from the bench of judicial science, and we call upon the Faradays, the Berzeliuses, the Liebigs, and the Dumas to eject us and occupy our place.[114]

It appears here that Brewster disqualified himself, at least rhetorically, as a judge, let alone the common man. He deferred to chemical expertise. But he pointedly disqualified 'all our anonymous craft', including presumably the anonymous reviewer who described Watt's theory of 1783 as 'unprofitable and worthless' (this was George Peacock) in much the manner that Harcourt dismissed the theory as 'an erroneous speculation'. Whewell was also quoted at length and associated with the interloping and unqualified judiciary. Watt's friends, we are

---

112 Brewster's words were: 'We are not able at present to refer to the original documents, but we had occasion some years ago, along with a distinguished chemist, to examine them with minute attention, and it was then our decided conviction, that the merit of the discovery of the composition of water belonged to Mr. Cavendish' (*Edinburgh Encyclopaedia*, vol. 18, at p. 786). Evidently, by 'original documents' Brewster could not have meant 'original published documents' since there would have been nothing preventing him consulting them 'at present'.

113 Brewster, 'Watt and Cavendish', pp. 474, 497, 503, 481.

114 Ibid., pp. 501–502.

told, 'can have no anxiety about the truth or worth of a theory [Watt's] which the members of the Royal Society received with high approbation, and which Black, and Robison, and Henry, and Berzelius, and Dumas have accepted as a great chemical truth'. Even Cavendish himself, Brewster claimed, stated that Watt's theory was the same as his own, 'with only an apparent difference'. Clinching his argument from chemical authority, Brewster noted that 'living chemists of high name, Professor Graham, of University College, for example', had shown Watt's theory to be '*exactly similar* to those entertained by the most distinguished philosophers of the present day'.[115]

There are two points to be noted here. The first is that by explicitly contrasting the views of chemical experts with those of Harcourt, Whewell and Peacock, Brewster challenged the chemical credentials of those three gentlemen. The readiness with which they *assumed* judicial functions, whether in the writing of scientific history or in the adjudication of current claims (including some of Brewster's own), was under attack here. The second point is that Brewster, in the manner of Watt Jr or Muirhead, marshalled chemical expertise behind the idea of the sameness of the theory of Watt and the conclusion of Cavendish. This meant that his arguments – he does make arguments despite having disqualified himself – are now very much the arguments from circumstantial evidence favoured by the Watt camp.

In the last three pages of his review, Brewster manages to link the institutional state of science in Britain, the treatment of Watt by the Royal Society in the 1780s and, implicitly, his own situation. Returning to the themes of his declinist writings of nearly twenty years earlier, Brewster attributed the problems to the reliance in Britain upon the voluntary principle in forming scientific institutions. He described the Royal Society as an 'unnatural union ... a copartnery of men of station and men of genius, – a collection of atoms of such opposite and incongruous properties, that even the electric spark of royal favour cannot effect their combination'.[116] In countries where talent was drawn from whatever station and properly supported in pursuing research, science prospered much more effectively, Brewster claimed. In Britain the voluntary principle led to the domination of the Royal Society by metropolitan and Oxbridge élites and by those wealthy gentlemen who could afford the fees and leisure required to participate in its forums. This meant, in Brewster's view, that the function of the organization 'must be performed in committees of various shades of capacity and knowledge'.

> The clashing interests of universities, castes, and professions, are all more or less represented and fostered in these judicial enclaves: But the provincial philosopher has no representation there, and whether he be a competitor for medals or fame, he will have little chance of success against an university or a metropolitan rival. And even if he is ambitious only of a niche for his discoveries in the Philosophical Transactions, or desires a testimony to the priority of his labours, he will succeed in neither, if some influential leader in the society, or some upstart member of a committee has been pursuing the same

---

[115] Ibid., p. 503. Roping in Thomas Graham in this way was a marvellous piece of mischief since he was at this time president of the Cavendish Society and of the Chemical Society of London. See Chapter 9, note 36.

[116] Ibid., p. 506.

train of research ... From these observations, our readers will understand how the claims of Mr. Watt must have fared in a body thus constituted, and thus managed.[117]

So it was that Brewster, like his fellow Gentlemen of Science, but in a way quite contrary to them, linked the substance of the water controversy to arguments about the basic character of science in Britain.[118] Brewster now simply abandoned the convenient metaphysics of 'theory' versus 'discovery' that earlier seemed to provide him with a way of reconciling his convictions regarding the water question with his loyalty to his old friend Watt. He now adopted a quite different model of discovery, that of 'synonymity and priority', in his embrace of 'outsider' politics and the campaign against 'judicial enclaves' in British science, past and present.

Conclusion

The Gentlemen of Science who rallied around Harcourt and the cause of Cavendish exercised enormous power in various ways within the British scientific community. One way was in setting the scientific research agenda. This was done directly, as we have seen, through control of funds awarded by the British Association for research projects, and more indirectly by the creation of ideas about exemplary work. We will see in Chapter 9 how the figure of Cavendish became important to these people in the sense of providing an exemplar of scientific research and in developing an ideology of the relationship between abstract research and industrial change. The Gentlemen of Science also played a prominent part in public science through their contributions to the reviews and their role in scientific publishing generally. We have already seen a further instance of this in the way that the Gentlemen of Science and their friends shaped the reputation of Arago.

The battles in the reviews, and in particular the multi-strung tension between Whewell and the other Cambridge men, on the one hand, and Brewster on the other, indicate how the water controversy was conducted amidst an ideological maelstrom. Brewster's dramatic conversion to the Watt camp and the way that he managed it (and effectively explained it) confirms this. We have noted that Brewster's conversion was accompanied by liberal use of legal language in discussion of the discovery question. He was adopting, at least in part, the approach taken by three fellow Scots who were, both literally and figuratively, the advocates of Watt.

---

117 Ibid., p. 508. Though he does not name them, Brewster is apparently referring to the Royal Society dissensions of the 1780s here.

118 John Christie has diagnosed Brewster's tendency in all his historical writing to make very explicit links with his own obsessions. Writing about Brewster's *Memoirs of Sir Isaac Newton*, Christie notes that Brewster 'impose[s] upon the chronological narrative a dynamic oscillating structure, the reader being switched back and forth between past and present ... A kind of egotistic teleology governs the movement of this pendulum: frequently, Newtonian history culminated in contemporary Brewsterian action.' See J.R.R. Christie, 'Sir David Brewster as an historian of science', in Morrison-Low and Christie (eds), *'Martyr of Science': Sir David Brewster 1781–1868*, p. 55.

Chapter 8

The Advocates of Watt: Brougham, Jeffrey and Muirhead

The water controversy at various times assumed the nature of a legal contest, with cases being made for the prosecution and the defence of the claimed priority of Watt. This might simply have been so because Watt's camp included a number of men whose professional training was in the law. However, the matter went beyond that. A particular understanding of the nature of discovery, what we have called the synonymity and priority model, lends itself to a legal approach in that its adherents assume the identity of the discoveries and contest priority purely on the grounds of circumstance. The cognate issue of patents of invention was very much to the fore in the period that concerns us, and this approach to discovery involved the perception of numerous and important analogies between discovery 'rights' and patent rights. Brougham and Muirhead gave considerable attention to the patent issue. Although I group these characters, together with Jeffrey, as advocates of Watt, and find similarities in many of their conceptions and argumentative strategies, they are also clearly individuals with differing reasons for involvement in the water controversy and in debates about Watt's reputation more generally. I will deal with each of them in turn.

Brougham

In the autumn of 1834, as Arago was making plans to travel to Edinburgh, and the British Association 'managers' were putting the final touches to arrangements for the meeting in that city, the government in which Henry, Lord Brougham had served was in disarray. Brougham was at a turning point. Since 1830, as Lord Chancellor in Earl Grey's government, he had played a crucial role in the passage of the Reform Act of 1832 and made significant strides in his law reform programme. Now Grey had resigned and the press, which Brougham had used so expertly for so long, had turned against him. Brougham was criticized for his self-obsessed ramblings during his speech at the Edinburgh dinner in honour of Earl Grey (also attended by Arago) after the British Association meeting and for the 'promotional' tour of Scotland that he took before and after it.[1]

In the wake of all this controversy Brougham retreated to Paris at the end of the year and was present at the meeting of the Institut on 8 December 1834 at which

---

[1] Robert Stewart, *Henry Brougham 1778–1868. His Public Career*, 1985, pp. 316–19; Ronald K. Huch, *Henry, Lord Brougham. The Later Years 1830–1868. The 'Great Actor'*, 1993, pp. 116–31; Morrell and Thackray, *Gentlemen of Science: Early Years*, p. 137.

Arago delivered his *éloge* of Watt. Even as his whole political future lay in the balance, Brougham could find time for this. Breakfasting with Arago and Pentland the next morning, Brougham remarked on the peculiar failure of Great Britain to honour Watt in his lifetime. The former Lord Chancellor vowed that if he were to return to that office, as he expected to do, it would probably involve a creation of peers and he intended to ensure that those creations did not neglect the descendants of both Watt and Arkwright.[2]

Brougham was always a compulsive writer as well as speaker. Sidney Smith cruelly but wittily referred to Brougham's literary productions as always long, 'like the penis of a jackass'. Even at the height of parliamentary business and chancery proceedings Brougham had contrived to maintain broader literary output. Sometimes, reputedly, when 'hearing' cases in chancery he was hard at work on essays for the *Edinburgh Review*, indifferent to the strenuous pleadings of the lawyers appearing before him. With his new-found freedom after the fall of the Grey administration he launched into a number of projects, among them his investigations into the 'water question' and the biographical inquiries that emerged later in his *Lives of Men of Letters and Science*.

By the 1830s Brougham could not be counted as more than an observer of the scientific scene although, characteristically, this did not hinder authoritative pronouncements. In his youth he had, no doubt, a remarkable command of the science of his time. Even as a student in Edinburgh he debated expertly with the professors of the university. In the late 1790s, his optical researches were published in the *Philosophical Transactions* of the Royal Society of London and he was the leading figure in the Academy of Physics in Edinburgh, a student society at the university that enjoyed a brief but stellar existence from 1797 to 1800. The pattern and tenor of their activities spoke of an 'inductivist egalitarian view of science'.[3] They were critical of the Tory-dominated Royal Society of Edinburgh and saw their Academy as an antidote to the senior body. A number of the Academy members, including Brougham and Francis Jeffrey, went on to be involved with the *Edinburgh Review*, which took a similar oppositional stance.

Brougham's output via the *Edinburgh Review* always contained a strong measure of commentary on scientific subjects, as did the *Review* itself in the early years. Indeed, Brougham's first public statement on the issues involved in the water controversy was made in an article for the *Edinburgh* in 1803. This was a review of the *Lectures* of Joseph Black that had just been published under the editorship of John Robison. As we have seen, this was a key document, albeit one requiring careful interpretation, in the historiography of the 'Scottish School' of chemistry in the late eighteenth century. What did Brougham make of the *Lectures*?

There are two major points to notice about Brougham's contribution at this stage. First he delineated a method discourse that he attributed to Black, to Black's pupil, colleague and editor, Robison, and that he, Brougham, also endorsed.[4] Second, he

---

2 J.B. Pentland to James Watt Jr, 12 December 1834, Watt Papers (Doldowlod), W/10.

3 G.N. Cantor, 'The Academy of Physics at Edinburgh 1797–1800', *Social Studies of Science* **5**, 1975, 133.

4 Cantor placed Brougham within a 'Scottish methodological tradition' strongly rejecting hypotheses involving unobservable entities (such as the ether) and explained Brougham's early tussles with

8.1   Henry, Lord Brougham

made some remarks about the significance of Black's discovery of latent heat and contrasted the mode of that discovery with the most common mode, one that applied, for instance, to the discovery of the composition of water.

The method discourse that Brougham endorsed might be characterized as 'cautious induction'. Black's own experimental work was treated as an example, and Brougham emphasized that Black was very cautious about theory and the erection of system. Black's teaching was also designed to be accessible and his points derived from clear, common, observable facts wherever possible so as to cater to his students. Black was quoted on the way in which he progressively integrated the work of Lavoisier into his lectures, refusing, on methodological and pedagogical grounds, to present Lavoisier's ideas as a system. Instead he interpolated particular facts and discoveries into his old lectures. Black made a virtue of the older material in the lectures:

> It will make the students acquainted with the chemistry of former years, which is far from being unworthy of the attention of a philosopher. Newton, Stahl, Margraaf, Cramer, Scheele, Bergmann, were geniuses not below the common level. But the person who learns chemistry by Lavoisier's scheme, may remain ignorant of all that was done by former chemists, and unable to read their excellent writings.[5]

Brougham himself endorsed this idea. He believed that the love of system had gone too far in France, in chemistry as in other areas, in seeking to obliterate the past. As he put it:

> The dogmatical spirit, indeed, with which the new nomenclature, and, in general, the new system, was promulgated, had a tendency to obliterate much very valuable information, contained in the writings of the elder chemists: and we conceive, that the present publication, if it serves no other end, would be highly important as a collection of things not to be met with in the works of the new school.[6]

However, sweeping away previous ideas was not just dangerous pedagogically and historically; it was also a threat to chemical progress. For, Brougham claimed, there was great danger in assuming that the new system could adequately account for all the facts. He praised Robison's notes to the *Lectures* for revealing where love of system has overcome careful induction from the facts. Brougham warned his readers against 'that implicit confidence in the universal truth of the antiphlogistic theory, which is derived from an unphilosophical carelessness about the facts, and a predetermination to learn the system synthetically'.[7]

Thomas Young over the wave versus corpuscular theories of light in terms of methodological differences. See G.N. Cantor, 'Henry Brougham and the Scottish methodological tradition', *Studies in the History and Philosophy of Science* **2**, 1971, 69–89.

5 Joseph Black, *Lectures*, vol. 1, p. 549. The words are given by Robison as a direct quotation from a conversation with Black.

6 Brougham, 'Lectures on the elements of chemistry', *Edinburgh Review*, **2**, 1803, 22.

7 Ibid., 24. It should be noted that Robison puts these precise sentiments into Watt's mouth also during the discussions leading up to his editorship of the *Lectures*. See John Robison to George Black, 18 October 1800, Edinburgh University Library, Special Collections, Gen 874, VI, 11–12: 'Mr Watt

As a specific example, Brougham noted that Lavoisier's system did not cope inductively with light and heat: 'Lavoisier and his followers maintain, that the light and heat extricated during the combustion of inflammable bodies, come entirely from the oxygenous gas.' In maintaining this, Brougham claimed, they overlooked numerous chemical phenomena that seemed inconsistent with that idea.[8] Brougham was here pointing to a set of phenomena in the emission of heat and light in chemical processes that he believed the older chemists had treated differently and that Lavoisier and his followers had not adequately accounted for.

At this early date of 1803, then, we can see that the methodological stance taken by Brougham, consciously within the tradition of Black and Robison, gave only a limited welcome to the new system of chemistry. Brougham cautioned that much of value was in danger of being overlooked in the spirit of system. This left the door open for people to appreciate earlier ideas, including those about the composition of water, in their original integrity.

When he discussed the composition of water specifically, however, Brougham's approach was not that of an ardent advocate of Watt's priority claim. This is perhaps not surprising since Watt himself was scarcely making a fuss about the issue at that time. Brougham discussed the composition of water as an example to illustrate a more general point about discovery, that in most cases discoveries are the result of extensive work by a wide range of people. In the case of the composition of water, the doctrine was arrived at by 'many insensible gradations' from numerous contributed facts:

> some ingenious men, particularly Mr. Watt, reasoning from all these facts, concluded that this fluid is a compound of the two airs, deprived, by their union, of a considerable portion of their latent heat, the quantity (viz.) which is necessary for maintaining the elastic aeriform state. This idea was verified by the accurate experiment of Mr. Cavendish, in which the quantity of water formed was compared with the quantities of air burnt; and the French chemists added new proofs of the proposition by the analytical process. This chain of investigation is evidently so long, and of such slow formation, that we cannot, with any degree of correctness, appreciate the comparative merits of those who severally extended it; nor point out the particular link upon which the grand discovery hangs. And the same distribution of praise is strictly proper in almost all the other instances of successful physical research.[9]

---

has given me another Notion of the subject [Black's lectures] from what I had allowed myself gradually to form. He considers it as a <u>History of Chemistry</u> for forty years, by one of its greatest Masters. Dr Black never attempted to give a <u>System</u> of Chemistry. He was unfriendly to all systems of an experimental Science ... Dr Black pretended no such thing – but to make his hearers good Chemists – not able to talk about theories, but able to examine the Chemical properties of bodies, and to apply their knowledge ... The philosophers, who want only refinements and new discoveries, will perhaps be disappointed – the System mongers will throw the book aside. But the public will be instructed ... Such is the view that Mr Watt entertains of the Work ... '. If this was indeed Watt's view, it reinforces the idea that after the first phase of the water controversy Watt retreated to the empirical world of chemical improvement. Perhaps there was a sense in which he had been there all along. To say so, however, would be to take sides!

[8] Brougham, 'Lectures on the elements of chemistry', 24–25.

[9] Ibid., 11–12. It should be noted that here Brougham gives the discovery as Watt conceived it and has Cavendish confirming it. Brougham thus rendered the doctrine of the composition of water

A point of contrast with this usual feature of discovery was, Brougham contended, Black's discovery of latent heat. Brougham claimed that in the case of latent heat, and of universal gravitation, the discoveries 'followed this *law of continuity*, in so slight a degree, that they may almost be allowed to form a case of exceptions to its operation'.[10] Black was thus put in Newton's company as not only a cautious but also a consummate inductive philosopher.

Brougham's earliest mention of the water question was thus non-committal as to priority, although it did give a prominent place to Watt. His discussion of Black in relation to the New Chemistry is, however, important in the light that it throws on the programmatic development of the science of chemistry at this time. Brougham was clearly prepared to see virtue in ideas and contributions that preceded, and in some ways lay outside, the new system of chemistry. We do not encounter Brougham engaged again with the water question, or with Watt's reputation more generally, until the 1820s. By this stage Brougham was functioning more conventionally as an advocate of Watt. He conducted his case less on matters of chemical substance, as it were, or methodological propriety, than on matters of literary circumstance and documentary evidence concerning it.

In the 1820s Brougham deployed Watt as a symbol in promoting the education of working men through the Mechanics' Institute movement. For example, in April 1825, on his installation as Lord Rector of the University of Glasgow, Brougham invoked the career of the great engineer. In doing so he perpetuated the notion of Watt as the pupil of Black in a way that would not have pleased Watt Jr but which made the connection between scientific education and the lower classes that Brougham sought. Noting that he spoke in an institution devoted to 'but a select portion of the community', Brougham nevertheless observed that

> from this classic ground have gone forth those whose genius, not their ancestry, enabled them; whose incredible merits have opened to all ranks the temple of science. I speak in that city where Black having once taught, and Watt learned, the grand experiment was afterwards made in one day, and with entire success, to demonstrate that the highest intellectual cultivation is perfectly compatible with the daily cares and toils of working men ...

Brougham contended that the more widely knowledge was spread, the 'more Watts and Franklins will be enrolled among the lights of the world, in proportion as more thousands of the working classes, to which Franklin and Watt belonged, have their thoughts turned towards philosophy'.[11]

Watt was invoked in other contexts too. Brougham was a central figure in patent reform, seeking to improve the lot of the patentee. The patent law was discussed in his famous law reform speech of 1828, much to the delight of his old friend David

---

differently from the way it was rendered in the Lavoisian system and effectively denied that the discovery of the composition of water had to be part and parcel of Lavoisier's New Chemistry.

[10] Ibid., 12.

[11] Henry Brougham, 'Inaugural discourse on being installed Lord Rector of the University of Glasgow, 6 April 1825', in *Speeches of Henry Brougham*, 4 vols, 1838, vol. 3, pp. 95–96. For further examples of the invocation of Watt, see Brougham's speeches to the Liverpool Mechanics' Institute and the Manchester Mechanics' Institution in July 1835, in *Speeches*, vol. 3, pp. 165–66 and 579–80.

Brewster, who was also agitating the issue.[12] Various Bills had been before Parliament in the 1820s and early 1830s without issue.[13] The failure of the 1833 Bill saw Brougham become more directly involved, and he subsequently introduced his own. Brougham's Bill was less ambitious than its predecessors. Its main provision was to employ the Judicial Committee of the Privy Council to decide on applications for the extension of patents. Such extensions previously required an Act of Parliament and that was an expensive process. Brougham also saw the Judicial Committee as dealing with disputes over priority of invention. In addition the Bill allowed changes to be made to specifications by disclaimer. It passed by a very narrow majority and was given Royal Assent on 10 September 1835. Some patent law reformers felt that the Bill did not go far enough. In particular, it did not deal with the cost of patents. Others believed, with Brougham, in the necessity of gradual reform, and welcomed the measure. It was after all the first successful piece of legislation on patents since the Statute of Monopolies. Brougham was also heavily involved in the Patent Law Amendment Act, which became law on 1 July 1852. This granted many of the provisions wished for by the invention interest, such as cheaper patents, a single patent for England, Scotland and Ireland, as well as changes designed to reduce the cost of litigation.

What interests us at this point is that Brougham, and others, used the example of James Watt's experience with patents to argue their point. The Select Committee of the House of Commons which sat in 1834 taking evidence on Brougham's Bill was shown, according to Brougham, that if Watt's statutory term in the patent had applied, he would have lost financially and that even when the patent was extended by Act of Parliament he spent many years out of pocket. The members of the Committee were advised that Watt would probably have fared better financially had he not taken out a patent in the first place.

> The Act which I introduced in 1835, grounded mainly upon that evidence [that is, the evidence relating to Watt], has removed some of the greatest defects in the law, and it has enabled, when coupled with the subsequent Act of last Session [an 1844 amendment], an inventor to obtain, at a very inconsiderable cost, his extension for any additional period, not exceeding the duration of the original patent.[14]

Brougham left no doubt that Watt was a scientific inventor who had deserved better protection from pirates and from mischievous assaults on patent specifications. Brougham took great interest in the process of patent specification. In 1828 he had personally drawn up the specification for J.B. Neilson's patent on the hot-blast technique. Neilson's case was regarded as having many parallels with that of Watt. We will see that J.P. Muirhead was also interested in the Neilson case, and inclined to see those same parallels.

---

[12] Michael Lobban, 'Henry Brougham and law reform', *The English Historical Review*, **115**, 2000, 1184–215; Brewster to Brougham, 10 March 1828, Brougham Papers, University College London, 26,606; David Brewster, 'Decline of Science in England', *Quarterly Review*, **43**, 1830, 305–42.

[13] The following relies on H.I. Dutton, *The Patent System and Inventive Activity during the Industrial Revolution, 1750–1852*, 1984, pp. 42–51, 57–65.

[14] Henry, Lord Brougham, *Lives of Men of Letters and Science, who Flourished in the Time of George III*, 1845, pp. 378–79.

Both Brougham and Muirhead defended rights to invention and scientific discovery rights in the same kind of way. To them there was no material difference. First of all there was no moral concern, as there was in other quarters, about the contamination of scientific activity by commercial gain. The likes of Brougham and Muirhead could see no reason whatever why those who had sought and made commercial gain should not also partake of scientific fame.[15] Priority was to be defended in similar ways against those who would seek to exploit, on the one hand, gaps in the specification of a patented invention or, on the other, niceties of philosophical difference relating to discovery. For the Watt camp, the sly circumvention of a patent specification was of the same order as piracy of discovery by the fine metaphysical distinctions indulged in by the likes of Harcourt and Whewell as they sought to elevate Cavendish's conclusions above Watt's theory of the composition of water.

Brougham's direct involvement in the water controversy now needs to be outlined. We have seen that he had considered the water question as far back as 1803. He had been supplied with details concerning it by Watt Jr during the course of writing inscriptions for the Watt monuments. However, Brougham appears to have turned to the question seriously only after attending the delivery of Arago's *éloge* to the Institute in early December 1834. Brougham inserted a footnote concerning Watt's priority in his *Discourse of Natural Theology*, published in the following year, where he stated:

> Dr. Priestley drew no conclusion of the least value from his experiments [on the explosion of inflammable air]. But Mr. Watt, after thoroughly weighing them, by careful comparison with other facts, arrived at the opinion that they proved the composition of water. This may justly be said to have been the discovery of that great truth in chemical science. I have examined the evidence, and am convinced that he was the first discoverer, in point of time, although it is very possible that Mr. Cavendish may have arrived at the same truth from his own experiments, without any knowledge of Mr. Watt's earlier process of reasoning.[16]

From the mid-1830s, Brougham made a number of investigations into the water controversy. He located original papers in the Royal Society archives, discovering interpolations in Blagden's hand in Cavendish's original manuscript of his paper 'Experiments on Air'. These interpolations were significant, he believed, in resolving circumstantial questions about who knew what when, and, in particular, in revealing an effort by Blagden (and presumably Cavendish) to disguise the fact that Cavendish had reached no conclusions until he heard about Watt's theory. Brougham also gained access to the Cavendish manuscripts themselves, and Watt Jr had these inspected by W.T. Brande and Charles Hatchett. The chemists reported that they could find no evidence of clear conclusions in Cavendish's papers. Brougham finished work on a 'Historical Note' on the water question and it was agreed that it

---

15 For debates on this issue see Iwan Rhys Morus, *Frankenstein's Children. Electricity, Exhibition and Experiment in Early-Nineteenth-Century London*, 1998, especially ch. 6.

16 Henry Brougham, *A Discourse of Natural Theology*, second edn, 1835, pp. 169–70. This note appeared as part of a discussion of induction in which Brougham used the analysis and synthesis of water as an example.

would be appended to Arago's *Eloge*. Watt Jr inspected the document and added a couple of footnotes that were printed in the final version. It was seen also by Muirhead.

Brougham's argument in the 'Historical Note' conformed substantially to the 'synonymity and priority' model of discovery. He assumed that the conclusions announced by Cavendish in his 1784 paper and Watt's theory were 'identical, with the single difference that Mr. Cavendish calls dephlogisticated air, water deprived of its phlogiston, and Mr. Watt says that water is composed of dephlogisticated air and phlogiston'.[17] The Note then relied upon the statement of a number of circumstantial facts leading to the conclusion that Watt had first put the conclusion in writing, that he did so without any conclusion being communicated from Cavendish, and that it was uncertain when Cavendish drew his conclusions. An interesting argument made by Brougham relied on an examination of Cavendish's publication practices. He claimed to show that Cavendish habitually published his experimental results and conclusions in the *Philosophical Transactions* quite soon after their prosecution. On the strength of this, Brougham suggested that Cavendish had no conclusions from his 1781 experiments at the time, otherwise he would have communicated them well before 1784.[18]

As of late 1839, when Arago's *Eloge* appeared (in French and in translation) with Brougham's 'Note' appended, Brougham had provided the most detailed and circumstantial case for Watt's priority. Although his later writings were to generate a good deal of reaction, they did not add substantially to his case. The account of Watt published in the *Lives* in 1845 reprinted the 'Historical Note'. The main text devoted less than three pages to the water question. It is notable for two things. The first was Brougham's denial that he had ever intended to insinuate 'a suspicion of Mr. Cavendish's having borrowed from Mr. Watt'.[19] The second notable comment addressed the unequal experimental activity of Watt and Cavendish:

> It must on no account be supposed that Watt cannot be considered as having discovered the composition of water, merely because he made no new experiments of particular moment, like Cavendish, to ascertain that capital point. No one refuses to Newton the discovery of gravitation ... and yet he made not one of those observations upon which his theory rests ... In like manner, Lavoisier, who discovered no gas, and made no original experiments of the least value in pneumatic chemistry, is universally admitted to have discovered the true theory of combustion and calcination, by reasoning on the facts which others had ascertained. Watt's happy inference from the facts discovered by Warltire and Priestley was just as much entitled, and for the same reasons, to be regarded as the discovery of the composition of water.[20]

---

[17] Henry Brougham, 'Historical Note', as reprinted in *Lives*, at p. 396. Brougham also portrayed *both* Watt and Cavendish as in the thrall of phlogiston theory. Two footnotes from Watt Jr extended the latitude given to identity by claiming that Watt's 1783 theory was essentially the same as even his earlier idea about water being convertible into air.

[18] Ibid., pp. 398–99. It was not claimed that Cavendish always published his work but rather that, when he did publish, he did so quite soon after performance of the investigation.

[19] Brougham, *Lives of Men of Letters and Science*, p. 381.

[20] Ibid., pp. 381–82.

This was, of course, a response to the arguments put forward by Harcourt, but also by Brewster, that Cavendish's experimental work gave him a claim of a type different in kind to that of Watt.[21] We will examine in Chapter 10 the detailed involvement of Brougham in the controversy during the mid-1840s.

For the moment we can say that Brougham was a powerful and important advocate of Watt. His involvement with the patent issue squared with a tendency to treat the water question as an analogous case to be argued on circumstantial evidence rather than on the minutiae of the specification. However, Brougham regarded himself as enough of a natural philosopher to be able to argue on chemical grounds also. When he did this he abandoned the preferred terms of engagement of Watt Jr and Muirhead. They believed that to enter the chemical arena was to concede too much to the chemical experts, like George Wilson, and the élite arbiters of science, like Whewell. Brougham's position was also complicated by his political relations with the Cavendish family and by his involvement with David Brewster in putting the case for a corpuscular theory of light against the dominant view supported by the leadership of the British Association and the Royal Society. In so far as it was possible for the Cavendish supporters to hold Brougham's scientific pretensions up to ridicule, Watt Jr's and Muirhead's decision about the grounds on which to fight their case was perhaps justified. Although they valued Brougham's support, they were also upset on more than one occasion by his cavalier approach to 'the facts'.

Muirhead

James Patrick Muirhead (1813–98) was born in Hamilton, Lanarkshire, the son of Lockhart Muirhead LLD, Regius Professor of Natural History at Glasgow University. Muirhead's mother was Anne Campbell and his maternal grandmother was a first cousin to James Watt. Muirhead was educated at Glasgow College and at Balliol College, Oxford. He was admitted advocate in Edinburgh in 1838 and spent eight years practising law there. He appears to have done work as a patent lawyer. In 1844 he married Katharine Elizabeth Boulton, second daughter of Matthew Robinson Boulton. Muirhead was thus doubly related to the Boulton & Watt concern.

Muirhead abandoned the law in 1846 and settled at Haseley Court in Oxfordshire in 1847. He had got to know James Watt Jr in the mid-1830s when he visited Aston Hall in the vacations during his studies at Oxford. Even at this stage Muirhead, who worked in the library at Aston Hall, seems to have fallen naturally into the role of a literary *aide-de-camp* to Watt Jr.[22] Watt Jr's plans of writing a memoir of his father

---

[21] It should be noted that the artful linking of experimental results and conclusions of the kind that Harcourt and Brewster referred to might be judged differently than Brougham does. It could be claimed, for example, that although Lavoisier's experiments were rarely entirely novel, his *linking* of experiment and theory was. It might also be argued that the tradition of physical astronomy within which Newton worked had long since institutionalized a division of labour between observers and theorists. I make these points simply to indicate the interpretative flexibility available in such an argument.

[22] Muirhead to Watt Jr, 11 November 1834, 27 January 1835, Muirhead Papers, MS GEN 1354/265, 269.

were eventually transferred to Muirhead and this became his primary occupation for many years. Muirhead, too, participated at one remove in the filial spirit. When he was called to the bar Muirhead produced, as required, a Latin dissertation. He dedicated this to Watt Jr for his 'many kindnesses'. The dedication read: 'viri clarissimi filio claro', which Muirhead hoped that Watt Jr would like, because he knew well 'your feelings of veneration and love for your father's memory, and that it has always been deemed by you as a principal object of your life to preserve his fame in undiminished brightness ... '.[23] In his capacity as chief historian to the filial project Muirhead produced first, in 1839, his translation of Arago's *Eloge* with original notes and appendix, then, successively, *The Correspondence of the late James Watt on his Discovery of the Theory of the Composition of Water* (1846), *The Origin and Progress of the Mechanical Inventions of James Watt* in three volumes (1854) and finally, *The Life of James Watt* (1858).

Muirhead's first major literary project with Watt Jr was his translation of Arago's *Eloge* of Watt. This came about in a rather odd way. Arago and Watt Jr had both agreed that Robert Jameson should publish a translation of the *Eloge* in the *Edinburgh New Philosophical Journal*, which Jameson edited. It appears that the initial plan was for Muirhead to help with the translation of the *Eloge* for Jameson's *Journal*. Rather quickly, however, Muirhead's translation became an independent venture. He expressed his aims as different from Professor Jameson's, given the rather limited readership of the *Journal*:

> first to gratify many individuals in the upper classes, who perhaps never see the Philosophical Journal; and secondly, to put the Memoir into the hands of the hundreds – I should rather say thousands, of intelligent mechanics, to whom it would be certainly very interesting and most probably very useful.[24]

In fact this bid for a more popular work directed not to experts but to the interested reader across the social scale, though consonant with the Watt camp's cause, was probably precipitated by a mix-up. Whilst Watt and Muirhead had understood that Jameson had agreed to Muirhead helping with the translation, Jameson himself professed no knowledge of the arrangement. He only learned of it, he claimed, when he had already received a full translation from another translator to whom he was now committed. Apart from undertaking the translation, Muirhead had added an extensive series of notes in elucidation of various points. Jameson saw the value of these and offered to add them to the other translation. Muirhead, however, resolved to publish separately as a distinct pamphlet. When Muirhead's project was well advanced, he was dismayed to learn that Jameson too was intent on publishing his translation of the *Eloge* as a separate pamphlet and not just in his *Journal*. Muirhead saw an advertisement for this work on 21 September 1839 and immediately went to see Jameson about it. Jameson and the publisher (Black) denied any knowledge of the venture while blaming each other! Muirhead was chastened and disillusioned about the motivations at work in the

---

[23] Muirhead to Watt Jr, 12 June 1838, Muirhead Papers, MS GEN 1354/280.

[24] Muirhead to Watt Jr, 31 July 1839, Muirhead Papers, MS GEN 1354/290. Muirhead also noted that his two audiences might require two forms of publication – a 'handsome 4to' and a 'practical 8vo'.

world of philosophical publishing.[25] Muirhead's translation duly appeared and was widely circulated by the translator and Watt Jr. In this way it became, as we have seen, one of the key documents in the water controversy.

Muirhead's next major project was the *Correspondence* on the water question itself. This had always been seen by Watt Jr and by Muirhead as the definitive answer to doubters and to the claims of Harcourt and his supporters. The evidence for Watt's priority lay in the sequence of letters between him and Priestley, De Luc and others that was eventually to be reproduced in the *Correspondence*. Watt Jr, though, was not over-eager to publish it. As we have seen, over the years he had shown it privately to many individuals and used it quite effectively as a behind-the-scenes lever of opinion. By the mid-1840s Watt Jr professed himself ready to release this major documentary source upon the world. He was exasperated by the persistent contrariness of Harcourt and his allies in the face of what Watt Jr took to be self-evident truths. His policy had been to let out only a little information at a time, but now he decided that the correspondence should become public to settle the matter once and for all. Unfortunately, by this stage Watt Jr's health was not good. His eyesight in particular was very poor. So he decided to entrust his faithful assistant Muirhead with the task of editing the correspondence. Watt Jr himself would supply a prefatory letter but Muirhead edited the correspondence and provided a substantial introduction to the work. That introduction became one of the most significant, and carefully crafted, statements of the case for Watt's priority.

How, then, did the editor Muirhead argue the case for Watt's claim to the discovery? To what extent did he engage with the arguments that Harcourt had tried to develop? To what extent did he retain a simple, empirical account of discovery strengthened by the 'revelatory' impact of the correspondence being introduced into the public domain?

Muirhead began by marshalling testimony to Watt's powers as a natural philosopher and, especially, as a chemist. Though self-taught, his natural powers gave him insight: 'How intently he watched the phenomena, how deeply he penetrated into the causes of chemical action … '.[26] Muirhead performed a delicate balancing act with regard to the chemical company that Watt should keep. Although anxious, in line with Watt Jr's sentiments, to show Watt as self-taught and not, at least formally, a student of Joseph Black, Muirhead nevertheless sought to assimilate Watt to Black rather than Priestley. According to Muirhead, Black was 'calm and reflective', conducting his experiments in a simple fashion. He was neat and accurate, and proceeded 'with all the force of exact demonstration'. Priestley, by contrast, was thrown to the wolves: though zealous and capable of great perseverance, Priestley was disordered and had 'an imperfect acquaintance with the true first

---

25 Jameson had a long history of sharp dealing, including a feud with David Brewster in the early years of the *Edinburgh Philosophical Journal*. See W.H. Brock, 'Brewster as a scientific journalist', in A.D. Morrison-Low and J.R.R. Christie (eds), *'Martyr of Science': Sir David Brewster 1781–1868*, 1984, pp. 38–39. In 1826 Jameson became sole editor, for Constable, of what was then styled *The Edinburgh New Philosophical Journal*. Brewster promptly founded, with Blackwood, a new *Edinburgh Philosophical Journal* that survived until 1832 and was the main vehicle for his 'declinist' writings.

26 J.P. Muirhead, 'Introductory Remarks', in Muirhead (ed.), *The Correspondence of the late James Watt on his Discovery of the Theory of the Composition of Water*, 1846, p. xx.

principles of science'. He proliferated experiments but had little sense of how to interpret them. Muirhead quoted Priestley's analogy between experimental philosophy and the beating of the ground during hunting as evidence of the crudity of Priestley's conceptions.[27]

Having consigned Priestley to the sphere of vagueness into which Harcourt and Peacock had sought to pitch Watt also, Muirhead now conjoined Watt and Black as the true Baconians:

> [W]e may perhaps question the propriety of applying language which conveys the idea of something vague and even fortuitous, to that system which Bacon first illustriously taught, and which Black and Watt so worthily exemplified; by which the present age has been guided to very many of the more remote and occult parts of nature, with the same certainty and safety, with which the compass has directed the course of navigation to the discovery of new regions of the globe.[28]

Thus for Muirhead, as for the other chief participants in the controversy, the alignment of their candidate discoverer with methodological propriety was of signal importance. As Brougham had done, Muirhead located methodological propriety in the likes of Joseph Black and his supposed method, one that was taken to involve cautious inductive procedure in the manner of Newton. Proceeding 'scientifically' was seen by both sides of the controversy as a crucial characteristic in a discoverer. Where they disagreed, of course, was in what it meant to so proceed.

The next step in arguing Watt's case was to frame the questions with which the discovery was concerned. Muirhead, as we saw in Chapter 2, rendered them thus:

> [W]ho first explained the real cause of the formation of the water, by drawing and stating the conclusion that water is composed of two gases, which unite in the process of their combustion, or explosion ... Who was in point of fact the first to make public that theory, after having formed it altogether independently of the idea of others[?][29]

We noted in our discussion of the nature of discovery that framing the question in this way involved a number of presumptions about the criteria for 'discovery'. First, the conclusion that is to count as a discovery *must not only be drawn first, but it must be stated first*, by which is meant the making public of the conclusion. On this criterion, even if Cavendish had drawn the conclusion at the time of his 1781 experiments and even if he had stated the conclusion in his laboratory notes at the time, he would not qualify as the discoverer. Muirhead was framing the question in a way that played to his strong suit — whatever else might be said, Watt seemed to have pretty clear priority in drawing a conclusion *and* communicating it to others in writing.[30]

---

[27] Ibid., p. xxvi.

[28] Ibid. On the varieties and uses of 'Baconianism' see Richard Yeo, 'An idol of the marketplace: Baconianism in nineteenth-century Britain, 1830–1917', *History of Science*, **23**, 1985, 251–98.

[29] Muirhead (ed.), *Correspondence*, p. xxxiv.

[30] This of course can be and was complicated by various factors. Thus it can be asked whether communication in a private letter counts; whether communication to the Royal Society counts or whether the communication being read at a meeting or being published in the *Philosophical Transactions*

Second, the conclusion itself should refer to the uniting of 'two gases' on their combustion to form water. The phrase 'two gases' is significant. Muirhead was playing down the issue of what those gases were.[31] Reference to the *production* of water in the experiments was not, on this framing, enough to qualify someone as a discoverer. Those who had previously observed a dewy deposit (for example, Priestley and Warltire) had assumed it to be a deposit of water previously present in the airs rather than created by their combustion. On the other hand, this phrase hedges the question of the identity of the two gases, a significant point given that one of the grounds of those arguing for Cavendish was that Watt was mistaken about what the gases were. The phrase also uses the terms 'combustion' and 'explosion' unproblematically, thereby sidelining the issue of the precise role of heat in the process. This, as we have seen, could be made into a major issue of difference between Cavendish's and Watt's conception of the composition of water. Muirhead resisted such a move and all was reduced to matters of circumstantial evidence.

Muirhead, following Brougham, found that Cavendish's journal, as published in facsimile by Harcourt, had nothing to say about the origin of the water in his experiments. The whole contained nothing 'inconsistent with the notion ... of a mere mechanical deposit of the water'.[32] Cavendish's writings and communications, Muirhead argued, did not provide conclusions from the experiments until the published paper of July 1784. That paper contained the following passage: 'during the last summer [1783] also, a friend of mine gave some account of them [the experiments] to M. Lavoisier, as well as of the conclusion drawn from them, that dephlogisticated air is only water deprived of phlogiston'.[33] This passage, as Muirhead delightedly reported, was not contained in Cavendish's paper as read to the Royal Society on 15 January 1784 but was added later, before publication, by Blagden. Muirhead concluded:

> There is thus no statement put on record by Mr Cavendish, so far as we have yet gone, of his conclusions having been either drawn by himself, or made known to a single human being, previous to the summer of 1783; while the only intimation to be derived from the printed papers in the Philosophical Transactions, of his having drawn his conclusions at even so early a period, is contained in the ... passage, which was written by Blagden, interpolated after the paper had been read in January 1784, and then adopted by Cavendish.[34]

The lack of plausibility of Cavendish having drawn conclusions was confirmed, in Muirhead's view, by the fact that his paper's title, 'Experiments on Air', made no

---

is the real point at which the 'making public' occurs. The difficulties here are precisely those involved in deciding whether Merton's norm of communalism has been adhered to. In the end this is a matter for interpretation and negotiation. However a rule or norm is stated, a variety of actions can be made out to be in accordance with it. See Michael Mulkay, 'Interpretation and the use of rules', *Transactions of the New York Academy of Sciences, Series 2,* **9**, 1980, 111–25.

[31] Compare especially the approach of George Wilson discussed below.

[32] Muirhead (ed.), *Correspondence*, p. xxxvi.

[33] Cavendish, as quoted in ibid., p. xxxvii.

[34] Ibid., pp. xxxviii–xxxix.

mention of the key discovery that it supposedly reported. This contrasted with Watt's paper, which stated directly that it contained 'Thoughts on the Constituent Parts of Water, and of Dephlogisticated Air'.

The next phase of Muirhead's argument was devoted to showing that Cavendish, Blagden and Lavoisier were involved in purloining Watt's theory and trying to present it as their own. Then Muirhead hoed into Harcourt, regaling the reader with the latter's mistakes and inconsistencies. A similar demolition of George Peacock followed. Muirhead observed at one point (concerning the views of Dr Henry and the use made of them by Harcourt) that 'the question has become one of evidence much more than chemistry'.[35]

This last observation was true of Muirhead's whole argument. For him, at least publicly, there was no complexity involved in the chemical issues. The nature of the discovery itself was treated as very straightforward. The complexities lay in issues such as who knew what when, acts of commission and omission in communication, and consistency, or otherwise, of statement. Muirhead was impatient with those who indulged in nice distinctions. Harcourt was castigated for worrying unnecessarily and unproductively about what Watt understood by the term 'phlogiston'. Brewster was considered to be drawing distinctions too fine to worry about when he maintained that the priority of the *hypothesis* concerning the composition of water lay with Watt but the discovery of the *theory* of the composition of water lay with Cavendish.[36]

Muirhead, like Brougham and Jeffrey, came from a legal background.[37] All our legal writers were taken to task by their opponents for being unfamiliar with the requisite science. Both Brougham and Jeffrey privately relied on others, including George Wilson himself, to keep them on the scientific straight and narrow.[38] Jeffrey remarked to Wilson in the course of discussions of the water controversy in their correspondence: 'I know I am but a child in your mind in any question of chemistry and I have nothing but my poor Logic to combat your Science with. But (unluckily perhaps) I have taken up a strong impression that the question we have to consider is much more a question of logic than of science ... '.[39] Where Muirhead, Brougham and Jeffrey did have an advantage, or so they felt, was in the argument of a case. This was why Muirhead sought to frame the controversy as a case involving an issue of evidence more than of chemistry.[40] James Watt Jr,

---

[35] Ibid., pp. lxxxiv–lxxxv, cxvii–cxviii.

[36] Ibid., p. cxviii. Francis Jeffrey shared Muirhead's view of Brewster's fine distinctions. Jeffrey said of Brewster's distinction between awarding the *theory* to Watt and the *discovery* to Cavendish: 'The metaphysics of this principle of distribution seem to me as questionable as the application of the expressions is arbitrary and obscure.' (Jeffrey to George Wilson, 6 April [1847], Special Collections, University of Edinburgh Library, Dk.6.23/1/14–15.)

[37] Wilson, *Life of the Honourable Henry Cavendish*, 1851, constantly refers, deliberately, I think, to 'the advocates of Watt'.

[38] For Wilson's assistance to Brougham see, for example, Muirhead to Wilson, 18 March 1846, Muirhead Papers, MS GEN 1354/212, and for Wilson's help to Jeffrey see Jeffrey to Wilson, 11 September [1847], Dk.6.23/1/34 and n.d. [1847] Dk.6.23/1/38–39, Special Collections, Edinburgh University Library.

[39] Jeffrey to Wilson, n.d. [1847] Dk.6.23/1/37, Special Collections, University of Edinburgh Library.

[40] It must be acknowledged, though, that by the height of the controversy, Muirhead was probably as well versed in the chemistry of the controversy as anyone. He certainly considered himself to be.

in assigning the editorship of his father's correspondence on the water question to Muirhead, stated: 'As a question of evidence, this falls peculiarly within the sphere of your pursuits ... '.[41] Muirhead concluded his most sustained account of the affair by drawing an analogy between the contest over priority of discovery and a patent case.

> Had Mr Watt's discovery of the theory of the composition of water been, like very many of his inventions, directly available for the increase of his own wealth, and, as such, protected by a patent, most certainly no case has been made out, on the part of Mr Cavendish, of such public use, or prior invention, as could have invalidated that patent.[42]

Muirhead then asked rhetorically whether the institution of science should be satisfied with any criteria in the award of priority of discovery less strict than those that apply in the award of a patent. Given the jealousy with which scientific fame is guarded and valued above pecuniary reward, the answer must, Muirhead contended, be no, and so a test of discovery modelled on the test of a patent he regarded as appropriate. So the claim was:

> First, that Mr. Watt formed the original idea in his own mind, and thus was A DISCOVERER of the true theory of the composition of water.
> Secondly, that being a discoverer, he was also THE FIRST PUBLISHER of that true theory.
> Thirdly, that being both a discoverer, and also the first publisher, he must therefore be held to be 'THE TRUE AND FIRST INVENTOR THEREOF'.[43]

An important feature of this rendition is that Watt is described simply as *a* discoverer. He need not be the *first* discoverer. Under the law of patents 'the prior discovery of an invention will not prevent another independent discoverer from obtaining a valid patent if the earlier inventor kept the secret to himself, the law holding that he is the "true and first inventor" who first obtains a patent'.[44] This legal definition of the true inventor is paralleled by analogy with the true discoverer. If the true inventor is defined by the act of taking out a first patent by *a* discoverer, then, by analogy, the true discoverer is defined by the act of first publishing an idea arrived at independently, though not necessarily first.

---

[41] Muirhead (ed.), *Correspondence*, p. ii.

[42] Ibid., p. cxxi.

[43] Muirhead stated that he was adopting the form of Godson on patents, pp. 27–30. The work in question is Richard Godson, *A Practical Treatise on the Law of Patents for Inventions and of Copyright*, 1823, 2nd edn, 1840. There are clear resonances between the water controversy and the patent controversy of this period, not least because Watt figured in both. See Christine MacLeod, 'Concepts of invention and the patent controversy in Britain', in R. Fox (ed.), *Technological Change. Methods and Themes in the History of Technology*, pp. 137–53. Each controversy also drew upon and shaped wider debates on the philosophy of discovery. These resonances were there in the beginning also. Thus Watt's correspondence in 1783 reveals his near simultaneous concern about plagiarism of steam-engine designs by Parisians and plagiarism of his ideas on water by Cavendish. See James Watt to Joseph Black, 3 February 1783 and Watt to Black, 21 April 1783 in Robinson and McKie, *Partners in Science*, pp. 121–22, 124–27.

[44] Article 'Patents', in *Encyclopaedia Britannica*, ninth edn, vol. 18, p. 355.

The link between the water question and concerns about patents was a very real one for Muirhead. Throughout the period when the water controversy was at its height, Muirhead seems to have closely followed the fate of James Neilson in the latter's defence of his patent on the hot-blast technique.

James Beaumont Neilson (1792–1865), who was Glasgow born, was an engineman in the coal industry until, in 1817, he was appointed foreman of the Glasgow Gasworks. He promoted a variety of improvements in gas manufacture but is best known for his development of the hot-blast technique in iron making. He had investigated the smelting of iron and in 1825 read a paper at the Glasgow Philosophical Society on his findings. In 1828 he was granted a patent on the process of heating the air blast between the engine and the furnace. The patent specification was actually drawn up by Lord Brougham, who had performed similar services for Boulton & Watt.[45] With difficulty (because conventional wisdom was that the colder the air the better), Neilson persuaded the Clyde Ironworks in Glasgow to try out the technique. It proved very successful. Widespread adoption of the technique followed. Neilson entered into partnership with Charles Macintosh and Colin Dunlop to exploit the patent and promote the process. The patent was widely challenged and became the focus of litigation, first in 1832. From 1839, over five years, 'some twenty actions were proceeding in Scotland, and several in England. Three juries sat upon the subject at different times, and on three occasions appeals were carried to the House of Lords.'[46] In the Lords, Brougham participated, unperturbed, in deliberations on the validity of the patent that he had drawn up.[47]

During the height of the water controversy, the Neilson case was one of the key patent disputes. On 1 February 1845 Muirhead attended a victory dinner given for Neilson by his patent partners. Held in the Council Hall, Glasgow, the dinner was attended by almost one hundred, including 'all the most intelligent engineers, and nearly all the great ironmasters, of the neighbourhood, or, indeed, of the country'. Muirhead had been asked to give a toast to the memory of Watt, Arkwright and Murdock. He felt that someone not a relative of Watt might do this better, but agreed, on the understanding that he would not be required to eulogize at length. He need not have worried:

> the constant tribute of praise which was paid in the early part of the evening to your Father's memory, and the rapturous applause with which allusions to his discoveries

---

[45] Archibald and Nan L. Clow, *The Chemical Revolution. A Contribution to Social Technology*, 1992 (originally published 1952), p. 355. Neilson must have seemed to be the ideal type of the adult-educated working man putting his knowledge to important use. Neilson had studied at the Andersonian Institution, whose founder, Dr George Birkbeck, was instrumental with Brougham in launching the Mechanics' Institute movement in the mid-1820s. In fact Neilson was instrumental in inaugurating the Glasgow Mechanics' Institution. He gave an address at the opening of its new rooms in 1825 in which he used Watt as an example of what could be achieved. See Thomas B. Mackenzie, *Life of James Beaumont Neilson F.R.S.*, 1928, pp. 9–10.

[46] Samuel Smiles, *Industrial Biography: Iron Workers and Tool Makers*, 1863, pp. 158–59. See also R.D. Corrins, 'The great Hot-Blast affair', *Industrial Archaeology*, 7, 1970, 233–63.

[47] See, for example, the report of Household Iron Co. v. Neilson on appeal before the Lords, in P.A. Hayward, *Hayward's Patent Cases, 1600–1883*, vol. 4, 1987, pp. 532–79.

were received, saved me the necessity of saying more of the merit which I most deeply felt than you will find in the Notes which I enclose.[48]

Enclosed was a copy of Muirhead's speech. In it he linked Neilson, his activities and his patent struggle with the case of Watt:

> reflecting on the achievements which are inseparably connected with that most Illustrious and most Beloved Name [Watt], it cannot, I think, fail to strike us how similar in many particulars has been the course, how kindred in some respects must have been the spirit, of James Neilson, and James Watt. Born in the same district of country; – the science of both cradled in the same City; – their merits recognised and fostered by patrons of similar eminence and similar benignity; – both in like manner observing, considering, and investigating the nature, – the marvellous nature, and properties of Heat; both with like felicity deducing consequences important and beneficial to Man; – with like perseverance elaborating and perfecting their respective inventions; – threatened alike with repeated illegal infringements of their just rights, and both alike, after an arduous contest, finally and triumphantly successful: – I know not what is wanting to the truthfulness and completeness of the parallel ...[49]

There can be little doubt from this that Muirhead considered that the *legal* defence of Neilson and the *historical* defence of Watt were complementary. According to his account, both inventors based their insights upon rigorous scientific investigation and not upon ingenuity alone. Both were investigators of nature, especially the nature of heat. Their claims to their discoveries were grounded in the same way.

Later, in his *Life of Watt* (1858), Muirhead was to remark on the way in which Watt's involvement in the patent contests 'sacrificed and consumed' the 'leisure and tranquility of a philosophic mind' and thus deprived humanity of 'further discoveries of refined beauty or extensive utility'.[50] Muirhead there also credited the law reforms introduced by Brougham with much improving the situation for contemporary investigators.

Jeffrey

Francis Jeffrey was less centrally involved in the water controversy than the other two advocates. His major public intervention was to write the article 'Watt or Cavendish?' for the *Edinburgh Review*, published in January 1848. The date is significant because some years earlier, Jeffrey, whose most recent contribution to the *Review* had appeared in 1840, had considered himself well enough retired to issue a four-volume *complete* compilation of his numerous contributions to that journal.[51] Jeffrey's first biographer, Lord Cockburn, had this to say:

---

48 Muirhead to Watt Jr, 2 February 1845, Muirhead Papers, MS GEN 1354/775.

49 Enclosure in Muirhead to Watt Jr, 2 February 1845, MS GEN 1354/775.

50 J.P. Muirhead, *The Life of James Watt, with Selections from his Correspondence*, 1858, p. 403.

51 Francis Jeffrey, *Contributions to the Edinburgh Review in 4 volumes*, 1840. In the Preface, Jeffrey stated: 'I wrote the first article in the first number of the Review in October 1802: – and sent my last contribution to it, in October 1840!' The review of the 'water question' was, in fact to become his 200th contribution to the *Edinburgh Review*.

During the autumn of this year [1847] he contributed his last article to the Review. It was the able and elaborate paper on the claims of Watt and Cavendish as the discoverers of the composition of water, which was published in January 1848. It would have been better perhaps if his final effort had been on a subject more congenial to his favourite tastes. But whether he shall turn out to be right, or to be wrong, in assigning the palm to his friend Watt, there can be no question as to the ability with which the evidence is discussed. He was always skilful in the art of arraying scientific proof.[52]

So there was a sense in which the judicious Jeffrey came out of retirement in order to adjudicate between Watt and Cavendish. However, this was not so strange as Cockburn found it. Jeffrey had a long prior involvement as an active participant in the 'reputational entrepreneurship' surrounding the figure of James Watt.[53]

The early days of the *Edinburgh Review* saw Jeffrey, as its editor, cooperate on at least one occasion with Watt Jr and others in a piece of reputational manipulation. It is sufficient here to recall that, according to Watt Jr, the *Review* was used in 1809, with Jeffrey's active cooperation, to publish a response to a group challenging Watt's engine improvements and hostile to the Soho engineering establishment.[54] A decade later, Jeffrey penned the obituary of Watt in *The Scotsman*, a much-quoted piece that most agreed did great justice to the departed engineer in both content and style. Watt Jr, in particular, admired the account and, when he wrote the brief sketch of his father's life for the *Supplement* to the *Encyclopaedia Britannica* in the mid-1820s, he agreed that Jeffrey's obituary should be appended to it. Watt Jr's diffidence as an author was matched by his admiration of Jeffrey's masterpiece.[55] This early association with the filial project helped to ensure Jeffrey's continued involvement in it. He was consulted extensively on the inscriptions for monuments to Watt that Brougham worked on, and took most of the credit for.[56] Watt Jr and Muirhead turned to Jeffrey, it seems, whenever they produced a new contribution to the literature.[57] Jeffrey was admired in part as a consummate stylist, but he was also greatly valued because, as Cockburn put it, he was so 'skilful in the art of arraying scientific proof'. Jeffrey was, after all, a judge, and, unlike his old friend Brougham, was also judicious. Whether handling evidence on paper, or people in conflict, Jeffrey was a polished performer. His skills as an editor, literary stylist, judge and

---

[52] Lord Cockburn, *Life of Lord Jeffrey with a Selection from his Correspondence*, 1852, 2 vols, vol. 1, pp. 402–403.

[53] On 'reputational entrepreneurship' see Gary Alan Fine, *Difficult Reputations. Collective Memories of the Evil, Inept, and Controversial*, 2001, pp. 12, 16.

[54] Watt Jr referred to this as the response to the 'Olynthiad'. See Watt Jr to Muirhead, 15 December 1844, Muirhead Papers, MS GEN 1354/766. The article, ostensibly by Playfair (and so attributed since), was, according to this letter, written initially by Watt Jr in consultation with his father and Mr Ambrose Weston and then edited by Playfair. See discussion in Chapter 5, above.

[55] See Watt Jr to Francis Jeffrey, 11 January 1824, Watt Correspondence C6/10, which also asks Jeffrey to look over and revise the article. This he did, according to Napier to Watt Jr, 4 February 1824, Watt Correspondence, C6/10.

[56] See Jeffrey to Brougham, 28 April 1832 and 1 November 1832, Brougham Papers, 43,083 and 15751, ff. 181–92.

[57] On Jeffrey's advice on Muirhead's notes to his translation of the *Eloge* see Muirhead to Watt Jr, 22 October 1839, Muirhead Papers, MS GEN 1354/380.

diplomat were placed at Watt Jr's disposal. Thus, he not only advised upon much of what Watt Jr and Muirhead wrote, but he also assisted in negotiating the complex world of the *Reviews*. He helped them to manage people, most notably his old friend Brougham, who frequently required containment. As we have seen, in the case of Brewster's 1840 review in the *Edinburgh*, Jeffrey was briefed by Muirhead and acted as a go-between with the editor, Napier, trying to put pressure on Brewster via Napier to shape a favourable outcome for the Watt camp.

Jeffrey's letter to Napier on this matter is a fine example of his mastery of what we would now call 'spin'. Having noted that there is to be an article on Arago's *Eloge* of Watt, Jeffrey continued

> the existing (or filial) Watt is in a great pucker and flurry lest you should take part against the paternal shade on the question as to the composition of water, and is most anxious to have that part of the subject carefully, and, in so far as possible, *favourably* handled. He says Brougham was anxious to do it, but that you had already entrusted the subject to another, and he fears that other may be Brewster, who has (it seems) in some measure prejudicated the question in his *Encyclopaedia*. Now I, without pretending to *know* the whole merits of the controversy, confess that I participate in those feelings, and am confident that you, both as a Scotchman and a friend of so many of Watt's friends, must also have a leaning in their favour, though you, no doubt, have a *judicial* function to perform, on which favour can have no influence. The short of the matter, however, is that I wish you, if you have no objection, to tell me *who* your reviewer is to be, and whether he is to be for or against Watt upon this question. If he is against him, I shall merely report to W. that you decline giving him any information, and that he may rely on justice being done; while, if he is in his favour, perhaps you would not object to my letting him know that you incline to think such will be the view of the matter. At all events, you may rely on my silence and discretion as to whatever you may please to communicate; and though I should rather like to relieve the fat man, I really take no very eager interest in the matter. From the slight review I have taken of the subject, I incline to think that Priestley has fully as good a title to the discovery as either Watt or Cavendish.[58]

Watt Jr, from whom Jeffrey distanced himself in this letter by gently mocking him, had a very different impression of what was going on, as did Muirhead. From their perspective Jeffrey was their man, engaged in extracting as much information as possible from Napier about the reviewer and applying pressure for favourable treatment. It does seem that Jeffrey was feigning indifference in order to do this.

Jeffrey's major public contribution to the 'water question' in 1848 was thus, contra Cockburn, *not* on a topic distinct from his interests. It was in a cause with which Jeffrey had identified at least since the great engineer's death. Not only the article itself but also the immediate, private circumstances whereby Jeffrey came to write it, exemplify the judiciousness, and cunning, that made him such a valuable member of the Watt camp. Whilst there was a tradition of real and ritual obeisance to Jeffrey in early nineteenth-century Scottish literary circles,[59] Watt Jr's and

---

[58] Francis Jeffrey to Macvey Napier, 20 October 1839, in Macvey Napier Jr, *Selection from the Correspondence of the late Macvey Napier, Esq.*, 1879, p. 305.

[59] On recapturing Jeffrey's early nineteenth-century reputation see James A. Greig, *Francis Jeffrey of the Edinburgh Review*, 1948, pp. 1–13.

Muirhead's estimation of him, and the value that they attached to his assistance, were quite genuine.

Jeffrey's essay of 1848 is interesting not least because it was produced at a time when there was considerable pressure on the Watt camp to supplement their empirical approach and address the chemical arguments of the other side. In doing this, chemical advice was sought and gained, as we have seen, from George Wilson. It had been intended that Wilson write the review in the *Edinburgh*, but the deal fell through and Jeffrey took on the task himself. It was agreed, however, that Jeffrey could make use of some of Wilson's material and we find the middle part of Jeffrey's article devoted to the 'charcoal argument'. This had been initiated by Harcourt and was to be a central focus of Wilson's *Life of the Honble Henry Cavendish*. Without Wilson's aid Jeffrey could not have made this departure from his 'natural' mode of operation.

The article does, however, conform to the empirical, synonymity and priority, approach in most respects. It begins with a rehearsal of the key events of the 1780s and of beliefs about the claims of Watt and Cavendish as expressed in various subsequent publications. Jeffrey gradually assembled what he called 'testimonies'. He suggested that were the matter to be decided by authorities, it would be easy to resolve with the names of Henry, Brande, Davy, Brougham, Brewster, Arago, Dumas, and Berzelius on one side, and 'on the other, those only of Harcourt, Peacock and Whewell'.[60]

> But let the chemists say what they will, it is *not* a question of science or authority half so much as of Logic and Evidence; and if we did not think it one which might be fairly left to the judgment of educated men, with but a moderate reference to a few admitted facts and principles of chemistry, we should scarcely have presumed to judge it for ourselves, – and certainly should never have thought of submitting it to the judgment of our readers. As it is, however ... upon the evidence now before us, we confidently expect to satisfy all who will take the trouble to follow us ...[61]

So Jeffrey, in line with his legal brethren and others of the Watt camp, asserted the eligibility of everyman to judge such a question against the Cavendish camp's exclusion of popular judgement.

Jeffrey's article does read like a legal brief in many respects. However, on the parallels between a legal case and contests over scientific priority, Jeffrey added some important caveats: 'we can by no means adopt those narrow and jealous canons of evidence derived from the rigid maxims of law, or the precedents of cases of Patents, by which both M. Arago and Sir D. Brewster seem anxious to limit the inquiry'. In a court of law, Jeffrey explained, the object was not the truth as such but rather the 'import of the evidence that *is legally admissible*'. So in the law, for example, evidence from closely concerned parties may be inadmissible. In a case like the question between Watt and Cavendish, before a public tribunal 'no evidence is inadmissible'.[62] So the analogy between the water question and a legal question

---

[60] Francis Jeffrey, 'The discoverer of the composition of water; Watt or Cavendish?', *Edinburgh Review*, **87**, 1848, 86.

[61] Ibid.

[62] Ibid., 87

was limited. Even more limited, in Jeffrey's view (though clearly not in Muirhead's), was the analogy with the law of patents. This is because a patent is granted to the first to disclose an invention to the public and cannot then be invalidated by someone subsequently claiming prior invention. Where the glory of discovery is concerned, however, 'the palm of priority … may be justly awarded to one who has been forestalled in the publication'.[63] Jeffrey clearly regarded Muirhead's argument from analogy with patents as an insecure one. Whether it was or not depended upon what was regarded as publication. If the time of actual appearance in a journal was used (which might seem logical by parallel with the public disclosure of a patent specification), then Cavendish would have the advantage. Perhaps because his argument depended upon Watt's priority in less formal communication, namely his letters of April 1783, Jeffrey questioned the analogy.

Having demonstrated that Watt was 'an original and independent discoverer of the theory which he propounded in April 1783' because Watt claimed it then and Cavendish had no demonstrable prior claim, Jeffrey turned to a matter of science. What was Watt's theory and did it present a 'true explanation' of the nature and composition of water? On the face of it the answer was yes it did, since, according to Jeffrey, Watt's statement of the theory and Cavendish's were expressed in '*the very same terms*'; even Cavendish had said as much. However, Harcourt (and Wilson) had brought up the so-called 'charcoal argument'. This was directed at the meaning of 'inflammable air' as used by Cavendish and Watt. For their explanation to be seen as true, inflammable air had to be read as interchangeable with 'hydrogen'. This was certainly reasonable so far as Cavendish was concerned, because the inflammable air in his experiments had been prepared by the action of mineral acids upon zinc or iron. Priestley, however, whose experiments Watt relied upon, did not always make inflammable air in that way. Sometimes he made it by heating charcoal in closed vessels. Whilst Priestley made little distinction between the two types of inflammable air, we know that only one constituent, the hydrogen, can be converted in its entirety into water. Whilst the charcoal gas would contain a proportion of hydrogen produced from the water adhering adventitiously to the charcoal, it could not possibly all be converted to water on explosion with dephlogisticated, or atmospheric, air. It was, therefore, impossible for Watt to infer the correct theory from Priestley's experiments.

Jeffrey's response addressed the, illegitimate, assumption in Harcourt's charcoal argument that the only experiments from which Watt drew his conclusions were experiments done with charcoal gas. On the contrary, Jeffrey argued, Priestley did perform combustion experiments with hydrogen (inflammable air prepared from zinc or iron and dilute mineral acid) and Watt plainly based his conclusions on those. In this respect, then, they were no different from Cavendish's experiments.

On another point, Jeffrey conceded that Watt's discovery was 'somewhat obscured and embarrassed' by his adhesion to phlogistic doctrine. This was scarcely a unique position, however, since Black, Kirwan and Cavendish himself were also adherents of it. Harcourt's attempts to suggest that Cavendish was somehow more free of phlogistic doctrine than Watt, Jeffrey found unconvincing.

---

[63] Ibid., 88.

After this long chemical excursion, Jeffrey returned to the business of circumstantial evidence of priority and independence of discovery. Much of this argument hung on whether Cavendish had drawn conclusions at the time of his experiments. Jeffrey made a range of ingenious arguments that turned on complex inferences from the statements of individuals. For example, the fact that Blagden began an account of the history of Cavendish's discovery in spring 1783 was significant, Jeffrey concluded, because Blagden, Cavendish's closest confidant, would surely have been told about it if the discovery were contemporaneous with the 1781 experiments, as Harcourt claimed. Here we see Jeffrey the barrister, cross-examining his historical witnesses in a virtuoso display of logical inference from evidence. When Jeffrey took on Harcourt's contention that the experiments of 1781 patently involved the conclusions and that Cavendish then drew them, we see Jeffrey's effective appeal to the psychology of belief, as if arguing before a jury:

> Now, we do not deny that there is, at first sight, something plausible and taking in this view of the matter; especially when addressed to a generation which has always been familiar with the conclusion, and with the universal assent of mankind in the sufficiency of the evidence referred to. Yet it requires but a moderate acquaintance with the actual history of the progress, even of the most obvious truths, and of the tenacity and vitality of prejudices and errors, to make us cease to wonder at the incredulity with which what is at last felt to be a demonstration, is often at first received.[64]

The plausibility of inertia in situations of potential radical discovery is argued in order to plead, contra Harcourt, that at a psychological level at least experiments cannot involve conclusions. Rather, people would believe that 'there must be a mistake somewhere, and the arrogant would scoff, and the thoughtful suspend their judgment accordingly'.[65] This is typical of Jeffrey's appeal to the judgement of plausibility of claims by 'everyman' against the 'expert' assertions of the likes of Harcourt.

Conclusion

In conclusion, we can say that the advocates of Watt brought their legal perspective to the water controversy. They favoured the model of discovery that dovetailed well with their legal approach and expertise. During the 1840s the question of the relationship between discovery and invention was open to negotiation and contest. Watt was a symbol of their legitimate proximity. Muirhead argued explicitly that the legal forms used to define the rights to an invention could also be applied to the matter of discovery. When they were, according to him, the dual claim of Watt to his steam-engine improvements and the discovery of the composition of water was secured. Jeffrey was as sure of those joint claims and also employed the empirical model of discovery. He was, however, involved in a long excursion over the charcoal argument, by way of defending the essential sameness of Cavendish's and Watt's

---

[64] Ibid., 128.
[65] Ibid., 129.

views. This move into chemical argument was made possible by Wilson's advice and involvement, even though Wilson took the argument in other directions. Jeffrey left the Watt camp's favoured territory of argument, but he did so only to defend the contention that such chemical arguments were unnecessary and inconsequential and to return the question to a matter of logic and evidence. Though Jeffrey felt that his colleagues sometimes took the legal analogies of the case too literally, he certainly argued as if before a jury, and asserted the legitimacy of public judgement of the matter.

We turn now to the Cavendish camp to consider ways in which Cavendish, like Watt, served as a symbol, but of a different understanding of discovery, its meaning and significance.

Chapter 9

The Defence of Cavendish: Character, Precision and Discipline

Cavendish, the millionaire, lives in a stable, eats nothing but mutton, and amuses himself – oh, solely for his private delectation – by anticipating the electrical discoveries of half a century. Glorious eccentrics![1]

Introduction

Was the Honourable Henry Cavendish honourable or not? This, as we have seen, was an important issue in the water controversy. The most contentious aspect of that controversy was the suggestion of dishonest dealings on Cavendish's part. Inevitably, then, the defence of Cavendish tended to be preoccupied with matters of character. However, even if the accusations of dishonesty had not been made, personal character would still have been a crucial issue because, for his defenders, it was intimately bound up with Cavendish's 'philosophical character', his precise mode of scientific work, and therefore was a basis for his claim to discovery.

Aldous Huxley placed the Honourable Henry Cavendish among the great English eccentrics. His peculiar behaviour and habits were widely remarked on in his lifetime and invariably mentioned by obituarists and early biographers. They remain a significant feature of historical folklore, no doubt rehearsed in school classrooms and university lecture halls to leaven discussions of the science that Cavendish pioneered.[2] Such accounts find significance in Cavendish's eccentricities mainly by way of illustrating the 'human aspect of science'. Probing a little more deeply, the connection is also often made between Cavendish's eccentricity and his genius and creativity. In this way, eccentricity becomes pathology, an organic condition of mind, and therefore plausibly linked to the creativity of that same mind. Taken to inhabit the nexus of genius and eccentricity, Cavendish was sometimes referred to as diseased. The chemist Thomas Thomson, for example, remarked in 1813 that Cavendish was 'shy and bashful to a degree bordering upon disease'.[3] Oliver Sacks

---

[1] Aldous Huxley, *Crome Yellow. A Novel*, 1952, p. 72. First published 1921.

[2] A colleague has recorded his memory of receiving a variant anecdote, involving sausages rather than mutton, at school, and I too recall this. See David Oldroyd, 'Social and historical studies of science in the classroom?', *Social Studies of Science*, **20**, 1990, 751 and 756, n1. Educational websites relating to Cavendish and 'the Cavendish experiment' in particular often convey the anecdotes regarding Cavendish's character and must have greatly increased the prevalence and currency of these conceptions.

[3] Thomas Thomson, 'A biographical account of the Honourable Henry Cavendish', *Annals of Philosophy*, **1**, 1813, 6.

193

recently added Cavendish to his stable of oddly enlightening characters by tentatively diagnosing him as suffering from Asperger's Syndrome:

> Many of the characteristics that distinguished Cavendish are almost pathognomic of Asperger's syndrome: a striking literalness and directness of mind, extreme single-mindedness, a passion for calculation and quantitative exactitude, unconventional, stubbornly held ideas, and a disposition to use rigorously exact (rather than figurative) language – even in his rare nonscientific communication – coupled with a virtual incomprehension of social behaviors and human relationships.[4]

Sacks based his diagnosis on George Wilson's detailed portrayal of Cavendish's eccentricities.[5] He finds this evidence 'almost overwhelming', unlike the rather thin evidence for other recent claims that Einstein, Wittgenstein and Bartok were autistic. Sacks claims that George Wilson had 'a wondering admiration and sympathy for his subject'. Perhaps so, but Wilson also stated that he found Cavendish hard to like. In investigating the water question, even as Wilson became more and more convinced of Cavendish's claim to priority, he liked Watt more and Cavendish less. Wilson was an intensely religious, but also a highly sociable and fun-loving, personality despite severe bodily infirmities and illness. He found Cavendish's cold, clear intelligence admirable in its results but also inhuman.

Jungnickel and McCormmach's impressive revisionist account of Cavendish's work and character was inspired in part by what they regarded as the serious imbalances and deficiencies of Wilson's *Life*. They were disappointed that Wilson devoted so much space to the water controversy in a way that, in their view, distorted the overall picture of the great natural philosopher. They also disagree with Wilson's diagnosis of Cavendish as a man lacking passion and they argue that Cavendish was in fact a passionate and a social man within the delimited bounds of the experimental life. To react only to Cavendish's surface demeanour is to profoundly misrepresent Cavendish, in their view.[6] Although I am significantly persuaded by, and much indebted to, this work in various ways, my perspective is very different. I am concerned not so much to establish the reality of Cavendish's character as to deal with perceptions of it, and ideological uses of those perceptions in the nineteenth century. In seeking to understand the ideological uses of depictions of Cavendish's character I am pursuing a case employed in different ways by Robert K. Merton and by Steven Shapin.

In his work on the normative system of science, Merton frequently invoked the case of Cavendish.[7] He did so in two main connections: ambivalence about secrecy in science and the conduct of priority disputes. In Merton's account the stories

---

4 Oliver Sacks, 'Henry Cavendish: An early case of Asperger's syndrome?', *Neurology*, **57**, October 2001, 1347. Not surprisingly, given its appeal to the trope of the eccentric scientist, Sacks's story was picked up in the media. See for example, Erica Goode, 'Was scientist more than just odd?', *The Sun-Herald* (Sydney), 14 October 2001, p. 37.

5 George Wilson, *The Life of the Honble Henry Cavendish*, 1851.

6 Christa Jungnickel and Russell McCormmach, *Cavendish. The Experimental Life*, 1999, pp. 10–15.

7 See Robert K. Merton, *The Sociology of Science. Theoretical and Empirical Investigations*, 1973, pp. 274, 288, 291, 357–58.

about Cavendish's reclusiveness and his failure to publish much of his work produce ambivalence among fellow scientists. Although Cavendish was very productive, his secretiveness and failure to publish violated the norm of communalism and must therefore attract disapproval from those who might have earlier profited from his work. Indeed, all people who have the optimal functioning of the institution of science as a value must be critical of Cavendish on that score. Thus, in Merton's work the anecdotes about Cavendish were linked to what he regarded as basic regulative features of the scientific community. It would be possible, though inappropriate in my view, to apply this perspective to Cavendish in the context of the water controversy.

Another use of the stock of Cavendish anecdotes, particularly those relating to his supposedly peculiar dietary habits, is made by Steven Shapin in exploring those cultural forms or tropes that link bodily asceticism with the production of scientific knowledge. Shapin is interested in the way in which notions of disembodied knowledge so important to conceptions of objectivity are reinforced by tales, norms and stipulations about the bodily habits of natural philosophers. Isaac Newton and Robert Boyle provide probably more, and tastier, stories, but from the late eighteenth century Cavendish became a very popular subject and remained so through the nineteenth and into the twentieth centuries.[8]

Merton and Shapin, in their different ways, remind us that it is important when studying the uses made of Cavendish's character in the water controversy to recall that wider traditions and tropes were being drawn upon. It is also vital, however, to remain alive to the *particular* circumstances in which invocations of character were made. In this way, variations in the significance attached to the trope and the springs of ambivalence about Cavendish's character are in some way accounted for. As we will see, accounts of Cavendish's character, its significance and its consequences for his science generally and for the water controversy specifically, all involved interpretative flexibility. Different sides in the dispute were able to make quite convincing but opposing interpretations.

A key moral issue with Cavendish's character – one that Huxley was clearly referring to when he remarked on Cavendish amusing himself with research for 'private delectation' – was his failure to publish much of his research. It became apparent as Cavendish's private manuscript papers were examined that he had kept a great many of his important research findings to himself. The full extent of this secrecy so far as the electrical researches were concerned was revealed with their publication in 1879, under the editorship of James Clerk Maxwell.[9] However, aspects of the treasure trove had been revealed earlier by various scientists who had had access to Cavendish's manuscripts.

The Cavendish family in the early nineteenth century were interested in having Henry Cavendish's papers published. The then Duke of Devonshire entrusted the papers to James Hudson in about 1830 with a view to their being prepared for

---

[8] Steven Shapin, 'The philosopher and the chicken: On the dietetics of disembodied knowledge', in S. Shapin and C. Lawrence (eds), *Science Incarnate. Historical Embodiments of Natural Knowledge*, 1998, p. 41.

[9] James Clerk Maxwell (ed.), *The Electrical Researches* (1879), included as vol. 1 of J.C. Maxwell (ed.), *The Scientific Papers of the Honourable Henry Cavendish, F.R.S.*, 1921.

publication, but Hudson appears to have held them for ten years or more without doing much with them.[10] William Cavendish, Lord Burlington, had been educated at Cambridge and, as we have seen, he became the major point of contact between the 'Gentlemen of Science' and the Cavendish family. In the aftermath of the Birmingham 'Address' it was via Burlington that Harcourt sought access to the Cavendish papers. Harcourt wrote on 23 September 1839, enclosing a copy of *The Athenaeum* of 31 August that contained an account of his 'Address', and formally requested access to Henry Cavendish's papers. In reply, Burlington noted that he had discussed this with the duke and learned that the papers were with Hudson, who had now been requested to send them to Burlington without delay.[11]

Harcourt had obtained access by January 1840 because he reported then to James David Forbes that the papers were

> exceedingly curious, in respect to the vast range of subjects which his [Cavendish's] inquiries embraced from the theory of the laws of motion & abstract questions of mathematics down, thro' the laws of heat electricity magnetism, sound etc., to more accurate geological observations than I believe anyone knew to have been made at that time. In his elaborate, & I imagine, unpublished exp^{ts} on heat which go back as far as the earliest of Black, there seems to be much deserving a more attentive perusal than I have yet been able to give them.[12]

Of course, Harcourt's primary purpose was to use Cavendish's experimental records to reinforce the case for his priority in the water question. We have seen how Harcourt did this. What interests us now is that in the published version of his 'Address' to the British Association Harcourt had a good deal to say about Cavendish's character. This is not surprising, since the 'Address' was a reaction to Arago's *Eloge*, which contained, according to the Cavendish camp, a scandalous set of aspersions on that character.

In comparing Cavendish and Watt, Harcourt stated that 'one stands as high in the discovery of natural facts, as the other does in their useful application'. In assigning them in this way to separate spheres of endeavour Harcourt also contrasted their genius while claiming not to place one above the other: 'let us hold a just and even balance between genius that rises superior to the pressure of circumstances, and that which reaches to at least equal intellectual heights, unseduced by rank and riches'.[13] This was Harcourt's interpretation of Cavendish's obsessive, solitary researches. They were not to be regarded as exhibiting a weakness of character because they were not always communicated publicly, but rather taken as an indication of strength of character in one whose wealth and station could have diverted him from the search for truth. In this interpretation Harcourt echoed Davy[14] and, notably, Cuvier, who had stated in his *Eloge* of Cavendish delivered in 1811 that:

---

[10] James Hudson was Assistant Secretary of the Royal Society of London for many years.

[11] Harcourt to Burlington, 23 September 1839 and Burlington to Harcourt, 28 September 1839, printed in *Harcourt Papers*, vol. xiv, pp. 98–99.

[12] Harcourt to James David Forbes, 11 January 1840, Forbes Papers, Incoming Letters, 1840, item 2.

[13] William Vernon Harcourt, 'Address', in *Report of the Ninth Meeting of the British Association for the Advancement of Science; held at Birmingham in August 1839*, 1840, pp. 6–7.

[14] Davy stated in 1810: 'in estimating the character of Mr Cavendish … his grand stimulus to

celui dont nous allons vous entretenir a eu le mérite bien plus rare, et probablement bien plus grand, de ne pas se laisser vaincre par ceux de la prospérité. Ni sa naissance qui lui ouvrait un chemin facile vers les honneurs, ni de grandes richesses qui vinrent subitement lui offrir l'appât de tous les plaisirs, ne purent le detourner de son but; il n'eut pas même en vue la gloire ou les distinctions; l'amour désintéressé de la vérité fut son unique mobile.[15]

Recounting his examination of the Cavendish manuscripts, Harcourt noted how Cavendish had 'travelled over the whole range of natural philosophy', producing much undisplayed knowledge that the manuscripts could now reveal. Leaving the mechanical, meteorological, magnetical and electrical works to others, Harcourt ventured to say a little about the gems found in his examination of the chemical and geological papers, mentioning in particular Cavendish's observations and recording of geological strata, his deduction of all the laws of the 'generation and destruction of heat' including numerous determinations of specific heat, his elucidation of the chemistry of arsenic ten years before the published experiments of Scheele, and his priority in distinguishing nitrogen from other forms of unrespirable and incombustible gases.[16] Thus, Harcourt found in the manuscripts much material of scientific as well as of historical interest. He reproduced and extracted some of this material, remarking that it was 'calculated to throw a strong light on the character of Cavendish, a character never very common and – least of all now – that of a man pursuing truth for its own sake, communicative of it to his friends, but caring nothing for public fame'.[17] Harcourt's lament about the scarcity of such persons in the present gives a clue to one aspect of Cavendish's symbolic importance for the 'Gentlemen of Science'. The latter were keen, even as they argued for the utility of science, to protect and promote non-utilitarian research. Cavendish could be held up as an example of purity in less complex times.[18]

Cavendish's failure to publish could therefore be interpreted in a variety of ways. Whilst it might be seen as reprehensible, and certainly was so seen by Arago, for example, it could also be seen more positively. Harcourt's account of Cavendish made a virtue of it and many may have been persuaded. Michael Faraday was one. Thanking Harcourt for a copy of his 'Address', Faraday remarked: 'What a contrast does Cavendish present to those whose craving is so

---

exertion was evidently the love of truth and knowledge: unambitious, unassuming, it was often with difficulty that he was persuaded to bring forward his important discoveries ... he was, as it were, fearful of the voice of Fame.'

15 G. Cuvier, 'Eloge historique de Henri Cavendish', in *Eloges Historiques*, third edn, 1874, pp. 201–21, at p. 201 (The *éloge* dates from 1811). A translation is available in Eduard Farber (ed.), *Great Chemists*, 1961, pp. 229–38, which renders this passage as follows: 'The man who is the subject of our present discourse had the rare and probably greater merit of not permitting himself to be overcome by the obstacles of prosperity. Neither the accident of his birth, which made fame and honour easily attainable, nor great riches, which offered him the temptation of pleasure, could turn him away from his goal. He did not aspire to glory or distinction; the disinterested love of truth was his motivating force.'

16 Harcourt, 'Address', pp. 30–32.

17 Harcourt to Lord Burlington, 21 October [1840], Devonshire Collection, Chatsworth, 230–0.

18 See Morrell and Thackray, *Gentlemen of Science: Early Years*, pp. 423–24.

great for fame that it leads them almost to the verge of honesty. With what dignity his character shines forth!'[19]

The issue of Cavendish's general character, and through it his 'philosophical character', assumed great importance in the water controversy, and not only because his honesty was attacked by Arago and Brougham and defended by Harcourt and Wilson. According to Cavendish's supporters, the great man's character, his indifference to fame and his thoroughness in particular, allowed the controversy to happen in the first place. Cavendish did not publish his 1781 experiments and conclusions at the time because he felt that more experiments were required before he could make a definitive statement. Thus his thoroughness before being willing to publish created the gap that allowed Watt's claim room and *prima facie* plausibility. However, Cavendish's thoroughness and caution also meant that his work was, as Davy put it, 'finished', and did not have to be repeated, retraced or recalled. The argument was that it was better to have such superbly executed and secure work in due time than rushed incomplete contributions as they were first glimpsed. The comparison with the style of Priestley was an obvious one.

Cavendish's supporters also argued that his character made it impossible that he could have engaged in the duplicity of which Arago and others accused him. George Wilson in the *British Quarterly Review* in 1845 put it this way:

Of all her illustrious philosophers, he was, without exception, the very last in reference to whom it was possible to believe that the accusation [of fraud] could be true. A man to whom applause had ever been hateful, and who had systematically avoided and declined the honours which his countrymen would willingly have conferred upon him, was not likely suddenly, and on a single occasion, to grow covetous of distinction, and to seek to gain it by fraud.[20]

The contrast between the approach of the Watt camp and that of Cavendish's supporters is that the former claimed to make no assumptions about Cavendish's character but rather to infer what his character must have been from examination of documents and events. Character was, they argued, something to be derived from the evidence. For the Cavendish camp, on the other hand, character was taken as given and therefore as itself evidence that the accusations of dishonest dealing must be mistaken. For them, too, the scientific consequences of his character were largely positive. Although it meant that some work was not published, it also gave the work that was published its 'finished' quality because of the thoroughness that Cavendish's general character engendered in his 'philosophical character'. George Peacock noted this feature of the man when he stated that Cavendish had 'the most cautious habits of reasoning, and never committed himself to a conclusion which his experiments and observations did not appear fully to justify'.[21]

---

[19] Michael Faraday to William Vernon Harcourt, 24 October 1840, printed in Frank A.J.L. James (ed.), *The Correspondence of Michael Faraday. Volume 2*, 1993, p. 699.

[20] George Wilson, 'Lord Brougham's Men of Letters and Science', *British Quarterly Review*, 2, 1845, 249.

[21] George Peacock, 'Arago and Brougham on Black, Cavendish, Priestley and Watt', *Quarterly Review*, 77, 1845, 114.

By the time Sir Joseph Larmor wrote a Preface to his 1921 revision of Maxwell's edition of the *Electrical Researches*, Cavendish's work could be portrayed in an intriguing way:

> Careless though Cavendish was of scientific reputation, intent on pressing on to new solitary achievement, to the neglect of publication, due as it would seem as much to the habit of continual postponement of final preparations for the press as to the fascination of exercising his powers of discovery – and even, as it has proved, as a consequence of his recluse and self-centred life – there are perhaps few investigators of the first rank of whose work and aims and procedure we have now more complete knowledge than of his.[22]

Were we to conclude, perhaps, that Cavendish's work was successfully communicated precisely *because* he had been so tardy and inefficient in doing so in his lifetime?!

The Cavendish Experiment

For his supporters and admirers in the 1830s and beyond, Cavendish was not just a historical figure but a person of contemporary scientific reckoning and example. The Cambridge connection was important. After Newton, Cavendish came to be seen as that university's favourite scientific son. Like Newton, whose reputation was also a busy construction site at this time,[23] Cavendish became a powerful symbol. Beyond this, his work provided an exemplar of procedure and reasoning via experiment and mathematical representation. His legendary precision was something against which the best scientists of the age sought to test themselves. This was particularly the case with regard to the attempt to replicate Cavendish's measurement of the density of the earth. A number of individuals among the 'Gentlemen of Science' devoted much time to this. There was also a great deal of symbolic capital invested in it as exemplary. Successful replication would ratify and assist the major thrust of work in 'physique du globe' in Britain that was sponsored by the Gentlemen of Science at this time. Equally, aspersions upon the character and reputation of Cavendish presented a potential threat to this venture being pursued 'in his name'. This is one reason why the defence of Cavendish on the water question was a matter of some moment in Birmingham in 1839 and beyond.

The physics of the earth was a major focus of interest in British science from the 1820s. The conduct of pendulum experiments to determine the figure of the earth, the making of measurements of terrestrial magnetism and its variations, and the study of the tides were a focus for a confluence of interests among the Cambridge

---

[22] Joseph Larmor, 'Preface' in James Clerk Maxwell (ed.), *The Scientific Papers of the Honourable Henry Cavendish, F.R.S. Volume 1. The Electrical Researches*, 1921, pp. vii–viii. These exculpations of Cavendish's secrecy are fine examples of the interpretative flexibility of the 'norm' of communalism in science. On this flexibility see Mulkay, 'Interpretation and the use of rules'.

[23] On Newton and constructions of his 'genius' at this time see Patricia Fara, *Newton: The Making of Genius*, 2002, pp. 202–30.

Network, scientific servicemen and mathematical practitioners.[24] Much of the lobbying of government by the leadership of the British Association, and a good deal of their expenditure of grant money for investigations, was related to these sorts of activities. The ventures were also characterized variously by the need to amass and control large quantities of data, to assess their reliability, and to take great pains in correcting results and adjusting them in the face of small but crucial sources of measurement, or experimental, error.

Within this context, Henry Cavendish's 'last experiment', his determination of the density of the earth, published in the *Philosophical Transactions* of the Royal Society in 1798, became one of great material and symbolic importance. Occupying fifty-seven pages in the *Transactions*, this paper is notable for its conception, its cautious prosecution and the insistence at all stages upon anticipating, and correcting for, potential errors in order to achieve the greatest accuracy possible.[25] Jungnickel and McCormmach make a crucial link between Cavendish's character and this experiment:

> Those traits that in his casual contact with people gave rise to anecdotes about his eccentricities were precisely the traits that in his scientific work made him extraordinary. To do science, Cavendish did not have to overcome his extreme diffidence but only to adapt it to science. The experiment on the density of the earth, *the* Cavendish experiment, is arguably not Cavendish's most important experiment, but if it is looked at for what it tells about the experimenter – as if it were a diary, which Cavendish did not keep, or a formal portrait, which he did not allow – it is the most revealing of his experiments.[26]

His most recent biographers thus consider the Cavendish experiment to determine the density of the earth as peculiarly revealing of the man's experimental life. As we have noted, their theme, contrary to those nineteenth-century and more recent accounts of Cavendish's 'coldness' and lack of passion, is that Cavendish led a passionate life of experiment, and even an active social life if one appreciates the importance to him of the small scientific circle with whom he interacted during the course of his experiments. Despite this, their perspective on Cavendish seems quite close to that of the 'Gentlemen of Science' in the 1830s and 1840s. Jungnickel and McCormmach believe that as well as working out his 'private destiny' through the experiment on the density of the earth, he also 'acted as the able representative of a general development in science' that being the 'drive for precision'. They mention that the new editor of the *Annalen der Physik*, L.W. Gilbert, in a 1799 foreword to

---

24 See David Philip Miller, 'The revival of the physical sciences in Britain, 1815–1840', *Osiris*, new series, **2**, 1986, 107–34; M.S. Reidy, 'The flux and reflux of science: the study of the tides and the organisation of early Victorian science', University of Minnesota, unpublished PhD thesis, 2000.

25 For accessible accounts of the Cavendish experiment that also have some historical sensibility see: P.F. Titchmarsh, 'The Michell–Cavendish experiment', *The School Science Review*, **47**, March 1966, 320–30; B.E. Clotfelter, 'The Cavendish experiment as Cavendish knew it', *American Journal of Physics*, **55**, March 1987, 210–13; Isobel Falconer, 'Henry Cavendish: The man and the measurement', *Measurement Science and Technology*, **10**, June 1999, 470–77.

26 Jungnickel and McCormmach, *Cavendish. The Experimental Life*, p. 453. See also Russell McCormmach, 'The last experiment of Henry Cavendish', in A.J. Kox and D.M. Siegel (eds), *No Truth Except in the Details. Essays in Honor of Martin J. Klein*, 1995, pp. 1–30.

the journal, called for the best work in physics in Germany to sit side by side in the journal with the best work from abroad. Gilbert cited Cavendish's experiment as an exemplar because of its wonderful exactness.[27] It was in the name of that development, its pursuit and institutionalization, that Cavendish became such a vital symbol for early Victorian science. This was especially so for those among scientific leaders ambitious to preside over education in the sciences and the increasingly organized prosecution of research.

In 1835, as the pursuit of physics of the earth gathered pace in Britain, the Council of the Royal Astronomical Society, on the suggestion of Augustus De Morgan, set up a committee to investigate the practicability of repeating the Cavendish experiment. The work was supported by a £500 grant from the government in 1837 to help defray costs. The person who took charge of the effort was Francis Baily, a retired banker, a founder of the Astronomical Society of London, and member of the Council of the Royal Society and of the inner circle of the British Association. Baily was the obvious person to engage in the kind of work involved in replicating the Cavendish experiment. He was the archetypal representative of thorough, precise and laborious work in science during this period. He devoted a great deal of time and energy to the reduction of astronomical observations and the collation of pendulum experiments undertaken to determine the figure of the earth. He was also centrally involved in determinations of the standard length. Baily has been accurately described as the 'perfected type' of the 'solid and sober, rather than brilliant' men who were so important to the Astronomical Society and, I would add, to ventures in the physics of the earth.[28]

The experiment almost defeated even Baily, who felt besieged by mysterious sources of error. A number of his friends were consulted on the experiment, including George Airy, the Astronomer Royal. In the end a suggestion from J.D. Forbes enabled Baily to obtain what he regarded as a satisfactory result.[29] The perceived importance of this result and the processes leading to it within the élite scientific community of the time are testified to in various ways. The Astronomical Society devoted the entire 14th volume of its *Memoirs* to the report of the experiments. Baily received the Society's Gold Medal in recognition of the work.[30]

We can see from this that the reputation of Cavendish was enhanced by the demonstrated difficulty of performing the Cavendish experiment to the degree of

---

[27] Jungnickel and McCormmach, *Cavendish. The Experimental Life*, pp. 453, 456.

[28] See J.L.E. Dreyer and H.H. Turner, *History of the Royal Astronomical Society 1820–1920*, 1923, pp. 87–88; Timothy L. Alborn, 'The business of induction: Industry and genius in the language of British scientific reform, 1820–1840', *History of Science*, **34**, 1996, 91–121.

[29] See J.D. Forbes to George Airy, 18 April 1840; J.D. Forbes to Francis Baily, 3 August 1840, 2 March 1841 and 22 March 1843, all in Forbes Papers, Letterbook III, pp. 94–95, 117–19, 210–11, 504–505. As Harry Collins among others has taught us (*Changing Order*), the business of experimental replication is a complex one and the decision that an experiment has been successfully replicated is underdetermined by the experimental set-up and outcomes alone. The Cavendish experiment would make a good case study of such questions.

[30] Francis Baily, 'Experiments with the torsion rod for determining the mean density of the Earth', *Memoirs of the Royal Astronomical Society*, **14**, 1843, 1–120. It is notable that Baily actually defended Cavendish against some criticisms made by Dr Charles Hutton of the conduct of the original Cavendish experiment (pp. 88–92). Dreyer and Turner, *History of the Royal Astronomical Society*, pp. 91–92.

precision that he obtained. For Baily, and the other 'Gentlemen of Science' engaged in these ventures in the physical sciences, Cavendish was not just a historical figure but a ghostly leader and exemplary practitioner moving among them, a genuine scientific presence. Knowing this can help us to understand the sensitivity of that group to any attack upon Cavendish's standing within the wider community.

The Chemists and Cavendish

The fact that Cavendish had come to symbolize precision and best practice in natural philosophy was important not just to exponents of mathematical physics and *physique du globe* but also to members of the nascent chemical community in early Victorian Britain. It is at first puzzling that, with the notable exception of George Wilson, members of the developing chemical community of the 1840s did not play a significant part in public agitation over the water question. The reason for this may lie in the fact that the institutional development of chemistry was relatively late and problematic. Particularly vexed was the issue of the relations between 'pure', academic chemistry and practical chemical work. Those engaged in trying to build these delicate disciplinary structures in the 1840s were, I suggest, wary of public controversy, or perhaps too busy to engage in it, and were on the whole happy for the élite 'Gentlemen of Science' to carry the torch for Cavendish. At a time when there were strong centrifugal tendencies in the infant chemical community it would have been unwise for its leadership to engage too strenuously in a debate on the rival merits of Watt and Cavendish. It was however useful for the academic chemists, in maintaining their *de facto* leadership of the community, to identify with the disciplinary precision associated with Cavendish. The negotiation of curricula in particular, and defence of the idea that a generalist chemical curriculum could serve people destined for a wide range of occupations, including practical ones, acted out in microcosm the arguments over the utility of pure science. Cavendish was used by members of the chemical community to symbolize research pursued outside the trammels of practical exigency yet simultaneously of great potential and actual practical importance.

The 1840s was a key decade of institutional development in chemistry. The Chemical Society of London was established in 1841, as was the Pharmaceutical Society, institutionalizing the difference between the chemist 'proper' and the high street variety. The Royal College of Chemistry was founded in 1845. It has been convincingly argued that the composition and activities of the Chemical Society, and the curriculum and educational philosophy promoted in the Royal College of Chemistry, reflected the same institutional dilemma. This dilemma was how to achieve unity at some level among diverse academic, consulting and manufacturing chemists. Bud and Roberts depict the character of Victorian chemistry as an outcome of the relations between these three principal groups.[31] The second half of the

---

[31] Robert F. Bud and G.K. Roberts, *Science versus Practice: Chemistry in Victorian Britain*, 1984. See also G.K. Roberts, '"A Plea for Pure Science": The ascendency of academia in the making of the English Chemist, 1841–1914', in David Knight and Helge Kragh (eds), *The Making of the Chemist. The Social History of Chemistry in Europe, 1789–1914*, 1998, pp. 107–19.

nineteenth century saw institutional fission with the foundation of the Institute of Chemistry in 1877 and the Society of Chemical Industry in 1881, the former catering particularly to the professional qualifying concerns of chemical consultants and experts, the latter to the interests of industrial chemists and manufacturers. Yet despite this fission, the leadership of all these bodies retained a strong academic complexion. In effect, academic hegemony was maintained, moderating the centrifugal tendencies of the community.

Crucial to the establishment and maintenance of this hegemony was the articulation of the concepts of 'pure' and 'applied' science and their linkage with the notion of a liberal education in chemistry. 'Pure' science was research undertaken in pursuit of the facts of nature without concern for practical objectives. The knowledge gained thereby was to be regarded as valuable in itself but also of potential utility. 'Applied science' drew upon the stock of pure science in order to apply it in practical areas such as agriculture, industry, commerce or public health.[32] The educational philosophy supporting this – the idea of a liberal education in chemistry – maintained that a core academic education in chemistry could prepare budding chemists equally well, no matter what technical area they might subsequently enter. Disagreement and contention about whether this educational structure was indeed appropriate for the cadres of new technical personnel required in government institutions from the 1850s created the tensions leading to the split in the Chemical Society of London and the foundation of the Institute of Chemistry. However, in this case, as also in that of the Society of Chemical Industry a few years later, no serious challenge to the academic conception of appropriate education was established.

The Devonshire Commission of the early 1870s gave the academic conception a further boost with its recommendation for the establishment of science colleges in the provincial industrial areas. (That Commission was, of course, chaired by William Cavendish, Duke of Devonshire, who, as the Earl of Burlington, had represented the Cavendish family in the water controversy in the 1840s.) This was a vital step in the establishment of what became civic universities in centres such as Manchester, Liverpool, Newcastle, Birmingham and Leeds. Initially, however, students in these provincial colleges submitted to the University of London examinations. Further developments in technical education, especially in the 1890s, meant a fourfold increase in the number of students undertaking the chemistry examinations of the Department of Science and Art, from 5800 in 1876 to 24,000 in 1895. Within this expanding system, the training of technical specialists and of teachers alike partook primarily of the academic model.

James Donnelly has shown that student demand at the Royal College of Chemistry, at Owens College, Manchester, at University College, London and King's College, London was mainly motivated by interest in practical training. In the face of this there was mounted what Donnelly describes as

---

[32] G.K. Roberts, '"A Plea for Pure Science"', pp. 108–10. The categories of 'pure' and 'applied' science should not be thought of as watertight. No piece of chemical activity automatically identified itself as one type or the other. The deployment of these concepts should be treated as contingent boundary work of the sort discussed by Tom Gieryn, *Cultural Boundaries of Science: Credibility on the Line*, 1999.

a campaign by the embryonic academic community of chemistry, and some of its 'lay' supporters, to exploit the utilitarian impetus for chemistry education and 'research' whilst retaining control and independence in relation to curricula and research ... At the level of publicly-articulated ideology a battle was fought to uncouple the benefits of research and education from any immediate orientation to technical problems.[33]

Many of the leading chemists of the middle to later nineteenth century participated in this process: at University College London, Thomas Graham, Alexander W. Williamson and William Ramsay; at the Royal College of Chemistry, A.W. Hofmann and Edward Frankland; at Owens College, Manchester, Frankland, then Henry Enfield Roscoe. As students of the Royal College of Chemistry themselves moved into a variety of teaching positions, so the educational philosophy and chemical curriculum within which they had been trained was propagated.

So far as the water question in the 1840s was concerned, that cluster of chemists whose leadership intersected the Chemical Society of London, Section B of the British Association and the Cavendish Society found Cavendish an apposite figurehead as a pioneer of sophisticated, but cautious experimentation and quantification in chemistry and also as the most disinterested investigator imaginable. George Wilson, who had suggested that the chemical publishing society mooted by the London chemists be called the 'Boyle Society', took its naming instead after Cavendish as a sign that those same London chemists intended to support Cavendish in the water question.[34] This, however, was not a matter of individual predilections but rather a choice greatly influenced by the situation of the chemistry discipline at the time and, specifically, by the concern to unify its disparate groupings under the banner of 'pure science', 'applied science' and a hierarchical relationship between them.[35]

Wilson was amused that Thomas Graham was dragged publicly into the water question by David Brewster:

> I was highly delighted with the allusion to Professor Graham in the N.B. [*North British Review*] The poor professor will be astounded and seek in vain for the passage in all his works. He will be, moreover, terribly annoyed at being compelled in this strange way, to support Watt & take a side! He the cautious trimmer and President of the Cavendish! Unfortunately he is not a reader of reviews.[36]

---

[33] James Donnelly, 'Industrial recruitment of chemistry students from English universities: A revaluation of its early importance', *The British Journal for the History of Science*, **24**, 1991, 8.

[34] George Wilson to J.P. Muirhead, 28 November 1846, as copied in Muirhead to Watt Jr, 30 November 1846, Muirhead Papers, MS GEN 1354/1055. See also W.H. Brock, 'The Cavendish Society's wonderful repository of chemistry', *Annals of Science*, **47**, 1990, 79.

[35] Among leading chemists the penchant for Cavendish seems to have prevailed regardless of other divisions within the chemical community. For example, it seems to have transcended the tension between those who emphasized the role of electricity in chemical phenomena and those who saw that concentration in British chemistry as a drag on the enterprise, and a reason for its failure to keep up with continental developments. See Bud and Roberts, *Science versus Practice*, pp. 40–45.

[36] Wilson to Muirhead, 27 February 1847, Muirhead Papers, MS GEN 1354/222. The article discussed is David Brewster, 'Watt and Cavendish', *North British Review*, **6**, 1846, 473–508. Brewster contended that Watt's theory had been shown by 'living chemists of high name, Professor Graham, of University College, for example ... to be *exactly similar* to those entertained by the most distinguished philosophers

Wilson's amusement stemmed from Graham's known shyness of such conflicts. However, whatever personal dislike Graham may have had of public conflict, he had additional reasons for wanting to avoid being dragged publicly into the Watt versus Cavendish split and, indeed, for wishing that that conflict would go away. He and his colleagues sought a unifying symbolism, not a clash of cultures. Graham must have perceived a very real danger that the Watt cause might become a rallying point for those who rejected the ideological position being advanced by the chemical leadership with himself at their head.

We will see in some detail in the second attributional survey (Chapter 11) that the chemical texts produced by and for the burgeoning chemical community paid routine obeisance to Cavendish. Although leading members of the British chemical community tended to stay clear of public involvement in the water controversy, their texts provide some insight into their opinions. There was a tendency in certain quarters to grant at least a measure of credit to Watt, especially in the late 1840s and the 1850s, in the wake of the main period of controversy. However, the dominance of the pro-Cavendish position, and of attributions of the discovery to him, was quite clear.

In many ways George Wilson (1818–59) straddled the communities that supported Watt on the one hand and Cavendish on the other.[37] He was the most prominent, qualified British chemist to enter the controversy directly. Wilson was the son of an Argyllshire wine merchant. In 1832 he entered Edinburgh University as a medical student and in 1837 passed the examination of the Royal College of Surgeons in Edinburgh. During his studies he acquired a particular taste for chemistry. In 1838 he travelled to London (where his older brother Daniel was based) and worked as an unpaid assistant to Thomas Graham. In Graham's laboratory Wilson prepared his doctoral thesis on 'haloid salts of the electronegative metals'. Wilson failed to settle in London. He returned to Edinburgh and proceeded MD in June 1839. Importantly for our story, Wilson attended the British Association meeting in Birmingham that year, at which Harcourt delivered his defence of Cavendish. Wilson had been a close friend of the naturalist Edward Forbes since his student days and he was part of Forbes's circle in the Association. The members of this circle, though in many respects very critical of the organization's leadership, tended to share idealist views that would ally them with Harcourt and Whewell's camp.[38]

---

of the present day' (p. 503). The reference is almost certainly to work on the catalytic decomposition of water at high temperatures that was pursued in various ways by Graham, by William Grove and by George Wilson. Brewster indulged in a sleight of hand here in creating the impression that it is Watt's theory of 1783 that is receiving confirmation. The parallel, which Wilson also pointed to, was with Watt's *early ideas* about the convertibility of water into air by the action of heat. Wilson referred to Grove's work as an 'exact confirmation of Watt's early views'. See Wilson to Muirhead, 1 February 1847, Muirhead Papers, MS GEN 1354/218.

[37] On Wilson see: Jessie Aitken Wilson, *Memoir of George Wilson*, 1860; R.G.W. Anderson, '"What is Technology?": Education through museums in the mid-nineteenth century', *The British Journal for the History of Science*, **25**, 1992, 169–84; Charles D. Waterston, *Collections in Context: The Museum of the Royal Society of Edinburgh and the Inception of a National Museum of Scotland*, 1997.

[38] Wilson was a member of the 'Universal Brotherhood of Truth' (or Oineromathic Brotherhood), an informal association formed by a group of students at Edinburgh University and led by Edward Forbes. The members of this group maintained strong links during their later careers and displayed strong

Wilson abandoned medicine. He declined a minor chemical lectureship in London and began in 1840 to build himself a career as a lecturer in chemistry at various Edinburgh institutions. He worked hard and long hours to earn a living from his lecturing and writing. In 1845, for example, he reported writing ten lectures a week for four classes of students in the months before Christmas. As demand for his writings grew, he supplemented his income by publication. He advised a correspondent that he had undertaken the writing of a simple chemical text in order to pay the rent of his summer cottage.[39] The financial springs of his literary ventures should not be overlooked. Wilson's career reached its high point in his appointment in 1855 as Director of the Scottish Industrial Museum and, later in the same year, as Regius Professor of Technology in Edinburgh University. Wilson was best known for his work on colour blindness and for his *Life of Cavendish* (1851), which is, of course, the major source of our interest in him.

How did Wilson come to write this *Life*? It may be that his interest in Cavendish was sparked by his attendance at Harcourt's address to the British Association in 1839. Another connection was through Thomas Graham's circle. Graham was President of the chemical book publishing society established in 1846 and named the 'Cavendish Society', in whose series Wilson published the *Life of Cavendish*. W.H. Brock has explored the history of the Cavendish Society and believes its title 'was probably a deliberate anglophilic vindication of Henry Cavendish's work … '.[40] By the mid-1840s, when Wilson began a series of biographical sketches of leading chemists for the *British Quarterly Review*, he was also, apparently, in negotiation with the Cavendish Society for the opportunity to write the *Life* of the great philosopher. He told his close friend Daniel Macmillan, the publisher, tentatively about the commission in September and October 1846.[41] The opportunity may have come through George Day, the Secretary of the Cavendish Society, a friend of Wilson's from the London years in Graham's laboratory.

---

idealist commitments. For Forbes and others these commitments manifested themselves in transcendentalist views of anatomy and natural history. It is likely that Wilson's chemical views were shaped by this philosophical outlook and that they were allied with Whewell's idealist treatment (including its application to chemical composition) of the philosophy of science in his *Philosophy of the Inductive Sciences*. See Philip F. Rehbock, *The Philosophical Naturalists. Themes in Early Nineteenth-Century British Biology*, 1983, pp. 68–91; Hannah Gay and John W. Gay, 'Brothers in science: Science and fraternal culture in nineteenth-century Britain', *History of Science*, **35**, 1997, 425–53 (428–31); E. Janet Browne, 'The making of the *Memoir* of Edward Forbes, F.R.S.', *Archives of Natural History*, **10**, 1981, 205–19. On the Forbes circle's tense relations with the BAAS leadership see Morrell and Thackray, *Gentlemen of Science: Early Years*, p. 138.

[39] See George Wilson to Daniel Macmillan, 5 June 1848, Macmillan Papers, British Library, Add. MSS 55,089, ff. 101–102: 'At present I am writing a wee book for Robert Chambers on Chemistry, a thing to pay for Summer Lodgings, & warrant having no class.'

[40] W.H. Brock, 'The Society for the Perpetuation of Gmelin: The Cavendish Society, 1846–1872', *Annals of Science*, **35**, 1978, 605. In line with my general argument, the anglophilia involved may have been secondary, not least given the prominence of Scottish-born chemists among the leadership of the Cavendish Society.

[41] See Wilson to Daniel Macmillan, 17 September 1846 and 3 October 1846, Macmillan Papers, British Library, Add. MSS 55089, ff. 77–79, 80–83.

9.1   Professor George Wilson

Wilson was also connected, if more recently, with the Watt camp. He was on good terms with Muirhead after their meeting in February 1846. He helped with chemical advice to Muirhead and James Watt Jr and also on Lord Brougham's writings.[42] Muirhead and Lord Francis Jeffrey made strenuous attempts to recruit Wilson as a reviewer of Muirhead's book on the water controversy for the *Edinburgh*

---

[42] See the discussion of their relationship in Chapter 10.

Review. The review of the *Correspondence* was of course of great importance to the Watt camp and the process was carefully watched and engineered. Wilson's competence was respected and he would be a valuable person from whom to secure a positive review. This was because he was a graduate of Thomas Graham's group and therefore one of the 'New Chemists'. Also, as an Edinburgh chemical lecturer, Wilson was in a position to influence chemical opinion.[43] While Muirhead and Francis Jeffrey were keen to recruit Wilson, Watt Jr appears to have gone along rather reluctantly, not least because he doubted the wisdom of making the water question a chemical one.

Wilson did accept the commission and produced an article for the *Review*. But Francis Jeffrey, who had taken it upon himself to deal with this in the 'interregnum' between the death of Macvey Napier, the *Review*'s editor, and the appointment of his successor, considered that Wilson's effort failed to give Watt sufficient credit. Jeffrey tried to induce Wilson to make suitable additions, but Wilson seems to have refused any such compromise. Wilson eventually withdrew the article but was paid for it and subsequently advised Jeffrey on the latter's own version of the article.[44] Watt Jr felt that his reservations about 'the Edinburgh Lecturer on Chemistry' had been well founded. As he remarked to Brougham:

> After the numerous professions of impartiality made by the Edinburgh Lecturer on Chemistry, we could not have anticipated such conduct on his part, and his dogged obstinacy [in refusing to be persuaded of Watt's case] surpasses all belief ... As to an intended use of it in any other ways he had best be cautious, as he may otherwise meet with worse usage than the dreaded displeasure of Harcourt, Whewell & the Dean of Ely [Peacock] could have caused.[45]

It seems most likely that Wilson's work on the piece that so annoyed Watt Jr did become the kernel of the later *Life of Cavendish*, perhaps partly explaining the narrow focus of the work. In his negotiations with Jeffrey and Muirhead, Wilson was happy enough to praise Watt in the sense of acknowledging that he had much merit in the affair. Wilson insisted, however, that Cavendish's claims to the discovery were firmly established and he totally resisted the implication by Arago and Brougham of dishonesty on Cavendish's part.[46] In fact Wilson authored a swingeing attack on Brougham in these terms in the *British Quarterly Review*. He was more cautious, however, about affronting others involved in the controversy. In declining at one stage to undertake the review of Muirhead for the *Edinburgh Review*, Wilson, who had just read Brewster's 'conversion' article in the *North British Review*, stated: 'The N.B. [*North British*] article will be highly gratifying to Arago, Dumas, & Lord Brougham:

[43] Although the review would have been anonymous, news of authorship frequently circulated quite freely and so any endorsement that Wilson might give to the Watt case would have been a real one.

[44] This account is reconstructed from Francis Jeffrey's letters to Wilson and from the Muirhead/Wilson correspondence; see particularly Jeffrey to Wilson, 10 August 1847, Dk.6. 23/1/16–17 and Jeffrey to Wilson, n.d. [1847], Dk.6. 23/1/37, Special Collections, Edinburgh University Library. The review that was finally published was [Francis Jeffrey], 'The Discoverer of the Composition of Water; Watt or Cavendish?', *Edinburgh Review*, **87**, 1848, 67–137.

[45] James Watt Jr to Henry Brougham, 17 September 1847, Brougham Papers, 29,218.

[46] See Wilson to Muirhead, 18 December 1846, Muirhead Papers, MS GEN 1354/214.

and grievously vexatious to Harcourt & Whewell. It were best then to "let well alone" as I cannot afford like Sir David to make these last transgressors my mortal foes, and I am unable unfortunately to satisfy the first illustrious three.'[47] Here is clear evidence that the ideological stance and power of the 'Gentlemen of Science' continued to shape the controversy for subsequent key authors.

Wilson's career as a chemical lecturer in Edinburgh depended upon recruiting students from among those engaged in medical studies in the town. A significant number were former Cambridge men, whom Wilson described as keeping him on his toes.[48] Figures such as Whewell and Peacock would have exercised considerable influence over the choice of lecturers by Cambridge men studying in Edinburgh. Thus there were rather direct, career-related, reasons why Wilson could not afford to make foes of Whewell and Harcourt. Although Wilson's *Life of Cavendish* was not a 'party' production, it was inevitably shaped by the larger ideological battle.

We gain insight into Wilson's relations with Cambridge people from his correspondence with his old friend Daniel Macmillan, who was intimately involved in the Cambridge scene. Wilson on the one hand appeared very concerned about what the Cambridge people thought about him, especially Whewell and Peacock.[49] Yet he was also quite willing to criticize them, albeit privately. The *History of the Inductive Sciences* was found to be inaccurate. Wilson, having been informed by Macmillan of the views around Cambridge of Scottish universities and the talk that the productions of 'Scotchmen' were never very accurate, wrote a humourous reply worth quoting at length:

> In sober seriousness my good Daniel what tempted you to repeat these 'havers' about Scotch ignorance. Most true it is that Scotchmen are not 'very accurate'. Neither are Frenchmen, nor Germans, nor Dutchmen, nor Poles, nor Russians, nor Norwegians, nor Swedes, nor Persians, nor Chinese, nor Turks, nor Caffres, nor Esqimaux. Only Rome is infallible. Oxford perhaps which casts sheeps' eyes towards the Seven Hills may put in a claim that way also. But I never heard that Cambridge could.[50]

The scoffers in Cambridge need not go across the Tweed 'or even across the Cam' to find examples of not very accurate men. He proceeded to enumerate examples of mistakes in Cambridge mathematical texts. Then, writing of Whewell, he said:

> Dare one scoff at him? Can the Head of Trinity be a blunderer? Is it possible that he is a Scotchman? He must be, for he is "very inaccurate". His presumptious history of the

---

[47] George Wilson to J.P. Muirhead, 1 February 1847, Muirhead Papers, MS GEN 1354/218.

[48] Jessie Aitken Wilson, *Memoir of George Wilson MD, FRSE*, 1860, pp. 245, 254. Wilson considered himself in 1840 as 'pretty certain of getting the Cambridge men, one and all' in his lecture course. It is likely that by the time he was getting embroiled in the water controversy he had built a steady clientele from that source.

[49] See, for example, Wilson to Macmillan, 6 August 1847, British Library, Add. MSS 55,089, ff. 93–94, in which Wilson told Macmillan about his forthcoming *Edinburgh Review* article (which of course never actually came forth!) and asked to be told whatever Macmillan could learn about Whewell's and Peacock's reaction to it.

[50] Wilson to Macmillan, 11 April 1847, Macmillan Papers, British Library, Add. MSS 55,089, ff. 90–92.

Inductive Sciences is wofully [*sic*] shamefully inaccurate. I do not say throughout, but on the subjects I know slightly, I pity the still slighter knowledge, & most pretentious ignorance of Master W.

Nor did Peacock escape:

Can he be Scotch also? Depend upon it he is, for how else can his blundering be accounted for[?] About a year ago, I was consulted as to the merits of an Article on the Water Question, which appeared in the Quarterly Review. I did not know its Author, but I was compelled to acknowledge that though it advocated my views, it was full of most discreditable chemical inaccuracies. It has since been acknowledged by Dean Peacock, who poor man is very proud of it.[51]

This captures well the attitude of Wilson, the true chemical expert and 'Scotchman', to the ideologues of Cambridge. Yet he was careful, and wise, to express such views privately, and then only to close friends.

The arguments presented by Wilson on behalf of Cavendish were detailed, complex and thorough. In a systematic fashion Wilson examined not only the writings and actions of the major protagonists in the original controversy but also *every* argument mounted in the subsequent literature by Watt Jr, Muirhead, Brougham, Arago, Harcourt, Brewster, Jeffrey and others. My chief concern is with Wilson's approach to the issue of 'discovery'. What distinguished Wilson's work, and what also makes it extremely difficult to read, is that he went to great lengths to contextualize both the knowledge and actions of protagonists. For example, we learn much more from Wilson than from anyone else about the experiments of Cavendish, Priestley, Lavoisier and others. In particular, Wilson was very concerned to show what Cavendish and Priestley *really meant* by such key terms as 'phlogiston', 'inflammable air' and 'air'. In doing this he entered into their intellectual life-worlds in a way that is much in tune with modern empathic historiography.[52] Yet no sooner had Wilson done this than he engaged in presentist scientific judgements about whether the protagonists' knowledge was sound or not, and whether it could have been sound given what they *really* had physically in their apparatus.

In the same vein as Harcourt, but in much more detail, Wilson argued that Priestley's experiment, because he used charcoal in preparing his inflammable air, could not have produced the pure mixture of gases in the correct ratio to produce only water on combustion. Therefore, in so far as Watt's inferences were correct (that too is disputed but can be left aside for the moment), they *could not have been properly drawn* from Priestley's experiments. Thus, either we say that Watt drew

---

[51] Ibid.

[52] A good example of Wilson's sometimes impeccable historical practice is provided by the way he deals with the question of what can be concluded from Cavendish's laboratory notebook. Watt's supporters, such as Brougham, made a good deal of the fact that Cavendish's notebooks do not contain any claim to draw a conclusion about the composition of water from the experiments they record. Wilson shows through an elaborate analysis of Cavendish's method of working that he *never* entered conclusions in his notebook of such a significant kind. The absence of conclusions about the composition of water is thus normal practice and does not indicate that Cavendish hadn't drawn any conclusions. (See George Wilson, *The Life of the Honble Henry Cavendish*, 1851, pp. 366–72.)

his inferences from Cavendish's experiments as imperfectly transmitted via Priestley's attempt to replicate them (and thus give Watt's inferences some basis in sound experimental practice at the expense of attributing to him knowledge of Cavendish's experiments that he didn't have at the time), or we cut Watt's inferences adrift from a sound experimental basis altogether and they become groundless, if inspired, speculations. Either way, the idea that Watt inferred a theory of the composition of water by a sound method is made to look suspect.

Wilson went further than his fellow Cavendish supporters in acknowledging an important problem with this line of argument. Whatever nice distinctions between the conceptual and experimental bases of Watt's views and those of Cavendish can be made in retrospect, these were not known, and in some cases could not have been known, by their contemporaries. So, Wilson seems to concede 'the issue of priority is to be decided by date alone'. In the end, however, Wilson cannot divorce the 'what' from the 'when' because his case for Cavendish having drawn conclusions on the basis of his experiments prior to Watt had to be built on *indirect* evidence. Wilson acknowledged that we do not have any explicit statement of a theory of the composition of water from Cavendish before his published paper. So Wilson's case was based on a hermeneutic analysis of Cavendish's programme of experimental work. Wilson sought to show that the direction, course, strategy and tactics of Cavendish's experiments on air from 1781 to late 1783 *only made sense* if he had drawn conclusions about the composition of water at a stage prior to Watt.[53]

While engaging in these complex hermeneutic arguments Wilson often seems to be adopting a radically contextualist account. He wanted to grant great credit to Watt, whose contemporaries might justly have regarded him as a discoverer in this case. Wilson conceded that Watt assisted in 'inducing belief in the compound nature of water', that his work did service 'at a certain epoch in the progress of discovery, and has a place in the history of science, whether it pleases us that it should have such a place or not'.[54] In the end, however, Wilson believed that the issue of discovery could and should be decided on his own knowledge of the true state of affairs. And that true state of affairs centred most clearly on the sustained experimental programme of Cavendish, and his careful, judicious and accurate method of working:

> Had [Cavendish] never experimented, or had he never reported his results to Priestley, there is no reason to suppose that Watt would have conjectured, even remotely, that water is a compound of oxygen and inflammable air. *He was not on the track of such a discovery.* His speculations on the convertibility of steam into a permanent gas by the change of all its latent into sensible heat, did not point in that, but in exactly the opposite direction. He was following Priestley in all his devious wanderings, and going astray along with him ... when Priestley's repetition of Cavendish's experiments (in which all

---

[53] See ibid., pp. 317–79. Other evidence is appealed to. If there were no conclusions drawn, then what could Lavoisier have pinched from Cavendish, via Blagden? The latter claims to have made known to Lavoisier in the spring of 1783 not only Cavendish's experiments but also his conclusions. Of course the assumption of bad faith on Blagden's and/or Cavendish's part can undermine this. But Wilson's whole analysis insists on assuming the good faith of all involved. Wilson's life philosophy involved always assuming the best about people.

[54] Wilson, *Life of Cavendish*, p. 437.

that was true and significant was Cavendish's) arrested him in his mistaken course, and enabled him to approximate to the true theory of the composition of water.[55]

In depicting Watt as 'not on the track' of the discovery of the composition of water, Wilson effectively deconstructed the 'identity claim' made by the supporters of Watt. Their easy assumption that Watt's theory was essentially the same as Cavendish's conclusions was undermined by Wilson's careful depiction of Watt's intellectual world, of the pedigree and context of his ideas. When it came to Cavendish, however, Wilson was not quite so thorough. He did acknowledge that Cavendish remained in the thrall of phlogiston theory. Wilson even conceded that Cavendish saw half of the water in the vessel at the conclusion of sparking experiments as condensed rather than produced. Crucially, however, Wilson contended that Cavendish did regard the other half as produced and therefore genuinely compounded from the original gases.[56] On this basis Wilson argued that Cavendish could claim the discovery. It is important also, however, to recall Wilson's and Harcourt's overall conception of what the discovery of the composition of water consisted in and what its significance was. That significance was not confined to showing that water is a compound rather than an element. It involved the typification of a whole class of chemical reactions and therefore the establishment of the basis of modern chemical practice. On this conception, the discovery could only be properly found in the wider context of a disciplined and sustained programme of research of the kind, and the range, pursued by Cavendish and not so readily attributable to Watt. In this sense, Wilson's whole account of the controversy was predicated on a concern to assert the standards of modern chemical discipline that Cavendish was taken to prefigure. 'Discovery' was treated within that framework of disciplinary concerns and heritage.

Wilson's biography of Cavendish was published, of course, in the year of the Great Exhibition. In the wake of that Exhibition a series of lectures on its results was given before the Society of Arts at the initiative of Prince Albert. Two of these are of particular interest to us. On 26 November 1851, William Whewell spoke on the 'General Bearing of the Great Exhibition on the Progress of Art and Science'. He concentrated on the relationship of Art and Science and noted that with regard to chemical processes and products, 'science has not only overtaken Art, but is the whole foundation, the entire creator of the art'. He continued: 'The great chemical manufactories which have sprung up at Liverpool, at Newcastle, at Glasgow owe their existence entirely to a profound and scientific knowledge of chemistry. These arts never could have existed if there had not been a science of chemistry; and that, an exact and philosophical science.'[57] Whewell having set out in general terms the value of science to Art, most especially in chemistry, the lecture of 7 January 1852 was given by Lyon Playfair, a major architect of the transformation of science education. Playfair addressed 'The Chemical Principles involved in the Manufactures of the Exhibition'. He warmed to the theme, declaring that 'The discoverer of

---

55 Ibid. (my italics).

56 Ibid., pp. 387–89; J.R. Partington, *A History of Chemistry*, vol. 3, 1962, p. 335.

57 William Whewell, 'The general bearing of the Great Exhibition on the progress of art and science', in *Lectures on the Results of the Great Exhibition of 1851, Delivered before the Society of Arts, Manufactures and Commerce, at the Suggestion of H.R.H. Prince Albert*, 1852, p. 28.

abstract laws, however apparently remote from practice, is the real benefactor to his kind; in reality, far more so than he who applies them directly to industry.'[58]

> The cultivators of abstract science, the searchers after truth, for eternal truth's sake, are – to borrow a simile, I believe from Canning – the horses of the chariot of industry; those who usefully apply the truths are the harness by which the motion is communicated to the chariot. But is the chariot drawn by the horses or the harness? Truth to say, in this country of ours, – and mark you well, in no other country in Europe, – we honour the harness, but neglect the horses ...[59]

Playfair argued that one could examine the work of abstract philosophers and trace from them numerous applications. He then identified Cavendish as the archetype:

> The very impersonification of abstract science was Cavendish ... yet, this man, destitute of passions and of sympathies ... has by his mind, which still lives, conferred more real material benefit upon Industry than any of the so-termed 'practical' men who have succeeded him. His discovery of the composition of water has given to Industry a vitality and an intelligence, the effects of which it would be difficult to exaggerate.[60]

Playfair had read, and referred to, Wilson's biography. He and Wilson had met in Thomas Graham's laboratory in the 1830s and remained close acquaintances. It was to be partly thanks to Playfair's influence that Wilson obtained his appointments as Director of the Royal Scottish Museum and the Professorship of Technology at the University of Edinburgh. Playfair's lecture shows how the connection was made between Cavendish the abstract philosopher and the burgeoning industrial strength of Britain in the 1850s.

By the time Wilson published his *Life* of Cavendish, the ideological convenience of Cavendish being reaffirmed as the discoverer of the composition of water was enormous. Chemistry was being described (by Whewell among others) as the archetypal science of science-based industry, as *the* example of the power of abstract science as an industrial force. If someone as remote as Cavendish could be convincingly portrayed as having such industrial impact, then the case for the value of abstract science was made. Social and, where appropriate, governmental support ought to follow for the promotion of scientific research and science education, but, crucially, on the terms desired by the leadership of the scientific community and

---

[58] Lyon Playfair, 'The chemical principles involved in the manufactures of the Exhibition', in *Lectures on the Results of the Great Exhibition of 1851, Delivered before the Society of Arts, Manufactures and Commerce, at the Suggestion of H.R.H. Prince Albert*, 1852, p. 190.

[59] Ibid.

[60] Ibid., pp. 192–93. The most extreme claim of this type for Cavendish that I have come across was made by Sir William Harcourt, then Home Secretary, on 14 October 1884, when he presented the prizes to students of the central school of science in Derby: 'In chemistry Derbyshire can boast of one of the earliest and one of the greatest of all the discoverers in chemistry ... Henry Cavendish, the discoverer of the composition of water ... Little could Henry Cavendish know how much that discovery of his would tend to the greatness and the wealth of the country to which he belonged. What he discovered was the foundation to a great degree of all Watt did, and the discovery of the steam engine and the uses of steam which have revolutionized the world' ('Sir William Harcourt at Derby', *The Times*, 15 October 1884, p. 7).

granting autonomy, as well as control of their diverse community, to those pursuing abstract scientific investigations.

Conclusion

I have argued that Cavendish's claim to discovery of the composition of water, and his scientific character more generally, was important to a number of constituencies in early Victorian Britain. He symbolized a kind of fundamental, quantitative research pursued in a thorough, cautious fashion that was important to the scientific self-image of his supporters. The chemists also appear to have adopted Cavendish as a figurehead, and one of their number, George Wilson, constructed a complex chemical rationale for awarding the discovery of the composition of water, that centrepiece of the New Chemistry, to him. Both the ideologues of the British Association and members of the élite chemical community found in Cavendish a useful symbol in negotiating the boundaries of abstract and practical science. By the 1850s the argument was being made more insistently that abstract science was, in the end, the source of the most significant practical benefits and so worthy of national support. Abstract science also needed to be protected from the stifling effects of a focus on immediate practicality. The choice between Watt and Cavendish portended much. In Lyon Playfair's terms, to choose Watt was to honour the harness; to choose Cavendish was to honour the horses.

Chapter 10

The Controversy Joined, 1840–60

Introduction

In preceding chapters we have learned in detail about the various individuals and groups who participated in the water controversy and about the springs and character of their involvement. However, except incidentally in order to help in their characterization, we have not pursued the progress of the controversy proper as it was fought out in private and in public over almost two decades following the release of Arago's *Eloge* and Harcourt's rejoinder to it at Birmingham.

In 1858, Muirhead rehearsed once again the arguments at the heart of the controversy but also ventured a history of the controversy itself. He asserted that, by 1848, when Francis Jeffrey published his article on the question in the *Edinburgh Review*, the controversy was essentially over. In his view it was over and settled in favour of Watt.[1] Muirhead regarded the publication of the *Correspondence* in 1846 as the decisive move. He believed that it removed all obstacles to a general recognition of Watt's priority. Watt Jr had regarded this as his trump card right from the beginning. Muirhead reinforced the idea of the *Correspondence* as decisive by recounting its role in Brewster's 'conversion':

> As an instance of the change which was wrought by the force of the truth on the convictions of others equally distinguished, we may mention a most eminent philosopher [Brewster], who having, at a former period, on the imperfect information then open to him, been disposed to support the claims of Cavendish, on fully studying the fresh evidence which the correspondence of Mr. Watt first made public, unhesitatingly professed his entire conversion; and ... publicly announced, as the conclusion at which he had arrived, that the argument for Mr. Watt's priority 'had now been placed on a sound and impregnable basis'.[2]

Unsurprisingly, this view was not shared by the Cavendish camp. We have seen already that Whewell, far from treating the publication of the *Correspondence* as decisive, considered that it did not contain 'any reason for withdrawing' what he had previously stated in his *Philosophy of the Inductive Sciences*. Cavendish's experiments and conclusions, Whewell maintained, conformed to the model of sound scientific practice whilst Watt's decisively did not. This was tantamount to saying that no evidence of a circumstantial kind could ever resolve the controversy

---

[1] See J.P. Muirhead, *Life of James Watt*, 1858, pp. 379, 383.

[2] Ibid., p. 378. We saw above in Chapter 7 that there are reasons to doubt that Brewster was in fact dramatically converted by the evidence of the *Correspondence*. However, it was clearly to the Watt camp's benefit to go along with Brewster's fiction.

in Watt's favour since it had already been settled in philosophical principle for Cavendish. For Whewell, too, the controversy was over, but the *Correspondence* had nothing to do with that situation. Such a stance did not encourage a sanguine view of the likely productivity of debate. Whewell believed that he had the correct philosophical test for identifying discoveries as such. Nothing else was needed.

It is probably true that, as a live debate, the water controversy effectively ceased in the late 1840s. This would help explain why the most substantial treatment of it, George Wilson's *Life of the Honble Henry Cavendish*, created little stir on its publication in 1851. Whilst there could be many other reasons for this – it was a long and complex book, not many copies were printed, it was not widely reviewed – it may well be that the controversy was already running out of steam by the time Wilson's book appeared. The clash of interests that sustained the controversy was perhaps attenuating.

So, let us follow our cast of characters from 1839 in their public exchanges and their private reflections in order to ascertain what they saw as the life of the controversy, how their positions changed (if at all), and at what stage the controversy came to be regarded as resolved or no longer of great moment. The main bursts of activity were, first, in the immediate wake of the publication of the *Eloge* and, second, in 1845–46, when a spate of significant publications appeared, most of them triggered by the writings of Henry Brougham.

In the Wake of the *Eloge*

Harcourt's rejoinder to Arago's *Eloge* of Watt came so quickly that many people would have learned of the one from the other. Muirhead's translation of the *Eloge*, and the translation done for the *Edinburgh New Philosophical Journal*, quickly appeared also. The Watt camp moved on a number of fronts. Muirhead was able to develop a brief response to Harcourt in the notes to his translation of the *Eloge*. This was difficult, however, because apart from the testimony of those who had heard the Address, there were only accounts in *The Athenaeum* and in the press to rely upon in reconstructing exactly what Harcourt had said.

In his note Muirhead chided Harcourt for attacking an absent foreigner (Arago) and for failing to engage with the evidence in Brougham's 'Historical Note' to the *Eloge*. Muirhead argued that Arago, as Secretary of the French Academy of Sciences, was by virtue of his character and his position to be 'exempted from all suspicion of indifference to the intellectual glory of his nation'. How much more credible then was Arago when he dropped any claim for Lavoisier in the water controversy and sought to form 'an impartial estimate of the respective claims of two Englishmen'.[3] Muirhead noted that Harcourt's main argument was founded on Cavendish's character and reputation but maintained that, whatever Cavendish's merits as an experimentalist and a philosopher, his behaviour according to the facts unearthed by Arago and Brougham was the only basis for judgement. To stories of Cavendish's diffidence and modesty Muirhead replied with similar accounts of

---

[3] François Arago, *Historical Eloge of James Watt ... Translated from the French by James Patrick Muirhead*, 1839, p. 114.

Watt's demeanour. He responded briefly to other claims about Watt's view of the nature of phlogiston but otherwise Muirhead professed himself startled at the lack of any evidence in Harcourt's rash production. By this, as we have argued, Muirhead meant the lack of evidence on dates. Harcourt 'not daring to grapple with the priority of publication ... expends himself in tedious sophistical declamation on the merits of the respective explanations of their theories'. Finally, Muirhead challenged Harcourt's taste in making his attack in Birmingham, an action that 'has left no impression so strong, as that of general DISGUST'.[4]

Privately the Watt camp speculated about whether Harcourt's attack was a lone effort, or, more likely, they thought, a product of 'conspiracy' involving other leading British Association and Cambridge figures. They also moved to try to secure a friendly review in the *Edinburgh*. We saw that this was unsuccessful. Frustrated by Macvey Napier, the Watt camp had Brougham's note of invective against Harcourt rejected for publication and the review of Arago's *Eloge* entrusted to the unreliable Brewster. The latter, of course, set about pleasing everybody, and his ingenious compromise position published in January 1840, ended up pleasing no one.

Watt Jr and Muirhead had become aware soon after the publication of Arago's *Eloge* that in London the naturalist Robert Brown was taking an interest in the water question, particularly in the aspersions cast on Cavendish's character by Arago and Brougham.[5] Watt Jr appeared confident in the knowledge that Brown had been 'charged by the Cavendish family to prepare an answer'.[6] Brown would have been widely regarded as well placed to investigate the water question. He had, after all, known Cavendish well during his years as Librarian to Sir Joseph Banks and had inherited the charge of the Banksian collections and papers, which he had supervised from his post at the British Museum. Brown had remained active in science. He had supported the cause of reform with the Cambridge men in the 1830 Royal Society election and had received an honorary DCL (Doctor of Civil Law) at the Oxford meeting of the British Association in 1832. By 1839 Brown was an elder stateman of science better placed than most to investigate happenings in the early days of the Banksian regime.

We do know that in October and November 1839 Brown, with the assistance of J.J. Bennett, did a good deal of work on the history of the discovery of the composition of water, the outlines of which can be followed in Brown's papers at the British Library.[7] Brown investigated printed sources of many sorts from the 1780s. In August and September 1839 he had visited Paris and gained access to the register of the Académie, where the meeting at which Lavoisier and Laplace recounted their experiments was recorded.[8] Given the involvement of Blagden in the affair, many would have assumed that the Banks letters would contain information relevant to his contentious activities and therefore hold a key to the question of

---

[4] Ibid., note on pp. 115–16.

[5] The following relies on, while clarifying, the account in David Mabberley, *Jupiter Botanicus. Robert Brown and the British Museum*, 1985, pp. 337–39.

[6] Watt Jr to Henry Brougham, 28 November 1839, Brougham Papers, 20,135.

[7] British Library, Add. MSS 33,227.

[8] Ibid., f. 59.

priority and, in particular, whether Cavendish had known of Watt's ideas and taken them as his own.

In the coffee room of the Athenaeum Club in London sometime in mid-October 1839, Brown met Charles Hampden Turner, an old friend of Watt Jr's. Turner was on a mission to discover what light, if any, the Banks–Blagden letters might throw on the controversy. For his part, Brown was interested to see the Watt correspondence on the water question that, as Turner confirmed, Watt Jr was considering publishing. Correspondence at the time reveals that initially Watt Jr was quite happy for Brown to consult his father's letters on the water question, and tentative arrangements were made for him to do so. However, Brown had fallen foul of Arago during his Paris visit. Arago, for whatever reason, was upset that Brown had accessed the archives of the Académie without his (Arago's) knowledge. So, when Watt Jr decided to consult Arago and Brougham on the wisdom of giving Brown the chance to see Watt's water correspondence, Arago suggested that Brown be denied it. A game of cat and mouse ensued, with Brown trying to gain access to correspondence between J.B. Pentland and Aston Hall explaining the reasons for this ban. Turner read some extracts to Brown but refused him a copy of the letter that would have explained Arago's reasons.[9] Watt Jr accepted Arago's and Brougham's advice not to allow Brown to see the Watt correspondence and, importantly, not to publish it at that point. Their concern was a strategic one with which Watt Jr agreed: 'I certainly have all along been of opinion that there will be advantages attending its coming out after our opponents have set forth their case.'[10]

Brown's intervention and his subsequent fading from the scene are interesting in a number of respects. Brown was clear that he became involved only because of the 'moral' question, that is, the charge of foul play against Cavendish. In a statement written after the publication of the Watt Correspondence, Brown acknowledged that if the question had been entirely chemical then he would not have become involved because of his 'imperfect acquaintance' with that science. However, because, with the publication of Arago's *Eloge*, the question became partly a moral one, affecting Cavendish's reputation, he and Bennett became interested in the question, which did not seem to require chemical knowledge beyond their reach.[11] Thus Brown took a rather different tack to Harcourt and Whewell, who were pursuing a primarily chemical argument. Brown was chasing empirical matters of priority, seeming, in fact, to adopt the same model of discovery as the Watt camp members. He invested enormous labour in determining dates, and the movements of key people. Harcourt subsequently relied on Brown for information on such questions. Brown read the proofs of Harcourt's 'Address' and offered advice on dates and interpolations.[12]

---

[9] Brown recounts his version of events in 'Memorandum written Decr 4th 1839 of the substance of what has passed between Mr Hampden Turner and myself on the subject of the controversy respecting the discovery of the composition of water', Correspondence of Robert Brown, British Library, Add. MSS. 32,441, ff. 336–37 and also see ff. 338–39.

[10] Watt Jr to Muirhead, 16 November 1839, No. 2, Muirhead Papers, MS GEN 1354/430.

[11] British Library, Add. MSS 33,227, ff. 76–79.

[12] See copy of Harcourt to Brown, 8 September 1839 in BL Add. MSS 33,227, ff. 87–88 and Brown to Harcourt, 14 June 1840 [Draft] in BL Add. MSS 33,227, f. 93. It appears also that Brown engaged in what I have called an 'attributional survey' of publications.

Brown had intended to publish something on the water question himself, and there was certainly an expectation among the Cavendish and Watt camps in late 1839 that he would do so. In the event nothing appeared, though Brown did continue to quietly advise Harcourt.[13] It seems likely that Brown acceded to the approach taken by Harcourt and Whewell. By March 1840, Muirhead was stating confidently that Brown had cold feet, that he was 'not known to be doing anything, and is believed to be doing and intending to do nothing. He is considered a cautious man, who will not unnecessarily argue a bad case, or attempt to extract any arguments in his favour, from facts which are all against him.'[14] An aspect of Brown's work did surface publicly, and posthumously in 1859, of which more below. Otherwise, he played no further identifiable role in the controversy.

Aston Hall, meanwhile, looked for reaction to Harcourt from across the Channel. Muirhead was 'full of interest and hope in the approaching crucifixion of Harcourt' in 'our Chief's speech'.[15] It was Arago's account, after all, which had been attacked by Harcourt. Arago, as usual, was threatening dire revenge. He wrote in November invoking the idea of a clerical conspiracy at about the same time as he advised against showing the correspondence to Robert Brown. Arago's main public response, however, came on the occasion of the presentation of a copy of Muirhead's translation of the *Eloge* to the Académie des Sciences. Whilst noting the larger problems with Harcourt's argument, Arago dealt with what he described as Harcourt's two principal objections. One concerned whether Priestley had weighed the gases prior to explosion and the dew produced by it and found them equal. The other matter was Arago's use of the term 'hydrogène' for the word 'phlogistique'. Harcourt had attacked this as a sleight of hand. In response, Arago presented to the Académie an autograph letter of Priestley to Lavoisier, dated 10 July 1782, in which the English philosopher stated the identity of inflammable air and phlogiston. This, Arago contended, showed that the substitution was entirely justified. After this characteristic piece of theatre from Arago, Dumas spoke. He advised the Académie, it was reported:

qu'après avoir examiné attentivement l'argumentation de son confrère; qu'après avoir fait aussi à *Aston-Hall*, près de *Birmingham*, chez M. *Watt* fils, une étude scrupuleuse de la correspondence de l'illustre ingénieur, il adopte complétement, et dans toutes ses parties, l'histoire que M. *Arago* a écrite de la découverte de la composition de l'eau. 'Mes opinions sur ce point sont tellement arrêtées, dit M. *Dumas*, que je désire voir ma déclaration consignée dans le *Compte rendu* de cette séance.'[16]

Muirhead communicated the substance of this to Watt Jr, commenting triumphantly:

---

[13] See drafts and copies of Brown to Harcourt, 7 February 1846 and Harcourt to Brown, 10 February 1846, BL Add. MSS 33,227, ff. 96 and 98, which deal with advice that Brown gave to Harcourt about his paper dealing with Brougham in the *Philosophical Magazine*.

[14] Muirhead to Watt Jr, 28 March 1840, Muirhead Papers, MS GEN 1354/481.

[15] Muirhead to Watt Jr, 17 January 1840, Muirhead Papers, MS GEN 1354/466. The 'Chief' was, of course, Arago.

[16] 'Correspondance. Histoire de la chimie', *Comptes rendus hebdomadaires des séances de l'Académie des Sciences*, **10**, 1840, 109–11.

There is a declaration which will be viewed, throughout Europe, among all the paltry shuffling of Brewster and suchlike, – 'velut inter ignes Luna minores'. Arago, Brougham, and Dumas, are a worthy triumvirate to maintain the certainty of evidence and the rights of your father, against Harcourt, Brewster, and Brown![17]

There was still, of course, no printed version of Harcourt's Address. As we noted, Harcourt had received some assistance from Robert Brown in working the speech up for publication. He received more assistance, though, from William Whewell, as we discussed in Chapter 7. Whewell helped to provide a philosophical framework for Harcourt's argument while the Cavendish family provided him with access to Cavendish's experimental notebooks. The latter gave Harcourt what he regarded as decisive proof that Cavendish had drawn conclusions from his experiments before Watt had his idea. Writing to J.D. Forbes in January 1840, Harcourt, who had felt somewhat under siege immediately after the 1839 meeting, was newly buoyant and confident. This new material would arm him against 'any of your philosophers, seduced in an unlucky hour by the good fare of the Soho works, or by that sympathy which is the one thing, according to Johnson, stronger than truth in a northern bosom'.[18] Harcourt described his valuable find to Whewell in March 1840:

> I have got from the Duke of Devonshire, thro' Lord Burlington, Cavendish's Mss and luckily found among them his day book of the exp[ts] in question, regularly dated, & shewing beyond further question that <u>one and all</u>, including those by which he first discovered the composition of Nitric acid as well as of water, were made, and the whole investigation completed, between two and three months before Priestley ... gave occasion to Watt to speculate on the subject ... So preposterous a claim to another man's discovery never was set up, as that which Arago, unhappily for Watt's character for candor, has revived.[19]

Watt Jr and Muirhead saw the published version of Harcourt's 'Address' in late August 1840. They had spent almost a year demonizing him. Now, here, finally was

[17] Muirhead to Watt Jr, 18 February 1840, Muirhead Papers, MS GEN 1354/473.

[18] Harcourt to Forbes, 11 January 1840, Forbes Papers, Incoming Letters, 1840, item 2.

[19] Harcourt to Whewell, 16 March [1840], Whewell Papers, Add. Ms.a.205[138(1–2)]. The Cavendish family supported Harcourt's efforts. Harcourt had sent a copy of the *Athenaeum* report of his Birmingham speech to Lord Burlington. Returning thanks for it, Burlington advised Harcourt that he had been making inquiries after any Cavendish papers 'which would assist in vindicating his character'. Burlington considered that his family 'ought to feel deeply indebted to you for having vindicated Cavendish's character on so public an occasion; I take great shame upon myself for having been hitherto so passive on the subject, but I hope you will be so good as to let me know if you think I can be of any further use to you, or if any other mode occurs to you in which I might be able to assist in obtaining information'. (Burlington to Harcourt, 28 September 1839, *Harcourt Papers*, vol. 14, pp. 98–99.) William Cavendish (1808–91), Lord Burlington, was educated at Trinity College, Cambridge graduating as 2nd Wrangler and 1st Smith's Prizeman in 1829. He served as MP for Cambridge University from 1829 to 1831 and became second Earl of Burlington in 1834. He served as President of the British Association in 1837–38. Subsequently he was to become the 7th Duke of Devonshire and Chancellor of the University of Cambridge. It is perhaps not surprising that Burlington served as the main intermediary to the family archives recording the work of his distinguished ancestor.

the fully documented argument, including the extensive, and presumably expensive, lithographs from Cavendish's notebooks. Muirhead was not impressed: 'Harcourt's flourish of trumpets led me to apprehend that he had discovered in the MSS so carefully lithographed, something decisive as to the <u>conclusions</u>. But on reading the facsimile carefully over, I cannot find a word of those conclusions in the whole of them.'[20] Muirhead found in the lithographs only proof that Cavendish 'never suspected the real nature of the process' by which water was formed until he heard Watt's deductions. The notebook showed, he claimed, that Cavendish believed in a mechanical deposit of water that he described as 'condensed'. The detail and scrupulousness of the journal meant that if conclusions had been drawn by Cavendish they would be there: 'it is impossible to suppose that notice of the celebrated <u>conclusions</u> would be altogether omitted, if they had existed in Cavendish's own mind at the time during which he conducted the expts'.[21]

Even as the Watt camp digested Harcourt's efforts, the next meeting of the British Association was imminent. The worthies of Glasgow had been pulling out all the stops. The enthusiasm of the locals threatened to bring ongoing private rumblings over water to the surface again. In December 1839, the Glasgow local committee had added Brougham to their number, in an honorary capacity, and they thought it a good idea to ask him to chair Section A. The locals were apparently unaware that there might be reasons for the volatile Brougham to continue the controversy at the Glasgow meeting. Murchison stepped in and resolved the matter. J.D. Forbes became President of the Section.[22]

Murchison and Edward Sabine, the General Secretaries, gave the Address at Glasgow in lieu of a Presidential Address. They invoked the genius of Watt but left ambiguous the extent to which he was to be seen as a 'man of science':

> raised through the industry and genius of her sons, to a pinnacle of commercial grandeur, well can this city estimate her obligations to science! ... she feels how much her progress depends upon an acquaintance with the true structure of the rich deposits which form her subsoil; and great as they are, she clearly sees that her manufactures may at a moment take a new flight by mechanical discoveries. For she it is, you all know, who nurtured the man whose genius has changed the tide of human interests, by calling into active energy a power which (as wielded by him), in abridging time and space, has doubled the value of human life, and has established for his memory a lasting claim on the gratitude of the civilized world. The names of Watt and Glasgow are united in imperishable records![23]

At the dinner given for the Association by the Magistrates and Town Council of Glasgow, the list of toasts included an early one to 'The Memory of James Watt, and the other eminent men of Great Britain who have contributed to the Advancement

---

[20] Muirhead to Watt Jr, 31 August 1840, Muirhead Papers, MS GEN 1354/502.

[21] Ibid.

[22] Morrell and Thackray, *Gentlemen of Science: Early Years*, pp. 215–16. See also Murchison to Harcourt, 22 March 1840 in Morrell and Thackray (eds), *Gentlemen of Science. Early Correspondence*, pp. 330–31.

[23] 'Address by Roderick Impey Murchison and Major Edward Sabine', *Report of the Tenth Meeting of the BAAS Held at Glasgow in August 1840*, 1841, p. xxxv.

of Science'.[24] The wording of this so as to include Watt among men of science must have caused a little nervousness in some quarters about what else might be to come, though it was safely proposed by General Tscheffkine.

After the Glasgow meeting in 1840 the water controversy seems to have been successfully buried, so far as the meetings of the Association were concerned, for all of fifty years, until Edward Thorpe raised it again at the Leeds meeting in 1890.[25] By then the chief issue was to defend Cavendish's secure claim against a revival of that of Lavoisier.

The stir created by the publication of the *Eloge*, translations of it, Harcourt's 'Address', Brewster's review in the *Edinburgh Review*, and Arago's and Dumas's brief response before the Académie, had died down by late 1840. The next few years were to be a period of relative quiet. This does not mean, of course, that nothing was going on behind the scenes. Watt Jr spent a good part of the period 1840–42 on estate and business affairs. His Welsh estates were expanded and improvements such as planting, fencing and building preoccupied him. This was also the time when the partnership between Watt Jr and M.R. Boulton was dissolved and new partners were taken on. The transition went well and eventually gave Watt Jr more leisure to spend at Doldowlod, but for the moment it was time consuming. The water question took a back seat for a while but was never far from view. Watt Jr appears to have assumed, now that the publication of Watt's water correspondence had been postponed for tactical reasons, that the next step lay with Arago and Brougham. They, after all, were the chief targets of Harcourt's broadside. Brougham had been stymied in access to the *Edinburgh Review* and an effort was made to encourage him to write an article on Watt and water for the *Quarterly Review*. Brougham did write more for the *Quarterly* in the 1840s as his relations with Napier and the *Edinburgh* continued to deteriorate, but the Watt article never materialized. Brougham was unwell through much of the early 1840s, plunged into depression by the death of his daughter.

The lack of a substantial response to Harcourt from Arago and Brougham worried Watt Jr and Muirhead. By 1843 they had decided to make a concerted effort to induce a response from their distinguished friends. In March 1843, Muirhead visited Brougham in London at his Grafton Street house. He was carrying a selection of papers relating to the water question, which he presented to his host. Brougham began to fulminate against Harcourt, Brewster and Davy. He accused Harcourt of 'insolent presumption and folly' in opposing Arago on a scientific question and himself (Brougham) in a matter of evidence. It had been agreed that Brougham, Muirhead and Arago would meet in Paris with a view to the two older men working together to produce, in short order, the definitive response to Harcourt. Muirhead would assist with his knowledge of the case and would provide documents. For his part, Watt Jr would stay at Aston Hall, delaying his journey to Doldowlod, so that he would be able to supply any further documents that might be needed at short notice.

---

24 The list of toasts in reproduced as Figure 23 in Morrell and Thackray, *Gentlemen of Science: Early Years*.

25 See T.E. Thorpe, 'Presidential Address, Section B', *Report of the Sixtieth Meeting of the BAAS held at Leeds in September 1890*, 1891, pp. 761–71.

Muirhead crossed the Channel with a portmanteau full of books and documents not long after his meeting with Brougham. The latter had asked Muirhead to ensure that Arago was 'primed' for Brougham's arrival a week or so later. Arago seemed enthusiastic, saying that they would 'arranger M. le Chanoine, et nous l'arrangerons bien!' Brougham duly arrived, meetings were held and work was done, but Brougham left before anything was completed. Arago promised to finish the task and send the resulting article for Brougham, Watt Jr and Muirhead to examine. Prior experience with the *Eloge* would not have induced high hopes at Aston Hall and, sure enough, months passed with nothing from Arago. In February 1844 Muirhead was in Paris again, where he saw Arago, who was ill in bed from overwork. That illness, together with Arago's known aversion to writing, Watt Jr believed, would explain the lack of progress.[26]

Brougham decided to go it alone. He wrote to Watt from Chateau Eleanor (named after his daughter) in Cannes on 22 November 1844:

> I have resolved to add a 4th vol. to my Statesmen of Geo III, and to make it consist wholly of men of science and letters. The two first of those of science are my illustrious master Black and my no less illustrious friend your father. I have nearly finished Black and I shall immediately begin the other. If I do not correct all opposition on the controversial points I shall be much disappointed.[27]

Thus was Brougham launched on the work that became the focus of a second period of intense controversy in 1845–46, and that ultimately precipitated the publication of the Watt correspondence on the composition of water.

Sweeping up after Brougham

Early in 1845 Muirhead and Watt Jr were waiting with growing anxiety for communication from Brougham about the life of Watt that he was to publish in his *Lives of Men of Letters and Science*. On 18 March Muirhead reported receiving proof sheets from Brougham. Less that a fortnight later, having conferred with Watt Jr over the proofs, Muirhead arrived in London, heading straight for Brougham's house in Grafton Street. He bumped into Brougham on the doorstep as his Lordship returned to dress for a dinner. The two fell into a heated argument, leaving Brougham late for his evening engagement.

The argument concerned, first of all, Brougham's failure to abide by an agreement that his life of Watt would not be printed without Watt Jr's corrections. Brougham had begun printing before proofs had been sent to Aston Hall. There was also dispute over a number of substantive issues. The most important was the character of Cavendish. Muirhead reported to Watt Jr that Brougham

> Spoke of the perfect honor &c &c of Cavendish: stated that he had already found he was wrong in asserting that Arago had not assailed it: that he has done so in the most

---

[26] Watt Jr to Brougham, 18 February 1844, Brougham Papers, 29,204.

[27] Brougham to Watt Jr, 22 November 1844, copied in Watt Jr to Muirhead, 3 December 1844, Muirhead Papers, MS GEN 1354/764.

abominable manner: – that he has no ground for it, does it only because Cavendish was <u>a</u> <u>Lord</u>, is detested throughout Europe and the World for his foul accusations of every one who has a drop of good blood in their veins …[28]

Muirhead and Brougham argued about the insertions in Cavendish's 1784 paper and especially whether Cavendish named Watt and so acknowledged Watt's paper read earlier to the Royal Society. When Muirhead reminded Brougham that the correspondence was 'quite explicit on the <u>silence</u> observed as to yr Father's name at the <u>reading</u> of C's paper', Brougham 'professed to believe that there is no correspondence on the subject which has not been printed'. Muirhead's response was to offer to show the correspondence to Brougham once again, with Brougham's own annotations upon it!

Muirhead was 'certain of the <u>animus</u> with which he [Brougham] now considers the conduct of Cavendish, and Arago has proved right in his prediction. But I shall hope for some effect, – "<u>veteris vestigia flammas</u>" – to be produced tomorrow by his reperusal of the correspondence; and vivid representations shall not be wanting on my part.'[29] The following day, Muirhead found Brougham more receptive and took him through the passages in the correspondence 'conveniently marked by himself' dealing with the water question. In all they spent seven hours on the business. Muirhead achieved his objective in that Brougham agreed to have the whole of the life of Watt reprinted and to do this under Muirhead's superintendence.[30] They also discussed the writing of the life of Cavendish. Brougham had noted the contents of a dozen of the letters in the correspondence and said he considered them most important. Clearly entering into the spirit of the Watt camp again, Brougham suggested that the whole correspondence should be published after this selection had been let out 'as a pioneer, and to draw out anything that may come out from the other side'. Muirhead exulted to Watt Jr

And where do you think the mine is to explode, but in the very heart of the life of Cavendish, of which I sent you a Proof of the commencement last night!!! <u>Is it not</u> <u>delicious?</u> He fell to work upon it just as I left him tonight and I am very much mistaken if it does not blow Captain Harcourt and all his crew out <u>of the Water</u>.[31]

An examination of Brougham's life of Cavendish reveals, however, that the mine did not, in the end, explode there – this, even though a published promise was made, in a footnote in Brougham's life of Watt, that material from Watt's correspondence would be used in the life of Cavendish.[32]

It appears that although Brougham cooperated regarding Muirhead and Watt's suggested insertions[33] in the life of Watt, he did not follow through entirely as

---

[28] Muirhead to Watt Jr, 29 March 1845, MS GEN 1354/791.

[29] Ibid.

[30] Muirhead also had discussions with Brougham's publisher, Charles Knight, who expressed himself glad that Muirhead and Watt Jr had intervened. Knight was worried about Brougham's accuracy and said he would not charge for the corrections (Muirhead to Watt Jr, 3 April 1845, No. 2, MS GEN 1354/800).

[31] Muirhead to Watt Jr, 30 March 1845, MS GEN 1354/792.

[32] See Henry Brougham, *Lives of Men of Letters and Science*, pp. 380–81.

[33] A list of these is appended to Muirhead to Watt, 30 March 1845, MS GEN 1354/792. Muirhead's

intended in the life of Cavendish. Some of the more plainspoken letters were condemned by Brougham as too inflammatory. An example was Black's letter to Watt warning him to beware of 'Blockheads' and 'Rogues' misunderstanding or stealing his discoveries.[34] Muirhead thought that he had persuaded Brougham to include such material but he was still showing resistance to 'moves that affect the Cavendish name'. Overall, however, Muirhead and Watt Jr were happy with the result of their 'management' of the backsliding Brougham. Watt Jr placed the following inscription in Muirhead's copy of Brougham's *Lives*:

> To James Patrick Muirhead, Esq. This volume containing a life of James Watt is presented by his Son, in grateful testimony of zealous & able cooperation in investigating facts and documents, and of critical censure and exposure of attempts to misrepresent & mislead. Aston Hall. 19 April 1845. James Watt.[35]

These custodians of the 'true facts' considered that their management of Brougham was a job well done. By November 1845 Brougham was dutifully submitting proof sheets of his life of Lavoisier to Watt Jr and Muirhead well in advance.[36] Other publications, notably reviews of Brougham, were now clamouring for attention from Aston Hall. These were to precipitate, finally, the decision to publish the *Correspondence*.

The articles in question we now know to have been written by George Wilson and George Peacock, the former in the *British Quarterly Review* and the latter in the *Quarterly Review*.[37] However, these were issued anonymously, of course. The Watt camp were outraged at their contents, but left guessing initially as to the authors' identities. Muirhead learned of the *British Quarterly Review* article in mid-November 1845, finding it 'long and very offensive' and looking 'very much as if <u>Harcourt himself</u> had written the sophistical' piece.[38] Muirhead had immediately recognized the style of argument – one using detailed chemical considerations to challenge the identity of Watt's and Cavendish's conclusions and thus skate over what Muirhead regarded as the key question of chronology. In his view the author

---

list also includes the footnotes referring the reader to the Cavendish essay. Watt Jr also lamented Brougham's statement that Watt Sr had studied at the College of Glasgow: 'If there is any one part of my fathers history more remarkable than another and upon which he had more occasion to pride himself, it was that of his being, with the exception of the time he passed with Mr Morgan in Cornhill, entirely self taught upon this head my perfect recollection of the uniform tenor of his conversation leaves me not the slightest doubt, and I trust his Lordship will not contradict him' (Watt Jr to Muirhead, 1 April 1845, MS GEN 1354/796).

[34] As reported in Muirhead to Watt Jr, 4 April 1845 MS GEN 1354/801. The Black letter to Watt, 13 February 1783, is reprinted in Robinson and McKie, *Partners in Science*, pp. 123–24.

[35] The inscription is copied at MS GEN 1354/811.

[36] See Muirhead to Watt Jr, 30 April 1845 and 3 November 1845, MS GEN 1354/815 and 857. Muirhead considered that Brougham's life of Lavoisier was excellent, needed little correction and asserted Watt's claims very well. Muirhead to Watt Jr, 2 December 1845, MS GEN 1354/875.

[37] [George Wilson], 'Lord Brougham's *Men of Letters and Science*', *British Quarterly Review*, **2**, 1845, 197–263; [George Peacock], 'Arago and Brougham on Black, Cavendish, Priestley and Watt', *Quarterly Review*, **77**, 1845, 105–39.

[38] Muirhead to Watt Jr, 14 November 1845, MS GEN 1354/859.

of the review exhibited 'the most ignorant, wanton, and foolish disregard of dates and everything else, or the most cunning concealment of their bearing upon the facts of the case ... '. Muirhead believed that Harcourt had supplied the reviewer with 'his own lying account of the matter'. He did find, however, one, and only one, 'palliating sentence in all his wretched scribbling'. In this the anonymous reviewer qualified ever so slightly his agreement with Harcourt: 'With Harcourt's views in the main we entirely agree, only we think that in his anxiety to vindicate Cavendish, he has done Watt less than justice as a chemist.'[39] The predilection of the anonymous reviewer to do justice to Watt brought him and the Watt camp into an unlikely, almost comical, alliance.

Muirhead wondered whether the anonymous reviewer was worth responding to. After all, the *British Quarterly Review* was a new, relatively unknown, publication with a small circulation and so unlikely to do much damage to the cause. Responding to it might simply bring it to undeserved notice. The situation was complicated, however, because David Brewster had already responded to it and done so in the scientific press, namely *The London, Edinburgh and Dublin Philosophical Magazine*.[40] Brewster took exception to a sentence in the *British Quarterly Review* article that criticized his *Edinburgh Review* essay of 1840 for treating the question between Watt and Cavendish as a matter of national honour and awarding his countryman (that is, Watt) the lion's share of merit. In reply Brewster vehemently denied being under the influence of nationalistic feelings, and disagreed that he had favoured Watt: 'Although Mr Watt was my countryman, and my personal friend and correspondent ... I have at three different times of my life come to the decision that he was not, and that Cavendish was the discoverer of the composition of water.'[41] To Muirhead this was the most annoying outcome of the episode:

> I confess I should like to have a touch at Sir David, on whom, as assuming to be a judge in the matter, and in place of honouring the name of your father, doing what he can (under the mask of friendship) to disgrace it, I look with continually increasing contempt.[42]

Muirhead now suggested to Watt Jr that the crucial step should be taken – the water correspondence should be published. Brougham had been recommending this since his recent sight of the material. Brougham's *Lives* appearing first had been intended to bring out any hostilities and had clearly done so. Muirhead suggested that they aim for publication the following spring. Watt Jr agreed and authorized Muirhead to proceed.[43]

No sooner had this decision been taken than the *Quarterly Review* article appeared. This was a paean to Cavendish calculated to hit the Watt camp hard. It is worth

---

[39] In Muirhead to Watt Jr, 15 November 1845, MS GEN 1354/862. The sentences quoted from the *British Quarterly Review* article at p. 250.

[40] Sir David Brewster, 'Observations connected with the discovery of the composition of water', *The London, Edinburgh and Dublin Philosophical Magazine*, **27**, September 1845, 195–97.

[41] Ibid., p.197. There was a response to Brewster: Anon, 'Sir David Brewster and the British Quarterly Review', *British Quarterly Review*, **2**, 1845, 575–78.

[42] Muirhead to Watt Jr, 15 November 1845, MS GEN 1354/862.

[43] Muirhead to Watt Jr, 15 November 1845, MS GEN 1354/862 and Watt Jr to Muirhead, 21 November 1845, MS GEN 1354/864.

looking at activity in the Cavendish camp leading up to this publication. Members of that camp had learned of Brougham's work on his *Lives*. The news may have come from the Duke of Devonshire via Lord Burlington, for in early March 1845 Burlington informed Harcourt that Brougham had applied to the duke for letters and anecdotes of Cavendish to use in the *Lives*. Burlington continued:

> The Duke has no private letters whatever, but has consulted me whether he should let Brougham see the scientific papers. I have told him that I do not think they are what Brougham wants, as I imagine he merely means to write sketches, such as his political characters written a few years ago, and I have recommended him not to send them to him. It has occurred to me, however, whether it might be advisable to shew him the particular papers (of which you made use) relative to the composition of water. He will, of course, have occasion to speak of this; and from the recollection of the part he took a few years ago, he may, perhaps, not be inclined to take a very fair view of the case. An inspection of the papers might tend to remove any false impressions from his mind. I am sorry he has taken up the matter at all, but that cannot be avoided.[44]

The Cavendish camp were expecting a sketch from Brougham and yet also hoping against hope that he might change his mind on the water question after examining complex documentary evidence in Cavendish's scientific papers. But even as they considered this, Brougham was already virtually in print. By early May Peacock had read Brougham's book and his statement on the controversy, and questioned Harcourt as to whether 'anything be more unfair (I had nearly added superficial) than his statement of it?'[45] Spurred by this, Peacock had read numerous documents connected with the subject and entirely concurred with Harcourt's view. He believed that Watt's claim could not be established 'without violation of all the principles of scientific ownership, which have been hitherto recognized'. To do as Brougham had done and to put the 'vague views' of Watt on a par with the 'distinct and unequivocal statements' of Cavendish, was totally unacceptable. Peacock thought that the matter could not be allowed to rest and that a good way to 'make the evidence popular' would be through a review in the *Quarterly*. He volunteered to do this if Harcourt would help with some of the chemistry. In a move reminiscent of the Watt camp's resolve to publish the Watt correspondence on the water question, Peacock also said that he would urge Lord Burlington to publish the chemical, physical and mathematical manuscripts of Cavendish. Peacock felt that Harcourt was the man to do this:

> You have done so much to vindicate Cavendish from the charges which have been prepared at Aston House [*sic*] and presented to the world through Lord Brougham and Arago, that I think you are the proper person to go on with the subject and to put a final extinguisher upon a claim which, in the form in which it has appeared, can do nothing but harm the memory of Mr. Watt.[46]

Peacock duly set to work on his piece for the *Quarterly Review*. By September 1845 he had completed it, but the editor, Lockhart, had advised him that it was

---

[44] Burlington to Harcourt, 1 March 1845, printed in *Harcourt Papers*, vol. 14, pp. 185–86.

[45] Peacock to Harcourt, 3 May 1845, in ibid., pp. 186–88.

[46] Ibid.

unlikely to appear before July the following year. Peacock was glad of the delay since he had written hastily during a period of illness and depression. He welcomed the chance to revise the piece. His examination of documents had further convinced him that Arago had been precipitate and Brougham just plain ignorant: he doubted whether Brougham 'ever wrote a single page of a scientific statement without a serious error'.[47] His study of contemporary chemical writers had persuaded Peacock that Harcourt's analysis of the chemical history was accurate and full. However, he had arrived at an interpretation of Watt's theory somewhat different from Harcourt's:

> it appears to me (if I rightly understand his paper, which is not easily done) that his elementary heat was considered as a chemical constituent, and that its action with the same elements in different proportions produced bodies with permanently different qualities. It was his first conception that steam if heated sufficiently, or if imbued with such a quantity of elementary heat that its latent might become sensible heat, would be converted into a permanently elastic fluid: we then find that he supposed in abstract the combination of one portion of elementary heat with oxygen and hydrogen would produce water, with another portion it would produce fixed air: if this view be correct, and I think it is, the pretended announcement of the true theory of the composition of water would be a retrograde and not a progressive movement in correct views of chemical theory.[48]

Watt's ideas were, Peacock felt, in a confused state because the transformation of bodies one into another occurred through the agency of an element (the elementary heat) that could not be 'chemically appreciated'.[49]

By October 1845 the publication schedule of Peacock's review had changed again, and he now lamented the lack of time for him to receive Harcourt's corrections to the proofs. Peacock advised, somewhat nervously, that he had been very severe on Brougham's 'insolence' and 'ignorance', in part because of Brougham's attack upon Harcourt. Peacock swapped notes with Harcourt, who was now working on his 'Letter to Brougham', about Brougham's failings. He felt that many of Brougham's mistakes derived from his reliance on Robison's *Lectures*, which was a 'singularly inaccurate book'.[50] Peacock also agreed with Harcourt that Watt himself abandoned the claim to the discovery soon after the publication of his paper, and that errant filial piety could explain its resuscitation: 'most of the recent attempts to revive this claim are referrible [*sic*] to the profuse hospitality of Aston Hall: there is

---

[47] Peacock to Harcourt, 24 September 1845, ibid., pp. 188–90.

[48] Ibid., pp. 189–90.

[49] I might observe here that, in terms of my own understanding of Watt's ideas, Peacock seems 'spot on' in his contextual interpretation of what Watt's notions 'meant' at the time they were developed. This does not mean, however, that I want to label Peacock 'right' in his participation in the controversy. That is not my role as historian. In any case I would be obliged to label Peacock 'wrong' in his blithe assumptions about Cavendish's ideas and his 'failure' to provide a similarly contingent understanding of them. In Mulkay and Gilbert's terms, Peacock used the 'empiricist repertoire' when describing Cavendish's ideas and the 'contingent repertoire' when describing Watt's. He engaged in selective deconstruction. (See G. Nigel Gilbert and Michael Mulkay, *Opening Pandora's Box. A Sociological Analysis of Scientists' Discourse*, 1984, p. 40.)

[50] Peacock to Harcourt, 25 October 1845, *Harcourt Papers*, vol. 14, p. 196. This raises suspicions that Peacock may have been the source of the Cambridge talk about Scotchmen as inaccurate that Daniel Macmillan reported to his friend George Wilson. See Chapter 9.

little doubt but that Arago was seduced by it'. This was typical of the Cavendish camp's view of its opposition as misguided by filial piety, influential through wealth, and scientifically uninformed, or out of date.

Before Peacock's review was published, the editor, Lockhart, intervened to remove passages likely to be offensive to Brougham. Peacock seemed somewhat relieved at this, though there remained much for Brougham and the Watt camp to object to.[51] When we read the review we see that Peacock certainly did hit hard. Cavendish, rather than Black, was given credit for the discovery of 'fixed air' and Cavendish's method of working was lauded to the skies. By contrast Watt's water hypothesis was condemned as 'unprofitable and worthless' and both Brougham and Watt Jr were roundly condemned for their interference. However, a key feature of Peacock's article, which it shared with Wilson's in the *British Quarterly*, was that it brought the chemical discussion to a new level. Specifically, Peacock gave a long history of phlogiston theory and of the relationship of heat theory to chemical thinking. He then claimed to show how, even as Cavendish floated above the mêlée because of his impeccable method and adherence to a non-material theory of heat, Watt mistakenly gave heat a central place in the *chemical* processes he was describing. For Peacock this incorporated into Watt's account 'the phlogiston theory in its most vague and inconclusive form'.

Peacock contrasted his own account, and Harcourt's, with Brougham's and Arago's. He pictured the latter two authors as paying little attention to documents and arguments. Brougham, he says, tossed these aside 'with a sneer':

> he examines no documents, he corrects no errors – but thinks it sufficient to give the sanction of his name to a statement drawn up by Mr James Watt, the son of the great engineer, which is not perfectly correct in the general outline of its facts, and is singularly partial and unjust in the conclusions which it deduces from them. Lord Brougham seemed to have forgotten that much might be pardonable in the fondness of a son which would be highly reprehensible in one exercising the function of a judge.[52]

The Watt camp had received advance notice that an article was to appear in the *Quarterly*. At first they were optimistic because they believed that Murray, the publisher, would not allow anything injurious to Watt's fame to appear. In the very last days of 1845, Muirhead finally received the *Quarterly* in Edinburgh, its shipping having been delayed by violent storms along the coast. When he saw it, Muirhead was outraged, complaining to Watt Jr that the author, whoever he was, was certainly an 'Ass' and 'a Liar, and one of the first water'.[53] They speculated about the authorship. It might be Robert Brown working with Harcourt, or possibly Dr John Davy. Brougham, characteristically, claimed to have inside information about the reviewer:

> I have ascertained that superlative Ass Whewell to be the author of the Q.R. A greater or more notorious blunderer exists not. His numberless books on all subjects he understands

---

[51] Peacock to Harcourt, 8 November 1845, *Harcourt Papers*, vol. 14, pp. 197–98.

[52] [George Peacock], 'Arago and Brougham on Black, Cavendish, Priestley and Watt', p. 138.

[53] Muirhead to Watt Jr, 27 December 1845, Muirhead Papers, MS GEN 1354/882.

nothing about, are the ridicule of Cambridge. But a first rate mathematician and <u>friend of his own</u> tells me he never heard him give a lecture on his own subject, without fear & trembling for his inaccuracies, which are quite habitual.[54]

Muirhead, though he must have been mightily amused by Brougham's detection of such faults in another, was not surprised at the news. He recalled that in 1841 Wordsworth had spoken to him of Whewell as 'one of the Carrion crows'. Muirhead was sure that the Reverend gentleman 'would have no objections to be also a "Chanoine d'York". I am afraid your respect for the Cloth is not increased by what we thus learn of its Members'.[55] This anti-clerical sentiment pervaded the Watt camp's discussions of their chief opposition whom they identified as an aristocratic, clerical interest. The implication, of course, was that Whewell was currying favour with the Canon of York and ecclesiastical authorities in the hope of preferment.

Muirhead and Watt sought to rouse Arago, who had been quiet for some time. Muirhead wrote to the Frenchman appraising him of the content of the *Quarterly Review* article with its 'accusations of inaccuracy, partiality, and prejudice' against Arago. Whewell was identified as the author and as the same man

> who nine years ago endeavoured to rob Black of the discovery of latent heat, <u>you</u> [Arago] of the discovery of the phenomena of Newton's rings when produced between a glass lens and a metallic reflector, as well as of the merit of the experiments undertaken at the desire of the French Government on steam at elasticities higher than eight atmospheres.

Whewell had also '<u>uniformly</u> deprived <u>Scotchmen</u> of any credit (so far as depended on him) for any invention or discovery whatever, and in the whole three volumes of his *History of the Inductive Sciences*, devotes but one sentence to the immortal labors of James Watt'.[56] Muirhead encouraged Arago to reply to these calumnies and also hoped that Dumas would assist the cause by giving them his criticisms of the chemical blunders that Whewell and Harcourt had committed.

Then a further production of the Cavendish camp appeared in the form of the letter to Lord Brougham by Harcourt in the *Philosophical Magazine* in 1846. This response had been encouraged by Peacock, even as the latter worked on his *Quarterly Review* article.[57] It repeated much of the material in Harcourt's 'Address' with, as Muirhead perceived it, 'more of the same sort of stuff, if possible still more confused, drivelling and miserable'.[58] Prominence was given to the charcoal

---

54 Brougham to Muirhead, 28 January 1846, copied in Muirhead Papers, MS GEN 1354/898. Brougham's anti-Whewellian invective mounted as he accused Whewell of 'audacious toad eating of the Archbishop' in his praise of the Archbishop's son Harcourt.

55 Muirhead to Watt Jr, 30 January 1846, MS GEN 1354/898.

56 Muirhead to Arago, 2 February 1846, Muirhead Papers, MS GEN 1354/901.

57 George Peacock to Roderick Murchison, 7 May 1845, Murchison Collection, Geological Society of London: 'I have been attempting to stir up Harcourt to attack Lord Brougham's most unfair & shallow publication.'

58 W.V. Harcourt, 'Letter to Henry Lord Brougham, F.R.S., &c., containing remarks on certain statements in his Lives of Black, Watt and Cavendish', *Philosophical Magazine*, **28**, 1846, 106–31, 478–525 ; Muirhead to Watt Jr, 5 February 1846, Muirhead Papers, MS GEN 1354/903.

argument, according to which Priestley's 'inflammable air' would have contained carbon monoxide, making it impossible for Watt to infer a 'true' theory. One particular piece of 'insolence' from Harcourt incensed Muirhead greatly: Harcourt described Watt as 'having been unable to examine abstract principles!'.[59] This stung precisely because it depicted Watt as an empiric. Harcourt also, rather cleverly, remarked upon Arago's silence on the water question for a number of years, implying that this was a result of Arago's having been persuaded by Harcourt's arguments in the 'Address'. It thus became important for the Watt camp to elicit some further response from Arago, so as to demonstrate his continued adherence to the cause. The situation was made more difficult, however, because of the falling out between Arago and Brougham.[60] In so far as Brougham was a primary target of the articles by Wilson, Peacock and Harcourt, there was little hope that Arago would leap to his defence.

The trio of pro-Cavendish articles published in 1845 and early 1846 did create a certain pressure on the Watt camp to enter into the chemical issues even as they challenged the capacity of Watt's supporters to do so.[61] There were moves, as we have seen, to enrol the further services of Dumas. Brougham, who was as sceptical of getting anything from Dumas as he was of anything from Arago, suggested that they find an Edinburgh chemist. Muirhead advised Brougham to recruit Professor Thomas Graham of University College London, but there were political difficulties in this. Besides, Graham was inclined to disagree with Arago's statement of the water question. Dr Fyfe at Edinburgh was considered but there were doubts as to his reputability and he had, it was discovered, published in support of Cavendish, albeit very briefly.[62]

Significantly, as this pressure towards involvement in chemical arguments was felt, Muirhead protested to Watt Jr:

> Now entre nous, a chemical analysis of either Whewell or Harcourt, is much more his [Brougham's] business than it is ours. For, as you know, we depend on the dates, and care nothing for absurd endeavours to make two theories which are identical (except as to heat) appear different. When your father said half a dozen times over that by phlogiston he in April 1783 meant inflammable air, I don't care though Harcourt talk of charcoal to

---

[59] Muirhead to Watt Jr, 6 February 1846, Muirhead Papers, MS GEN 1354/905.

[60] Arago felt that Brougham had been unsupportive politically. Brougham saw it this way: 'Arago's unaccountable spleen towards me is on account of my not taking part in his crazy politics, and complaining that he lets his crazy brother go about the world levying money on Arago's friends.' (See Brougham to Muirhead, 7 February 1846, Muirhead Papers, MS GEN 1354/906, Copy.)

[61] Harcourt concluded his long response to Brougham: 'I hope I may have persuaded you that it is at once more safe, and more just, for those who have not had leisure to pursue chemical studies to their foundation, to leave chemistry and chemists to themselves – at least so far as regards the minutiae of the science, and arbitrations of the rights of discovery … ' (Harcourt, 'Letter to Henry, Lord Brougham', p. 524).

[62] On Graham see: Muirhead to Brougham, 10 February 1846 (copied in MS GEN 1354/910); Brougham to Muirhead, 12 February 1846 (copied in MS GEN 1354/915) and 16 February 1846 (copied in MS GEN 1354/918). On Fyfe see Watt Jr to Muirhead, 14 February 1846, MS GEN 1354/915. Andrew Fyfe's *Elements of Chemistry* (1827), as Watt Jr noted, gave the major credit for discovery of the composition of water to Cavendish rather than Watt.

all eternity; (where he may perhaps find himself getting enough of it, for telling lies and disgracing his holy vocation in this world). As a question of evidence my case is already complete, and I am satisfied to treat it so.[63]

Brougham's situation was different, Muirhead recognized, because he had been attacked directly in both the *Quarterly Review* and the *Philosophical Magazine* and accused of 'numberless errors in the physical sciences wholly irrespective of the water question, and which I should be sorry to see mixed up with it'. Through all this Muirhead had been hard at work on his long introduction to the *Correspondence* and he was inclined to treat that introduction as one thing and Brougham's defence of himself against charges of scientific incompetence as another.[64] Muirhead seemed determined to keep the Watt Camp's case on its firmest ground of circumstantial evidence. However, Watt Jr was keen to assist Brougham, and Muirhead dutifully went along with this. He was eventually to find a person who seemed like the ideal chemist, but one who ultimately caused the Watt camp a great deal of trouble. This was none other than Dr George Wilson.

Wilson swung into the Watt Camp's view by courtesy of a friend of Muirhead's, Dr Allen Thomson.[65] Thomson, according to Muirhead, had 'a great liking for Brougham, considers Whewell a presumptuous puppy, and would do anything in his power to aid the cause'. If Thomson sought an assistant, he knew of a young man, Mr Wilson, who had taken Fyfe's place at Edinburgh and was well spoken of. It was envisaged that the joint labours of Thomson and Wilson as chemists-for-hire would be rewarded by a sum of about 20 guineas.[66]

On the evening of 23 February 1846, in Edinburgh, Muirhead, accompanied by Allen Thomson, met George Wilson for the first time. He reported the meeting to Watt Jr the following day. Muirhead was both startled and gratified by the encounter. He was startled because he learned that Wilson was in fact the author of the article in the *British Quarterly Review*, 'in which Cavendish's claim is upheld, his honor defended, and Lord Brougham assailed on a thousand points with the severest criticism!' Despite this, Muirhead had left the meeting highly gratified because he had 'succeeded in enlisting that active and dangerous enemy in our service, an exploit which has given me the greatest satisfaction, and will I believe greatly aid our cause'.[67]

There were many signs of Wilson's great potential usefulness: he was a man of considerable attainment in science; he had a strong understanding of the history of chemistry; he was regarded by all as highly able and trustworthy; he desired to be impartial. Given that Wilson had, as Muirhead recalled, praised Watt as a chemist

---

63 Muirhead to Watt Jr, 9 February 1846, MS GEN 1354/908.

64 Ibid.

65 Thomson (1809–84) was successively in the 1840s Professor of Physiology at Edinburgh and of Anatomy at Glasgow. He was the son of Dr John Thomson, whose translation of Fourcroy, with notes, was published in 1798–1800. On both see *DNB*. As we saw in Chapter 4, these notes sought to set Fourcroy right on the water question. Allen Thomson brought his father's work to Muirhead's attention, who duly noticed it in his Introduction to the *Correspondence*.

66 Muirhead to Watt Jr, 19 February 1846, MS GEN 1354/919.

67 Muirhead to Watt Jr, 24 February 1846, MS GEN 1354/922.

in the *British Quarterly* article, Muirhead thought it worth a try to convert Wilson. A long discussion revealed the young doctor to be fully conversant with the details of the water question. Muirhead believed that Wilson was of a very different mind when the meeting ended. He also learned that Wilson was working on lives of English chemists, among whom he ranked Watt high. Wilson was eager for information, had decided to wait for the *Correspondence*, and agreed to submit to Aston Hall the proofs of any life of Watt that he might write. Finally, Muirhead was convinced that Wilson merely wanted to get at 'the Truth'.[68]

Muirhead wrote to Brougham, not naming Wilson or Thomson, advising that two able men were working on the *Quarterly Review* and *Philosophical Magazine* articles. By now Wilson had become 'our principal chemical operator' and was finding numerous errors in the *Quarterly*. The chemist, Muirhead advised, was 'animated by a cordial detestation of Whewell, whom he considers as blundering as he is presumptuous'.[69] However, both the chemist (Wilson) and Forbes doubted Whewell's supposed authorship of the *Quarterly* article.[70] It was now becoming clear that Peacock rather than Whewell was the author.

As Muirhead spent more time with Wilson he was further convinced that he had converted him:

> There is in fact no difference now between us, excepting that he, like some other chemists, appears still to think it much more probable that Cavendish drew his conclusions in 1781 than that he did not. The grounds on which he is inclined to be of this opinion, are entirely chemical; and he does not feel by any means certain that he is right. The priority of publication, and complete originality on the part of your Father he most fully admits.[71]

Even Watt Jr seemed to overcome his reservations, suggesting that Wilson be shown, confidentially, Watt's correspondence on the water question. He also thought that if Wilson's work proved satisfactory then he might be the ideal person to review the *Correspondence*, once published, for the *Edinburgh Review*.[72]

Over the next few months Muirhead and Watt Jr's attention was focused on the introduction that Muirhead had written to the *Correspondence* and also on a note that Brougham had produced in response to Harcourt and Peacock. Muirhead saw Brougham in London about both documents. He travelled to Paris with Brougham, where he saw Arago. Although Arago was as usual overworked, he met with Muirhead to discuss the water question and assured him that he was as strongly in support of the Watt cause as ever.[73] Muirhead had to deal carefully because Arago

---

[68] Ibid.

[69] Muirhead to Brougham, 25 February 1846, copied in Muirhead to Watt Jr, 25 February 1846, MS GEN 1354/923.

[70] Forbes to Muirhead, 28 February 1846 and Muirhead to Forbes, 28 February 1846, both copied in MS GEN 1354/927 (Muirhead to Watt Jr, 28 February 1846).

[71] Muirhead to Watt Jr, 26 February 1846, Muirhead Papers, MS GEN 1354/925.

[72] Watt Jr to Muirhead, 27 February 1846, Muirhead Papers, MS GEN 1354/926.

[73] Characteristically, Arago was full of dire threats that when he next wrote on the question he would be much more severe: 'il faut ecraser, abinier, tous les trois [Harcourt, Whewell and Peacock] je les abimerai tout entier; il faut mettre les pieds sur ces messieurs la, et danser sur ces carrons' (Arago, quoted in Muirhead to Watt Jr, 4 April 1846, Muirhead Papers, MS GEN 1354/951).

and Brougham were still feuding. This could have been disastrous, but Muirhead was relieved that the only effect seemed to be a tendency on Arago's part to condemn Brougham's writings as weak and on Brougham's part a resistance to backing Arago on the question of Cavendish's dishonesty over the interpolations and dates. In Paris, Muirhead also saw Dumas, who professed his continuing support of the Watt cause. Dumas saw nothing resembling conclusions in the facsimiles that Harcourt had published of Cavendish's diary, and even if they had been there, Watt was entitled 'as the first publisher of it in writing, before a learned body, to the priority, on all the principles recognised among scientific men'.[74]

John Murray, who had published the translation of the *Eloge*, was chosen as the publisher for the *Correspondence* on the prospect that he would obtain a better circulation than Charles Knight. The fact that Murray was the publisher of the *Quarterly Review* was not held against him, the editor Lockhart being blamed for letting Peacock's article through. Murray reportedly sided himself with the Watt camp, and felt that Peacock's review had done the *Quarterly* harm. He held out the prospect of a 'counter article' even as he denied any influence over the editor or the *Review*.[75] By June 1846 proofs were being corrected. At this stage the second part of Harcourt's letter to Brougham appeared in the *Philosophical Magazine* and was referred to Wilson for comments but was thought to offer little new, except a lame defence of Peacock's review.

As of September 1846, Watt and Muirhead were monitoring the reports of the British Association at Southampton. They were interested in whether Dumas countenanced the meeting and were glad when it became evident that he was not there. They lampooned what they regarded as the 'Tomfoolery' of the meeting, the admission of ladies as philosophers to swell the coffers, and the lack of gentlemanly behaviour. They rejoiced that *The Times*, too, criticized the Association. In response to Muirhead's criticism of the Southampton meeting, Watt Jr objected to 'the assumption of superior knowledge by their sagacious promoters. The bubble cannot hold together much longer.'[76] Watt Jr and Muirhead no doubt anticipated that publication of the *Correspondence* would contribute to the bursting of the bubble not least by bringing the 'facts' before every reasonable man and revealing the sophistry of the self-appointed élite of the Association.

The *Correspondence* was ready by late November, and Muirhead, Watt Jr and Murray professed themselves happy with it. They began to distribute complimentary

---

[74] Muirhead and Watt Jr also thought that Brougham's backsliding on Cavendish was a problem. See Chapter 8 above. On Dumas's views see Muirhead to Watt Jr, 6 April 1846, Muirhead Papers, MS GEN 1354/954.

[75] Watt Jr to Muirhead, 30 March 1846, Muirhead Papers, MS GEN 1354/946 recounts Watt Jr's meeting with Murray: 'he distinctly denies any authority over or interference with any of the Articles, & said that book after book published by his father and himself had been blown all to pieces, to their great pecuniary loss, but without their venturing to interfere. I however rowed him well for it, and told him it w[d] never have happened in his father's time, which he seemed to think too sharp a cut. We parted good friends, he assuring me that he would do his best to gain the book circulation, and that if the Editor should be satisfied by our publication that the Reviewer [Peacock] had been wrong in either his facts or conclusions, he would readily admit a counter article.'

[76] Watt Jr to Muirhead, 26 September 1846, MS GEN 1354/1032, in reply to Muirhead to Watt Jr, 24 September 1846, MS GEN 1354/1029.

copies. The scale of this is revealing. A publisher's account from September 1847 indicates that 170 copies had been sold to that point but more than 200 copies had been given away by Watt Jr and the editor.[77] The first responses came from close allies. Brougham thought the volume 'capital' and was 'amazingly pleased with the figure we cut'.[78] Wilson's reaction was positive. Muirhead described him as 'an enthusiastic convert' and as expressing deep conviction of Watt's originality, priority of publication, and sagacity. Wilson's view of Cavendish's fame had reportedly changed by examining the letters.

> Deprived of the discovery of the comp^n of water, he [Wilson] justly says that Cavendish will no longer be looked on as marvellous in the extent either of his observations or deductions; and although I think he has a lurking belief that C. may have drawn the conclusion in his own mind in 1781 or 1782, he is candid enough to admit that we have no evidence ... [79]

Muirhead considered this as much as one could expect from any chemist.

J.D. Forbes delayed any reply regarding the *Correspondence*, but Wilson reported meeting him accidentally. Forbes said he was still reading but did not like many of the things that were said about his friend Harcourt. Muirhead was apprehensive since Forbes, as Secretary of the Royal Society of Edinburgh, might use the meeting of that body to make some remarks on the copy of the *Correspondence* presented to the Society. Muirhead decided to attend the meeting prepared to give battle. He would be ready to use an *ad hominem* argument by reminding Forbes 'that in his own discoveries, he has only gleaned where others, greater than he, had reaped. His proceedings as to both Melloni and Agassiz are so well known here, that I shall easily silence him.'[80] Muirhead hoped and believed that the 'popular view' would be that expressed by 'honest John Smith' of Glasgow who thanked Muirhead for the 'lucid statement' in his introduction to the *Correspondence* which, in his view, made it 'impossible to doubt, to whom the world was indebted for the discovery; any more, than the usefulness of bringing these records to light, which establish the righteous claim of the real philosopher'. Relaying Smith's words to Watt Jr, Muirhead rejoiced: 'What would Forbes say if he heard this last, unkindest cut, at his idol Cavendish? On the whole, I see no reason to doubt that the work will be attended with its due effect.'[81]

All awaited anxiously for a response from Jeffrey, who was mysteriously silent. When he finally replied, on 7 December, the delay was explained: the envelope had

---

[77] Muirhead to Watt Jr, 27 September 1846, Muirhead Papers, MS GEN 1354/1150.

[78] Brougham to Muirhead, 3 December 1846, copied in Muirhead to Watt Jr, 5 December 1846, MS GEN 1354/1056.

[79] Muirhead to Watt Jr, 7 December 1846, MS GEN 1354/1058.

[80] Ibid. The reference to Macedonio Melloni (1798–1854) concerns the closeness of his and Forbes's experimental work on radiant heat. That to Louis Agassiz (1807–73) concerns his controversy with Forbes about their theories of glaciation. See on the latter Frank F. Cunningham, *James David Forbes. Pioneer Scottish Glaciologist*, 1990, pp. 93–110.

[81] Muirhead to Watt Jr, 10 December 1846, MS GEN 1354/1061. In reply Watt Jr expressed little surprise at Forbes's behaviour: 'I should as little expect a candid admission of his errors from Harcourt as from his servile admirer. Dr Smith's opinion is worth a hundred such and I trust with you may be the general impression.' I have been unable to identify Dr John Smith definitely.

looked so much like that used to distribute the Bannatyne Antiquarian publications that he had put it on one side unopened! Jeffrey had only glanced at the work but had already been in touch with Napier to remind him of his promise to find a competent reviewer. He asked Muirhead for suggestions. Muirhead, who with Watt Jr had long had Wilson in mind, immediately saw Wilson and Jeffrey. Jeffrey was proposing to ask Sir John Herschel to recommend someone. There was doubt whether Wilson, for all his qualifications (which Muirhead advanced as substantial) was a skilful enough writer for Jeffrey's taste. Eventually, Wilson *was* chosen, but that was only to be the beginning of the story.

Wilson's situation at this point in late 1846 was an intriguing one. His much-vaunted impartiality wove a complex web. Publicly, in so far as his identity as the reviewer in the *British Quarterly Review* (and indeed the article itself) was known, Wilson was identified with the Cavendish camp. Privately he had worked as a hired chemical 'gun' for Muirhead and Watt Jr, and therefore indirectly for Brougham, whom he had criticized harshly in his review. Wilson's work for the Watt camp was to develop a critique of the chemical competence of the articles by Harcourt and Peacock, and thus to strike at the heart of the Cavendish camp's case. Now, even as he negotiated with Muirhead about undertaking the review of the *Correspondence* in the *Edinburgh Review* as the 'nominee' of Watt's supporters, Wilson was approached by the Cavendish Society to write the life of Cavendish for them!

As Wilson told the story to Muirhead, he had been approached to be the Edinburgh agent for a chemical book club being founded in London. He had liked their objectives and suggested that the club be called the 'Boyle Society'. He was surprised to learn, on receiving a prospectus, that the decision had been made to call it the 'Cavendish Society'.

> In September I received a letter from one of the Secretaries, informing me that the Society had some thoughts of asking me to write Cavendish's Life. I wrote in return to say, that unless I was left quite uncontrolled in writing the book, I should not care to undertake it. I have heard no more about it.
> It is manifest, however, that the London Chemists intend to take C's side, otherwise they would not have named their Society after that Observer.[82]

Whilst relations between the Watt camp and Wilson were good at this point, the year 1847 was to see a major saga enacted between Wilson, Muirhead and Francis Jeffrey over the proposed *Edinburgh Review* article on Watt's *Correspondence*. In early December 1846 Wilson was reading the *Correspondence*, by which he professed to profit greatly. On 18 December, however, he wrote to Muirhead having had second thoughts about the wisdom of undertaking the review. Wilson claimed to be in no doubt about the claims set up for Watt, and he believed that his treatment would satisfy Watt Jr and Muirhead in that regard. However, his view of Cavendish's rights in the matter would not. Wilson also could not praise Arago and Brougham

---

[82] George Wilson to Muirhead, 28 November 1846, copied in Muirhead to Watt Jr, 30 November 1846, Muirhead Papers, MS GEN 1354/1055. This remark supports Brock's surmise about the significance of the name 'Cavendish Society'. See W.H. Brock, 'The Society for the Perpetuation of Gmelin: The Cavendish Society, 1846–1872', *Annals of Science*, **35**, 1978, 599–617.

or denounce Harcourt in the way that Muirhead and Watt Jr would wish. He felt that Harcourt had made important contributions to the debate and that Brougham was blameworthy as a chemist. Wilson was convinced by the Neptune business that Arago was 'not a safe or impartial judge, in a question of scientific priority'. Muirhead replied that so long as they agreed on Watt's claims, that was the main concern. Otherwise he was happy for Wilson to exercise his own judgement and hoped that, if Jeffrey made the offer of the review, Wilson would accept it.[83]

Wilson and Muirhead were on the best of terms as the new year began. Wilson wrote Muirhead a letter of introduction to his old friend George Day, the Secretary of the Cavendish Society, asking him to tell Muirhead all he could about the intended life of Cavendish.

> Mr M. is of course a supporter of Watt, & takes what some of you will consider a strong view of matters. He is however a liberal Critic, and probably the only person in Europe who understands the documentary details of the Watt and Cavendish dispute. Although Mr. Muirhead and I hold different opinions ... we both think ourselves entitled to be considered impartial judges & discuss amicably together the points on which we cannot agree.[84]

Wilson even asked that Day keep Muirhead's inquiries a secret from the Cavendish Society people. He sent him as a private friend to learn what he could about the Cavendish biography and 'the feeling in London about the Watt affair'. Wilson assisted in other respects too, advising Muirhead and Watt Jr about how to send copies of the *Correspondence* to key chemist–historians, Frederick Hoefer and Hermann Kopp.[85]

In their next communication, however, Wilson again told Muirhead that he could not write the *Edinburgh Review* article. The reason now was David Brewster's article in the *North British Review*. He shared the concern behind Brewster's treatment of Watt, but felt that justice had not been done to Cavendish. Enumerating the reasons why he should be relieved from the task of the review, Wilson argued first that what he had to say of Watt's merits in the affair would fall short of what Brewster had said. Surely Muirhead would not want 'an uncertain sound' from the *Edinburgh* when the *North British* had sounded 'so distinct & exhalting a note'. His second concern was the polarization that Brewster would rekindle:

> The N.B. article will be highly gratifying to Arago, Dumas, & Lord Brougham: and grievously vexatious to Harcourt and Whewell. It were best to 'let well alone' as I cannot afford like Sir David to make these last transgressors my mortal foes, and I am unable unfortunately to satisfy the first illustrious three.[86]

---

[83] Wilson to Muirhead, 18 December 1846, Muirhead Papers, MS GEN 1354/214 and Muirhead to Wilson, 19 December 1846, Muirhead Papers MS GEN 1354/215.

[84] Wilson to George E. Day, 12 January 1847 (Copy), Muirhead Papers, MS GEN 1354/216(b).

[85] Wilson to Muirhead, n.d. [12 January 1847] and n.d. [January 1847], Muirhead Papers, MS GEN 1354/216(a) and 217. Kopp's history was close to completion, and he had already dealt with the water question in volume 3 published in 1845. See Kopp, *Geschichte der Chemie*, 1843–47, vol. 3, pp. 259–72. Wilson thought that Kopp would be interested and might publish a second edition at some stage.

[86] Wilson to Muirhead, 1 February 1847, Muirhead Papers, MS GEN 1354/218.

Wilson, as we have seen, was reluctant to alienate the Cambridge men by public disagreement. He was happy to praise Watt, but he would have to defend Cavendish against the charges of theft and falsehood. Muirhead, however, still encouraged Wilson to make himself available to write the review.[87]

In mid-February Macvey Napier died and the editorship of the *Edinburgh Review* was thereby thrown open. Jeffrey now formally took up a caretaker role and it was agreed that Wilson would write the piece. Wilson was immediately inundated with offers of assistance from Muirhead, Watt Jr and Jeffrey! He agreed to have them all correct his proofs. There was a similar offer, via Muirhead, from Brougham also, which Wilson politely declined:

> it were best that his Lordship left me alone, and I do wish you would tell him so. Say I am a <u>dour</u>, perverse, dogged Scotchman, not like him a Giant in Genius, and an Encyclopaedia in learning, but a one-sided Chemist who can not be got to see more than that Oxygen & Hydrogen form water.[88]

In early summer Wilson was still working on the review and exchanged friendly, detailed queries with Muirhead about such matters as the precise publication process for the 74th volume of the *Philosophical Transactions*. Much turned on this so far as the interpolations in Cavendish's paper and the misdating of reprints were concerned. They shared other information. Wilson reported an interview with Jeffrey in which he received valuable advice on the handling of the subject. When Wilson told Jeffrey that although he had different views about Cavendish from Muirhead's estimation, he was not a partisan of Cavendish and had no desire to do injustice to Watt, Jeffrey smiled and replied 'I'll not let you do that.'[89] It is indicative of the spirit of goodwill prevailing that Wilson found nothing sinister or disturbing in this remark.

By early August, a copy of Wilson's manuscript review was in Muirhead's hands, having been sent to the new editor of the *Edinburgh*, William Empson, and to Jeffrey somewhat earlier. This left Muirhead very little time, since the aim at this point was to publish in the October number of the *Review*. Wilson anticipated Muirhead's reaction with some concern since he thought it 'cannot be acceptable to you & Mr Watt'.[90] Wilson and Jeffrey were now trading statements about the balancing of merit between Watt and Cavendish. Jeffrey developed two long statements that Wilson found he had to 'totally dissent' from.[91]

Muirhead arrived in Edinburgh on 18 August and spent that evening preparing a 'full <u>Written</u> statement of the <u>anti-charcoal</u> argument'. The following morning he was with Jeffrey and Empson at Craigcrook expounding that argument:

> They were of course at first disinclined to believe me, in opposition to a professed chemist, on such a point; but I completely satisfied them both, and had the pleasure of

---

87 Muirhead to Wilson, 8 February 1847, Muirhead Papers, MS GEN 1354/219.

88 Wilson to Muirhead, 27 February 1847, Muirhead Papers, MS GEN 1354/222.

89 Wilson to Muirhead, 24 June 1847, Muirhead Papers, MS GEN 1354/225.

90 Wilson to Muirhead, 12 August 1847, Muirhead Papers, MS GEN 1354/229.

91 Jeffrey to Wilson, 10 August 1847, Special Collections, Edinburgh University Library, Dk.6. 23/ 1/16/17.

astonishing, upsetting, and <u>flammergasting</u> these two quick and able men, to my heart's content.[92]

Muirhead was able to inform Watt Jr that Jeffrey would now insist that Wilson alter his paper and, if he would not, then Jeffrey would take the article on himself. Muirhead reassured Watt Jr that 'we shall stand <u>no nonsense</u> from any Doctor on the face of the earth'.[93]

At this point, Wilson, who was at his summer cottage in Dirleton, east of Edinburgh near North Berwick, invited Muirhead to visit him. On 20 August, when Muirhead received the invitation, he arrived that same morning by train from Edinburgh at Drem and was then met by Wilson's gig, which took him down to Dirleton. The two men evidently had heated discussions of the charcoal question – what had Watt known about Priestley's mode of preparing inflammable air? Muirhead did not partake of the country dinner and wine that had been offered, leaving at 3pm. It was shortly after this that Muirhead brought the disagreements to a head:

> It is very evident that notwithstanding all our endeavors to prevent them, misapprehensions have prevailed, with all of us on several important and indeed fundamental points: – not only as to your Sentiments on the great point in dispute but also on the extent to which you feel yourself bound to support preconceived opinions, and so far to be unfitted for the office of an absolutely impartial judge. You now write exactly as I have heard you talk before the publication of Mr. Watt's correspondence: – whereas I had understood that the perusal of that volume, and the repeated Study of the Appendix, had very materially altered your view; – and I certainly was not prepared for the mode of argument adopted in one part of your able and interesting paper, in which I must say, however unwillingly that I do not think that full justice has been done to the claims of Mr. Watt.[94]

Muirhead intimated that any remedy for the misunderstandings might well be beyond reach. He was unwilling to negotiate further and suggested that Wilson sort the situation out with Jeffrey. Wilson's terse reply returned a piece of correspondence between Jeffrey and Muirhead, as requested, and asked that Muirhead send his 'argument against the affirmation of Watt's knowledge that Priestley used the Charcoal gas'. This was important because Lord Jeffrey was adopting Muirhead's views 'but does not state articulately on what grounds'. Wilson felt that he was being denied the information necessary to respond to the criticisms that had created the impasse between the parties.[95] The dispute deepened, Wilson demanding justice, Muirhead expressing outrage at the implication that it had been denied, and

---

[92] Muirhead to Watt Jr, 19 August 1847, Muirhead Papers MS GEN 1354/1115.

[93] Muirhead to Watt Jr, 22 August 1847, Muirhead Papers, MS GEN 1354/1118.

[94] Muirhead to Wilson, 27 August 1847, Copy, Muirhead Papers, MS GEN 1354/234. Jeffrey, too, had begun to characterize the disagreement as unmendable: 'What startles me most, I must confess, and quite fills me with misgivings as to the issue of this misunderstanding, is what you now tell me as to the extent to which you are already committed, in honor and consistency, as to the decision of this controversy ... I certainly was under a very opposite impression when I first ventured to press you to take this task upon you ... '. (Jeffrey to Wilson, 23 August 1847, Special Collections, Edinburgh University Library, Dk.6. 23/1/23–26).

[95] Wilson to Muirhead, 28 August 1847, Muirhead Papers, MS GEN 13354/235.

introducing a legalistic tone into the correspondence. Muirhead's demand that no copy of the correspondence between Jeffrey and himself be retained by Wilson was met by Wilson's pointed 'request as a favour' that the manuscript copy of his review article that Muirhead held be returned without any copy in whole or in part being made! Accusations of rudeness began to fly.[96] Amidst all this Jeffrey decided that Wilson's paper was to be withdrawn from the *Edinburgh Review*.

The correspondence between Wilson and Muirhead took a conciliatory turn quite quickly, beginning on 10 September when Wilson sent a long letter 'seeking to remedy the present difference between us'.[97] Wilson rehearsed the course of the disagreement and speculated about why Muirhead had taken offence. He traced it to a disagreement about the charcoal question during their discussion at Dirleton when they both became heated. Wilson assumed that it must have been his request for Muirhead's argument in writing that offended. Wilson explained that he requested this only because he felt that Muirhead's views on the charcoal issue were weighing with Lord Jeffrey's response to the article: 'However greatly Lord J. exceeds us in a thousand particulars, it is paying ourselves no very grand compliment to say, that we know the facts of the water-question better than he does. He looks to us for the facts, & changes his views, as he took the former from you or from me.'[98] Wilson was resigned to Jeffrey's decision not to publish his article, but he doggedly sought to continue the discussion of the charcoal argument with Muirhead. The latter declined, rather wearily, while accepting that the dispute and offence between them were now over. Muirhead forwarded a present of a small writing desk from Watt Jr to Wilson's sister (who acted as a faithful copyist for her brother) as thanks for her efforts in transcribing the manuscript: 'I can wish her its employment in further less thorny themes that that which so lately engaged her pen.'[99]

Muirhead and Wilson maintained friendly, though more distant, contact. Jeffrey and Wilson retained a strong mutual regard.[100] With Wilson taken off the *Edinburgh Review* assignment, an agreement was struck that he would be paid for the article and that Jeffrey would be able to make use of it in his essay. Jeffrey set to work and produced a judicious assessment, though clearly pro-Watt, which appeared in the January 1848 number of the *Review*. We have already examined the content of this piece in some detail. Suffice it here to note that Jeffrey's paper did take a long excursion into the charcoal argument, though only to dismiss it. Muirhead spent some time tutoring Jeffrey in chemical issues to this end. Soon after Jeffrey took the article over, Muirhead described to Watt Jr a session with him:

> I was with him most of the day; and among other things, read over to him, with explanations, Dumas' very elegant paper; from which I showed him that it can be proved, that Cavendish used neither perfectly pure nor perfectly dry hydrogen, nor could the water he obtained have been perfectly pure either. So much for the system of

[96] Wilson to Muirhead, 2 September [1847], Muirhead Papers, MS GEN 1354/239.

[97] Wilson to Muirhead, 10 September 1847, Muirhead Papers, MS GEN 1354/243.

[98] Ibid.

[99] Muirhead to Wilson, 11 September 1847, Muirhead Papers, MS GEN 1354/244.

[100] Jessie Aitken Wilson, *Memoir of George Wilson*, 1860, pp. 320, 338, 358–59.

attempting to carry back the chemistry of this century into the last! Wilson's absurd objections can thus be further met.[101]

For his part, Wilson focused his energy and ingenuity upon what was to become the life of Cavendish in which these arcane chemical arguments were to assume an important role.

This saga enacted between Wilson, Muirhead and Jeffrey represented a rapprochement between, then a collision of, opposing models of discovery. Muirhead, against his better judgement that the dates were everything, allowed Wilson to draw him into detailed chemical argument. There, inevitably, he grew frustrated with the fact that Wilson, who had earlier appeared convinced by the circumstantial materials published in Watt's *Correspondence* on the water question, seemed now to have reverted to the position that he had held when they had first met, and Wilson was fresh from writing his *British Quarterly Review* article. Their respect for each other as 'liberal critics' could not, in the end, bridge the conceptual gulf that separated them. In many ways, however, these tense exchanges marked the end of 'live' controversy over the water question. It is to the final ripples that we now turn.

The Controversy after 1848: The Final Ripples

In 1848, C.R. Weld's *History of the Royal Society* was published, the second volume of which contained an account of the water controversy.[102] The account is located in the section dealing with the years 1780–85, but, not surprisingly, draws widely upon subsequent evidence and opinion. It appears that overall Weld's account was designed to pour oil on the waters of controversy. This tendency may well have been assisted by the chemists whom Weld thanked for 'revising the following pages relating to this subject', the chemists being Professors Graham and Miller and Mr Brande.[103]

Weld went out of his way to be even-handed. He did not enter into chemically based judgements. Instead he listed attributions of the discovery made by Arago, Dumas, Brande, Hatchett, Berzelius, Rees's *Cyclopaedia*, Whewell's *Philosophy of the Inductive Sciences*, Peacock and Brown. He tried to take the sting out of some of the key accusations. Thus, while he dealt with the interpolations of Charles Blagden in Cavendish's paper, even going to the length of printing facsimiles of the handwriting of Cavendish, the author of the interpolations, and of Blagden for purposes of comparison, he defused the notion of a conspiracy based on the interpolations. He pointed out that, after the reading of Cavendish's paper, in accord with the then practice, an abstract of it was composed to be read at the next meeting. This abstract, Weld argued, would have been a prime opportunity to fiddle the dates of discovery, but it was not taken. In particular there was no effort to

---

[101] Muirhead to Watt Jr, 11 September 1847, Muirhead Papers, MS GEN 1354/1138.

[102] Charles Richard Weld, *A History of the Royal Society, with Memoirs of the Presidents compiled from authentic documents*, 2 vols, 1848, vol. 2, pp. 170–85.

[103] Ibid., vol. 2, p. 170, note 16.

assert the 1781 date of Cavendish's experiments.[104] The import of this was that the actions of Blagden and Cavendish may have involved some genuine mistakes but no intentional fraud or conspiracy against Watt.

At another point Weld dealt with the issue of open scientific communication by discussing not Cavendish's failings in that regard but Watt's. Referring to Watt's withdrawal of his paper and the fact that he did nothing until spurred into action by Cavendish, Weld commented that 'Watt's silence was the extreme of caution'. Weld reported conversations with Faraday in which the latter argued that Watt deserved blame for not communicating immediately a theory that he believed to be true.

> If, for argument's sake it be assumed, that the discovery of the composition of water was of a nature to confer a great and immediate benefit upon mankind, it must be allowed that Cavendish, by his open communication of it to the Royal Society for insertion in the *Philosophical Transactions* ... was the first to make it generally known; whereas Watt did not come forward until Cavendish had made the discovery public.[105]

Given Arago's concern with *Cavendish's* lack of communication, this does smack very much of a desire to balance the scales, to show that there were faults on both sides. Weld's balance was impeccable. He concluded his account by first quoting Whewell's categorical denial of the discovery, and even understanding of it, to Watt, and then immediately endorsing the factual accuracy of the key dates in the affair as set out by Muirhead in his introduction to the *Correspondence*. Finally Weld expressed himself gratified to find 'upon the testimony of the present Mr. Watt' that 'when his father became a Fellow of the Royal Society, in 1785, he formed the personal acquaintance of Mr. Cavendish, and lived upon good terms with him. How greatly is it to be desired that all scientific rivalries might terminate in so amiable a manner!' Weld's clear message was that enough was enough, and the water controversy should be laid to rest.

'The present Mr. Watt', who had in fact shown little sign of wanting to terminate the scientific rivalry, was himself laid to rest at about this time. During the production of the *Correspondence* Watt Jr's failing health was apparent. He was effectively blind and had pain in his legs which affected his mobility. By May 1848 he was in terminal decline and died on 2 June. As the events of the 1848 Revolution rocked Paris, events that his old friend Arago was closely involved in, the affairs of the bachelor who so long ago had participated in the original Revolution were wound up. Brougham received a bequest of books from Watt Jr's library and sought a portrait of his friend, but Muirhead was unable to help with anything except a profile made in Paris in the eighteenth century. The one good portrait of him that existed was still hanging, inaccessible, at Heathfield House.[106] It transpired that Watt Jr had not paid the duty on his bequests. This meant that those receiving them, like Brougham, were left with the bill. Muirhead felt that 'the grace of all Mr W's bequests has been disfigured by the <u>posthumous economy</u>'. He had spoken to Watt Jr about this but the dying man

---

[104] Ibid., p. 173.

[105] Ibid., pp. 177–78.

[106] Muirhead to Brougham, 8 July 1848, Brougham Papers, 23,387. The then inaccessible portrait was almost certainly that reproduced in Figure 5.1.

had refused to do anything, all to save about £500. Muirhead wondered whether this was a 'money-mania', finding the psychology of it baffling.[107]

The most important bequest from Watt Jr's point of view would have been the charge of caring, as he had done over more than forty years, for the reputation of his father. This fell, inevitably, to Muirhead, who was Watt Jr's literary executor. Muirhead did see through the intended publishing project. The estate, however, passed into the Gibson family in circumstances that caused Muirhead some distress. He recalled for Brougham a trip to Wales 'to <u>Enthrone</u> young J.W. Gibson in his large estates there'.

> I found to my sad annoyance, that at the mature age of twenty-four, he was <u>plucked</u> for his degree at Cambridge, and at twenty-five, celebrated his majority under the Will, by a riotous party of young publicans and cock-fighters from the purlieus of Birm^m and Handsworth. And upon this <u>the Venerable Shade</u> was looking down from the wall at Heathfield![108]

It is clear that Muirhead's enthusiasm in the cause had faded somewhat in the 1850s even as he dutifully saw through the publication of *The Origin and Progress of the Mechanical Inventions* and of the *Life*. He probably felt that he owed this much to his old friend and benefactor, Watt Jr, but had no obligation beyond that. Muirhead described the *Life of James Watt* to Brougham as a 'rifacimento'. His literary enthusiasm seems to have been spent on the 'Woodcocks' project and a return to the affairs of the Bannatyne Club.[109]

We saw that Muirhead considered the water controversy to be essentially over after Jeffrey's article was published in 1848. He saw Wilson's publication of the *Life* of Cavendish as an anti-climax. Informing Brougham of its appearance, Muirhead noted its numerous serious misstatements, and detected 'the cloven hoof of Harcourt and Co. into whose hands I was aware that W[ilson] had latterly fallen'. The book, at least 500 octavo pages, was evidently the product of much labour but very imperfect. The imperfections could easily be spelled out, 'should it be thought worthwhile to do so'.[110] The clear implication was that noticing the work might not be worth it. The book was long, 'most unfair, but fortunately also most unreadable' and 'appeared to have fallen stillborn from the press'. To notice the work would only be to draw attention to it.[111] Muirhead thought that unless the Cavendish Society had presented it to the French Institute they should not 'run the risk of propagating error by sending anything to Paris'.[112] Muirhead had believed in

---

[107] Muirhead to Brougham, 14 August 1848, Brougham Papers, 23,391. Muirhead did use the term 'psychology'.

[108] Muirhead to Brougham, 16 February 1857 and 26 November 1858, Brougham Papers.

[109] Ibid. The Woodcocks project involved a highly contrived, and rather indulgent, literary venture in which a list of eminent contributors wrote poems and epigrams inspired by Sir Francis Chantrey's feat, in November 1829, of killing two woodcocks with one shot and by Chantrey's sculpture commemorative of the occasion. It was published as J.P. Muirhead, *Winged Words on Chantrey's Woodcocks with Etchings*, 1857.

[110] Muirhead to Brougham, 9 May 1851, Brougham Papers, 3929.

[111] Muirhead to Brougham, 14 February 1852, Brougham Papers, 12,826.

[112] Muirhead to Brougham, 18 February 1852, Brougham Papers, 12,827.

1848 that the controversy was effectively over. Wilson's publication did not seem to change his mind.

Wilson's *Life of Cavendish* was not, in fact, extensively reviewed. None of the major reviews dealt with it. The *British Quarterly Review* carried a favourable notice in its 'Criticisms on Books' section by Robert Vaughan, the editor – no doubt just reward for Wilson's contributions to that journal. The notice printed approvingly a long extract from Wilson's introduction and depicted Wilson as a lone rational voice against the irrationally pro-Watt pronouncements of other reviews.[113] The *Athenaeum* reviewed Wilson's book but concentrated on the issue of Cavendish's character and, so far as the water question was concerned, simply repeated the claim that it had made in reviewing the *Correspondence* – that Cavendish and Watt were to be regarded as joint discoverers who arrived at the discovery independently. This did no justice to Wilson's arguments, but was an understandable response to such a severe and complex book in a general journal of literature.[114] A favourable review, and very clear summary, had been arranged by Wilson's friend, Daniel Macmillan, to appear in his weekly magazine, *The Spectator*.[115] A notice in the *British & Foreign Medico-Chirurgical Review* was positive, praised Wilson's impartiality in the water question but contented itself with long quotations concerning Cavendish's character.[116] Wilson's book was thus not entirely unnoticed, and it did stimulate some other popular accounts of Cavendish, but its impact in the serious literary press was limited. In this sense it is understandable that Muirhead might consider it stillborn.[117]

Another sign that the controversy was regarded as effectively over comes in the form of a meeting between Muirhead and Harcourt in 1856. Muirhead described the occasion, rather jocularly, to Brougham:

113 'Review of *The Life of the Honourable Henry Cavendish*', *British Quarterly Review*, 21, 1851, 257–59.

114 'The Life of the Honorable Henry Cavendish', *The Athenaeum*, 13 December 1851, 1305–1306.

115 'Wilson's Life of Cavendish', *The Spectator*, **24**, 9 August 1851, 760–61. See George Wilson to Daniel Macmillan, 2 March, 1851, Macmillan Papers, British Library, Add. MSS 55089, ff. 135–36.

116 'Review of George Wilson, The Life of the Hon. Henry Cavendish', *British & Foreign Medico-Chirurgical Review*, **9**, April 1852, 533–36.

117 Among popular accounts, Cavendish's cold, faithless rationalism was a compelling topic. Following Wilson's line, its scientific results were admired even as its human consequences were lamented. For a fine example see: 'The Hon. Henry Cavendish', *The Leisure Hour. A Family Journal of Instruction and Recreation*, 4, 1855, 489–94. This article awarded Cavendish the discovery of the composition of water (among many discoveries) but also concluded: 'How mournful to think that a man with so many excellences stood aloof from that generous and ennobling faith which would have quickened his dormant affections, and superadded to his intellectual eminence the attractiveness of Christian love' (p. 494). It would be useful to pursue the response to the *Life* into the growing *scientific* press of this period, but I have been unable to do this. It seems likely that Muirhead's confidence would have been dispelled by what he saw there had he deigned to notice that sort of forum. As will become apparent in Chapter 11, a thorough survey of chemical texts would certainly have given him no grounds for complacency. Jessie Aitken Wilson, *A Memoir of George Wilson*, 1860, pp. 341–42 depicted the book as a success and as being widely appreciated as resolving the controversy in Cavendish's favour.

You will be amused to hear that I have not only broken bread with the Canon of York, (without, however, enquiring into the composition of the other article of prison fare), but that I count some of his family among my dear friends, and was staying with one of them the other day on a delightful visit! To do him justice, he appears to be very amiable, and, so far as I could observe, to bear no malice in his heart. So may all controversies end![118]

After the publication of the *Life of Watt* in 1858, Muirhead's only remaining substantive involvement in the controversy appears to have been occasioned by the death of the botanist Robert Brown.

It will be recalled that Brown had been a rather shadowy worker in the Cavendish vineyard in the wake of the publication of Arago's *Eloge* and Harcourt's response. Brown had in fact done considerable work on the water controversy. The traces remain in his papers, and constitute a very useful resource.[119] It had been expected that Brown would publish something on the water question in 1839–40, but nothing appeared. Brown had consulted a wide range of printed sources and also manuscripts in the Royal Society and the Académie des Sciences. He corresponded with Harcourt and was regarded as something of a behind-the-scenes expert whom Harcourt relied upon for advice on his 1846 letter to Brougham in the *Philosophical Magazine*.[120] Brown was one of the suspects when members of the Watt camp were trying to guess the identity of the author of the 1846 *Quarterly Review* article.

After Brown's death in June 1858, his collaborator and literary executor, J.J. Bennett, felt obliged to release the outcome of the researches on the water question. Indeed, he stated that the executors had received several requests for the release of this information. George Wilson had written that same month to *The Athenaeum* in response to its obituary of Brown. Wilson recounted Brown's interest in the water question and recalled two meetings with him when Brown had referred to documents in his possession which would put Cavendish's claim beyond dispute. When pressed for further information, Brown had simply smiled. Wilson assumed that the documents in question would be among the papers of Sir Joseph Banks that had passed down to Brown. He urged their publication after inspection by interested parties such as the Duke of Devonshire, the Cavendish Society, or himself.[121] In the event Wilson was quite wrong about the nature of the document. Bennett revealed its character and its believed import in a letter to the President of the Royal Society, Sir Benjamin Collins Brodie, which was read to the Society on 17 February 1859.[122]

---

[118] Muirhead to Brougham, 23 June 1856, Brougham Papers, 3937.

[119] See David Mabberley, *Jupiter Botanicus. Robert Brown of the British Museum*, 1985, pp. 337–39. British Library Add. MSS 33,227, 33, 441.

[120] Harcourt to Brown, 8 September 1839, 10 February [1840], 9 June [1840], Robert Brown Correspondence, British Library, Add. MSS 33,227, ff. 87–88, 92, 95; draft letters Brown to Harcourt, 14 June 1840, 7 February 1846, Add. MSS 33,227, f. 93, 98.

[121] George Wilson, 'Robert Brown and the water controversy', *The Athenaeum*, 26 June 1858, p. 819. Wilson's letter was dated 23 June. The obituary of Brown had appeared in *The Athenaeum*, 19 June 1858, p. 786.

[122] "'Statement of Facts relating to the Discovery of the Composition of Water by the Hon. H. Cavendish". In a Letter from J.J. Bennett, Esq., F.R.S. to Sir B.C. Brodie, Bart., P.R.S., dated February 12, 1859. Received February 14, 1859', *Proceedings of the Royal Society of London*, vol. 9, November 1857–April 1859, pp. 642–44; 'Letter from James P. Muirhead, Esq., to Sir Benjamin C. Brodie, Bart.,

Muirhead also wrote to Brodie, on 28 February, rebutting the argument made by Bennett, and he sought to have the letter read to the Society. There appears to have been some reluctance to air the other side of the argument, because it was only after some negotiation that a revised letter from Muirhead to Brodie (dated 8 March) was read to the Royal Society on 10 March. Bennett's and Muirhead's communications were also the subject of notices in *The Athenaeum*, together with a response by George Wilson.[123]

In this exchange the complexities of the arguments in the previous episodes in the water controversy were gone. Bennett's claim was that Brown had made a simple textual discovery that settled the matter. The man who arguably incited the first phase of the controversy in the 1780s by what he wrote to Watt, J.A. De Luc, became the focus of one of the last arguments in the 'live' controversy during the second phase. Specifically, Brown had found in De Luc's *Idées sur Meteorologie* a statement that appeared to show that Cavendish *had* drawn conclusions from his experiments before Watt. Muirhead's response was to set De Luc's words in the context of other things that he said in the same book in an effort to show that their meaning was not as Bennett and Brown claimed. This is an interesting reversal in the sense that the pro-Cavendish forces were now arguing in simple empirical mode whilst Muirhead's was a hermeneutic approach. Wilson's contribution to the exchange reaffirmed the empirical, common-sense perspective.[124]

Pres. R.S., Dated March 8, 1859, relating to the Discovery of the Composition of Water', ibid., pp. 679–81.

123 On Muirhead's negotiations with Brodie, see Muirhead to Brougham, 7 March 1859, Brougham Papers, University College London, 5527; *The Athenaeum*, 26 February 1859, p. 287 (Bennett); 12 March 1859, pp. 356–57 (Muirhead); 30 April 1859, pp. 582–83 (Wilson). Wilson had previously communicated his views in Edinburgh: 'On the recent vindication of the priority of Cavendish as the discoverer of the composition of water', *Proceedings of the Royal Society of Edinburgh*, vol. 4, November 1857–April 1862, pp. 205–208. (The paper was read on 18 April 1859.)

124 The arguments focused, according to Bennett, on the date and nature of Cavendish's communication to Priestley. Bennett quoted from the key document, which was De Luc's *Idées sur la Météorologie* (vol. 2, 1787, pp. 206–207). There De Luc recalled visiting Priestley towards the end of 1782. According to De Luc, Priestley spoke of Cavendish's communication to him about the explosion experiments: 'Il me communiqua alors, que M. Cavendish d'après une remarque de M. Warltire; qui avoit toujours trouvé de l'eau dans les vases où il avait brûlé un mélange *d'air inflammable* et *d'air atmosphérique*; s'etoit appliqué à découvrir la source de cette eau, et qu'il avoit trouvé, "qu'un mélange *d'air inflammable* et *d'air déphlogistiqué* en proportion convenable, étant allumé par l'étincelle électrique, se convertissoit tout entier en *eau*". Je fus frappé au plus haut degré de cette découverte.' The statement within De Luc's quotation marks is taken to be what Cavendish said to Priestley in late 1782, and the words 'se convertissoit tout entier' reveal that Cavendish believed that the airs were *converted* into water. Bennett regarded this evidence as conclusive of Cavendish's priority. Its credibility, he felt, was enhanced by the fact that it came from De Luc, Watt's 'amie zélé', and that it remained uncontradicted. Muirhead's response to Bennett quoted from other parts of De Luc's *Idées*, in which De Luc's statement could only make sense if Cavendish had made conclusions from his experiments known much later than late 1782. In addition, Muirhead noted that the passage from De Luc that Bennett relied upon was written some years after the encounter to which it refers, and from memory, and so is of doubtful reliability in directly quoting what Priestley told De Luc about what Cavendish had said to him. So much for clear empirical evidence!

We can only speculate about the reasons for this change of approach. It provided the Cavendish camp with a more accessible argument, a feature also of the argument from character increasingly used in the 1850s. Wilson himself was acutely aware of the dryness of his book on Cavendish and that it had not made as much impact as it might otherwise have done. Even experts in the field would have found some of Wilson's (and Harcourt's) historical arguments difficult of access. Learned chemists were increasingly removed from the era of phlogiston theory and would not necessarily have had it at their fingertips as an object lesson in bad science. This was one sign that the water controversy was becoming a truly historical problem by the 1850s, that is, a problem not so immediately driven by contemporary concerns.

Another indication of the declining saliency of the controversy is that opportunities to argue the respective cases were no longer so used. This was true of reviews of *The Origin and Progress of the Mechanical Inventions*, which was published in 1854, as well as of reviews of the *Life of James Watt*, when it appeared in 1858. Brewster's review of the former work did maintain Watt's claim on the water question but did so simply by referring back to his 1847 article.[125] Reviewers were more concerned with an overall assessment of Watt and his significance. They were happy to see him as an engineer, albeit a philosophical one. The urgency to make him a philosopher and a scientific discoverer was no longer so great. The case of Samuel Smiles's treatment of Watt is instructive in this regard.

Smiles contacted Muirhead in early 1858 via his publisher, John Murray, unaware that Muirhead's *Life of James Watt* was about to be published. He informed Muirhead that he had done considerable work on a life of Watt and requested access to the correspondence. He did not want to quote from it but 'to gather from the inspection of the letters, such traits of character & points of interest in reference to personal matters as often let in a flood of light on individual history & its development'.[126] Muirhead's reply was sharp and unhelpful:

> It is, I feel assured unnecessary for me to remind you that I am not only a kinsman of Mr Watt, but the literary Executor of his son; and I do not hesitate to say, that no complete or worthy Life of James Watt can ever be written by any one who is disbarred, as you would be, from the free use of both his Correspondence (whether published or in MS) and the Specifications of his Patents.
>
> Under these circumstances you will no doubt be ready to admit that the subject of your projected undertaking is already very decidedly and legitimately pre-occupied.[127]

Smiles retired calmly and courteously in the face of this rather curt rejection.[128] However, when Muirhead's *Life* appeared, Smiles took the opportunity to review it anonymously. His criticisms are of considerable interest as a discussion of how the life of a man such as Watt should be approached in the high noon of Victorian society. Smiles, perhaps getting his revenge, was critical of the hyperbole that

[125] David Brewster, 'Review of Muirhead's *The Origin and Progress of the Mechanical Inventions of James Watt*', *North British Review*, **23**, 1855, 193–231.

[126] Samuel Smiles to J.P. Muirhead, 4 January 1858, Muirhead Papers, MS GEN 1354/91(a).

[127] J.P. Muirhead to Samuel Smiles, 7 January 1858, Muirhead Papers, MS GEN 1354/91(b).

[128] Smiles to Muirhead, 9 January 1858, Muirhead Papers, MS GEN 1354/91(c) and John Murray to Muirhead, 5 February [1858], Muirhead Papers, MS GEN 1354/91(d).

Muirhead indulged in. He regarded it as inappropriate in any biography, but especially in Watt's case: 'The life of that sterling and thoroughly unaffected man ought to be a sterling and thoroughly unaffected book.'[129] Apart from attacking Muirhead's style, Smiles criticized the tendency to exaggerate the, admittedly colossal, impact of the Watt engine and to attribute the steam technology of the railways to Watt, when it belonged to George Stephenson. In another review attributed to Smiles, other 'corrections' were made, for example, to over-enthusiasm in discovering childhood genius in Watt and to the depiction of the idea of the separate condenser as a flash of inspiration rather than the culmination of a lot of hard work. Smiles gave the composition of water a sentence: 'it is now placed beyond a doubt that he was the first to promulgate the true theory of [water's] composition, though Cavendish had arrived by independent research at the same result'.[130] Here, as in the *Lives of Boulton and Watt* eventually published in 1865, Smiles gave little prominence to the water question and, when he mentioned it, pushed controversy firmly into the past while retaining a judicious, non-committal claim for Watt.[131] Stories about Watt were taking their place in Smiles's pantheon of heroic, human, and not necessarily scientific, engineers. Smiles was fond of Watt's garret workshop. It was illustrated in his *Lives of Boulton and Watt* and represented as the site and symbol of Watt's creativity. In 1874 Smiles wrote:

> One of the most remarkable things about engineering in England is, that its principal achievements have been accomplished, not by natural philosophers nor by mathematicians, but by men of humble station, for the most part self-educated … The great mechanics … gathered their practical knowledge in the workshop, or acquired it in manual labour.[132]

In the struggle between those propagating the narratives of 'genius' and of 'hard work', so active at this time, Watt the craftsman and engineer gained ascendency over Watt the philosopher.

In 1875 the chemist–historian T.E. Thorpe delivered a lecture on Henry Cavendish in the Manchester Science Lectures at Hulme Town Hall. When Thorpe came to what he called Cavendish's 'greatest discovery' he looked back on the water question.

> Not many years ago there was a great controversy concerning the question – Who was the discoverer of the composition of water? I am not now going to rake up the matter; for it is gradually being forgotten; but I think that every chemist now allows that the claims of Cavendish have been incontestably proved.[133]

---

129 Anon, 'James Watt', *Fraser's Magazine*, **59**, 1859, 318. This is, I think, attributable to Smiles.

130 [Samuel Smiles], 'Review of Muirhead, *Life of James Watt*, Muirhead, *The Origin and Progress of the Mechanical Inventions of James Watt* and George Williamson, *Memorials of the Lineage, Early Life, Education, and Development of the Genius of James Watt*', *Quarterly Review*, **104**, 1858, 447.

131 See Samuel Smiles, *Lives of Boulton and Watt*, 1865, pp. 377–81. Smiles states: 'Each was quite competent to have made the discovery; nor is it necessary for the fame of either to strip a leaf of laurel from the brow of the other. Moreover, we are as unwilling to believe that Cavendish would have knowingly appropriated to himself the idea of Watt, as that Watt would have knowingly appropriated the idea of Cavendish' (p. 380).

132 Quoted in Eric Robinson and A.E. Musson, *James Watt and the Steam Revolution*, 1969, p. 1.

133 T.E. Thorpe, 'Henry Cavendish', in T.E. Thorpe, *Essays in Historical Chemistry*, 1902, p. 95.

Thorpe was born in Manchester in 1845, when the water controversy was at its height. He studied under H.E. Roscoe at Owens College and then with Robert Bunsen at Heidelberg. The Chair of Chemistry at the Andersonian College, Glasgow, was his first appointment. In 1874 he moved to a chair at the new Yorkshire College of Science in Leeds. Just thirty years old when we meet him, he was a prime example of the thoroughly trained, actively researching, institution-building chemist of the last quarter of the nineteenth century.[134]

Thorpe was happy to see the water controversy forgotten and was convinced that the case for Cavendish had been victorious. He did note, however, that 'the time was ripe for this discovery'. The work of a number of Cavendish's contemporaries was tending, Thorpe said, in the same direction and, if Cavendish had not capitalized on his opportunities, then someone else would have made the discovery with little delay. Appealing thus to the phenomenon of simultaneous or multiple discovery, Thorpe effectively rendered the discovery of the composition of water as the product of the culture of late eighteenth-century chemistry. In this way he took the sting out of any contest and justified his decision not to rake it up. The chemical consensus on the water question went hand in hand with Thorpe's assessment of Cavendish's overall significance. Considering Cavendish's corpus of scientific work, Thorpe asked rhetorically 'what is the most obvious characteristic of all this labour?'. The answer was its thoroughly quantitative character:

> Weighing, measuring, calculating; such, indeed, was pre-eminently the essential nature of Cavendish's work. If, then, the claim of any one to be styled the founder of chemistry as a science rests upon his recognition of its quantitative relations, may we not also, and with equal truth, say that 'Chemistry is an English Science – its founder was Cavendish, of immortal memory'?[135]

This was, of course, a response to Adolph Wurtz's famous statement of 1869 in which he claimed chemistry as a French science whose founder was Lavoisier. Clearly, the iconic status of Cavendish remained very important to Thorpe and to many of his fellow British chemists in the later decades of the nineteenth century. Cavendish's claim to the discovery of the composition of water was secured, finally, by his identification with the very nature of the science of chemistry. That discovery was a central feature of the science. Chemistry was defined as what Cavendish did. Ineluctably, the discovery was his.

Thorpe defended this position against the claims of Berthelot, published in 1890 in his book *La Révolution Chimique, Lavoisier*.[136] This episode had interesting parallels with earlier events. Here was a Perpetual Secretary of the Académie, one

---

134 Thorpe went on to have two spells as Professor of Chemistry at the Royal College of Science, South Kensington (1885–94 and 1909–12), which sandwiched his tenure of the post of Government Chemist. He became FRS in 1876 and was President of the Society of Chemical Industry in 1895, of the Chemical Society (1899–1901) and Foreign Secretary of the Royal Society (1899–1903). His research concerned vanadium, phosphorus compounds, the relation of molecular weights to specific gravities, and the accurate determination of atomic weights. He was also to become well known for his work in the history of chemistry. (*DNB* (1922–30), pp. 842–43).

135 Thorpe, 'Henry Cavendish', p. 97.

136 M. Berthelot, *La Révolution Chimique, Lavoisier*, 1890, ch. 10.

of Arago's successors making strong claims on the water question, but this time in favour of Lavoisier. Thorpe, who was President of the Chemical Science Section of the British Association, responded at the Leeds meeting of that body in September 1890.[137] Berthelot essentially took the position that Lavoisier himself had taken in 1783, implying a smooth progress of Lavoisier's experimental programme gaining little from the news brought to Paris of Cavendish's experiments. Thorpe in response pointed to Lavoisier being on the wrong track, having abandoned phlogiston only to be led astray by *le principe oxygine* in looking for an acid as product of the combustion of inflammable air. Only the detailed news of Cavendish's experiments put Lavoisier back on track. Thorpe reproduced Blagden's letter to Crell's *Chemische Annalen* through which Blagden and Cavendish sought to set things right at the time. Thorpe noted that Lavoisier never responded to Blagden's letter, thereby tacitly accepting Cavendish's priority. So once again the water question was before the Association, some fifty years after Harcourt's 'Address', this time to defend Cavendish against Lavoisier rather than Watt.

On 11 March 1898, Thorpe delivered the Watt Anniversary Lecture to the Greenock Philosophical Society in the Watt Memorial Hall, the very building that Watt Jr and the worthies of Greenock had erected to Watt's memory. Thorpe was clear from the beginning that Watt was to be regarded as a 'scientific man, in the truest and noblest sense of that term'.[138] Before this audience, Thorpe ended up dividing the spoils: 'these eminent men [Watt, Cavendish and Lavoisier] took an independent and, we may say, an equally important share in the establishment of one of the greatest scientific truths that the eighteenth century brought to light'. The lecture was carefully judged in that its conclusion praised Watt's 'intellectual grasp', his 'mental vision' and his 'love of truth' even as the body of the lecture tied Watt's thinking on water firmly, more firmly so than Cavendish's, to old modes of thought. Thus in the conclusion we are told that Watt 'was the first, so far as we can prove from documentary evidence, to state distinctly that water is not an element, but is composed, weight for weight of two other substances, one of which he regarded as phlogiston and the other as dephlogisticated air'.[139] However, Watt reasoned from 'imperfect and altogether erroneous data' whilst Cavendish supplied the 'true experimental basis' of the discovery.

In the body of the lecture Thorpe argued that Watt's early ideas on the interconvertibility of air and water were grounded in ancient notions, a kind of intellectual hangover. Moreover, there were key continuities between Watt's early ideas on interconvertibility and those which he announced in his letters of 1783 and the *Philosophical Transactions* in 1784. The key continuity was that Watt still thought in terms of 'air' as a single sort of matter and that the different airs with which pneumatic chemistry was populated were distinguished by different modes

---

[137] T.E. Thorpe [Presidential Address, Section B], *Report of the Sixtieth Meeting of the British Association for the Advancement of Science held at Leeds in September 1890*, 1891, pp. 761–71, especially pp. 766–71.

[138] Thorpe, 'James Watt', in *Essays in Historical Chemistry*, p. 101. The lecture was printed, and its venue identified in 'James Watt, and the Discovery of the Composition of Water', *Nature*, **57**, 7 April 1898, 546–51.

[139] Ibid., 121.

of composition with heat. This was essentially the view of Watt that Peacock and Harcourt had expressed. Thorpe thus depicted Watt as doubly in thrall to phlogiston theory and to a material chemical theory of heat. Cavendish himself, Thorpe conceded before his Greenock audience, remained in the grip of phlogiston theory. The same point was not emphasized, however, in the account of Cavendish given in the Manchester Science Lectures. Even as the iconic status of Cavendish for the chemical community was maintained, concession to Watt's claims was still possible before other audiences as the occasion required. As the century closed, the calm modesty and love of truth exhibited by Watt could be maintained, even though, as Thorpe put it, 'the voice of envy and detraction has not been unheard amongst the strife of partisans in the Water Controversy'.[140]

Explicit controversy over the water question had certainly calmed by the 1860s. It had run out of ideological steam. The attributional process, of course, continued and we conclude the substantive examination of the controversy with our second attributional survey. We will see that the victory that Muirhead and Brewster felt had been won for Watt in the realm of the reviews was lost sight of in a wider attributional arena.

---

[140] Ibid., 122.

Chapter 11

Still Waters:
Attributional Survey, 1830–1900

Introduction

It was noted in connection with the first attributional survey in Chapter 4 that the line between the controversy proper and the ongoing processes of attribution is difficult to draw. In principle it is impossible to draw, since there is no line. The activities involved in the controversy itself are primarily processes of attribution. The difference, then, is one of perception. We might safely say that during the late 1830s and through the 1840s a literate observer of the British scientific scene would be aware that a controversy on the water question was going on. Books and pamphlets were appearing and articles in the reviews were carrying the arguments on. By the mid-1850s, however, it is not clear that the same literate observer would be aware of a current controversy. Relatively still waters prevailed, but there were undercurrents. As public controversy calmed, a number of beneath-the-surface moves were made in texts and other publications that, while not very visible contributions to an ongoing controversy, were important in the settling of the issue in an attributional sense. That settling process stretched out over several decades. Let us examine first what was happening in the important area of encyclopaedia coverage of these issues.

Encyclopaedic Interventions

The importance of the *Encyclopaedia Britannica* in the early history of the water question will be recalled. Articles on 'Water', 'Steam' and the 'Steam Engine' in the third edition were important in emphasizing Watt's philosophical character and gave him considerable credit for discovery of the theory of the composition of water. Thomas Thomson's articles on 'Chemistry' from the 1801 *Supplement* onwards redressed the balance very much towards Cavendish while still giving some acknowledgement to Watt. The key decision by Macvey Napier to invite Watt Jr to write the article on his father for the *Supplement* to the fourth, fifth and sixth editions of the *Britannica* created, as we have seen, an opportunity for the Watt camp's claims on the water question to reach the *Britannica*'s audience. Other encyclopaedias before 1830 commonly divided the credit for the discovery between Cavendish and Watt, though inclining towards Cavendish. Consistency was not a strong virtue of these publications, and contradictions between different articles in the same encyclopaedia were quite common.

The seventh edition of the *Britannica* was also edited by Napier but published by a new owner, Adam Black, who had purchased the *Britannica* from Constable for £6150 at auction in the late 1820s. Although Black had hoped to publish the new edition by 1830, it was not until 1842 that its twenty-two volumes were completed. These volumes retained many articles from earlier editions. Thomson's article on 'Chemistry' remained in a further revised form. It had less historical content than previously. The brief historical section firmly identified Cavendish as the discoverer of the composition of water.[1] No mention at all was made of Watt. Water was dealt with briefly and abstractly under 'Hydrogen', without history or attributions. The article on Cavendish was substantially unchanged from earlier editions, remaining largely a seriatim account of Cavendish's papers in the *Philosophical Transactions*. The article clearly and unequivocally characterized Cavendish's 1784 paper as containing the discovery of the composition of water. It also congratulated the British chemists for not being seduced by system: 'it must ever be remembered, to the honour of Mr Cavendish, and to the credit of this country, that we had not all been seduced, by the dazzling semblance of universal laws, to admit facts as demonstrated which were only made plausible by a slight and imperfect analogy'.[2] The article on Watt was still that written by Watt Jr, with its claim that Watt was the first to make known the theory that 'water is a compound of dephlogisticated and inflammable airs ... deprived of their latent or elementary heat'. The only textual differences are that in the concluding note Watt Jr is identified as the author of the article, and the reader's attention is drawn to Arago's recent 'admirable account' of Watt.[3] Thus, in the edition overall, mixed messages were still conveyed, although the strictly chemical articles had nothing to say about Watt.

Macvey Napier died in 1847 and in 1851 Black decided to publish a new edition, the eighth. Dr Thomas Stewart Traill, Professor of Medical Jurisprudence at Edinburgh University, was chosen as editor. John Leslie's dissertation on the progress of the mathematical and physical sciences was continued by Professor James David Forbes. In that dissertation Forbes was to change substantially the way in which the *Britannica* represented the 'water controversy'.

In some respects inertia still ruled the day in the eighth edition. The article on Cavendish was virtually unchanged. That on Watt was also substantively the same. However, an effort had been made to direct readers to counter-balancing material. A note at the beginning of the article on Watt clearly identified Watt Jr as the author, stated that some changes had been made in the article, and directed the reader to remarks on Watt in Forbes's 'Preliminary Dissertation'.[4] It will be

---

1 Thomas Thomson, 'Chemistry', *Encyclopaedia Britannica*, seventh edn, vol. 6, 1842, pp. 341–505. For the attribution to Cavendish see p. 349.

2 'Cavendish, Henry', ibid., pp. 262–63.

3 'Watt, James', ibid., vol. 21, 1842, pp. 818–19.

4 'Watt, James', *Encyclopaedia Britannica*, eighth edn, vol. 21, 1860, p. 773. The note reads: 'It may be interesting to the readers of the *Encyclopaedia Britannica* to know that the following article on JAMES WATT was contributed in 1823 by the son of the great mechanician, the late James Watt of Birmingham. A few necessary emendations have been made on it, chiefly drawn from *The Origin and Progress of the Mechanical Inventions of James Watt*, by his kinsman, James P. Muirhead, M.A., 3 vols., 1854; and from the *Life of James Watt* by the same author, 1858. The character of Watt appended

remembered also that Watt Jr had inserted a footnote in his original article referring to the confusion of dates in the papers in the *Philosophical Transactions*. In the eighth edition this footnote was carefully modified. The reference to Cavendish having circulated misdated copies of his paper was removed, as was Watt Jr's arch commentary. Instead we are told that the reason for the confusion has been cleared up and we are referred to Muirhead's *Life of James Watt* for details.[5] The obedient reader who turned to Forbes's 'Preliminary Dissertation' would find there a substantially changed picture of the water question.

Forbes was, as we have seen, a member of the gentlemanly élite of the British Association who cooperated with Baily on the Cavendish experiment, regarded Cavendish as a scientific hero, and supported Harcourt's defence of Cavendish at the Association's Birmingham meeting in 1839. In the 1840s and 1850s, rather quietly, Forbes published a number of items that began, as he saw it, to set the record straight in various respects.

In writing a life of John Robison for the Royal Society of Edinburgh,[6] Forbes had studied Robison's articles in the *Encyclopaedia Britannica* on 'Steam' and 'Steam Engine'. It will be recalled that those articles had given great credit to Watt, but that the engineer himself had subsequently edited them to assert his lack of indebtedness to Joseph Black in working through to the idea for the separate condenser. In 1855, when he was working on the section dealing with Watt in his 'Preliminary Dissertation', Forbes sought comments from George Wilson. Wilson encouraged Forbes to reassert Watt's debt to Black, thus, in his view, setting right both Watt himself and Muirhead, who had perpetuated Watt's view in his introduction to the *Correspondence*. He wrote to Forbes, 'your note corrects this revival of Watt's own misconception of his debt to Black ... '.[7]

On the water question itself, Wilson felt that it was 'much better the Controversy ... should be left untouched in Watt's Life'. This was because 'no praise of Watt will satisfy those Eulogists of his who have made his superiority to Cavendish the subject of contention till the necessity of subordinating the latter has become a monomania with them'. Wilson suggested that Forbes might notice with additional fullness Watt's knowledge of the chemistry of his time. He was, after all, a friend of Black and Priestley, helped to introduce chlorine bleaching, and was an experimenter himself. For these reasons Watt 'had claims to be called a Chemist as the recognized

---

to the biography is from the brilliant pen of the late Lord Jeffrey, who knew the engineer well, and enjoyed much of his esteem. Further information regarding Watt and his discoveries will be found in the SIXTH PRELIMINARY DISSERTATION, by Principal Forbes, prefixed to this work.'

[5] The note reads: 'There is a confusion of dates in the accounts of this affair. Mr Watt's letter to M. de Luc in the *Philosophical Transactions* appears dated 26th November 1784, which is evidently an error of the press. Mr Cavendish, in his letter, read 15th January 1784, speaks of Mr Watt's paper "as lately read before the Society", whereas the paper itself purports to have been read on the 29th April 1784. [This confusion has since been cleared up by the discovery that the 26th November 1784 of the *Philosophical Transactions* should be 26th November 1783. See p. 343 of the *Life of James Watt*, by J.P. Muirhead, London, 1858.]'

[6] 'Biographical Notice of Sir John Robison', *Proceedings of the Royal Society of Edinburgh*, vol. 2, 1846, pp. 68–78.

[7] George Wilson to J.D. Forbes, 17 October [1855], Forbes Papers, Incoming Letters, 1855, no. 128.

coadjutor of the Chemists of his day'.[8] Thus Wilson and Forbes sought to shape the chemical reputation of James Watt, at once granting his chemical credentials in his own time and yet, by depriving him of the discovery of the composition of water, denying him a place in the making of the New Chemistry.

Forbes, it must be realized, greatly admired Watt. He regarded him as a 'profound' engineer. It is worth dwelling on this terminology for a moment. It was important to Forbes that specialization be recognized and observed. He took issue with Macaulay's praise of superficial knowledge, drawing a distinction between knowledge and wisdom. The latter marked off, in Forbes's view, the 'profound' engineer or lawyer. One gets the impression that Forbes felt that to push Watt's original scientific pretensions too far was to paint him as superficial and, in fact, to detract from his reputation as a profound engineer. Watt's champion in the water question, Henry Brougham, had earlier been nominated by Forbes as the very type of the superficial man of knowledge:

> I cannot help fancying that the character of Lord Brougham is a perfect index to the grand distinction between Knowledge & Wisdom. Great & quick abilities – an unbounded literary appetite and memory, & probably a real taste for Science; a powerful constitution & latterly much leisure, have altogether failed to make his Lordship's head anything better than a vast storehouse of <u>knowledge</u>; but which has produced nothing great of its own. For I suppose it is allowed on all hands that he is profound neither as a Lawyer, a Statesman or a Man of Science. But he must be the very beau-ideal of Macaulay's 19th Century man.[9]

Watt was different. He was a profound engineer. He was also a respectable, but not a profound, chemist, since in that department he had not produced anything great of his own. In accord with Wilson's advice, the section of Forbes's 'Preliminary Dissertation' dealing with Watt's work made no mention of the composition of water.[10] Forbes contrived instead to deal with the water controversy in the section dealing with the work of Cavendish.[11] He made a number of points. First, he sought to put the water question into perspective by arguing that, despite the long and

---

[8] George Wilson to J.D. Forbes, 15 October 1855, Forbes Papers, Incoming Letters, 1855, no. 126.

[9] Forbes to Whewell, 29 October 1848, Whewell Papers, Add. Ms.a.2048[4]. For related correspondence on their respective responses to Macaulay see Forbes to Whewell, 19 October 1848, Add. Ms.a.2048[3(1)], 15 November 1848, Add. Ms.a.2048[5], and Whewell's letters to Forbes on this matter in Todhunter, *William Whewell*, 1876, vol. 2, pp. 346–50. Whewell and Forbes were reacting to a lecture given by Macaulay to the Edinburgh Literary Association in October 1848. For this episode as part of Whewell's and Forbes's concern to manage the forum of public debate about science, see Simon Schaffer, 'The history and geography of the intellectual world: Whewell's politics of language', in Menachem Fisch and Simon Schaffer (eds), *William Whewell: A Composite Portrait*, 1991, pp. 217–18.

[10] James David Forbes, 'Dissertation Sixth: Exhibiting a General View of the Progress of Mathematical and Physical Science principally from 1775 to 1850', *Encyclopaedia Britannica*, eighth edn, vol. 1, pp. 795–996.

[11] Forbes also apologized for inserting a biography of Cavendish 'into a chapter professedly on Heat … ' (p. 928, n 4). The section began with Forbes's version of the by now standard accounts of Cavendish's character: neither his nobility nor his wealth 'could withdraw him even for an hour from the course of study which he had marked out; and which constituted for him at once labour and relaxation, the end of living, and almost life itself' (pp. 928–29).

bitter controversy of recent times, the dispute 'hardly could be said to exist until the contemporary generation who witnessed the facts, and also the succeeding one had passed away'. Forbes contended that Cavendish until his death in 1810 and 'for nearly thirty years after' had the 'unquestioned tribute of at least the primary merit in so great a step in science'. Declining to analyse in detail a controversy 'purely personal, and which has almost filled volumes', Forbes proceeded to offer two considerations that he argued resolved the matter, one based on the behaviour of Watt, the other on the character of Cavendish.

Watt's behaviour in withdrawing his first letter to Priestley was not, Forbes stated, the behaviour of a man convinced of his ideas. Watt would not have revived his claim in public after this withdrawal 'had not the experiments and claims of Cavendish at home, and of Lavoisier in France, reanimated all his zeal for the assertion of his opinion'. Forbes doubted that we should allow Watt the advantage of 'anticipating the date of his matured conviction'. That is, we should not grant as a discovery at the time of its suppression a claim that Watt sought to suppress. Forbes also emphasized Watt's subsequent acceptance that Cavendish had a superior claim:

> Watt, in after life, may be said to have tacitly relinquished to Cavendish the honour which, in the first irritation of the conflict of their claims, he showed no disposition to do; it is, therefore, reasonable to infer that, on reflection, he saw good reasons for doing so. By this I mean that he suffered judgment to be passed in favour of Cavendish's claim in the writings of many of his eminent contemporaries, without attempting publicly to correct the all but universal impression which they made.[12]

Forbes believed that this argument (one also made by Harcourt) was clinched by Watt's behaviour in regard to Robison's article on 'Steam' in the 1797, third edition of the *Britannica*. When Watt edited and revised this he did nothing about a statement that it contained clearly attributing the discovery of the composition of water to Cavendish. Instead he 'permitted the fact to be thus transmitted to posterity'. Given this, Forbes believed, 'Watt's friends should have left the matter as he was content to leave it'.[13] Forbes was inclined to link the justice of attributing a discovery to a person with the degree to which they had worked and fought to lay claim to it. If they did not do that work, then, he argued, others should not take up the burden for them.

Having thus dealt with Watt's behaviour, Forbes turned, much more briefly, to Cavendish's character:

> it would yet be difficult to find in the whole range of scientific history (without excepting the venerable name of Newton), an individual so devoted to knowledge for its own sake, so indifferent to the rewards of discovery, so averse to the publication of what he felt to be important, and knew to be original, so insensible to the voice of praise when applied

---

[12] Forbes, 'Dissertation Sixth', p. 930.

[13] Ibid. Watt Jr, of course, would have disagreed with Forbes's assessment of his father's attitude. He stated quite clearly that Watt continued to maintain his claim but would not take steps to deal publicly with contrary statements because of his confidence that posterity would judge the facts of the matter in his favour. Watt's supporters took his failure to intervene as a positive sign of his modesty and his lack of concern about fame in his own lifetime. (See Chapter 5.)

to himself, so ardent in acquainting himself with the labours of others, and so liberal in assisting them.[14]

Forbes found it incredible that Cavendish would ever 'stoop even to the artifices of little minds for exalting his own reputation at the expense of others … '. From the perspective of the Watt camp there is something contradictory in this argument in that Watt's modesty is a ground for denying him the credit while Cavendish's modesty becomes the ground for granting it! Be this as it may, there was the argument in a nutshell. Forbes was aware, of course, of Wilson's reams of complex and convoluted argument and analysis exploring every aspect of the water controversy. In the end, however, the literate and even the scientific public that consulted the *Britannica* for its information needed only this argument from behaviour and character, needed only these indicators of truth. It is certain, given the limited circulation of Wilson's *Life* and the extensive circulation of the *Britannica*, that the attribution of the discovery to Cavendish was clinched in many more minds by Forbes's approach than by Wilson's.

The ninth edition of the *Britannica* contained new articles on 'Chemistry', 'Cavendish', 'Watt' and 'Water'. 'Chemistry' was contributed by Professor Henry Armstrong, Raphael Meldola and F.H. Butler. It contained no mention of Watt at all. The discussion of Cavendish's work described him as having 'discovered in 1781 that hydrogen and dephlogisticated air (oxygen), when exploded in a close vessel … produced pure water … Cavendish's discovery deprived it [water] of the rank of an element … and thus prepared the way for the acceptation of correct and definite views concerning the elementary bodies.'[15]

The article 'Cavendish' was an edited version of that in the eighth edition. It continued to describe the 1784 paper 'Experiments on air' as containing 'an account of two of the greatest discoveries that have ever been made in chemistry, – the composition of water, and that of nitric acid'. Although the work on composition of water was briefly described, interestingly, no effort was made to date the discovery as occurring in 1781. The usual depictions of Cavendish's character were provided and a new passage expressed his foundational importance in the history of chemistry: 'The splendid career of chemical investigation, which has since been pursued with a degree of success unprecedented in history, may be said to have been first laid open to mankind by his labours.'[16] Amidst all the enduring tropes about Cavendish's eccentricities this stands out as a key statement about the man. Cavendish was attributed that significance partly because of what he was taken to have discovered, but mainly because of the way that he discovered it. The rigorous, quantitative, extended train of research was the hallmark of Cavendish's work. It was the basis on which T.E. Thorpe designated him as the founder of modern chemistry.

When we turn to the entirely new article on 'James Watt' by Professor James A. Ewing, we do find, finally, some reference to the composition of water in the small print of the article. The small print mentions first some of Watt's minor innovations and then informs us:

---

14 Forbes, 'Dissertation Sixth', p. 930.

15 'Chemistry', *Encyclopaedia Britannica*, ninth edn, vol. 5, 1876, pp. 459–579, at p. 462.

16 'Cavendish, Henry', ibid., pp. 271–72, at p. 272.

In the domain of pure science Watt claims recognition not only as having had ideas greatly in advance of his age regarding what is now called energy, but as a discoverer of the composition of water. Writing to Priestley in April 1783, with reference to some of Priestley's experiments, he suggests the theory that 'water is composed of dephlogisticated air and phlogiston deprived of part of their latent or elementary heat'. It is difficult to determine the exact meaning attached to these antiquated terms, and to say how far Watt's suggestion anticipated the fuller discovery of Cavendish.[17]

In this way the engineer's account of Watt, though going so far as to mention the water question, simply opted out of it. Watt was *a* discoverer but one with impenetrable and antiquated ideas. No such trouble was hinted at so far as the 'fuller discovery' of Cavendish was concerned, though, as we have seen, if Cavendish had been placed in context, this too could have been made out as antiquated. So far as the ninth edition of the *Britannica* was concerned overall, the place of Watt in the discovery of the composition of water was a historical curiosity and no more. Indeed, even the curiosity was limited!

Apart from the *Britannica*, another encyclopaedia of some consequence in the scientific world was the *Encyclopaedia Metropolitana*. This is best known to historians of science as the repository of two major treatises by John Herschel. Herschel wrote the almost 250-page treatise on 'Light' and also the one on 'Sound'. The former in particular was at the cutting edge of scientific work in 1828 when it was published and was an important document in the ongoing debate about the wave theory of light.[18] The articles 'Chemistry' and 'Electricity' for the *Metropolitana*, each of over 150 pages, were written by Herschel's Cambridge friend, the Reverend Francis Lunn.[19]

The main section on Cavendish in Lunn's 'Chemistry' recounted his major work in this fashion:

> The more prominent facts which were brought to light by the high talents of Mr Cavendish, most assiduously, yet cautiously exerted, were the compleat knowledge of hydrogen gas, which, though the substance had been obtained before, was quite disregarded until his time. These researches led him to the brilliant discovery of the composition of water, which he laid before the Royal Society in 1784 (Vide ELECTRICITY. Art 167). Thus was the synthesis of water accomplished.[20]

This statement conveys Cavendish's talent, his 'brilliant discovery' in unequivocal terms. There is no mention of Watt at all. If, however, we follow the advice to see the article 'Electricity', also written by Lunn, then we find a more detailed and extensive account incorporated into the section on electrolytic decomposition and

---

[17] 'Watt, James', ibid., vol. 24, 1888, pp. 412–14, at p. 414.

[18] Richard Yeo, *Encyclopaedic Visions*, pp. 274–75.

[19] Francis Lunn (1795–1839) was a student with Herschel at St John's College, Cambridge. He was elected FRS in 1819 and was an early member of the Astronomical Society of London. He had assisted E.D. Clarke in experiments to isolate cadmium from zinc, and had been a candidate for the Professorship of Mineralogy at Cambridge in 1822. From 1828 to the end of his life he was Vicar of Butleigh in Somerset. (See Venn, *Alumni Cantabrigiensis*, Part I, vol. 4, p. 235.)

[20] Francis Lunn, 'Chemistry', *Encyclopaedia Metropolitana*, vol. 4, 1845, pp. 587–762, at p. 595.

composition of water. This in itself is interesting because it shows that by the 1830s and 1840s the water question, for contemporary chemists, was part of a rather different constellation. It had shifted from pneumatic chemistry to electrochemistry and had therefore been placed in a tradition that included later workers such as Davy, Faraday and, in the 1840s, William Grove, George Wilson and others. The statement made under 'Electricity' began with a clear attribution to Cavendish:

> In 1781, after some attempts made by Mr Warltire and Dr Priestley, who fired mixtures of common air and hydrogen in close vessels, and remarked an appearance of dew on the inner surfaces; the complete and satisfactory synthesis of water was performed by Mr Cavendish, to whom the honour of this discovery is generally and justly ascribed ...[21]

The competitors were then mentioned but quickly sidelined. First Watt was dealt with:

> although it appears that Mr Watt, who had reasoned upon Priestley's experiments, had arrived at a similar conclusion, which he communicated to Dr Priestley by letter, dated April 26, 1783. Mr Cavendish, in 1781, burned 500,000 grain measures of hydrogen, and having collected 135 grams of pure water, ventured upon the bold conclusion, that water was composed of the two gases, oxygen and hydrogen.[22]

For someone aware of the detailed arguments bruited in the water controversy, even as this encyclopaedia article appeared, the rhetorical finesse of this statement would be apparent. First there is the impression given of timing: Cavendish's deeds were in 1781, Watt's in 1783. Cavendish's 'bold conclusion' is located in 1781, Watt's 'reasoning' in 1783. Then there is the matter of what they arrived at: Watt reached a 'similar conclusion'; Cavendish reached the modern view. Moreover he did so in a quantitative fashion. The impression conveyed is that Watt failed to quite get there, whereas Cavendish hit the bull's eye. Finally Lavoisier was dealt with: 'The celebrated Lavoisier having had a different object in view, though he made many experiments on these substances, did not arrive at the true composition of water, until he was informed by Sir Charles Blagden of Mr Cavendish's result, which he immediately verified on a larger scale.'[23] Lavoisier was reduced to verifying that which Cavendish had discovered.

We have seen that other, more complex, more equivocal stories than that given here could be told. The evidence that Cavendish drew any conclusion in 1781 was indirect. Harcourt and Wilson had had to run long, elaborate arguments of a hermeneutic kind to make their cases for Cavendish's priority. This is not to say that the arguments were not good ones. However, once we know the need for those arguments, the short-cuts taken in briefer accounts become clear to us. As the statements move through different literary forms they become simplified (of necessity), and what was equivocal and uncertain becomes unequivocal and definite.

---

[21] Francis Lunn, 'Electricity', ibid., vol. 5, 1845, pp. 41–172, at p. 109.

[22] Ibid., p. 109.

[23] Ibid.

Whether such simplification is justified is, in the end, a matter of judgement. Lunn was among those who, by gaining access to the *Metropolitana*, could make his judgement count.[24]

The evolving stance on the water question taken in various articles and editions of the *Britannica* and the *Metropolitana* was a predictable one given the affiliations of those writing and editing them. However, what eventually found its way into an encyclopaedia could also be, and often was, a matter of accident or happenstance. One should not expect clean consistency in such matters.

The *Penny Cyclopaedia* is a case in point. Whereas the *Britannica* was directed under Napier and Traill primarily to a scientific and learned audience, with the 'ordinary reader' catered to as a second priority, the *Penny Cyclopaedia* was directed to the lower classes.[25] It was published by the Society for the Diffusion of Useful Knowledge (SDUK). The Chairman of the SDUK's committee and, of course, one of the organization's founders was Lord Brougham. However, the *Cyclopaedia* did not clearly represent views on the water controversy in line with Brougham's. Whether through accident, inattention or design, the article on 'Water' offered only a few lines on the water question. We are simply told that 'The subject of the discovery of the composition of water has lately excited considerable discussion; we are however of opinion that the claim of Mr Cavendish as the author of this great discovery, and which has been for some years assigned to him without dispute, is rightly so attributed.'[26]

Here Watt was not mentioned and Cavendish awarded the discovery. However, in the article 'Watt, James'[27] a different, rather odd, story was told. First it was noted that 'little can be said here' about Watt's share in the discovery. He was stated to have been working on the question at the same time as Cavendish and Lavoisier. The curious were then referred to Arago's *Eloge* and to Brougham's 'Historical Account' appended thereto. Finally, the following strange statement was offered:

> it may suffice to observe that the great and pressing claims of Watt's professional avocations, together with his modesty and retiring habits, may in a great measure account for any difficulty that may arise in tracing the progress and extent of his discoveries in this, by no means the least important of the many subjects to which he addressed his comprehensive mind.[28]

This statement under 'Watt' is, as a whole, clearly pro-Watt, unlike that under 'Water'. This is evident from the authorities quoted – Arago and Brougham, Muirhead and Watt Jr are referred to, all of whom take Watt's part. Yet the oddly non-committal air to the statement is puzzling. Why, if pro-Watt, does the author bring up the 'difficulty' referred to at the end? Reading Arago, Brougham, Muirhead and

---

[24] See Stephen Hilgartner, 'The dominant view of popularization: Conceptual problems, political uses', *Social Studies of Science*, **20**, 1990, 519–39.

[25] Yeo, *Encyclopaedic Visions*, pp. 277–78.

[26] See 'Water', *The Penny Cyclopaedia*, vol. 26, 1843, p. 110.

[27] 'Watt, James', ibid., vol. 24, 1843, pp. 135–43.

[28] Ibid., pp. 135–43, at p. 141.

Watt Jr would supply plenty of evidence for Watt's claim. So where is the difficulty? Perhaps the writer believed that there was little direct published evidence of Watt's inquiries in this area, inquiries that he supposed or knew to be *more* extensive than indicated in public accounts. The point, then, was that Watt's business preoccupations, his modesty and retiring habits prevented him from laying a more substantial public paper trail of his discoveries in the area. Given Brougham's and the SDUK's predilection to broadcast the achievements of men of modest backgrounds, it is surprising that more was not made of Watt's claims. This reminds us that, given the exigencies of production of these accounts, we should not necessarily expect coherence, consistency or clarity in them.

An important, and popular, work of the later nineteenth century was *Chambers's Encyclopaedia*. In its early editions this work trumpeted itself as 'A Dictionary of Universal Knowledge for the People'. It subsequently dropped its democratic designation in the 1895 edition, being content simply with 'Universal Knowledge'. Coverage of the water question shows an interesting shift when we compare the articles on 'Watt', 'Cavendish', and 'Water' in successive editions.[29] Table 11.1 summarizes the key changes.

The 1895 revision of the article on Watt suggests that a conscious decision was made to depict him as an engineer rather than as a 'man of science'.[30] The 'header' shows this clearly in its removal of that very term and the substitution of a narrow designation. The account of the experimental basis of Watt's steam-engine improvements (which had been highlighted in earlier editions) gave way to a moment of engineering inspiration. In concert with this, Watt's wide-ranging interest in, and contributions to, the physical sciences were replaced by the account of his garret workshop at Heathfield. In all editions the issue of Watt and the composition of water was referred to the article 'Water'. The referral in the 1895 edition placed his claims to priority firmly in the past whilst earlier editions treated them as current. When we examine the articles on 'Water', we find that Watt's claim was subordinated to that of Cavendish in all cases. If anything, the 1895 edition is more generous to Watt, although it does clearly give the priority to Cavendish and once again it tends to encapsulate the question as a historical curiosity. The article on 'Cavendish' changed more decisively, shifting from acknowledgement that Watt had a claim to dismissal of that claim.

Other encyclopaedias of the later nineteenth century exhibited similar, rather perplexing, inconsistencies. *The National Encyclopaedia*, published in fourteen volumes in 1884, had no entry for Henry Cavendish. The article 'James Watt' did mention his scientific pursuits. It had this to say on water: 'Concerning Watt's share in the discovery of the composition of water, an investigation in which he, Cavendish, and Lavoisier were engaged about the same time, we must refer those who are curious to Arago's Life of, or Eloge upon Watt, and to the "Historical Account of

---

[29] 'Watt, James', *Chambers's Encyclopaedia*, vol. 10, 1868, pp. 105–106 and vol. 10, 1895, pp. 578–79; 'Cavendish, Henry', ibid., vol. 2, 1861, p. 696 and vol. 3, 1895, pp. 36–37; 'Water', ibid., vol. 10, 1868, pp. 84–88 and vol. 10, 1895, pp. 563–71.

[30] This was in line with other later nineteenth-century writings about Watt, including those of Samuel Smiles, already noted, which downplayed the 'philosopher' in the engineer and emphasized the craftsman and the hard work.

11.1 Comparison of articles in editions of *Chambers's Encyclopaedia*

Article	1860–68, 1874 & 1883 editions	1895 edition
Watt, James	'WATT, JAMES, mechanician, engineer, and man of science ... '	'WATT, JAMES, improver, and almost inventor, of the modern steam engine ...'
	Contain extensive accounts of Watt's steam experiments as leading to separate condenser idea.	Account of steam experiments removed and replaced by simple statement: 'he hit upon the expedient of the separate condenser'.
	'He had a most extensive and accurate knowledge of the physical sciences, to several of which he made important contributions, and an almost unsurpassed fund of general information.'	Reference to physical sciences dropped and replaced by: 'The attic room at Heathfield Hall ... where he used to work alone, is still preserved ... Here he was perfectly happy working with his turning-lathe, and amongst his tools and models ... He had a quickness of apprehension, a powerful memory, and an immense store of well-digested miscellaneous information outside his own domain ... Watt stands at the head of all inventors ... '.
	'His claims to be considered the discoverer of the composition of water are considered in the article WATER.'	'Watt's claims to be the first discoverer of the composition of water were long and strenuously maintained (see WATER, p. 565)'.
Cavendish	'he ascertained that water resulted from the union of two gases – a discovery, however, to which Watt (q.v.) is supposed to have an equal claim'.	'he ascertained that water resulted from the union of two gases – a discovery which has erroneously been claimed for Watt (q.v., see also WATER)'.
Water	Substantial section gives details of Cavendish's and Lavoisier's work and a history of the nineteenth-century controversy in some detail. At the end of this section: 'As we have no space to discuss Watt's real claims, we may here state that Dr George Wilson, whose *Life of Cavendish* is in reality a strictly impartial history of the water controversy, maintains on very solid grounds that in reality Watt was informed of Cavendish's discovery through Priestley, as Lavoisier was through Blagden.'	'The question as to who was the discoverer of the composition of water – the great Water Question – takes rank in the history of chemistry as the controversy as to the discovery of the calculus and of the planet Neptune in other sciences. Brougham, Brewster, Kopp, Arago, Dumas, and many others have maintained one or other of the theses; and the claims of Cavendish, James Watt, Priestley, and Lavoisier have been canvassed and defended. Research seems inclined to give the priority to Cavendish, while allowing that Watt made independent experiments and came to similar results soon after.'

the Discovery of the Composition of Water" by Lord Brougham.'[31] Obviously, the reader following this referral would be exposed to a strongly pro-Watt account. The entry on 'Water', however, told a very different story:

> Cavendish, by a series of ingenious experiments in the year 1781, demonstrated its [water's] chemical composition. He came to the conclusion that water consisted of dephlogisticated air (or oxygen) united with phlogiston (or hydrogen), and a similar conclusion was arrived at by James Watt, and by the French chemist Lavoisier. The attention of the former was directed to the subject by the account of Cavendish's experiments, which he received from Dr. Priestley, and the latter was stimulated by a similar account derived from Blagden. Attempts have most ungenerously been made to deprive Cavendish of the honour of the discovery, and fix it either upon the Frenchman or the Scotchman. But Dr. George Wilson, in his 'Life of Cavendish', and Dr. Whewell, in his 'Inductive Sciences', have successfully controverted these claims, and proved that all the credit should fairly be given to the great English philosopher.[32]

This time the authorities cited are strongly pro-Cavendish and the claims for Watt (and for Lavoisier) seen as ungenerous.

As a final example, consider *The Globe Encyclopaedia of Universal Information*, which was edited by John M. Ross and published in Edinburgh in the late 1870s. The article 'Chemistry' nominated Cavendish as the discoverer, as did the article on the great man himself. Neither so much as mentioned Watt. However, the article on Watt informed readers that Watt was 'quite at home' in the more theoretical departments of science and was 'an independent discoverer' of the composition of water, though Cavendish had the priority. The article 'Water' also had Cavendish proving its composition in 1781, but noted that Watt had a claim and that a bitter controversy had occurred. In the end, however, the priority was given to Cavendish, though Watt was recognized as an independent researcher on the topic.[33]

We can conclude that in the more erudite encyclopaedias and many of the popular ones, the standard stories in the later nineteenth century gave priority to Cavendish though retaining in some cases reference to the claims of Watt. Whatever lessons were learned about the water question by generations of students and general readers in the late nineteenth century, one can say that these lessons were neither entirely consistent nor uniform. In some senses, then, as a matter of 'public opinion' the water controversy remained partially open in the encyclopaedic realm, though overall the balance of credit certainly lay with Cavendish. In many cases the character of relevant articles might well owe much to 'scissors and paste' treatments of prior publications, but there is some evidence, especially in

---

31 'Watt, James', *The National Encyclopaedia. A Dictionary of Universal Knowledge*, 1884, vol. 14, pp. 370–71, at p. 371.

32 'Water', ibid., pp. 361–63, at p. 361.

33 *The Globe Encyclopaedia of Universal Information*, 6 vols, 1877–79. See 'Cavendish, Henry', vol. 2; 'Chemistry', vol. 2, pp. 109–14, at p. 109; 'Water', vol. 6, pp. 476–77, at p. 477; 'Watt, James', vol. 6, p. 482. Another encyclopaedia consulted was *The Oracle Encyclopaedia. Profusely Illustrated. Containing the most Accurate Information in the most readable form*, published in 5 vols in London by George Newnes Ltd in 1895 and edited by R.W. Egerton Eastwick B.A. of the Middle Temple. The articles on Cavendish, Water and Watt were taken verbatim from *The Globe Encyclopaedia*.

the case of the eighth edition of the *Britannica* and *Chambers's Encyclopaedia*, for conscious crafting.

We now turn to a more extensive body of literature which also played an important part in fixing opinion on the 'water question' – chemical textbooks.

The Water Question in Textbooks of Chemistry

The relationship between textbooks and history is an interesting and important one. Historical accounts of scientific work can be used as introductions to the current state of play. Priestley's writings would be an example. History can also be used consciously as a pedagogic device or to serve didactic or nationalistic purposes.[34] But more frequently, perhaps, history is used simply in the 'who, what and when' mode in which a brief, obligatory mention is made of the first person to do something. This process is part of the process for allocating credit in science. Through it succeeding generations of students pay homage to their scientific forebears and students and practitioners of a science acquire basic historical navigational beacons. There is usually no room or desire in such accounts for long, complex or equivocal historical disquisitions. Thus, whatever the state of play in a contested allocation of credit, the author of the text will feel pressure to close that contest for himself and his readers.[35] Because of this, a popular, widely employed text can be enormously influential among large bodies of people, almost silently resolving controversies and contested points that may persist in more arcane forums less directly relevant to disciplinary practice.

Chemical texts of all kinds proliferated in the later nineteenth century as the teaching of chemistry in universities, colleges and schools expanded enormously. My concern is to gain a sense of how the water question was dealt with in this literature. In so far as the literature dealt with the question at all it ought perhaps to reflect sentiment within the chemical community. Equally the ideas propagated concerning the water question would themselves bear, in ways and to an extent perhaps hard to determine, upon the career of the controversy itself. A survey of this literature is, then, in the nature of a test of the hypothesis that the views of the controversy in expert circles eventually found their way to other 'levels'.

I have examined a large sample of texts and the summary results of that examination are presented in the Appendix. The sample consists of chemical texts with 'chemistry' in the title listed in the main catalogues of the National Library of Scotland and the Edinburgh University Library, and published between 1830 and 1900. To make the task more manageable, I screened out specialist works and texts intended for particular groups of students (such as medical students), or dealing with specialist aspects of

---

[34] See Colin A. Russell, '"Rude and Disgraceful Beginnings": A view of history of chemistry from the nineteenth century', *The British Journal for the History of Science*, **21**, 1988, 273–94. Part of Russell's aim in this paper is to question some of the knee-jerk dismissals of the work of chemist–historians of the nineteenth century.

[35] This is a line of thought no doubt inspired by Latour and Woolgar's discussion of statement types and the addition and removal of 'modalities'. See Latour and Woolgar, *Laboratory Life*, 1979, pp. 81–86.

chemistry, including those dealing exclusively with organic chemistry. The remaining works I have examined for statements of relevance to the water controversy. 'Influential' works that merit more detailed attention can be identified by their multi-edition status. Some were popular because they were texts certified in some way. Thus, for example, in 1859 there were twenty-eight chemistry texts on the recommended list of the Department of Science and Art because they were regarded as particularly suitable for use in schools.[36] There exist other sorts of recommendations. For example, in 1886, William A. Tilden, Professor of Chemistry at the Mason College of Science in Birmingham, produced a set of desiderata for the Birmingham Reference Library.[37] For 'the science of chemistry as it now is' Tilden recommended as larger textbooks Roscoe & Schorlemmer, Miller, Fownes, and Bloxam. These all covered both experimental and theoretical chemistry. He recommended Hofmann's *Modern Chemistry*, Wurtz's *Atomic Theory*, and Remsen's *Principles of Modern Chemistry* as elementary works in theoretical chemistry. He suggested M.M. Pattison Muir's *Principles of Chemistry* as perhaps more for the teacher than for the student and identified Lothar Meyer's *Die Modernen Theorien der Chemie* as the most important general treatise. He also referred to Ostwald's *Lehrbücher*. In suggesting model original works that students should read he included Dumas's work on the composition of water in the *Annales de Chimie* of 1843. Thus as well as conducting an overall survey of texts and their attributional tendencies, it is also possible to isolate smaller samples of 'influential' works so identified in various ways.

My survey of chemical texts does reveal certain obvious patterns that should be apparent on perusal of the tabulated information in the Appendix. First, it must be said that a significant proportion of elementary chemical textbooks showed little concern with attribution, let alone history. Of ninety post-1840 texts surveyed, thirty-nine made no attribution for the discovery of the composition of water in their accounts of its synthesis and analysis. In the style of catechisms or recitations of facts and principles, they stuck strictly to the chemical subject matter. They named hardly any names. There was no concern to attach the facts presented to any particular discoverer. Understandably, the overwhelming concern was to convey the facts about the composition and properties of water rather than to even hint at the water question.

While this seems disproportionately true of elementary texts, it is also true of many more advanced ones. Large, systematic texts such as D.B. Reid's *Elements of Chemistry, Theoretical and Practical* adopted a strict 'universal' form. The section on water reads thus:

SECT. 1. – WATER
Symb. H; Eq by W., 9; by volume □ (one measure). Specific gravity, 1.000. One cubic inch weighs 252.458 grains at 62° Fahr., Bar. 30°; it is about 815 times heavier than air,

---

36 See James Tilleard, *On Elementary School Books*, 1860, p. 4. (This work was reprinted from the *Transactions of the National Association for the Promotion of Social Science*, 1859.)

37 William A. Tilden, *Books on Chemistry. Birmingham Reference Library Lectures*, 1886. It is worth noting that Tilden prefaced his remarks on texts by a brief survey of the history of chemistry. Noting key advances that had established chemistry as a science, he included 'The examination of hydrogen (1766) and the experimental proofs of the composition of water (1781) both due to Cavendish … '. He gave Wilson's *Life of Cavendish* as his reference.

and when converted into vapour at 212°, it expands to 1696 times the volume it occupies at its greatest density. The specific gravity of steam (air at 212° being 1) is 0.625, or 0.484; air at 60° = 1 ...[38]

And when the explosion experiment is described it is again in very neutral terms:

> When a mixture of half a measure of oxygen gas (□) with one measure of hydrogen (□) is inflamed in a dry glass vessel, both gases entirely disappear, and the interior surface of the vessel is found bedewed with moisture, formed by the condensation of the watery vapour that results from the combination.[39]

This text would have been widely used by Reid's students at the Edinburgh School of Arts and in his practical chemistry classes at the University of Edinburgh.

William Gregory's *Outlines of Chemistry, For the Use of Students* was designed for his own students at the University of Edinburgh and for similar groups. In explaining the form of his work Gregory emphasized, in 1845, the crowding of the curriculum and took the historic step, especially for a Professor of Chemistry at Edinburgh in direct line from Black, of removing any treatment of the 'Imponderables', that is, Heat, Light, Electricity and Magnetism. These belonged to physics, he said, but the main reason for leaving them out was 'because the enormously increased extent and importance of Chemistry, especially of Organic Chemistry, rendered every moment of time, in a course of lectures ... precious in the highest degree'.[40] Gregory was the man who completely rewrote the article 'Chemistry' for the eighth edition of the *Encyclopaedia Britannica* in an entirely systematic way, removing virtually all historical treatment, and, in the process, attributions of discoveries. For a character such as Gregory, the pressures of pedagogy decisively crowded out attributions, of which there are hardly any in his book, and none concerning the composition of water.

Works that responded to the escalation of possible content rather differently also often had a different attitude to 'extraneous' attributional and historical material. Albert Bernays's *First Lines in Chemistry* is an example. In justifying his text, Bernays explained that he had 'vainly sought a manual for his pupils with a clear and simple exposition of the leading facts and principles of the science, unencumbered by a mass of information, of no service except to advanced students'.

> The plan adopted by most manuals of Chemistry in our language, of discussing in a long introduction, which is never read, the most recondite laws of the science, and the most intricate facts, before the student has mastered the simplest, is one that I have never been able to see the advantage of ...[41]

It seems probable that his selectivity and thoughtful pedagogy was linked to Bernays's decision to include a good deal of modest historical information throughout

---

[38] D.B. Reid, *Elements of Chemistry, Theoretical and Practical*, 3rd edn, 1839, p. 31.

[39] Ibid., p. 99.

[40] William Gregory, *Outlines of Chemistry, For the Use of Students*, 2 vols, 1845.

[41] A.J. Bernays, *First Lines in Chemistry. A Manual for Students*, 1855, p. vii.

his text. Thus his discussion of 'Hydrogen' begins: 'Discovered by Paracelsus in the 16th century, but first properly investigated by the illustrious Henry Cavendish in 1781. It is the base of water … '.[42] The treatment of water positively overflowed with historical information:

> Water was long considered as an elementary substance; it was even supposed capable of being converted into earth, till Lavoisier proved the earth to be derived from the vessels in which the operation was conducted. The composition of water was first demonstrated by Cavendish in 1781, and almost about [*sic*] the same time by Watt, in so far as both proved that water was always formed when hydrogen was inflamed in oxygen. Subsequently Lavoisier decomposed water into its elements.[43]

Without more detailed research it is impossible to state categorically why Bernays's approach differed so substantially from Reid's. Besides his more selective and relaxed approach to pedagogy, we might point to the texts he relied upon and also to the tradition within which he trained. He had studied for his PhD under Liebig at Giessen, and it is noticeable that authors of texts who shared this experience also seemed sensitive to historical matters.[44]

Robert Dundas Thomson was an example, going to Giessen in 1840 after having trained for the medical profession in Edinburgh and Glasgow, and having studied chemistry at Glasgow under his uncle, Thomas Thomson. He assisted his uncle in lecturing on chemistry at Glasgow University from 1841, but failed in a bid to succeed to the Chair of chemistry in 1852. In his *School Chemistry*, Thomson systematically included historical information in a rather telegraphic form. For example, under 'Hydrogen' we find:

> *History* (Mayow 1674) Inflammable air (Boyle, Hales and Cavendish before 1766) Phlogiston. Hydrogen … (Lavoisier, 1787) …
> *Preparation.* The source of hydrogen, in whatever manner it be prepared, is water, which is composed, as Watt suggested from Warltire and Priestley's experiments (1781) and as Cavendish demonstrated (1781), of oxygen and hydrogen.[45]

Although his uncle was regarded as an 'enemy' by the Watt camp, the nephew seems to have been unusually generous in his acknowledgement of Watt in a school text.

One of the most successful of nineteenth-century chemical texts was George Fownes, *A Manual of Elementary Chemistry. Theoretical and Practical*. First published in 1844, the work went through its eleventh edition within thirty years, helped, no doubt, by the favour it found with the Reverend Henry Moseley, Chief

---

[42] Ibid., p. 27.

[43] Ibid., p. 33.

[44] Bernays described his book as founded on 'the manuals of Berzelius, Gmelin, Regnault, Brande, Liebig and Turner, Woehler, Fownes, Gerhardt and others'. Bernays also wrote popular texts such as *Household Chemistry*, 1852, gave numerous public lectures, and was interested in 'social matters'. See *DNB*, **22**, Supplement, pp. 183–84.

[45] Robert Dundas Thomson, *School Chemistry: or, Practical Rudiments of the Science*, 1848, pp. 47–48.

Inspector of Schools in the Education Office.[46] Fownes had studied under Professor Thomas Everitt at Middlesex Hospital and then undertaken a PhD at Giessen. He worked as an assistant to Thomas Graham in the laboratory at University College London, where his path would have crossed that of George Wilson, who was a student there at the same time. Fownes resigned in 1840 to become a lecturer on chemistry at Charing Cross Hospital. He became Professor of Chemistry to the Pharmaceutical Society in 1842 and in the same year succeeded Everitt at Middlesex Hospital. In 1845 he resigned from his hospital appointment because of illness but in 1846 took up the Professorship of Practical Chemistry in the Birkbeck Laboratory at University College. At the time of his death in 1849, he was Secretary of the Chemical Society.

The two editions of Fownes's *Manual of Elementary Chemistry* that were published during his lifetime (in 1844 and 1848) and the third edition of 1850, published shortly after his death, made an apparently quite unequivocal statement on the water question. Under 'Hydrogen' we find:

> It appears that the composition of water was first demonstrated in the year 1781 by Mr Cavendish, but the discovery of the exact proportions in which oxygen and hydrogen unite in generating that most important compound has from time to time to the present day occupied the attention of some of the most distinguished cultivators of chemical science.[47]

This is an interesting statement. Although making the attribution to Cavendish in a manner not surprising in an upwardly mobile young chemist serving as Secretary of the Chemical Society in the 1840s, it is carefully worded. Whilst the neophyte would probably take away from this simply the attribution of discovery to Cavendish, the informed reader would learn more, or perhaps we should say less, because the information would be more equivocal. The 'It appears' would signal knowledge that there was an issue here, that there was a water question. The 'first demonstrated' would indicate Fownes's awareness of key criteria of attribution lying in demonstration, as opposed to merely having an idea. The remarks about the composition of water continuing to engage some of the best chemists perhaps conveyed the idea that Cavendish's work, in this as in other areas, was still live and challenging.

By the seventh edition of 1858, with H. Bence Jones and A.W. Hofmann now editing the work, an interesting addition had occurred in the form of a footnote to the paragraph quoted above. After Cavendish's name an asterisk now led the reader to the following footnote:

> *A claim to the discovery of the composition of water, on behalf of Mr James Watt, has been very strongly urged, and supported by such evidence that the reader of the controversy may be led to the conclusions that the discovery was made by both parties, nearly simultaneously, and unbeknown to each other.[48]

---

[46] See David Layton, *Science for the People. The Origins of the School Science Curriculum in England*, 1973, pp. 99–100 on Moseley's emphasis on the importance of teaching chemistry in schools and his favoured texts.

[47] George Fownes, *A Manual of Elementary Chemistry, Theoretical and Practical*, 1844, p. 105.

[48] Fownes, *A Manual*, 7th edn, 1858, p. 123.

Again the reasons for this change involve speculation. Had the agitations of the 1840s finally become too much to ignore? Was one of the editors a Watt supporter? Whatever the case, this formulation remained unchanged until the tenth edition of 1868. There the following remark was added at the end of the above footnote: 'See the article "Gas" by Dr. Paul in Watts's *Dictionary of Chemistry*, ii, 780.' The keen student who followed up this apparently innocuous further reference would find a surprisingly long and complex essay on the water question. Dr Paul thoroughly contextualized both Watt's claim and Cavendish's 'discovery' and, on the basis that Cavendish's true meaning on the composition of water fell short of the mark, ended up giving the major credit to Lavoisier since Cavendish did not do 'anything more than supply the evidence of the composition of water'.[49]

Paul dealt decisively with any claim for Watt, stating that such a claim 'appears to involve a disregard of what really constitutes a title to be considered as a discoverer'.

> Watt certainly was the first to put forward, in 1783, the opinion that water was a compound of inflammable and dephlogisticated air; but that opinion was merely an hypothesis, based upon data furnished to him by Priestley, and unsupported by any experimental observation of his own. In fact, he never appears to have laid claim to anything more than having put forward this view as a speculation; and though, for a time, he believed he had been unfairly treated, his only complaint was that his 'ideas' had been pirated, and that no mention had been made of his 'theory', either by Cavendish or Lavoisier ...[50]

Paul's remarkable article disappeared from the edition of *Watts' Dictionary of Chemistry* that was revised and entirely rewritten by Pattison Muir and Foster Morley in 1894. The article 'Gas' was removed, and discussion of the history of the composition of water was shifted back to the article 'Water'. Now, in a few column inches, Cavendish's archaic interpretation of his own experiments was subordinated to Lavoisier's accomplishment. Watt had disappeared.[51]

The career of the treatment of the water question through the many editions of Fownes's work and Watts's *Dictionary* is unusual. I have argued on the basis of the course of the 'live' controversy and treatments in major encyclopaedias that the categorical case for Cavendish was being established by the 1850s and 1860s. Yet

---

[49] B.H. P[aul], 'Gas', in Henry Watts (ed.), *A Dictionary of Chemistry and the Allied Branches of Other Sciences*, 1864, vol. 2, pp. 773–82, esp. pp. 779–82. Henry Watts had been involved with the editing of Fownes for some time. Dr Benjamin Horatio Paul (1827–1917) was trained in pharmacy, subsequently gaining his PhD with Leibig at Giessen in 1848, and also studying with Thomas Graham. He was elected FCS in 1868 and became editor of *The Pharmaceutical Journal* in 1870. He worked as a consulting chemist. See 'Benjamin Horatio Paul', *Journal of the Chemical Society*, **113–114**, 1918, 334–36.

[50] Ibid., p. 782.

[51] M.M. Pattison Muir and H. Foster Morley, *Watts' Dictionary of Chemistry. Revised and Entirely Rewritten*, 1894, vol. 4, pp. 859–60. The tone is captured in the following: 'Cavendish established the fact ... but he stated this fact in language that no longer carries a definite meaning with it. Lavoisier added to the experimental basis whereon the fact rested, and he expressed the fact in language that still is clear, definite, and descriptive' (p. 860).

here we have an example where a categorical case (if a carefully worded one) was modified in the 1850s to give *more* credit to Watt. It was then further modified in the 1860s to pull the rug out from under *both* Watt and Cavendish in order to install Lavoisier as discoverer. Whatever the reason for this, through Fownes's *Manual* Watt's claim would have been kept alive to some degree for generations of chemistry students, even if, by the late 1860s, the more diligent of them who followed through to Dr Paul's article might end up as supporters of Lavoisier, as would readers of Watts's *Dictionary*!

Fownes was one of the texts recommended by Tilden in 1886. Another was Roscoe and Schorlemmer, a more advanced text, and one that contained the most extensive treatment of the water question, and of chemical history generally, of any textbook examined. Having stated in the Preface that their aim was 'to place before the reader a fairly complete, and yet a clear and succinct, statement of the facts of Modern Chemistry', Roscoe and Schorlemmer explained their use of history:

> The volume commences with a short historical sketch of the rise and progress of chemical science, and a few words relative to the history of each element and its more important compounds prefaces the systematic discussion of their chemical properties. For this portion of their work, the authors wish here to acknowledge their indebtedness to Hermann Kopp's classical works on the History of Chemistry.[52]

In their Historical Introduction, Roscoe and Schorlemmer depicted the discovery of the composition of water as being associated forever with the name of Cavendish. They argued that he was the first to actually set out to determine the nature of the water in the explosion experiments. They also stated that Cavendish was the first to show that the only product of the explosion of pure dephlogisticated with pure inflammable air is pure water. His accomplishment, as they put it, was to 'distinctly prove the fact of the composition of water'.[53] Beyond this, though, it appeared to them that Cavendish did not hold 'clear views' that water is a chemical compound of its two elementary constituents: 'On the contrary, he seems to have inclined to the opinion that the water formed was already contained in the inflammable air, notwithstanding the fact that in 1783 the celebrated James Watt had already expressed the opinion that "water is composed of dephlogisticated and inflammable air".'[54]

Their opinion on the controversy simply quoted Kopp to the effect that Cavendish 'first ascertained the facts' that were the basis of the discovery, whilst Watt was the 'first to argue from these facts concerning the compound nature of water', though he did not specify the components properly. Again, along with Kopp, they nominated Lavoisier as first clearly recognizing the compound nature of water and determining its components exactly.[55]

What happens in Roscoe and Schorlemmer when we turn from the nuanced Historical Introduction to the historical material presented in conjunction with the

---

[52] H.E. Roscoe and C. Schorlemmer, *A Treatise on Chemistry. Volume 1. The Non-Metallic Elements*, 1877.

[53] Ibid., p. 21.

[54] Ibid.

[55] Ibid., pp. 30–31.

treatment of elements and compounds? Under 'Hydrogen' we find the following statement:

> It has already been stated (see Historical Introduction) that water was long supposed to be an elementary or simple substance, and it was not until the year 1781 that Cavendish proved that water was produced by the union of oxygen and hydrogen gases, whilst Humboldt and Gay-Lussac first showed in 1805 that these gases combine by volume in the simple relation of one to two.[56]

At this level, as expected, the statement is much more categorical and of the simple form 'in 1781 ... Cavendish ... proved', but the reader is referred to the Historical Introduction. The same is done in that portion of the text dealing with the 'Formation of Water':

> The question of the discovery of the composition of water, a substance which up to the last century was considered to be a simple body, has been fully discussed in the historical introduction. We there learned that Cavendish first ascertained that by the combustion of two volumes of hydrogen and one volume of oxygen, pure water and nothing else, is produced. Warped, however, as his mind was with the phlogistic theory, he did not fully understand these results, and the true explanation of the composition of water was first given by Lavoisier in 1783, when the French chemist repeated and confirmed the experiments of Cavendish. The apparatus, of much historical interest, used by him for proving that hydrogen gas is really contained in water is seen in facsimile in Fig. 60.[57]

Notice, first, that in neither of the two extracts quoted above is Watt mentioned. At this level of historical information, one candidate for credit falls out of the picture. We seem to be left with Cavendish, at least to judge from the material under 'Hydrogen', but then, when we get to the formation of water, another twist occurs. Here the criteria are tightened and Cavendish's priority is presented as clouded by his archaic theoretical ideas. The 'true explanation' is now reserved for Lavoisier. It is not made clear whether the 'discovery' is to be regarded as his. This depends on how the term is to be used. It is notable that the term discovery is not linked to a particular person in either of these passages: Cavendish first 'proved' or 'ascertained' are the verbs used, not 'discovered'. Lavoisier too did not discover, but rather offered the 'true explanation'. It may well be that Roscoe and Schorlemmer were consciously and systematically avoiding attributions of discovery as such.

It has not been possible to explore in detail what was going on behind the attributions made in the texts highlighted above. Getting behind the texts would involve extensive consultation of manuscript materials outside the scope of the current project. However, whatever personal and institutional stories might be told about individual texts, there is a level at which the attributional process was 'genre

---

[56] Ibid., p. 99.

[57] Ibid., p. 202. Roscoe and Schorlemmer were among those authors of chemical texts who also wrote histories of chemistry. Thus: H.E. Roscoe, *John Dalton and the Rise of Modern Chemistry*, 1895; H.E. Roscoe and A. Harden, *A New View of the Origin of Dalton's Atomic Theory*, 1896; C. Schorlemmer, *The Rise and Development of Organic Chemistry*, 1879. Other prominent British examples included Thomas Thomson, M.M. Pattison Muir, William Tilden, T.E. Thorpe and W.A. Shenstone.

driven'. That is, the exigencies of chemical text composition and publishing inevitably limited the historical information that could be presented. This, I suggest, in itself favoured simple attributions to Cavendish despite the occasional availability of historically complex and subtle discussions such as those by B.H. Paul and by Roscoe and Schorlemmer. The necessities of simplification and condensation led to a large volume of chemical literature opting for a totally 'pared-down' view that Cavendish discovered the composition of water.[58] The common concern to present chemistry through the medium of experimental demonstration also clearly favoured Cavendish over Watt since the latter's work provided no clear experimental exemplar for pedagogic purposes.

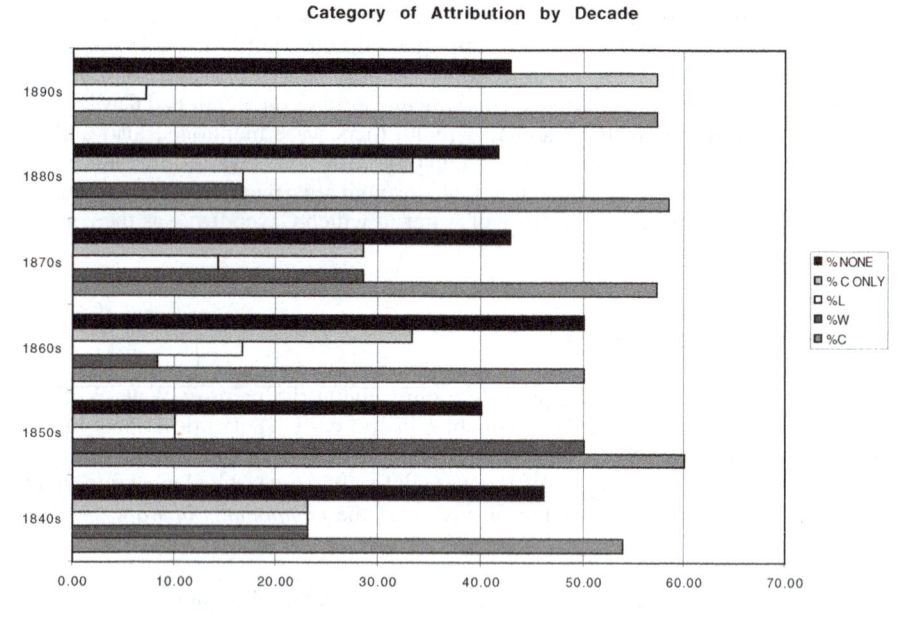

Category of Attribution by Decade

11.1 Attributions of the discovery of the composition of water in a sample of chemistry textbooks, 1840–99

Figure 11.1 shows, for all texts in my sample between 1840 and 1899, the types of attributions made relating to the discovery of the composition of water. The attributions made in each category are indicated as a percentage of the total number

---

58 The formulaic historical snippets included in many later nineteenth-century texts can be seen as the demise of a 'true' historical approach. Colin Russell cites Frankland and Japp's *Inorganic Chemistry*, which included a routine history section for all major compounds, as setting a pattern for generations of textbooks. Russell believes that this trend 'accelerated the dehistoricisation of chemistry'. See Colin A. Russell, '"Rude and Disgraceful Beginnings"', *The British Journal for the History of Science*, **21**, 1988, 285, 292.

of texts in each decade. Thus the top bar in each cluster indicates the percentage of texts that made no attribution, the second bar the percentage that attributed the discovery to Cavendish only, and so on. Given that some texts make attributions to more than one person, the percentages do not add to 100.

The following points are notable. Whilst the percentage of texts not making any attribution is reasonably constant, varying between 40 per cent and 50 per cent over the whole period, there is a clear tendency for attributions made to 'Cavendish only' to increase. By the 1890s almost 60 per cent of texts surveyed made the attribution to Cavendish alone. The variation in the percentage of attributions to Lavoisier is too small to read anything into it. We can say that Lavoisier did have a small following among historically conscious British chemists of the late nineteenth century, though their views were rarely if ever expressed in textbooks.[59] However, the variation in the figures for Watt are significant. We see clearly a rise in his fortunes in the 1850s but a decline in subsequent decades until, in the 1890s, none of the texts surveyed made an attribution of the discovery to him. It must be remembered that 100 per cent of texts making *any* attribution mentioned Cavendish; the only variability is in the extent to which others were mentioned also and in some cases given priority over him, or equality with him. Overall, the survey of chemistry textbooks clearly indicates that, through this medium, generations of students of chemistry imbibed a story of water in which Cavendish was the central figure.

Further Popular Attributions

There is a notable Scottish strand of literature giving the palm to Watt. William Anderson's *The Scottish Nation,* published in the early 1860s, described James Watt as 'a celebrated natural philosopher and civil engineer' and gave thanks to Arago for rightly establishing for Watt the credit for the 'greatest and most important discovery in modern chemistry, the discovery of the *components of water*'.[60] The entry also found it:

> Not less remarkable – and proof of the complacency of Watt's disposition – that beyond securing the reading of his paper and its insertion in the volume of the Journal referred to, – confiding in the justice of posterity, – he took no steps to vindicate the originality of his announcement even although urged to do so, than that so many years should have elapsed during which the merit of it has generally been assigned to others, until a foreign biographer, invoking that justice, has secured for him its recognition.[61]

---

[59] Apart from B.H. Paul, M.M. Pattison Muir is notable. See his *Heroes of Science. Chemists,* 1883, pp. 77–78, 92 and also Muir, *A History of Chemical Theories and Laws,* 1907, pp. 43–47, which described Cavendish as 'trammeled by the theory of phlogiston'. Lavoisier was 'the greatest of all chemists' in whom 'the power of destroying and the power of reconstructing are united in so extraordinary a degree' (p. 47).

[60] 'James Watt', in William Anderson, *The Scottish Nation,* 9 vols, 1882, vol. 9, pp. 613–22, at p. 620. This was first published in the early 1860s.

[61] Ibid., p. 620.

Unlike Forbes, who found Watt's modest behaviour a sign of his lack of seriousness in his claim, this author argued the opposite case.

It is well known that another famous Scot, Andrew Carnegie, wrote a biography of Watt (for the 'Famous Scots' series), which was published in 1905. Carnegie's treatment of the water question is remarkably decisive. The volume makes no mention of Cavendish at all even though the water question is dealt with in a number of places. At one point we are advised almost casually amidst an explanation of latent heat that 'water passed as an element until Watt found it was a compound'.[62] In another passage, the year 1783 was described as a good one for Watt because '[h]is celebrated discovery of the composition of water' was published then. Moreover, 'the attempts made to deprive him of the honour of making this discovery ended in complete failure. Sir Humphry Davy, Henry, Arago, Liebig, and many others of the highest authority acknowledged and established Watt's claims.'[63]

Yet another genre worth dipping into in order to see what was said about the water question is the literature of uplift so prevalent in the middle decades of the nineteenth century, much of it intended for young readers. Many examples of this genre emphasized the way in which success had been achieved in the face of great difficulty. An example of this was *The Pursuit of Knowledge under Difficulties* by G.L. Craik.[64] The work was first published by the SDUK in 1830 without Craik's name upon it. Both Watt and Cavendish received attention. The few pages on Cavendish appeared in the second of two chapters headed 'Advantages of Wealth', and also pursued the theme of Cavendish rising above the distractions that his wealth might have induced. The discovery of the composition of water was also atributed to Cavendish, and remarks were made about his 'cautious and scrutinizing observation by which alone truth is to be detected'. The chapter on Watt and the steam engine made no mention of the water question at all.

The new edition of *Pursuit*, published in revised and enlarged form in 1858, this time explicitly under Craik's authorship, included a number of crucial changes. The section on Cavendish still remarked upon the importance of his contributions to pneumatic chemistry, but continued 'if we may no longer assign to him the undisputed glory of the great discovery of the composition of water ... he will certainly for ever be remembered as the chief author of the experimental investigation which led to it'. A long scholarly footnote, rather out of place in the work as a whole, recounted the saga of the water controversy and its various interventions. The claim for Watt was carefully circumscribed as 'merely the merit of having been the first to perceive the full import of Cavendish's decisive experiment ... and his statement ... is certainly the earliest on record'. It was further acknowledged that Watt had been gestating this idea for some time. But the limitations of Watt's experimental contribution were noted, as were the doubts entertained about the 'absolute correctness' of his theory. Also, Cavendish's independence of Watt in drawing his own conclusions was asserted. Nevertheless, overall in this case the controversy had ensured that previously straightforward attributions to Cavendish

---

[62] Andrew Carnegie, *James Watt*, 1905, p. 36.

[63] Ibid., pp. 114–15.

[64] [G.L. Craik], *The Pursuit of Knowledge under Difficulties*, 2 vols, 1830 in the SDUK 'Library of Entertaining Knowledge'.

were now complicated and given more nuanced expression in at least some cases. Although I have no documentary evidence to support the idea, it does seem possible that the SDUK, the author Craik and the publisher Charles Knight may in some combination have been swayed to make these changes because of the intimate part their 'leader', Henry Brougham, played in the water controversy as a key member of the Watt camp.

Another volume, *Perseverence under Difficulties as shown in the Lives of Great Men*, published by the Society for Promoting Christian Knowledge in 1862, discussed similar issues. Having noted that Watt was self-taught in chemistry as in all else, the author stated that Watt's chemical reputation 'rests principally on an important discovery that he made – *the composition of water*'.

> Watt was the first person to discover that [water] was composed of two different kinds of gases, namely oxygen and hydrogen ... The honour ... was claimed by other people besides Watt, among whom were the eminent philosopher Mr Cavendish, and M. Lavoisier a great French chemist; and there were many disputes and controversies on the subject ... After a careful comparison of dates it has now been proved for certain that though Mr Cavendish and others may have made a similar discovery a short time later, the fact that water was a compound of two gases was first found out by Watt ... If Watt had had nothing to do with steam, his great scientific attainments, and this discovery especially, would justly entitle him to the character of a great natural philosopher and man of science.[65]

This, in pure form, is the kind of popular account of Watt as scientific discoverer that people such as Whewell and Forbes were intent upon stamping out. It is identifiably drawing upon the synonymity and priority argument of the Watt camp, admitting of no significant difference between Watt's views and those of Cavendish and Lavoisier. It also sees no problem in identifying Watt as a great natural philosopher and man of science. It is evidence that in popular forums Watt as discoverer proved remarkably long-lived. Ironically, however, this rump of popular support for Watt probably helped to secure the discovery of the composition of water as a natural event for which Cavendish was responsible. The transparently nationalist literature, certainly, provided a useful object lesson in how nationalist sentiment could distort 'true' appreciation of the facts about discovery. The historiography of the water controversy readily imbibed this asymmetry.

Conclusion

It must be said that, taken together, the career of accounts in encyclopaedias, and the overwhelming tendency of historical renderings proffered in textbooks, helped to close the water controversy as all but a historical curiosity. Although the claims of Watt were kept alive to a perhaps surprising extent in the learned and technical literature, and a minority of British chemists plumped for Lavoisier, claims for Cavendish dominated. Only in certain pockets of nationalistic and self-help literature

---

65 *Perseverence under Difficulties as shown in the Lives of Great Men*, 1862, pp. 210–11.

was Watt the heroic discoverer of the nature of water kept alive into the new century. By the time of the Watt centenary celebrations in 1919 those charged with the commemoration of his life showed little or no interest in the water question. The official centenary volume, by Dickinson and Jenkins, is a massive work, but it contains only a few references to the water question and those are bibliographical ones.[66] The focus of the centenary meetings themselves was upon engineering and upon Boulton & Watt engines. Official parties attended a garden party at Heathfield House and were taken to view the carefully preserved workshop above the kitchen where Watt the craftsman had spent so many hours during his later years.[67] It was this Watt, the engineer and craftsman, not the philosopher and man of science, who emerged from the plethora of writings about him in the late nineteenth and early twentieth century.

---

[66] H.W. Dickinson and Rhys Jenkins, *James Watt and the Steam Engine. The Memorial Volume Prepared for the Committee of the Watt Centenary Commemoration at Birmingham 1919*, 1927, pp. 59, 361, 367, 370.

[67] Ibid., pp. 401–404.

Chapter 12

Conclusions

From a modern perspective one might question the need to take the water controversy at all seriously. The Watt case is usually thought to be rather weak. In terms of the scientific credibility of their supporters, Watt and Cavendish appear to the modern eye unequally matched in this delayed-priority dispute. Cavendish commanded the BAAS leadership and the emergent chemical élite. Watt, by contrast, had Watt Jr, Muirhead, Brougham, Jeffrey and latterly Brewster in his corner and also Arago, with more distant support from Dumas. The filial thrust and the pleadings of Watt's advocates lacked scientific credibility. Indeed, in adopting the empirical conception of discovery and seeking to shift the terms of the contest to approximate to a purely evidential matter, the advocates of Watt tacitly, and sometimes explicitly, acknowledged their lack of scientific credibility.

Perhaps we too should simply admit that the case for Watt was simply a short-lived exercise in 'hype' with little of substance going for it. Although I have declined in this work to give a full account of the first phase of the water controversy, the story told in Chapter 3 and in the first attributional survey does make a number of relevant points. First it indicates that when looked at in context, the contributions of both Watt and Cavendish were credible ones. There is no intrinsic reason why Watt should not have come out of that situation with recognition as a discoverer. However, the retrospective recasting of Cavendish's work, which began in the 1780s, had gone a long way by the 1830s. His work had been 'modernized' to accord strongly with the New Chemistry in ways that Cavendish himself had not intended or hardly accepted. Watt, partly because of his own lack of ongoing involvement in the chemical debates, attracted much less attention of this sort, so that his ideas were much easier to restore to their original context. For this reason, the Watt camp in the second phase of the controversy faced a steep interpretative gradient.

Watt's strength lay not just among his immediate supporters, who openly and publicly participated in the water controversy. It was also among a much wider constituency of 'labourers in the vineyards' and industrially linked middle class. There were various reasons why Muirhead's texts appealed to such characters. Watt's symbolic importance to ideas about industrialization, political economy and the patent question must not be forgotten as we explore the intriguing ins and outs of the water controversy. That controversy was sustained in part by its resonance with these other, larger questions. Watt's reputation was what linked them. If Watt could be claimed as a natural philosopher, then certain positions in those larger ideological struggles were easier to sustain. This was why Watt's claim to the discovery of the composition of water (and his claim to be independent of Black in his steam-engine improvements) assumed such importance. They were both vital to

his *independent* philosophical reputation. On the other hand, to diminish Watt's independent philosophical reputation, as the supporters of Cavendish did, both in the water controversy proper and in the matter of Watt's relations with Black, was to reassert distinctions between 'pure' and 'applied' science and the hierarchical scientific/technical order that those distinctions sustained.

Along the way we have seen various broader cultural contexts within which, and through which, the water controversy was given life. In the case of Arago it was French industrialization and the attempted democratization of scientific institutions, in the sense of making them more publicly accountable, that stimulated the presentation of Watt as a philosopher and an engineer of humble origins transforming his national economy. In the case of Brougham the fight for worker education, the promotion of useful knowledge and the issue of patent reform were all causes in which the philosophical Watt was an asset. The chemists were preoccupied with issues of disciplinary identity and character to which the competing icons of Cavendish and Watt were very important. The 'Gentlemen of Science' also were fighting other battles closely related to the 'water question' – seeking the dominance of their kind of science and preferred mode of scientific organization via debates on issues such as Newton's character and the controversy over the discovery of Neptune. Their dominion in British science in the 1840s and 1850s depended upon a distancing of scientific discovery from industrial application, upon a link between the two that was mediated, or at least acknowledged to be so mediated, by themselves and not others.[1]

The contest over discovery and its fundamental contestability has been the other chief concern of this study. Great confidence was exhibited by the actors in the second phase of the controversy (and has also been shown by historians) about the certainty with which the true discoverer could be identified. My stance has been to question this certainty, to show the inherent instability and contestability of empirical and more complex philosophical criteria of discovery. Whatever criterion of 'discovery' or 'discoverer' we might set up, it can always be shown to be wanting in a logical point of view. In fact neither reason nor 'nature' (in this case meaning historical action treated naturalistically) can operate as external determinants in the identification of discoverers. The case remains, however, that controversies such as the water question are conducted as if such external determinants do operate. I have seen it as my task to take the reader behind the discovery accounts of the historical actors in the controversy in order to lay out the rhetorical character of those accounts and to indicate the grounding of rhetorical strategy in circumstance. The arguments in the water controversy were interested arguments. They were made because more than 'the truth' was at stake. It mattered in a variety of ways whether Watt or Cavendish (or Lavoisier, for that matter) was identified as the discoverer of the composition of water.

My efforts to place the arguments of the protagonists in context have been driven by the desire to identify the interests at play in the story. The identification of

---

[1] The publication of *Vestiges of the Natural History of Creation* was the other great challenge to the interpretative primacy of scientific elites in negotiating, in that case the theological, relations of science. On this see James A. Secord, *Victorian Sensation. The Extraordinary Publication, Reception and Secret Authorship of* Vestiges of the Natural History of Creation, 2000.

interests is itself a difficult exercise. Accounts that rely upon unidimensional and static interest stories are certainly unsatisfactory. In the case of the water controversy, nationalism has often been appealed to, the struggle between the supporters of Cavendish and of Watt being portrayed as driven by English versus Scottish nationalism. (The usual subtext of this sort of explanation had been that only such irrationalisms as nationalism could explain why the controversy kept going when it was obvious that Cavendish had the stronger claim.) There is no doubt that national feeling was an element in the story. There were junctures, mainly on the Watt side, for example, where individuals privately expressed or validated such sentiments. Watt Jr, for example, privately expressed the view that his father's case might benefit and should benefit from national sentiment. David Brewster, more than anyone, linked the controversy to national feeling by invoking what he regarded as a Cambridge conspiracy against all 'Scotchmen'. National feeling is also shown by the way in which attributions in popular culture in the late nineteenth century and subsequently include a strong national component in the case of Watt. The latter attributions are perhaps fairly pure instances of national feeling in action. But in the midst of the controversy, national feeling is not a good guide to allegiances. Brewster himself long supported the Cavendish case, albeit in his own distinctive fashion. George Wilson, his teacher Thomas Graham, James David Forbes and numerous other Scottish chemists and natural philosophers participated in the controversy on the side of the Englishman.

So national feeling as an interest is cut across, if not obliterated, in many cases by other interests and concerns. Notable here are what Barnes calls 'professional vested interests'. The state of chemistry in the 1840s in Britain as a field of inquiry, its social position and the aspirations of its practitioners, informed a set of professional vested interests. Those interests were in having chemistry seen, at the élite level, as a quantitative discipline and an abstract science not to be equated with the empirical methods of the practical chemist. Yet in creating such a distance from practical chemistry, the élite did not want to divorce themselves from practical outcomes. Far from it, they wished to portray their abstract chemical work as ultimately the basis of major practical innovations of economic importance. For characters such as Thomas Graham, George Wilson or Lyon Playfair, this sort of professional vested interest as a chemist cut across and ultimately overrode any nationalist sentiment in favour of Watt. For them, in displaying their field in public forums, the association with Cavendish was the more desirable. For them, Cavendish personified the careful, cautious, quantitative, exact and abstract science with which their careers and their institutions were tied up. Watt might well be admitted as a competent chemist in his own time. Wilson was happy, for example, to admit and propagate that idea. But Cavendish (suitably abstracted from *his* context) was treated as a chemist in advance of his times who prefigured the chemistry of the mid-nineteenth century and became, in Thorpe's hands, its founder.

The case of David Brewster provided an interesting test case for my approach. Here was a prominent natural philosopher who changed sides in the controversy. After arguing for many years for Cavendish, against his national inclinations, Brewster suddenly switched to the Watt side. He did this after the publication of the Watt *Correspondence* and used this as his pretext, behaving as if he had been converted by the 'new' documents. In fact the documents were not new to him at all

– he had seen them privately before and drawn the opposite conclusion. What had changed were his relations with the British scientific élite. Long-standing tensions with the Cambridge group, especially Whewell and Airy, came to a crisis point in the early 1840s when Brewster's optical research was finally effectively excluded from the *Philosophical Transactions* of the Royal Society of London. Brewster subsequently made little effort to publish in outlets controlled by the scientific elite. He diverted his publications to the *Proceedings* of the Royal Society of Edinburgh. Brewster opted for 'outsider' status. He appears to have decided, when the opportunity arose with the publication of the *Correspondence*, that he could best promote his objectives by supporting the Watt cause in the water controversy and linking Watt's 'suppression' to the ongoing failings, as he saw them, of British scientific institutions, notably the Royal Society of London.

The Cambridge men were not a uniform 'interest group'. Certainly Whewell and Peacock, the clerical branch, to which we might add the clerical but non-Cambridge Harcourt and the Cambridge but non-clerical Airy, were very strongly pro-Cavendish. They were willing to take up the fight actively. They also fought most fiercely for hierarchical control of the scientific community, engaged in strenuous boundary-work at the pure–applied science border, and promoted an idealist model of discovery. Charles Babbage, although he did not become conspicuously involved in the water controversy, was clearly pro-Watt, and this squares well with his radical views on questions of scientific organization and the relations between science and technology. John Herschel was, as in much else, in a position intermediate between Babbage and Whewell. He was inclined to emphasize the place of experimental proof in scientific work and as a criterion of discovery. He was less of a hard-liner than his clerical friends on science–technology hierarchies, and more inclined than them to distribute credit between Cavendish and Watt. The Cambridge men, then, did not form a phalanx. Though if forced to choose on the water question, all except possibly Babbage would put Cavendish's claim above Watt's, there was subtlety and variability in their stances. That variability reflects their demeanour within the politics of science at this time. The same can be said for James David Forbes, a man who admired James Watt as a scientifically informed engineer of great profundity but found the work of Cavendish to be in tune with his own specialized ambitions and activities.

The pro-Cavendish camp were not just defending Cavendish's claims; they were defending their own status as the arbiters of science in early Victorian Britain. They claimed the expertise to pronounce on scientific questions and on historical questions of discovery. In many ways the chief danger that Watt Jr, Brougham, Muirhead and the like represented was that they challenged that claim. They did so, as did Brewster after his conversion, with circumstantial arguments and a model of discovery that they contended were accessible to all reasonable men.

Watt Jr, Muirhead and Brougham made clear occasionally some of the deeper currents of their opposition to the Cavendish camp. Whewell, Harcourt and Peacock they regarded as part of a presumptuous gang of ambitious, corrupt, clerical *arrivistes* deferring to old aristocratic forms of governance in carving out their careers. The British Association was also much denigrated as involving a kind of whipping up of the scientific mob in a way dangerous for scientific credibility and commercial integrity.

By the time that live controversy was winding down in the late 1840s and 1850s it was possible for both sides to be confident that they had been victorious. Members of the Watt camp were confident that they had had the best of the argument in the reviews and had secured a good deal of popular support. The members of the Cavendish camp were convinced that they had demonstrated the scientific case, whatever popular sentiment might judge. In many ways, however, the victory was still in the making. It came through the attributional processes that we surveyed in Chapter 11. It is notable that the Cavendish camp changed their argumentative strategy in more public forums in the 1850s. Perhaps wisely, they no longer appealed to the complex chemical arguments that formed the basis, or detailed rationale, of their own convictions. Instead they used the argument from Cavendish's character or, in the case of the 'Brown discovery', a more empirical mode of argument. Crucial to the success of the Cavendish camp was their control of the training of students and of the popularization of science. Chemists educated in Britain in the 1840s and the 1850s were trained to revere Cavendish as a founder of their discipline. When they in their turn came to write textbooks and the like, Cavendish was securely and unproblematically identified as the discoverer of the composition of water. Through such texts and popular accounts in encyclopaedias, and increasingly through historical works, the Cavendish gospel was propagated. In these accounts, any sense of the rhetorical and interested character of arguments in the water controversy was lost, as they thoroughly naturalized Cavendish's 1781 experiments as the discovery event, and reified the great natural philosopher as the discoverer. Watt supporters were generally less well placed to influence students and wider audiences. In this way the day was won for Cavendish amongst expert and popular opinion. Although Watt's claims did not die, and were propagated in much biographical literature with a nationalist leaning, the victory was Cavendish's. So it was that I, along with thousands of other young twentieth-century students of chemistry, thought we were following in the footsteps of Cavendish alone when we set out to blow ourselves up trying to synthesize water. For us, of course, James Watt was an engineer.

Appendix
Attributional Survey Database

The listing gives attributions of discovery of the composition of water as made in chemistry textbooks of 1840 to 1900.

Author	Title	Edition	Date	Attribution								
				C	W	L	C>W	C=W	W>C	L>C	C>L	None
Hoblyn, Richard D.	A Manual of Chemistry		1841									x
Kane, Robert	Elements of Chemistry		1841									x
Turner, Edward	Elements of Chemistry	6	1842	x							x	
Baxter, W. Raleigh	The Hand Book of Chemistry		1843									x
Daniell, J.F.	An Introduction to the Study of Chemical Philosophy		1843	x								x
Balmain, William H.	Lessons on Chemistry		1844									x
Fownes, George	A Manual of Elementary Chemistry	1	1844	x								
Gregory, William	Outlines of Chemistry		1845									
Sparkes, George	An Easy Introduction to Chemistry		1846									
Brown, J.C.	Lectures on Chemistry		1846	x	x	x					x	
Parkes, Samuel	An Elementary Treatise on Chemistry		1848	x	x							
Thomson, Robert Dundas	School Chemistry		1848	x	x			x				
Gmelin, Leopold	Hand-Book of Chemistry		1848	x	x	x	x					
White, W.	Chemistry for Students		1851									x
Reid, D.B.	Rudiments of Chemistry		1851									
Regnault, M.V.	Elements of Chemistry	4	1852			x				x		
Thomson, Robert Dundas	Cyclopaedia of Chemistry		1854	x	x			x				
Bernays, Albert J.	Household Chemistry	3	1854	x	x			x		x		
Bernays, Albert J.	First Lines of Chemistry		1855	x	x					x		
Glover, Robert Mortimer	A Manual of Chemistry		1855									x
Fownes, George	A Manual of Elementary Chemistry	7	1858	x	x			x				
Buckmaster, J.C.	The Elements of Inorganic Chemistry		1858									
Bidlake, J.P.	Text-Book of Elementary Chemistry		1858									x
Miller, William Allen	Elements of Chemistry Part II	2	1860									
Odling, William	A Manual of Chemistry		1861	x								
Pope, George	A Class Book of Rudimentary Chemistry		1864									x
Williamson, Alexander W.	Chemistry for Students		1865									x
Hudson, Fearnside	Inorganic Chemistry for Science Classes		1865									x
Hofmann, A.W.	Introduction to Modern Chemistry		1865									x
Roscoe, H.E.	Lessons in Elementary Chemistry		1866		x							
Bloxam, Charles L.	Chemistry Inorganic and Organic		1867	x								

Author	Title	No.	Year							
Fownes, George	A Manual of Elementary Chemistry	10	1868	x	x	x		x		x
Naquet, A.	Principles of Chemistry Founded on Modern Theories		1868	x	x			x		x
Barff, F.S.	An Introduction to Scientific Chemistry	2	1869	x					x	
Gill, C. Haughton	Chemistry for Schools		1869	x						
Kay-Shuttleworth, U.J.	First Principles of Modern Chemistry	2	1870	x			x			
Hart, H. Martyn	Elementary Chemistry		1870							
Grundy, Cuthbert C.	An Introduction to the Study of Chymistry		1870							
Rodwell, G.F.	A Dictionary of Science		1871	x		x		x		x
Roscoe, H.E.	Chemistry		1872				x			
Meldola, Raphael	Elementary Inorganic Chemistry		1873		x					
Rigg, Arthur	An Easy Introduction to Chemistry		1873							
Jamieson, Thomas	Inorganic Chemistry		1874							x
Brown, Alex Crum	Chemistry		1875							x
Valentin, William George	Introduction to Inorganic Chemistry	3	1876	x						x
Tilden, William A	Introduction to the Study of Chemical Philosophy		1876	x		x		x		x
Roscoe, H.E. & Schorlemmer, C.	A Treatise of Chemistry; Vol 1		1877	x	x	x		x	x	x
Thorpe, T.E.	A Manual of Inorganic Chemistry; Vol 1	2	1877	x	x	x	x	x		
Kemshead, W.B.	Inorganic Chemistry		1877	x						
Morris, David	A Class-Book of Inorganic Chemistry	2	1880			x	x			
Greville, H. Leicester	The Student's Hand-Book of Chemistry		1881							
Faulkner, George R.	Elementary Chemistry		1883		x					
Frankland, Edward & Japp, F.R.	Inorganic Chemistry		1884	x		x		x		x
Anderson, J.H.	The Public School Chemistry		1885	x						x
Maybury, A.C.	The Student's Chemistry; Part I		1886						x	
Shenstone, W.A.	A Practical Introduction to Chemistry		1886		x			x	x	
Taylor, R.L.	Chemistry for Beginners	1	1887	x			x			x
Muir, M.M. Pattison & Slater, C.	Elementary Chemistry		1887	x						
Jago, William	Inorganic Chemistry Theoretical and Practical	9	1888	x					x	x
Meyer, Lothar	Modern Theories of Chemistry		1888	x						x
Mixter, William G.	An Elementary Text-Book of Chemistry	2	1889	x						x
Bloxam, Charles L.	Chemistry Inorganic and Organic	7	1890	x						x
Ward, Robert Avey	Elementary Chemistry for Science Schools		1890							x
Ramsay, William	A System of Inorganic Chemistry		1891	x						x

Author	Title	Edition	Date	C	W	L	C>W	C=W	W>C	L>C	C>L	None
									Attribution			
Ramsay, William	Elementary Systematic Chemistry		1891	x								x
Fisher, W.W.	A Class Book of Elementary Chemistry		1891	x								x
Watts, W. Marshall	A Practical Introduction to the Elements of Chemistry	2	1891	x								x
Luff, Arthur P.	A Manual of Chemistry		1892									x
Lilley, H.T.	A Lecture Course in Elementary Chemistry		1892									x
Furneaux, William S.	Elementary Chemistry, Inorganic and Organic		1892									x
Cox, E.J.	The Standard Course of Elementary Chemistry		1892									x
Taylor, R.L.	The Student's Chemistry		1892	x								x
Briggs, William	A Synopsis of Non-metallic Chemistry		1892									
Roscoe, Henry	Inorganic Chemistry for Beginners		1893	x								x
Mills, John	Chemistry for Students		1893	x								
Harrison, W. Jerome & Bailey, R.J.	Chemistry for All		1893	x		x						
Snaith, W.A.	Inorganic Chemistry for Elementary Classes	23	1894	x								
Cooke, Samuel	First Principles of Chemistry	6	1895	x								
Sexton, A. Humboldt	Elementary Inorganic Chemistry	4	1895								x	
Clowes, Frank	A Treatise of Practical Chemistry	6	1895								x	
Trotman, S.R.	Elementary Non-Metallic Chemistry		1896	x								x
Perkin, W.H. & Lean, B.	An Introduction to the Study of Chemistry		1896	x		x						
Vernon Harcourt, A.G. & Madan, H.G.	Exercises in Practical chemistry	5	1897							x		
Muir, M.M. Pattison	A Course of Practical Chemistry		1897								x	
Jones, Chapman	Practical Inorganic Chemistry		1898								x	
Bailey, G.H.	Advanced Inorganic Chemistry		1898	x							x	
Newth, G.S.	A Text-Book of Inorganic Chemistry	7	1899								x	
Willson, Rivers	Chemistry: For the use of Students …		1899									
Roscoe, Henry E. & Harden, Arthur	Inorganic Chemistry for Advanced Students		1899									
Ramsay, William	Modern Chemistry: Theoretical		1900	x							x	
Shenstone, W.A.	The Elements of Inorganic Chemistry		1900	x							x	

Key:
C Cavendish   W Watt   L Lavoisier   > favoured over   = equal to

Bibliography

Note: The nineteenth-century chemical texts forming the basis of the survey in Chapter 11 are included here only if they are individually discussed in my text and/ or notes. For details of the rest see the Appendix.

Aikin, A. and C.R. Aikin (1807), *A Dictionary of Chemistry and Mineralogy*, 2 vols, London: John & Arthur Arch and William Phillips.

Alborn, Timothy L. (1988), 'The "End of Natural Philosophy" revisited: Varieties of scientific discovery', *Nuncius: Annali di Storia della Scienza*, **3**, 227–50.

—— (1989), 'Negotiating notation: Chemical symbols and British society, 1831–1835', *Annals of Science*, **46**, 437–60.

—— (1996), 'The business of induction: Industry and genius in the language of British scientific reform, 1820–1840', *History of Science*, **34**, 91–121.

Anderson, R.G.W. (1992), '"What is Technology?": Education through museums in the mid-nineteenth century', *The British Journal for the History of Science*, **25**, 169–84.

Anderson, Wilda C. (1984), *Between the Library and the Laboratory. The Language of Chemistry in Eighteenth-Century France*, Baltimore: The Johns Hopkins University Press.

Anderson, William (ed.) (1882), *The Scottish Nation*, 9 vols, Edinburgh: A. Fullarton & Co.

Anon. (1851a), 'Review of *The Life of the Honourable Henry Cavendish*', *British Quarterly Review*, **21**, August, 257–59.

—— (1851b), 'The Life of the Honourable Henry Cavendish', *The Athenaeum*, 13 December, 1305–306.

—— (1851c), 'Wilson's Life of Cavendish', *The Spectator*, **24**, 9 August, 760–61.

—— (1855), ' The Hon. Henry Cavendish', *The Leisure Hour. A Family Journal of Instruction and Recreation*, **4**, 489–94.

—— (1859), 'James Watt', *Fraser's Magazine*, **59**, 318–29.

—— (1927), 'A day with Wordsworth', *Blackwood's Magazine*, **221**, 728–43.

Appel, Toby A. (1987), *The Cuvier–Geoffroy Debate. French Biology in the Decades before Darwin*, Oxford: Oxford University Press.

Arago, François (1839), *Historical Eloge of James Watt by M. Arago ... Translated from the French with Additional Notes and an Appendix by James Patrick Muirhead*, London: John Murray.

—— (1840), 'Eloge historique de James Watt', *Mémoires de l'Académie Royale des Sciences de l'Institut de France*, **17**, lxi–clxxxviii.

—— (1857), *Biographies of Distinguished Scientific Men, translated by W.H. Smyth, Baden Powell and Robert Grant*, London: Longman, Brown, Longmans & Roberts.

Ash, Marinell (1986), 'New Frontiers: George and Daniel Wilson', in J. Calder (ed.), *The Enterprising Scot: Scottish Adventure and Achievement*, Edinburgh: HMSO, pp. 40–51.

Ashworth, William J. (1996), 'Memory, efficiency, and symbolic analysis: Charles Babbage, John Herschel, and the industrial mind', *Isis*, **87**, 629–53.

Baily, Francis (1843), 'Experiments with the torsion rod for determining the mean density of the Earth', *Memoirs of the Royal Astronomical Society*, **14**, 1–120.

Barnes, Barry (1982), *T.S. Kuhn and Social Science*, London: Macmillan.

——, David Bloor and John Henry (1996), *Scientific Knowledge. A Sociological Analysis*, Chicago: The University of Chicago Press.

Baxter, Paul (1985), 'Science and belief in Scotland, 1805–1868: The Scottish evangelicals', unpublished PhD thesis, University of Edinburgh.

Beddoes, Thomas (1794–95), *Considerations on the Medicinal Use and on the Production of Factitious Airs, and on the Manner of obtaining them in Large Quantities. In two parts. Part I By Thomas Beddoes M.D. Part II by James Watt, Esq.*, Bristol: J. Johnson and H. Murray, 3rd edn, enlarged, 1796.

Bellamy, Martin (1994), 'P.S. *Caledonia*: Denmark's first steamship', *The Mariner's Mirror*, **80**, 54–65.

Bennett, J.J. (1859), 'Statement of facts relating to the discovery of the composition of water by the Hon. H. Cavendish. In a letter from J.J. Bennett, Esq., F.R.S. to Sir B.C. Brodie, Bart., P.R.S., dated February 12, 1859. Received February 14, 1859', *Proceedings of the Royal Society of London*, **9**, November 1857–April 1859, 642–44.

Bensaude-Vincent, B. (1983), 'A Founder myth in the history of science? – The Lavoisier case', in L. Graham, W. Lepenies and P. Weingart (eds), *Functions and Uses of Disciplinary Histories*, Dordrecht: Reidel, pp. 53–78.

—— (1990), 'A view of the Chemical Revolution through contemporary textbooks: Lavoisier, Fourcroy and Chaptal', *The British Journal for the History of Science*, **23**, 435–60.

—— (1993), *Lavoisier: Mémoires d'une révolution*, Paris: Flammarion.

—— (2001), 'A genealogy of the increasing gap between science and the public', *Public Understanding of Science*, **10**, 99–113.

Bernays, Albert J. (1855), *First Lines in Chemistry. A Manual for Students*, London: John Parker.

Berthelot, M. (1902 [1890]), *La Révolution Chimique Lavoisier*, Paris: Felix Alcan.

Berzelius, J.J. (1845), *Traité de Chimie*, Paris: Firmin Didot Frères.

Black, Joseph (1803), *Lectures on the Elements of Chemistry delivered in the University of Edinburgh by the late Joseph Black, M.D. ... Now Published from his Manuscripts by John Robison, LLD*, 2 vols, Edinburgh: William Creech.

Bloor, David (1976), *Knowledge and Social Imagery*, London: Routledge & Kegan Paul.

Brande, William Thomas (1821), *A Manual of Chemistry*, 2nd edn, 3 vols, London: Murray.

Brannigan, Augustine (1979), 'The Reification of Mendel', *Social Studies of Science*, **9**, 423–54.

—— (1981), *The Social Basis of Scientific Discoveries*, Cambridge: Cambridge University Press.

Brewster, David (1830), 'Decline of science in England', *Quarterly Review*, **43**, 305–42.

—— (1835), 'Report of the first, second and third meeting of the British Association', *Edinburgh Review*, **60**, 363–94.

—— (1837), 'Whewell's *History of the Inductive Sciences*', *Edinburgh Review*, **66**, 110–51.

—— (1840), 'Life and discoveries of James Watt', *Edinburgh Review*, **70**, 466–502.

—— (1842), 'Whewell's *Philosophy of the Inductive Sciences*', *Edinburgh Review*, **74**, 265–306.

—— (1845), 'Observations connected with the discovery of the composition of water', *London, Edinburgh and Dublin Philosophical Magazine*, **27**, 195–97.

—— (1846), 'Watt and Cavendish – Controversy respecting the composition of water', *North British Review*, **6**, 473–508.

—— (1855), 'Review of Muirhead's *The Origin and Progress of the Mechanical Inventions of James Watt*', *North British Review*, **23**, 193–231.

Brock, W.H. (1978), 'The Society for the Perpetuation of Gmelin: The Cavendish Society, 1846–1872', *Annals of Science*, **35**, 599–617.

—— (1984), 'Brewster as a scientific journalist', in A.D. Morrison-Low and J.J.R. Christie (eds), *'Martyr of Science': Sir David Brewster 1781–1868*, Edinburgh: Royal Scottish Museum, pp. 37–42.

—— (1990), 'The Cavendish Society's wonderful repertory of chemistry', *Annals of Science*, **47**, 77–80.

Brooke, John Hedley (1977), 'Natural theology and the plurality of worlds: Observations on the Brewster–Whewell debate', *Annals of Science*, **34**, 221–86.

Brougham, Henry (1803), 'Lectures on the elements of chemistry', *Edinburgh Review*, **2**, 1–26.

—— (1835), *A Discourse of Natural Theology*, 2nd edn, London: Charles Knight.

—— (1838), *Speeches of Henry Brougham*, 4 vols, Edinburgh: Adam and Charles Black.

—— (1845), *Lives of Men of Letters and Science, who Flourished in the Time of George III*, London: Charles Knight and Co.

Browne, E. Janet, 'The making of the *Memoir* of Edward Forbes, F.R.S.', *Archives of Natural History*, **10**, 205–19.

Buchanan, R.A. (1989), *The Engineers. A History of the Engineering Profession in Britain, 1750–1914*, London: Jessica Langley Publishers.

Bud, Robert F. and G.K. Roberts (1984), *Science versus Practice: Chemistry in Victorian Britain*, Manchester: Manchester University Press.

Buttmann, Günther (1970), *The Shadow of the Telescope. A Biography of John Herschel*, New York: Charles Scribner's Sons.

Buxton, H.W. (1988), *Memoir of the Life and Labours of the Late Charles Babbage*, edited and introduced by Anthony Hyman, Cambridge, MA: MIT Press.

Cannon, Susan Faye (1978), *Science in Culture: The Early Victorian Period*, New York: Dawson and Science History Publications.

Cannon, Walter Faye (1964), 'Scientists and Broad Churchmen: An early Victorian intellectual network', *Journal of British Studies*, **4**, 65–88.

Cantor, G.N. (1971), 'Henry Brougham and the Scottish methodological tradition', *Studies in the History and Philosophy of Science*, **2**, 69–89.

—— (1975), 'The Academy of Physics at Edinburgh 1797–1800', *Social Studies of Science*, **5**, 109–34.

—— (1983), *Optics after Newton: Theories of Light in Britain and Ireland, 1704–1840*, Manchester: Manchester University Press.

—— (1975), 'The reception of the wave theory of light in Britain: A case study illustrating the role of methodology in scientific debate', *Historical Studies in the Physical Sciences*, **6**, 109–32.

Cardwell, Donald (1971), *From Watt to Clausius: the rise of thermodynamics in the early industrial age*, Ithaca, N.Y.: Cornell University Press.

Carnegie, Andrew (1905), *James Watt*, Edinburgh and London: Oliphant Anderson & Ferrier.

Cawood, John (1979), 'The Magnetic Crusade: Science and politics in early Victorian Britain', *Isis*, **70**, 493–518.

—— (1985), 'François Arago, homme de science et homme politique', *La Recherche*, **16**, 1464–71.

Chapman, Allan (1988), 'Science and the public good: George Biddell Airy (1801–92) and the concept of a scientific civil servant', in N.A. Rupke (ed.), *Science, Politics and the Public Good: Essays in honour of Margaret Gowing*, Basingstoke: Macmillan, pp. 36–62.

Chen, Xiang and Peter Barker (1992), 'Cognitive appraisal and power: David Brewster, Henry Brougham, and the tactics of the emission–undulatory controversy during the early 1850s', *Studies in History and Philosophy of Science*, **23**, 75–101.

Christie, J.R.R. (1984), 'Sir David Brewster as an historian of science', in A.D. Morrison-Low and J.R.R. Christie (eds), *'Martyr of Science': Sir David Brewster 1781–1868*, Edinburgh: Royal Scottish Museum, pp. 53–6.

Clotfelter, B.E. (1987), 'The Cavendish experiment as Cavendish knew it', *American Journal of Physics*, **55**, 210–13.

Clow, Archibald and Nan L. Clow (1992 [1952]), *The Chemical Revolution. A Contribution to Social Technology*, Philadelphia: Gordon and Breach Science Publishers.

Cobbett, William (1817), *The Parliamentary History of England from the Earliest Period to the Year 1803*, London: Longman, Hurst, Rees, Orme & Brown.

Cockburn, Lord (1852), *Life of Lord Jeffrey with a Selection from his Correspondence*, 2 vols, Edinburgh: Adam & Charles Black.

Cole, William A. (1982), 'Manuscripts of Joseph Black's Lectures on Chemistry', in A.D.C. Simpson, *Joseph Black 1728–1799. A Commemorative Symposium*, Edinburgh: The Royal Scottish Museum, pp. 53–69.

Collins, Harry (1985), *Changing Order. Replication and Induction in Scientific Practice*, Beverly Hills: SAGE Publications.

—— (1991), 'Captives and victims: Comment on Scott, Richards, and Martin', *Science, Technology, & Human Values*, **16**, 249–51.

Corrins, R.D. (1970), 'The great Hot-Blast affair', *Industrial Archaeology*, **7**, 233–63.

Coulter, Moureen (1992), *Property in Ideas: The Patent Question in mid-Victorian Britain*, Kirksville, MO: Thomas Jefferson University Press.

Craik, G.L. (1830), *The Pursuit of Knowledge under Difficulties*, 2 vols, London: Charles Knight.

Crosland, Maurice (1978), *Gay-Lussac, Scientist and Bourgeois*, Cambridge: Cambridge University Press.

—— (1967), *The Society of Arcueil*, London: Heinemann.

—— (1992), *Science under Control: The French Academy of Sciences 1795–1914,* Cambridge: Cambridge University Press.

—— (1994), *In the Shadow of Lavoisier: The* Annales de Chimie *and the establishment of a new science*, Chalfont St Giles: The British Society for the History of Science.

—— and C.W. Smith (1978), 'The transmission of physics from France to Britain, 1800–1840', *Historical Studies in the Physical Sciences*, **9**, 1–61.

Cunningham, Frank F. (1990), *James David Forbes. Pioneer Scottish Glaciologist*, Edinburgh: Scottish Academic Press.

Cuvier, Georges (1874), 'Eloge historique de Henri Cavendish', in *Eloges Historiques*, 3rd edn, Paris: Ducrocq, pp. 201–21.

Daumas, Maurice (1955), *Lavoisier, théoriecien et expérimentateur*, Paris: PUF.

Davie, George (1964), *The Democratic Intellect: Scotland and her Universities in the Nineteenth Century*, 2nd edn, Edinburgh: Edinburgh University Press.

Davis, John L. (1998), 'Artisans and savants: The role of the Academy of Sciences in the process of electrical innovation in France, 1850–1880', *Annals of Science*, **55**, 291–314.

Davy, Humphry (1812), *Elements of Chemical Philosophy*, London: J. Johnson & Co.

Davy, John (ed.) (1839), *The Collected Works of Sir Humphry Davy, Bart. LL.D. F.R.S. Edited by his Brother John Davy, M.D. F.R.S.*, 9 vols, London: Smith, Elder & Co.

Dickinson, H.W. and Rhys Jenkins (1927), *James Watt and the Steam Engine. The Memorial Volume Prepared for the Committee of the Watt Centenary Commemoration at Birmingham 1919*, Oxford: Clarendon Press.

Donnelly, James (1991), 'Industrial recruitment of chemistry students from English universities: A revaluation of its early importance', *The British Journal for the History of Science*, **24**, 3–20.

Donovan, Arthur (1975), *Philosophical Chemistry in the Scottish Enlightenment. The Doctrines and Discoveries of William Cullen and Joseph Black*, Edinburgh: Edinburgh University Press.

—— (1984) 'The Chemical Revolution revisited', in Stephen H. Cutliffe (ed.), *Science and Technology in the Eighteenth Century: Essays of the Lawrence Henry Gipson Institute for Eighteenth Century Studies*, Bethlehem, PA: Lawrence Henry Gipson Institute for 18th-Century Studies, Lehigh University, pp. 1–15.

—— (1993), *Antoine Lavoisier. Science, Administration, and Revolution*, Oxford: Blackwell.

—— (1995), 'The new nomenclature among the Scots: Assessing novel chemical claims in a culture under strain', in B. Bensaude-Vincent and F. Abbri (eds),

Lavoisier in European Context. Negotiating a New Language for Chemistry, Canton, MA: Science History Publications, pp. 113–21.

Donovan, Arthur (ed.) (1988), *The Chemical Revolution: Essays in Reinterpretation*, in *Osiris*, **4**, 5–231.

Doyle, W.P. (1982), 'Black, Hope and Lavoisier', in A.D.C. Simpson, *Joseph Black 1728–1799. A Commemorative Symposium*, Edinburgh: The Royal Scottish Museum, pp. 43–46.

Dreyer, J.L.E. and H.H. Turner (eds) (1923), *History of the Royal Astronomical Society 1820–1920*, London: The Royal Astronomical Society.

Durand, M.J. (1986–87), 'Le Travail mathématique de George Peacock (1791–1858)', *Sciences et Techniques en Perspective*, **11**, 91–151.

Dutton, Harold I. (1984), *The Patent System and Inventive Activity during the Industrial Revolution, 1750–1852*, Manchester: Manchester University Press.

Dyck, David R. (1967), 'The nature of heat and its relationship to chemistry in the eighteenth century', unpublished PhD thesis, University of Wisconsin.

Edelstein, Sidney M. (1948), 'Priestley settles the Water Controversy', *Chymia*, **1**, 123–37.

Eller, Johann Theodor (1764), *Physikalisch–Chymisch–Medicinische Abhandlungen aus den Gedenkschriften der König*, Berlin.

Enros, Philip C. (1981), 'The Analytical Society (1812–1813): Precursor of the renewal of Cambridge mathematics', *Historia Mathematica*, **10**, 24–47.

Erdman, David V. (1986), *Commerce des lumières: John Oswald and the British in Paris, 1790–1793*, Columbia, MO: University of Missouri Press.

Falconer, Isobel (1999), 'Henry Cavendish: The man and the measurement', *Measurement Science and Technology*, **10**, 470–77.

Fara, Patricia (2002), *Newton: The Making of Genius*, London: Macmillan.

Farber, Eduard (ed.) (1961), *Great Chemists*, New York: Interscience Publishers.

Farrar, W.V. (1973), 'Andrew Ure F.R.S., and the philosophy of manufactures', *Notes and Records of the Royal Society of London*, **27**, 299–324.

Fine, Gary Alan (2001), *Difficult Reputations. Collective Memories of the Evil, Inept, and Controversial*, Chicago: The University of Chicago Press.

Forbes, J.D. (1846), 'Biographical notice of Sir John Robison', *Proceedings of the Royal Society of Edinburgh*, **2**, 68–78.

Fourcroy, A.F. (1788), *Elements of Natural History and of Chemistry ... Translated into English, with Occasional Notes, and an Historical Preface by the Translator*, 4 vols, London: G.G.J. and J. Robinson.

—— (1800), *Elements of Chemistry and Natural History to Which is Prefixed the Philosophy of Chemistry, 5th edition with notes. By John Thomson, Surgeon, Edinburgh*, 3 vols, Edinburgh: Mundell & Son.

Fownes, George (1844) *A Manual of Elementary Chemistry. Theoretical and Practical*, London: John Churchill.

Gale, W.K.V. (1961–62), 'Soho Foundry: Some facts and fallacies', *Transactions of the Newcomen Society*, **34**, 73–87.

Gay, Hannah and John W. Gay (1997), 'Brothers in science: Science and fraternal culture in nineteenth-century Britain', *History of Science*, **35**, 425–53.

Gieryn, Thomas F. (1983), 'Boundary-work and the demarcation of science from

non-science: Strains and interests in professional ideologies of scientists', *American Sociological Review*, **48**, 781–95.

—— (1999), *Cultural Boundaries of Science: Credibility on the Line*, Chicago: The University of Chicago Press.

Gilbert, G.N. and M. Mulkay (1984), *Opening Pandora's Box: A Sociological Analysis of Scientists' Discourse*, Cambridge: Cambridge University Press.

Gillispie, Charles C. (1960), *The Edge of Objectivity*, Princeton, NJ: Princeton University Press.

Godson, Richard (1840), *A Practical Treatise on the Law of Patents for Inventions and of Copyright*, London: Saunders and Benning.

Golinski, Jan (1992), *Science as Public Culture: Chemistry and Enlightenment in Britain, 1760–1820*, Cambridge: Cambridge University Press.

—— (1992), 'The Chemical Revolution and the politics of language', *The Eighteenth Century*, **33**, 238–51.

—— (2002), 'Conversations on Chemistry: Talk about phlogiston in the Coffee House Society, 1780–1787', in T. Levere and G.L'E. Turner (eds), *Discussing Chemistry and Steam. The Minutes of a Coffee House Philosophical Society, 1780–1787*, Oxford: Oxford University Press, pp. 191–205.

Gooding, David (1985), '"He who proves, discovers": John Herschel, William Pepys and the Faraday Effect', *Notes and Records of the Royal Society of London*, **39**, 229–44.

Gordon, Mrs Margaret Maria Brewster (1869), *The Home Life of Sir David Brewster*, Edinburgh: Edmonston and Douglas.

Gregory, William (1845), *Outlines of Chemistry*, London: Taylor and Walton.

Greig, James A. (1948), *Francis Jeffrey of the Edinburgh Review*, Edinburgh: Oliver & Boyd.

Gross, Alan G. (1998), 'Do disputes over priority tell us anything about science?', *Science in Context*, **11**, 161–79.

Grosser, Morton (1962), *The Discovery of Neptune*, Cambridge: Cambridge University Press.

Guerlac, Henry (1976), 'Chemistry as a branch of physics: Laplace's collaboration with Lavoisier', *Historical Studies in the Physical Sciences*, **7**, 193–276.

—— (1982), 'Joseph Black's work on heat', in A.D.C. Simpson (ed.), *Joseph Black 1728–1799. A Commemorative Symposium*, Edinburgh: The Royal Scottish Museum, pp. 13–22.

Guttridge, George H. (ed.) (1961), *The Correspondence of Edmund Burke, vol. III*, Cambridge: Cambridge University Press.

Harcourt, E.W. (ed.) (1880–95), *The Harcourt Papers*. Oxford: privately printed.

Harcourt, William Vernon (1840), 'Address', *Report of the Ninth Meeting of the British Association for the Advancement of Science held at Birmingham in August 1839*, pp. 3–69.

—— (1846), 'Letter to Henry, Lord Brougham, F.R.S., &c., containing remarks on certain statements in his Lives of Black, Watt and Cavendish', *Philosophical Magazine* **28**, 106–31, 478–525.

Hayward, P.A. (1987), *Hayward's Patent Cases, 1600–1883, vol 4 (1842–1844)*, Abingdon: Professional Books Limited.

Heilbron, John L. (1993) 'A mathematicians' mutiny with morals', in Paul Horwich

(ed.), *World Changes: Thomas Kuhn and the nature of science*, Cambridge, MA: MIT Press, pp. 81–129.

Herschel, J.F.W. (1830), *A Preliminary Discourse on the Study of Natural Philosophy*, London: Longman, Orme, Brown, Green and Longman.

Hilgartner, Stephen (1990), 'The dominant view of popularization: Conceptual problems, political uses', *Social Studies of Science*, **20**, 519–39.

Hilken, T.J.N. (1967), *Engineering at Cambridge University 1783–1965*, Cambridge: Cambridge University Press.

Hills, Richard L. (2002), *James Watt. Volume 1: His time in Scotland, 1736–1774*, Ashbourne: Landmark Publishing Ltd.

Horn, Jeff and M.C. Jacob (1998), 'Jean-Antoine Chaptal and the cultural roots of French industrialization', *Technology and Culture*, **39**, 671–98.

Hounshell, David A. (1980), 'Edison and the pure science ideal in 19th-century America', *Science*, **207**, 8 February, 612–16.

Huch, Ronald K. (1993), *Henry, Lord Brougham. The Later Years 1830–1868. The 'Great Actor'*, Lewiston: The Edward Mellen Press.

Humboldt, Alexander von (1860), *Letters of Alexander von Humboldt, written between the years 1827 and 1858 to Varhagen von Ense*, London: Trubner & Co.

Huxley, Aldous (1952), *Crome Yellow. A Novel*, London: Chatto & Windus.

James, Frank A.J.L. (ed.) (1993), *The Correspondence of Michael Faraday. Volume 2*, Stevenage: The Institution of Electrical Engineers.

Jeffrey, Francis (1840), *Contributions to the Edinburgh Review in 4 volumes*, London: Longman, Brown, Green and Longman.

—— (1848), 'The discoverer of the composition of water; Watt or Cavendish?', *Edinburgh Review*, **87**, 67–137.

Jeremy, David J. (1977), 'Damming the flood: British government efforts to check the outflow of technicians and machinery, 1780–1843', *Business History Review*, **51**, 1–34.

Jones, Peter M. (1999), 'Living the Enlightenment and the French Revolution: James Watt, Matthew Boulton, and their sons', *The Historical Journal*, **42**, 157–82.

Jungnickel, Christa and Russell McCormmach (1999), *Cavendish. The Experimental Life*, Lewisburg, PA: Bucknell.

Kendall, James (1952), 'The first chemical society, the first chemical journal, and the Chemical Revolution', *Proceedings of the Royal Society of Edinburgh*, **63A**, 346–58, 385–400.

Knight, David (1986), 'Accomplishment or dogma: Chemistry in the introductory works of Jane Marcet and Samuel Parkes', *Ambix*, **33**, 94–98.

—— (1988), 'Revolutions in Science: Chemistry and the Romantic Reaction to Science', in W.R.Shea (ed.), *Revolutions in Science. Their Meaning and Relevance*, Canton, MA: Science History Publications, pp. 49–69.

Koertge, Noretta (1982), 'Explaining scientific discovery', in P.D. Asquith and T. Nickles (eds), *PSA 1982: Proceedings of the 1982 Biennial Meeting of the Philosophy of Science Association*, East Lansing, MI: Philosophy of Science Association, vol. 1, pp. 14–28.

Kopp, Hermann (1843–47), *Geschichte der Chemie*, 4 vols, Braunschweig: F. Vieweg und Sohn.

—— (1875), 'Die Entdeckung der Zusammensetzung des Wassers', in H. Kopp, *Beiträge zur Geschichte der Chemie*, Drittes Stück, Braunschweig: Vieweg und Sohn, pp. 237–310.

Kuhn, T.S. (1962), 'Historical structure of scientific discovery', *Science*, **136**, 760–64.

Latour, Bruno (1983), 'Give me a laboratory and I will raise the world', in K.D. Knorr-Cetina and M. Mulkay (eds), *Science Observed*, Beverly Hills, CA: SAGE Publications, pp. 141–70.

—— (1987), *Science in Action: How to Follow Scientists and Engineers through Society*, Milton Keynes: Open University Press.

—— and Steve Woolgar (1979), *Laboratory Life: The Social Construction of Scientific Facts*, Beverly Hills, CA: SAGE Publications.

Laudan, Rachel (1993), 'Histories of the sciences and their uses: A review to 1913', *History of Science*, **31**, 1–34.

Layton, David (1973), *Science for the People. The Origins of the School Science Curriculum in England*, London: George Allen & Unwin.

Levere, Trevor and Gerard L'E. Turner (eds), (2002), *Discussing Chemistry and Steam. The Minutes of a Coffee House Philosophical Society 1780–1787*, Oxford: Oxford University Press.

Lobban, Michael (2000), 'Henry Brougham and law reform', *The English Historical Review*, **115**, 1184–215.

Mabberley, David (1985), *Jupiter Botanicus. Robert Brown of the British Museum*, Braunschweig: J. Cramer.

Mackenzie, Thomas B. (1928), *Life of James Beaumont Neilson F.R.S.*, Glasgow: The West of Scotland Iron & Steel Institute.

MacLeod, Christine (1996), 'Concepts of invention and the patent controversy in Britain', in R. Fox (ed.), *Technological Change. Methods and Themes in the History of Technology*, Amsterdam: Harwood Academic Publishers, pp. 137–53.

—— (1998), 'James Watt, heroic invention and the idea of the Industrial revolution', in M. Berg and K. Bruland (eds), *Technological Revolutions in Europe. Historical Perspectives*, Cheltenham: Edward Elgar, pp. 96–116.

MacLeod, Roy (1983), 'Whigs and Savants: Reflections on the reform movement in the Royal Society, 1830–1848', in I. Inkster and J. Morrell (eds), *Metropolis and Province. Science in British Culture 1780–1850*, London: Hutchinson, pp. 55–90.

Marcet, Jane (1817), *Conversations on Chemistry; in which the Elements of that Science are Familiarly Explained and Illustrated by Experiments*, 2 vols, 5th edn, London: Longman, Hurst, Rees, Orme and Brown.

Marsden, Ben (2002), *Watt's Perfect Engine. Steam and the Age of Invention*, Cambridge: Icon Books.

Martin, Brian, Evelleen Richards and Pam Scott, 'Who's a captive? Who's a victim? Response to Collins's method talk', *Science, Technology, & Human Values*, **16**, 252–55.

Maxwell, James Clerk (ed.) (1921), *The Scientific Papers of the Honourable Henry Cavendish, F.R.S.*, Cambridge: Cambridge University Press.

McCormmach, Russell (1990), 'Henry Cavendish on the Proper Method of Rectifying Abuses', in Elizabeth Garber (ed.), *Beyond History of Science. Essays*

in Honor of Robert E. Schofield, Bethlehem, PA: Lehigh University Press, pp. 35–51.

—— (1995), 'The last experiment of Henry Cavendish', in A.J. Kox and D.M. Siegel (eds), *No Truth Except in the Details. Essays in Honor of Martin J. Klein*, Dordrecht: Kluwer Academic Publishers, pp. 1–30.

McDowell, R.B. and John A. Woods (eds) (1970), *The Correspondence of Edmund Burke, Vol. IX*, Cambridge: Cambridge University Press.

McEvoy, John G. (1992), 'The Chemical Revolution in context', *The Eighteenth Century: Theory and Interpretation*, **33**, 198–216.

—— (1997), 'Positivism, Whiggism, and the Chemical Revolution: A study in the historiography of chemistry', *History of Science*, **35**, 1–33.

McMullin, Ernan et al. (1980), 'The rational explanation of scientific discoveries', in T. Nickles (ed.), *Scientific Discovery: Case Studies*, Dordrecht: Reidel.

Mertens, Joost (2000), 'From Tubal Cain to Faraday: William Whewell as a philosopher of technology', *History of Science*, **38**, 321–42.

Merton, Robert K. (1973), *The Sociology of Science. Theoretical and Empirical Investigations*, Chicago: The University of Chicago Press.

Metzger, Hélène (1930), *Newton, Stahl, Boerhaave et la Doctrine Chimique*, Paris: Félix Alcan.

Miller, David Philip (1981), 'The Royal Society of London, 1800–1835: A study in the cultural politics of scientific organization', unpublished PhD thesis, University of Pennsylvania.

—— (1986), 'The revival of the physical sciences in Britain, 1815–1840', *Osiris*, new series, **2**, 107–34.

—— (1997), 'The usefulness of natural philosophy: The Royal Society of London and the culture of practical utility in the later eighteenth century', *The British Journal for the History of Science*, **32**, 185–201.

—— (2000), '"Puffing Jamie": The commercial and ideological importance of being a "philosopher" in the case of the reputation of James Watt (1736–1819)', *History of Science*, **38**, 1–24.

—— (2002a), '"Distributing Discovery" between Watt and Cavendish: A reassessment of the nineteenth-century "water controversy"', *Annals of Science*, **59**, 149–78.

—— (2002b), 'The Sobel effect', *Metascience*, **11** (2), July, 185–200.

—— (forthcoming), 'True Myths: James Watt's Kettle, his Condenser and his Chemistry', *History of Science*.

Morrell, J.B. (1971), 'Professors Robison and Playfair and the *Theophobia Gallica*: Natural philosophy, religion and politics in Edinburgh, 1789–1815', *Notes and Records of the Royal Society of London*, **26**, 43–63.

Morrell, Jack and Arnold Thackray (1981), *Gentlemen of Science: Early Years of the British Association for the Advancement of Science*, Oxford: Clarendon Press.

—— (eds) (1984), *Gentlemen of Science. Early Correspondence of the British Association for the Advancement of Science*, London: The Royal Historical Society.

Morris, Robert J. (1972), 'Lavoisier and the caloric theory', *The British Journal for the History of Science*, **6**, 1–38.

Morus, Iwan Rhys (1989), 'The politics of power: Reform and regulation in the work of William Robert Grove', unpublished PhD thesis, University of Cambridge.

—— (1991), 'Correlation and control: William Robert Grove and the construction of a new philosophy of scientific reform', *Studies in History and Philosophy of Science*, **22**, 589–621.

—— (1998), *Frankenstein's Children. Electricity, Exhibition and Experiment in Early-Nineteenth-Century London*, Princeton, NJ: Princeton University Press.

Muir, M.M. Pattison (1883), *Heroes of Science. Chemists*, London: SPCK.

—— (1907), *A History of Chemical Theories and Laws*, London: Chapman and Hall.

—— and H. Foster Morley (eds) (1894), *Watts' Dictionary of Chemistry. Revised and Entirely Rewritten*, 4 vols, London: Longmans, Green and Co.

Muirhead, J.P. (1854), *The Origin and Progress of the Mechanical Inventions of James Watt*, 3 vols, London: John Murray.

—— (1857), *Winged Words on Chantrey's Woodcocks with Etchings*, London: John Murray.

—— (1858), *The Life of James Watt with Selections from his Correspondence*, London: John Murray.

—— (1859), 'Letter from James P. Muirhead, Esq., to Sir Benjamin C. Brodie, Bart., Pres. R.S., Dated March 8, 1859, relating to the discovery of the composition of water', *Proceedings of the Royal Society of London*, **9**, November 1857–April 1859, 679–81.

—— (ed.) (1846), *The Correspondence of the late James Watt on his Discovery of the Theory of the Composition of Water*, London: John Murray.

Mulkay, Michael (1980), 'Interpretation and the use of rules: The case of the norms of science', *Transactions of the New York Academy of Sciences*, Series 2, **9**, 111–25.

Murray, John (1802), *Elements of Chemistry in Two Volumes*, Edinburgh: William Creech.

—— (1819), *A System of Chemistry*, 4th edn, London: Longman, Hurst, Rees, Orme & Brown.

—— (1822), *Elements of Chemistry in Two Volumes*, revised by John Murray, Edinburgh: Adam Black.

Musgrave, Alan (1976), 'Why did oxygen supplant phlogiston? Research programmes in the Chemical Revolution', in Colin Howson (ed.), *Method and Appraisal in the Physical Sciences. The Critical Background to Modern Science, 1800–1905*, Cambridge: Cambridge University Press, pp. 181–209.

Musson, A.E. and Eric Robinson (1969), *Science and Technology in the Industrial Revolution*, Manchester: Manchester University Press.

Napier Jr, Macvey (ed.) (1879), *Selection from the Correspondence of the late Macvey Napier Esq*, London: Macmillan and Co.

Nicholson, William (1790), *The First Principles of Chemistry*, London: G.G. & J. Robinson.

Nicholson, William (1795), *A Dictionary of Chemistry*, 2 vols, London: G.G. & J. Robinson.

Nickles, Thomas (1990), 'Discovery', in R. Olby et al. (eds), *Companion to the History of Modern Science*, London: Routledge, pp. 148–65.

Oldroyd, David (1990), 'Social and historical studies of science in the classroom?', *Social Studies of Science*, **20**, 747–56.

O'Sullivan, Abigail (2001), 'Henry Dale's Nobel Prize Winning "Discovery"', *Minerva*, **39**, 409–24.

Outram, Dorinda (1978), 'The language of natural power: the *Eloges* of Georges Cuvier and the public knowledge of nineteenth-century science', *History of Science*, **16**, 153–78.

—— (1987), *Georges Cuvier*, Manchester: Manchester University Press.

Parkes, Samuel (1818), *The Chemical Catechism*, 18th edn, London: Baldwin, Cradock & Joy.

Partington, James R. (1928), *The Composition of Water*, London: G. Bell and Sons Ltd.

—— (1962–64), *A History of Chemistry. Vols 3 and 4*, London: Macmillan.

Paul, B.H. (1864), 'Gas', in Henry Watts, *A Dictionary of Chemistry*, 4 vols, London: Longman, Green, Longman, Roberts and Green, vol. 2, pp. 773–82.

Peacock, George (1845), 'Arago and Brougham on Black, Cavendish, Priestley and Watt', *Quarterly Review*, **77**, 105–39.

Perrin, C.E. (1982), 'A reluctant catalyst: Joseph Black and the Edinburgh reception of Lavoisier's chemistry', *Ambix*, **29**, 141–76.

—— (1981), 'The triumph of the Antiphlogistians', in Harry Woolf (ed.), *The Analytic Spirit. Essays in the History of Science In Honor of Henry Guerlac*, Ithaca, NY: Cornell University Press, pp. 40–63.

Playfair, John (1809), 'Account of the steam engine', *Edinburgh Review*, **13**, 311–33.

Playfair, Lyon (1852), 'The chemical principles involved in the manufactures of the Exhibition', in *Lectures on the Results of the Great Exhibition of 1851, Delivered before the Society of Arts, Manufactures and Commerce, at the Suggestion of H.R.H. Prince Albert*, London: David Boyne, pp. 159–208.

Playfair, William (1819), 'Memoir of James Watt Esq. F.R.S.', *New Monthly Magazine*, **12**, December, 576–84.

—— (1819), 'The late JAMES WATT, Esq, F.R.S. &c &c', *Monthly Magazine*, 1 October, 230–39.

Pollard, Sidney (1965), *The Genesis of Modern Management*, Cambridge, MA: Harvard University Press.

Popper, Karl (1959), *The Logic of Scientific Discovery*, London: Hutchinson & Co.

Powell, Baden (1856), 'The life and works of Francis Arago', *Edinburgh Review*, **104**, October, 301–37.

Rehbock, Philip F. (1983), *The Philosophical Naturalists. Themes in Early Nineteenth-Century British Biology*, Madison: The University of Wisconsin Press.

Reid, D.B. (1839), *Elements of Chemistry, Theoretical and Practical*, 3rd edn, Edinburgh: Machlachlan Stewart & Co.

Reidy, M.S. (2000), 'The flux and reflux of science: The study of the tides and the organisation of early Victorian science', unpublished PhD thesis, University of Minnesota.

Roberts, G.K. (1998), '"A Plea for Pure Science": The ascendancy of academia in the making of the English chemist, 1841–1914', in D. Knight and H. Kragh

(eds), *The Making of the Chemist. The Social History of Chemistry in Europe, 1789–1914*, Cambridge: Cambridge University Press, pp. 107–29.

Roberts, Lissa (1991), 'A Word and the World: The significance of naming the calorimeter', *Isis*, **82**, 198–222.

Robinson, Eric (1954), 'Training captains of industry: The education of Matthew Robinson Boulton (1770–1842) and the younger James Watt (1769–1848)', *Annals of Science*, **10**, 301–13.

—— (1954–55), 'An English Jacobin: James Watt, Junior, 1769–1848', *Cambridge Historical Journal*, **11**, 349–55.

—— (1956), 'James Watt and the tea kettle. A myth justified', *History Today*, **6**, April, 261–65.

—— and Douglas McKie (eds) (1970), *Partners in Science. Letters of James Watt and Joseph Black*, Cambridge, MA: Harvard University Press.

—— and A.E. Musson (1969), *James Watt and the Steam Revolution*, New York: Kelley.

Robison, John (1822), *A System of Mechanical Philosophy*, 4 vols, Edinburgh: John Murray.

Rocke, Alan J. (1992–93), 'Pride and prejudice in chemistry: Chauvinism and the pursuit of science', *Bulletin of the History of Chemistry*, **13–14**, 29–40.

—— (2001), *Nationalizing Science. Adolph Wurtz and the Battle for French Chemistry*, Cambridge, MA: The MIT Press.

Roscoe, H.E. (1895), *John Dalton and the Rise of Modern Chemistry*, London: Cassell.

—— and C. Schorlemmer, (1877), *A Treatise on Chemistry. Volume 1. The Non-Metallic Elements*, London: Macmillan & Co.

—— and A. Harden (1896), *A New View of the Origin of Dalton's Atomic Theory*, London: Macmillan.

Russell, Colin A. (1959, 1963), 'The electrochemical theory of Sir Humphry Davy', *Annals of Science*, **15**, 1–25; **19**, 255–71.

—— (1988), '"Rude and Disgraceful Beginnings": A view of history of chemistry from the nineteenth century', *The British Journal for the History of Science*, **21**, 273–94.

Sacks, Oliver (2001) 'Henry Cavendish: An early case of Asperger's syndrome?', *Neurology*, **57**, 1347.

Sarjeant, W.A.S. and J.B. Delair (1980), 'An Irish naturalist in Cuvier's laboratory. The letters of Joseph Pentland 1820–1832', *Bulletin of the British Museum of Natural History (Historical Series)*, **6**, 245–319.

Schaffer, Simon (1986), 'Scientific discoveries and the end of natural philosophy', *Social Studies of Science*, **16**, 387–420.

—— (1990), 'Measuring virtue: Eudiometry, enlightenment and pneumatic medicine', in Andrew Cunningham and Roger French (eds), *The medical enlightenment of the eighteenth century*, Cambridge: Cambridge University Press, pp. 281–318.

—— (1991a), 'The eighteenth brumaire of Bruno Latour', *Studies in the History and Philosophy of Science*, **22**, 174–92.

—— (1991b), 'The history and geography of the intellectual world: Whewell's politics of language', in Menachem Fisch and Simon Schaffer (eds), *William Whewell: A Composite Portrait*, Oxford: Clarendon Press, pp. 201–31.

—— (1994), 'Making up Discovery', in Margaret Boden (ed.), *Dimensions of Creativity*, Cambridge, MA: MIT Press, pp. 13–51.

—— (1994), 'Babbage's Intelligence: Calculating Engines and the Factory System', *Critical Inquiry*, **21**, 203–27.

Schofield, Robert E. (1964), 'Still more on the Water Controversy', *Chymia*, **9**, 71–76.

Schorlemmer, C. (1879), *The Rise and Development of Organic Chemistry*, Manchester: J.E. Cornish.

Schuster, John and Richard Yeo (eds) (1986), *The Politics and Rhetoric of Scientific Method*, Dordrecht: Reidel.

Scott, Pam, Evelleen Richards and Brian Martin (1990), 'Captives of controversy: The myth of the neutral social researcher in contemporary scientific controversies', *Science, Technology & Human Values*, **15**, 474–94.

Secord, Anne (1994), 'Science in the pub: Artisan botanists in early nineteenth-century Lancashire', *History of Science*, **32**, 269–315.

Secord, James A. (2000), *Victorian Sensation. The Extraordinary Publication, Reception and Secret Authorship of* Vestiges of the Natural History of Creation, Chicago: The University of Chicago Press.

Shairp, J.C., P.G. Tait and A. Adams-Reilly (1873), *Life and Letters of James David Forbes, F.R.S.*, London: Macmillan & Co.

Shapin, Steven (1984), 'Brewster and the Edinburgh career in science', in A.D. Morrison-Low and J.J.R. Christie (eds), *"Martyr of Science": Sir David Brewster 1781–1868*, Edinburgh: Royal Scottish Museum, pp. 17–23.

—— (1984), 'Pump and Circumstance: Boyle's literary technology', *Social Studies of Science*, **14**, 481–520.

—— (1984), 'Talking History: Reflections on discourse analysis', *Isis*, **75**, 125–28.

—— (1988), 'Following scientists around', *Social Studies of Science*, **18**, 533–50.

—— (1998), 'The philosopher and the chicken: On the dietetics of disembodied knowledge', in S. Shapin and C. Lawrence (eds), *Science Incarnate: Historical Embodiments of Natural Knowledge*, Chicago: The University of Chicago Press, pp. 21–50.

Shattock, Joanne (1989), *Politics and Reviewers: The* Edinburgh *and the* Quarterly *in the early Victorian Age*, Leicester: Leicester University Press.

Smeaton, W.A. (1971), 'Some comments on James Watt's published account of his work on steam and steam engines', *Notes and Records of the Royal Society of London*, **26**, 35–42.

Smiles, Samuel (1858), 'Review of Muirhead, *Life of James Watt,* Muirhead, *The Origin and Progress of the Mechanical Inventions of James Watt* and George Williamson, *Memorials of the Lineage, Early Life, Education, and Development of the Genius of James Watt*', *Quarterly Review*, **104**, 410–51.

—— (1863), *Industrial Biography: Iron Workers and Tool Makers*, London: John Murray.

—— (1865), *Lives of Boulton and Watt*, London: John Murray.

Smith, Crosbie (1998), *The Science of Energy. A Cultural History of Energy Physics in Victorian Britain*, London: The Athlone Press.

Smith, Robert W. (1989), 'The Cambridge Network in action: The discovery of Neptune', *Isis*, **80**, 395–422.

—— (1991), 'A national observatory transformed: Greenwich in the 19th century', *Journal for the History of Astronomy*, **45**, 5–20.

Stansfield, Dorothy A. (1984), *Thomas Beddoes M.D. 1760–1808*, Dordrecht: Reidel.

Stansfield, Dorothy A. and Ronald G. Stansfield (1986), 'Dr. Thomas Beddoes and James Watt: Preparatory work 1794–96 for the Bristol Pneumatic Institute', *Medical History*, **30**, 276–302.

Stewart, Larry (2002), 'Putting on Airs: Science, medicine and polity in the late eighteenth century', in T. Levere and G.L'E. Turner (eds), *Discussing Chemistry and Steam. The Minutes of a Coffee House Philosophical Society 1780–1787*, Oxford: Oxford University Press, pp. 207–55.

Stewart, Robert (1985), *Henry Brougham 1778–1868. His Public Career*, London: The Bodley Head.

Tann, Jennifer (ed.) (1981), *The Selected Papers of Boulton and Watt, Volume 1*, Cambridge, MA: The MIT Press.

Theerman, Paul (1985), 'Unaccustomed role: The scientist as historical biographer – Two nineteenth-century portrayals of Newton', *Biography*, **8**, 145–62.

Thomson, Robert Dundas (1848), *School Chemistry: or, Practical Rudiments of the Science*, London: Longman, Brown, Green & Longmans.

Thomson, Thomas (1813), 'A biographical account of the Honourable Henry Cavendish', *Annals of Philosophy*, **1**, 5–15.

Thorpe, T.E. (1891), 'Presidential Address, Section B', *Report of the Sixtieth Meeting of the British Association for the Advancement of Science held at Leeds in September 1890*, London: John Murray, pp. 761–71.

—— (1902), *Essays in Historical Chemistry*, London: Macmillan & Co. Ltd.

Tilden, William A. (1886), *Books on Chemistry. Birmingham Reference Library Lectures*, London: Simpkin, Marshall and Co.

Tilleard, James (1860), *On Elementary School Books*, London: Longmans, Brown, Green, Longmans and Roberts.

Titchmarsh, P.F. (1966), 'The Michell–Cavendish experiment', *The School Science Review*, **47**, 320–30.

Todhunter, Isaac (1876), *William Whewell, D.D. Master of Trinity College Cambridge: An Account of his Writings with Selections from his Literary and Scientific Correspondence*, 2 vols, London: Macmillan.

Torrens, Hugh (1994), 'Jonathan Hornblower (1753–1815) and the steam engine: A historiographic analysis', in D. Smith (ed.), *Perceptions of Great Engineers: Fact and Fantasy*, London: Science Museum for the Newcomen Society, National Museums and Galleries on Merseyside and the University of Liverpool, pp. 23–34.

Ure, Andrew (1821), *A Dictionary of Chemistry on the Basis of Mr Nicholson's*, London: Underwood.

Waterston, Charles D. (1997), *Collections in Context: The Museum of the Royal Society of Edinburgh and the Inception of a National Museum of Scotland*, Edinburgh: National Museums of Scotland.

Watt, James (1784), 'Thoughts on the constituent parts of water and of dephlogisticated air; with an account of some experiments on that subject. In a letter from Mr James Watt, Engineer, to Mr. De Luc, F.R.S.', *Philosophical Transactions of the Royal Society of London*, **74**, 329–53.

Watt Jr, James (1824), 'Watt, James', *Supplement* to the fourth, fifth and sixth editions of the *Encyclopaedia Britannica*, **6**, 778–85.

Watts, Henry (1864), *A Dictionary of Chemistry and the Allied Branches of Other Sciences*, 4 vols, London: Longman, Green, Longman, Roberts and Green.

Weld, Charles R. (1848), *A History of the Royal Society, with Memoirs of the Presidents, compiled from authentic documents*, 2 vols, London: John W. Parker.

Whewell, W. (1837), *History of the Inductive Sciences, From the Earliest to the Present time*, London: John W. Parker, 3rd edn, revised, 1857.

—— (1840), *The Philosophy of the Inductive Sciences*, 2 vols, London: John W. Parker.

—— (1841), *The Mechanics of Engineering. Intended for Use in Universities, and in Colleges of Engineers*, London and Cambridge: John W. Parker and J. & J. Deighton.

—— (1852), 'The general bearing of the Great Exhibition on the progress of art and science', in *Lectures on the Results of the Great Exhibition of 1851, Delivered before the Society of Arts, Manufactures and Commerce, at the Suggestion of H.R.H. Prince Albert*, London: David Boyne, pp. 3–34.

Williams, Robert B. (1995), 'Accounting for management as an expression of eighteenth century rationalism: Two case studies', unpublished PhD thesis, University of Wollongong.

Williamson, George (1840), *Letters Respecting the Watt Family*, Greenock: privately printed.

Wilson, George (1845), 'Lord Brougham's Men of Letters and Science', *British Quarterly Review*, **2**, October, 197–263.

—— (1851), *The Life of the Honble Henry Cavendish*, London: The Cavendish Society.

—— (1858), 'Robert Brown and the water controversy', *The Athenaeum*, 26 June, 819.

—— (1859), 'On the recent vindication of the priority of Cavendish as the discoverer of the composition of water', *Proceedings of the Royal Society of Edinburgh*, **4**, 205–208.

Wilson, Jessie Aitken (1860), *Memoir of George Wilson MD, FRSE*, Edinburgh: Edmonston & Douglas.

Woolgar, Steve (1976), 'Writing an intellectual history of scientific development: The use of discovery accounts', *Social Studies of Science*, **6**, 395–422.

—— (1980), 'Discovery: Logic and sequence in a scientific text', in K. Knorr, R. Krohn and R. Whitley (eds), *The Social Process of Scientific Investigation*, Dordrecht: Reidel, pp. 239–68.

Wurtz, Charles Adolphe (1869), *Dictionnaire de chimie pure et appliquée*, Paris: L. Hachette.

Yeo, Richard (1985), 'An idol of the marketplace: Baconianism in nineteenth-century Britain, 1830–1917', *History of Science*, **23**, 251–98.

—— (1988), 'Genius, method and morality: Images of Newton in Britain, 1760–1860', *Science in Context*, **2**, 257–84.

—— (1993), *Defining Science: William Whewell, Natural Knowledge, and Public Debate in Early Victorian Britain*, Cambridge: Cambridge University Press.

—— (1996), 'Alphabetical lives: Scientific biography in historical dictionaries and

encyclopaedias', in M. Shortland and R. Yeo (eds), *Telling Lives in Science: Essays on Scientific Biography*, Cambridge: Cambridge University Press, pp. 139–69.

—— (2001), *Encyclopaedic Visions: Scientific Dictionaries and Enlightenment Culture*, Cambridge: Cambridge University Press.

Index

Académie des Sciences 7–8, 40, 105–9,
    114, 218–19, 245
  Comptes rendus of 110
Adams, John Couch 13–14, 110, 124
Aikin, A. 66
Aikin, C.R. 66
air 54, 210, 250
  dephlogisticated 14, 28, 42, 56, 68, 78,
    190, 250, 271
  inflammable 14, 28, 42–3, 54, 56, 68–9,
    77, 190, 210, 271
  nitrous 55
  phlogistication of 55–6
Airy, George 24, 138–9, 201, 282
  Astronomer Royal 143
  engineering and 143
Albert, Prince Consort 212
Alborn, Timothy L. 138 n. 27
Andersonian Institution 74
Annales de Chemie et Physique 123
Apothecaries Act (1815) 75
Arago, Dominique François Jean 1, 7–8,
    22–3, 38, 83, 89, 91, 103–27, 129,
    159, 169–70, 197, 218, 222–3, 230,
    233 n. 73, 241–2, 254, 274
  Brewster and 159
  Cavendish and 110, 242
  character of 122–4
  discovery and 109–10
  early years 108
  éloge of James Watt (1834) 105–7, 111,
    113, 114–17, 119
  Eloge of James Watt (1839) 1, 21, 98,
    103, 106, 109, 111, 121, 126, 160,
    177, 216
  French industrial development and 105–
    7, 280
  Muirhead visits 223, 233–4
  Perpetual Secretary of Académie 106–8,
    123
  political activities 107, 109, 114, 117,
    123–6
  portrait of 108

reform of Académie and 105, 107, 109,
    280
  reputation in Britain 123–6, 140, 237
  response to Harcourt 219
  uses of éloges 105–7, 109, 122
  visits Watt Jr 103, 106, 111–12
Arkwright, Richard 120, 170
Armstrong, Henry 258
Ashworth, William J. 138 n. 27
Athenaeum (Club) 218
Athenaeum (Journal) 244–5
attributional model, *see* discovery

BAAS, *see* British Association for the
    Advancement of Science
Babbage, Charles 8, 123, 125, 136–40, 142,
    282
  patents and 140
Bacon, Francis 157, 181
Baily, Francis 140–41, 255
  Cavendish experiment repeated by 201–
    2
Banks, Joseph 30–32, 44–6, 100, 245
  'Banksian Learned Empire' 8, 137
Barnes, Barry 6, 13, 16, 281
Barrow, John 94, 96
Beddoes, Thomas 53–4, 78
Bennett, J.J. 217–18
  executor of Brown 245
  letter to Royal Society of London 246
Bensaude-Vincent, Bernadette 37–8
Bernays, Albert 267–8
Berthelot, P.E.M. 7, 249–50
Berthollet, Claude Louis 107
Berzelius, Jöns Jacob 42, 167, 241
Biot, J.B. 108–9
Birmingham
  Soho Engine Manufactory 88, 90
  Soho Foundry 88
Black, Adam 254
Black, Joseph 29–30, 35, 38, 47, 50–51, 60,
    69–70, 77, 79 n. 66, 90, 93, 158, 167,
    180–81, 190, 225, 229

Brougham praises 170–74
career 47 n. 60
Edinburgh lectures of 50, 69, 75–8, 115, 172 n. 7
Glasgow lectures of 75
latent heat 48 n. 61, 49, 115, 172
Lavoisian system and 53–4, 76, 172
relations with Watt 75, 79, 80 n. 71, 158, 180–81, 255, 280
students of 79
work on heat 48–51
Blagden, Charles 31–2, 33 n. 21, 38, 46–7, 57, 100, 110, 114, 126 n. 82, 119, 191, 217, 250, 260
Brougham accuses of deceit 176
modifies Cavendish's manuscript 182, 241
visit to Paris (1783) 41
Blake, Henry Wollaston 89
Bloor, David 5 n. 8
Boulton, Matthew 51, 84, 85 n. 6, 86, 90, 93 n. 33, 96
Boulton, Matthew Robinson 86, 88–90, 96, 114, 117, 120, 178, 222
Boulton, Watt & Co. 83, 86, 88, 91
Boyle, Robert 195, 236
Brande, William Thomas 63, 73, 74 n. 53, 176, 241
Brannigan, Augustine 6, 13, 15 n. 6, 16
Brewster, David 8, 22, 32, 57, 97, 102, 112, 129, 140–41, 150, 159 n. 90, 168 n. 118, 183, 204, 226, 247, 281
article on Watt in *Edinburgh Encyclopaedia* 112 n. 22, 158–9, 165
'Cambridge Network' and 153, 155, 163–4
career of 154–5
conversion to Watt 153, 164–8, 215, 281
debates on light 156, 282
distributes discovery between Cavendish and Watt 153, 162
edits Robison's *System* 157
North British Review article (1846) 153, 164–7, 237
patents 140, 154–5
portrait of 165
review of *Eloge* 153, 159–62, 217
Watt and 158–9
Watt camp and 153, 157–8, 163
Whewell and 155 n. 76, 156–7, 164
British & Foreign Medico-Chirurgical Review 244

British Association for the Advancement of Science (BAAS) 1–2, 8, 116, 129, 200, 204–5
'boundary-management' and 141, 143–5
Brewster and 155–6, 162
experts and lay publics 152
'Gentlemen of Science' and 8, 133, 138, 140, 142 n. 38, 153, 168
hot blast technique and 144–5
mechanical sciences and 141–2, 145
meetings 8, 103, 105, 111–12, 116, 123, 136–7, 159, 205, 221–2, 234, 250
patents and 144
research funds of 140–41
voluntarist tradition and 140
British Quarterly Review 206, 208, 225–6, 229, 236, 241, 244
Brock, W.H. 206, 236 n. 82
Brodie, Benjamin Collins 245–6
Brooke, John Hedley 155
Brougham, Henry 2, 8–9, 21–3, 83, 89, 91, 110, 114, 120, 125–6, 136, 144, 153, 169–78, 183, 207, 221–7, 231–2, 242, 276
Brewster and 154–5, 163
Cavendish and 177–8, 223–4, 227
Discourse of Natural Theology 176
discovery and 173–4, 177
Edinburgh Review and 170
Forbes on 256
Harcourt attacked by 153 n. 69
hears Arago's *éloge* 169
'Historical Note' to *Eloge* 104, 106, 119, 121, 161, 176–7, 216
inscriptions for Watt monuments 61 n. 5, 97–8, 103, 176
Lavoisian system and 173–4
life of Cavendish in *Lives* 224–5
life of Lavoisier in *Lives* 225
life of Watt in *Lives* 223–4, 229
Lives of Men of Letters and Science 101, 170, 223, 226
Lord Chancellor in Grey government 169
Neilson patent and 144, 175, 185
optical experiments with Brewster 178
patent laws and 119, 174–6
Peacock on 228–9
portrait of 171
review of Black's *Lectures* 170, 172
scientific work of 170
SDUK and 261–2
water controversy and 173 n. 9, 176–8

Watt Jr and 223–33
Watt and 158 n. 87, 178
Watt used as symbol by 174–5, 280
Wilson on 232, 238
Brown, Robert 136, 229, 241, 246
advises Harcourt 218, 245
death of 245
denied access to Watt's correspondence
218
water controversy and 217–19, 245
Buckland, William 111, 140
Bud, Robert 202
Bunsen, Robert 249
Burke, Edmund 85–6, 118–20, 122, 161
Burlington, Lord, *see* Cavendish, William
Butler, F.H. 258
Butterfield, Herbert 34

caloric 40
Cambridge Network 138–40, 155, 199–200,
238, 282
engineering and 142–3
Cambridge, University of 138, 199
Campbell, Anne 178
Campbell, Miss Jane 116
Campbell, Mrs Marion 116–17
Cannon, Susan Faye 138
Cantor, Geoffrey 170 n. 4
Carnegie, Andrew 275
Cavendish Society 24, 204–6, 236–7, 243,
245
Life of Cavendish and 206
Cavendish, Henry 1–4, 19, 25, 29, 32 n. 17,
35–6, 38–47, 54, 60, 62–70, 72–8, 80–
81, 92, 99, 101, 126–7, 131, 149–50,
160–62, 173, 182, 190–91, 236, 242,
248, 260, 271
Asperger's Syndrome and 194
Cavendish experiment 199–200
Chambers's Encyclopaedia on 262–3
character of 9, 133 n. 10, 134, 193–200,
216, 244, 257–8
chemists and 202–5, 249, 258, 281
Electrical Researches of 199
Encyclopaedia Britannica on 69–72,
254, 257–8
experimental journal of 182, 220–21
'Experiments on Air' 28–32, 55–6, 119,
176, 182
Forbes' idol 235
'Gentlemen of Science' and 199–202
honesty of 198, 234

image of 5, 24–5, 35, 66–7, 150, 168,
197, 199–202, 213 n. 60, 214, 249,
251, 275, 281, 283
Lavoisian system and 55
misdating of paper 33 n. 20, 101, 126 n.
82, 238, 255
Peacock on 229
precision of 20, 199–201, 249, 258
unpublished work of 195–8, 227
Wilson on 194, 212, 235, 243–4, 247
Cavendish, William (Lord Burlington, later
7th Duke of Devonshire) 163, 196,
203, 220, 227
Cawood, John 106
Chantrey, Francis 97, 111, 115, 136
Chaptal, J.A. 107
Chemical Revolution 6, 27, 35, 47, 56; *see
also* chemistry
composition of water and 39–47
constructivist perspectives 36
historiography of 27, 34–9, 57
Chemical Society of London 24, 137, 202–
4, 269
chemistry 34–9, 70; *see also* Chemical
Revolution
as 'English science' 249
British chemical community 202–5, 281,
283
defined by Black 48
defined by Whewell 147–8
discipline of 9, 40, 204, 212, 280
French 38, 53, 60, 73, 76–7, 172–3, 249
German 38
industry and 213
lectures on 61, 75–80
practical training 203
textbooks 7, 21, 61, 64–7, 205, 265–74
Christie, J.R.R. 168 n. 118
Cockburn, Henry 186–7
Collins, Harry 21, 61, 201 n. 29
composition of water 2, 14, 28–32, 50–54,
68; *see also* water controversy
Cooper, Thomas 85
core set 21, 61
Corrie, John 102, 165
Crosland, Maurice 34, 107, 110
Cullen, William 49, 79 n. 66
Cuvier, Georges 107, 109–111
Eloge of Cavendish 121 n. 66, 196–7

Daguerre, L.J. Mandé 109, 126
Dalton, John 42, 60, 79

Daumas, Maurice 40
Davy, Humphry 37, 54, 60, 66–7, 73, 75,
  131–2, 134, 196, 260, 275
  Cavendish and 66–7, 102–3, 196 n. 14
  composition of water and 132 n. 7
  Greenock monument meeting 102
  visits Watt Jr 102, 132 n. 7
Davy, John 229
Day, George 206, 237
De Luc, Jean André 30–32, 45–6, 51–2, 75,
  84, 100–101, 246
De Morgan, Augustus 201
Derby Philosophical Society 85
Devonshire Commission 203
discovery 1, 11–16, 25–6, 41–2, 73, 109,
  133, 272; *see also* priority; Neptune
  attributional model of 5–6, 12–22, 37,
    59, 283
  Brewster on 156, 168
  Brougham on 173–4, 177
  Brown's approach to 218
  composition of water 14, 27, 42, 59, 67,
    132, 212
  discourse analysis and 15–16
  'expert' vs democratic judgement of
    151–2, 166, 189, 191, 282
  finitist account of 6, 280
  Forbes on 150, 164, 257
  Herschel on 139 n. 31, 149, 150 n. 61,
    164
  invention and 158 n. 87, 184, 191
  Kuhn on 12–13
  legal approach to 101, 103, 160 n. 96,
    166, 169, 183–4, 189–90
  Muirhead on 18, 180–83, 241, 246
  multiple 249
  myths 26 n. 28
  objectivist account of 11–12, 280
  Popper on 12
  social process of 1
  Whewell on 18–19, 148, 152, 215–16
  Wilson on 19–20, 132 n. 9, 210, 246–7
Donnelly, James 203–4
Donovan, Arthur 41–2, 50 n. 66
Dumas, Jean Baptiste 37, 39, 167, 219–20,
  231, 234, 240–41
Dunlop, Colin 185
Dyck, David R. 50, 53

Earth
  physics of 199–200
Edelstein, Sidney M. 44–5, 47

Edinburgh Academy of Physics 170
Edinburgh New Philosophical Journal 21,
  116, 122, 216
Edinburgh Philosophical Journal 154
Edinburgh Review 9, 22, 91, 124, 152–3,
  156–7, 159–60, 164, 170, 186–9, 207–
  8, 215, 217, 222, 233, 237–8, 240
Edinburgh School of Arts 267
Edinburgh, University of 48, 61, 79, 154,
  205–6, 267
  Chemical Society 77–8
  Natural History Society 77, 78 n. 65
Edison, Thomas 24 n. 27
Eller, Johann Theodor 51
Empson, William 238
encyclopaedias 7, 9, 21, 61, 67–74, 253–65
  Chambers's Encyclopaedia 262–3, 265
  Edinburgh Encyclopaedia 154, 158–9
  Encyclopaedia Britannica 48, 53–4, 67–
    72, 80, 94–6, 99–102, 115, 157,
    253–9, 261
  Encyclopaedia Edinensis 72
  Encyclopaedia Metropolitana 259–61
  Globe Encyclopaedia 264
  London Encyclopaedia 63, 72
  National Encyclopaedia 262, 264
  Penny Cyclopaedia 261
eudiometer 28, 55–6; *see also* air
Ewart, Peter 113
Ewing, James A. 258–9

Fairbairn, William 142, 144
Fara, Patricia 150 n. 61, 199 n. 23
Faraday, Michael 115, 149, 197–8, 242,
  260
finitism 13–14, 280
Forbes, Edward 134, 205
Forbes, James David 24, 98–9, 151, 163,
  196, 201, 220–21, 235, 275–6, 281–2
  Brewster and 155
  Brougham and 256
  Cambridge Network and 140
  Cavendish and 257–8
  discovery and 150
  'Dissertation' in *Britannica* 151, 254–8
  Watt and 256–7
Fourcroy, Antoine François de 61–3, 66, 73,
  85
Fownes, George 268–9
Fox–Talbot, W. Henry 109
Frankland, Edward 204
Freiberg School of Mines 84

French Revolution 85–6
Fry, Joseph 32
Fyfe, Andrew 231–2

Gay–Lussac, Joseph Louis 107, 123
Geological Society of London 137
Gibson, J.W. 243
Gibson, James 117
Gieryn, Tom 24
Gillispie, Charles 34, 39–41
Glasgow 48, 185, 221–2
Glasgow Philosophical Society 185
Glasgow, University of 49, 97, 268
Gleig, George 70
Godson, Richard 184 n. 43
Golinski, Jan 2, 79 n. 66
Gooding, David 149
Graham, Thomas 24, 167, 204–6, 213, 231,
    241, 269, 281
Great Exhibition (1851) 212–13
Greenock 118
    Arago visits 115
    monument meeting 102–3
Greenock Grammar School 97
Greenock Philosophical Society 250
Greenock Public Library 83
Gregory, Olinthus 91, 157
Gregory, William 81 n. 74, 267
Grove, William 204 n. 35, 260
Guerlac, Henry 41

Hales, Stephen 38
Hall, A. Rupert 45
Hamilton, Gilbert 24, 30, 89
Harcourt, William (Home Secretary) 213 n.
    60
Harcourt, William Vernon 1–2, 18–20, 24,
    55, 105, 124, 141–7, 178, 183, 196–8,
    226–31, 237, 251, 260, 282
    Address (1840) 130 n. 2, 134, 152, 196,
        220–21
    address to BAAS (1839) 8, 126 n. 82,
        129, 134–5, 145, 152, 216
    Brougham attacked by 230
    Cavendish and 129–32, 148, 196, 220
    Cavendish family and 220 n. 19
    charcoal argument 20, 190, 230–31
    early years 129
    founder of BAAS 140
    'Letter to Brougham' 230–31, 234, 245
    Muirhead meets 244–5
    Peacock and 227

portrait of 130
    Watt and 196, 220, 231
    Whewell assists 220
Hartop, Henry 144
Hatchett, Charles 176, 241
Henry, William 102, 114, 165, 167, 183
Herschel, John 8, 123, 125, 136, 138, 236,
    259, 282
    discovery and 139 n. 31, 149, 164
Herschel, William 109–10
Hills, Richard L. 4 n. 7, 48 n. 62
Hodgkinson, Eaton 144
Hoefer, Frederick 237
Hofmann, A.W. 204, 269
Hope, Thomas Charles 48, 50, 53, 75–7, 79,
    102, 158, 164–5
    Edinburgh lectures of 80, 81 n. 74
Horner, Leonard 115
Hudson, James 195–6
Humboldt, Alexander von 125
Huxley, Aldous 193, 195

Institute of Chemistry 203
Institution of Civil Engineers 91–2
    Airy and 143
    BAAS and 142
iron production
    hot blast technique 144, 185

Jameson, Robert 116, 122, 154, 179–80
Jeffrey, Francis 8–9, 22–3, 91, 159, 169–70,
    183, 191–2, 208, 215, 235–6
    article on water controversy 186–91, 240
    Edinburgh Review and 186, 238
    filial project and 187
    legal approach to controversy 189–91
    Napier and 188
    obituary of Watt 94, 187
    Watt Jr and 187–8
    Wilson and 238–40
Jeremy, David J. 112 n. 17
Jones, Peter 84, 86, 90
Jungnickel, Christa 3, 47, 55–6, 194, 200

Keir, James 54
King's College, London 203
Kirkaldie, George 78
Kirwan, Richard 190
Knight, Charles 224 n. 30, 234, 276
Knight, David 60, 63, 66 n. 19
Kopp, Hermann 43, 237, 271
Kuhn, Thomas 12, 36

Lakatos, Imre 36
Laplace, Pierre Simon 30, 66
Larmor, Joseph 199
latent heat 50–52, 68, 115; *see also* Black, Joseph
Lavoisier, Antoine Laurent 1, 7, 14, 19, 25, 30, 32–3, 35, 37–41, 47, 50, 54, 57, 62–7, 69–71, 73, 75–7, 85, 100, 177, 222, 250, 260, 270–72, 274
    image of 37–9
    'Memoir on Heat' 41
    theory of combustion 40
    Traité élémentaire de chimie 37
    view of Priestley 41
Leslie, John 254
Leverrier, Urbain Jean-Joseph 13–14, 110, 124, 126
Liebig, Justus 268
Lockhart, J.G. 229, 234
Lunar Society of Birmingham 45, 85
Lunn, Francis 259–61

Macaulay, Thomas Babington 256
Macintosh, Charles 185
MacLeod, Christine 4 n. 7
Macmillan, Daniel 206, 209, 244
Macquer, Pierre Joseph 62, 66, 70, 73
Manchester Constitutional Society 85
Manchester Literary and Philosophical Society 85
Marcet, Jane 65
Marsden, Ben 4 n. 7
Maty, P.H. 32 n. 14
Maxwell, James Clerk 195
McCormmach, Russell 3, 31, 47, 55–6 194, 200
McEvoy, John 34, 38
McKie, Douglas 34
Mechanics' Institutes 8, 91, 174, 185 n. 45
Meldola, Raphael 258
Merton, Robert King 3–4, 166, 194–5
    Cavendish and the norms of science 133 n. 10, 195
Miller, Margaret 84
Morrell, Jack 138, 140–42
Moseley, Henry 268–9
Muir, M.M. Pattison 274 n. 59
Muirhead, James Patrick 2, 8–9, 18–19, 22–4, 44, 65, 71, 74, 83, 90, 101, 122–3, 134–5, 144–5, 159, 161, 163–4, 166, 169, 175–6, 178–86, 188, 190–91, 207–8, 215–17, 219–26, 229–41

Arago's *Eloge* praised by 216
argues from synonymity and priority 180–84
Brougham and 223–5
Cavendish and 182
charcoal argument and 238–9
discovery viewed empirically by 183, 231, 241
early years 178
edits *Correspondence ... composition of water* 179–80, 232–3
filial project and 179, 243
Harcourt and 216, 221, 245
legal approach 183–4
letter to Royal Society of London 246
Life of James Watt 186, 243, 245, 247, 255
marries Katharine Elizabeth Boulton 178
orchestrates response to Harcourt 222–3
Origin and Progress of the Mechanical Inventions of James Watt 243, 247
response to *British Quarterly* article 225–6
speech at Neilson dinner 185–6
translation of *Eloge* 136, 152, 179, 216
Watt Jr and 178
Whewell and 230
Wilson and 232–3, 238–40
Wilson's *Life* and 243–4
Muirhead, Lockhart 178
Muirhead, Robert 116
Mulkay, Michael 133 n. 10, 181 n. 30, 199 n. 22
Multhauf, Robert 34
Murchison, Roderick 124, 135, 221
Murray, John (publisher) 229, 234–5, 247
Murray, John Jr 64
Murray, John MD Sr 64
Musgrave, Alan 36

Napier, Macvey 71, 94–6, 153, 159, 188, 208, 217, 222, 236, 238, 253–4, 261
Neilson, James Beaumont 144, 185
    patent on hot blast technique 144, 185
    victory dinner for 185–6
Neptune
    discovery of 13–14, 110, 124–5, 237, 280
Newton, Isaac 35, 133, 172, 174, 177, 181, 195, 199, 257, 280
Nicholson, William 62–3, 73–4

Owens College, Manchester 203–4, 249

Oxford University 140

Papin, Denis 118, 122
Parkes, Samuel 65
Partington J.R., 27, 34, 42–5, 47, 54–5
patents 118–19, 161, 169, 174–6, 184–6,
    189
  BAAS and 140–41, 144
  Brewster on 155
Paul, Benjamin H. 42, 270, 273
Peacock, George 24, 55, 99, 124, 138–9,
    145, 183, 198, 209–10, 227, 228 n. 50,
    233–4, 241, 251, 282
  on Cavendish 131 n. 4, 229
  on filial project 228–9
  on Watt 131 n. 4, 228
  Quarterly Review article by 210, 225,
    227–9
Peel, Robert 90
Pentland, Joseph Barclay 111, 114–17, 120,
    170, 218
Perpignan 116
Perrin, C.E. 76
Pharmaceutical Society of London 202
Phillips, John 140
Philosophical Magazine 230, 232–4, 245
phlogiston 2, 33–6, 40, 42–3, 53, 56, 67,
    69, 78, 131, 133, 162, 183, 190, 210,
    229, 247, 250–51, 272
Playfair, John 91, 157
Playfair, Lyon 214, 281
  Cavendish and 213
  Society of Arts lecture by (1851) 212–13
Playfair, William 93
Popper, Karl 12
Powell, Baden 124–5, 140
Priestley Jr, Joseph 84
Priestley, Joseph 20, 28–33, 35–6, 38–42,
    44–7, 51–2, 55–6, 60, 62–4, 66, 68–
    71, 73, 75–7, 100, 131, 133, 265
  compared with Cavendish 198
  Harcourt on 133
  image of 180–81
  inflammable air 190
  Wilson on 210–211
priority 151, 184, 191; *see also* discovery
  'argument from difference' 17–18
  'argument from synonymity and priority'
    17–18, 22, 54, 99, 135, 167, 177,
    189, 211
  invention and discovery compared 176
  open communication and 110, 181 n. 30

politics of 149

Quarterly Review 99, 222, 226–7, 229–30,
    232–4

Ramsay, William 204
Rennie, George 112–13
Rennie, John 92, 94, 96, 115
Roberts, G.K. 202
Robinson, Eric 84, 116 n. 39
Robison, John 49, 53–4, 69, 70 n. 53, 75–6,
    78–9, 80 n. 71, 94, 97–9, 115, 157–8,
    167, 170, 172–3, 228, 255
Roscoe, Henry Enfield 204, 249, 271–2
Royal Astronomical Society of London 137
  Cavendish experiment repeated by 201
Royal College of Chemistry 202–4
Royal Institution 67, 75
Royal Society of Edinburgh 170, 235, 255,
    282
Royal Society of London 8, 30–33, 44–5,
    62, 119, 137, 156, 245–6
  archives of 103, 176, 245
  Brewster and 164, 167
  Copley Medal of 123
  dissensions of (1783–4) 31, 45, 167, 168
    n. 117
  Philosophical Transactions 22, 28, 31,
    52, 68, 79, 100, 161, 170, 177, 200,
    242, 282
  Weld's *History* of 241–2
Russell, Colin 273 n. 58

Sabine, Edward 221
Sacks, Oliver 193–4
Schaffer, Simon 16–17, 25, 56 n. 83, 151 n.
    65
Scheele, C.W. 70
Schofield, Robert E. 45–7
Schorlemmer, Carl 271–2
science
  cultural politics of 137–52
  'pure' and 'applied' 203–4, 214, 280, 282
  relationship with technology 8, 104, 107,
    144 n. 42, 212, 280
  textbooks and 265
  transformations in 8
Science and Art Department 203, 266
Scottish Industrial Museum 206, 213
SDUK, *see* Society for the Diffusion of
    Useful Knowledge
Secord, James A. 280 n. 1

Shapin, Steven 155 n. 73, 194
    Cavendish and dietetics 195
Smeaton, John 115
Smiles, Samuel 126, 247
    image of Watt 248, 262 n. 30
    Lives of Boulton and Watt 248
    refused access to Watt papers 247
    reviews Muirhead's *Life of James Watt*
        247
    water controversy and 248 n. 131
Smith, Sidney 170
Smyth, W.H. 125
Society for Promoting Christian Knowledge
    276
Society for the Diffusion of Useful
    Knowledge (SDUK) 261–2, 276
Society of Arcueil 107–8
Society of Arts, Commerce and
    Manufactures 212
Society of Chemical Industry 203
Southern, John 79, 158
Spectator 244
Stewart, M.S. 102–3

Tann, Jennifer 88
Taylor, John 115
Telford, Thomas 115
textbooks, *see* chemistry
Thackray, Arnold 138, 140, 142
Thomson, Allen 232
Thomson, John 63
Thomson, Robert Dundas 268
Thomson, Thomas 24, 70–71, 74, 193, 253,
    268
Thorpe, T.E. 222, 249, 258, 281
    career of 249–50
    lecture on Cavendish 248
    Watt Anniversary lecture (1898) 250
Tilden, William A. 266, 271
Torrens, Hugh 92
Traill, Thomas Stewart 151, 254, 261
Tuffen, John 85
Turner, Charles Hampden 97, 218

University College, London 203–4
Ure, Andrew 74, 79

Vaughan, Robert 244
Volta, Alessandro 28

Walker, James 91–2, 142
Walker, Thomas 85

Warltire, John 28, 46, 56, 62, 66, 68, 70,
    73
water, *see* composition of water; water
    controversy; air
water controversy 2; *see also* composition
    of water
    attributional model and 17, 253
    attributional survey 6–7, 9, 59–81, 251,
        253, 255–75
    Brewster on 161
    Carnegie on 275
    charcoal argument 20, 29, 46, 190, 210,
        238–40
    chemists and 204–5
    course of 215–51
    'expert' and 'popular' forums 22, 276
    Forbes on 256–8
    Herschel on 139 n. 31
    historiography of 5
    ideological struggles and 152, 168, 281
    legal approach to 23–5, 169, 176, 183–4,
        189–91
    literature of uplift and 275–6
    nationalism and 3, 25, 153, 188, 226,
        274–6, 281, 283
    phases of 3, 25, 46, 54, 57, 60, 129, 241,
        279
    resolution of 6, 25, 216, 248, 251, 253,
        283
    Smiles on 248 n. 131
    textbooks and 265–74
    Watt correspondence about 93–4
    Whewell's approach to 147–9
Watt Jr, James 2, 22–4, 61, 65, 67, 74, 153,
    158, 163, 176, 180, 184, 188, 207–8,
    217–18, 224, 232, 239, 281
    article on Watt in *Britannica* 71–2, 94–6,
        99–102, 115, 158–9, 187, 253–5
    BAAS and 92, 137, 141, 143–4, 234,
        282
    Brewster and 159–60, 163
    Brougham and 225
    communications with Arago 105, 113–22
    death of 242
    discovery viewed empirically by 83, 99–
        101, 104
    early years 83–5
    engine experiments 89 n. 15
    engineers and 91–2
    family business and 86, 88–90, 117 n. 44
    filial project 7, 83, 92–104, 126, 157–8,
        223, 228–9, 243

French Revolution and 84–6
Harcourt's address and 135
health fails 180
portrait of 87, 242
Preface to *Correspondence* 101–2
Radnorshire estates 91, 114, 117, 121 n.
  63, 222
relations with his father 84, 86, 121 n. 63
visits Paris 114, 117, 120
will of 242–3
Wilson and 233
Watt, Gregory 86, 88
Watt, James 1–5, 18–21, 27, 29–33, 39–54,
  57, 59–65, 67–81, 83, 86, 93 n. 33,
  100, 131, 160, 170, 173, 182, 184,
  190, 205, 215, 227, 242, 276–7
air and 43 n. 48, 46 n. 57, 51–4
Anniversary Lecture 250
Black and 48 n. 61, 75, 79, 80 n. 71, 158,
  180–81, 255, 280
Britannica on 68–72, 259
Brougham and 174–5, 178, 280
Centenary celebrations of 277
Chambers's Encyclopaedia on 262–3
chemistry of 48 n. 62, 50–54, 250–51
Correspondence ... composition of water
  99, 101, 112, 164, 166, 225, 235
death of 92
elected FRS 33
experiments 48–9, 80, 177
ideas on composition of water 50–54, 68,
  228 n. 49
image of 4, 25, 83, 98–9, 103–4, 113,
  121, 133, 136, 174, 180–81, 185,
  216–17, 221, 247–8, 255–6, 261,
  274–5, 277, 279, 283
kettle myth and 116 n. 39
Memorandum concerning his youth 116,
  118
monuments to 83, 97, 102–3
natural philosopher 32 n. 16, 180
Newcomen Engine 49
notes on Robison's *System* 157, 158 n.
  86, 257
patents and 175, 186
Peacock on 228–9
pneumatic apparatus designed by 54
relationship between science and
  technology and 104, 214
retires from business 88
separate condenser 49
Thorpe on 250

'Thoughts on the Constituent Parts of
  Water' 32 n. 14, 52, 161, 183, 228,
  242
Watt Jr and 84, 86
Wilson on 211–12
workshop of 248, 277
Watt, Jessie 53, 86
Webster, Thomas 142
Weld, C.R. 241–2
Westminster Abbey 61, 97
Whewell, William 8, 18–19, 24–5, 51, 55,
  111, 137–9, 141, 145, 148 n. 55, 151,
  166, 168, 178, 209, 219, 230, 242,
  276, 282
Brewster and 155–7, 164, 166, 168, 282
Brougham and 230 n. 54
Cavendish and 148–9
chemistry and 147, 212, 231
discovery and 18–19, 148, 152, 215–16
engineering and 142
Forbes and 151
History of the Inductive Sciences 19, 25,
  145, 147, 151–2, 156, 162, 209–210
misidentified as author 229–30, 233
Muirhead on 230
Philosophy of the Inductive Sciences
  147–8, 164, 215, 241
portrait of 146
science and practice and 145
Society of Arts lecture by (1851) 212
water controversy and 19, 148, 215
Watt and 51, 147–9
Wilkinson, John 84, 88
Williamson, Alexander W. 204
Wilson, George 2, 9, 19–20, 23, 43–4, 178,
  183, 192, 194, 198, 202, 204–12, 235–
  8, 255–6, 260, 281
British Quarterly Review article 208,
  225, 229, 236, 241
Brougham attacked by 208
Brown and 245
Cambridge links of 209–10, 237–8
career 205–6
Cavendish Society and 236
charcoal argument and 210, 239
chemical lecturer 206
discovery and 19–20, 210, 246–7
hermeneutic case for Cavendish 211
Life of Cavendish 19, 189, 194, 206,
  208–9, 213, 216, 236, 241, 243–4
Muirhead and 233, 239–41
portrait of 207

Professorship of Technology, Edinburgh
    213
relations with Watt camp 207, 232–3,
    236–9
review of *Correspondence ...
    composition of water* 208, 236, 238–
    40
Watt Jr's opinion of 208, 233

Watt praised by 211, 235
Whewell's *History* 209
Wordsworth, William 90, 230
Wurtz, Charles Adolphe 38

Yeo, Richard 145, 155 n. 83
Yorkshire Philosophical Society 129
Young, Thomas 72

Made in the USA
Coppell, TX
27 September 2020